50 Years After *Brown*:
The State Of Black Equality In America

African Americans' Continuing Pursuit of
14th Amendment Rights

Anthony Asadullah Samad

50 Years After *Brown*:
The State of Black Equality in America

African Americans' Continuing Pursuit of 14th Amendment Rights

Anthony Asadullah Samad

www.Kabilipress.com

KABILI PRESS
Los Angeles, CA

50 Years After *Brown*: The State
of Black Equality In America

Copyright © 2005 by Kabili Press, Inc.

Library of Congress Cataloging-in-Publication Data
     50 Years After *Brown*: The State of Black Equality In America/ Anthony Asadullah Samad
         p. cm.
     Includes bibliographical references and index.
     ISBN 0-9723880-2-8 (cloth: alk. Paper)
1.   African American Studies-United States
2.   Race Relations-United States
3.   African Americans-Civil Rights
4.   Politics-United States
5.   History-United States

Samad, Anthony Asadullah 1957-
   50 Years After *Brown*: The State of Black Equality In America
   Authored, January, 2005

Printed in the United States of America

1 2 3 4 5 6 7 8 9 0

This book is dedicated to my mother, Margaret Davis, who on the evening of September 15, 1963, after news of a church bombing in Birmingham, sat my sister, Shawn, and I down with tears in her eyes and explained to us that some people in America didn't like us because of our race, and to always remember that we were no better than anybody else-but nobody was better than us, that we are all equal in God's eyes and God is the only one that counts. Our first life lesson on race and equality in America.

It is also dedicated to my in-laws, James and Dorothy Ward, my grand-parents, Bill and Thelma Mosley, grandma, Ma'Dear Chinn, my Uncle "Buddy" and Aunt Reba, and all those who lived under the constraints of Jim Crow segregation in America. May we never see the return of "Separate But Equal" and hope that future generations can achieve true racial equality in the United States.

Lastly, this book, in part, is dedicated to the memory of my closest mentor, Oscar Morgan, an Louisianian raised in segregation but had a dignity that quietly exemplified the statement, I AM A MAN. Thank you for teaching me to be a Man, in a land that would still call black men, "boy" if they could. Your lessons are life sustaining and will never be forgotten.

Other Books by Anthony Asadullah Samad:

Souls For Sale: The Diary of An Ex-Colored Man

Acknowledgments

I'd, first like to give thanks to God for the presence of mind to write this book, and the gift of writing to articulate the subject of this work in the most substantive matter possible. I'd like to thank my wife and life partner, Debra Ward-Samad, for her intelligence, depth of insight and support in my studies. It is sincerely appreciated. I'd like to thank my children, Kellie, Gabby, Tony and DeShawn and their work in Kabili Press. Its success will be the fruits of your labor. Keep looking to the future. I'd like to thank my doctoral dissertation committee at Claremont Graduate University, Dr. Jean Schroedel, Dr. Joyce Perkins and USC Professor, Dr. Michael Preston, for your guidance and advice in helping me in my comprehensive study of *Brown v. Board of Education*. Your advisement to "dig deep" on this topic and move past *Brown*, as "icon" to *Brown* as complicated legal and social policy, opened up a body of literature and related study that led to this in depth study on the question of black equality in America. Your support of my graduate study, this dissertation topic, and this work is appreciated.

I'd like to thank those who helped this project come together. I'd, first, like to thank my, editor, Kamau Ramsey, for your handling of this project and your professional eye in insuring the highest quality writing we could produce. I would especially like to thank Dr. Mamie Clayton, and the Mamie A. Clayton Library (a division of the Western States Black Research and Education Center) for the archival photographs that give life and substance to African Americans' struggle for equality in America. Your collection is truly a phenomenal assembly of historical evidence to the pride, pain and suffering of the African American experience in America, and I am proud to represent just a sample of your collection in this book. It was a wonderful addition. Thank you, again, Dr. Clayton.

I would like to thank Nahid Jambelameli for design of this book cover. The response has been overwhelming, and thanks for your page design on the photo inserts and the care you showed to Dr. Clayton's collection. Your effort I thank Narvela Santiago-Samuels for your design of the dust cover and the marketing collaterals in support of this book project. You took the project to another level, and it's appreciated. I'd like to thank Pamela Bright-Moon, Alisa Bass-Covington and AngelRose Productions for your work on the accompanying documentary project. While it is a work in progress, I'm excited about the possibilities. Thank you for your honest input and your persistent efforts to cover this complex topic in film.

I'd like to thank several friends whose advice made this a better project from its inception; Fred Rasheed, Dr. Mark Ridley-Thomas, Denise Pines, Atty. Carmen Hawkins, Kwame Cooper, Donald Lancaster, Toni Bradshaw, and Greg Brandon. Thanks for helping build on the success of the first book. Thanks to those who reviewed the drafts of this book project and for the critiques offered. I'm honored that you took the time to give your prestige, scholarship and expertise in response to this work.

And lastly, thank you to all of you who support my writings, both the weekly commentary and the first book. You are an inspiration for me to keep on writing and offering critical analysis on how we change the world for a new generation of thinkers and social engineers, and lift up the race in the process. God bless you.

AAS

CONTENTS

CONTENTS

(continued)

INTRODUCTION

Equality, is the central tenet of a truly democratic society. The United States of America was founded on the basic principle of egalitarianism, and sought to engage democratic practices based on universal suffrage, majority will and limited government that placed constraints on the activities of the majority to protect the rights of statistical minorities. The American "experiment" of democracy was supposed to represent how the benefits of liberty, equality, and property, without limit-under free market principles-could advance a "society of equals." The flaw in the American experiment was its engagement in the Trans-Atlantic Slave Trade, and its use of enslaved persons, as a form of labor to transform its initial society into an agricultural economy that traded with the world. What started as indentured service turned into one of the most vile and abusive forms of permanent slavery-an institution almost wholly made in America-as other countries abolished their forms of slavery by the start of the 19th Century, and the Trans-Atlantic Slave Trade ended in 1808. America, on the other hand, transitioned its involvement in the slave trade, to a home-bred institution that became almost exclusively African, categorized humans as property, and stripped enslaved persons of the rights and privileges for the duration of their lives. This is where America's legacy of inequality began.

The Fourteenth Amendment, passed in 1868, was meant to set straight the inequalities created during America's slavery era, particularly, its "three-fifths" designation of "all other persons," that came about as a last minute compromise to save the Constitutional Convention of 1787. Such a designation was reserved for, not indentured servants, but enslaved persons of African descent. The Fourteenth Amendment is considered "the equality amendment," because, for the first time in America's history, it clearly defined anyone born in the United States as a citizen-something previously taken for granted-and gave equal protection, under the law, to all persons living in this country. It took America 86 years to settle the question of equality for American born Africans in the United States.

Not until the case of *Brown v. The Board of Education of Topeka, KS, et al.*, did the United States Supreme Court admit that equal treatment had not been given to African Americans, and that a social derivative of slavery, de Jure segregation, that legally separated only African Americans from the rest of American society, and offered less than equal benefits, and privileges to them, existed in the previous 58 years to the *Brown* decision. Even 10 years after the *Brown* decision, until the passing of the 1964 Civil Rights Act, African Americans were treated as second class citizens in the United States. Yet, *Brown v. Board of Education* is a significant benchmark, for a number reasons.

First, *Brown* was the case that ended "American Apartheid," de Jure segregation, representing a legal race caste system that imposed harsh penalties on African Americans, for violating the private spaces of Caucasian Americans, and certain public spaces that they frequented, restricting their freedom of movement, limiting access to social, political and economic benefits, and enjoyment to tangible and intangible societal privileges.

Second, the *Brown* decision offered up the first legitimate legal interpretation of the Fourteenth Amendment in the Twentieth Century. It was the first since the amendment was passed, that gave full equality consideration to the African American, without society seeking to differentiate between legal or political equality and social equality.

Third, *Brown* ignited America's social change movement, a time as volatile as any since America's Civil War, as each was ignited out of America's racial conflict. Just as the cause of the Civil War was the expansion of slavery, and the freedom rights of enslaved Blacks, the 20th Century Social Change Movement came about out of a fight for civil rights, and true social equality for segregated Blacks.

Lastly, the *Brown* decision, as law and policy, represented the most serious challenge to America's racial hierarchy since Reconstruction. In the 50 years since *Brown*, there has been an ardent attempt to reconcile the pain of segregation, and the memories of the equal rights struggle, which included some horrendous assassinations of some of the most visionary individuals of the 20th Century. During that same period, *Brown* forced the country to deal with the realities of the racial divide, social and economic disparities born out of the barriers imposed during America's segregation era. In selected periods since *Brown*, there have been policy initiatives that have attempted to rectify racial disparities. There also were policy initiatives to stall "equalization" efforts, and many more to keep African Americans subordinate to Whites, within American society, and keep the disparities of the racial divide in place.

More than about eliminating desegregation in public schools, *Brown* represented the elimination racial inequality created out of disparate racial policies. Lost in the discussion about *Brown*, is the discussion about equality. Specifically, what equality meant before *Brown* and what equality has meant after *Brown*. More critically, was that the elimination of racial segregation policies brought about the elimination of racial discrimination, and brought about the type of societal access in American society that produces the benefits of racial equality.

Thus, this book looks at the subject of equality, in a full historical context, from the founding of America, through its civil war, and through the period that was supposed to represent the dawning of a new day in America, the day the Supreme Court put the legal race caste on hold-for the sake of truly making all in American society, equal, under the law. However, obtaining equality in America, for the African American, has not been a simple and forthright engagement. It has been replete with shifts in social attitudes, conditions, norms and ideology that impeded the intent of the *Brown* decision, and, at times, purposely undermined the goals to achieve racial equality. And there has been a re-entrenchment, in terms of strategies to prevent African Americans, in the collective, from realizing equality.

Born out of the author's doctoral study, examining the complexity of the *Brown* decision, as law and policy, this book establishes equality as the fundamental premise of the desegregation cases. Societal disparities in wealth, jobs, education, housing, political empowerment, social enjoyment and freedom of movement were all functions of the restrictions placed on Blacks by "Separate but Equal" policy. The tenets of the *Brown* cases sought to prove, through a preponderance of evidence-first, in the equalization cases, then, in the sociological arguments, that public policy in the South, meant to separate the race, actually was meant to discriminate between the races. The basis by which the *Brown* case, and its preceding cases, were tested, and proven, were simply-all measures of equality. Inequalities in education, in teachers' salaries, in employment opportunities, in voting access were simple matters of fact. Inequalities in social networks, systemic benefits, institutional access, economic opportunity and personal privileges were complex matters of dispute, that were ultimately proven through intangible means, principally, the psychological effects of racial discrimination raised in the *Brown* cases.

The most difficult question raised in the *Brown* decision wasn't the matters of fact-the inequities were what they were, but the matters in dispute-the intangible benefits of racial privileges that produce outcomes of inequality, benefits that were more difficult to measure, more difficult to ascertain, more difficult to regulate. The U.S. Supreme

Court was able to rationalize matters of fact, and put a stop to the stated inequalities of de jure segregation. However, it had to take the matter of remedying the unstated inequalities of systemic access and societal privileges under submission. In short, the Supreme Court had no answer for how to address the racial etiquette of segregation, and did not want to facilitate a second Civil War, creating a reaction similar to that created after the *Dred Scott* decision, by providing immediate relief to African Americans. So, they waited, over a year, and came forth with a relief that was, essentially, no relief at all, "with all deliberate speed."

From May 17, 1954 to May 31, 1955, the country was in a quandary over how to best bring about an equality remedy for African Americans that would not offend white Americans. Once the *Brown II* case came down, America recognized that the Supreme Court simply put it in the hands of the local communities to work out remedies to address racial inequalities, as long as, they did not violate the newest interpretation of the Fourteenth Amendment, holding that equality and equal protection, for all, as the law and the societal guideline. The next fifty years after the *Brown* decision has been spent trying to decipher what equality was, and what it wasn't; what equality should be, and what it shouldn't be; and how racial equality should be achieved, and, of course, how it shouldn't (and wouldn't) be achieved.

What this writing does is set out a chronology of the equality efforts of African Americans over the past two centuries, analyzes what the impediments to racial equality have been over the past five decades, and draws conclusions that suggest that racial equality has not been achieved in the 50 years since *Brown I* (or *Brown II*), for very specific reasons documented in this book.

Lastly, this book analyzes what the current impediments to racial equality are, and how they should be viewed, in terms of the historical barriers that have been central themes in promoting a racial divide in America. The state of black equality in America is a continuing pursuit, in how best to address a redistribution of societal benefits, that were disparate from the outset, are still disparate and, not intended to be distributed equally, heretofore, based on current attempts to forestall the question of how best to address racial inequalities. Moreover, the legal interpretations of the Fourteenth Amendment, interpretations stemming from the *Brown* decision, are now being used to enforce "individual rights, and maintain the racial divide in American society, under the guise of promoting a truly egalitarian "colorblind" society. Equality, in America, is still a highly contested proposition, where the benefits ascribed are disparate and evasive, and devoid of remedies to allow those historically denied it, a true opportunity to redeem lost equality, or to achieve real equality. Thus, is the state of black equality in America.

1

Haunting Legacies In The Fight For Black Equality:

The "Three-Fifths" Compromise & the *Dred Scott* Decision

"I say then I am not, nor ever have been in favor of bringing about in any way the social and political equality of the white and black races,--that I am not nor ever have been in favor of making voters or jurors of negroes, nor of qualifying them to hold office, nor to intermarry with white people; and I will say in addition to this that there is a physical difference between the white and black races which I believe will forever forbid the two races living together on terms of social and political equality. And inasmuch as they cannot so live, while they do remain together there must be the position of superior and inferior, and I as much as any other man am in favor of having the superior position assigned to the white race."

Abraham Lincoln, Sept. 18, 1858, during the fourth debate with Senator Stephan A. Douglas

The legacy of *Brown versus the Board of Education* is grounded in a continuing societal debate as to whether America ever intended for Blacks to be considered equal to Whites in this country, and the legal, social and political pursuits in which Blacks have engaged, over the larger part of the last two centuries, to achieve such "equality status." The creation, promotion and subtle continuation of a race caste system in the United States today is rooted in the early socio-economic attitudes and political behaviors of those who founded this country, who intentionally skirted the question of "equality for all," when it came to the status of African bondage in America, as well as, those born in America of African (or part African) descent. Slave or free, the social and political status of Blacks didn't matter, because the social pecking order that would become America bore its roots in that of Europe, where economic subjugation, repression of wealth and suppression of property rights, served as the basis for which the "New England" markets would be established. Through unbridled wealth accumulation and the exploitation of non-European cultures, the new experiment called the United States of America would seek to perpetuate economic imperialism, under the guise of free market capitalism, and narcissism under the guise of democracy. Equality was the basis by which it sought to build relationships within the society, without having to address issues of class standing that permeated European societies. Those relationships in British America, however, were defined and differentiated early, according to a social construct, in which race was the primary determinate of where one stood in the society. The treatment of America's friends and enemies alike, in the pursuit of commerce, in the pursuit of justice, and in the pursuit of equality, has been, and forever would be, differentiated by race. The treatment of people of color, in particular, the African American, stems from the originating definitions of Africans in America's colonial experience that would subsequently be grandfathered into America's social construction of nationhood.

2

The African American experience, in pursuit of equality in America, has been predicated on the politics of "white supremacy" domination. Socialization in the U.S. has been a replication of social and political encounters that gave advantages to the founding dominant culture, of what became known as the United States of America, and fostered a social pecking order that has been in place, starting with its initial engagement in race relations with the indigenous people of "the new land," the so-called American Indian. Policy initiatives established against the Native American in the 17th and 18th Centuries served as a volatile demonstration of self-interested choices and the societal constraint practices imposed on the African by the dominant culture. Co-signed by the American government, these initiatives employed a lasting social legacy by which future equality policy was dictated.

The most lasting legacies of America's race politics were two significant "equality" decisions designed to impact African Americans in ways to disenfranchise them, demean their humanity and differentiate them, separating Blacks from the mainstream society. One, was a legislative policy choice to define the status of the African in comparison to Whites. The other, a politically tainted judicial decision that sought to refine societal perception of the status of Blacks. The latter action was a demonstration in how far government sanctioned perceptions could reach in deconstruction of black humanity, perception that still provide modern day indictments on black humanity that continue to carryover massive disparities in social, political and economic equality. Moreover, the residual effects in how Blacks perceive equality in relation to how Whites receive equality in America are still present today. Most critically, those perceptions represent the basis for "unequal-ness" that has served as the essence of the inequality stand for which the *Brown* cases was born, fifty years ago, and whose vestiges are still seen today.

The two societal decisions that has created the longest lasting legacies and most far-reaching impressions of unequal perceptions in the social status of Blacks were the "Three-fifths" resolution of the 1787 Constitutional Convention in Philadelphia that brought forth the United States of America, as we know it, and the 1857 U.S. Supreme Court judicial decision where a man sought freedom from slavery on grounds of favorable legal precedent in a test of the American legal system. This case was the *Dred Scott* decision.

To understand how America established and reinforced its perspective on equality, particularly as it relates to the African American, would require a chronological analysis as to how early America constructed its domestic race relations, and how that construct has been carried forward, through key social and/or political events every twenty years or so. These events either reinforced the construct, or redressed and regressed a shifting construct. Race always has been a foremost consideration in the development of America's societal construct and socio-political relationships, in defining rights and privileges in American society, and in the authoritative allocation of resource distribution as it relates, to what Harold Laswell subsequently surmised as one of the purest definitions of American politics, "Who gets what, when and how."

From purely commercial, though destructive, relationships with the Native Americans (labeled as Indians) to the later proprietary, though absolutely dominative, relationships with American born Africans (labeled as Negroes), equality in these relationships were subordinated with the aim of establishing white settlements that were self-

3

sustaining. Largely through the expropriation of land (from Indians) for their own use and the extraction of labor (from Africans) for their own economic benefit, Europeans claimed and built a nation to serve their own interests. It ultimately had an impact on American/Indian relations that degenerated into genocidal slaughter, and later affected how European Americans would refuse to allow Native Americans to integrate into their society unless they agreed to acculturation. At the same time, European turned "Americans" constricted how African "Americans" would assimilate and acculturate into society as "partial citizens."[1] Peaceful relations with America had been predicated largely on Indians subordinating its indigenous culture to that of American culture, and tribes relenting, by force, to America's increasing land demands. Peaceful relations with Africans had been predicated largely on Africans submitting to the absolute authority of white Americans and acceptance of the restrictions of the socio-political construct defined for them. In fact, the intentions (and pretenses) of future United States' policy positions that sought to address equal protection under the law can be seen in America's first "race policies" toward Native Tribes. U.S. race relations, and equality policy rooted in America's 400 year dealings with Africans, were created out of a desire on the part of the "Founding Fathers of America" to establish citizenship benefits and social privilege rights, whereby those who were not of the society's lineage would have no claims to any of the rights and privileges that were heretofore established.

Key in understanding American Indian policy in the United States between 1790 and 1830, was that most policy decisions were driven by the Manifest Destiny aspirations, interjecting "God's will" into its commercial ambition, of a new government beholden to European values, dominated by a white electorate, whose own interests required expansion of cultural settlements-consistent with their values and cultural interests-into territories previously negotiated and reserved for Indian nations.[2] Relations with Africans in America during that same period provided the free labor that developed the land, much of which, was taken from the Indians, and fueled an agricultural economy that provided large economic benefits and allowed the new nation to compete in global commerce at a minimal economic cost. It was not the intent of the European influence that founded this country to incorporate non-European, non-Christian values into their culture. Nor was the intent to have the indigenous Natives, or the enslaved African populations to be an integral part of the formulating societal structure (beyond involuntary material contributions). Nor was it their desire for Africans (nor Indians) to receive economic benefits from their individual or collective labor resources and land assets.

Neither African nor Native "equality" was part of the original "equation" that was to make up the racial or "cultural" composition of what became known as the United States of America. But aside from the cultural intent, a fundamental part of the United States "equation" was the installation of egalitarian values that sought to make America a "society of equals," except for those who were not intended to be included in the equation. The initial engagements in race relations with Blacks and natives represented a common denominator, factors, if you will, used to achieve desired outcomes to fulfill expansion and capitalistic goals. Clearly, it was a strategy whose end goal was an advancement of a "white supremacy" social construct that would ultimately facilitate a domestic "cultural" conversion, and domination that would bring about a "white man's country" in mindset and practice.

A few years prior to 1790 was this nation's first engagements in "race" policy. However, at the new nation's Constitutional Convention, with Anglo-Saxon empowerment fully engaged and its cultural conversion now part and parcel to the formation of nationhood, the confliction over the issue of non-white egalitarian policy, caused the deliberations to become stalemated. The issue at hand was an attempt on the part of large states' interest to marginalize Southern states' desire to include slaves in its population enumeration. Indians were never considered, because Native tribes never acquiesced to being part of the new "arrangement," and thus separated themselves from having to deal with what Natives considered to be "folk tongue" diplomacy. Blacks, however, had been acculturated into a subordinated role in American society, or "seasoned," by virtue of their dominant presence in involuntary servitude-an existence of force on the part of Africans, and an existence of necessity on the part of Whites-that eventually would become systemic and institutional in form and practice.

In advocating for government representation based on proportionality versus small state interest of being equal in stature to their larger counterparts, the humanity, and thus, the equality of the African in America was called into question. To complicate the argument of the proposed structure even more, the South was currently engaged in the importing benefits of the transcontinental slave trade whereby its "peculiar institution" was positioned to grow given that slavery, though not a focal point of the convention, was seen as something that would just disappear over time. Enslaved Blacks, who had been historically defined as chattel property, now saw their humanity being embellished for the purpose of empowering the South, as it attempted to bolster its population enumeration to maintain equity in a nation of voting equals.

While the British colonies had engaged legislative and judicial laws targeted at Africans and Indians throughout the 18th Century, the true test for how egalitarian societies function came about in this convention. Specifically, how each person's contribution in the society was valued in relation to another's. Those of African lineage in America had no equal standing among whites at this conjuncture in the nation's existence. In fact, they had no standing in American society whatsoever. Yet, consideration was being given to their standing as a person for the political expediency of the South. Citizenship status and, more importantly, class status represented indelible characteristics of accepted and protected persons in the social construct nearly invisible to the discussion of both personal value and societal contribution of Africans.

The slave, be they Africans brought to America or those of African descent born in America, who numbered nearly one quarter of the four million inhabitants of the newly formed United States of America. Slaves were not seen as part of the construct, and were left both unaccepted and unprotected in the formation of a new Constitution. Yet the condition of the slave and his status in society was not totally invisible since he was acknowledged as necessary to sustain the agricultural economy of the South. Still unaccepted on equal standing in the societal construct, the African in America then served as the center focus as to how the North and the South would define American culture, and resolve American conflicts over the structure of the new government and the limits (or constraints) of representative democracy. Specific focus was given to whom would be represented, and counted, in the representation body of the new legislature called the House of Representatives.[3]

The convention itself had stalled over the enumeration question. On July 12, after rejecting a motion by South Carolina's General Charles Cotesworth Pinckney to allow their slaves to be counted as "whole men," a discussion was pursued on whether Blacks should be counted as less than whole. In a resounding demonstration of the consensus of thought with respect to the social status of the slave in America, General Pinckney's motion failed, eight states to two. Thus, to move the process away from the "full stop" stalemate of the prior day, a compromise was offered by Connecticut's Roger Sherman based on resolution discussions that had taken place earlier in the convention.[4] America's House of Representation enumeration would be based on every man, woman, child, and "three-fifths of all other persons."

It is called America's "Great Compromise," whereby had it not occurred, there was a great likelihood that a Constitution would not have passed, and thus the United States would not have been formed-at this convention, or any other convention-where the issue of counting slaves would have been taken up.[5] What this so-called "compromise" put in place was a not so subtle acknowledgement that a formal societal race caste, not only existed, but was subtly ingrained in the consciousness of Whites their status in American society, and the privileges that would be inherently tied to their skin color. Their "whiteness," if you will. It also signaled that this race caste would be tolerated by, and even perpetuated in, the new government.

Even in its very neutral language, this "three-fifths" designation would serve as the basis for establishing a race caste system that, while having no biological basis, would have social standing that benefited the psychological and sociological purposes of both elite and working class Whites. The term "three fifths" only refers to the enumeration of Blacks in national census count and the subsequent apportionment of representation in one body of Congress and directing taxation on the states. However, the impression indelibly left on the minds of the public who would ratify this historic document was that the "Founding Fathers" had given sanction to the caste, and even in their silence of not speaking against the institution, seemed "destined to cast a long shadow" in how future generations would apply equality in American society. Under the shadow of being defined as "three fifths" of a human being, Africans in America (then) were cast outside of the egalitarian values Europeans were establishing for themselves in this new experiment called the United States. It also set the political, social and economic baseline for both unequal and preferential treatment of groups of people from which America would never retreat, and for which America, particularly African Americans, have yet to recover. Two hundred and seventeen years later, both Whites in America and Blacks in America, are still under the shadow of the mindset cast by the "three-fifths" resolution.

The "three fifths" resolution was more than about defining governing policy. "Three fifths" was even more than about unconscionably quantifying the humanity of a people. "Three fifths" was a clear attempt

7

to differentiate Blacks from Whites. The principle condition of the overwhelming number of Blacks during that period-involuntary servitude-was secondary, because all Blacks were treated as if they were slaves, or "three-fifths" of whites, even if they were free. "Three fifths" was formal continuation of the establishment of the racial boundaries set up by a society, emulating European influences. Over 100 years earlier, the colonies, defined such racial boundaries through courts, laws and preferential policies that subsequently turned indentured service into "lifetime" servitude-applicable only to African men and women coming to America. The indentured servants that came to Jamestown in 1619 all had contracts. This meant that though the first 20 Africans brought to America may have come against their will, they were bound to the same contractual arrangement that bound Whites. Human cargo were to be legally held only as indentured servants, sold freely to "a bidder" (later called a Master) for a specified period of time after which time "a bindee" would go free. However, because the Africans could not communicate, there was no end date to their contract .[7]

Over the ensuing fifty years, the status of Africans went from indentured servants to slaves and from human to chattel. But one thing was for sure, policies and laws directed at Africans were not applied to any other indentured servants of European descent. At first, just non-Christian Africans were defined as "slaves for life" by a Virginia court in 1670.[8] Soon there was no distinction between blackness and slavery, as far as whites were concerned, and such "slave" status was never applied to any non-blacks whatsoever.

In the decades following the Constitution's ratification, white indentured servants actually went through great lengths to differentiate themselves from this slave status assigned to Blacks, setting in place their own social pecking order that was being evidenced in the emergence of class stratification among whites. White indentured servants called themselves hired hands (paid wages emphasizing both freedom and choice) as opposed to a non-compensated, "free" hand in bondage. Poor Whites defined themselves as "laborers," as opposed to being called servants, taking titles like mechanics or tradesman or freeman (which encoded egalitarian values that gave emphasis to the economic and political independence not afforded to slaves) which represented redefined societal labels of the skilled working class associated with their "whiteness."[9] (Blacks had skills developed in slavery, yet, they were excluded from taking the title of mechanics, and the like). Lastly, indentured, poor and working class whites referred to their hirers as

8

"boss" versus "Master" to avoid having their labor efforts viewed in comparison to the evolving institutionalization of slavery that was to take place over the next 75 years following Constitutional ratification.[10]

The fundamental perpetuation of a race caste reflected society's perceptual differences in equality between being Black and being White in British America. These perceptual differences were carried over into the new society, the new democracy. Practices by the new government implied that Blacks had not been equal to Whites in Colonial America up to this point, and that they wouldn't be seen as equal, nor treated as equal in the newly formed democracy.

"'Three-fifths' is the boundary designated for you, and your lot (slavery) is what it is," the framers seemed to say by their actions. Thus, "three-fifths" became the signification by which future race relations between Blacks and Whites in America would be measured, and enacted. This compromise on slavery served as a catalyst for the extended discussions around the economic and political differences of Northerners and Southerners. Those discussions would have never come about had not the racializing policy of "three-fifths" sought to, first, arrest the concerns of Whites of various socio-economic status around how to best use public policy to protect their property interest. Second, it sought to empower those Whites who lacked wealth and power, willingly accepting their lower class standing by sharing the egalitarian status of "whiteness"-a right that would be foremost in societal recognition and upheld in the courts "as a property right." Thus, the "three-fifths" compromise set a precedent under which Black rights were subjugated, subordinated and at times-as history has proven-totally sacrificed to further the interest of Whites.[11]

In this regard, the "Three-fifths" resolution also came to signify the privileges that would be afforded in accordance with boundaries assigned to a particular racial group. In America, laws are enacted for very specific purposes, largely to establish and maintain social order as well as serving to set societal boundaries-of enjoyment, of privileges, of tolerance, of security, of equality. In a free, egalitarian society, laws are set by the people, accepted by the people and changed by the people. The limits to which societal boundaries are set offer those in society the opportunity to decide what they will accept, what they will reject and what they will remain indifferent to. The framers of the American Constitution cast broad boundaries to ensure the fullest enjoyment of freedom, liberty and the pursuit of happiness that "an equal" in a society of equals could enjoy. Yet, by virtue of their discussions and enact-

9

ed resolutions, they deliberately and consciously set the lowest boundary for the African American (then the African in America). By assigning the race a "less than equal" status in society, a less than egalitarian value of "three fifths," less than equal access in society-a less than equal privilege in society, the African American was assured to be "less than equal" in comparison to their white counterparts. At the time, the framers of the Constitution remained indifferent to the "peculiar" institution that a significant number of delegates at the Constitutional Convention had moral misgivings about.

"Three-fifths" was the most fundamental flaw of the new Constitution, a "white mark" if you will, against the integrity of democratic ideals on which this country was founded, and against those in the convention that argued that the United States would be a nation of equals, whereby "All men are created equal." By ignoring the slavery provisions in the Constitutions, the framers sought not to give significant credence to an institution that 1) they thought was dying a slow death and would eventually collapse under its own weight, and 2) affected only non-whites, in particular, Africans, who were perceived as inferior beings, that brought forth no moral outcry over their enslavement.[12] Given that there is little merit to rationalizations that the compromise was nothing more than the crisis of the time and prevailing thought, one can only surmise that what the framers truly meant, by passing the "three-fifths" resolution, was that, All white men were created equal, and that equality is defined by white men, for white men, and could only be interpreted by other white men.

* * *

Thomas Jefferson, the principle author of the Declaration of Independence, who penned these famous words on July 4, 1776:

"We hold these truths to be self-evident, that God created all men equal, that they are endowed by their Creator with certain unalienable Rights, that among these are Life, Liberty and the pursuit of Happiness."

Jefferson sought to introduce the societal notion of an universal equality by framing it in the context of Lockean theory, whereby, freedom and equality were viewed as being essentially God-given-directed under a "natural law" that was superior to any man-made law, first and foremost, as the basis for proposing revolution against the

10

imperialist Monarchy of Britain. Establishing the equality of men was imperative to eliminating class and the problems created in societies with formalized class stratifications. Not only was total universalism the primary objective in a nation of equals-total universalism, meaning universal equality of man, universal human rights and universal liberty-but egalitarians, such as Jefferson, needed to cause a shift in the public discourse that unify the new nation as to what equality meant and what it was worth.[13] Egalitarians also shared the Enlightenment Period view of the world that subscribed to the notion that all mankind stemmed from the same creator. Slavery was a conflict in enlightenment thought, inasmuch as, it went, not only against the equality of man espoused in Lockean thought but, against the state of nature that taught all mankind that one man should not own another, or be subordinated to another, or have their liberties destroyed by another, stated thusly:

"The state of nature has a law of nature that governs it, which obliges every one, and reason, which is that law, teaches all mankind, who will but consult it, that being all equal and independent, no one ought to harm another in his life, health, liberty or possessions: for men being all the workmanship of one omnipotent, and infinitely wise maker; all the servants of one sovereign master, sent into the world by his order, and about his business; they are his property, whose workmanship they are, made to last during his, not one another's pleasure: and being furnished with like faculties, sharing all in one community of nature, there cannot be supposed any such subordination among us, that may authorize us to destroy one another, as if we were made for one another's uses, as the inferior ranks of creatures are for ours."[14]

Therefore, in seeking to define the rights and privileges of America's new democratic society, that accepted "the subordination of man" (slavery) as part of its culture, and qualified one's status as property, and caused the creation of "inferior ranks," those who sought to define equality in American society were fraught with ideological and moral conflicts. The subordinated "slave status" of Blacks made it difficult for European elites to see them as their equals. However, their enlightened beliefs wouldn't allow them to see slaves totally as chattel property, though they had been so legally defined.

Though the framers had obvious contradictions about counting slaves as whole persons that would essentially equate enslaved black people with free white persons, they were forced to acknowledge that under American laws, slaves were considered both as persons and property. "In some respects, as persons, and in other respects, as property," James Madison once wrote, the compromise of the African represented the compromise of egalitarianism, since counting slaves as full persons would mean to either value Blacks as equal to Whites, or diminish the value of being counted as a free person. Since slaves could not live as free persons, the framers determined that they would not be counted as free persons and their status in the Constitution would be of "mixed character of person and property" as Madison would state it, "their (slaves) true character."[15] While race, at this point, didn't affect the representation and taxation status of free Blacks, because civil status (free or slave) dictated enumeration and taxation, race ultimately would be introduced, again in conflict with Enlightened thought. Race was viewed as a natural component of self-identity. The subordination of the African's status in American society was tied to the entrenchment of slavery, and the subsequent redefinitions of racial categorizations that assigned superior and inferior status to Whites (free or indentured) and Blacks (free or slave) respectively.

As Jefferson Republicanism began to take root, the promotion of egalitarian values were used to build the virtues of "the common good," namely equalities in income, wealth, utility and life chances, as well as equal consideration among classes and equality of rights as basic privileges of all citizens in a true democracy. These values were the first lessons political "white men" learned in founding this country.[16] Egalitarian practice in America social and political order allows for the distribution of social, political and to a lesser degree, economic privileges that allowed poor Whites to lay claims to the benefits of being "American." Egalitarian practice that emphasized race instead of class served as the best way to define equality of citizenship in America.

The fact that equality applied only to citizens, and liberty and property remained consistent with the promotion of civic virtues and the "common good" egalitarian interests of free Whites, Blacks had one of two options; 1) to deny that equality applied only to citizens, or 2) assert the citizenship of Africans living in America. Armed with both "Natural law" and liberties guaranteed to birth-right, Whites then used capability of self-government as the dividing line for conferring citizenship and establishing "racial boundaries." Simultaneous to establishing the virtues of Republicanism in the new government, the U.S. Congress also passed the first of its "racialized" policies, a naturalization law in 1790, limiting naturalized citizens to "free white persons."[17]

Jefferson was also one of the first to analyze the potential for a multi-racial society of equals and provide an analysis (his analysis) of the capacity of Blacks to function in a society of Whites. Jefferson rationalized that while Blacks were inferior to Whites "in the endowment both of body and of mind," he was part of a greater global examination of the equality of the Negroes that sought to suggest that they (the Negro) of a "distinct race" capable of socializing with Europeans, a concept that was associated with atheism and blasphemy in the context of 18th Century Anthropology study.[18] Predicating the social Darwinism that would become prevalent in the 19th Century, European scholars sought to differentiate the African from the human species, in thought, in anatomical structure, that left the Negro as an "intermediate species between the white man and the ape."[19]

The anatomy of both Black men and women was of particular interest to Anthropologists, who frequently noted their sexual differences in both scientific and erotic context; the largeness of the Negro Male's penis, or the length of the Negro woman's clitoris, or the size and length of African (Hottentot) women's buttock's or breasts, citing these and other characteristics as proof that Negroes were intermediate between Whites and apes. Public discourse focusing on the comparative humanity of Whites and sub-humanity of Blacks served to rationalize racial equality, initially based on observed biological differences and perceived sexual aggression-a stereotype that would become part of black-white xenophobia over the next three centuries.

Jefferson called out many of the same anatomical observations and suggested that the sexuality of the slave was more innate than whites, suggesting that Black males were less likely to be able to control their sexual urges, observing that "They (Male slaves) are more ardent after their female; but love seems with them to be more an eager desire, than a tender delicate mixture of sentiment and sensation."[20] This assessment coming from a man that history has shown was both enamored and conflicted in his own emotions and intimate desires over his relationship with his personal slave servant, Sally Hemings, who also became his life long companion and confidante, as well as his concubine with whom he fathered at least two children that he freed-along with three other half relatives born out of Jefferson and Hemings' 38 year "contract."[21] Sally's love was only partially reciprocated by Jefferson-for upon his death, her years of loyalty, service and companionship (intellectual and sexual) did not earn Sally her freedom, an ultimate demonstration of Jefferson's confliction over perceived humanity and equality differences between Blacks and Whites.

13

The contract was "a life of servitude" for Sally, in exchange for freedom of her (their) posterity. Jefferson, even in death, insured that the contract was upheld, disregarding Sally's own humanity-to not only serve him, but whoever else his estate sold her to. She was, in effect, not withstanding all other emotions, his property-a privilege of which was of benefit to him and not to her. All Sally could do was hope that any benefit (favor) that she had earned with Jefferson, be passed on to her children-and it was. They were freed, but they weren't equal.

Still, Jefferson's views were consistent with the constant indictments on the humanity of the African, suggesting inferiority that focused on perceptions of the African's (slave or free) intellectual capacity, emotional stability, sexual proclivities, and the ability of Africans to engage in social civility protocol. More importantly, the social constraints (of miscegenation) justified the twisted rationality that Blacks were less equal than Whites. By acknowledging the human capacities of Africans in America, but juxtaposing them against sub-human assertions, and in some instances- tying Africans to beastly and animalistic (ape-like) qualities, white thinkers even stepped past their own evolutionary origins to dehumanize the African.

Thus, suggesting that emancipating slaves and allowing them to intermix with civilized (and in their minds, highly socialized) whites, on the basis of mixing superior and inferior persons, had inherent risks that America could not (more likely, would not) take, inferring that slavery just might be justified and the enslaved status of Africans was appropriate. While Jefferson saw many similarities in a physical sense, and saw Blacks as potential candidates for self-government, given Blacks capacity to learn, he also saw prejudices playing a significant role in dividing Blacks and Whites into parties, "and produce convulsions which will probably never end, but in the extermination of the one or the other race." Given these prevailing feelings rooted in supremacy rhetoric, equality status for the African in America was defined on some intermediate status, somewhere between "man and ape," "person and property," "three-fifths of all other persons" in the United States.

*   *   *

The conflicts of Lockean "natural law" theory, egalitarianism among whites and equality rights of Blacks resurfaced in a prominent way 70 years later. The Dred Scott case sought to challenge the inter-

14

pretation of equality and the status of people of African heritage in America, again in a way, that forced Whites to assess their own rights and privileges in relation to those afforded to Blacks in and out of bondage. No other case in the history of America, up to that point (and many suggest, since that time), sought to take head on the equality status of the African American in American society and the property rights of Whites held therein. The 1857 Supreme Court decision of *Dred Scott v. Sanford* (actually recorded as *Sandford*, but never corrected in the court record)was still America defining "on the record" statement, in terms of, attempts to sort out the Constitutional interpretation of the intentional racial disparities of the unequal protections meant by the framers, who sought to silently cement society's rights and privileges as exclusive to whites, and to the exclusion of Blacks, without specifically controverting their own words of "All men are created equal," and "equal protection under the law." Unlike any case before or since, the *Dred Scott* case broke the silence of what America (Whites in society) really thought of Blacks and, moreover, where America (again, these same Whites) really meant for Blacks to belong in the permanent context of its society.

In a nation that had become increasingly conflicted over the economic benefits and moral detriments of slavery, so much so, that the unity of the Union became jeopardized, the *Dred Scott* case would proved to be the litmus test for black freedom, black citizenship, the right of government to limit slavery expansion and the egalitarian rights of slaveholding whites to take their property wherever they pleased-with the expectation that their property rights would be protected.

One legal case, a seemingly insignificant legal case, at a critical juncture in America's history, wove its way through the Missouri state and federal court systems some five years to address each of these very political questions. Slavery and the global demands of America's agricultural monopoly on cotton presented the executive, legislative and judicial branches of the United States with five largely sectional political controversies, the Missouri Compromise, the Texas acquisition and subsequent Mexican War debates, the Compromise of 1850, the Kansas-Nebraska Act and, the *Dred Scott* decision, each of its own volition were of such voracity that it tested the limits of the U.S. Government, but it totality presented such a volatile climax that it left "Americans" no other alternative, but to turn on each other, in defense of what each section believed in, thus bringing about Civil War.[22]

15

While the first four of the controversies were of significance to the political and geographic interests of the United States, the *Dred Scott* decision touched each of these controversies indirectly, but more specifically focused solely on the constantly tenuous state of White-Black relations. This case forced the issue, in terms of defining the status of the one truly undefined commodity in American society, the American Negro, and his continuing conflicts, free or enslaved, in the American public-individual and collective-to establish equality.

Slavery was the most politically volatile issue of the 1850s. Not only had the slave population quadrupled since the turn of the century (from 1,002,000 in 1800 to 3,638,000 in 1850), literally doubling from 1,777,000 in 1820 to 1850, but, the value of slaves also significantly rose over that same time period having increased by 150%. The average price of a field hand rose from about $800 in 1820 to almost $2,000 in the late 1850s, making it more difficult to allow slaves to be set free, or just escape without just compensation. To set a Black slave free in 1820 was a slight loss, offset by relief from the burden incurred of supporting a slave for life, or beyond their most productive years.

By 1860, Blacks in slavery were seen as appreciating capital assets whose value rose as the cotton became more reliant on slave labor. Most of the appreciation took place with the rise of the cotton industry in the South, during the volatile 1850s, when discussions regarding both the abolition and expansion of slavery were at the highest and broadest reach. Slaves had become such valuable property that slaveowners could not just give them away or let them walk away. Those that didn't use their slaves in agricultural endeavors hired them out. Those who left slaveholding territories for the land grant incentives of western and northern expansion took their slaves with them, claiming their property rights traveled with them even in anti-slavery and "free soil" territories. Contesting the property rights of whites over the freedom rights of their human chattel had come to a point of a national stalemate, of which the sectional balance of power between the anti-slavery North and the pro-slavery South rested.

No single case weighed so much on a single institution as did this lawsuit, and no individual litigant in American constitutional history has equaled the fame of *Dred Scott*.[23] While constitutional questions relating to the rights of Negroes attracted the attention of the courts as early as the era of the American Revolution, the issue of property rights, particularly, inheritance and estate rights, such as passing on slaves to beneficiaries, have also been of primary Constitutional con-

16

cern.

The *Dred Scott* case came to signify a challenge of both the property rights of property owners and an equality challenge for the social status of Blacks, whether they were, free or slave, to sue whites over their own rights of "natural law" in court systems set up to eradicate disputes in a land of equals. So who was this Dred Scott, and how did his case come to be of such national importance? Moreover, how did his case get into the court system that was, by and large, reserved for whites, and why was the *Dred Scott* case significant in terms of future claims of equality and equal protection for Blacks?

Historically, Dred Scott, who has been described as someone "whom the burden of servitude rested rather lightly...nobody directly concerned with him wanted him as a slave...as a chattel he was a liability rather than an asset. One published report described Dred Scott as "illiterate but not ignorant," while another called him a "small, pleasant-looking negro with an imperial beard, wearing a seedy black suit and looking somewhat the worse for wear and tear." The inference, of course, was to focus on what white society was dismissing as a frivolous act, deemed the insignificance of a single slave, not the significance of a single legal case, which Dred Scott himself could not have known the impact of, but was, in deed, a lightening rod, given the nation's political turbulence, as well as, the shifting of key actors in both the Presidency and the Judiciary, at the time the case was heard.

Dred Scott, for most of his adult life, had actually lived longer in free territories than he had in slave territory, having been born in slavery what historians estimate to be around 1795 in Southampton County, Virginia. Dred Scott had six masters during his lifetime. He moved north to St. Louis with his first master, Peter Blow in 1927. Blow died in 1931 and Scott became the property of Blow's daughter, Elizabeth. Scott's second master for two years, Elizabeth Blow sold him in 1833 to an army surgeon named Dr. John Emerson, Scott's third master, who took him on duty stops in Rock Island, Illinois and to Fort Schilling, then in what was called the Wisconsin Territory. Slavery was illegal in Illinois and outlawed in the Northern Missouri-Wisconsin territories, so for five years, Scott lived on free soil.[24] Emerson died in early 1839, leaving Scott to his widow, Irene Sanford Emerson, Scott's fourth master, who moved to New York, and left him in St. Louis. She hired Scott out to the sons of Scott's original owners, Henry and Taylor Blow, who were anti-slavery activists. Henry Blow, who helped organize the Free-Soil movement, wanted to see Scott free, so being a lawyer, in 1846, he financed and helped Scott put a case together in the Missouri courts to declare himself free, under the state case of, *Scott, a Man of Color, v. Emerson.*

Blow became Scott's sixth master after the Supreme Court's decision came down in 1857, when he bought Scott from Emerson's brother, John F.A.Sanford. Sanford, Scott's fifth master, received the ownership title to Scott from his sister, Irene, when the original lawsuit was revived, over discussions involving challenges to slaverholders' property rights in the Missouri Compromise of 1820, then transferred to the federal court docket to be heard by the U.S. Supreme Court, as *Dred Scott v. Sandford.* "Sandford," instead of Sanford, was a misspelling on the court docket. Henry Blow then set Scott free, his purpose with Scott having been served-to put the anti-slavery discussion on the national agenda. The *Dred Scott* decision became the impetus for the discourse and was the match that lit the fuse to a future Civil War explosion.

The irony of Dred Scott, the person, was that he asserted his rights to freedom, but never challenged the property rights of the Whites that owned him. He had survived two masters, had two inherited owners that really didn't want him, but didn't let him go either, for property wasn't to be just given away, yet he never ran away. Given that Scott was never really heavily supervised, and had much freedom of movement as a hired out slave of absentee owners the last twenty years of his life, "stealing away to freedom" wouldn't have been much of a challenge, via the Underground Railroad, which was becoming a common vehicle for slave escapes in the 1840s and 1850s. Each time being bequeathed or "transferred" to a descendant of his legal owner, Scott never questioned his "natural rights" against the property rights of the six people who had "held title" to him. None of those "legal" owners, except the last, had the will to manumit Scott. Each could have given their slave freedom, yet it was the law of the land that protected the property rights of each, and gave him or her their right to dispose of their property freely.

"Freedom rights" were passed on in Scott's case and in many others, by virtue of will-less estates that caused the fate of a slave to be determined by the next of kin. Slavery, after 1640, became enduring for the natural life of the slave, not the master. This practice was understood, in as much as it was common social protocol exclusive to African slaves, having begun within five years of Africans having set foot in the colonies in 1619. It was further solidified by a Virginia court, in 1670,

18

who decreed that the status of non-Christian African men and women coming to America "shall be as slaves for their entire lives," thus distinguishing Blacks from any other indentured servants, and obliterating the line between blackness and slavery in the eyes of America's white population.[25]

Two centuries of having bartered Blacks in slave auctions and private sales, and treating blacks as property, had certainly established, even in the minds of enslaved Africans, that the enslaved could not win freedom on the basis of challenging a slaveowner's ownership claim. Money was exchanged, titles given and property rights were legally conferred. No court in the land would overturn documented property claims. Freedom was best obtained by getting into territories where slavery was not tolerated, and thus, the state courts of the land would not honor human property claims, because owning another man or woman was illegal.

Escaped slaves often sought out anti-slavery territories like Ohio or Philadelphia, or even Canada, because they understood that once on "free soil," the law was most likely to be on their side. So Dred Scott never challenged his freedom rights, based on ownership conflicting with natural law, or having to surrender himself, based on his masters having "a right" to pay for his unassuming personage. Scott never contested his chattel status in the context of being a property right of his respective masters.

Instead, Dred Scott chose to test what egalitarians were arguing amongst themselves, the Constitutionality of boundaries imposed on slavery. Dred Scott chose to contest the integrity of the laws that said slavery was restricted to certain geographical locations, and beyond those locations, slavery was prohibited. Scott contested his freedom rights, based on where his masters had taken (and left) him, territories the United States had designated as "slave-free" lands. Since before the 1787 Constitutional Convention, operating under the Articles of Confederation, the old Congress of the Confederation of the United States passed, and later reaffirmed under the new Constitution in 1788, the Northwest Ordinance that prohibited slavery and involuntary servitude in all American territories to the north and to the west of the Ohio River, which currently represent the states of Ohio, Indiana, Illinois, Michigan, Wisconsin and the eastern portion of Minnesota.

Sectional conflicts came to a head in 1819, when the territory known as Missouri requested statehood. Northerners in Congress argued that Missouri was included in the Northwest Ordinance because it was largely geographically located north and west of the southern-most point of the Ohio River, and thus should be a Union state. However, Southerners argued that Missouri was included in the lands that were part of the Louisiana Territory purchased from France in 1803, and that the Northwest Ordinance only applied to lands by the United States in 1787, that the Ohio River ended when it flowed into the Mississippi and that the Ordinance only applied to land east of the Mississippi River. Since Missouri was west of the Mississippi, Missouri wasn't part of the ordinance, and should be admitted as a slave state.

When Congress finally settled the debate of Missouri statehood in 1820, it came about as a part of the Missouri Compromise, that had three parts; 1) Maine, then part of Massachusetts, would be admitted as a free state, 2) Missouri would be admitted as a slave state, 3) Slavery was "forever prohibited" in all the federal territories north and west of Missouri, including all that territory ceded by France to the United States, not included within the limits of Missouri. Having lived in both the Illinois and Wisconsin territories, at least twice, Dred Scott had lived in "free soil" territories covered under the Missouri Compromise where slavery was illegal, thus calling his slave status into question.

The fact that slavery was deemed illegal in the land where his masters lived at the time of their demise, allowed Dred Scott to test his equality against the arguments occurring in debates "among equals" as to what was free soil and what was slave soil. Scott declared that he was free of slavery, based on geographical conditions and legal precedents (anyone living in a free jurisdiction, thus comes free and once free, always free) that reinforced those conditions. In other words, Dred Scott put himself in the middle of a white male "family fight," and the sectional questions white Northerners and Southerners were wholly debating, including, "Did property rights have geographical limits?" Meaning, could the government tell individuals where they could take their property, and could that property be invalidated if it was in a place where slavery wasn't sanctioned?

In doing so, the resulting question came about, "what rights did the Negro have to declare himself free of anything?" Well, of course, "natural law" gave him such rights "to be free," if it were, in fact, applied to a white indentured servant. However, the status of Blacks was such that the laws questioned any Black that wasn't "vouched for," or one that didn't "have papers" to prove that they were legally free (through documented manumission papers). Their status could be challenged at any time, and they could even be remitted back into slavery at the behest of any white person, if a claim came down to the word of a white person versus the word of a Black. This was, by the way, a common practice of slave catchers chasing runaways, and confronting the first stray Black they met, when crossing into the Northern States and so-called "free land" territories, after the passage of a more vigorous Fugitive Slave Act of 1850.

By raising the question as to whether or not he was free, Scott called attention to his own social status, as perceived by Whites, and his legal status was then called into question, as well as the legal validity of the government's so-called "free-soil" territories. From a legal perspective, Dred Scott was correct. He was entitled to his freedom, based on what had become common law among court decisions that addressed whether a slave who once lived in free territory could be considered free. This legal precedent was first set in the British judicial system, upon which American case law was established, in the 1772 case of *Somerset v. Stewart*, where in the court stated that a person was only considered a slave when there was specific legislation to support it. In the absence of such legislation, "The state of slavery is of such a nature, that it is incapable of being introduced on any reasons, moral or political...it's so odious, that nothing can be suffered to support it, but positive law." This meant that when a master took a slave into a jurisdiction that lacked laws establishing slavery-the slave reverted to his "natural status" under natural law, meaning that of a free person. Once that status was gained, it could not be taken away.[26] Thus, legal support for the theory, "Once free, always free."

This actually became known as common law, both to Whites and to enslaved Blacks, and commonly followed judicial order in other slave states including Kentucky, Louisiana, and Mississippi where courts freed Blacks on this very important precedent. In Missouri, the jurisdiction of Scott's case, there were about a dozen precedents of "Once free, always free" cases, where slaves sued and won on the same basis as Scott-having lived and/or worked in free territories.

Starting in 1824, in the case of *Winney v. Whitesides*, the Missouri Supreme Court freed a slave taken to neighboring Illinois, and some ten other cases over the next 13 years, where slaves gained their freedom in the Missouri courts, by having worked or resided in free jurisdictions, making Missouri one of the most liberal states in the nation on this question.[27] Scott initially sued for his freedom in the Missouri lower court (St. Louis Circuit), under the case docket, *Scott v. Emerson*, in June, 1847. After dismissal on a technicality, a re-file and attempts to challenge the case's retrial order, the case was heard in January, 1850. This was the same year the Compromise of 1850 strengthened the Fugitive Slave Act of 1850 that put the issue of slave runaways and "Once free-always free" on the national agenda. The judge in Scott's trial instructed the jury on the "Once free, always free" precedent, and stated that if they determined that Scott, in fact, lived in free jurisdictions, that it terminated his slave status, and that he should be set free. They, the jury, did find that Scott had lived in free territories, and they did set him free, consistent with legal precedent. Irene Emerson appealed the case, then remarried and left the state. When the case was heard before the Missouri Supreme Court in 1852, the politics of popular prejudice had replaced the basis of legal precedent, and in overturning 28 years of Missouri precedents, reversed the lower court decision, remanding Scott back to slavery.[28]

Missouri Supreme Court Chief Justice, William Scott, made no attempt to hide his disdain for the Compromise of 1850 and the national politics involving the limits placed on slavery. He introduced three "new principles" to guide future decisions. The court viewed that "Times are not now what they were when the former decisions on this subject were made" justified as the basis for the shift in precedent; one, being that "every state has the right to determine the scope of application of its comity (respect for the law of other states), the second being that "a state cannot take the property of its own citizens by the command of other states' law, and third being that "slavery was a godly business to place uncivilized Negroes 'within the pale of civilized nations.'"[29] It was this third principle that offered race as a guiding measure instead of the equal justice and equal protections under the law that common law practice is intended to portray. Rather than convey to Scott his due entitlement, judicial review changed its interpretation of the law and its degree of activism-for this one case.

As such, the *Dred Scott* case, for all intent and purposes, was considered, dead-as a legal issue, given the jurisdiction that both the State of Missouri had on the question of citizenship, as it related to court standing, and the last word the Missouri Supreme Court had on the question of Scott's current "in-state" slave status. He was still a slave and there was little he could do about it. However, part of the storied legacy of the *Dred Scott* decision was that it was a case "brought back from the dead"-having laid dormant for six years-for political reasons, to address political societal issues. One in particular, had to do with rights of equality in relation to the "national" social standing of

Blacks beyond the scope of individual states. What did federal law say about the social standing of Blacks and how would this issue be addressed if raised by Blacks in non-slaveholding states. It wasn't until the *Dred Scott* case was revived that its political reach and usefulness became obvious to both anti-slavery and pro-slavery forces. Ultimately it became, not only a referendum on the "property rights" status of slaveholders within, and without, the now transcendental state of slavery, but a referendum on the social and political definition of Blacks, enslaved or free.

Dred Scott's master in the federal case, John Sanford, responded not by challenging Scott's prior residencies in free soil territories, where legal precedence was highly in Scott's favor. Rather, he chose to challenge Scott's constitutional personhood, and the validity of Scott's standing in the courts, by questioning his status as a citizen. This placed the *Dred Scott* case squarely in the middle of the national debate about slavery and the limiting of property rights for Southern property owners seeking to take their property into lands governed by the U.S. By contesting Scott's social and legal standing, Sanford asked the courts, on the part of slaveholders everywhere, to define their chattel, and then to qualify whether that chattel could be forfeited simply by taking it, or having it run away, into territories where slavery was illegal.

The Supreme Court on the other hand, could have avoided this case altogether by simply stating that Scott's federal case lacked jurisdiction due to the fact that it was a state case, that Missouri law controlled Scott's status declaring that he was still a slave, and thus, as a slave he could not sue in the federal courts.[30] In fact, had Scott's original case, *Scott v. Emerson*, been revived, as the most direct way to get into the federal courts, it probably would have been dismissed for lack of jurisdiction.[31]

Scott's case had been consolidated with a petition for freedom on behalf of his wife, Harriett, who initially had a separate case in state court, as well as, enjoined their two daughters in the suit that now gave full recognition to their marital contract, and their standing as a family. With new attorney's representing their case, the Scotts filed a new case in federal court under the U.S. Constitution's diversity of citizenship clause, due to the fact that it involved "citizens" of different states, with his master, Sanford, living in New York while the Scotts still resided in Missouri.[32] While the claims of trespass Scott filed in the Circuit Court of the United States in the District of Missouri (federal court) were similar to those he had filed in the state courts seven years

23

earlier, there were some differences of note, including filing under common law instead of statutory law. Common law enhanced his "once free, always free" claim that had come to be known as "common practice" throughout the nation, and didn't require a petition for permission to sue from the court, avoiding possible quash motions that arose in earlier petitions.[33] The Scotts also increased their request for damages, from ten dollars in the state case to nine thousand dollars in the federal case while Sanford filed a plea of abatement that challenged the federal courts' jurisdiction.

At this point, attention was called to Scott's claim of citizenship not being true, as "Dred Scott is not a citizen of the State of Missouri, as alleged in his declaration, because he is a negro of African decent; his ancestors were of pure African blood, and were brought into this country and sold as negro slaves."[34] The Scott's new attorney, Rosewell Field, filed a demur petition challenging Sanford's plea, his lack of showing sufficient cause in his claim, that the court lacked jurisdiction and most critically challenged Sanford's ascertion that Scott was not a citizen, just because he was of African descent.[35]

Scott's case was heard by Judge Robert W. Wells. Although a slaveholder most of his life, Wells was considered an Anti-slavery judge given his position of gradual emancipation. He upheld the demurrer, denied Sanford's claims of jurisdiction, and gave special notice to Sanford's claim that Blacks had no standing in court, by saying that Blacks, though not citizens were native born, could not be held to a "special privilege and immunity that whites didn't enjoy. Thus, Blacks could sue if they could be sued and had the same standing as foreign born alien Blacks who were permitted to sue in court.[36] The trial was set over for the next term.

In April, 1855, a jury trial found in favor of Sanford, because Judge Wells gave jury instructions that biased the jury, giving Scott grounds for appeal. The instructions Judge Wells gave the jury stated that "upon the facts in this case, the law is with the defendant (Sanford)," when he should have given an instruction consistent with what Scott's attorney had requested, "That upon the facts agreed by the parties, they ought to find for the plaintiff."[37] Thus the error was in what the jurors might have interpreted Judge Wells instructions, as Scott not being entitled to his freedom, if the facts were found in his favor, and that is exactly how they ruled. The appeal was accepted by the U.S. Supreme Court in December, 1854, held over through the 1855 court term, and opening arguments were heard in February of 1856.[38]

There was essentially four questions before the court; two dealing with the status of Blacks-which spoke directly to Scott and the issues at hand, and two deal with the overarching issue of the limits and boundaries of slavery, as they related to a slaveholders property rights-an issue that the court was not necessarily required to take up, but felt compelled to. So the first question was dealing with the issue regarding the plea of abatement; was this a case between two "citizens," according to Missouri state law, thereby subject to appellate review? The second question was an issue specific to Scott, were Negroes of African decent considered citizens according to the U.S. Constitution? The third question dealt with issues, as to whether Congress had the power to enact the Missouri Compromise, and whether Congress could prohibit slavery in territories not under their authority? The fourth question dealt with the issue of challenging "once free, always free," in determining whether the laws of Missouri allowed for Scott's reversion back into slavery, after living in free territories? [39]

The first set of briefs and oral arguments lasted four days, and focused on the "Black" citizenship question, Congress' prohibitive powers relative to slavery and non-state territories, and the Constitutionality of the Missouri Compromise.[40] The U.S. Supreme court elected not to render a decision in that term, and put it off until the following year.

Meanwhile, the national discourse around slavery was worsening, and the profile of the case was heightening, as a newly elected President, James Buchanan, who was more concerned about the Court disposition on the Missouri Compromise and its impact on slavery, than the outcome of the Scott family's freedom rights. Buchanan wanted the Court to rule on the Missouri Compromise's legitimacy, because he held that view that slavery was rooted in the Constitution, and therefore, could not be legislated out of existence, even in the new territories. Leaving it intact would aggravate the ever widening schism between the North and the South that threatened to bring about the secession of the South-a concern that became reality three years later in his administration, when seven states would leave the Union to form the "Confederate States of America."[41]

Buchanan, who took office before the *Dred Scott* decision was rendered, tried to get a hint on which way the court was leaning. He wanted to use his inauguration address to give political cover to the Supreme Court, in the event that it chose to address the Missouri Compromise question. By publicly suggesting on the question of whether slavery could be lawful in the territories "is a judicial question, which legitimately belongs to the Supreme Court, before whom it is now pending and will, it is understood, be speedily and finally settled," gave rise to the suspicion that he may have had prior knowledge on the court's decision.[42] Since the constitutionality of the Missouri Compromise had not been raised before any of the courts, state or federal, in either of Dred Scott's cases, in any cases that had been already ruled on by the courts, nor had the Supreme Court asked for argument on the question, the Missouri Compromise wasn't necessarily an issue that the court had to address, because it wasn't an issue before the Supreme Court.[43]

Northern Congressmen, and even the Northerners on the high court, suggested that the Missouri Compromise was a political question that should be addressed by the legislature, and that the court should bring a narrow decision that excluded the "territory issue," and focus on whether or not Dred Scott should be "reverted" to slavery, by affirming the lower court decision.[44] Dred Scott's slave status could have been easily upheld without the high court commenting on the constitutionality of the Missouri Compromise, or the rights of free Blacks, but the Southern composition of the Supreme Court, and the pro-slavery sentiment didn't allow for the slavery expansion issue to be ignored. This brought the Dred Scott case into the national debate on slavery, and utilized law to preempt all political discussion and debate on the festering conflicts among the state's on the issue of slavery in banned territories.[45]

The balance of the Supreme Court also became an issue of discussion as to how the decision might fall. Five of the justices; James Wayne of Georgia, John Catron of Tennessee, Peter V. Daniel of Virginia, John A. Campbell of Alabama, and Chief Justice, Roger B. Taney, were from slave states. The other four justices; John McLean of Ohio, Robert C. Grier of Pennsylvania, Samuel Nelson of New York, and Benjamin R. Curtis of Massachusetts, were from northern states and had always lived in "free states" absent of slave presence. Though the high court appeared, on its face, to be as balanced, geographically, as it possibly could be with a slight Southern majority, five to four, with all five coming from slaveholding families, the balance was misleading, because only one justice had been appointed by a Republican President. The rest were appointed by Democratic Presidents. All except two justices were appointed by Southern, slaveholding Presidents-two Northern justices considered "doughfaces," northern men with southern principles.[46]   Clearly, the focus of the high Court was Chief Justice, Roger B. Taney.

Roger B. Taney, was appointed to the Supreme Court in 1835, as Chief Justice, by "Ole Hickory," President Andrew Jackson, after serving as Attorney General in part of his first and second administrations (1831-1833).[47]   Taney, either seventy-nine or eighty (depending on the various sources), at the time the *Dred Scott* decision was announced, had been Chief Justice from twenty years, succeeding at the time of his appointment the most influential personality ever to sit on the Supreme Court, Chief Justice, John Marshall. Marshall, who was responsible for heightening the influence and prestige of the high court as the final interpreter of the Constitution in cases such a *Madison v. Marbury*. He established the Court's power of judicial review over state government in cases such as *McCulloch v. Maryland*, giving the federal government (Congress) the authority of establishing a national bank under the Constitution's "elastic clause" (Article I, Section 8, Clause 18)-a power that Taney, as Attorney General, would have a major role in undoing when he convinced President Andrew Jackson to veto the recharter of the second Bank of the United States in 1832.[48]

As the longest serving Chief Justice in American history (34 years), Marshall, called "The Great Justice," for being a defining force of judicial activism in making the Constitution "a living document" by "interpreting it in ways the framers were unable to foresee," brought unity and order to the Court, influenced the Court's majority to speak with one voice (which it hadn't done prior to Marshall's appointment) and reserved his greatest opinions for protecting private property rights as a foundation of individual liberty.[49] By the time Marshall died (on the high bench), he had transformed the Supreme Court from the weakest branch of government-that caused John Adams' first choice, John Jay (the first Chief Justice) , to decline reappointment, which Adams then offered to Marshall-to, in many respects, the strongest branch to which the other branches of government looked to for guidance on Constitutional questions. This was the mantle of power, influence and prestige being handed to Taney, and twenty years later, in the tradition of John Marshall, his successor wrote an opinion in a very tumultuous period, on the ultimate "property right" question, a slaveholder's right to take his property, even if that property is human chattel, where he pleased, without out fear of losing that property, because of the limits imposed by government.

With seven of the associate justices being partisan Democrats,

27

the other one a Whig, and along with Chief Justice Taney, the Supreme Court had an overwhelming "pro-slavery" majority.[50] However, several justices on the high court wanted to write a narrow opinion, dealing just with the issue of Scott's freedom-which they felt when juxtaposed against the property rights issue would have remanded Scott back to slavery. Because only the five Southern justices were originally prepared to deal with the territorial issue, the justices collectively felt that the public would see this court as more swayed by personal and political views than by judicial discretion supported by legitimate legal argument.[51] The two Northern justices, Nelson and Grier, also wanted the high court to avoid the Blacks as "citizens" question for the same reason.

To avoid this geographically "partisan" position and give the pro-slavery leaning "credibility," President-elect Buchanan convinced his fellow Pennsylvanian, Grier, to side with the Southern justices, giving credence to the historical notion that Buchanan had prior notice of the decision and spoke with reassuring confidence in his inaugural address that he would "cheerfully submit" to whatever the court's decision would be.[52]

Whatever Buchanan knew, however, could, in no way, give hint to what the Supreme Court, Chief Justice Taney in particular, was about to do, in what was considered a bombshell opinion for the pro-slavery forces, that even they couldn't anticipate, and a boondoggle of a decision for the anti-slavery movement. It became clear from the time the court took the bench, that Dred Scott and his family had now become a side bar to the larger societal issues of territorial limitations of property rights, the challenge of slavery as a cultural institution and the qualifications of citizenship, as it related to African lineage in America, none of which were issues before the court, nor did they seem necessary to decide.

When the court came forth with a majority, 7-2, decision, the news dispatched from the courts announced that Chief Justice's Taney's opinion took three hours to deliver and covered three "important points…listened to with profound attention in a crowded courtroom."[53] The points were dispatched in the following order, according to the *St. Louis Leader*, March 7, 1857;

First, *"negroes, either slave or free, as men of the race, are not citizens of the United States by the Constitution."*
Second, *the Ordinance of 1787, after the adoption of the Constitution, could*

"not confer feedom or citizenship within the Northwest Territory" to Negroes.

Third, the "Missouri Compromise in so far as it undertook to exclude negro slavery…was a legislative act exceeding the powers of Congress, and void and of no legal effect."[54]

While the news may have been clear and concise on the decision, it in no way conveyed the passion and contextual power of Taney's statement. What future Supreme Court Justice, Oliver Wendell Holmes called the public's "immediate overwhelming interests" were so great and over-encompassing in scope, that the public virtually forgot about why the case was in court, and what the real decision was supposed to be about. The actual decision on Dred Scott and his family was referenced as one of the court's "incidental points" in the decision.[55]

Dred Scott was then, and always has been, cemented as an incidental tool of a much greater social and political agenda, on both sides of the case-never being granted the freedom that both law and legal precedent set in his favor-because that freedom presented much greater stakes to the cultural institutions that threatened to divide this country. Dred Scott's case was the venue to address this cultural divide. Dred Scott, himself, and the fate of his family, was just a by-product, history's most famous by-product, made famous by the timing of the case and the significance of the issues that Taney included in his opinion.

In Taney's eyes, Dred Scott, the individual, came to signify several things; the audacity of Blacks to try and equalize themselves to whites; the insidious attempt on the part of Blacks to utilize the federal court system to act as citizens, in suing whites and using case law and legal precedent as a tool to achieve freedom; using the irreverence abolitionists and Northern Radicals had for slavery, as an institution, to exploit the legal caveats associated with non-slavery territories to legally escape slavery; and to subtly strip Whites of their property rights, through loopholes in the legal system.

However, *Dred Scott*, the case, represented an opportunity to embellish the power of the court over the power of Congress; embellishing the institution of slavery at a time when Congress was challenging its expansion in the Kansas and Nebraska territories, leaving the high court's imprints on the "popular sovereignty" debate; and the opportunity to make a statement on the property rights of slaveholders and Congress' attempt to limit those rights to slaveholding states. While the reinforcement of slavery was the larger issue for the South, Taney's characterizations of the African American, their biological and

29

intellectual status in comparison to Whites, the commonality of treatment and social practices, and the intent of framers of the Constitution, gave the South (and some in the North) the justifications they needed to keep Blacks in the social and political caste allotted for them.

Taney's vilification of Blacks stemmed from his background, not just as a one-time slaverholder (Taney had manumitted his slaves by the time he was appointed Jackson's Attorney General), but, as firm supporter of the right to own slaves, an uncompromising supporter of slavery and a staunch opponent of racial equality and black rights, which made him a formidable foe of the Republican Party and anti-slavery movement.[56] Thus, Taney sought to make this opinion a boost to all his personal sensibilities, and a stab at everything despised, about the attack on America's "way of life."

Taney outlined his opinion according to the two leading questions presented by the record: 1) Had the Circuit Court of the United States jurisdiction to hear and determine the case between the parties? 2) If it had jurisdiction, was the judgment given it erroneous or not? The Chief Justice first sought to establish the Circuit Court in error for setting aside the Plea in Abatement that challenged Scott's assertion of citizenship and was the basis for the diversity of citizenship petition that got the case into the federal courts.

Taney reasoned that the Circuit Court bought the fact that Scott and his family asserted themselves "citizens" of Missouri, and proceeded in this suit, based on citizenship for which they were not entitled. Missouri state law prohibited him from being a citizen. In addition, the fact that Scott was a Negro of African descent, whose ancestors were of pure African blood, brought to this country and sold as slaves, in Taney's view, meant that Scott was of a lineage that were never entitled to citizenship rights or citizenship privileges. Therefore, Scott was still a slave, and therefore, was not free. Under Missouri law, Scott was still a slave as long as he resided in the state, and Taney gave no credence to the fact that Scott had lived in free territories, stating that Congress had only those powers associated with the right to acquire territory and prepare it for statehood, and that "no word could be found in the Constitution which gives Congress a greater power over slave property than property of any other description..." Thus all territorial restrictions on slavery were dead, on the basis that to exclude slavery would violate the due-process clause of the Fifth Amendment.[57]

Then, Taney turned his attention to the question of black

"citizenship." Though the Constitution made no distinction between free persons, only free persons and "all other persons," that codification for enslaved persons to be counted as three-fifths, Taney sought to separate the status of free Blacks from free "Whites" by offering his own interpretation of "national" citizenship versus the citizenship status offered by the states, producing a "duel citizenship" which he suggested, with no evidence, that it was never the intent of the framers to offer "national citizenship" to Blacks.[58]

Taney suggested that his position was based on the "fact" that the framers intentionally excluded Blacks as persons-personhood transcending to citizenship, by categorizing them as "all other persons," but assigning them "three-fifth" designation in enumeration and representation factors that made them less than Whites, who were counted as full "citizens." Taney's theory then being, how can Blacks be citizens if they not even considered persons? Taney's southern sensibilities would not allow him to consider that free Blacks in the North and South had been enumerated and included in representation apportionment from the very outset. This didn't matter to Taney, who then cited the different social statuses of Blacks in the various states, some allowing Blacks to be citizens, other allowing Blacks restricted "forms" of citizenship, pointing out that Blacks were not entitled to the privileges and immunities of "national citizenship" as Whites were. Taney reasoned that once Blacks left a certain state, their citizenship rights ceased to exist, according to whatever the next state allowed.

In this regard, Taney was correct. Most Blacks did not have freedom of movement. However, the point that Taney was asserting that Scott was allowed to sue under the "diversity of citizenship" provision of the Constitution, reserved for cases between citizens of two states, and since states could fix citizenship status of Blacks, they had no "national citizenship" to fall back on, and since Missouri still considered Scott a slave, he was three-fifths a person and not a person, therefore not a citizen. As far as he was concerned, there was no such diversity of citizenship for a Black, and thus Scott had no standing in his court.

But the Court's decision would have been the same as it applied to Scott, had he been a free man, under Taney's position, even though he ignored two critical facts; One, that the Constitution did not exclude free Blacks from either state or national citizenship, and two, that several states, before and after the Constitution's ratification, allowed Blacks to vote and exercise other political rights.[59] Essentially,

Taney's theory of America's "dual citizenship"-one for Whites and one for Blacks-was a figment of his cultural imagination that made its way into his judicial interpretation of the Constitution.

Taney, in no way, sought to moderate his views in defense of slavery, and instead used his opinion in the most inflammatory terms possible, rendering the *Dred Scott* decision, as what can only be described as, "a pro-slavery manifesto."[60] Moreover, because Dred Scott had brought his suit under the "diversity of citizenship" provisions of the federal courts, he and other Blacks suing for freedom could assert equal footing with Whites under the protections of citizenship, if the court failed to address the issue-though it was not a question before the court. Taney revived Sanford's objection to Scott's citizenship claim under the Court's authority to review the merits of the case, and "whole record of the proceedings in the courts below."[61]

While Taney sought to remain true to his "pro-slavery roots," by not avoiding the questions that, most agree, had no standing in the court, the issues of slavery and the constitutionality of restricting its expansion in the Missouri Compromise-in dedicating twenty-one pages to his legal analysis-this, by no means, was the object of his primary focus.[62] Taney gave "his full vent" to his deeply held beliefs that Blacks were inferior to Whites, and should not share in any of the Constitutionally guaranteed rights enjoyed by Whites.[63]

With all the power of the Chief Justice of U.S. Supreme Court behind him, Taney sought to become the prevailing authority on the status of Blacks in America, by squarely addressing the issue of Negro citizenship, and black equality in the courts, and thus, set a new precedent on the constitutional definitions of citizenship. Taney devoted the largest portion of his opinion, twenty-four of fifty-five pages, to the question of black citizenship and whether or not the framers of the Constitution ever meant to include Blacks as citizens.[64] He qualified that portion of his opinion by giving a construct of American culture, asserting Blacks:

"had for more than a century before been regarded as beings of an inferior order, and altogether unfit to associate with the white race, either in social or political relations; and so far inferior, that they had no rights the white man was bound to respect; and that the negro might justly and lawfully be reduced to slavery for his own benefit."

Thus, in making the cultural realities of the "inferior order" status and lack of social and political standing that Blacks in America had endured, heretofore, as a positive, absolute fact, backed by a court of

32

from case law and legal precedent, the most wrongful eradication of Black equality rights and the most significant causation of commonly accepted racial dogma that brought about the subsequent undermining of equal protection under the law for Blacks, in particular, ever publicly witnessed and carried out by an American court.

The *Dred Scott* decision is still one of the most enduring legacies of racial discrimination affirmed by American law and American societal practices. It's racializing dogmatism burned into the conscience minds of both Whites and Blacks, not so much as justified law-but, as cultural fact established through societal practice. It was a cultural fact that Whites did not consider Blacks as their equal, nor sought to recognize them as citizens in their society. If the "three-fifths" clause established Black-White inequality as a constitutionally supported cultural fact, the *Dred Scott* decision sought to reinforce the inequity as cultural practice through court backed case law. Moreover, the *Dred Scott* decision heightened the stigma on black equality, and subsequently-Black people in America, that many felt gave rise to, and carried over into the Civil War. The fight for "black rights" as it was called, became the fight to "check slavery" that had been unleashed by the Supreme Court in the *Dred Scott* decision, leading to the loss of prestige for the high Court for years to come.

This mindset, much of which was carried into cultural practice, would be carried over into two-thirds of the 20th century. The tenets of the *Dred Scott* decision, though legally discredited over time, would resurface almost forty years later in the case of *Plessy versus Ferguson*. The *Plessy* decision revived and legalized the racial caste that *Dred Scott* decision sought to affirm as cultural practice. It was these same set of cultural practices that the *Plessy* decision recreated as de jure, segregation law, and it was these same set of cultural practices that would give birth to the *Brown* case, which sought to redress, on some level, and overcome, nearly one hundred years later. All residual vestiges of the "three-fifths" and its successor, *Dred Scott*, the inequality phenomena set in place from the very outset of America formation, still haunts Blacks in America, long before and even fifty years after the *Brown* decision became case law.

35

2

Abolition of Slavery, "Black Codes" and the Equality of Citizenship

I am not in favor of a caste, nor a separation of the brotherhood of mankind and would willingly live among White men as Black, if I had an equal possession and enjoyment of privileges, but I shall never be reconciled living among them subservient to their will.

- Martin Delany, 1852

The outbreak of the Civil War proved to be the only time this country fell out over differences in opinion, over what the property rights of egalitarians should be about. It also represented a demonstration of how far principled men, principled in the sense that whether it was right or wrong-they stood up for what they believed-were willing to go, to protect their cultures and "way of life." As immoral and unprincipled as the practice of slavery was in America, Southerners believed in it, and believed that it was the destiny of Blacks to serve Whites.

Arguments over whether the Civil War was over slavery or "states rights" have become more blurred, as history has retold the story. One thing is for sure-"the irrepressible conflict" was about a conflict of loyalties of which no man knows whether his final allegiance was due to his state, or to the federal union of states.[1]

If the Civil War wasn't about the inability of a nation to peacefully coexist "half-slave and half-free," then it was most certainly about the rights of the states, in particular, the slave states, to define the property rights of their states and the welfare of its citizens, guaranteed under the Constitution.

Frederick Douglass, the pre-imminent anti-slavery spokesperson of the 1850s and 1860s surmised the underlining role of slavery very concisely when he stated,

"Now, evade and equivocate as we may, slavery is not only the cause of the beginning of this war, but slavery is the sole support of the rebel cause. It is, so to speak, the very stomach of this rebellion. "[2]

Lincoln, himself, acknowledged the same while attending a public meeting where Christian denominations passed a memorial in favor of emancipation in Chicago. When questioned on, "why emancipation?" Lincoln responded, "I admit that slavery is the root of the rebellion, or at least its sine qua non (indispensable or essential question)."[3]

The Civil War represented a fundamental breakdown of Article IV of the Constitution, where the "relations among the states" were undermined by the failure of the Northern States to give "full faith and credit" to the property rights of Southern slaveholders, and the Southern states failure to give "privileges and immunities" to Northern Whites and free Blacks seeking to destroy their way of life, as they knew it and perceived it.

The South's "peculiar institution" was at the center of the conflict, if not the actual conflict itself. Slavery was to be tolerated, not escalated or accelerated. The conflicts of culture, of moral and political philosophy, and of the future territorial direction of the country made "a house divided against itself" turn on itself in a battle of wills for the type of democracy they would ultimately uphold. A democracy that would try to live up to the stated Constitutional origins of professed egalitarian values and allow slavery to die, or one that would ignore the basic tenants of human equality and allow for slavery's expansion.

The notion that the slavery had to expand or die was driven partially on the fact that the economic imperative of slavery required fresh lands to maintain its profitability, and further growth of a plantation economy required an enormous investment in human capital, thus the need for slavery to survive.[4] The South's political economy (condoning of slavery to drive its plantation economy) benefited the nation as a whole, but its expansion into the northern and western territories politically threatened the nation's stability.

As much as white males had to gain in the future direction of this "land of laws," the African in America had so much more to gain. At stake was his freedom, his national status and his political enfranchisement, all currently denied at the start of the war. The Civil War, by most accounts, lasted four years. Some establish the date of the outbreak of Civil War in December of 1860, when the first state, South Carolina, seceded. Other historians suggest it was February of 1861, when seven of the "deep South" states (South Carolina, Mississippi, Florida, Alabama, Georgia, Louisiana, and Texas) formed the Confederate States of America-an obvious signal to a newly inaugurated Lincoln in the way the founders had notified Britain of its intentions with signing of a Declaration of Independence in 1776.

Most historians, however, signal the start of the war on April 13, 1861, with the attack on federal troops at Fort Sumter in Charleston, South Carolina. President Lincoln's immediate response, by presidential proclamations on April 15th, was to summon federal militia to suppress "the combinations" in the seven lower states. Lincoln followed that mandate up with proclamations on April 19th and 27th, which launched federal blockade of southern ports. That action forced four more states (Virginia, Arkansas, Tennessee, and North Carolina) to join the Confederacy between April 17th and May 20th.

Whatever event set off the war, it was clear to Lincoln that the South was now prepared to turn on the federal government to defend its way of life. While Lincoln and North had, and probably would have, tolerated slavery for another 50 years while it "died its slow death," the new President could not tolerate federal insurrection. He sought to take control to defend the national government's federal rights while the states sought to assert their rights.

Both sides believed that they were upholding the Constitution, and that this was just a minor scurmish, a conflict in political philosophies-though a serious one. Both sides also thought the war to be shortlived and would end by the winter of 1861.[5]

Four years later, the philosophical battle over a clash of sectional cultures was still raging.

There is no controversy, however, over when the Civil War ended, starting with Gen. Robert E. Lee's surrender to Major General Ulysses S. Grant at Appomattox, Virginia, on April 9th, 1865, with total surrender being completed on May 26th, 1865. The total number of Confederate troops that surrendered and paroled between April 9th and May 26th was 174, 223.[6] The terms of surrender initiated by Grant and followed through the process by were considered quite lenient, even by 19th Century standards-demonstrating a cordiality emblematic of brothers at a family fight-but moreover reflective of a family that was ready to come back together after the fight that had gone on too long and had lost its focus.

Demoralization occurred on both sides, as the war became more hostile over what was each side really fighting for. In attempts to preserve the Union, the North found themselves in the midst of advocating for, and incorporating emancipation and recognition of black humanity and citizenship into their goals of winning the war.[7] Union soldiers who started out fighting to protect the Union became more conflicted over this, and ended up demoralized that they were fighting to "free Negroes." Confederate soldiers who started out trying to save slavery property rights, became conflicted that Lincoln was using their own slaves against them to win the war, and were demoralized that they had lost everything they believed in, along with all property rights, by virtue of having turned traitorous to their country.

Even though Confederates were viewed as treasonous, they were treated with all the dignity of family gone astray, permitted to just return home, with their sidearms and their horses, on the promise of no further insurrection.[8] Privileges white men, even in conflict, never afforded Native Americans or enslaved Africans, but accorded themselves as a demonstration that such goodwill might one day lead to a reconstructed society and a new nation-without slavery.

One thing both sides were not willing to do and remained conflicted about throughout the war, and even during the reconstruction that was to follow, was to afford equality status to Blacks on the same level as Whites. And as confused as Blacks were about the war, they were not confused about their rights to equality. The

39

question was, who most likely would help them get there. Between 1861 and 1865, four million plus slaves and free Blacks were forced to reckon with their feelings about their places in society. The stakes were higher for them as Blacks, particularly black men, because the racialization of society had began to implicate them, regardless of "free" or "slave" status.

One side viewed them as sub-human, incapable of socialization, while the other viewed Blacks as intellectually inferior and not capable of self governance. Blacks now had to choose who they were going to place their bets with, in terms of whether they would remain loyal to their "owners" and a way of life that would keep them in bondage as chattel, or shift loyalties to the uncertainties of a new reality called freedom in the north, in a society that viewed them less than equal.

The fight was a twofold one for Blacks, to become an equal in a society, free of slavery, in the South and to become free of stereotypes that dehumanized their status in the North. The choices weren't as clear cut as they would seem. The obvious choice, freedom, wasn't an option many Blacks considered. The slave system under which African Americans had been forced to live did not produce an independent, self-reliant citizen often celebrated in 19th Century American democratic political thought.

Because slavery was based on "absolute control," aimed at controlling every aspect of black life in order to extract maximum profits from its laborers, Blacks released from bondage were impoverished, illiterate and highly dependent on their former slave masters, most of whom despised any Black with whom they came in contact.[9] Many enslaved Blacks were afraid of the unknown and actually found comfort in the relative "security" of slavery.

The South actually used this relatively small segment of the slave population to justify claims that Blacks were actually happy in slavery. Thousands of freed Blacks returned to their former slave masters, requesting to work their fields for free, in exchange for rented land and food.

This came to be known as sharecropping, that lasted for another 100 years, well into the 1960s. Those enslaved Blacks were the exception, and not the rule. An overwhelming number of enslaved Blacks chose freedom and were anxiously trying to discern how they could fit into this war. Southerners expected their enslaved to help them fight the insurgent North and they were actually winning until Lincoln began to ponder a novel idea, Emancipation.

White Northerners were just as conflicted. While slavery was a moral wrong they couldn't condone, they weren't quite ready for Lincoln's proposed emancipation policy. Most Northern Democrats were opposed and unequivocally opined that slavery was the best status for Blacks, while the Republicans were being egged by abolitionist to fulfill an anti-slavery pledge, but were cautious to follow Lincoln's lead. Lincoln had to proceed slow, because of the constitutional, political and military implications of moving too quickly.[10]

At issue here was two questions, What did emancipation mean, in terms of who would be freed? And, What would occur after emancipation, in terms of how and where these "freed" Blacks would fit in their new roles in society?

For years, decades, even a century, Lincoln's emancipation proclamation was seen as some benevolent act of kindness, some pursuit of rightness, some righteous departure of the politic of the day, when in reality, it was nothing more than a tactic of warfare, to turn the tide of the war in favor of the Union forces, because emancipation was limited to just those states in rebellion against the Union.

However, Lincoln knew the ramifications of a partial "freeing of the slaves." The President, who could care less about "saving or destroying slavery," by just wanting to save the Union, understood that emancipation would lead to a total abolition of slavery, and another fight within the Union's slaveholding states could pose risks in losing the war. Emancipation was also inevitable, largely because of the mass defections of enslaved Blacks that were taking place in the South. There would be no way to put that genie back in the bottle after the war.

Enslaved Blacks, by and large, continued to work the farms and plantations, at the beginning of the war, in spite of the absence of white males who were off to war, choosing to stay in place rather than taking on the suicidal task of trying to escape past armed Confederate forces. The fact that they did not rebel didn't mean they acquiesced either; for as soon as they caught sight of Union troops making deep penetration in the South, loyalties shifted. True feelings were made known-that feeling being the desire to fight with the Union army and taking their chances on a permanent freedom.[11]

After waiting a while to see if the war was real, and what would happen in, what obviously had to look like an indistinguishable family fight, wherein picking sides could be dangerous either way they went, over two hundred thousand enslaved Blacks ran to Union lines to "fight for freedom and what historian James McPherson surmised as, the war's turning point.

This suggested that the North would not have won the war as soon, if at all, if not for the massive defection of enslaved Blacks,"38,000 of whom would die fighting for the Union's cause."[12] Most crossed over to the Union side, only to be designated as "contraband of war" (property of war, not prisoners of war) until Lincoln decided how he wanted to use them, or to let them go. Letting them fight, and kill white Southerners, wasn't an option either.

Intertwined with the emancipation issue, was another crucial issue for Lincoln to ponder, the right of Blacks, free in the North and escaped in the South, to bear arms in defense of the Union. When Lincoln called for volunteers to join the Union army, thousands of free Blacks stepped up to try to liberate their brothers in the South-using the war as a means to end slavery.

Lincoln rejected their offer initially. However, so many enslaved Blacks, 900 by count, came forward when news spread that the Union was holding contraband who aided in building Confederate fortifications across the Chesapeake Bay, that the North soon saw it as a way to strip the South of its labor force and using it for their war labor purposes, without having to commit to emancipation.[13] Apparent that the North was not willing to let the escaped Blacks fight, nor willing to set them free (because they considered them property of the South), Congress then passed the first Confiscation Act that forfeited property used to aid the rebellion, meaning the enslaved Blacks that were being held as contraband, which now the Secretary of the Navy, Gideon Wells, would employ to fight against the Confederate troops, as long as, they didn't receive a rating or pay higher than "boys" fighting at $10 a month (white privates received $13 a month).

This form of economic subjugation represented one of the first demonstrations of what life in America would be for Blacks, in terms of unequal treatment under the law-not just prior to emancipation-but for the next 140 years. However, this particular act of unequal compensation wasn't corrected until June, 1864 when Congress passed a law granting equal pay for black soldiers.[14]

Still many Union soldiers refused the help of escaped bondsman, and Union troops even returned some of them back to their Southern plantation owners when claimed.[15] This behavior caused the rebuke of abolitionists and Northern Black leaders like Douglass, who stated that "the great and grand mistake of the conduct of the war thus far, is the attitude of our [Union] army and Government towards slavery."[16]

Within the first year of the war, however, both the North and the South were employing Blacks in some strategic non-fighting engagements, be they as laborers or as guides. However, by summer, 1862, Union losses shifted opinions about arming escaped Blacks, "fugitive slaves" as the South referred to them. Congress passed a second Confiscation Act in July of 1862, that allowed the President to move closer to emancipation, by emancipating enslaved Blacks who had escaped from rebel states. The act also cracked the door to allowing enslaved Blacks to fight, by allowing the President to use his discretion in that regard, if it became necessary.[17]

Still resisting the arming of Blacks, Lincoln sought to use his emancipation strategy as a first resort (and the arming Blacks as a last resort). He was forced to countermand an emancipation order of one of his generals earlier in the year (May) who was following the lead of acts of Congress, that forbade military officers from returning escaped Blacks back to their masters. A month later, 3,000 enslaved Blacks were freed, compensating slaveowners up to $300 a slave in a abolishment plan in the District of Columbia.[18] However, Lincoln had yet to play his emancipation card and was attempting to pass his own compensated emancipation plan that would include the Border States in the Union. His was a two-fold plan, however. Lincoln's plan involved not only compensating slaveowners, but also compensating emancipated slaves, and free Blacks, to leave America under a U.S. sponsored colonization policy.

The ideology behind Lincoln's plan was a resignation on the part of the President that Blacks and Whites would never be able to live together in America on equal footing, and that conflict would follow wherever Whites and Blacks were forced to share common

43

societies. Lincoln clearly understood the race politics of America, historically and in its present context, and sought to avoid the question of "Negro equality," which he and most other white males, North and South, repudiated on a right regular basis.

What did equality for Blacks mean at this critical juncture in America's history? Well, for Blacks-it meant principally three major points on which to lobby Lincoln; permitting Blacks to join the Union army, freeing enslaved Blacks from bondage-declaring slavery illegal, and supporting equal suffrage for Blacks, namely in the right to vote.[19] Direct concerns of black-white relations precipitated the Civil War, and carried over into the War, as a political issue without end. Opponents of Lincoln's Republican Party charged that the party advocated for equality-even amalgamation of the races, while Lincoln and the Republicans defended themselves against being promoters of Negro equality by professing their own allegiance to white supremacy.

At the same time, the North criticized slavery's sexual politics and accused the South of promoting the growth of the black population throughout the United States by virtue of slavery's closet misogynistic behaviors.[20] While condoning inequality toward Blacks, and at times even endorsing many of the discriminating laws that excluded Blacks from suffrage, making them non-citizens in the north, many Republicans, including Lincoln advocated colonization and deportation of Blacks, as the only solution to the race problem.[21] This was the only way Lincoln could get Union men in the slaveholding Border States to accept full and total emancipation.[22]

However, Congress, particularly Congressmen from the border states, rejected Lincoln's compensation plan (to slavemasters) as cost prohibitive, at a projected $478 million to be paid over thirty years. Congress did give Lincoln $600,000 to set up a plan for colonizing Blacks, free or enslaved, if he could get Blacks to agree to do it.[23] Lincoln then arranged a much publicized meeting at the White House with a select group of Negro leaders. This too would represent a future source of division for African Americans, the competition to be the "selected spokesperson" for Black America before the power seats of white America. On this occasion, Lincoln picked a five person delegation, whom he met with on August 14, 1862 on the question of colonization.

44

While Lincoln thought the group might be excited over the notion that he was seriously considering emancipation, he was speaking with Northern Blacks that owned homes and had long-standing roots and birthrights in the their communities as free men. They owned assets in the millions, in aggregate, and saw Lincoln's offer as a sucker's deal to leave a secure lifestyle, as unequal as it was, for an insecure offer to relocate in another country-not by any agreement that they had fashioned, but one that the U.S. Government brokered. Why would they accept a colonization offer? In protest meetings in various cities, Blacks rejected such a plan to forsake "their land," only to appease the racial attitudes of what they called "traitors in arms," and said so in a published rebukes of Lincoln's offer.[24]

This didn't stop Lincoln from signing colonization agreements with the governments of Colombia (the Chiriqui Province, located in Panama) in Central America, the independent Caribbean Island of Haiti-home of the successful slave revolution led by Toussaint L'Ouverture in 1791, and later the African country of Liberia. All of these colonization experiments were unsuccessful and full of potential embarrassments.[25]

Inasmuch as not many Blacks took the governments offer, and of those who did take the deal suffered various health and social calamities, Lincoln still felt his colonization plans would eventually materialize and moved forward anyway, issuing a preliminary proclamation in September of 1862, stating that, effective January 1, 1863, slaves in areas held by rebels would be free.[26]

Reinforcing that the Emancipation Proclamation was nothing more than a tactical measure of war strategy, despite the pleasure of free Blacks and abolitionists in the North, more than 800,000 enslaved Blacks remained in bondage by the Union border states and hundreds of thousands, if not millions, remained enslaved in the Confederacy, until federal troops could carry forth the message some months later[27]-as the Confederate government of the South didn't recognize any proclamations of the Union.

An enraged Confederate President, Jefferson Davis, threatened to overturn the Emancipation Proclamation and re-enslave the 250,000 free black people still living in the South at the time of the order. He perceived the policy as a shrewd move on the part of Lincoln to keep Britain from siding with the Confederacy, on the basis that cotton shortages were impacting British free trade, by 1862. Britain might have interceded because the port blockages represented an issue of "freedom" for the South's free trade rights, but Britain could not, and would not intercede on the side of slavery.[28]

The impact of the Emancipation Proclamation was been perceived as minimal in a historical context, largely because of the confusion as to whom the proclamation applied. Slavemasters held back on freeing their property, until they could get further clarification (which usually meant seeing the actual proclamation), while enslaved Blacks stayed put, because they didn't know if emancipation was rumor or fact.

This confusion ensued, because while the proclamation was targeted at the rebellious states in the South, there were pockets of "allegiance" throughout the South, where plantations had taken oaths of loyalty to the federal government. This included plantations in specific portions of Virginia, Louisiana as well as the Mississippi Valley, that were clearly posited in rebellion states, but emancipation didn't apply to them.[29] Nor did it apply to the Union's border states, whose slaves were getting the word second hand, overhearing the outrage of their masters, that Lincoln had emancipated the slaves-not knowing the complete details that excluded them.

Most critically, the compliance with emancipation most often came with notification and the presence of Union soldiers, communicating the order themselves. Enslaved Blacks usually heard about it for the first time from a Union officer. For enslaves Blacks in the South, freedom that was tied to the emancipation proclamation, from a legal perspective, was limited in scope, because it came only as fast as the progress of Union troops into rebel territory, and the enforcement powers that accompanied them.[30] There is no misperception of the importance of the emancipation proclamation, in terms of its effect of dramatically weakening slavery, however. It opened the door for slavery's quickly approaching abolition.

Though the news of the emancipation proclamation traveled slowly amongst the slave population, it traveled like wildfire amongst the Confederate soldiers and civilian population, who called the constitutionality of Lincoln's action into question. The issue was not whether, or not, Lincoln had the power to do it, in the context of war strategy. Clearly, he did have executive power standing. The issue here was whether Lincoln had constitutional standing to suspend, confiscate and emancipate folks' "property rights" beyond the war. Lincoln freed some slaves, but had not abolished slavery.

Absent of law, where was the legal ground on this emancipation, given that some areas of the country were still slaveholding? With *Dred Scott* Chief Justice Roger Taney still on the bench, Lincoln knew, as did Congress, that his order could not withstand constitutional scrutiny. Soon, there was a groundswell to create a Constitutional amendment to settle the slavery question, once and for all, by making Lincoln's order "colorblind," and providing for a federal law that would not give legal recognition of whiteness, nor an inferior status of Blackness.

In the first, and only, attempt to address the issue of racial status through legislation, Congress sought to legally prohibit racial classifications in the Constitution,[31] by resurrecting a pre-war resolution proposed in February, 1861 to abolish slavery and reintroduce it, by resolution, as the 13th Amendment in December of 1863. It took 15 months to work its way through Congress. It became an issue in the 1864 election, but by February of 1865, the 13th Amendment to abolish slavery was locked and loaded.

The Confederate army overwhelmed by the 200,000 plus soldiers already fighting in the Union army, saw the writing on the wall (of both losing the war and losing slavery). Confederates finally relented, less than a month before its final surrender, to allow enslaved Blacks to fight, under conditions of a "well-digested plan of gradual and general emancipation" of its own.[32] In an attempted to match the North's use of its property against them, the Confederate Senate introduced a bill in January, 1865, calling for the enlistment of 200,000 enslaved Blacks, who would receive their emancipation, if they remained loyal to the Confederacy through the end of the war.[33]

By the time Confederate President, Jefferson Davis, signed the bill March 13, 1865, Confederate troops were already in retreat or suffering defeats in Virginia, Tennessee, North Carolina and Alabama.[34] As the North began to gain a distinct advantage in the war, and various surrenders of Confederate troops began to take place, it became obvious that slavery was on the way out, when pledges to uphold the Emancipation Proclamation and support the 13th Amendment became negotiating tenets for the conditions of surrender. In each negotiated surrender of Confederate troops, upholding the status of the newly "freedmen," and freeing the rest of those in bondage had to be accepted before the "terms" of surrender were complete.

Acceptance of the abolishment of slavery as a condition of surrender, by no means, meant a surrender of white soldiers' position on black equality, however. The irony of Grant's generous surrender terms of Lee and 26,000 white Confederate soldiers on the steps of the Appomattox Courthouse on the 9th of April, 1865, would be historically juxtaposed against the mostly notably vile inflexible surrender terms given to Union black soldiers a year earlier. As was most often demonstrated in Southern war policy, black soldiers were not afforded the diplomacies of war in what was considered a white man's fight over democracy philosophy. Black soldiers were generally captured and forced into slavery, or outright killed-even in surrender.[35]

In one of the biggest atrocities in American history, on April 12, 1864, white soldiers, led by a field commander, the future founder of the Ku Klux Klan, General Nathan B. Forrest, slaughtered a regime of Negro soldiers at Fort Pillow, after they had waved a white flag of surrender and agreed to be taken as prisoners of war and be humanely treated, as Lincoln had insisted, according to the protocols that had been established for prisoners during the war. Forrest, instead, refused their surrender-not permitting them to do so, and didn't hesitant to kill 262 black Union soldiers (several historical sources document the number as closer to 300 or more). Some were even burned alive.[36]

They were viewed as traitors to the rebel cause and Confederate way of life, even as the South, themselves, were being viewed as treasonous while in rebellion against the United States of America. A form of vigilante justice was extracted upon Negro soldiers that enraged Lincoln, and even prompted thought of retaliation by Union Officers, (future U.S. President) Ulysses Grant and William T. Sherman, though the latter defended the rights of black soldiers never used them in combat.[37]

On the "rumor" of a wholesale massacre of Negroes having taken place, Lincoln said, "if there has been the massacre of 300 there, or even the tenth part of 300, it will be conclusively proved; and being so proved the retribution shall as surely come."[38] Lincoln promised a full and complete investigation of the murders at Fort Pillow, though he understand more than anyone, that these were only a sample of the type of racial conflicts America would endure under the attempts to equalize the black and white races.

A Congressional Committee of Inquiry was appointed with special reference to the Fort Pillow massacre of "colored soldiers." The reports findings gave support to the "indiscriminate slaughter" after surrender. Yet, follow-up did not uphold Lincoln's promise of retribution. Sherman's findings did not support the political leanings of the report, and events suggested that, while more of the defenders were killed than should have been, that the battle was just that, a battle. Thus, no retaliation was ever ordered.[39]

Both Lincoln and Congress knew that the claims of slaughter were closer to the truth than claims of battle, but they also knew that enslaved Blacks that would take up arms against white men were viewed as the ultimate threat, particularly on the battle field that would eventually carry over into a post Civil War society-whatever that would look like.

Yet, when the Union, upon the instructions of Lincoln, offered the Confederacy "generous terms" of surrender, they included allowing all Confederate soldiers to lay down their war weapons on the steps of the Courthouse (or leave them wherever they were). Officers could keep their personal side arms, and the soldiers kept their horses (to work their small farms-those that had not been confiscated), and were instructed to return to their homes (unescorted).[40] Most Confederate soldiers, after laying down their arms, were allowed to walk home.

Within a week of Lee's surrender, Lincoln was assassinated by one of a group of Southern conspirators that sought to assassinate the President, the Vice President, Andrew Johnson, and Secretary of State, William H. Seward (who was stabbed by one of the co-conspirators on the night Lincoln was shot).[41] John Wilkes Booth's actions that night included a leap from the Presidential box where Lincoln was sitting to the stage, where he cried out, "Sic simper tyrannis! The South is avenged," thus giving support to a prevailing theory that Lincoln's own assassination was motivated by a man inflamed over the Emancipation Proclamation, who perceived Lincoln as a traitor to Whites and white interests.

There is, by and large, consensus that the Northern aboli-

49

tionists' promotion of "black equal rights" and Lincoln's capitulating to Radical Republicanism in freeing the slaves, thus destroying "the Southern way of life" during the war, were the root sources of the plot to kill, not just Lincoln, but Union leadership.[42]   Clearly, Booth's sentiment was not a fringe minority view. It was widespread, almost equal to those who may have favored emancipation as a war tactic to give the Union some advantage.

However, frustration of freeing Blacks was not to be underestimated. For soldiers on both sides, desertion rates rose significantly, after the issuance of the Emancipation Proclamation, because it than changed the nature of the war, in the eyes of white men, from preserving the Union to a "nigger war" (fighting for the freedom of slaves and equal rights for freed Blacks).[43]

Lincoln did not live to see the 13th Amendment enacted. Ratification was announced by Secretary Seward, who on December 18, 1865 stated that Lincoln's "war measure" had been passed "by the legislatures of twenty-seven states, constituting three-fourths of the states of the Union," allowing the amendment to "become a valid part of the Constitution."   Again, even in post mortem, Seward found the need to clarify and reinforce Lincoln's purpose in the minds of Whites, as to why this-the freeing of Blacks-was occurring. Nobody knew better than the late president himself that abolishing slavery would not confer Blacks the full rights of citizenship.[45]

The 13th Amendment made Blacks free from slavery, but as they would soon find out, it did not make them equals. The Reconstruction Period, which many historians believed started January 1, 1863, with Lincoln's Emancipation Proclamation, but is by and large, associated with the civility of the physical and political reconstruction that took place with the readmission of the former confederate states back into the Union, (1866 through 1870) probably looked more like what Lincoln would had envisioned, inclusive of the racial emersion difficulties, had he lived through his second term of office. However, Lincoln could not have envisioned the depth of hostility that would take place over the twelve years following his assassination. America's social (race) reconstruction would be nowhere near as civil.

*   *   *

50

After the war, the federal government put armed troops in the Southern states to avoid the possible reoccurrence of Confederate insurrection, but more critically to give protection to its newest "citizens," African Americans, who were not legally designated as citizens-by virtue of Congressional act-until the passing of the first Civil Rights Act of 1866. The immediate post war activity focused on rebuilding the South, and integrating four million formerly enslaved persons into a resistant society. The last staple of the pre-war "black equality" triad, suffrage, became the primary focus of societal discussion. The question simply was, "Did freedom equate to citizenship?" Blacks thought it did, while Whites thought that it didn't. Parts of the federal government, Congress, thought that it did, while other parts of the federal government, the President, and most of the re-admitting state governments thought that it didn't.

President Andrew Johnson did as much to fuel the confliction over the equality of citizenship issue, when he initially vetoed the 1866 Civil Rights Act. His justification was that this would also allow Chinese, Indians (Native Americans) and Gypsies to be made citizens. President Johnson also reasoned that it was the rights of the states to confer citizenship. Therefore, a person could be a citizen in the country, but not in the state, and with eleven of the then thirty six states not represented in the Congress, it wasn't wise to pass this act.[46]

51

W.E.B DuBois, in his post analysis of the Reconstruction Era some 70 years later, captured both African American and some Republican sentiment when he wondered aloud what President Johnson expected Negro status in society to be; they were not to be citizens, and they were not to be voters, yet they were to be free.[47] This inferred that freedom and citizenship was not necessarily one and the same. While Congress over-rode the President's veto, allowing the act to still represent "Blacks as citizens," it did little to ease the nation's confliction over the status of Blacks beyond offering some Constitutional protection of Blacks as "persons."

This caused mass hysteria throughout the south, because most Whites still did not view Blacks as equals, and citizenship was viewed as a privilege of "whiteness." Even Republicans, who advocated for the abolishing of slavery, were conflicted as to what comprised citizenship for Blacks. While they most certainly supported political equality for Blacks, the party was split on the issue of social equality, causing them to avoid the issue as one "beyond the realm of government consideration. "[48]

Leaving the interpretation of citizenship to the states however, didn't offer Blacks any true solace. Many states were quite emphatic that freedom didn't necessarily equate to citizenship. Mississippi's new Governor, at this phase of Reconstruction, was an unpardoned ex-Confederate brigadier general named Benjamin G. Humphreys, who succinctly stated that "The Negro is free, whether we like it or not...To be free however, does not make him a citizen, or entitle him to social and political equality with the white man."[49]

The mass exodus out of slavery meant that Blacks had to go somewhere other than the plantation (though many stayed after they were free). However, many states passed laws prohibiting the entry of Blacks into their state, restricting Blacks' "freedom of movement," requiring Blacks to put up "responsibility bonds" (post bond that they'd be responsible citizens, while in their state or town), requiring Blacks to be "vouched for" (by a White who know them), before they could work in a state, limiting their work to apprenticeship roles, being arrested for vagrancy, and loitering when they couldn't work-even being remanded to what equated to be slavery, for limited periods of time, as part of their sentence. Moreover, those laws sought to deny the "national citizenship" that was argued in the *Dred Scott* case, and the state citizenship that Chief Justice Taney ultimately ruled on. While some states may have recognized black citizenship, other states didn't have to.

These laws, that became widespread throughout the South, and even in parts of the North, came to be known as "the Black Codes." Black codes, while varying from state to state and in their varying provisions, forbade Blacks to vote in some states, or to hold office; Blacks could not serve on juries, nor testify against Whites in a court of law; Blacks were not eligible for military service; Blacks could not assemble in public without a permit issued by local law; Blacks were required to carry passes when they moved from place to place; Blacks had to be employed at all times, and when they refused to work, they could be fined or hired out as laborers. Black codes generally restricted "black rights" of movement, working and earning capacity, property ownership and inheritance of property, suing and being sued in courts, personal socialization, public enjoyment and marriage.[50]

These were the common restrictions of the Black codes, and often represented blatant demonstrations in the differences in societal treatment afforded Whites and Blacks. Some of the more extreme codes included prohibitions against inter-racial marriage, inter-racial sex, hiring skilled black labor, admitting Blacks into labor unions, prohibiting drinking and gun ownership.[51]

There was no other purpose for these laws except to control the masses of Blacks that were no longer under the "absolute authority" of slavery. Many of the laws were passed under the guise of seeking to regulate both the behaviors of former Confederate soldiers and former slaves. They were supposed to be equally applied, since few of the laws specifically mentioned race, but the differences in penalties and discrepancies in the severity of punishments invoked on Blacks clearly demonstrated for whom the laws were intended.[52]

For instance, in North Carolina, the legislature in 1866 passed a decree that attempted rape, not actual rape, but attempted rape, of a white female by a Negro was punishable by death; whereas rape (not attempted rape, but rape) of a woman of any color by a white man was punishable by fine and the lash.[53] In Mississippi, Blacks (freed, free or mulatto) were hired under service contracts and required to fulfill their obligations of that contract. If they quit before the contract was up, any white person could arrest them. White laborers worked at their discretion and the length of contracts was at the laborer's discretion.[54]

The proliferation of such laws made it understood, among both the white and black populations, that under Reconstruction, the states and their local governments did not intend to let the federal government dictate how freedom would be interpreted, and how equality would be defined. President Johnson, himself, remained quiet on the practice of Black codes, though he knew that the codes denied Blacks their civil rights. As Southern states were re-admitted, he silently sided with their conflicting state's rights, because of his own perception that Blacks were not capable of self-government, and thus needed closer regulation.[55]

Clearly though, it became plain to Congress that the Blacks codes attempted to nullify the effect of civil rights legislation and differentiate treatment between "white citizens" and "black freedmen," now called citizens. This brought about the need for another constitutional amendment to define the tenants of citizenship, what citizenship meant, and how citizens were to be treated, meaning given their "due process," to pursue the rights of freedom and to be "equally protected" under the law. For the very first time in the history of the United States, Blacks would be defined as citizens, by constitutional law, and so stated in the Constitution of the United States.

The prevalence of Black Codes led Congress to put a check on the unequal treatment of Blacks in the remaining non-readmitted Confederate states. Congress passed the 1867 Reconstruction Act, which divided the south into five military regions and sought to insure that they would not be re-admitted to the Union until they first ratified the 14th Amendment, that put a stop to Black code laws by stating that, "no state shall make or enforce any law which shall abridge the privileges or immunities of citizens of the United States; nor shall any state deprive any person of life, liberty, or property, without due process of law; nor deny to any person within its jurisdiction the equal protection of the laws.[56]

Finally, 81 years after the Constitutional Convention first framed the definition of Africans in America as "three-fifths of a human being," this partial designation was repealed and replaced by the definition of "citizens," as anyone born in America, including Blacks, who shall be equal to Whites-with the rights and privileges of Whites-with an emphasis on "equal protection under the law," became a part of the U.S. Constitution for the very first time in the history of America.

54

3

The 14th Amendment and Its Roots of Resistance to Equal Treatment

"We are four million, out of 30 million who inhabit this country, and we have rights as well as privileges to maintain and we must assert our manhood in their vindication."

Pinkney P.S. Pinchback, 1837-1921
First Black U.S. Governor during Reconstruction

The passing of the 14th Amendment represented a defining moment, not only for Blacks but, for America. It sought to set straight the flawed and benign language of the Constitution's framers, by addressing the fractional language of "three-fifths" of all other persons that came to be silently, but commonly, associated with the status of Blacks. It also established a baseline for defining equality, equal treatment for all, due process and equal protection under the law. This brought forth a resistance to acknowledging the equality of Blacks, as well as, a pattern of societal attitudes and social behaviors that sought to differentiate Blacks from Whites, in the context of citizenship.

While one could argue that "three-fifths" was most specifically associated with the enumeration of slaves, the social construct both in the North and the South was such that Blacks were not seen as equal to Whites, whether their status was slave or free, and in many instances, free Blacks were often treated no different than slaves. The body politic of America was such that the question of citizenship, and U.S. Supreme Court Chief Justice's Roger B. Taney's declaration in the *Dred Scott* decision that "Blacks are not citizens..." had become a matter of fact in the eyes of most Whites, and a constant point of contention, for newly freed Blacks in that period of Reconstruction.

Just as Lincoln's Emancipation Proclamation was celebrated in the north, and in nations abroad, as an act of decency and good will-though it was more a strategy for colonization of Blacks than the liberation of Blacks, it was perceived as an assault against whiteness, or as interpreted by the South, as "a great violation of faith" that ought to exist between leading classes, between people of the same blood. Confederate President, Jefferson Davis, called it "...a measure by which several millions of human beings of an inferior race, peaceful and contented laborers in their spheres, are doomed to extermination, while at the same time they encouraged a general assassination of their masters, by the insidious recommendation to 'abstain from violence unless in necessary self-defense" in a speech to the Confederate Congress, two weeks after Lincoln's decree.[1] The 1866 Civil Rights Act was also passed by Congress, in an attempt to confer "official" citizenship rights on Blacks. This was, particularly in the South, where states sought to hold to its Civil War racist character regarding the equality of Blacks and sought to extend those views and attitudes well into Reconstruction.[2]

The Radical Republicans controlling Congress, on the heels of passing the 13th Amendment abolishing slavery, sought to give legislative protection to the four million freed men and women, in the midst of a states rights movement to impair the equality edicts of the federal government, through the passing of slavery-like state laws enforced as Black Codes. The issue at hand was simply, "did freedom for Blacks mean equality for Blacks?" If so, then the second question, succinctly put, was, "how would black equality be demonstrated?" Congress surmised that it would be demonstrated in the form of citizenship rights.

At the same time Congress was trying to give legislative Reconstruction protection to vulnerable Blacks, the newly sworn in President, Andrew Johnson, was advancing a reconstruction plan of his own, which included restoring the citizenship rights of Confederate soldiers. In the first of two proclamations issued on May 29, 1865, President Johnson offered a blanket pardon and amnesty to all participants in the rebellion against the Union (except 14 classes of

56

Southerners who had to apply to him individually). These included Confederate officials and owners of taxable property (worth more than $20,000) who pledged loyalty to the Union and support for the end of slavery. Their oath would restore their citizenship rights, and have return to them all property confiscated by the Union during the war-except for enslaved persons.[3]

While history has reflected this action on the part of Johnson as resisting efforts of Congress to repatriate Blacks, Johnson's pardons were really only one of the many policy initiatives proposed to be carried out by Lincoln, had he lived. Lincoln, attempting to stem the rage and demoralization of Whites in rebel states over the Emancipation Proclamation, announced his plans for reconstruction. In December, 1863, he issued a proclamation, called the Proclamation of Amnesty and Reconstruction. This proclamation, commonly called Lincoln's "Ten-Percent Plan," offered full pardon and full restoration of all rights to white southerners who pledged total loyalty to the Union and accepted the abolition of slavery.

Like his successor's plan, Lincoln's plan excluded high-ranking political and military Confederate leaders. Once the newly sworn Southern loyalists in any rebel state reached ten percent of the number of voter's in the 1860 election, they could call a convention and establish a new state government to replace the old government, as long as, its new constitution included the abolition of slavery.[4] However, Lincoln's plan offered caveat's that slavery-type laws could be temporarily passed to control freed slaves "consistent…with their present condition as a laboring, landless, and homeless class."[5] Johnson, in some regard, was only carrying out the will of Lincoln, with his own unique twist, of course-that being, restoration of property.

This, of course, put those former confederates directly at odds with freedman and women, who were receiving confiscated lands distributed through the Bureau of Refugees, Freedmen and Abandoned Lands (historically known as the Freedman's Bureau), created by the Freedman's Bureau Act, passed (also vetoed by President Johnson and further overridden) by Congress, at the same time the 1866 Civil Rights Act was passed. The second proclamation set up a provisional government in the state of North Carolina that became the model of governance for the rebel states of Mississippi, Georgia, Texas, Alabama, South Carolina and Florida, while each was negotiating re-admittance to the Union.[6] This would directly pit the President's plan against the efforts of Congress, inasmuch as the President would appoint the

Provisional Governors loyal to his view of the role the federal government should play in and how Blacks and their rights were to be perceived in the society.

Using his State of the Union address in January, 1866, President Johnson suggested that the restoration of civil government represented what he saw as the end of Reconstruction efforts, and that nothing more needed to be done, except to admit southerners back into the national government.[7] Johnson sought to ignore the state of over four million Blacks that had been released from centuries of bondage, without so much as a dime. However, Congress sought to acknowledge and rectify, on some small level, the social and economic state of Blacks by passing the nation's first Civil Rights Act, as well as, the Freedman's Bureau to help Blacks adjust to freedom, and assist in the social and economic transition that would be required to make Blacks equal.

Johnson disagreed and vetoed both the Civil Rights Act and the Freedman's Bureau, because he thought that the act gave preference to Blacks, while discriminating "against the white race." He surmised that the Bureau wasn't necessary, since civility had returned to the South. Furthermore, the federal government wasn't in the business of providing food, clothing, shelter and education to Blacks.[8]

Africans born in America had not received any financial considerations during, or upon release from slavery-not even the minimal stipends that were paid to American enslaved Africans when slavery was abolished in the District of Columbia. President Johnson duly noted that Congress had engaged in a social welfare role for Blacks that it had never done before, not even for Whites. At the same time, he refused to acknowledge that no other race, including indentured Whites, had experienced such an institutional system of bondage, and that such a social role was necessary to repair some of slavery's damage. Johnson resisted that argument. Instead, he chose to focus on the benefits that freedman would derive from the government's assistance to their new status. This was not lost on Johnson, who, born of the poor white laborer class, stated pointedly at the actions of his party's Radical Republicans; "Congress has never felt itself authorized to spend public money for renting homes for white people honestly toiling day and night, and it was never intended that freedmen should be fed, clothed, educated and sheltered by the United States. The idea upon which slaves were assisted to freedom was that they become a self-sustaining population."[9]

Certainly at the forefront of Johnson's objections was the land

grant discussions, the famous (or infamous) "40 acres and a mule" proposal, making its way through the Congress. The discussion, led by
Pennsylvania Radical Republican Congressmen, though reflective of
only a small group of Whites, was a resurrection of the action taken by
Union Army General William T. Sherman. After winning major war
victories and confiscating Confederate land in Savannah Georgia, up
through the coasts of South and North Carolina, Sherman issued
Special Field Order No. 15, temporarily granting each freedman's family forty acres of land to be permanently bestowed to them by
Congress.[10] Some 40,000 former slave families received this forty acres,
and actually settled on abandoned and confiscated land of former slaveholders for several months, until President Johnson negated the order
with his Reconstruction plan pardons. In less than a year, some 7,000
pardons were granted that allowed many former property owners to
reclaim their lands from freedmen-many forced off their "homes" at
bayonet point, by the same Union soldiers they had fought with to
return the South to the Union.[11]

This time, Thaddeus Stevens, in arguing for land reform and
armed with statistics to back his proposal, suggested that one million
freedman families should be given 40 acres of land from the 394 million
acres held in ex-Confederate states by 70,000 of the richest slaveowners, as well as publicly held federal lands.[12] The 40 million acres that
would be granted to ex-slaves would be only a fraction of what would
still be retained by the states, Stevens argued. This didn't include the
homesteads then being offered in the Western territories at 160 acres
per settler-four times what Stevens' proposal was offering freedmen.[13]

In comparison, the Homestead Act of 1862, was passed by
Congress to encourage western expansion and the development of the
country, by giving any person (in this instance, male or female) 160
acres of free land, if they were willing to live on the land for a minimum
of five years and improve the land. The act sought to provide "every
poor man" a farm, and Congress granted 80 million acres to a half million families under this act.[14] The Homestead Act, however, targeted
largely White and Eastern European immigrants (Russian, German,
Scandinavian). Blacks were generally ignored for two reasons: First,
because the citizenship rights (including property rights) were still new
and being called into question by most Whites as well as state and local
governments. Secondly-and most importantly-most of the country
resisted selling property to Blacks, even federal government controlled
property. Whites in general asserted, in the collective, societal attitudes

that sought to maintain a racial status quo that objected to the notion of a class of property holding Blacks.[15] Property, of course, has been the historical basis for "an American's" full citizenship rights, including voting and holding office.

President Johnson's assertion that Congress had never done anything of the such for poor Whites wasn't exactly true. He just didn't want anything of the such, whether it was on an equal or unequal basis, done for the benefit of Blacks, particularly as an act of Congress, thereby attempting to racialize his argument to gain support from those who held similar sentiments. In this regard, he succeeded, as most of the members of Congress couldn't see giving every ex-slave family land and thus, "the forty acres and a mule" proposal never gained momentum enough to be even brought to the House floor for a vote. Granting land to all former slaves was even too radical for the majority of Radical Republicans, but support for the Freedman's Bureau held, and its land distribution program would serve as the basis for addressing some of the land needs of Blacks.

A point to note, however, is that Blacks did not get completely locked out of government homestead programs, as they understood that acquiring land was crucial in securing both their economic and social parity with Whites. As the federal government opened up public lands in southern areas where Blacks were more populous, they were able to access land grant programs.

At the same time that Johnson was fighting Congress' Reconstruction Plan, in particular--the Freedman's Bureau Act and the Civil Right Act of 1866, Congress also passed the Southern Homestead Act in June of 1866. This particular law specified that those southern public lands were not to be distributed to southerners who had taken up arms against the North, and designed principally to benefit former slaves "to let them [the Negroes] have land, in preference to people from Europe, or anywhere else."[16]

Under this act, Alabama, Mississippi, Louisiana, Arkansas and Florida offered eighty acres of land to the head of each family, regardless of race. In the first year, former slaves not only held homesteads in all of the southern states covered under this act, but made significant land acquisitions; 160,960 acres of homesteads in Florida, 116 out of 243 homestead in Arkansas, and by 1874, black families owned more than 350,000 acres in Georgia.[17] However, the homesteads were relatively small in size, which meant that they were not attractive to northern Whites or immigrants, and they were generally of poor quality. As a result, only 4,000 of four million Blacks in the south made application for homesteads covered under the 1866 act.[18] These land acquisitions were nowhere near enough, and nowhere close to what Blacks were entitled. The biggest "equality" barriers Blacks faced in Reconstruction were in purchasing land and in voting-Johnson's other worry.

In President Johnson's opposition to the 1866 Civil Rights Act, he argued that Congress was doing for Blacks what it had not done for "numbers of intelligent, worthy and patriotic foreigners" who must wait five years, become familiar with American institutions and demonstrate "good moral character" before being naturalized as citizens.[19] President Johnson, couching his biased views in a "equal treatment" discrimination argument, further cited that the "avenues of freedom and opportunity" were being "suddenly" opened to Blacks, before their penchant for self-governance could be demonstrated. President Johnson, who didn't see freedom as citizenship, nor Blacks as equals, or potential voters, rationalized, as if also predicting the future, that if Congress could legislate a citizenship act enumerating civil rights for Blacks, it would lead to Congress legislating other equality-based franchise rights such as the right to vote, and the right for Blacks to hold office.[20]

Thus, he viewed the Civil Rights Act of 1866 as a slippery slope that would not stop at citizenship. Arguing for the wrong reasons, he was correct in his assessment of Congress' legislative intentions and the ultimate outcomes that would be derived from those intentions. The bill was declared a step toward concentrating all legislative power in the national government, and an attempt by Congress to use "Social Equality" to over-ride state jurisdictions, on the question of race and equality between Whites and Blacks.[21] Thus, declaring that the bill provided "for the security of the colored race safeguards which go infinitely beyond any that the General Government have ever provided for the white race," Johnson promised a sure veto, if Congress sent it forward. Which they did.[22]

The language of the Civil Rights Act of 1866, which was actually the Civil Rights Act of 1865, but was vetoed, as promised, by President Johnson, and not over-ridden until early 1866, gave specific and directed emphasis to the newly acquired social and political status of Blacks, as persons-not property, as well as, the others rights therein conferred. For the first time in the history of the United States of America, an American law directly stated that Blacks were citizens.

The act also delineated and detailed what that meant, in terms of Blacks having the right "to sue, be parties, and give evidence; to inherit, purchase, lease, sell, hold, and convey real and personal property," as well as, the right to "full and equal benefit of all laws and proceedings, for the security of persons and property, as is enjoyed by white persons," which Congress assumed included voting. The act could not have been plainer, put in its simplest terms, that BLACKS WERE NOW EQUAL TO WHITES. Most Whites, however, rejected that notion, both in the North and the South-particularly in the South.

As social and political reaction to black societal inclusion attempted to racialize citizenship and rationalize whether or not freedom meant equality, the Civil Rights Act of 1866 sought to eliminate any rationalizations that sought to differentiate equality rights by clearly stating that there was no difference in citizenship rights. Simply stated, Black's rights were the same as White's rights. Of course, Whites didn't see it that way, and challenged the constitutionality of the 1866 Civil Rights Act, the first of its kind in the history of the United States. Thus, Whites in the South, and in the North, continued to create social and political barriers to challenge Black's right to work, right to vote and right to full enjoyment of the benefits of an open and free society.

This caused Congress to institute one its most drastic legislative attempts to assert equal protection for Blacks under the law, the Reconstruction Act of 1867. This action on the part of Congress divided the rebel Southern states into five military districts, under federal authority, whose interim governments served at the pleasure of President Johnson, with the instruction that they were to be re-admitted to the Union after they had ratified the Fourteenth Amendment.[23] It became more evident to the Radical Republicans that their efforts to legislate equality could not override established prejudices, including those of President Johnson. Johnson chose provisional governors in the unconstructed states who were typically among the old Whig elite. They favored few changes in the South's pre-war society. None of whom supported civil equality for Blacks-and as a result, none of the "Johnson Governments" allowed any Blacks to vote, not even a handful of property holding Blacks (as Johnson had initially instructed).[24]

Continuing with suppressive doctrines like the Black Codes and biased social attitudes that demonstrated a high animus toward Blacks, Congress proposed and initiated the ratification process for the Fourteenth Amendment, to reinforce the language of the 1866 Civil

Rights Act, in affirming the citizenship rights of Blacks.[25] That meant that black citizenship was not just a federal law, but part of the U.S. Constitution, ratified by the states, and its acceptance would also be the defining stipulation for outstanding rebellion states (of which there were still negotiating with the terms of Reconstruction) to be readmitted to the Union. All post Civil War definitions of equal treatment and equal protection of citizens, and in some instances-non-citizen legal residences, visiting residents and illegal residents-stem from the 14th Amendment.

Aside from the Bill of Rights, the Fourteenth Amendment is considered the most legally defining, the most articulate and constitutionally enforced piece of legislation in American society today. Certainly, it is the most relied upon for interpreting the lengths and limits of individual rights and government protections, within a society of equals. The Fourteenth Amendment, proposed in Congress, at the same time as the Civil Rights Act of 1866, but ratified two years, later in 1868, is five clauses long. The time of its ratification was the longest supplement ever added to the U.S. Constitution. It is written as follows:

Section 1: All persons born or naturalized in the United States, and subject to the jurisdiction thereof, are citizens of the United States and of the State wherein they reside. No State shall make or enforce any law which shall abridge the privileges or immunities of citizens of the United States; nor shall any State deprive any person of life, liberty, or property, without due process of law; nor deny to any person within its jurisdiction the equal protection of the laws.

Section 2: Representatives shall be apportioned among the several States according to their respective numbers, counting the whole number of persons in each State, excluding Indians not taxed. But when the right to vote at any election for the choice of electors for President and Vice President of the United States, Representatives in Congress, the Executive and Judicial officers of a State, or the members of the Legislature thereof, is denied to any of the male inhabitants of such State, being twenty-one years of age, and citizens of the United States, or in any way abridged, except for participation in rebellion, or other crime, the basis of representation therein shall be reduced in the proportion which the number of such male citizens shall bear to the whole number of male citizens twenty-one years of age in such State.

Section 3: No person shall be a Senator or Representative in Congress, or elector of President and Vice President, or hold any office, civil or military, under the United States, or under any State, who having previously taken an oath, as a member of Congress, or as an officer of the United States, or as a member of any State legislature, or as an executive or judicial officer of any State, to support the Constitution of the United States, shall have engaged in insurrection or rebellion against the same, or given aid or comfort to the enemies thereof. But Congress may by a vote of two-thirds of each House, remove such disability.

Section 4: The validity of the public debt of the United States, authorized by law, including debts incurred for payment of pensions and bounties for services in suppressing insurrection or rebellion, shall not be questioned. But neither the United States nor any State shall assume or pay any debt or obligation incurred in aid of insurrection or rebellion against the United States, or any claim for the loss or emancipation of any slave; but all such debts, obligations and claims shall be held illegal and void.

Section 5. The Congress shall have power to enforce, by appropriate legislation, the provisions of this article.[26]

64

The first two clauses of the Fourteenth Amendment give specific focus to America's social reconstruction, as it relates to the citizenship status, rights and privileges of Blacks. While, the second two clauses give specific focus to America's political reconstruction and the status of affairs associated with former Confederates serving the newly reconstructed Union, and absolving the Confederacy's war debt. The first two clauses of the amendment were of the most historic significance. The first clause placed new restraints on the states for the first time since the Constitution was ratified in 1790, and it put in place constitutionally protected procedures and safeguards that prohibited the states from treating any individual or class of people as inferior to any other.[27] The second clause, while not giving Blacks the right to vote (as Congress would ultimately be forced to do with a 15th Amendment, two years later in 1870), it gave incentives for allowing Blacks to vote (in the South). It also set in place sanctions against the states that didn't comply-again, largely targeting the race politics of the Southern states while almost ignoring the subtle but effective disenfranchisement of Blacks in the North, due to their fewer numbers.[28]

In exchange for social reconstruction compliance, Congress

allowed pardoned Confederates to hold federal office, and forgave the Confederacy war debt, by picking up the tab on rebel soldiers war pensions and widow's benefits. This still didn't allow the 14th Amendment to gain the support of President Johnson who sought to fire officials he accused of "Africanizing the South."[29] His firing of Secretary of War, Edwin Stanton, in defiance of Congress' recently passed Tenure-of-Office Act, caused Johnson to become the first U.S. President to be impeached, as politically motivated as it was, tried in the Senate, and almost removed from office. This was the beginning of the end for Johnson, who was almost assuredly a one-timer. Equal rights for Blacks, including full suffrage, would guarantee that Blacks would play a significant role in electing a new President in the upcoming elections of 1868.

The 14th Amendment, however, represented much more than the reinforcement of citizenship for Blacks, and the elimination of the "duality," "plurality" and other degrees of citizenship-i.e., federal versus state citizenship or free (White) versus freed (Black)-in this gray period of America's social and political Reconstruction. Though just five simple clauses, this one amendment covered and reinforced a breath and depth of authority for the federal government in extending the federal "Bill of Rights" over the rights of states (the Supremacy Clause), and the right to enforce and give protection to anyone in need of having their rights defended. It defined privileges and immunities with respect to all citizens, including suffrage (voting) for all male adults. It set penalties for states in Congressional representation that failed to allow for universal suffrage, as well as, defined what due process is, and what represents in the context of equal protection under the law.

With clarity of equal rights law seemingly in place, Whites sought to use different methods to marginalize black equality. The most common was through the redefinition of social norms, meaning the social attitudes and behaviors that were meant to usurp the intent or meaning of the law without actually breaking the law (or where it could be proven that the law was broken).

The resistance to black equality and equal treatment under the law found its new roots, quite quickly, as a result of the class conflict of the rich and poor that was taking place in the latter 19th Century Agrarian movement, in what Howard Zinn termed as the "other Civil War."[30] Free market capitalism was being challenged, and subsequently overtaken, by monopoly capitalism in the Industrial Revolution.

65

Blacks sought to advance their social, economic and political agendas, which started during the pre-Civil War abolitionist movement. Inasmuch as, black abolitionists sought to go beyond white abolitionists' endorsement of black freedom and humanity, to assert their own humanity positions. Some suggested this was a "black militant" position, that included, 1) demanding black economic and political acceptance (integration) into America's government and economy, and 2) accepting Blacks as equal to Whites-fully capable of independent self-development and self-governance.[31]

Working class and poor Whites, by contrast, sought to try to find a place for themselves in this shifting egalitarian society that now forced them to compete for jobs and resources with rich capital interests on one hand, and four million former slaves on the other. Societal elites and industrialists whose main pursuits were building monopolies and concentrating capital, while forcing farmers out of their dominate position in the American economy, demonstrated a great deal of sensitivity to poor Whites on this issue on race equality.

The elimination of citizenship dualism facilitated a racial dualism that promoted a racialized hierarchy symbolic of the *Herrenvolk* democracies of Europe, where white men of a certain social or class standing were the only ones privileged enough to retain full citizenship rights in the society.[32] *Herrenvolk Democracy*, denoted ideology used in the United States and Apartheid South Africa, espouse full democracy for that society's dominant culture, or "master race" as it was then called, but was tyrannical for statistical minorities in the society. This partially describes the juxtaposing of gains by poorer Whites in political rights against the loss of rights by free and freed Blacks in the 19th Century.[33]

In this same context, the practice of *Herrenvolk Republicanism* began to emerge in the Reconstruction period, where fear of plots by the rich against those of the bottom strata of society where egalitarianism evaporates and class structures are reinforced. To eliminate the potential for class conflict, Blacks were moved out of the ranks of the producers, thus making it easier to deflect those differences between rich and poor Whites, and focus more on those differences between Blacks and poor Whites. *Herrenvolk Republicanism*, in a systemic and institutional application, had the advantage of fostering social attitudes that reassured poor Whites, whose biggest fear was downward social mobility, that one might lose everything in this period of capitalization and industrialization, except their *whiteness*.[34]

While not necessarily equal to them, rich Whites understood that America was founded on *herrenvolk* principles, and had, heretofore, been "white man's country" in its cultural mores, values and traditions, and that working class Whites were a part of that tradition. Blacks and their historical contributions, in their former "traditional" role as chattel property, in building this country, during slavery, while acknowledged as a "three-fifths" legacy, were, by and large, ignored, as was that notion that Blacks would now have rights equal to a white person-any white person. Thus, the resistance to equal treatment began.

Differential treatment of Blacks would come about in two ways (that are still, largely, in effect today), by contact and by contract. In his book, *The Anatomy of Racial Inequality*, economic theorist, Glenn Loury, details the specific strategies of creating inequities between Blacks and Whites that found its roots in the inter-racial competition of the Reconstruction Period. In what he calls "elemental distinctions" in these two kinds of behaviors, Loury explains the term: Discrimination in contract "is meant to invoke the unequal treatment of otherwise like persons on the basis of race in the execution of formal transactions-the buying and selling of goods and services, for instances, or interactions with organized bureaucracies, public and private. Discrimination in contract, in other words, is a standard means by which reward bias against Blacks has been effected." Loury explains the second term, discrimination by contact, as "the unequal treatment of persons on the basis of race, in the associations and relationships that are formed among individuals in social life, including the choice of social intimates, neighbors, friends, heroes and villains. It involves discrimination in the informal, private spheres of life.[35]

Part of that "discrimination by contact" strategy was perpetuated through a constant barrage of distortions about Blacks, their ability to be civilized (challenges to their humanity), their ability to be socialized (mainstream interface with Whites), their ability to be intellectualized (educated) and their ability to control their passions with respect to Whites (anger over slavery, sexual fascinations or innate desires stemming from slavery's sexual politics). Reconstruction had not eliminated the race caste established during slavery. Slavery in its various manifestations, from voluntary servitude to involuntary servitude, from indentured (contract) slavery, that included Whites to permanent slavery that was exclusive to Blacks, and the transition of enslaved persons from humans to chattel property, created a separateness between Black and White that both Presidents Lincoln and Johnson were forced to acknowledge. In recognizing the inevitable (the fall of slavery), both sought to avoid the question of how to equalize a society that no longer permitted Whites to have absolute control over Blacks. Lincoln sought to avoid the question of equality through colonization. Johnson sought to avoid the question of equality through racialization, or maintenance of the status quo-meaning the promotion of societal control, economic domination, and political power vested in white supremacy.

The origins of white supremacy were rooted in the superior/inferior relationship of racial inequalities between Whites and Blacks in the Antebellum era where slavery dictated inter-racial politics. Whites' resistance to equal treatment during Reconstruction was largely centered in the superior/inferior complex that carried over into society from slavery. The mindset of Whites remained as it had been in the past, in terms of feeling that they were better than Blacks, irrespective of this new shift in legislative protocols. The attitudes of Whites, with respect to Blacks were still tied to slavery, even though there were no more slaves. It was a mindset in the South that associated freedmen as "once a slave, always a slave" because slavery had transitioned into a "white master/ black slave" institution. Slavery inextricably associated whiteness with power, blackness with powerlessness; whiteness with goodness, blackness with badness; whiteness with intelligence, blackness with stupidity; whiteness with morality, blackness with immorality; whiteness with beauty, blackness with ugliness; whiteness with adult behavior, blackness with child-like behavior, and most importantly, which speaks to the ideology of white superiority and black inferiority in the establishment of a hierarchy associated with the race caste Whites were seeking to continue in Reconstruction, whiteness was associated with competence, while blackness was associated with inadequacy.[36]

Though Whites knew and understood that the freedmen were smart and competent enough to run their plantations and be hired out as skilled servants during slavery, Blacks in Reconstruction were suddenly intellectually inferior and socially inadequate to Whites, if it meant they would be allowed to compete in society as equals. Thus, Blacks were stigmatized in ways that created doubt about their societal capacities in the more gracious cases, and created outright fear in the common cases. Southern Whites, who were quite familiar with Blacks in the former master-slave relationship during slavery, suddenly became xenophobes in the Reconstruction era, whereby Blacks became foreigners and strangers in their own country-one they were seeking to claim ownership of, but was socially rejecting in its equality claims.

In avoiding contact with Blacks, when at all possible, and by stigmatizing their presence in society as over-dependent, undesirable, unsophisticated, and incapable of public trust and self-governance, small farmers and poor Whites were able to separate their agrarian social and political interests from those of Blacks, though they were of the same economic class. Different treatment by contract resulted in Whites imposing disparate, unequal and revocable conditions on Blacks in any agreement Whites would have with Blacks, thereby marginalizing how Blacks could engage on a free and equal basis in their social, political and economic dealings during Reconstruction. These contact and contract barriers would be set up in every facet of the new society, not because the federal government wanted these barriers to exist-but because social attitudes of the period caused them to exist, and many got their cues from the attitude of the President of the United States himself. W.E.B. DuBois' assessment of President Johnson's treatment of Blacks in his book, *Black Reconstruction in America, 1860-1880*, capsulized the nation's hostility against Blacks and black equality in a nutshell, stating,

"For the Negro, Andrew Johnson did less than nothing, once he realized that the chief beneficiary of labor and economic reform in the South would be the freedmen. His inability to picture Negroes as men made him oppose efforts to give them land; oppose national efforts to educate them; and above all things, oppose their rights to vote. "[37]

The right to work, the right to be educated, and the right to vote all became "separation points" that allowed Whites to receive "inherent" social benefits, differentiating their citizenship as unquestionable "inalienable rights" while Blacks were forced to pursue legal and legislative remedies to derive and openly receive such citizenship benefits. Further resistance to equal treatment for Blacks was centered in a racial animus (innate racial hostility) that carried over from the slavery and the Civil War into the Reconstruction Era, whereby the prejudices Whites had for Blacks would be magnified in the public discourse-in print, in commercialization of products. This allowed Blacks to become socially stigmatized in ways that undervalued their social capital and alienated their participation in even the most basic public enjoyments.

The politics of this process known as "Jim Crowism," which will be discussed in the next chapter, transitioned the legislative politics that were straightforward in context, but were either being ignored,

69

or misinterpreted, in ways that forced Blacks to seek clarification in the public discourse, in the legislature and in the courts. During the implementation of a largely invisible systemic process, Blacks' very presence amongst Whites became highly scrutinized, and subsequently came to be disdained, if the social interface between Blacks and Whites were not on an unequal basis. Race equality was decried, and the new culture of raceless egalitarianism was subtly (at first) being transformed into a culture of race based superiority-through the engagement of social behaviors and attitudes that would ultimately bring about a more rigid and vicious society of racial supremacy, politically and economically advantageous to Whites, while being socially and humanly demeaning to Blacks. Blacks in Reconstruction were not totally ignorant of what was taking place. In witnessing the legislative/executive branch conflicts around a series of Radical Reconstruction Acts passed in the first six months of 1867, each overriding a prior Presidential veto, including the Freedman's Bureau authority to distribute land to Blacks at a fair price, Frederick Douglass asserted that it was the duty of the federal government to assure that freedman had a place to go in this period of so-called freedom and equality, and that Blacks were politically and economically protected from the racial animus directed toward them, stating:

"The Negro must have a right to the land. Without land, he would be completely dependent upon the old slave owners whose object was 'to get as much work for as little pay as possible.' It was impossible for the freedman to obtain land on any fair terms from the former slave owners. These men don't want them to have land. They want to keep them poor and dependent."[38]

Douglas then went on to urge Congress to legislate easy payment terms for the masses of freedmen to purchase land, asserting that it was the duty of the government "to see not only that the Negro has the right to vote, but that he has a fair play in the acquisition of land; that when he offers a fair price for the land in the South, he shall not be deprived of the right to purchase, simply because of his color."[39] Douglass, and others, knew that the "play" was, if left up to Southern Whites to advance equality rights for Blacks, including rights to compete with them for land and vote, it would never happen. There was too great an animus present for most 19th Century Whites to see clearly in regard to this equality politic.

Racial animus, as studied in the 20th Century, is reflected as an intangible factor in measuring biased behaviors and racial attitudes that come out at certain times when inter-racial dynamics occur. For instance, in the case of a white-black encounter, a white voter voting for a white candidate over an equally or better qualified black candidate, or a white juror determining guilt of a black defendant, or a white employer interviewing an equally qualified black job candidate, or a white salesperson waiting on a black customer. While one could generally deny any outward racial prejudices, their unconscious choices, predisposed actions and innate biases, would indicate otherwise. In the example of the white/black interface, the animus surfaces when Whites are given a choice other than Black-be it White, Asian or Latino. They will make a choice, ordered according to their racial preferences, irrespective of other considerations like qualifications or facts in evidence.

Yet, in the 19th Century, such animus came about as a variant of several factors; First, the Civil War and Blacks fighting in the Union cause; second, hostility over the abolition of slavery and anger due to the loss of land and chattel property that ensued; and third, but most importantly, the competition that arose between freeman (Whites) and freedman (Blacks, with little differentiation given to those Blacks who had always been free and those Blacks who had been freed by manumission, emancipation or the abolition of slavery). White indentured servants and those poor Whites of the working class went through great lengths to differentiate themselves from the politics of slavery, any designations associated with slave labor, and any association with any terms that suggested they were or had been a slave. Thus, the use of language in society became a vital tool in establishing the barriers of "equal treatment" resistance.

As it became more necessary to distinguish one's self as suitable for labor in a transitioning economy, the term "mechanic," whose original definition in the 1829 Webster's Dictionary was neutrally descriptive as "a person whose occupation is to construct machines or goods," by Reconstruction had become a term pridefully applied to white workers, though there was little denying that black workers, former slaves and free Blacks could do craft labor.[40] In the Antebellum period, white mechanics sought to define their status in the labor force through the use of terms like "hired hands" instead of servants, and called employers "boss," instead of "master," to establish clear differences between those who were free to contract out their skills to whomever they pleased, and those who were leased out for labor. By establishing themselves in society as freemen, an evolving identity that suggested that inherit "payoffs" of whiteness, and at the same time, fighting for the term, *freeman* (versus *freedman*) in defining their status in society, making it impossible to not use race in the construction of class identity.[41]

This was key in establishing differences in equal treatment, "by contract," because skilled labor received higher wages than unskilled labor. As the formation of unions came about to protect the *right to work*, as well as workers rights against the suppression of wages by industrial capitalists, *freemen* gained membership, while *freedmen* were excluded. When Blacks were allowed to work, it was under disparate constraints and for less money than would be paid to Whites. Economic subjugation strategies used to justify paying Blacks less and marginalizing their wealth building capacities was principally centered in limiting Blacks to sharecropping and other roles as dependent agricultural workers, while excluding Blacks from the industrializing sector of the economy. The transformation of the black slave to the black sharecropper was strategic, inasmuch as it involved everything from creating myths that Blacks were not equipped to work with machines, to establishing a principle way of differentiating white and black laborers, via the degree of mechanization involved, to putting in *de facto* bans on the hiring of Blacks in factory work.[42] This point will be examined in more detail in chapter four.

Discrimination "by contact" was largely imposed in two key areas; First, through the exclusion of Blacks in societal memberships (unions, churches, business and fraternal groups) that build social, political and economic networks. Blacks were not seen as "brothers" in the labor movement, and were often put at odds with white workers, both in competition and collective bargaining situations. It also put a limit on what Michael C. Dawson, in his book, *Behind The Mule: Race and Class in African-American Politics*, terms as "life chances," those opportunities that allow for empowerment, be they political, social or economic, that come about as a result of racial groups seeking to pursue racial group interests. As in discrimination by contract, economic subjugation played just as much a significant role in contact discrimination, by insuring that racial group interests were maximized by and for Whites, while suppressing the economic group interests of Blacks, by socially, and when possible-politically, isolating them.

This pattern of economic subjugation, and the political basis for which such patterns existed, in terms of the social consequences that were directed at Blacks that pursued "equal" economic interests-particularly economic interests that crossed racial lines, became fixed during the Reconstruction Period; and were seared into the memories of African Americans, well into the 20th Century.[43] The quickest way to bring danger or death, to an individual, or even a whole Black township, was to compete for "white" jobs, or pursue what was considered "white wages," in attempts to "live white," meaning for Blacks to try to live equal to Whites.

These tenets of racial inequality didn't always work then, nor do they in the 20th and 21st Century, but they worked enough to create barriers that established clear and distinct differences in treatment between Whites and Blacks, and ultimately created social and economic gaps in the quality of life between Whites and Blacks. Political empowerment was viewed then, as in present day, the best way to close social and economic gaps. Clearly, this was the focus of the Radical Republicans legislative agenda. They may not have wanted to make Blacks equal, but they did want to close the gap and attempted to make Blacks self-sustaining for a limited period in time.

Efforts to gain full voting franchise rights for Blacks during this highly racialized period brought forth a host of stigmatizing images, meant to incite white passions and conjure up the worst possible characterization of the African American and his/her roles in the general society. Because Blacks were banned from being educated during slavery, African American illiteracy rates were 95% at the time slavery was abolished in 1865.[44] Their lack of literacy and their educational ignorance became issues that Whites used as justifications for black inequality. Black socialization and their ability to adapt to the social protocols were questioned, as well as, whether or not Blacks had the emotional self-control to be self governing and socially responsible.

This assertion was centered in what Southern Whites, in particular, saw as a desire on the part of black men, oversexed, as a result of the breeder mentality that was part of the sexual exploitation and economic (property) benefits immersed in the domestic slave trade (after the Trans-Atlantic Slave Trade was banned in 1808) to miscegenate. Thus, the black man's forced sex labor orientation now made him a threat to the civility of America's social order. Once mostly viewed as docile and trustworthy during slavery, the black man was seen just a for years later as violent and unpredictable, and whose only preoccupation was to miscegenate with white women. Thus, no white woman was safe from the beastly oversexed passions of the former slave, less she be raped and stripped of her societal purity. An image of the black man that Frederick Douglass late in his life, would call "a myth" and a societal ploy to disenfranchise African Americans, in order keep

73

a low public esteem for the moral character of black people, thus inhibiting their social elevation and entitlement to full citizenship.[45]

Other images of Blacks, like "Jim Crow," which came to signify the racial protocols of the Post Reconstruction social construct, representing southern Blacks in an Antebellum context as lazy, shiftless and irresponsible, and "Zip Coon" that made mockery of northern Blacks' attempts to educate, acculturate and assimilate themselves into white society, created a stigmatization of the black image that became prevalent throughout the Reconstruction Era, and well into the 20th Century.

Whether commercialized on food and household products, or humored in traveling minstrel shows, the African Americans' attempt to acquire a dignity in citizenship was undermined. Particularly in entertainment, where art and life often imitate, and even transcend, one another.

Never was this more demonstrated than in minstrel shows, where blackface white entertainers provided solace and relief to poor white workers in the midst of an industrial revolution that challenged their egalitarianism, but not their Anglo-Saxonism. Blackface whiteness, devoid of positive content, that both delighted and unified wage-earning urban masses, was seen as an invisible way of undermining the black image because, as entertainment, it could be respected as everything-rowdy, rebellious and respectable, or it could be denied that it was anything-in terms of its intent to deconstruct the dignity of the black citizen.[46]

One thing that could be said about the appeal of blackface and the post-Civil War 'coon songs" that they promoted; that minstrels popularity stemmed from their ability to project those Black values and action that aroused both fear and fascination among Whites.[47] But at the end of the show, minstrels could always clean up and return to their white selves, into a society that embraced what David Roediger called a "common whiteness." The blackface gave the minstrel stage the ability to foster ethnic diversity, even during periods of anti-immigrant hysteria.[48] Minstrel shows promoted, even prided "ethnic" whiteness while racializing, even condemning, through mockery, the conditions and circumstances of blackness. Thus, Blacks, in the relational context to Whites, were to be either feared or mocked, but under no circumstance were they to be considered equal to Whites, even if their social, economic and political lots were the same.

In the final analysis, what stigmatizing the black image sought to do was to vilify notions of black equality as ridiculous and absurd-and provide rationalization for the argument against black suffrage. By casting African Americans in the most extreme social context and imagery possible, white society was inferring that "they are not like us; they are not equal to us, and they should not be able to vote with, and/or govern us." That was the underlining message. The vote for Blacks was clearly in jeopardy. Public sentiment was only about to take a turn for the worse, because of two events; the re-admission of most of the rebel states, and Blacks voting in their first national Presidential election. Both were seen as threats to the current Reconstruction "status quo," one in a negative way, the other in a positive way.

By Spring of 1868, with seven states having satisfied the conditions of returning to the Union, principally ratifying the 14th Amendment in their newly seated state legislatures, the United States Senate voted to re-admit Alabama, Arkansas, Florida, Georgia, Louisiana, and the Carolinas at the end of June, leaving Mississippi, Texas and Virginia still in limbo, but having enough votes, after seating the new representatives to declare the 14th Amendment ratified.[49] However, with the readmissions of the southern states came the return of states rights, and the powers enjoyed with the return of home rule. America has always been a "states rights" nation, giving the states to formulate and maintain their "local cultures," which is what gave rise to and the protection of slavery for 250 years-up to that point.

With states now in control of their own governments, the southern states were also in control of the rights and privileges states enjoyed before the Civil War, and whatever forms of governance the states set up for themselves. Whatever qualifications the states had set up for voting, including how they allowed Blacks to vote, were no longer under federal jurisdiction and therefore, of no legitimate concern. The public sentiment among Northerners was that the South would use state powers to institute a new reign of white supremacy.[50]

These concerns were valid and, the premonitions correct. It would have a negative impact on universal black suffrage down the line. Objections to black suffrage was still fragmented. Blacks understood that their voting rights were, and had been, under siege during the Johnson administration. The platform position of the Democrats for the 1868 Presidential election advocated against universal male suffrage (black men voting). Yet, Blacks were position to use their vote, as sporadic as it was-and in the face of rising intimidation factors (that will be discussed in the next chapter), to support of the Republican

75

Party candidate, Ulysses Grant-for several reasons.

First, the Democratic nominee, Horatio Seymour, went on record condemning the Republican party's policy of Reconstruction, and gave specific criticism to the notion of Negro suffrage, calling it "unconstitutional," "revolutionary," and void." This made Grant, literally, the only choice for Blacks.[51] This posture also went against what was occurring in the newly re-admitted state conventions being held to replace the military governors appointed by the Reconstruction Act of 1867, for the purpose of writing new constitutions that would meet requirements set by Congress. One of which was that all male citizens of the state be registered to vote before the convention be held, and then when their own newly elected legislatures, by universal suffrage, had ratified the 14th Amendment.[52]

In nine Southern states-Alabama, Arkansas, Florida, Louisiana, Georgia, North Carolina, South Carolina, Virginia and Mississippi, some of the most progressive state constitutions in the history of the south were being drawn up in convention that included black and white delegates, as well as, franchising to common people regardless of race or color, public education and social legislation for the poor.[53] While actions taken by these former rebel states were seen as progressive, they were not necessarily actions taken by southerners themselves. The new governments were controlled by what historians have called "Alien Republican Party governments" that were controlled by three elements: white Northerners-called "Carpet baggers" because of their carpet sack luggage-who came South to take advantage the land homesteads; a minority of Southern born Whites-called "Scalawags," because they were openly sympathetic to black equality, and were-supportive of the newly imposed federal military government, seen by most southerners as an alien authority over former confederates to insure no further insurrection; and newly enfranchised black men, many, who had been free-rather than slaves-before the war.

This constituted the "new southern majority" that gained the majority legislative seats, largely, because the bulk of the south's "true" white residents sat out the federally mandated and military supervised state elections. This was due to the fact that, since they could not control the election-they knew they couldn't win these elections, nor maintain their pre-war political/social norms.[54]

Secondly, the 1868 election represented a referendum on progress of Reconstruction and support for the continuance of the new southern governments. A vote for Seymour meant a vote against "the new way," and a return to the old ways of the South, that weren't necessarily beneficial to poor Whites either. Thirdly, this election represented an affirmation of the black vote, the first of its kind and a demonstration that Blacks could determine the future of the country through public discourse and directed action.

Blacks no longer had to appeal to the sentiments of progressive Whites to carry their varied interests. The interests of Blacks were now interlocked with the interests of common Whites, representing an opportunity to elect Grant, with such a decisive victory, and such an overwhelming majority, that any sentiments of confederate traditions would be put to an end. The duty of progressive Americans was to produce a vote, in the words of Frederick Douglass, "so pronounced and overwhelming as to extinguish every ray of hope to the rebel cause."[55]

Lastly, and most importantly, this election represented an opportunity for Blacks to demonstrate their loyalty to Grant, in a way that Grant would be reciprocal, in appointing Blacks in his administration, and provide for an incentive for Grant to preserve Reconstruction and black suffrage, whereby no future governments would exist in America without the political involvement of African Americans. Grant did, in fact, make giving Blacks suffrage and protecting them in the process a priority, as well as, trying to convince Southern Whites to accept a "racially mixed society," while also getting Northern Whites to accept moderate Reconstruction policies, without alienating them.[56] Grant knew what Congress also knew that Reconstruction efforts to enfranchise Southern Blacks didn't impact Northern Blacks, where much of the disenfranchisement barriers that existed in the south, were pervasive in the North.

To address the inequities of this "Northern Hypocrisy" being imposed on Southern states, which allowed the prevention of Blacks from voting in the North without the same level of scrutiny that the South received, Congress proposed the 15th Amendment. By adding this amendment to the list of requirements to be re-admitted, and affirming "the right of citizens of the United States to vote shall not be denied or abridged by the United States or by any state on account of race, color or previous condition of servitude," most of the Southern legislatures ratified it. Although, significant states like California, Delaware, Kentucky, Maryland, Oregon and Tennessee did not.[57] Without the Southern states, the 15th Amendment would not have been ratified, giving further credence to the lack of passion the Northern states had for black suffrage. The North's push for so-called black equality, the abolition of slavery, the establishment of citizenship, in the final analysis, was not tantamount to pushing for black voter enfranchisement. The true Southerners, in recognizing the North's passivity-even insincerity-in this regard, didn't take long to find ways to undermine the direct intent of empowering Black voters. By the time the 15th Amendment was ratified in 1870, Whites were clearly resisting the "black equality" movement, on many fronts. One way was to continue to demean Blacks in ways to separate them from Whites, by not giving them the respect of social entitlements and personal salutations afforded to each other.

The protocols of Whites addressing each other as "Mister," "Madame," and "Miss" were not extended to Blacks. Because the deviations from the historical traditions of the south that had governed regular racial interfaces angered and even frightened Southern Whites, many reverted to addressing Black men as "boy," Black women as "girl" (or "gal"), and it was not uncommon to provoke racial confrontations by referring to Blacks as "niggers."[58] Not only did Whites seek to create unequalness by referring to Blacks vis-a-vis informalities that were common during the Antebellum period, such as calling Blacks by their first name with no salutation acknowledgement, many agitated Blacks by repeating the offenses as Blacks sought to engage the equal respect that Whites were not only afforded, but expected. It was not uncommon during this period to hear Black men correct, and even demand that they also be called, "Mister."[59] This represented a refusal on the part of White to acknowledge equality and the refusal on the part of Blacks to accept inequity.

It was these confrontations that caused some Southern Whites to suggest that Blacks were becoming "Uppity," as a result of these new rights, and began to bring forth a societal resistance that would lead to the end of the Reconstruction.

4

"Redeemers:" the Ku Klux Klan
And the
Compromise of Reconstruction

They can put him in a smoking car or baggage car-take him or leave him at a railroad station, exclude him from inns, drive him from all places of amusement or instruction without the least fear of the national government interfering for the protection of his liberty.

- Frederick Douglass

The benefits of Reconstruction, in spite of inconsistent applications of equality policies and frequent spurts of societal resistance, produced significant gains for the status of the African American. The Reconstruction Amendments; the 13th Amendment abolishing slavery, the 14th Amendment extending citizenship to Blacks, as well as due process and equal protection under the law, and the 15th Amendment, guaranteeing the right vote, offered the necessary constitutional protections to make Blacks full and equal partners in American society. The gains Blacks received were many. Congress, led by the "Radical Republicans" and the legacy of Lincoln-aside from the fact that colonization, not equalization, was the late President's desired legacy for addressing "the Negro Problem"-sought to legislate equality, equal treatment and equal protection under the law in every way they could.

Aside from making acceptance of the Reconstruction Amendments mandatory conditions for re-admittance to the Union, Congress passed several critical pieces of legislation that made enslaved

Blacks' transition from slavery to freedom a lot easier than it wouldn't have been had the legislation not existed, or had popular, though silent, sentiment on the new status of Blacks prevailed.

From the outset, at the end of the war, Congress sought to address the question of black citizenship by passing the Civil Rights Bill of 1865 (passed in 1866 as a veto over-ride). Also in 1865, the Freedman's Bureau, was set up to support refugees-Black (employment, education and homes for freedman), and White (transportation and home for those displaced by the war). Although, initially not funded by Congress, the bureau provided far-reaching benefits for Blacks, that included furnishing supplies, providing medical services, establishing schools, supervising labor contracts between freedmen and their employers, and managing the leasing and selling of confiscated or abandoned lands to former slaves.[1]

Between 1865 and 1869, the bureau had issued 21 million rations of support-five million rations going to Whites, 15 million plus going to Blacks, set up 46 hospitals-with bureau staffed physicians, surgeons and nurses-spending more than $2 million to treat more than 450,000 cases of illness, and spent more than $5 million in the schooling of 247,333 ex-slaves in 4,329 schools set up by the bureau.[2] Schools set up during this period included money to set up teaching colleges and vocational schools, including Howard University, that allowed a first generation of Blacks to pursue professional and industrial career with some level of academic certification and/or credentialing-which was important, as Blacks were being forced to apprentice in skilled professions, even though they had years of experience.

The federal government issued in 1865, a vehicle for Blacks to set their wages in a banking institution, similarly named the Freedmen's Bank. This first attempt to engage the African American in the mainstream economy of Reconstruction America would serve as a sampled demonstration of the collective economic capacity of Blacks. The bank was established specifically for Blacks-though headed by a white man appointed by the federal government, William Booth, and staffed by all white cashiers in its first few years. It had thirty four branches throughout the nation, with only two branches in the North (in New York and Philadelphia), and totaled $3,299,201 in deposits by 1874.[3] The bank aided Blacks in financing land loans and facilitating business start-ups.

Reconstruction forced Blacks onto the voting rolls in every state in the Union. With the assistance of the Freedman's Bureau and the army, by 1867, universal franchise was complete throughout the South. African Americans totaled over 700,000, in comparison to about 600,000 Whites, with five states; Alabama, Florida, Mississippi, Louisiana, and South Carolina having more black registrants than white, even though, Blacks only represented a majority of the population in the last three of those five states.[4]

Blacks immediately understood the power of the vote. When the states held their elections to call for constitutional conventions and to select delegates, while many southern Whites boycotted the election, in protest of Carpetbagger-Scalawag-Black coalition seeking to install a new southern social order. However, Black voter turnout was nearly 80% and out of 1,000 state convention delegates elected in the various states, 265 were Black. 107 of them born into slavery.[5]

By the time the 15th Amendment was passed on March 30, 1870, the full inclusion of Blacks was so euphorically celebrated that it was heralded as everything from "the Nation's second birth," to a "greater revolution than that of 1776," accomplished by a 100-gun salute in the nation's capital on the day ratification was announced.[6] The political empowerment that followed was a demonstration of full equality, in the truest sense, as African Americans elevated their social status through the engagement of political representation-an extension of their newly guaranteed voting power. The sudden and, in some cases, massive appearance of the black elected official, while sporadically in evidence prior to 1870, came about as a direct result of the full empowerment of the 15th Amendment. Between 1869 and 1901, two black U.S. Senators, Hiram R. Revels and Blanche K. Bruce, the only Black to be elected to a full term in the state during the 19th Century-both were from Mississippi-and twenty black House members served in the Congress.[7]

Blacks made their first appearance in the Forty-first Congress in 1869 when three Congressmen were elected. Five were elected in the 42nd Congress. Seven were elected in both the 43rd and 44th Congresses-which represented the peak of black representation in the federal legislature.[8] In all, almost three-fourths of the Blacks in Congress during the 19th Century, 14 House members and both Senators, were elected at the height of Reconstruction, after the passing of the 15th Amendment. Hundreds of Blacks were elected to state legislatures and statewide offices. Blacks held a majority in the lower house of the South Carolina state legislature. They were closely equal to Whites in the Louisiana state legislature, where Blacks also elected

81

three lieutenant governors, including one, P.B.S. Pinchback who served as governor for 43 days in 1873, when the elected governor, Henry C. Warmoth, was removed from office.[9] Mississippi also elected several black statewide officials, including A.K. Davis as lieutenant governor, James Hill as secretary of state, and T.W. Cardozo as superintendent of education, all elected in the same year of 1873.[10] Black legislators focused their legislative efforts on initiating public school systems, to address high levels of illiteracy, creating greater relief through the Freedman's Bureau, reforming state jury systems, improving voter education and suffrage (ballot) access for Blacks

    As much of an opportunity for equality as legalizing voting, via the 15th Amendment, may have created, it still did not offer African Americans the total protection necessary to bring about full access. Though Reconstruction would not end until five years later, when President Rutherford B. Hayes withdrew federal troops from the South, offering no civil rights protections to Blacks, as early as 1872, Northern reconstructionist had grown weary of the fight to give full protections to Blacks.

    As President Grant began to send federal troops less frequently to respond to acts of violence and violation of the rights of Blacks, the less protection they had from residual hostilities of former Confederates. While Blacks' civil rights were being denied, the restoration of civil rights was given to, less a small few ex-officers and government officials of the former Confederacy, the overwhelming majority of ex-confederates. The last institutional support mechanism to provide federal support to Blacks, the Freedman's Bureau, was abolished. This period of what was seen as "federal coercion" of giving Blacks equality was slowing coming to an end.[11] Northerners became increasingly preoccupied with what Historian, Howard Zinn, called "the other Civil War," the rise of Industrialism, and the class battle between egalitarian, agrarian interests and rich industrialists who were buying up the 50 million acres of land Congress had set aside under the 1862 Homestead Act that made land available at $1.25 an acre--$200 minimum, more than most common interests could afford, and tailor-made for speculators and railroad interests.[12] Combined with focusing on the politics of Western expansion, Northerners finally were more willing to allow Southern Whites to become the arbiters as to the limits of Black rights, and solvers of its own race problems-absent federal intervention.[13]

    Southern Whites, on the other hand, had great resentment for the Republican Radicals who instituted political and social reform by

82

force. Southerners saw Radical policy initiatives as "Yankee-inspired" and punitive toward the South, particularly new programs to raise taxes on real estate that had been lightly taxed before the Civil war. It was most difficult for Southern Whites to accept the Republican dominated state governments that were reflective of a new racial regime that conflicted with the 250 year traditions of slavery that made it difficult for them to accept a black person as political equals to Whites.[14]

The South became the battleground between political forces of the "Pre" and "Post" Civil War eras, the former-all white, all southern traditionalists, all slave, and anti-equality; the latter, Black and White, anti-slave, anti-southern tradition, and pro-equality. Those Radical governments that succeeded, for a while, in bringing change to those states where Southern traditions were most deeply entrenched, and black political representation was most in evidence-namely, Alabama, Mississippi, Texas, Florida, Louisiana, and South Carolina, began to lose their hold as efforts increased to "redeem" the South from what southerners viewed as "Black Republicanism."[15]

The politics of "Redemption" involved southern conservatives seeking to drive out Republican influence in the South by taking control of the newly redeemed state legislatures and local governments. They called themselves, Redeemers, and they used the power of "home rule," constitutional powers reserved for the state, in ways that neutralized the influence of the Radical Republicans at the federal level, while using local influence to strategically defeat Republicans within the state. Redeemers understood that local governance and local cultures were such that the federal government could not supervise every facet of state. Redeemers understood the new state power demands, and constraints on the federal government, of dual federalism that made the feds and the states sovereign in their respective spheres of authority. In ridding Southern urban cities, with large black populations, of Republican control, conservative, mostly Democratic Party driven policies in the state legislature was seen as the single most important factor, if urban Redeemers were to triumph. Cities were the creations of the states, and final power rested within the state's political sphere of authority-not the federal government's.[16]

The process of redemption, started by southern conservatives and national Democrats, determined to "redeem" southern states, was not just from Radical Reconstruction, but from the politics of black equality, and specifically with the intent of shifting social, political and economic benefits back in the control of the various societal forces of

83

"white supremacy." The most blatant lawful technique used by Redeemers was simply to remove Radicals from office, and either appoint their replacements, or provide for new elections. This strategy was used against Southerners, the precedent established by the military, when setting radical controlled governments during Congressional Reconstruction.[17] The objectives of redemption were accomplished by a mixture of fraud, intimidation and, most importantly, legislative manipulation, with the goal being the severely weakening of black political influence, through a return of a targeted disfranchisement of Blacks.[18]

Redeemers gained office by the use of changing voting procedures in local elections. They made allegations of illegal Negro voters (out of town/state) that couldn't be verified as a means to restrict Black voters. Local election laws were thereby repealed, disempowering Blacks. State legislative gerrymandering was used to change local district boundaries, and local law enforcement and election officials arrested Blacks and white Radicals who allegedly gave false information or, for interfering with officers in the conduct of their duty-when challenged, only to have the charges dropped after elections.[19] Gerrymandering was clearly the most effective technique to undermine the Radicals, and disenfranchise Blacks. It excluded them from familiar districts or voting places, and was made even more effective by state supported legislative changes in the requirements for voting.[20]

State powers were used to create barriers to voting, which included grandfather clauses, poll taxes and selective literacy tests, mostly imposed on Blacks. An array of reasons were used to keep Blacks, and sometimes Radicals, from voting, by tightening voting requirements, like voting at a specific site, establishing residency in the state six months before elections, in the county three months before election and the voting ward (district) fifteen days before election. If any step was missed, voting was denied.[21] These changes in voting policy were rarely made public to Black communities until election day.

Redeemers used trickery and technicalities to discount votes in black precincts in some elections, while in other elections, they used straight out fear-xenophobic fears that the alleged inferiority of Blacks was not being emphasized enough. Although, in its absence, racial peculiarity-the notion that the presence of Blacks among Whites and the push to empower them in roles of authority over Whites, was outside the cultural norms of the majority population who regarded America as "White Man's Country." America was meant to be a government and a society run by, and for the benefit of, Whites who actively sought to exclude Blacks by denying them power, wealth and position, and even condoned mistreating Blacks by perpetuating racial violence, riots and lynching-was advanced in its stead.[22] The promotion of thought that Blacks were, in fact, peculiar-if not inferior-not only stressed the racial differences between Blacks and Whites, but also stressed innate inequality differences which legislation sought to close, but that many Whites viewed as useless, given the perception of differences in human nature and social incompatibility held by Whites. The fear created by impending federal legislation that would provide public enjoyment rights for Blacks that would, in effect, "force" Whites to socialize with Blacks, in most instances, against their will, heightened social stigmatization of Blacks, and provided further justification for Whites to act against "equalization" policies that promoted racial interaction.

This fear of association with Blacks called, "Negrophobia," as it was written in *the Independent*, "is a prevalent characteristic of the white American mind."[23] Public attitudes, fueled by southern "Redeemers" clearly (if not silently) affirmed sentiments that increasingly weary and apathetic Northerners, who had advocated for black freedom but, did not view Blacks as their equal. Suddenly, public discourse turned to how this incessant prejudice toward African Americans could be solved. And just as during the slavery abolition discussions, colonization, though more impractical as a solution to "the Negro problem" than it was during slavery, represented the broadest discussion. There were some segments of the public discourse that felt that subjugation (subordinated citizenship under the authority of Whites) was the surest preventative measure to all out "race war" or extermination, if the races could not be kept separated, public sentiment being that "the extermination of the Negro is as sure as that of the Red Man."[24]

As Republicans sought to continue to push enforcement legislation on the federal level, two things occurred. First, Senator Charles Sumner, who was considered Blacks biggest advocate of equal rights in the Congress, died on March 10, 1874. Sumner, who had sought to make Blacks "whole" after slavery by introducing land reparations legislation into Congress (which was defeated), was considered one of the last of the "old guard" Radical reformist, that left a huge void in the Republican reform agenda. There was no readily identifiable successor, and thus, his passing represented a changing of the guard, of sorts. The Republican party's past advocacy regarding the status of the Negro had died with Sumner and had rested into a present state of indifference.[25]

The second thing to occur was a massive shift in party control of former Republican strongholds in the elections of 1873 and 1874, where Democrats claimed both Congressional and State offices, both legislative and executive, in states that were once radically sensitive to "equalization" issues of the African American. Elections in Connecticut, Ohio, New York and Wisconsin produced election gains for the Democratic Party. Republican voters expressed their lack of confidence in their party by staying home or voting Democratic, demonstrating that, in spite of the beating Democrats took in 1872, their message of exploiting racial issues was proving effective.[26] This strategy proven particularly effective in upper South borderline states. Democrats regained control of the Arkansas state legislature, and recaptured both the governorships and legislatures of Texas and Virginia, setting the stage for what Republicans feared would be major losses in Congress in the North, stemming from the "bad odor" of advocating for "black rights."[27]

By 1875, redemption had reclaimed almost every local city and southern state in the Union. The impact of the redemption period was the spread of antebellum racial attitudes, and the promotion of unspoken racial sensibilities, even in the North. However, redemption encompassed the embitterment of the South who saw the presence of the freedman as "an impudent personal insult added to the ignominy of defeat," and viewed Northerners who turned their world upside down, "the bottom rung on top-the former slave now master," as Yankees who "hug and kiss the niggers, promenade the streets with them, and carry the black babies in their arms," in ways "to make a Christian curse."[28] Treating Blacks as equals was something white Southerners would never get used to, nor was the prospect of Blacks' voting, largely because both were viewed as acts of enfranchisement that were functions of Northern vindictiveness intended to humiliate and enfeeble the South.[29]

While this brought out a more flagrant practice of racism in the South, Southerners knew that, while Northerners were tolerating black political equality, they did not believe in social equality, harbored some of the same social prejudices and practiced some of the same forms of racial discrimination as were present in the South.[30] The politics of redemption helped bring these prejudices out. However, redemption would have not been as effective, without an enforcement mechanism, to serve as an object of focus, in demonstrating white resistance to the forced acceptance of black equality. This weapon was established early in the redemption movement and lasted throughout the 19th and 20th centuries.

A major weapon of "redeemers" was the Ku Klux Klan. Founded in 1866 as a Confederate veterans "social club," the Ku Klux Klan quickly turned into an anti-Black, anti-Radical organization that dawned hoods, mounted horsed and swooped down in the middle of the night, making fearsome noises and firing guns as they torched black homes, attacked and beat black militiamen, ambushed both black and white Radical leaders, intimidated black voters and initiated a phenomenon called "lynching." Lynching was an act of vigilantism, whereby legal due process was by-passed in exchange for society imposed "justice," largely imposed on Blacks accused of committing crimes.[31]

The origins of the Klan have been documented as starting in a law office in Pulaski, Tennessee around May or June, 1866, by six young Confederates from "good or well educated families," some of whom became lawyers and state legislators, who were in pursuit of the "excitements of wartime."[32] Formalization of their "club" came in its second meeting, and eight to ten members came together to establish a name and rituals for the organization. They wanted their name and identity to stand out and inspire query, to "attract attention without specifically asking for it, so they chose "Ku Klux Klan, "because of its alliterative content, and its uncertain meaning.[33] The name is a derivative of the Greek word, kuklos, "Ku Klux" meaning "circle or band," and Klan was redundant but added to catchy alliteration that founders wanted to get attention.[34]

The ritual of the Ku Klux Klan was also influenced by the Greek liberal arts curriculum. A host of academic and social fraternities throughout America's colleges drew on Greek names and rituals, and included Medieval titles like Grand Cyclops (President), Grand Magi (Vice President), Grand Turk (Marshal), Grand Exchequer (treasurer), and two Lictors (guardians of the meeting place-called the Den), as well as a uniform called "regalia" that consisted at the outset of a white mask with holes for the eyes and nose, a high conical cardboard hat, making the wearer seem taller and a long flowing robe. Membership, meeting places and rituals were sworn to secrecy to all persons of "the order," and their existence would come to the attention of outsiders only as they made their appearances in public, and in disguise.[35]

The genesis of the Ku Klux Klan was centered in a desire, on the part of southern white men, to find a place in the new Radical culture of the south, while creating a desire to belong to a more tradition-al southern culture of "days gone by" where white men, who ran the South, came from southern stock, and "niggers knew there place," refer-ring to the lack of social status and political standing Blacks had in the Antebellum period. Formalized as a "social club" to romanticize that period, the first years of the Klan are hazy, largely based on oral histo-ries.[36] But, in essence, while desiring to change local in its founding year, culture, there is no record of its members engaging in any of the violent activities that the Klan would become known for, though vio-lent sentiments were clearly present. At that point, members were nothing more than a bunch of local yokels coming together in small towns throughout Tennessee to celebrate the ambitions of the failed Confederacy. Although they had a desire to influence civic and politi-cal affairs, the Klan contributed little in its infancy, and its public pres-ence reflected "outrage [that] were relatively scattered and unorganized, by no means numerous," in contrast to what they would be in years soon to come.[37] As men of prestige and "Southern honor" sought to join their ranks, the Ku Klux Klan's stature and membership also rose. It wasn't until a year later, at a reorganization meeting in Nashville, around April of 1867, that the Klan sought to spread its influence beyond the borders of Tennessee, and more importantly to become a conservative symbol for "the redemption" of the southern states from Republican control.[38]

88

The one man that history has most commonly given credit to founding the Ku Klux Klan, and its rise to national prominence, is for-mer Confederate General Nathan Bedford Forrest. Soon after the reor-ganization meeting (though not present), Forrest assumed a three year term as the Klan's first state president, with a title called, the Grand Wizard. Forrest's qualification for the post was heralded, as he was the only one even considered-outside of former U.S. President Andrew Johnson, though the retired President's nomination for the post was more rumor than fact-because of his success as a cavalry leader during the war and one of the ablest field commanders of the Confederate Army, as well as subscription to the conservative doctrine of his peers that often, and forcefully, expressed which represented "a perfect embodiment of the Southern chivalric ideal and a perfect leader for the quixotic crusade projected by the Ku Klux Klan."[39]

Forrest's presence brought forth other Bourbon and ex-Confederate leaders, making its reach appear more widespread, more fully organized, more highly connected than it actually was, for the

Klan hardly extended beyond the state of its birth (Tennessee) and a few counties of north Alabama, before 1868.[40] However, that didn't stop the appeal the Klan had to the masses of men who heard about a secret society of white men seeking to "redeem" the south back into the control of white men. Many heard about the Klan through their Masonic affiliations, and because of the similarities of secret codes, grips, signs and passwords used by both groups, while having no direct connection, the two "orders" frequently overlapped in membership.[41]

The reorganization of the Klan under Forrest brought forth many changes, including a membership application process that sought to purge applicants and affirm ideology to the groups founding principles. Applicants were asked a series of ten questions, of which every member had to answer every question favorably, in the opinion of the order, to be admitted. Membership was restricted to eighteen years of age, and applicants had to be recommended by a present member and pass an oral examination. Once surviving "the screening process," the applicant had to take an oath of absolute secrecy regarding the order and those who belonged to it-under penalty that those who betrayed the secrets on purposes of the order would incur "the extreme penalty of the order's 'law.'"[42]

The questions were framed to elicit responses to whether an applicant ever belonged to, or subscribed to the principles of the Radical Republican Party, the Loyal League, or the Grand Army of the Republic; whether an applicant served in the federal army during the war and fought against the South; whether they favored, or opposed Negro equality-both social and political; whether they favored a "white man's government;" whether they supported re-enfranchisement of white Southerners and in directing animosity toward the federal government, applicants were asked whether they favored "Constitutional liberty, and a Government of equitable laws, instead of a Government of violence and oppression;" whether applicants favored "maintaining the Constitutional rights of the South"; and believed in "the inalienable right of self-preservation of the people against the exercise of arbitrary and unlicensed power."[43]

While it was Forrest's desire, and attempt, according to his own Congressional testimony a few years later, to be careful to select its membership among responsible white southerners, emphasizing that "the Klan admitted no man that was not a gentleman," and excluded men that were "rowdies and rough men...men who were in the habit of drinking, boisterous men, or men liable to commit error or wrong," and

89

the purpose, was to empower disenfranchised Whites with the right to vote, not eliminate Blacks right to vote.[44]

However, the Klan had become over-run with common men who saw the group as a tool to exact their frustrations out on Blacks and white supporters of Reconstruction and of black equal rights. Violence and lawlessness soon became associated with Klan activity. So much so, that Forrest resigned in 1868, over many of the acts Klansmen were being accused of, and sought to disband the group in 1869, soon after his departure, calling the Klan a band of "wild young and bad men."[45] But the group refused to disband, as white southerners had adopted a position to do whatever it had to do, extralegal and blatantly illegal, what they had not been allowed to do by law; return to a position of absolute control over Blacks, drive Blacks and their Carpetbagger/Scalawag partners from power in Southern government, and establish a social doctrine called "White Supremacy" that would not question their authority. The Klan, thus, had become too powerful and too useful a tool for southern Whites, to be easily destroyed.[46]

One of the first indications of the future impact and ultimate influence the Klan (and groups like the Klan) would have, came to light, in terms of extorting violence and intimidation, in efforts to repeal the black vote, and subsequently black equality. In the weeks leading up to the 1868 election, Southern Whites, having begun to create this "atmosphere" aimed at redeeming the South, began using "social groups" to influence civic engagements, like running local and state elections, and discouraging Blacks from going to the polls, by forming a number of groups that sought to re-instill a pre-war white supremacy.

The Ku Klux Klan wasn't the only group formed to play obstructionist roles in black enfranchisement. Other groups took names like the White Brotherhood, the Council of Safety, the Constitutional Union Guard, the Pale Faces and the Knights of the White Camellia, who was a secret order that was also very powerful in their own right-but clearly, the most frightening, fastest growing, most wide-spread and long lasting of these groups, by far, was the Ku Klux Klan.[47]

During the 1868 Presidential elections, Klansmen assassinated an Arkansas Congressmen, three members of the South Carolina legislature and several Republican members of state constitutional conventions. What further empowered the Klan was that many of their outrages went unchecked. Law enforcement could not deal with the totality and frequency of the violence, largely due to the fact that witnesses to these acts were often scared off from testifying.[48] Masked and hooded Whites rode through Republican strongholds, targeting Blacks and wielding knives, axes and guns, killing masses of Blacks, including women and children as many freed slaves still went to the polls in spite of white intimidation. These acts of the Ku Klux Klan were frequent enough to suppress Blacks' voting in Tennessee, Alabama and South Carolina, below 1867 voting levels, and created so much havoc in Louisiana and Georgia, that Republican officials rejected Grant's presidential campaign to prevent the further killing of Blacks.[49]

The Klan's anonymity and violent ferocity added to its stature, and because most of its acts were committed against Blacks and black sympathizers, there wasn't a huge public outcry from anybody, other than Blacks themselves. Under Union readmission came a Southern home rule, now under the influence of Redemption, that provided Blacks little choice but to seek protection from local law officials or the courts, many of whom were either part of the Klan's anonymity, or felt intimidated themselves, thereby acting complicitly, and reinforcing both the Klan's actions and its ultimate aim, the restoration of white rule and the maintenance of white control over Blacks, at all cost.[50] In many instances, when no governmental protection came, Blacks resorted to their constitutional right of self-protection by forming militias among black civilians and war veterans, many of whom retained their military weapons, to protect their communities. Others resorted to the same sort of tactical aggressions that the Klan imposed, including retaliations such as lynching the white killer of a black civilian in Victoria, Texas, and the shooting of a Confederate veterans in South Carolina, after he stabbed a black sergeant who refused to leave the railroad car where he was seated among white women, refuting historical speculation that Blacks were unwilling and unable to defend themselves.[51]

By 1870, the Ku Klux Klan had literally become synonymous with the Democratic Party in the South. With no visible ties, two organizations gained respectability, because Blacks and Republicans saw them as one and the same. Both groups took a public position against the equality rights of Blacks, that gave an aura of power that included lawlessness and vigilantism used to frighten supporters of black societal inclusion. The Democratic Party benefited from its loose association with the Klan, who was one of the biggest supporter and interest groups within the party, because the KKK served as an informal type of underground military that reinforced the two principle goals of both groups; 1) To return Blacks to the subservient role in the South's

91

labor force; 2) to end black suffrage through intimidation of Blacks, and by politically destroying supporters of Negro suffrage in the Republican Party.[52]

As a result of the constant barrage of death, threats, intimidation, outright trickery and violence that faced Blacks who sought to vote freely, Congress put in place a series of "enforcement" acts, detailing what authority the federal government had in enforcing the Fifteen Amendment. The first act passed was the Enforcement Act of May 31, 1870, banning the use of force, bribery, or any intimidation that interfered with the right to vote because of race. This focused on disfranchisement activity on the state and local levels, where refusal to count black votes, or miscount non-existent votes might occur, as well as, outlawing groups who might seek to travel on public highways, or on private property for the purpose of trying to injure or intimidate voters. If such allegations occurred and were brought to the federal courts, federal officials and military troops could intercede in local elections to supervise them and make arrests where necessary.[53]

The second act passed was the Enforcement Act of July 14, 1870, which gave greater strength that allowed for the monitoring of Congressional elections in cities of at least 20,000 in population, with policing authority to make arrests without warrants. The third act was passed on February 28, 1871, required written ballots and allowed federal judges to appoint election supervisors in each precinct in elections serving 20,000 or more. The fourth, and only "force act" to be directed at a specific segment of the population, was called the Ku Klux Klan Act or the Enforcement Act of April 20 1871. It outlawed the Klan and other groups that conspired to deprive citizens of their civil and political rights by interfering with their voting, or the due process trial rights to seek their rights in court. The fifth and last act, the Enforcement Act of June 10, 1872, gave election supervisors the right to monitor rural elections, but restricted their involvement to observing, lacking authority to arrest violators, or to interfere with local authorities who were carrying out the election process.[54]

Congress also launched a federal investigation into the Klan that produced hundreds of arrests and indictments against some of the South's most prestigious citizens, including doctors, lawyers, ministers, college professors, businessmen and other professionals. These led to federal trials in Mississippi, South Carolina and North Carolina that forced many of the Klan's more blatantly violent activities underground, but did not discourage support of the South's most influential citizens from continuing the Klan's reign of terror.[55]

The combination of Redeemer politics and Klan intimidation was a prescription for political disaster for the Republican Party and Radical reconstruction. Saddled with economic depression, unpopular Reconstruction policies that sought to "equalize" Blacks and Whites, and charges of rampant corruption caused massive losses of Republican offices in the Congress and state legislators. However, President Grant took particular notice of the outcomes in the South, where eighty-nine were Democrats elected to Congress, and only seventeen Republicans, largely due to the widespread violence of the Klan, and a new white supremacist group, the White League, who practiced "Redeemer" politics, that kept Blacks from the polls in massive numbers.[56] If the off-year elections were any indication that Reconstruction was under assault, the Presidential elections of 1876 would solidify its demise as Redeemers, having quashed the Radical movement in taking over Congress, set their eyes on removing Radical influence on the Presidency.

As Reconstruction began to unravel, Blacks still sought to pursue equality to the extent they could, and tried to up hold the law, as they refused to submit to Klan violence. Where Blacks were in positions of authority to uphold the law, they did. Black judges issued arrest warrants for those involved in Klan activity, and black sheriffs and soldiers didn't hesitate to arrest, and even shoot Whites in authority who broke the law.[57] This effort on the part of Blacks to defend themselves against socially condoned violence initiated the first of a series of race riots that occured between 1866 and 1898. Most occurred in the two years before the 1876 Presidential elections, and pitted white anger and black frustration-as one segment of society sought to deny the other's equality, while the other sought to save its equality. This "great wave of riots" of 1874-76 accompanied the white Democratic drive to "redeem" the South of Radical control, but more critically, to remove Blacks from participation in government as officeholders, officers of the law and as voters, to hedge their fear of what redeemers called, black domination of the South.[58]

Redeemer's influence also reached in the North, as Northern Whites began to retreat on their inter-racial society practices, by shunning and separating themselves from Blacks publicly, treating them as lepers, through practicing de facto segregation in housing, recreation and education, as well as excluding Blacks from areas of public enjoyment, like first-class hotel dining rooms, theatres and opera houses.[59]

93

Economic subjugation became more pronounced in the areas of employment and wage compensation. Black men were restricted to menial jobs like porters, night-workers, painters and cooks, losing many of their former positions as coachmen, barbers and waiters to Irish and German immigrants.[60]

The black entrepreneurial class also began to suffer labor, wage and contract injustices, promoting various forms of subjugation. Black farmers and planters, in particular, became the targets of legal and extra-legal devices to limit their economic freedom, usually free market "restrictions" in their sharecropping and farm credit contracts that penalized them, civilly and criminally, from moving from plantation to plantation, because of laws imposed on contractors (usually White) prohibiting one employer from "enticing away" his neighbor's tenant (usually Black).[61] Once a Black laborer or sharecropper took an advance deposit from more than one employer, the others pressed charges for "intent to defraud," which was a minor but jailable offense, paid the black laborers fine, and the laborer became indebted to the employer until he worked off the debt-getting the laborer's work for less than he would have gotten it, had it been contracted, a peonage form of "semi-slavery," with debt servitude characteristics that were illegal. Black laborers were forced to work one contract (farm) at a time, when they clearly had the capacity to do more, a clear intention to limit the economic earning potential of the laborer.[62]

Black farmers and sharecroppers also suffered financial bondage, through a credit system that forced them to borrow money at higher rates of interest than charged white farmers, and take a lien on their crop that was impossible to clear by the end of the year, requiring a new agreement to be entered into with the same disadvantageous terms, almost insuring some involuntary labor benefits to be gained by the contractor, or jailed for debt.[63] Blacks had nowhere to turn to, financially, and their options were further complicated by the under-mining of the one banking system set up to aid them.

The Freedman's Bank, which prior to the start of the Depression of 1873, had thirty four branches-thirty of which were in the South, and by 1874, had deposits in all branches totaling $3,299,201.[64] The panic of 1873 that caused the big financial houses to fail, took its toll on the Freedman's Bank, as its directors speculated with the bank's assets, leaving it with a series of bad loans that caused the bank to fail. It closed its doors at the end of 1874, depriving its depositors, which included black churches, benevolent societies and many individuals, most of their savings.[65] The suspicious failure of Freedmen's Bank still represents one of Black America's biggest tragedies that would cause a mistrust of banks by African Americans well into the 20th Century. Even 128 years later, when California Congresswoman Juanita Millender-McDonald called for an investigation into the failure of the Freedmen's Bank, the principle question remained: "What happened to the money on deposit of the many African Americans who never received a cent from the bank's liquidation.

The absence of an economic support system was devastating to black farmers and land owners, as confiscation programs targeted black owned property, and vigilantism of the Klan targeted black businesses. The impoverishment of poor Whites drove many to do work that was once exclusively held by Blacks. That brought forth a segregation and economic compartmentalization (Blacks doing the least desirable work), while allowing Blacks and poor Whites to earn similar wages in a depression era, but did not afford Blacks the same protections and work guarantees, as workers began to unionize against industry. It excluded Blacks from many of the unions-pitting them against their "white brethren" as "scabs" and strike-breakers" in labor situations that turned racial quite quickly. The African American had clearly become an outsider in his own country, and the dream of equality was fading fast.

Alas, the election of 1876 ushered in the end of radical reconstruction, under the guise of what was termed, "Sectional Reconciliation." Whites were now prepared to forgo the equality of Blacks, to take on the challenges of industrialization and capitalism that were impacting both the North and the South, to bring about a new era of prosperity. In other words, it was time to make money again. Both were now prepared to acknowledge that the nation fell out over the slavery issue, and on the 100th anniversary of the nation's birth-it was time to "reconcile their differences." The primary difference was equality and protection under the law for Blacks, as well as, Whites.

The two sections had remained divided over the query of what should be the equality status of Blacks in the Post slavery era. The North had nowhere near the passion over the issue of black equality that it had in abolishing slavery-largely because they didn't agree with it. Equality for Blacks was never a true pursuit. Freedom was the true goal, and freedom for Blacks was achieved. Northern Republicans were now forced to acknowledge that it would never be able to dictate race relations to the South, and as long as Blacks remained free, that was the best they could hope for.

The South, however, had not only reclaimed its culture, it had reclaimed control of its politics. With the politics of redemption having sufficiently marginalized the black vote, Blacks were viewed as little help to the Republicans' Presidential re-election efforts. The Republican Party saw Blacks as a liability to the party, and the politics of saving reconstruction and saving re-election were not complementary at this point. The Republicans were in danger of losing all but four of the Southern states. The two states Republicans still held, Louisiana and Mississippi-two states with the highest black populations-were literally in a state of lawlessness over conservative attempts to change voting and district lines, where Grant had to send federal troops to intervene to protect black citizens from white supremacy groups.[66] Another state, South Carolina, where Blacks formed militias to protect themselves against the Klan and the White League, had several conflicts, including the Hamburg Massacre, where Blacks and Whites were killed as Whites sought to restore, in the words of one Klansman, "the eternal fitness of things-a white man in a white man's place, and a black man in a black man's place."[67]

The 1876 Presidential campaign was frequently marred with outbreaks of violence as the two Presidential nominees, Republican Ohio Governor, Rutherford B. Hayes,, and Democratic reformist Governor, Samuel J. Tilden, from New York, each tried to distance themselves from President Grant's intervention in the South, even in the face of Republican party claims that the tenets of reconstruction were being violated by the South's efforts to return the same "unreconstructed" leaders to power that guided the Confederate states out of the Union.[68] They were right. This southern policy became an issue, in an election, where many issues didn't separate the two presidential nominees.

Tilden was considered "the more dangerous man" to elect to the White House, because of the Democrat's past decisions and personal traits, that included his temperamental indecisiveness, and physical disability. He was perceived as an uninspiring leader, while Hayes was viewed as energetic, faithful to the Union, supportive of the 15th Amendment, and was seen as a levelheaded, sensible man who appeared safer and sounder on the "great" issues.[69] Those issues being a commitment to reconstruction policy, and the equal protection under the law for all citizens, guaranteed by the 14th Amendment.

The election was a virtual toss-up, though it had been a fore-gone conclusion that Tilden would win after 16 years of Republican dominance, with Hayes and Tilden finishing in a dead heat in the electoral college, largely due to Hayes winning his home state, Ohio, where black voter turnout helped him carry the state. However vote results in three states, Louisiana, South Carolina and Florida, had been contested, where Republican officeholders threw out returns from counties where Blacks had been denied the right to vote, while Democrats from those states insisted that their votes represented the true "will of the people," and should be validated by Congress.[70]

The country faced a constitutional crisis, as there was no clear constitutionally sanctioned process in place, and neither party trusted the other to suggest a remedy that would not be decidedly partisan, depending on the party of the person in charge of the process. Both parties finally agreed to appoint a fifteen member commission, consisting of five House members, five U.S. Senators and five Supreme Court justices–each party having seven commission members with the fifteenth being chosen from the court by the four other justices, two of each who professed democrat and republican ideology.[71]

The justices chose independent, David Davis, who stepped aside, in favor of Joseph P. Bradley, a Republican that tilted the vote in favor of the Republicans, who after several eight-seven votes along partisan lines, confirmed the Republican electors that made Hayes the next President of the United States. Democrats, feeling that they had been cheated, moved to block the final electoral vote count in Congress, which almost turned into a use of force, where both parties threatened to take up arms again.[72] Before another Civil War broke out, Hayes met with Democratic leaders to work out a deal that would allow Hayes to become President, but would also free the South of the last remnants of reconstruction, the presence of federal troops.

In a backroom deal called "the Bargain of 1877," the terms of which were never made public, but the intent of which was perfectly clear. The new administration's policy would, in the words of a Kansas Republican Committee leader, "conciliate the white men of the South-put "Carpetbaggers to the rear," and say, "Niggers take care of your-selves," leaving none to wonder what Hayes gave up to be sworn in as President, a few days later, and within months withdraw federal troops in Louisiana, South Carolina and the rest of the South as a first order of business, officially ending radical reconstruction of the Union.[73]

The infamous Compromise of 1877 literally sealed the fates of

Blacks in the South, who were handed over to the most racist elements of the South, the same elements that had already partnered with the Democratic party to launch a campaign of "terrorism" designed to disfranchise Blacks, and subject them to political domination, and without any real economic power to establish self-sufficiency.[74] The Southern Democrats, who played several roles in destroying Reconstruction and redeeming the South, were now credited with saving white supremacy from the threat of Black domination, invigorating the South's white population who bought into the Democrats' new "white master class society" ideology, and their racist idea of a white controlled "Solid South," causing Blacks to be abandoned by any "friends" that were vestiges of Southern republicanism-for the sake of sectional reconciliation.[75]

By 1880, nine of ten southerners in Congress had served the Confederacy, either in army "grays," or in its short lived government, including eighteen ex-Confederate generals (the last to be pardoned and have citizenship rights restored, including property, representation and suffrage rights, to get back into the Union) and the former commander of a prisoner of war camp.[76] While the South was unsuccessful in their effort to dissolve the Union, they won the battle of states rights (home rule) and state cultures (race lines)-refusing to let the North dictate the terms of peace, a bi-racial society that neither really wanted, and an equality neither thought Blacks really deserved. The loss of the war and the institution of slavery was offset by the gains of "white supremacy" redemption (expanded by a representation bolstered by a citizen count that included Blacks-more political power than when the South seceded), and a new labor system that allowed for the continued domination of black workers-clearly more lasting victories that outweighed their short-term losses in the four year Civil War.[77]

The ideological racism left over from slavery had succeeded and combined with the institutionalization of racism. Blacks had been condemned to the role of scavengers of monopoly capital that was now overtaking free market agrarian capital of small white farmers.[78] Already suffering from a depression, and not particularly sensitive to the plight of Blacks, nor the competition they brought, Whites separated their interest from those of Blacks through violence and mechanization of agriculture. This fostered a politically inspired disfranchisement and segregation that reduced Blacks to a virtual pariah in the South, forcing them to migrate to an industrialized North, that also exploited their labor, and housed them in segregated slums.[99] Blacks in the North, and in the South, began to experience a separation and alienation from the white world that "loosened the threads of black life," soon becoming "Nobody's Negro"-a termed used to attach a stigma to the uncertain meaning of "free Black" status, over the next two decades, as Blacks "lost their cultural center," and fell into a state of "disorientation," and became wanderers, as they sought to migrate to parts of the country that would accept their presence.[80] There were few, as a new period of racial radicalism brought social stigmatization, political marginalization, public isolation and economic subjugation, replacing the "equality rights" Blacks had merited, earned, and engaged during the now fading radical reconstruction.

The end of Reconstruction represented the end of two of the three significant phases of national debate around the issue of racial equality that took place in the last half of the 19th Century but would influence the whole 20th Century. Unfolding between 1865 and 1896, these three phases, Reconstruction (1865-70), Redemption (1871-80), and Separation (1881-96), would be influenced by three dominate voices; inegalitarian white supremacists, egalitarian republicans and African Americans, who used every venue possible in thousands of national and local public forums-including public lecture halls, floors of state legislatures, the chambers of Congress, the Presidency, the Supreme Court, in local newspapers, books and pamphlets-to argue their positions of conscious, of rhetoric and of deception to reinforce their respective "cultural" value systems around the national question of what was, and should be, the "state of equality" in America.[81]

The first, and most significant being, Reconstruction, which, for the first time since the United States was founded, the institution of slavery was not part of the national fabric. Constitutional equality was guaranteed to all people born in the United States, including African Americans. The Reconstruction period sought to legislate social change, through political advocacy, that fostered a constitutional equality, which involved the passing of three Reconstruction Amendments. Amendments that facilitated freedom, citizenship and equal protection under the law, and franchise (voting), that brought about representation, but didn't change attitudes about the status of Blacks in the mainstream society.

The public debate around whether freedom meant citizenship, and whether citizenship actually meant equality with Whites led to the second period of national debate, which was Redemption. Redemption was a period of cultural "mass" resistance to "black" equality rights, and the social mainstreaming of the African American, the first of several that would occur over the ensuing 120 years, which sought to renegotiate the cultural shift that constitutional equality had initiated. Redemption also represented a period of extremes, where the birth of a common "cultural" vigilantism, selective interpretation, and legal manipulation undermined the intent of laws, causing equality to be ignored, obstructing the application of equal justice for all. The third phase, Separation, which will be discussed in the next chapter, served as the basis for the de jure segregation politics that would dominate the 20th Century, finally being challenged in the *Brown* decision, but never being appropriately resolved whereby true equality could ever be achieved.

"Separate But Equal" doctrine, legal race separation policy, driven by white supremacy attitudes, legalized the race caste in America and reintroduced dual (second class) citizenship and social attitudes constructing racial inferiority of Blacks, as a cultural fact of living in the United States. Known as "Jim Crow" segregation, "Separate But Equal" doctrine, while largely a Southern institution-though commonly practiced in the North, represented the second most damaging institution to constitutional equality, after slavery. The effects of Jim Crow segregation have been just as long lasting. The whole notion of "Separate but Equal," its social standing, political impetus and legal legitimization could be summed up in one word... *Plessy*.

5

Plessy

*It always surprised me to hear Southern racists talk about the sancti-
ty of Jim Crow, as if he had been around forever. Actually, he didn't gain full
strength until the years after Plessy v. Ferguson.*

- Roy Wilkins, former NAACP Executive Secretary

The period following Reconstruction, and the Redemption
phase that ushered out Reconstruction policies and practices, sought to
immediately correct the cultural shift that had taken place during that
time, particularly, in the seven years between the ratification of the
14th Amendment, and the passing of the last Civil Rights Act of 1875,
which sought to introduce African Americans into the mainstream of
American society, and "equalize" them, in terms of rights and privileges
extended to all citizens. Rights and privileges were often the measurable benchmarks of voting, working, property rights and education
rights, and most important-the right of liberty, the right to choose what
they're lot in life would be, and the freedom to pursue it-including the
freedom to live where one chose (freedom of movement between the
states), and the freedom to contract for their trade (pursue entrepreneurial and capitalist interests). Each represented measurable tenants
that were enforced through policy initiatives, largely driven by social
attitudes that could be identified, assessed, tracked and stripped, and
easily manipulated, on various levels. While manipulation of policy was
at its minimal from 1868 through 1875, and though radical
Republicanism was in control of the Congress and the Presidency, the
seeds of redemption, and the attitudinal shift that accompanied it,
began to grow in 1872, and by 1876 had grown into full bloom.

The "Redeemers" influence on the deal that confirmed
Rutherford B. Hayes, as the 18th President of the United States, can-

not be understated. The Democrats may have lost the Presidency, but they regained control of the South, and the discretion in which they could reinstall their "Southern way of life," the antebellum culture of a race caste system that re-established clear delineated lines of racial superiority of Whites over Blacks.

Once state control was reasserted, with the pullout of federal troops in the South, the highest and foremost priority of Southern Whites, former Confederates now in control of the Union governments they tried to replicate under secession and defeat during the Civil War, was to regain social control over Blacks. The quickest way to achieve this control was to pull the plug on social equality, first, by disengaging from Blacks in all social interaction, then by causing public isolation and societal alienation.

The politics of disengagement and alienation pulled the plug on the access to the "prefabricated structure of white culture," built on the labor and unpaid fortunes, through the lives and legacies of enslaved Africans, that afforded Black people a social, political and economic framework within which they could rebuild and reshape their lives, in a meaningful way, after 300 years of slavery.[1] The disengagement of Blacks from the white ways of life began at a time when black life was rushing into the white mainstream in unprecedented mass and strength, and caused, not just a physical separation that reduced interracial contacts, but an intellectual separation that made it impossible for Blacks to maintain a high level of awareness of the ever-changing white world that dominated massive industrial, economic and political shifts that were occurring at that time.[2]

The principle strategy used in this disengagement was through "Jim Crow" politics, whereby Blacks weren't excluded from society, at least not immediately, but were gradually and systemically separated from interacting with Whites, through an initial wave of measures that created separate facilities for Blacks and Whites. Jim Crow methodology sought to create the illusion that equality was being carried out, as long as, similar opportunity, similar access, and similar facilities were created for both races. Fearing that the federal government would intercede, if Blacks were completely driven out of Southern society, Southerners chose to simply separate, or *disengage* Blacks from white society, by creating an overlay of equality-in effect, shaming the federal government in creating the semblance of equality to pretend to follow the intent of the law, which would satisfy the federal courts, but, changing the letter of the law, transitioning an inter-racial society into a segregated one.[3] This Jim Crow politic was essentially the architect of a policy that would become known as, "Separate but Equal."

Slightly more than a generation after Reconstruction's end, "Separate but equal" policy completely characterized Southern and border state life, spreading like a ground fog in hiding racial discrimination, while preserving the white South's antebellum way of life.[4] Jim Crow segregation essentially became law that re-enforced racial disengagement. Moreover, Jim Crow politics built a white supremacy infrastructure that preserved the old master/slave system, and re-integrated white superiority ideology throughout the political and social fabric of an entire region, whereby African Americans did have the capacity to challenge white supremacy and the Jim Crow policies that, from the end of Reconstruction until the *Plessy* decision in 1896, spread like a virus-from community after community, county after county, in state after state, until "the virus" had overtaken the entire South, starting out as "custom" but eventually turning into the full force of statutory law, making Jim Crow "law" synonymous with what it meant to be from the South, and in the South.[5]

The sudden reversal and adoption of the overt racism that Jim Crow politics exuded were centered in a number of factors that targeted Blacks, representing both attitudinal and societal industry shifts in white society. The attitudinal elements were reflected in white society's growing anxiety over the hysteria tied to Black male sexual attacks, and held over resentment toward Blacks in their Union role in the South's defeat that caused, what the South perceived as "Radical misrule" during Reconstruction. Whites conjoined black freedom with white defeat, and saw Blacks' behavior as Reconstruction inspired "misdeeds and buffoonery" that made them targeted "surrogates" for hatred directed at the North, but also served as the impetus for unrestrained anti-Negro engagements on the part of the white population that became reflexive of the South's mental landscape.[6] Society's industrial shifts against the Populist movement of the 1880s caused white agrarians, largely small farmers, who broke their bi-racial alliance with black small farmers, not only making black farmers a convenient scapegoat for the movements political frustrations, but, allowing the interest that white agrarians had in railroad reform to ease the way for Jim Crow restrictions as a form of railway regulation.[7]

The most direct trigger of the initial wave of Jim Crow legislation, however, was the increasing unwillingness of Blacks to defer to Whites and their refusal the informal racial etiquette Whites were try-

103

ing to impose. A new generation of Blacks raised outside of the confines of slavery and unacquainted with the antebellum protocols of the
South came of age in a way where Blacks asserted themselves in the
face of these changing attitudinal and societal changes, raising white
concerns about out of control "uppity" Negroes during this period.[8]
Thus, the thesis of Jim Crow segregation laws was not just to force the
disengagement of, and the separation from America's black population,
but also sought to debase the character and self-esteem of Blacks, in
order to re-direct them "to their assigned place" in American society,
which according to this period of racial radicalism-was a place inferior
to that of Whites in America's social "pecking order." This period
introduced law to re-formalize America's race caste.

   This period of disengagement did not go unnoticed by Blacks,
who began to develop cultural norms of their own, in schools, in land
and in religion-that were never institutions of a shared reality, but
desires on the part of Black people, to share material and spiritual
opportunities that were the cultural benefits of freedom and equality-as
practiced by Whites, in America. However, the institutions created by,
or, for Blacks under Reconstruction, and largely sustained by white
benevolence and governmental support, began to lose support under
disengagement. These institutions, particularly schools, suffered sharp
declines in per capita funding, as well as, a withdrawal of white teachers whose teaching models for achievement in American culture. It
caused a loss of capacity on the part of Blacks to clearly perceive "white
ideals," and a mass evaporation of the resources necessary to pursue the
dominant culture's ideals and an institutionalized alienation that
resulted in, and solidified, a clear "economic" and "knowledge" separation between the white and black worlds.[9]

   The patterns of social segregation in the 1880s and 1890s may
have been increased by black self-segregation, caused by the growth of
black prosperity-the first black "middle class, so to speak-while giving
black communities some level of economic growth in the "anti-Black"
business environment of industrialization, though small relative to
Whites, animated Whites minds into believing that Blacks were out-
achieving Whites in a period where "whiteness" had taken on public
qualities in ways that it never had before.[10] Middle and poor class
Whites, worried about the increasing gaps in wealth equalities amongst
Whites, exacted their fears toward race rather than class, and sought to
preserve the privileges of "whiteness," not just in going about their daily
activities of riding streetcars, drinking at water fountains and using

public toilets, but in heightening attention to the "racial body" itself, by heightening function of racial intimacy and passing laws concerned with the intimate contact of physical spaces and things, like beds, forks, cups, water fountains, toilet seats, telephone mouthpieces, anything that had to do with things you put in the mouth, and/or places where you were naked, or physically exposed, became part of the "new segregation" mindset.[11]

Disengagement of this nature was more common in the North, which was keeping pace with the South in its separation behaviors, in housing, in education, in the workplace, and in the marketplace. Everywhere in the North, Blacks were being treated with contempt, denial of civil liberties and subject to immediate violence at the slightest instigation.[12] Alienation was growing fast, and now transitioning the integration that Reconstruction had fostered, as Blacks lost access to white culture and were forced to fill places with other Blacks in social institutions that Whites once held. First in schools, but then it extended, at various rates, to religion, civic affairs, politics, on farms, in commerce, in industry. It spread to the professions, in public spaces such as libraries, music, drama, the opera, the arts, restaurants, bars, ice cream parlors, burial grounds, and in transportation.[13] Alienation became the social politic and the re-enforcing attitude as Whites sought to eradicate the presence of Blacks from their social spheres- even in passing them during transit. And when they did encounter Blacks, Whites wanted there to be a clear understanding that Blacks were to be in a position of showing and exerting deference to them on these chance encounters.

Segregation served the agenda of both disengagement and alienation, because it separated white society from Blacks, as often as possible, and asserted white superiority as customary deference extended to Whites in any social interface with Blacks. Segregation developed in an unusually diverse pattern in one major area of life, where chance encounters with Blacks were most likely to occur, transportation. Blacks were effectively excluded from the social mainstream simply by the white power structures providing of separate travel facilities in the racial radicalism era's two dominant forms of mass transportation, railroads and streetcars.[14] Tennessee, which was the first Southern state to engage "equal" accommodation laws in the Reconstruction era, was the first to legislated racially mandated segregation in public transportation rooted in the "Separate but Equal" ideology.[15]

Whites, during this period of "racial radicalism," seemed unit-

105

ed in taking it upon themselves to bring about this cultural shift to help Blacks "find their place," and control their whereabouts at all times, as they did during slavery. The biggest threat to this cultural shift was the Black that had no accountability, or was considered "loose," in the context that Blacks were roaming the countrysides of this nation, to find a place where their equality could be exerted, and their rights respected. The "strange Black" then became a focus of alienation, as many Blacks got squeezed off lands and out of work, and became wanderers or "Nobody's Nigger." This vestige of slavery brought forth a form of heightened xenophobia that suggested that Whites didn't fear those Blacks they knew and maintained social control over-"Their nigras," so to speak-but "your nigra," the one they didn't know; the strange Black who had escaped, or was out of the control of somebody, was society's biggest threat to the security of white sanctity. The "nigger loose,"-the one without place, without the restraining and taming of a Black that represented legitimizing the white man's social control link to the white world-became the worse of all social crises in Southern communities.[16]

The ultimate goal of this period after the Compromise of 1877, was to, not only regain social control of every Black in the South, but reintroduce a twisted sort of cultural identification tied to the passivity associated with Blacks during slavery, the Sambo mentality, which Conservatives assumed were part of Blacks inherent nature-a nature they incorrectly surmised made them inferior to Whites and naturally subservient.[17] Of course, out of the benefits of freedom, equality and social and political progression had emerged out of radical Reconstruction the birth of the "New Negro," the first generation of Blacks that were born free in America-never having felt the civilizing effects of slavery-of a different mindset, more mature, educated and whose capacity was unrestricted-his potential, still unknown. The 1880s brought forth an era of competition and opportunity for Blacks that gave them brief relief from the social shift, and some political benefit from 1888 elections, that saw Republicans gain control of both the Presidency and the Congress, and a last attempt to equalize public education through a "Blair bill," to provide federal funding to public schools that included Black children and a "force bill," by Henry Cabot Lodge, to ensure fairness in federal elections, through the use of federal election supervisors.[18]

This raised a flag for Democrats, who thought there might be a resumption of Reconstruction on the horizon. However, the recession

106

of the late 1880s, and the depression of the 1890s introduced a social-psychological politic that overwhelmed the socio-economic politics taking place on the national scene. Race relations soon turned bitter, as economic depression of the country brought a racial Conservatism that quashed the popular liberalism. Conservatism returned under the guise of a return to Victorian values. Where economic depression caused little separation between the conditions of poor Blacks and Whites, Southern white men saw themselves as providers and protectors of their families, and in the absence of such, men on the lower end of the economic scale in not being able to provide for their families financially-most sought to protect their families, particularly their women, against societal threats based on sex and race.

This "values" protection became of utmost importance. At the center of this values shift was the racial purity of the white race, the sexual piety of white women, and the rage against the "black beast rapist" that was part of the "nigger loose" national mindset of strange Black men wandering the countryside, waiting for the opportunity to violate white women's sanctity.[19] While it has never been demonstrated that this racial propensity even existed with sufficient frequency to cause mass hysteria, a national phenomena called lynching became a frequently used tool of "social control," and its rise from 1884 to the turn of the century was of significance-only because its use often went unpunished and deemed socially warranted. Reported lynchings (hundreds of lynched and missing Blacks went unreported during the entire time in which lynching statistics were kept) increased from 51 in 1884 to 113 in 1901, and over 100 for the next seven of nine years in the period preceding and seceding the *Plessy* decision, with the leading justification being black criminality, but highlighting black men's alleged desire to rape a white woman, or girl-given the period and severity of the penalty, in all probability, was the one charge least likely to be true-and be least challenged.[20]

By the time Conservative Radicalism took strength in 1889, the basic tenets of their philosophy was the "retrogression" of the Negro, and the obsession over how such deterioration of black life, and the "unchecked Negro" would impact white life. As opposed to seeking programmatic ways to lift Blacks up, as Liberals hoped to do, Radical Conservatives espoused programs designed to put Blacks down, introducing pseudo-science as the basis to assert rises in purported black criminality was possibly linked to education-because Blacks were innately bad and with education, smarter, and the smarter Black using

107

his education to do evil, and that education only heightened this potential for evil, thus causing some Whites to turn against any formal education at all for Blacks.[21] Combined with, in the radical mind, the single most significant manifestation of black transgression, the increasing frequency of sexual assaults on white women and girl children by black men. While not a common occurrence, one was too many and enough to revive the hysteria associated with the Nat Turner rebellion.

Despite that the country was suffering from very real political and economic realities, the politics of the new radicals, racial radicals, not to be confused with republican radicals, that defined the period of Radicalism that were in effect when *Plessy* became part of the national discourse, rose solely from the racial realities of black regression that were able to be observed, and the sexual images of Negro brutes roaming, without restraint, with "their breasts pulsating with the desire to sate their passions upon white maidens and wives."[22] The response to this most exaggerated form of stigmatizing a whole race, through the behaviors of a few, a true case of the "exception becoming the rule," was to separate Whites from Blacks, whenever and wherever possible, a phenomena that sought to reverse the trend of accepting the social company of Blacks without, hesitation or discrimination.

During the entire decade of the 1870s, while admission and patronage policies, in venues of public enjoyment (restaurants, pubs, theaters, hotels, publicly shared places, like parks and transportation vehicles) were generally a matter of choice for individual owners-some who selectively engaged restrictions, or refused Black patronage-there was no state in the Union, North or South, that had laws requiring separation of Whites and Blacks in place of public accommodation.[23] This was largely due to the passing of the Civil Rights Act of 1875 that sought to eliminate the infrequent behavior of refusing Blacks to socialize amongst Whites in various venues. Often represented in history of the Radical Republicans' "final protection," the act went beyond giving the political protections of the prior civil rights acts. In its preamble, it declared itself "an act to protect all citizens in their 'civil and legal' rights," as "the appropriate object of legislation to enact great fundamental principles into law."[24] Seeking to regulate people's social behaviors, as the driving "principle," the act said "it is the duty of government in its dealings with the people to mete out equal and exact justice to all, of whatever nativity, race, color, or persuasion, religious or political." In its first section (Section 1) it state that "all persons within the jurisdiction of the United States shall be entitled to the full and equal enjoyment of the accommodations of inns, public conveyances on land or water, theaters and other places of public amusement; subject only to the conditions and limitations established by law, and applicable alike to citizens of every race or color."[25]

Moreover, Section 2 tied civil and criminal damages to anyone violating the act. The penalties were considered federal offenses and varied from a $500 violation penalty paid to the aggrieved party, to a $500-$1,000 fine, to a 30 day to one year prison sentence, but any offense could be reviewed by the Supreme Court regardless of the amount in controversy.[26] The public reaction to the law was mixed, and did not stop discrimination by many venues that, either continued to refuse Blacks, closed their establishments or became private establishments to skirt the law. Southern states took the lead in legalizing "Separate But Equal," enforcing public separation of the races through legislation, or in passing local ordinances that set up second class facilities that admitted Blacks on a selective or separated (balcony, roped area) basis, though some establishments in the North and the West did the same, by enforcing local customs, or just ignoring the federal law, altogether, by commonly refusing Black patronage entirely.[27] Ironically, the racial resistance of refusing entry to Blacks in places of public enjoyment or Jim Crow discrimination become known as a southern phenomena, yet the first legal challenge to enforcement of "public enjoyment" equality would come out of the North-of all places, New York.

109

Tennessee became the first to pass legislation that moved toward mandated transportation segregation in 1881, in direct contradiction to the Civil Rights Act of 1875.[28] Nine states passed Jim Crow acts within a five year period, from 1887 to 1892 after the U.S. Supreme Court weighed in on the issue of the government's right to regulate public enjoyment in 1883. However, the main focus of each state's laws were railway travel-though some laws later added streetcars and steamboats-targeting public space where Blacks, Black men in particular, could most commonly come in contact with unescorted White women and children. The laws of importance enacted before *Plessy* during this period represented a first wave of legislation; in Florida (1887), Mississippi (1888), Texas (1889 and 1891), Louisiana (1890 and 1894), Alabama (1891), Arkansas (1891 and 1893), Tennessee (1891), Georgia (1891), Kentucky (1892). Then a second wave of legislation was passed after *Plessy* in South Carolina, North Carolina and Virginia (between 1898 and 1901), Maryland (1904) and Oklahoma

(1907).[29] Clearly, it was this first wave of "separation laws" that created the most concern for Blacks, and thus, served as impetus for the initial legal challenge to railway discrimination before segregation laws spread throughout the rest of society. These laws only represented the beginning of racial radicalism-whose true purpose was a political guise to achieve social means of regaining control of African Americans as a group, and as individuals.

The purpose of Radicalism, thusly defined, was to re-socialize Blacks, re-acclimate Blacks to an environment of intimidation and violence that would lower their self-esteem, and force them to accept this Radical mood, that, in effect, would usher in a new socialization for the New Negro, through speech inflections, pauses, rises and fall in speech pitch and volume, of body postures, relative positions, movement of hands and eyes, matters of dress and costume, of naming and titles, of place and setting, money in the bank, and talking down from the porch to the yard-things that they had never seen before, that hadn't been seen since slavery-that would install new social control mechanisms, verbal and non-verbal behaviors, and a new set of laws, to disenfranchise, separate-henceforth, segregate-and legally manage black existence.[30]

This is the socio-political environment that *Plessy* was set to usher in. The most significant event that opened the door for this attitudinal shift that produced the mentality of *Plessy* and its legalized doctrine of "Separate But Equal" de jure segregation, was, again-a U.S. Supreme Court decision to intervene a subject of national debate, and rule on-judicial interpretations of what "equal" meant, in a collaboration of public enjoyment discrimination lawsuits called, the *Civil Rights Cases of 1883*.

Starting with one event on the 22nd of November in 1879, when a black man named William R. Davis, Jr. and his "octoroon" girlfriend purchased two tickets to see Victor Hugo's *Ruy Blas*, and were refused entry. The doorkeeper, Samuel Singleton, told him that "these tickets are no good," but directed him back to the box office for a refund. Davis filed a criminal complaint against Singleton that the court upheld, however, the validity of the 1875 Civil Rights Act would soon be called into question.[31] Singleton was indicted on December 9th and the case was heard January 14, 1880, launching a national debate on the "division of opinion between the judges" surrounding the 1875 Civil Rights Act, as hundreds of such cases had caused federal judges in Pennsylvania, Texas, Maryland and Kentucky to rule the Act constitutional, although federal courts in North Carolina, New Jersey and California held the Act invalid and federal courts in others states, including Tennessee, Missouri, Kansas and New York were divided on questions of validity of the Act, thus certifying the issue, as one for Supreme Court intervention.[32]

By the time Davis' case reached the Supreme Court in 1880, as U.S. vs. Singleton, five other cases; *U.S. vs. Stanley*, Murray Stanley indicted for refusing to serve Blacks at his hotel in Topeka, Kansas; *U.S. vs. Nichols*, Samuel Nichols indicted for refusing to accept a Black as a guest in his Nichols House hotel in Jefferson City Missouri; *U.S. vs. Ryan*, Michael Ryan indicted for refusing to admit a Black man to the dress circle of Maguire's Theater in San Francisco; *U.S. vs. Hamilton*, train conductor, James Hamilton indicted for refusing to seat a Black woman holding a first class ticket in the ladies car of the Chatanooga & St. Louis Railroad; *Robinson vs. the Memphis & Charleston Railroad*, where the railroad company was sued, when the conductor, C.W. Reagin, refused to honor Mrs. Sallie Robinson's first class seat for part of the ride, but honored her companion's seat, traveling with her light skinned "white looking" nephew, Joseph C. Robinson, because he thought she was a prostitute traveling with a white man. Sallie Robinson was only allowed to move to the first class parlor, after Mr. Robinson had disclosed his race, but she sued anyway.[33]

Five of the six cases involved criminal matters related directly to the constitutionality of the Civil Rights Act of 1875. When the case was decided on October 15, 1883, the Supreme Court had ruled that the Civil Rights Act of 1875 was unconstitutional. Justice Joseph Bradley, in disposing five of the six cases, after denying the Hamilton case, wrote in his opinion for the 8-1 majority that the government (Congress) had the power to regulate wrongs of the state, but could not use the Thirteenth and Fourteenth Amendments to cover "social discriminations," when they were put in place to rectify and establish political rights.[34]

Opining that Congress had no power to regulate wrongs of the individual, as long as, those wrongs did "not deprive" [constitutionally protected] rights to vote, to hold property, to buy and sell, to sue in courts, but he may, by force or fraud, interfere with the enjoyment of the right; he may commit an assault against the person, or commit murder, or use ruffian violence at the polls, or slander the good name of a fellow citizen…he will only render himself amendable to satisfaction or punishment; and amenable, therefore, to the laws of the state where

111

the wrongful acts are committed..."The wrongful act of an individual, unsupported by any such authority (government mandated wrong), is simply a private wrong, or a crime of that individual..."[35]

Thus, the Constitution only protected civil rights, and state sanctioned civil wrongs-and when wronged by individuals, aggrieved persons had to pursue civil and criminal remedies outlined by state law for individual claims-not federal court. Bradley added one last twist, similar to the way Roger B. Taney had done just over 25 years earlier, stating, in effect that there must be a point at which the Negro ceased to be "the special favorite of the laws," and must take on "the rank of mere citizens."[36]

What Justice Bradley meant was the rank of mere citizens included determining the limits of your social contacts and the boundaries of private enjoyment, even in public, a person has a right to associate with women, to what extent he or she pleases. Bradley gave sanction to what white people had been saying since reconstruction, that government did not have the right to force Blacks on them in a social role. Republicans had forced political equality on the nation, but in trying to force social equality-they had gone one step too far. The government can legislate political equality but it can't legislate social enjoyment-nor force private establishment owners to open their doors to persons they do not desire to share their accommodations, company of its patrons, or the benefits of private enjoyments. "Open to the public" did not mean open to the public. It meant "opened to the welcomed public." All other "publics" stay away-a thinly veiled replication of the pre-war Constitution's reference to Blacks inferior status as slaves or "three-fifth's of all other persons."

In trying to separate from Blacks, Whites not only wanted to socially control Blacks, they wanted to control who they, themselves, socialized with, and if it meant to the exclusion of Blacks-it was a social wrong they were willing to accept. Thus, after 1883, there were a proliferation of laws seeking to disengage Blacks by engaging restrictive convenants in privately owned properties and establishments. Within five years, restrictive convenants had extended to public accommodations and public spaces. The first genuine "Jim Crow" law requiring railroads to Blacks in separate cars or behind partitions was adopted by Florida in 1887, and by 1892, eight other states had followed. Blacks, on the other hand, held no less than five national conventions in 1890, to focus on their social plights, and to develop strategies of protest, mostly in the forms of resolutions and confessions of helplessness.[37]

African Americans, understanding the attitudinal shift about to take place, engaged themselves in a number of organizations that were set to "test" laws targeting the integration and societal enjoyment rights of Blacks. One such organization was the American Citizens' Equal Rights Association of Louisiana Against Class Legislation, started by a group of Blacks of culture, education and wealth that had a heritage of several generations of freedom, stemming from the large mixed race ancestry of French, Native American and Black populations that had lived together for centuries. The group sent a protest letter to the Louisiana legislature to reject a Jim Crow separate car bill making its way through the state's General Assembly-a body that still had sixteen Black senators and representatives at this point because Blacks were still voting in large numbers.[38] The protest put the Black legislators on notice, but they had little power to block the bill itself. They did have the power to block another piece of legislation-a lottery bill, sponsored by the powerful Louisiana Lottery Company, who could have helped kill the separate car bill if it meant getting the lottery bill pass the black filibuster. The black legislators, however, separated on their interests, taking their individual "considerations" instead, voted for the lottery bill, and with no political leverage, were rendered helpless on the separate car bill, which was passed and signed by the Governor on July 10, 1890.[39]

113

Thus, the bill called "An Act to provide equal but separate accommodations for the white and colored races" became law in Louisiana. A second group of Blacks and Creoles from New Orleans set up another group called, the Citizens' Committee to Test the Constitutionality of the Separate Car Act. Their charge was to force this new law into the court system, by intentionally placing light skinned Blacks, not discernible from Whites, in white-only rail cars, having them declare their "blackness," get arrested and litigate the case on the basis of the 14th Amendment's Equal Protection and Due Process Clauses. The committee raised $1,400 in advance, and hired two attorneys.

The first "test case" was launched with a 21 year old black man from a prominent New Orleans Creole family named, Daniel F. Desdunes, who purchased a first class ticket from New Orleans to Mobile, Alabama on the Louisville and Nashville Railroad. The case of *the State of Louisiana v. Desdunes* worked its way through the state court system. However, the Louisiana State Supreme Court decided the case of *Abbott v. Hicks*, which said a ticket used for interstate travel, covered under federal law, meaning Louisiana's state law didn't apply to interstate passengers, setting a precedent in favor of the Desdunes case.[40]

Not wanting to be overturned on appeal, Orleans Criminal District Court Judge, John H. Ferguson dismissed the Desdunes case, setting the stage for the second test case with plaintiff, Homer Plessy, a local shoemaker, who also fit "the profile" for test cases, light enough to purchase a first class ticket without objection, but black enough to be recognized as "out of place" in a white-only riding car. The Committee then changed strategy to focus on intrastate travel, and had Plessy, a one-eighth black man (commonly called "octoroons") from New Orleans, who, like Desdunes, was from a family of historically free Blacks, purchase a ticket for travel entirely within the state of Louisiana. A week after the Desdunes case was dismissed, Plessy boarded the East Louisiana Railroad from New Orleans to Covington, Louisiana. The Committee had given notice to the railroad of Plessy's status and intents, and once seated and requested to move, upon Plessy's refusal-he was arrested June 7th, 1892.[42]

Indicted on July 20, 1892, on a criminal charge of violating the Separate Car Act, Plessy did two things that made the case difficult for state courts to hear the case, and made it appropriate for settlement in the federal courts. First, he did not enter a plea, and second, he did not respond to the court on questions about his race, instead having his attorney challenge the court's authority to hear the case, on the grounds that the Separate Car Act was a violation of the U.S. Constitution and Plessy's 14th Amendment rights, that guaranteed equal protection under the law.[42] The local prosecutor, Lionel Adams, allowed the case to go back to John Howard Ferguson, who had heard the earlier test case. Because of the unanswered questions by Plessy on his race and his guilt or innocence that provided absence of "fact" and questions of "law" to determine an outcome in the case, Ferguson postponed judgment that allowed the case to move forward to the Louisiana Supreme Court, as an *Ex parte* application for a ruling on questions in Plessy's behalf, giving rise to the belief that Ferguson may have also cooperated with the Committee to test the constitutionality of the separate car law.[43]

Ferguson was a Massachusetts native who came south after the civil war, married a daughter of a leading New Orleans attorney, successfully ran for state justice, and became part of the Southern power structure. He was, though, clearly one of the last remaining remnants of radical republican influence, which explains the high respect he

114

afforded Plessy's attorneys.[44] Ferguson was part of the carpetbagger movement that allowed the Radical Republicans to build a coalition with free Blacks, former slaves and "Scalawags" (Southern Union sympathizers) to take control of Southern politics. Absent of the sensitivity needed to advance the case, Ferguson had the power to rule on Plessy's race, based on what he, himself, was able to observe (as Whites often did), find him in opposition to the law, then rule on the law. But he chose to leave both questions open, rule against Plessy's question of constitutionality, leaving the path to appeal open for the higher courts to consider.

Once the case got to the Louisiana Supreme Court, Plessy's attorneys, faced with the dilemma of having the state high court not consider its claim on race-and remanding the case back to Ferguson to determine whether Plessy was right or wrong, versus whether the law was right or wrong-choose not to allow their client to remain silent as they had in the lower court. This time, they responded to questions on Plessy's race, identifying him as "seven-eighths Caucasian and one-eight African blood," and "that the mixture of colored blood was not discernible in him," making the case a single claim in question for the court, whether the law could be upheld or struck down, solely on the basis of a railroad company making "an insidious distinction and discrimination between citizens of the United States, based on race," which Plessy's attorney's asserted was "obnoxious to the fundamental principles of national citizenship."[45]

It was at this point that the *Plessy* case became a referendum on race, in terms of the extents by which the law protected, or rejected, race. The case became the ultimate test of what was...race and what were the privileges, the "equalities," accorded to one's race status? Was one's race defined as a matter of how light you were? Or, was race a matter of how *white* you were? It was during this period of time that whiteness became defined as a matter of pure racial linage, whereby any bloodline other than European could be called into question. Essentially, the real question that the court was putting to Homer Plessy, when it asked "what is your race?," was, "Are you white?" Plessy's response was, essentially, "I don't know? Am I, and does it make a difference in my constitutional rights?" Well, for white people, it did make a difference.

America was not about how light you were, though many Blacks had historically "passed" for white. It was how white you were and total whiteness became the badge for "all-access" privileges in

115

American society. The socially constructed "one drop rule" became "cultural fact" during this period. Because the sexual politics of slavery in the South had created millions of persons of mixed race linage, not all of whom were considered Black, and many of whose race could not be easily discerned, skin race often was used to assess the benefits of "whiteness," that were not intended for Blacks. Because "whiteness" had no real meaning beyond the historical "Black/White" paradigm of slavery that had no "gray lines" in distinction, who was Black, and who was white was a simple categorization that was eliminated with Reconstruction and the "equalization" of rights.

The populist movement worked to unite the white and black poor, eliminate segregation, and eliminate race as a social category, in favor of class. Mark Twain's 1894 novel, *Pudd'nhead Wilson*, was a tragedy (as Twain called it) that showed what could happen when bloodlines become entwined. It was a story of a mulatto slave girl, Roxana, who had a child by her slave owner-Percy Driscoll, who also had a child by his white wife, who then dies, leaving the young white child in Roxana's care. The two infants are indistinguishable. Fraught with the thought that her own child might be sold away-switches the babies, where the white child grows up a black slave "of good character," and the black child grows up white with no "known virtues and less sense."[46] Twain, popular among white readers, helped shift cultural attitudes toward the "gratitudes" of whiteness connected to Adam in the Bible, "the first great benefactor of our race," and whereas whiteness had no meaning prior to this cultural awakening, it became the physical marker that distinguished Whites from "others," and linage became the basis by which whiteness was traced and rewarded.[47] Thus, historical whiteness became of value, and its benefits grandfathered into society, at a time when those "passing" for white, as Plessy did, could net some of those same benefits.

What being "white" meant, more specifically-the societal rewards of whiteness, came into the national consciousness as the "perceptible reality of skin tone became the dream of racial essence," making the physical "metaphysical," making whiteness real-not imaginary, and by being able to determine whether one had even a drop of black blood pushed one's whiteness beyond appearance and into the past of known and unknown ancestors, where it took crucial social fact of ancestry to prove one's whiteness, a fine legal distinction meant to clarify a permanent system of, first-racial distinction, and secondly, basis for racial separation.[48] Thus, the one-drop rule looked at one's linage, and if there were any Blacks in that linage-no matter how far back, no matter how white you looked-one drop of black blood made you of the black race. Though Homer Plessy had more white blood in him than his "not discernible," black blood, in America, cultural fact made him a Negro, and not worthy of enjoying the company of Whites, which he bore closer resemblance to than the people for whom he fought.

What the Louisiana State Supreme Court wanted to know specifically, in asking Plessy's race, was, "Are you white?" If Plessy is white, then the court has a problem with why a white man was removed from a white riding car; if Plessy is not white, then the law has standing-and the court wants to know, why are we here? Plessy's, and the committee's, challenge was not to challenge the law, but challenge the state's definition of race. By conflicting America's definition of race, Plessy forced the court to recognize distinctions, or differences, that cause the law to be applied differently in each case of race-offering protections to one, and abstaining protections to the other. The question, in essence, then became not "Are you white, but who is white, and who assigns "whiteness?" Thus, justification for Plessy's seven-eighths response, which then flagged him to clarify what the other one-eighth was. In the eyes of Whites, and the standards of whiteness established during that period, you could't just be white (in terms of light), you had to be "all white." Anything else was subject to interpretation according to the "one drop rule." The fact that Plessy acknowledged that he was one-eighth Black made him, Black, and in violation of the law.

The state high court included the former Governor, Francis T. Nichols-then the Chief Justice, who had signed the Separate Car Act of 1890. Nichols was heralded as "the Redeemer Governor" who took Louisiana back from carpetbaggers in 1877, but had been "fair and just to colored men," and offered a degree of protection that had not been enjoyed even under Republican Governors.[49] Yet, now in the midst of a populist movement, driven by racial radicialism, Nichols views had shifted, consistent with the rest of the country, where concessions to racism were being made by conservatives of his upper class politic to divert the attentions of poor white farmers from economic reforms that would address redistribution of societal wealth, in making them equals amongst Whites.[50]

Thus, Justice Charles Fenner, speaking for the majority of the court, including Chief Justice Nichols, swept away all of Plessy's arguments against the law violating the 13th and 14th amendments, siding with the precedent of *Civil Rights Cases of 1883* that protected private

socialization rights of Whites. Further, Fenner opinion sought to specifically address Plessy's 14th Amendment claim of unequal-ness, stating
that the Separate Car law satisfied the Equal Protection Clause,
because it "impairs no right of passengers of either race, who are secured
that equality of accommodations which satisfies every reasonable
claim."[51] Fenner went on to say that the court must uphold race as a
legitimate basis for governmental distinctions, due to the absence of an
acceptable alternative. To nullify race in one legal distinction, would
nullify race in all other legal distinctions, such as schools and inter-
racial marriages, Fenner reasoned, and the Louisiana Supreme Court
upheld the Louisiana's Separate Car Law. Chief Justice Nichols did
clear the way for an appeal at a later hearing by granting Plessy's petition for a writ of error, permitting him to seek redress before the U.S.
Supreme Court and showing that he hadn't forgotten his roots of paternalism that caused him to denounce bigotry when he was Governor.[52]

The stage was set to test "race" in the highest court in the land.
After a three year wait, *Plessy v. Ferguson* was heard in April, 1896. The
state of Louisiana held its case on the basis of court precedent established in the *Civil Rights Cases*, and a second case also decided in 1883,
Pace v. Alabama, where the Supreme Court upheld race, or color, as a
basis for the state making distinctions in the most fundamental rights
of social enjoyment-interpersonal relations, therefore allowing
Alabama to outlaw interracial sex and marriage.[53] Louisiana had the
right to do the same. It did. The law was broken, and Plessy should pay
the fine, was the state's position. Plessy's defense was that the state
could not define race, and that race, since slavery, had been, not a physical, but a social construct, of which, the differences, in many state
laws, showed the many ways for which race could be manufactured.
Plessy's defense ignored the question as to whether he was colored or
white, but set to focus on whether they could reasonably categorize
Plessy when the U.S. Constitution made no distinctions among its citizens. The states varied on racial definition beyond rationality, where,
for instance, North Carolina used a rule where by a black person was
measured by "any visible admixture of black blood," and Ohio, used a
rule by which "the preponderance of blood" determined the race.[54]
Plessy's attorney's surmised Homer Plessy would have been ruled Black
in North Carolina and under his "seven-eighths" analogy, been ruled
White in Ohio.

Plessy's senior counsel, Albion W. Tourgee', asserted that the
Louisiana law was an exercise of white class privilege, a camouflage of

118

bias and an attempt, on the part of Whites, to assert an appearance of impartiality when, in fact, Separate But Equal" was designed to discriminate against colored citizens and that the logic of segregation operated in one direction, for the special privilege of Whites who claim a superior position in society. While the Separate Car Act created two separate crimes; the crime of black citizens refusing to enter a colored car, or leaving a white one; and the crime of white citizens refusing to enter a white car, or leaving a colored one, the law was only enforced one way, because the real object of the law, which was to keep Negroes out of one car, for the gratification of Whites, and to claim that the law was for the common advantage of both races was "farcical."[56]

Tourgee' summarized that the Constitution was "color-blind," and for the government to recognize color or race, in any way, led to "invidious distinction and discriminates between citizens of the United States..." "is obnoxious to the principles of national citizenship," to which, he concluded, "perpetuates involuntary servitude" that violates the 13th and 14th Amendments to the Constitution.[57] The Supreme Court didn't buy the argument, and five weeks later, on May 18th, 1896, ruled in a seven to one decision that separating on race was reasonable and constitutional.

In one of the most infamous decisions in the Supreme Court's history, social order dictated legal precedence be upheld (contradictory to the *Dred Scott* decision, where social order went *against* legal precedent to be upheld). Justice Henry Billings Brown of Massachusetts announced that Louisiana had acted within its power to express "the established usages, customs and traditions of the people," and that Louisiana did nothing more than recognize "the reality of race," which represented "distinctions based upon physical differences, race being a "fact of life and of law," which stymied Plessy's defense that race, as a physical construct, did not exist, nor was it real.[58] Brown stated that the segregation law recognized "facts" that "must always exist, as long as, white men were distinguished from the other race by color," and that Plessy's claims only assumes that the legal separation of the two races "stamps the colored race with a badge of inferiority," that nothing in the act reflects such designation, and that such assumption solely exists "because the colored race chooses to put that construction upon it."[59]

Justice Brown interpreted Plessy's plea, erroneously, as an attempt to force government to legislate social norms, to which he responded, in a very "Taney-istic" manner: "Legislation is powerless to eradicate racial instincts or to abolish distinctions based upon physical

119

differences, and the attempt to do so can only result in accentuating the difficulties of the present situation. If the civil and political rights of both races be equal, one cannot be inferior to the other civilly or politicalically. If one race be inferior to the other socially, the Constitution of the United States cannot put them upon the same plane," reinforcing Brown's conclusions that racial instincts were rooted in man's nature, and that such distinctions were "impervious to alteration through legal schemes."[60]

The biggest tragedy in the Supreme Court's majority decision against *Plessy* was that it was fraught with legal errors, first from recent state court laws that were becoming more common in the 1880s and 1890s-using state police powers to extend to segregating railway travel. Brown also cited the most controversial cases, *Roberts v. City of Boston* (1849) and *West Chester and the Philadelphia Railroad Co. v. Miles* (1867), the former of which was overruled by a Boston school committee who proceeded in integrating public schools, but contained language that reinforced Brown's conclusion when Justice Shaw opined that "since the law was not the cause of segregation, it could not be the solution."[61]

Justice Brown also used two Supreme Court cases that were contradictory; the first being, *Hall v. DeCuir* (1877), where the Supreme Court reversed a state judgment awarded when Mrs. DeCuir had been denied a first class cabin on a boat sailing between cities in Lousiana, citing that the 1869 Louisiana law forbidding race discrimination potentially violated Congress' power to regulate interstate commerce since the boat's ultimate destination was out of state; the second case was, *New Orleans & Texas Railway Co. v. Mississppi* (1890), where the Supreme Court upheld an 1888 Mississippi law fining a railroad for not providing racially segregated accommodations, a law the court interpreted to apply only to intrastate commerce-though the trains cross state borders-and closer to the Louisiana law in the *Plessy* case,"almost directly in point" to Plessy's circumstances in Brown's opinion, though Mississippi law had not ordered Blacks into separate cars as had the 1890 Louisiana law that Plessy challenged.[62]

These cases were a reach, as was most of Brown's case law cited from either pre-Civil war days or only incidentally touched areas of transportation and education, but none dealing with state-enforced racial segregation of passengers on riding cars or trains.[63] Brown, like Taney, almost forty years earlier, offered no clear legal precedent for the majority ruling, just racial innuendo and popular sentiment. Yet, the ruling legitimated segregation that brought what many consider one of the most brilliant legal dissents in Supreme Court history.

Justice John Marshall Harlan, one of history's longest serving justices (33 years), wrote a dissenting opinion, nearly as long as the majority opinion, in *Plessy* but offered a much more rational and legally supportive analysis of what segregation meant, and was intended to do. Harlan started with a very fundamental analysis of the Constitution, that all citizens were "equal before the law," that there is no caste system in America, that the "Constitution is color-blind (in support of Tourgee's term of analysis)"and tolerates "no classes among citizens." Harlan also concurred with Tourgee that the 13th and 14th Amendment revised the definitions of citizenship in this country that eradicated any "burdens" and badges of slavery and servitude, guaranteeing Blacks full equality before the law as well its negative-"exemption from legal discriminations, implying inferiority in civil society."[64] Harlan, clearly was knowledgeable of what was going on in the lower courts, citing numerous cases where the Court overturned state laws that excluded Blacks from jury panels, based on the revision of citizenship and the equal status.

Harlan then, in what would be a haunting prediction of the future lunacy of how far segregation could go, asserted that while people had a right to keep private company of their choosing, government could not prevent a white man and a black man from choosing to occupy the same conveyance on a public highway, if they chose to do so, without infringing on the personal liberty of each other. If they were allowed to do so, Harlan theorized, what is to prevent state power from keeping Whites and Blacks from walking on the same side of the street, or even from sitting on the same side of the courtroom, or extending such exclusions to Protestants or Catholics and setting aside separate railway accommodations for them?[65] Harlan explained the irrationality of this premise and how "pride of race" must be "reasonable," whereby its expression of such feelings cannot be permitted to undermine the rights of fellow citizens.[66] Harlan stated that equality in the Constitution recognizes the freedom of movement as a public right, a "civil freedom" for all, to include the public sphere, not just the political rights of voters and jury members, asserting that railroad travel does not confer social equality, and compares the separating of railway passengers as frivolous and sinister, as separating black and white jurors in separate jury boxes. Harlan stated that "the thin disguise of equal accommodations for passengers in railroad coaches will not mislead any one, nor atone for the wrong done this day," citing that the majority's judgment would promote inter-race violence, and that the destinies of both races were so linked that "the interests of both require that the common government of all shall permit the seeds of race hate to be planted under the sanction of law." Harlan then predicted that the same shadow cast on the *Dred Scott* decision would be cast on the *Plessy* decision, because they were one in the same. Inasmuch as, in the former case, Harlan stated, Justice Taney denied to the descendants of "Africans who were imported into this country and sold as slaves "their right to protection under the Constitution," instead terming them a subordinate inferior class of beings-without rights or privileges, but such as those who held the power and government might choose to grant them."

Whereas, in the latter case, Justice Brown's opinion was likely to stimulate aggressions upon "admitted rights of colored citizens," and encourage states to "defeat the beneficent purposes" of the Constitution, forecasting that this judgment would, in time, "prove to be quite as pernicious as the decision made of this tribunal in the *Dred Scott* case.[67] The flood of racial aggressions that Justice Harlan predicted did come to pass in the first half of the 20th Century. Of the 16,826 cases that Justice Harlan heard in his 33 years of service, this opinion would stand out as a beacon to guide future civil rights adjudication in the second half of the twentieth century.[68] But on this day, Homer Plessy would lose, pay the fine and like Dred Scott, become distinguished in name, as a historical footnote, and immortalized for the vicious inequities caused by the cases that would bear their names. There would be no social outrage, or no civil war, after the *Plessy* decision. Society would firmly and quietly settle into a formally recognized and accepted racial caste, based on white supremacy, that would legally subjugate Blacks socially, economically and politically. The battle would not come for another 30 years, and would take 25 years to overturn. *Plessy* would stand for 58 years total, and its effects would last another decade beyond that.

The Supreme Court ruled that race was "a fact of life," the same type of cultural reasoning, represented as matters of fact, that were in evidence in Roger B. Taney's opinion in the *Dred Scott* decision. The *Plessy* decision re-introduced Taney's "dual" citizenship theory, where Whites had national privileges, while Blacks' privileges varied from state to state. The *Plessy* decision turned whiteness from a privilege, which anyone could access, if they could pass for white, to a right for those who could prove they were white. Cultural fact, not necessarily being "legal fact," had been affirmed by a court of law, and was now cultural law deemed legal. *Plessy* rewarded whiteness and penalized blackness, and everything in between.

The *Plessy* decision reconnected America's culture of the present to its racial past, through the edict of the *Dred Scott* case, that "Blacks were so far inferior that they had no rights that Whites were bound to respect" had come full circle, almost 40 years later. Whites now did not have to give equal access, provide equal treatment, or give equal respect or provide comfort to Blacks in their spheres of public enjoyment. They only had to give acknowledgement, lip service, to some degree of "equal" accommodation outside their private view, and private space. Once again, cultural law as fact had now become "the law" under the Constitution of the United States, and legal separation of the races, known as segregation, was born. The legacy of *Brown* has its genesis in a case that became the longstanding precedent for racial discrimination, economic inequities and social control. A case called, *Plessy*.

6

Jim Crow & "Separate But Equal" Segregation:
"Just The Way It Was"

Racial Segregation, discrimination and degradation are no unantici-pated accidents in this nation's history. They stem logically and directly from the legacy that the founding fathers bestowed upon contemporary America.
- John Hope Franklin

If you make a man feel that he is inferior, you do not have to compel him to accept inferior status, for he will seek it for himself.

- Carter G. Woodson, cited in his book, *The Mis-education of the Negro*

After the *Plessy* decision in 1896, America had finally fash-ioned its legal doorway to a race-based society. A doorway cut on the back of black equality rights, with Whites ready and willing to enter a house built on race and racial differences. With the law firmly estab-lished on its side, White America took great steps to institutionalize white supremacy, and create systems that would, not only solidify a per-manent race caste, but hold it in place for decades to come. The system of "rights" suppression that evolved into multiple layered facets of sys-temic and institutional racial repression came to be known as, Jim Crow racism.

Jim Crowism has had a very mystic origin, and several transi-tional meanings, from when Thomas D. Rice wrote a minstrel dance song, imitating a black cripple's walk, called Jim Crow, to slaves seeking to skirt around some laws and church edits prohibiting dancing (dancing was considered crossing your feet) during slavery, in which slaves would sing;

> "I turn about and spin about and jump just so,
> Every time I turnabout, I jump Jim Crow."

Jim Crow transitioned from a noun, a term for a dance and song in 1832, to an adjective for minstrel shows that showed white "delineators," mimicking behaviors of Blacks in 1838.[1] The popularity of minstrel shows took off after the Civil War, when Whites used shows to romanticize the days of the Antebellum Period-a time when Blacks knew their place and Whites were in charge of the entire society. These shows also provided some sort of psychotic relief for Whites hard hit by post war economic depressions, brought on by industrialization, capital monopolies and competition. While much of the competition came from European immigrants and population growth, poor Whites focused on the rare prosperity of Blacks as the cause of their economic woes, thus bringing forward high racial anxieties.

These minstrel shows were made to entertain them, and help them forget about their economic troubles, finding a security in their whiteness. In that, no matter how bad things got-at least, "they weren't Niggers"-white society's subtle guarantee that one's whiteness would always stand for something, and would always stand above the plight of the American born African. Minstrel shows created and magnified images of African Americans in grotesque caricatures, and represented a critical part of the culturalization of America during this period that sought to elevate European cultural values during this period and, at the same time, sought to stigmatize Blacks in status, strip them of any public respectability and distort their imagery, by demeaning their public persona and degrading their humanity in ways that offered little, in terms of sociability and human dignity. In many of these shows, it was the first indoctrination many Whites had with Blacks, and the first impressions they took away of Black people, in relation to themselves, which of course, appeared inferior to them-exactly the message intended to convey-in order to uphold Jim Crow culture.

Exactly when the term Jim Crow transitioned to laws constricting the rights and movements of African Americans isn't exactly known. It is thought to have come into existence right after the Civil

125

War, with the advent of "black codes," in the mid-1860s and became a form of common practice in the 1890s. However, while the term was not yet associated with the practice, racial segregation with the backing of legal and extra-legal codes existed in the North and South to control free Blacks, and in free states in the 1840s and 1850s, and permeated all aspects of Blacks before the Civil War broke out in 1860.[2] Whites used these laws to prohibit Blacks from full enjoyment, and as a form of social control, in order to "keep Blacks in their place"-meaning rendering them "incapable of being assimilated politically, socially, or physically into white society."[3] These early laws included requiring Blacks to post bonds when traveling, to be vouched for when in the company of Whites, Jim Crow "social control" culture and the legal and extra-legal means (which also included illegal means) of accounting for Blacks, who didn't belong to somebody, or had freedom of movement, and/or equal or near equal liberties, offered a blanket "societal check" on the African American.

Jim Crow, as law, sought to deny the private and public rights of Blacks, where, under the guise of being equal, Blacks were systematically subordinated by private and public institutions in all areas of social and economic life. Jim Crow laws were also of a highly political nature, as they were used to impede the representation rights, voting rights, jury rights and trial rights of Blacks. While Jim Crow laws didn't necessarily cause or increase segregation, which has always existed on a de facto basis, a function of the cultural identification that caused people of different races to cluster, it didn't allow Blacks and Whites to come together, because these laws governed the terms under which Whites and Blacks came together, and strictly regulated the nature of interracial social contact.[4] "Separation" laws, more commonly known as segregation laws, formalized the White/Black divide, creating an American form of racial apartheid and served as the legal forerunner and cultural prototype to the form of governance installed by the government of South Africa in 1948. U.S. Apartheid laws preceded South African Apartheid laws by 50 years.

As "etiquette," Jim Crow practices were strict and punitive, as unspoken standards of interracial protocols, that sought to demean the individual dignity of every Black and belittle the societal standing of Blacks in the collective. It denied African Americans all forms of social standing and basic human dignities usually afforded all in a civil society, and required all Blacks of any age to show deference to all Whites-even children, stripping Blacks of all public salutations and titles of public respect such as "Mister," or "Misses" or "Madame" or "Sir"-instead replacing them with titles of adolescence like "boy," "girl," or "gal," or first names (not surnames) absent of any social formalities-even if the black person was the elder of the white person. Any attempt to insist on public honor or extract respect was usually met with admonishment or hostility followed by a reinforcement point, usually a verbal assault of some kind-most commonly the term, "Nigger."

Blacks were required to step out of the path of Whites to avoid any chance encounter, never challenge the word or question the authority of Whites, particularly white males. The word of a White was always more credible than the word of a Black and always supported by the community culture as necessary to quash due process, which also gave rise to outlandish accusations that fed the mob mentalities that fueled vigilantism. The protocol of Jim Crow racial etiquette was to keep Blacks in an inferior position to Whites at all costs and humiliated in their own self-image, that when combined, presented a double edged sword that offered a reinforced white supremacy, juxtaposed against a demanded inferiority of social status for Blacks and a lower placement than Whites, most times-the lowest placement of all societal population segments, in America's racial hierarchy.

Jim Crow, as extra-legal means, represented a "social check" against resistance to segregation or advocacy against the inequalities of Jim Crow, where extra-legal means could turn to illegal means rather quickly, when intimidation and violence against Blacks were usually deemed as necessary and warranted to keep the racial etiquette in check. Any one White, several Whites, or a mob could "check" any Black, group of Blacks, or even a township of Blacks, at any time. Blacks, in just standing up for their Constitutional rights, brought provocation "upon themselves," as unprovoked assaults of black men, rape of black women, abduction of black children and even the murder of Blacks were not considered crimes against society, but "means" to an end-the end being the subordinated social control of African Americans. "Separate But Equal" policy and racial etiquettes would become synonymous in meaning and practice, to where its was commonly known and accepted as the South's "Jim Crow" system of racial oppression. In its totality, what Jim Crow meant in the 20th Century was an "American Nightmare," as chronicled by Jerome M. Packard, represented "the legal, quasi-legal, or customary practice of disfranchising, physically segregating, barring and discriminating against black Americans, virtually the sole practitioners of such practices being white

Americans."[5] In the same way that enslaved Blacks used "Jim Crow" a term for shuffling feet as a way to circumvent dancing, white America used "Jim Crow" a term for "Separate But Equal" laws as a way to circumvent Constitutional equality, by claiming that all citizens were being given equal treatment-though separated-under the law a subterfuge to prevent Blacks from being equal in America. Jim Crow and its politics of white supremacy were not only born in America, Jim Crow was America, and represented what it stood for, for nearly 100 years (1864-1964). Segregation, only second to 300 years of institutionalized slavery, was the most degenerative social politic in the history of America, as it related to fairness, justice and equality.

Jim Crow racism took hold in a widespread manner after the *Plessy* decision, when Jim Crow laws sprung up everywhere, and enforcement of those laws took an aggressive turn for the worse. Whatever vestiges of Radical Reconstruction that survived the Redemption Period, were erased in the period following *Plessy*, as the Post Reconstruction Period (1877-1919) would go on record, save for slavery, as the most vicious period in American history, in terms of how white supremacy was re-introduced and reinforced in American society.

The very first targets of Jim Crow "separate but equal" policies in the public sector were political representation and education, the two most common vehicles for which equality could be obtained. Blacks, while marginalized in some states by the withdrawal of federal troops in the South in 1877, still maintained some political standing in Congress and in many state legislatures.

The principle "Jim Crow" laws used to marginalize black voting were "understanding" or "good character" clauses, which allowed poor Whites to be "grandfathered" into voting, based on the understanding that they qualified for certain loopholes that only white men could get through. A second law was poll taxes requiring payment to vote that was selectively applied as a "discouragement payment" for Blacks and poor Whites. Starting in 1895, in South Carolina, through 1910, all of the former Confederate states passed some form of literacy, character, or grandfather clauses, as well as poll taxes to impede black voting.[6]

Another common disfranchisement ploy was refusing to allow Blacks to vote in elections where popular decision choices amongst the largest pool of candidates were made, called "white primaries." In doing so, Whites were able to suppress (exclude) the black vote, while choosing the candidates most suitable to their interests and the next most suitable. By the time Blacks got to vote in the general elections, they didn't have much to choose from, in terms of candidates that were likely to push for, or uphold, black equality.

Mississippi, though not the first to approve the use of white primaries, was the first to elect a "Jim Crow" Governor through its use. Mississippi, the first state to impose black codes in 1865, the first state to initiate a "redemption plan" targeting both black majority counties and federal presence, in 1875 (called the "Mississippi Plan") and the first state to engage segregation laws, first with segregated waiting rooms in 1888, then with segregated cemeteries in 1890. Mississippi was a very poor state that never recovered from the Civil War, economically, and thus, only knew severest poverty of which both Blacks and Whites shared.[7] With only the narrowest strand of difference in the quality of Black and White living standards, the vote was the only difference of measure between Black and White. Though intimidation had increased significantly since 1877 to impede access to the ballot, formal restrictions appeared quickly as the progressive movement empowering the common man throughout the nation, worked against Blacks in the South, as "rednecks" (Whites with open hostilities toward Blacks) and poor Whites (those most in direct competition with Blacks) came together to adopt direct primaries that would exclude Blacks, until the choices were made-choices that would obviously serve "superior race" politics through "White Only" primaries.[8]

This practice was first approved in South Carolina, in 1896 (the year *Plessy* was decided), and was replicated throughout the rest of the South; in Arkansas, in 1897; Georgia, in 1898; Florida and Tennessee, in 1901; in Alabama and Mississippi, in 1902; Kentucky and Texas, in 1903; Louisiana, in 1906; Oklahoma, in 1907; Virginia, in 1913; and North Carolina, in 1915.[9] These primaries were in effect until outlawed by the Supreme Court, in 1944, at which time, Black voter influence had been completely demoralized. Black elected officials were left unprotected, when black voters were tricked, manipulated and intimidated at the polls and black representation diminished as the black vote dropped off, until there were, literally, none.

It even led to the election of Jim Crow candidates who openly campaigned on platforms to uphold Jim Crow laws that would impose and maintain the inferior status of Blacks, if elected. With the first "White Only" primary in 1903, Mississippi showed the power of Jim Crow's "racial message" when it elected the first "Jim Crow" Governor, James K. Valdaman, a race baiter of the worst kind, appealing to popular sentiment. Valdaman, a candidate from the Mississippi Delta, traveled around the state on an oxen drawn wagon making course and vulgar jokes, with Blacks and "negro equality" his target. Valdaman said things like; "The Negro, like the mule has neither pride of ancestry, nor hope of posterity;" "The way to control the nigger is to whip him when he does not obey without it;" and, in specifically addressing use of economic subjugation as a form of social control, " is never to pay him more wages than is actually necessary to buy food and clothing."[10] Vardaman came to recognize what the center of racism in America was, economic subjugation, and without the vote, and without money, Blacks simply could not be equal and would always hold a societal position inferior to that of Whites.

Candidates of this type surfaced in other states and became the prototype for the "Dixiecrat" in the 20th Century. This wasn't the only way Jim Crow laws were used to disenfranchise Blacks, and again, Mississippi, would lead the way over the next thirty years, "cementing the Negro in his place" by passing segregated streetcars, segregated hospitals and mandating black nurses for black patients, segregating taxis and even passing a law, in 1930, that prohibited "publishing, printing or circulating any literature in favor of, or urging inter-racial marriage or social equality."[11] Mississippi showed the power of "states rights" under the Post Civil War "dual federalism" posture of federal government, who just turned their heads to the various state's "cultural behaviors," as long as they weren't pervasive-which could've been interpreted as meaning, "as long as, such behaviors didn't abridge the rights of Whites."

The impact of *Plessy* was absolutely devastating to the political representation ambitions of African Americans in the early 20th Century. Townships, counties and states, one by one, began to adopt Jim Crow laws, such as grandfather clauses, white primaries, poll taxes, and literacy tests to disengage black suffrage. Blacks who insisted on voting and/or maintaining their full franchise rights were usually sunject to an encounter with Jim Crows' intimidation forces; legal (law enforcement), extra-legal (gerrymandering policies) and illegal (the Ku Klux Klan). While black representation had started its slide prior to the *Plessy* decision, it took a full scale drop-off after *Plessy*. To demonstrate how dramatic the impact of *Plessy* was, and how quickly its influence spread, take into consideration that when the federal government pulled out its troops in 1877, there were eight members (one Senator, and seven House Members) in Congress. At the time of the *Plessy* decision, that number had fallen to one (George W. Murray of South Carolina). There would only be one black Congressman elected after the *Plessy* decision, in 1897 (George H. White of North Carolina). Within five years of the *Plessy* decision, in 1901, when a white challenger came after White, there were no Blacks in Congress, and few Blacks in state legislatures. From 1901 to 1929, there was no political representation for Blacks-not one Black-in the United States Congress, until 1929, when Oscar DePriest was elected from Illinois. However, a Black Congressman would not be elected in the Upper South until Parren Mitchell from Maryland was elected in 1971. The deep South didn't elect another Black congressperson, until Georgia elected Andrew Young, and Texas elected Barbara Jordan in 1972,-76 years after *Plessy*.

This meant for nearly three-fourths of the 20th Century, the majority of the black population in the United States, 60% of Blacks still lived in the South by 1970, had no real political representation. Yet, with only the shadow representation of Dixiecrats and other anti-Black forces, Blacks were expected-even demanded-to comply with taxation measures, much of which represented an over-taxation known as "the black tax," just to be able to participate in a subordinated role in American society, while their political rights were not being enforced. This was, in essence, the very issue-taxation without representation-that brought on the Revolutionary War, which, in turn, created the United States of America. Yet, Britain's inegalitarian practices had taken on a life of its own here in America. This is how powerful Jim Crow took hold in the South, and it did not represent a voluntary withdraw of Blacks from the American political system. Blacks were run out of the political system through policy manipulation, social extremism, an original form of societal terrorism and through outright intimidation.

To further inbred segregation into Whites' cultural "way of life," and into the hearts and minds of their children, education became the breeding grounds for the segregationist mindset. The demonstrative affects of racial inequalities were based on numerous assertions from intellectuals, both Black and White. In education, separation efforts took extra-ordinary speed, when states moved to segregate public schools and higher education. Public school districts throughout the South became segregated schools. Prior to 1900, while there were disparities in funding and resources that favored Whites schools, there were no real differences between the black schools and white schools,

131

because public spending on education was so low that it really didn't permit for gross disparities, and Blacks were able to successfully resist proposals to divide school tax revenues according to race.[12]

However, after 1900, as Jim Crows influence grew, the tide of racial discrimination, the allocations in what white schools and Blacks schools received became dramatically more disparate. For example, percentages in school funding in North Carolina, where black children were 34% of the school population, shrank from 28% to 13% by 1915. While in South Carolina, spending ratios between white children and black children went from almost 6 (5.75) to 1, in 1900, to 12 to 1 by 1915. Black teacher's pay in Mississippi went from just fifty cents less than white teachers pay in 1901, to one-half of white teachers pay by 1910.[13] School officials even passed out and stored school books by race, which, in North Carolina and Florida, specified that books used by black students had to be maintained in a separate space from those of Whites.[14]

The major conflict in education came in the divide between higher education (learning colleges), and industrial education (vocational colleges). The first land grant college was established in Jefferson City Missouri in 1866 (Lincoln University), but Congress passed a second Morrill Act, that allowed a total of seventeen land-grant institutions to be funded that allowed higher education to begin the practice of segregating college students, as the former Confederate states used the land grant funds to build separate colleges specifically for Blacks.[15] Actually, the first Morrill Act, passed in 1862, had only provided for the establishment of land-grants colleges. It wasn't until 1871, that race became a factor, when Mississippi created the first college specifically for Blacks.[16] By 1896, the year *Plessy* was decided, every "Dixie" state (except Tennessee, who designated Tennessee Agricultural and Industrial as a Negro land grant college in 1919) had funded a land grant college for Blacks to attend, as well as, four "border" states, Kentucky in 1886, West Virginia in 1891, Delaware in 1895 and Oklahoma in 1897.

If Blacks wanted a quality education beyond high school, they had to, by and large, look to private institutions, as state funded colleges were generally segregated, and denied admission to African Americans. None of the Negro land grant colleges, as late as 1916, however, offered college level work.[17] This is where Jim Crow culture played its biggest influence in education, in determining curriculum rationalizations for black educational ambitions. During the 1890s, the focus of higher education shifted from the more esteemed liberal arts colleges, to what was called, "Industrial education," a catch-all term for what we now call vocational education. The essential difference between liberal arts colleges and industrial colleges was that one was for learning knowledge, while the other was for learning trades and skills. "Manual Labor" schools were colleges that specialized in the manual trades that included farming, home economics, shoemaking, printing, carpentry, bricklaying and any other "odd jobs" associated with manual labor.[18] The prevailing thought was that Blacks were better with their hands than they were with their minds, so send them to college to develop labor skills, not intellectual skills. Some of the very first successful black colleges that were manual labor and vocational institutes, including Tougaloo, Spelman, Hampton, and the model that would be held up as the promotion for the expansion of industrial education, Tuskegee Institute.

While industrial and agricultural education was viewed by abolitionists, free Blacks and freedmen as the best way to transition a nation of former bondsman into society, the popularity of the concept was widely adopted by philanthropists who encouraged it. Southern Whites saw it as a way of keeping Blacks in a subordinate position, by teaching them to work with their hands, rather than teaching them to work with their minds, in preparing Blacks for professional careers. [19] While competition with Blacks was of primary concern in both economic life and in the socio-economic class structure, Whites could not deny that they still needed black labor. Four-fifths of the South's black population lived in rural areas, most of whom earned their living farming white owned land as renters or sharecroppers.[20] Industrial education made sense as a legitimate way to gradually educate Blacks and include them in the national economy. The term was misleading and meant various things to various people.

For Washington, it was an opportunity to use Northern money to build black schools, educate Blacks in industrial education and beyond-even if they were separate but equal. For white Southerners, it meant providing Blacks with separate inferior schools with watered-down curriculum, and training in only rudimentary skills. For white Northern industrialists, it was a chance to bond with white Southerners on the question of education, in that they saw Reconstruction as a mistake, doubted that black intelligence was equal to Whites, skeptical about the value of higher education to Blacks and, not interested in supporting black "social equality" claims.[21] But the national discussion

133

on industrial education soon became the doorway to the "citizenship litmus test," as advocates of industrial education began to stress that it could prove to be a tool in the moral development of the African American, from which moral virtues could be implanted to build the Negro's progress, "as a man and a citizen."[22] This position operated on the thesis that there had been a "regression" in the state of the Black during the Post-Reconstruction Period, suggesting-according to those philanthropist and industrial education proponents, that it would be years-even centuries-before Blacks would be civilly and intellectually prepared to enjoy the rights of citizenship equally with Whites. Jim Crowism had bushwacked the national debate on where to direct the educational ambitions of, and how best to educate, Blacks.

Moreover, Jim Crow proponents had found their very first black spokesperson for industrial education, whose opinion was consistent with their own, in Booker T. Washington, founder of Tuskegee Institute, who saw black demands for equality as futile and antagonistic to the race politic. Whites did all they could to profile "the Tuskegee Idea," which, in effect, said that the vast majority of Blacks were not going to better their position by means of politics, protest or higher learning, and that their salvation rested in mastering basic work skills and applying them, with honest sweat, to the demands of the Southern agricultural economy. In doing so, Blacks would be able to earn the respect of Whites, which would then allow Blacks to pull themselves up "by their own bootstraps," erode white prejudice, and in time, Whites would willingly accord them full citizenship rights, including the right to vote.[23]

The Tuskegee Idea was centered in Washington's doctrine of vocational education for Blacks, and was the best suited strategy in a "go along to get along" interface with Whites. It was hailed in the North and the South as a formula for satisfactory social and economic equilibrium between the races, that would bring peace in the South.[24] When Washington offered his view that Blacks should stop fighting segregation, that "In all things that are purely social we can be as separate as the five fingers, yet one as the hand in all things essential to mutual progress," at the 1895 Atlanta Exposition, and, at a time when Whites thought that education was "ruining the Negro," suggested to make friends with Whites, by casting their buckets down "where you are," accepting roles in society as that would not agitate Whites, it made Washington unquestionably " *the* spokesperson for Blacks," until his death in 1915. Many viewed Washington's philosophy of getting along with the white man as his being the beneficiary of their philan-thropy-that also freed him from the school funding race politics of Alabama-as he urged Whites to help more "sensible Negroes," who understood "that the agitation of questions of social equality is the extremest folly."[25]

Blacks throughout the nation were outraged at the proposition that a black person, much less, one serving as a spokesperson against the fight for equality, would advocate for the subordination of Blacks, as a political strategy of what was called, "accommodation," to gain white trust and affirmation of an equality already guaranteed in the Constitution. In that outrage came a countervailing school of thought led by black intellectuals, newspaper editors and political thinkers, that said Blacks could succeed, by not focusing solely on manual labor and subordination, in achieving social equality.

Led by Harvard scholar and activist, William Edward Burghardt (W.E.B.) DuBois, who had no equal in terms of his intellect, articulation and forethought of what was required to advance the status of Blacks in the face of this emerging segregation movement, that said that Washington's politics of accommodation were bankrupt, because it allowed the white South to destroy the political and civil rights of Blacks, while offering no remedies to break the racial oppression and economic deprivation forging a poverty that engulfed the masses of Blacks. DuBois also saw Washington's educational programs as too narrow, as only serv-ing minimal economic interests for Blacks, while benefiting the larger economic objectives of Whites, and not addressing the intellectual and knowledge building interests of Blacks. DuBois, the first Black to earn a Ph.D. at Harvard in the same year Washington made his infamous Atlanta speech, attacked Washington's depreciation of higher education in his book, *Souls of Black Folk*, in 1903, as developing "money-makers," instead of men incapable of thinking beyond the realms of technical skills.[26] DuBois proposed instead a "talented tenth" that would excel in all areas, and lead the race to equality and self-sufficiency.

DuBois thought Washington's position helped fuel Jim Crow politics, because Washington had allowed himself to become "a compro-miser" between the South, the North, and the Negro (DuBois termed Washington 1895 speech "the Atlanta Compromise"), by extending the olive branch to white Southerners that resulted in the disfranchisement of Blacks, and the legal creation of a distinct status of civil inferiority that made it impossible, in the scope of true free market competition, for black artisans, businesspeople and property owners to defend their rights and exist without full suffrage.[27]

Industrial education, in DuBois' opinion, was only a subterfuge in the elevation of Booker T. Washington's status as a spokesperson for Blacks. In the eyes of W.E.B. DuBois, northern philanthropists, in the likes of Railroad Industrialists, Collis P. Huntington and William H. Baldwin, steel magnate Andrew Carnegie and oil magnate, Henry H. Rogers, gave Washington millions, and used him, as did white Southerners, to promote Jim Crow, and dismiss social equality as unreasonable and unattainable, making him, in DuBois' words, "the most distinguished Southerner since Jefferson Davis," in affirming the South's second "great divide" and helping facilitate its own separate nation in racial segregation.[28] The public higher education sector, meanwhile, turned its backs on Blacks altogether, as state funding laws made segregation a condition for funding.

In the private sector, racial segregation grew, as social norms had embraced racial etiquette with enduring voracity. A physical and omnipresent "the color line" began appearing in every form of social interface in the South that Whites could imagine. Hotels, theaters and restaurants, railroad trains, bus and train waiting rooms, restrooms, parks, swimming pools, all began to demand and enforce race caste accommodations that required Blacks to be accommodated in an "equal" but "separate" fashion. The most common definition of equal, whether it is noun, verb or adjective, is; "of the same measure, quantity, value, quality, number degree, or status as another," or in essence, the same or same value.[29] But that wasn't the fashion in which Jim Crow "equality" was implemented.

Signs designated "White Only," "Colored Only," "White Section," "Colored Section," "White Entry," "Colored Entry," "Whites Service Only," "Colored Served In the Rear," dominated society, and in each and every instance, with very few exceptions, whatever was deemed "colored" use was less than, smaller than, higher than, subordinate to, or behind whatever was deemed "white" use. Race equality was no longer objectively imaginative, it was subjectively definitive. Separation of the races was becoming an increasingly accepted protocol of American society, where black/white interaction literally shrank by the day.

The workplace became the most common reflection of the "separated Southern landscape, as Blacks and Whites who had historically worked together in relative (but not totally "conflict free") harmony in the offices, shops and factories, were suddenly mandated to keep away from each other-with the penalties directed at Blacks for violation-and were required to use separate doors, separate dressing rooms, separate lunch rooms, separate pay windows, separate toilets-even separate stair-ways and pathways.[30] Everything from libraries-where libraries were either segregated by building, (black libraries for Blacks) or section with-in the same building (but Blacks couldn't check books out), to prisons-where black and white inmates were barred from sharing cells, eating together, shackled together (when on the chain gang), and in some instances, even sharing the same prison; from insane asylums and men-tal hospitals, to cemeteries-where Whites were actually exhumed from any cemetery where Blacks were buried; from ticket lines to public phones; from separate entrances in almost every private place-in restau-rants and theatres (where Whites entered the front and Blacks entered the rear) to waiting rooms and traveling quarters; from the church where Blacks and Whites commonly worshipped under the same roof during slavery (though Blacks were most often in the balcony), only now to separate worship throughout the South (and in the North). Even "sin" was segregated in that whore houses sold sex (and bought) sex accord-ing to the color of one's skin-though white men could (and frequently did) patronage black bordellos while black men risked harm-even death-in "sex for hire" propositions solicited to white bordello houses.[31]

Racial etiquette laws seeking to maintain private segregated space were reinforced with stiff penalties. Fines and penalties were even legislated to target Blacks, constrain black behavior, or maximize pun-ishment for crimes most likely to be committed by Blacks. For instance, Alabama had 10 p.m curfews for Blacks that required them to be off the street, or be jailed, while Missouri made chicken stealing a felony pun-ishable by five years in jail for Blacks, where anybody else got a $200 fine.[32] In Georgia, black men who could not find work were arrested for loitering, then leased out by the local prison, under a convict lease sys-tem, to do work for lumber companies, brickyards, and plantations around Atlanta-for free. In 1905, Blacks represented 50,000 out of a total population of 130,000 (38%), yet Atlanta arrested 10,000 black men of a total of 17,000 arrests (59%), with a death attrition rate of about 10%.[33] Black men were, literally, worked to death while in jail. Criminalization policies were the most consistent form of socially con-trolling Blacks, particularly black men.

In a societal culture that wanted to assure absolute accountabil-ity for Blacks at all times, and had no tolerance for the "nigger loose" that could bring crime to the doorstep of Whites, and the threat of rape to white women, a bigger fear that drove inherent extra-legal means for communal protection, white males would leave nothing to chance, to

137

due process, if the racial protocols were violated in a way that assaulted the sensibilities of their women. Black hypersexuality, a necessary myth promoted by white males, was the most ardent justification against "social equality." The black rape threat was used to emasculate black men in ways that had nothing to do with criminality and everything to do with promoting a societal distrust that mitigated social contact and stripped away legal and equal rights.

The assertion that the worst case scenario of a crime, rape of a white woman, might occur, became justification for denying Blacks the right to vote, excluding them from juries, discriminating against black men in work, or segregating them in spaces and place where they couldn't work along side, or, in authority over, white women, traveling the presence of white women, sit at tables with white women, anyplace where a possible sexual relation could be approached or engaged. White Southerners essentially interpreted black claims to equality as an attempt to be in the company of, and subsequently engage some sort of attack on, white women.[34]

It was during this period of Post-Reconstruction that saw the rise of America's "strange fruit" phenomena, lynching. Lynching, from 1892, until well into the 20th Century, was the practice of hanging or killing a person by mob action, usually for an alleged crime or an observed breach of racial etiquette. It was usually from a tree, but it could also be from a building or a light post, and sometimes, even a burning cross. It had also become a largely black phenomena, although-like most behaviors and systems targeting Blacks-it didn't start out that way.

Lynching originated from the term, "lynch-law" named after American Revolutionary War Colonel, Charles Lynch of Bedford County, Virginia, who set up an "informal" court to deal with Tories (British loyalists) and criminals prior to the establishment of Virginia statehood in 1781.[35] "Lynch-law" had no connection to the death penalty, nor Blacks, in its inception, because Blacks had no standing in the courts. Punishment handed down by the "court" was limited to fines and whippings-and did not hand down death penalty verdicts-which the extra-legal form of punishment came to mean until 1850 when horse thieves and "desperadoes" were executed for their crimes by a vigilance committee.[36]

It wasn't until after the Civil War and during the Reconstruction Period that lynching obtained its modern meaning of death by mob. Early statistics in the 1880s had more Whites being lynched than Blacks. The first recorded statistics between 1882 and

1888, indicated 595 Whites were lynched in the United States, compared to 440 for Blacks in the same period. However, simultaneous to the culmination of racial radicalism in the Redemption Period in 1889 was the transition of lynching as a racial act against Blacks. Ninety-four Blacks were recorded in 1889 as lynched rising above Whites (76 Whites that year) for the first time. By 1892, the year Plessy was filed, clearly public sentiment toward Blacks had changed, and lynching had reached its highest point, with black lynchings (162) more than doubling that of Whites (69) and from 1906 to 1915-the start of America's period of political estrangement with Blacks-black lynchings were 10 times higher (620) than white lynchings (61).[37]

Lynching could be a mysterious act of vigilantism, or it could be a publicized public spectacle with women and children in a "picnic" like social gathering. The fact that lynching was most commonly performed by "persons unknown," though the community intelligentsia knew who were involved most of the time, prosecuting mobs-versus individuals-was much more difficult, and too overwhelming, to prove in court.[38] One of the origins of the term, picnic, allegedly stemmed from Southern folklore, as a gathering where a group of rowdies would "pick a nigger,"-any Black-who might be in the area, to lynch for their own entertainment.

Lynching didn't just involve hanging an individual. Many times, it involved the total mutilation of one's body, from burning the person alive while hanging, to decapitation, castration of limbs and genitals. Lynching also represented the extent of Jim Crow "zero tolerance policy" on race matters, a constant threat to those who might step out of bounds on racial etiquette, or get caught in a place where they weren't supposed to be, that this too might happen to you if you step out of your 'place' in this society. Blacks from the North, often unacquainted with the race politics of the South, could end up being lynched, and many Blacks from the South went North, at a moments notice, to keep from being lynched.

The difference in the volatility of race treatment in the North and the South separated around the practice of lynching. The three decades (from 1889 to 1918) that reflected the Post Reconstruction Period in America saw 88% of the lynchings that occurred during this period in fourteen Southern states.[39] Lynching represented black America's biggest threat from which no one was immune. The vile and demeaning form of torture replaced slavery's whip as the dominant form of social control, and was not a rare occurrence in the Post

139

Reconstruction Era. It was a frequent, even popular occurrence during some years in this era, where there was, at least, one lynching somewhere in America *every week.*

There were several social and commonly accepted patterns to lynching, such as, when lynchings were most likely to occur, July being the most favored month; favorite places for lynching to occur (a mountain, a town center, a park, someplace common to the populace); lynching was likely to occur in places undergoing rapid economic changes; lastly, lynching were likely to occur in places with strong local cultures, weak judicial systems and places where lynchings were frequent and less likely to be punished-in other words-accepted as part of the local cultural practice.[40] It wasn't uncommon for local mobs to break accused Blacks, awaiting due process, out of the custody of local jailers to lynch them-as many didn't trust the local judicial system to impose a satisfactory level of justice. Lynching was often viewed as "justice," and in some instances, such as a Black accused of rape, a simple lynching was seen as "too noble" of a death for such a vicious accusation.[41] Shooting, burning, and mutilation were likely to follow.

The common explanation to rationalize lynching was that "it was justified" to stem the urge of black men to rape white women. A study on lynching done in 1942, stated that from 1883 to 1941, there were 3,811 Blacks lynched in the United States, but only 641 (less than 17%) were even accused of rape, attempted or committed (same penalty for both).[42] Instead, black people were lynched for the simplest and most asinine reasons, such as poisoning a mule, writing an insulting note to a white girl, talking disrespectfully, and commonly for "acting white." "Acting white," as perceived by Whites, was essentially any Black who tried to live as Whites lived, by trying to own property, trying to vote, or encourage others to vote, expressing themselves in free speech as protected under the 1st Amendment, trying to protect themselves and their families as guaranteed under the 2nd Amendment, trying to work or compete with Whites both in labor and in business, trying to engage in the social enjoyments preferred by Whites (operas, theatres, fairs, etc.).[43]

"Acting white" was, in essence, trying to act equal to Whites, or showing no deference to Whites in public-which Whites accused Blacks of "acting above themselves," which is where the term, "uppity" originated. Simple contact with Whites, known as "bumping Whites" usually brushing a White, when refusing to step off a sidewalk, became reason enough to raise suspicion that a Black was "being uppity" and had committed a "crime" against race etiquette.[44]

For the first 71 years of record-keeping (until 1952, where according to a Tuskegee Institute, there was no known lynching of an African American), there was, at least, one *recorded* lynching in America (there were many that went unrecorded, because the bodies were never found).[45] This didn't end the practice, however. A secondary phase of the lynching phenomena accomplished the rise of the Civil Rights movements of the 1950s and 1960s, and there were regular lynching reports well into the 1970s, and even, on occasion, in the 1980s. Lynching is one of the truly "Made in America" commodities, and has found its place in American society as a useful tool to reinforce the social, political and economic agenda's forged out of *Plessy* and "Separate But Equal."

Lynching not only created deep physical pain, but created a deep emotional scar and psychological controls on black populations as lynching took on various forms to communicate various messages. Lynching ranged from hanging, with a quick break of the neck, to hanging with a slow strangulation, hanging and shooting, hanging and burning, hanging with a "slow burning," hanging, then dragging or mutilating the body, leaving a dead lynch victim for days "on display" (exhibition), taking "souvenirs" (fingers, toes, ears, teeth, bones and sexual organs were commonly seen in jars in offices and business owners' display windows), all meant to send messages to Blacks that Whites were in control, and this could happen to any Black who didn't know how to control themselves around Whites.[46] Government control, "cultural" control and compliance control (the ability to impose the will of Whites and make Blacks comply) made up the politics of Jim Crow. The threat of intimidation and actual practice of lynching was the final reinforcement that made Jim Crow stronger and more pervasive, as society began to understand its benefits in instilling fear in the black community, and controlling its more "radical" elements.

Jim Crowism had little or nothing to do with "equality" or "separatism" or respect in upholding the law or the Constitution. Jim Crowism had everything to do with societal benefits, or "privilege;" essentially defining what Whites were privileged to do versus what Blacks were privileged to do, where Whites were privileged to go versus where Blacks were privileged to go, and most important, who Whites were privileged to be versus who Blacks were un-privileged to be. In the end, the real privilege in Jim Crowism was in being "white," and its real purpose was in defining and maintaining the privileges of

141

"whiteness" in America, sole and simple, no mistake about it. Whiteness and blackness were juxtaposed against each other, as mats on a wall, and societal privileges represented an "either/or" proposition. White meant "entitled," Black meant "un-entitled." Entitlements would become a significant point of discussion in the latter 20th Century-in terms of "who is entitled to receive what from government"-but at this point in time, there was only one recipient of entitlement, and that belonged to Whites.

The legal test of *Plessy* was essentially about "who was white" in America. The category of "white," while clear on its face, was never absolute in its definition. Whiteness has always been a moving scale, but only to a point. *Plessy* sought to help clarify the point, or "draw the line." Geographical lineage could qualify one as white, but genealogical lineage could disqualify one as white. A white person was generally considered someone of European genetic stock, and on the moving scale of whiteness, full-blooded (unmixed) northern Europeans were seen as unquestionably white, while southern Europeans, many of darker skin tones, though white, weren't seen "as white." This became problematic when darker Southern Europeans intermarried with fairer northern Europeans, specifically the Germanic, Anglo-Saxon, or Scandinavian people-largely because the ruling mantra of America's racial society was "the whiter, the better" and social attainments, political power, and wealth accumulation accrued in direct proportion to the "indisputability of the whiteness of one's ancestry and physical features."[47]

Blackness, on the other hand, held many of the same complications, particularly in America because the term "black" had become synonymous with "slave" and African, the common term for Blacks throughout the world, didn't include all persons considered "black" by America's race caste. The term, black, commonly excluded super-Saharan Africans (Semitic or Arab Muslims) who didn't look like Black Africans (those most resembling the American Negro), while sub-Saharan Africans (Muslim and Christian Ethiopians), who looked much like their super-Saharan brethren were considered Black, and were actually a small group of the formerly enslaved population of America, thus the source of their designation.[48]

The sexual politics of slavery created a "new race," called, Mulattos, which allowed their offspring to claim European lineage, or "claims to whiteness." Many of those offspring actually more resembled their European bloodlines than their African bloodlines. By the end of slavery, a majority of American born Africans, whose complexions ranged from shades of Northern European "pink-white" to sub-Sarahan coal "blue-black," had some degree of European ancestry, or whiteness" in their genetic make-up.[49] American Africans, however, were excluded from geographical lineage or European kinship. There were plenty of "white" persons of African descent, whose African heritage could be hidden. It was called, passing, a practice many Blacks engaged in to escape the social penalties being black imposed-and constantly ran the risk of being uncovered and forced to assume the status of Negro, any black genes meant you were black and to be denied of the privileges reinforced by "race standards" in America.[50] As discussed in the previous chapter, the "one-drop rule" became the "race standard" in America, even if a person was of equal lineage of African and European (equally half-white and half-black). America's race standard did not allow for anything such as a "half-a-white, or even seven-eighths white-as Homer Plessy found out. You were either white, or you weren't. Being white had nothing to do with color, as mixed-race off-spring found out, and everything to do with separating black from white, and the exclusivity of privileges that being "all white" brings to those who possess such a birthright.

If "Separate But Equal" didn't have to do with societal privileges, it would not have had to be as aggressively enforced. If equal meant "equal," as long as Whites didn't get less than equal treatment, what Blacks got wouldn't have really mattered. But what we saw, in the historical context, was that since Whites never saw Blacks as "equals," it did matter what Blacks received, comparatively, in the eyes and minds of Whites-not just poor Whites, but all Whites. And if Jim Crow was just about being separate, there wouldn't have been a need to separate Blacks away from their Constitutional rights to vote, to sit on juries, to hold office and to run their communities. While Blacks could easily and equally provide themselves these rights, duties and opportunities, they would not have the privilege to do so under a Jim Crow system of white supremacy and racial discrimination. Legalized social separation and exclusion of Blacks from the electoral system, to strip African Americans of any influence over government policy, were the focus of privileges denied, the primary and secondary features of Jim Crow politics in the South, between 1890 and 1910.[51]

Whiteness was made a benefit in America, and to such benefit extended certain privileges-activities and opportunities exclusive to Whites. These activities and opportunities represented social, political and democratic privileges afforded to "Whites only." America was the land of opportunity for all, but it was based on privileges of liberty and justice extended to some-not all. That "some" of the whole, a part of society (not sum of the whole-total society), were white people, as defined by highly subjective and interpretive race "facts" of Jim Crow. This subsequently introduced forms of economic subjugation that created massive racial disparities in access to jobs, wages and long term employment rights.

As industrialization sought to monopolize jobs, lower wages and constrict collective bargaining, unionization became the most common vehicle to protect jobs and wages. Unions varied from craft unions to industrial unions, but what they had in common was that they were the basis for which "skilled" workers could protect their trade and exclude "outsiders" from practicing the trade-while at the same time-maintaining control over jobs, and even maintaining a monopoly over particular jobs essential to the growth and expansion of industrialization.[52] Few Blacks belonged to these unions, because they were thought to lack the necessary skills, or were kept out, mainly due to discriminatory policies that were set in place for racial purposes, as racial exclusion was seen as part of the larger design on the part of white workers to restrict competition-from unskilled workers and to preserve their own domination in the labor movement.[53]

This position created bitter conflicts between working class Whites and Blacks, as it became apparent that Blacks were being forced out of their jobs through unionization, and as employers saw large societal race conflict as a way to play one race against the other as a benefit to themselves, by using displaced black workers as strike breakers, when it was convenient to do so. This created fear and insecurity among white workers, who knew employers had "a reserve" of unemployed, job-hungry non-unionized black laborers to undermine their strike demands. It occurred enough between 1910 and 1930 to intimidate Whites into maintaining persistent racial animosities, that quickly could turn hostile, as Whites viewed Blacks as allied with union-busting employers-when, in fact, all they wanted to do was work and work consistently.[54]

Violation of the racial etiquette also involved a form of corporal punishment, strict and consistent, as it was during slavery. However, Jim Crow not only allowed the law, and legal law enforcement community, to enforce the racial etiquette, it allowed any white person who was offended by any black person, at any time, to enforce the etiquette, and it turned its head if the enforcement was overtly brutal, deadly, and most implicit, if the action was illegal. The government and the community were complicit, in its approval, in its silent affirmation of social controls that were limitless and undaunting, in ensuring that Jim Crow laws were upheld, and Jim Crow "culture" was obeyed. There was nothing that couldn't be done to black people during this period, though the more extreme actions were sought to be kept at a minimum, to keep the federal government from intervening. What "the minimum" was could and never would be discerned. It simply meant "to do whatever had to be done" to keep Blacks "in their place." That's just the way it was.

Those who redeemed the South back into the hands of race supremacist, which clearly was not the majority of Whites in the South-but a significant number of powerful people, mostly men, in the South-would establish Segregation's mantra as a reminder of its post civil war victory. It would state, "Segregation Yesterday, Segregation Today, Segregation forever." Segregation was able to profoundly suppress and regress the social, political and economic rights of Blacks, largely because the overwhelming number of Blacks were still in the South, directly under the thumb of the Jim Crow politic. As Jim Crow was taking hold at the turn of the 20th Century, according to the census of 1910, Blacks were overwhelmingly Southerners where nine of ten Blacks in the country lived in the South. They were largely concentrated in rural towns in such significant numbers, that three of every four Blacks in the nation lived in rural communities.[55]

Pseudo-science was introduced into the national discourse on race, to help justify Jim Crow. Again, with the maintenance of whiteness in mind, white theorists always suggested that cohabitation between a superior race and an inferior race would bring about a genetic threat that would not only bring down the superior race, but the regression of society as a whole. Thus, with the presence of black people, "New World" European society discouraged cohabitation (defined as sexual involvement with or without marriage) between Blacks and Whites. By the end of the 19th Century, it was sanctioned as an unacceptable practice termed, miscegenation ("racially unsound unions," according to Southern Whites), and though having occurred throughout the history of mankind, for the first time race mixture was made a key element within a major society.[56]

The close personal interaction between Whites and Blacks, 350 years of interaction by the turn of the 20th Century-300 years of which were the Master-slave interactions of the Antebellum South, created a one-sided forced miscegenation through master-slave sexual politics that produced hundreds of thousands, even millions, of mixed race off-spring which society termed, Mulattos, but played a key factor in changing the genetic make-up of the African-from full blooded African, "black" in their indigenous make-up to the American Negro, "brown" in their racially morphed make-up.[57]

The American Negro represented the making of a new being-an extension of its African roots and European captor combined, socialized as a European in identity, blended in their various color-producing genes, unique in its experience as full slave and half-free which conflicts memories of freedom in the continent of Africa, the slave trade and an existence in America as a compromised person. The Negro's condition, thus, made him a target for social engineering, where pseudo-scientists offered less than scientific "evidence" that suggested color (or race) was somehow indicative of a lower form of being, and the lighter a person, the more socially and intellectually advanced one was, and the darker a person was, the more intellectually inferior. While there was absolutely no basis for such theories, other than popular sentiment, Eugenics and Social Darwinism became the basis by which segregationist sought to validate white supremacy, and rationalize black inferiority.

The popularity of "scientific racism" and its emphasis on biological differences being the determinant of the natural capacities of, and destinies of racial groups, was the most obvious manifestation of Jim Crow racism, as Southern Whites openly embraced the pseudo-Darwinian concept that the struggle for existence in human life created a hierarchy or "contest" among human races that led to the survival and dominance of "the fittest race" who find it necessary to their survival to rule over inferior races with a firm hand.[58] Moreover, such antidotal analysis fed racial xenophobia that reinforced the politics of separation over fears that "race mixing" would lead to cohabitation and interracial marriages, that would breed mixed race children, thus leading to white America's ultimate obsession: "the mongrelization of the race," a theory that suggested that just by socializing with Blacks, Whites would eventually disappear from society, as they would become "mongrelized," as a result of mixing with an inferior race.[59]

Thus, separation was mandatory, and race-mixing could not be tolerated. In the 1890s, this school of thought in the 1890s evolved from Charles Darwin's "model of scientific predestination" that begun to overturn scientific beliefs on race in 1859, in psychology, sociology and economics, where statistical modeling was used to explain white

146

superiority over Blacks in terms of evoluntionary laws. By 1876, Dr. William Graham Sumner had integrated social Darwinism into the first sociology course in the United States-one that was rife with terms that described human beings as "strong" and "weak" which Sumner suggested were analogous to "the industrious" and "the idle," "the frugal" and "the extravagant," the "survival of the fittest" and the survival of the un-fittest, which was suppose to represent the laws of civilization and "anti-civilization," respectively.[60]

By the time renowned geologist, Joseph Le Conte published his views on race in 1892, Darwinian terms of "the fittest" and "un-fittest" were being framed in racial context, specifically Whites, as survival of the fittest, and Blacks as survival of the "un-fittest," and that laws determining the order of species among animals also applied to "races of men," where Le Conte clearly linked the condition of the Negro in terms of a "weaker variety of human...still in childhood that had not yet learned to walk alone in the paths of civilization.[61] " Le Conte surmised that Blacks were either destined to extinction, or relegation to a subordinate place in the "economy of nature," where they must either choose to return to slavery or extinction through "extermination or mixture-warning Whites that amalgamation weaken both Whites and Blacks because breeding between "pure types" produced the worst results. Le Conte concluded his theory, the broad acceptance of Whites, that if Blacks refused to submit to white control, Whites then must engage the law of self-preservation to save themselves, which would make the destruction of the Black race avoidable.[62]

The brutal firmness with which this mentality was enforced by Whites for the "survival of the race" purposes, if one believed in what Southern Whites subscribed to, but moreover was grounded in what a community of historians and scientists were calling "irrefutable laws of nature," tied to what they saw as the failures of Reconstruction, and the fact that in 25 short years, thirteen of which represented the massive resistance of the Redemption Period (1877-1889), Blacks had failed to do anything with their freedom, and had become more of a threat that Whites needed to ban together to oppose. By the 1890s, there was a community of historians portraying slavery, and the Civil war years, as years of national disaster. Now sectional elements, that were enemies thirty years earlier, were now "tragic brothers" in a struggle for "self-preservation," and more interested in national reconciliation than any theoretical advancement of sociological science.[63]

By the late 1900s, scientific racism was so pervasive it had

147

made its way into the public policy arena of Congress. In January, 1909, Florida Senator, William H. Milton, used the pseudo-science of so-called scientific racism to justify black inferiority as a legitimate basis for introducing federal legislation to ban inter-racial marriage. Milton submitted the following "evidence" into the Congressional record as the basis for black inferiority in supporting his legislation;

1.   Abnormal length of arms, averaging two inches more than the Caucasian.
2.   Projection of the jaw at a facial angle of 70 degrees, as against 82 for Caucasian.
3.   Average weight of brain, being for gorilla-20 ounces, Negro-35 ounces, European-45 ounces.
4.   Full black eyes with black iris and yellowish sclerotic coat.
5.   Short, flat snub nose, depressed at the base, broad at the extremity, dilating nostrils, and concave ridge.
6.   Thick protruding lips showing inner red surface.
7.   Exceeding thick cranium enabling him to butt with the head and resist blows that would break an ordinary European skull.
8.   Correspondingly weak lower limbs, broad flat foot, divergent and sometimes prehensile big and projecting heel.
9.   Complexion brown or blackish, due to abundance of coloring matter.
10.   Short black hair and distinctly woolly.
11.   Thick epidermis, emitting a peculiar rancid odor.
12.   Frame of medium height and sometimes out of perpendicular.
13.   The early ossification of the skull.[64]

The bill was tabled (not defeated) for future consideration. One introduced by another Florida Congress member, Frank Clark, in February of 1913, actually passed the House by a vote of 238 to 60 with 126 not voting. It didn't become federal law, only because the Senate didn't take up the bill.[65]   There were, at least, 21 anti-intermarriage bills, according to a study done by Sidney S. Tobin on such proposed legislation, between 1907 and 1923-two and a half times more than the anti-lynching bills presented in that same time period.[66]

Whites went so far to try and to scientifically prove that Blacks were subhuman, unequal and inferior to Whites, that in 1906, the New York Zoological Park went to Africa, imported a four foot, eleven inch Pygmy [sic], the infamous Ota Benga exhibit, and housed him in a cage with an orangutan where tourist could look at side by side comparisons of (Black) man and ape. To contribute to this horrendous assault on black humanity and an obvious attempt to humiliate Blacks, the *New York Times* saw fit to note some of the more "obvious points of resemblance (in the size of their heads, height, and facial grin)," a sign of the times in terms of how glaring white insensitivity was to any serious considerations of accepted equality between Black and White.[67]

This was the mindset that drove the lynch mentality. Whites refused to even allow Blacks to be compared to them, and most had so little regard for the quality of Black life-viewed not just as unequal, but so far inferior (to reflect on Roger B. Taney's words a half century earlier) that "Blacks had no rights Whites were bound to respect," a prospect that had become race reality after the turn of the century.

During the early years of 20th Century racial segregation, black life had no value to most Whites, who could decide at a moments notice that a Black person's life was not worth living, much less withstand a personal affront to the dignity of any White person. As challenging for equality rights became more risky, so did the notion that Blacks would somehow erode feelings of prejudice by subordinating themselves to Whites. The biggest proponent of this "politic of accommodation," Booker T. Washington, was quickly losing credibility for his inability to take justifiable stands on two very important "equality" challenges, Blacks' right to vote, and Blacks' right to life, liberty and pursuits of happiness.

149

Disfranchisement and lynching were Washington's two weaknesses in that he offered policy solutions that were disparate and condescending to Blacks. Washington favored educational and property qualifications to vote that would be disproportionately targeted at Blacks-literacy tests being the primary tool that eradicated the black vote in the early 1900s. The persistence of lynching undermined Washington's assertion that Whites could be counted on to protect Blacks, and even in the face of what clearly was a major contradiction for Washington, he seemed to lack the courage to denounce lynching with any real veracity or passion. Fact of the matter was that Washington was as vulnerable to lynching as any other Black, because his silence represented to the world that lynching was an acceptable form of social control in which the highest black person could be put at the mercy of even the lowest of Whites, and that, in essence, Blacks were not entitled to, not only equal protection, but any protection under the law.[68]

Many Blacks openly stated that Washington didn't speak for

them as they saw Washington's silence and avoidance of advocacy on the issue of lynching as deplorable and hypocritical. DuBois clearly understood Washington's politics of subordination and what it meant in the context of what the pseudo-scientists were trying to reinforce, in terms of black inferiority, as "a natural state" of order, as it related to black/white social equality. DuBois understood that this was a critical juncture in the state of America's race relations, and that the regression in the public discourse around black equality was being subjugated by the willingness of the nation's leading black spokesperson to accept a less than equal standing in American society. It was at a Pan African conference in London in 1900 that DuBois first made his most famous statement, one that was still being quoted over 100 years later at the turn of the Twenty-first Century, that:

"The problem of the Twentieth Century is the problem of the color line, the question as to how far differences of race, which show themselves chiefly in the color of the skin and the texture of the hair, are going to be made, hereafter, the basis of denying to over half the world the right of sharing to their utmost ability the opportunities and privileges of modern civilization."[69]

150

DuBois, himself a scholar of renown (not a "black" scholar of renown), wanted to help America and the world understand that the essence of equality in the United States was about opportunities and privileges being reserved for Whites only, and that the whole purpose of the resurrection of social-Darwinism and the American segregation movement was formulated out of the desire to return the African American to the conditions of slavery, by faith, by science, by politics, and by force if necessary-to serve the interests of Whites and to benefit the long term position of Whites as a "master race." Thus, the reason lynching had become the lynchpin for reinforcing the racial etiquette was because of the wholesale resistance to social equality on the part of Whites and the social conflicts that were going to occur, as Blacks resisted subordination.

To stem the tide of accommodation rhetoric that made Booker T. Washington Whites' favorite source of validation for their white superiority/black inferiority position, and the lynchings that provided the first and last line of defense for those who killed in the name of segregation, and were, by and large, going unprosecuted, black and white intellectuals, lawyers and activists began discussing the whole issue of lynching and the constitutionality of what "Separate But Equal" meant for Blacks, in terms of equal protection under the law. Frustrated by Washington's refusal to take the lead on opposing lynching and disfranchisement, and chasting him as a "sham" and a "traitor," many Blacks begin to identify the few progressive Whites they could find to set in motion a new movement to save the black vote, and to make lynching a federal crime.

In July of 1905, led by Harvard graduates, W.E.B DuBois, and William Trotter-a Boston editor and writer who was a vehement critic of Washington, a group of 29 black men had to leave the country and meet on the Canadian side of Niagara Falls to discuss strategies for leading a new movement to organize and fight for equality rights in the United States. Called the *Niagara Movement*, this was seen as, by and large, the launching of DuBois' *Talented Tenth* movement to save the race against what he and the others viewed as Washington's call to permanent racial subjugation. The group's core demand was to call and work toward "the abolition of all caste distinctions based simply on race and color."[70] The following year, DuBois put Washington on notice, and made all aware of the movement and its mission to demand equality at a meeting at Harper's Ferry (the site of John Brown's rebellion), stating:

"We will not be satisfied to take one jot or tittle less than our full manhood rights. We claim for ourselves every single right that belongs to a freeborn American, political, civil, and social; and until we get these rights we will never cease to protest and assail the ears of America."[71]

151

In spite of DuBois' charge, few of the "Talented Tenth" had the nerve to attend the Harper's Ferry meeting, and even fewer were demanding equality of any kind at that point. And though it was only embraced in theory, and never, en masse, as practice, the Niagara Movement is still viewed as the forerunner to the NAACP, in terms of its organized advocacy and focus on critical and pressing societal issues, specifically in defense of the rights of black people. However, conflicts between Blacks and Whites became ever more frequent as the politics of work, the politics of sex, and the politics of race became more intertwined. Whites became less tolerant of "equality talk" and more fearless in their assaults on Blacks, not just as individuals but, the black community in the collective sense, Blacks, period, became the society enemy when issues of race and demands for equality came to a head.

Whites attacked Blacks en mass when race was at the core of the dispute.

Race riots, six major ones between 1900 and 1910, in the North and the South, offered varying trials to whether Blacks could expect equal treatment and equal protection in situations where racial interaction became a prescription for racial catastrophe. Two riots in Springfield, Ohio in 1904, centered around a Black person killing a white police officer-under assertion that the Negro was defending himself. The fact that a white mob hung the Negro, riddled his body with bullets, then destroyed the Negro section of Springfield, was attributed to the latent hatred of Negroes by Whites.[72] In 1906, the Negro part of Greensberg, Indiana was destroyed in a riot, when a jury didn't convict a Black of an attack on a White. In Brownville, Texas, in August of 1906, a decorated regiment of black soldiers, who fought gallantly during the Spanish American War, was attacked by a mob, when one of the soldiers defended themselves, causing the whole town to riot and attack Blacks. President Theodore Roosevelt, who was supposedly a friend and ally of Blacks during that time, took the report from white commanding officers given to his inspector as fact and dismissed the entire battalion with dishonorable discharge, making them disqualified to receive military or civil service benefits.[73]

A race riot occurred in Atlanta in September of 1906, stemming from the race baiting that occurred after some Whites viewed a play based on Thomas Dixon's racially inflammatory book, *The Clansman*-which was made into a motion picture in 1915 by D.W. Griffith, called, *The Birth of a Nation* (triggering race riots all over the country), and set out in a spur of "spontaneous attacks" against "black rapists," though no specific rapist or accused rape event was ever identified. However, in Springfield, Illinois in August of 1908, the pattern of the true anatomy of the American race riot had been solidly congealed when a "legitimate" allegation of rape of a white woman against a Negro represented the nation's biggest fears, "Race War in North," as it was called in *the Independent* (considered one of the most important written accounts of the event). Though the woman stated the man in custody wasn't the man who attacked her, every black man came under assault. Even the state militia couldn't stop two Blacks from being lynched and the black section of town from being burned down.[74]

It was this riot that shocked the North, as if race riots were to be expected in the South, and spread of the lynching phenomena into the North, that served as the impetus for a meeting to be called in New York, on the one hundredth anniversary of the birth of Lincoln, that lead to the formation of the NAACP and a national campaign against lynchings. There were several reasons for the formation of the National Association for the Advancement of Colored People; 1) the Niagara Movement had begun to lose steam by 1908, and Blacks were desperate for a new voice-other than Booker T. Washington, who had been re-empowered after the riots, to advance the cause of black people; 2) Northern Blacks wanted to initiate a "progressive movement" that would redirect the resources of philanthropists from Washington's emphasis on accommodation advocacy to social change advocacy; 3) many Blacks felt that only a bi-racial effort could successfully defeat segregation of the "politics of lynching," and 4) it represented a "wake-up" call, a mobilization, to those Whites who still believed in racial equality.

The aim was to organize a "large and powerful body" of citizens to come to the aid of black people. On May 19th, 1909 in New York, the National Conference on the Negro was held. The nation's leading black spokesperson, Booker T. Washington, declined to attend as did Monroe Trotter, who was suspicious of the motives of white people, and most of the "young radicals" of the Niagara Movement. However, a distinguished gathering of educators, professors, publicists, bishops, judges attended including the likes of Ida B. Wells, John Dewey, Jane Addams, William Dean Howells, John Milholland, W.E.B. DuBois and two persons whose family ties back to America's first civil rights movement, the movement to abolish slavery, Mary White Ovington and Oswald Garrison Villard, the grandson of William Lloyd Garrison. The conference produced a permanent charge that would be called the National Association for the Advancement of Colored People, a plan of action and a pledge to work for the abolition of all forced segregation, equal education for black and white children, the complete enfranchisement of Black men, and the full enforcement of the Fourteenth and Fifteenth Amendments.[75]

A year later, in May of 1910, the "NAACP" was functionalized with the election of Moorfield Storey from Boston, as President, and William E. Walling, as Chairman of the Executive Committee, and the nation's first and oldest "civil rights" organization was born. There were no black officers in the NAACP's original officers slate, except W.E.B. DuBois, who was appointed director of publicity and research-responsible for starting up the organization's communication organ, called *The Crisis*. While DuBois was able to get the magazine up in the first year (to a national circulation of 100,000 by 1918), his presence branded the NAACP a target for Booker T. Washington, who was successful in keeping the Northern Philanthropists away, as well as, many Blacks who thought it too "radical" to be taken seriously.[76]   And the fact that the NAACP was organized, funded and run by mostly white people made it a target for criticism for people like Trotter, who had previously been a constant ally of DuBois (though most of his Niagara allies subsequently followed him into the organization).   However, it was undoubtedly the presence of DuBois and his influence on the organizations most visible literature, its monthly magazine, that established him as a force in the NAACP, and gave the most public assurance that the NAACP was truly committed to racial equality and truly served the interest of black people.[77]

The NAACP's first public charge was to wage a national campaign against lynching. The NAACP became the foremost lobbying interest in Congress to pass federal "anti-lynching" legislation, and nationally the most vehement voice against lynching, the very issue that caused DuBois to call the meeting in Niagara Falls. Every day one occurred, and on DuBois' insistence, the organization gave public notice of this fact. In its New York headquarters, each time a lynching took place somewhere in the United States, the NAACP would put out a black flag, with the words; *A Man Was Lynched Yesterday.*

154

It had become such a common phenomena of the period, it seemed that no one would take notice...until the NAACP made it a national issue. So was the state of segregation in America. During Jim Crow, that's just the way it was.

7

A New Black Resistance Movement:
Ode To Charles Hamilton Houston

"Whether elected or appointed, public officials serve those who put and keep them in office. We cannot depend upon them to fight our battles."
                                                    - Charles Hamilton Houston

"Charles Houston was the Moses who led us through the wilderness of second class citizenship toward the dimly perceived promised land of legal equality."

- William Hastie, First Black ever
  appointed to a federal judgeship

Once a formalized strategy to attack segregation was mounted through a mobilized thrust centered in a new organization called the National Association for the Advancement of Colored Association (NAACP), Black America formally began what would be a nearly 100 year pursuit of equality advocacy, with the first fifty years seeking to restore the basic dignities and fundamental humanity of the African American, and the last fifty years seeking to reconcile political, social and economic benefits and privileges, most of which were lost in the prior two centuries.

The single biggest influence on the strategic attack on the elimination of legalized segregation was the brainchild of a man who understood the crushing power of Jim Crow, in its ability to strip African Americans of their dignity and create feelings of inferiority in a nation of equals. His name is most often forgotten when talking about the ultimate victory of *Brown*, and the heroes that stem from this historic case. Thurgood Marshall is the person most frequently mentioned as the central figure in the new resistance's legal culmination, due to his heading the NAACP/Legal Defense Fund at the time of the *Brown* decision, as well as, his subsequent ascendancy to the U.S. Supreme Court. But, the man most responsible for "killing Jim Crow" is a man by the name of Charles Hamilton Houston, to whom this chapter is dedicated.

As the legal architect to overturn de jure segregation, he documented the inequities of racial separateness and exposed the fallacies of equal protection under law associated with "Separate But Equal." Houston formulated the twenty-five year legal strategy, recruited and trained the "legal army" to the fight, set up a law incubator for civil rights lawyers, then argued and won many of the predicate cases leading up to *Brown*. Charles Hamilton Houston was a child, intellectually birthed in the midst of this emerging resistance to Jim Crow.

However, twenty years before Houston's impact would be felt, the initial groundwork for advocacy had been laid by those resisting the inequities of "Separate But Equal" and its abuse of African American's 14th Amendment rights. All Houston did was lay down the legal groundwork that gave the advocacy force enough to make the change come about. It would take awhile. Plainly put, Blacks weren't treated as equal citizens, weren't given equal due process, and weren't given equal protection under the law. A "color" or race line was firmly in place by the start of the 1920s.

156

It was during this period that African Americans were essentially "niggerized" as noted scholar, Cornel West, surmised when a white colleague expressed to him a sense of insecurity he had, in being "unloved and unprotected," in the aftermath of the September 11, 2001 terrorist attacks on the United States. West told his colleague that he now knows what it is like to be "niggerized," a state that African Americans had felt during most of their presence here in America. This "state" of being "unloved and unprotected" was reinforced in the first quarter of the 20th Century, where a rise in anti-Black sentiment took enormous proportion, and a resistance to that sentiment emerged from amongst the African American population. It was during this time the "new Black Resistance movement" and its various ideological and literary strains were born. The initial advocacy focus was in putting the nation on notice about the politics of lynching, to get America to just stop killing black people in what the NAACP's first black Executive Secretary, James Weldon Johnson, called the battle to "save black America's bodies and white America's soul."[1] Johnson is credited for being the single most influential person in the NAACP's membership growth, particularly in the South, in his first years of service, as field secretary from 1916 to 1920, and in the vast reduction of lynchings in the nation during his tenure as Executive Secretary from 1920 to 1930. The one thing Johnson was not able to accomplish, as was no other black leader, within or without the NAACP, was to get the federal government, specifically the Congress and the Presidency, to outlaw lynching.

The federal government of the United States of America has never passed an anti-lynching law, per se, to protect African Americans, or anyone else, from the vicious and public debauchery of lynching. Because it had become largely directed at African Americans as a form of social control and hardly affected anyone else, it became "a black problem," for which only black leadership was prepared to advocate against for a protracted period of time. From 1918 to 1950, the NAACP advocated for the passing of an anti-lynching bill, and actually got three bills introduced into the House of Representatives-the first by Congressman L.C. Dyer of Missouri in 1922, as well as, a second bill in 1937 and a third bill in 1940. All three bills passed through the House, but never made it through the Senate.

The NAACP got President Harry S. Truman to set up a Committee on Civil Rights, who recommended in 1947 that Congress pass an Anti-Lynching law (causing a huge fallout, in which Southern Democrats, led by South Carolina's Strom Thurman, left the party to start the States Rights Party, and ran Thurman against Truman for President in 1948), only to have Congress refuse. It wasn't until 1966, with the disappearance of three civil rights workers in Mississippi (Goodman, Chaney, Schwartz in 1964), and frequent attacks on civil rights workers during voter registration campaigns in 1965 and 1966, that Congress introduced a civil rights housing bill, banning racial discrimination in the sale and rental of housing, that was amended to give federal protection to civil rights workers, and make it a federal crime to cross state lines to incite a riot-supposedly directed at traveling lynch mob activity. However, it was actually more in response to the other roving forms of violence-highway assaults, Klan marches and church bombings-that that came about in response to what southern Whites perceived as a "northern invasion" and other "outsiders" (even Dr. King was called an outsider when he traveled across county lines within the states where he lived) that history came to know "the freedom rides," where students and ministers from Northern states went South to educate, register and empower black voters.

The actual anti-violence (not anti-lynching) bill became known as the Civil Rights Act of 1968, and was hurriedly passed by Congress on April 10th, and signed into law by President Lyndon Johnson on April 11, 1968, only in the aftermath of (and in response to), the assassination of Dr. Martin Luther King, Jr. who had been murdered on April 4th. It contained very specific language that authorized federal action if two or more persons should conspire to intimidate a citizen in the "free exercise of constitutional rights, whether or not death ensued."[2] While lynching was never mentioned specifically, this part of the act was directed at the mob violence behavior associated with lynching mentality, and sought to criminally punish those involved-to the extent they could be identified.

Though lynching was no longer part of America's more popular cultural practices by the late 1960s, it was still part of America's race conflict mentality that raised its ugly head, from time to time, for the remainder of the 20th Century. Lynching, still one of the most stigmatizing terms in American society today, was never acknowledged as a societal problem, nor was it ever legally disavowed, in a direct reference, by the federal legislature during a consecutive seventy-one year engagement that ran from 1881 until 1952, the first year since records were kept that there was no known lynching of an African American in the United States.[3]

Still, beginning in 1916, James Weldon Johnson, W.E.B. DuBois and the NAACP, the organization Roy Wilkins, who succeeded Johnson's successor, Walter White, called "the most radical idea of this century," launched its legacy of civil rights advocacy by targeting lynching as a national problem. The NAACP was "the voice" most responsible for putting lynching on this country's legislative agenda, waging the widest "public campaign" against lynching, and raising the level of attention given to lynching, through the use of moral suasion, public pressure, editorial critique and legal intervention, to put an end to this most abrasive of extreme racial activity.[4]

Ironically enough, while lynching violated a person's Fourteenth Amendment rights to due process and equal protection under the law, the Fourteenth Amendment also gave protection to lynchers, because due process required clear proof to charge, a fair trial before a jury of one's peers and reasonable doubt to convict, something Whites were guaranteed and Blacks were denied by this very act. This made it difficult to pursue the prosecution of lynching, without a federal law to designate it as a federal crime, when states (some of whom had anti-lynching laws) and local governments, either were complicit in the act, as many were in either their soft investigation or prosecution of the crime, or were benign in upholding the rights of Blacks to participate in the criminal justice process, as witnesses or on juries, that made it easy for local white citizens to protect guilty parties within the community or state cultures. Blacks further understood the games that were being played by state officials, with federal government, as well as, with themselves, as many state's began to hide behind "state's rights" proclamations that put prosecuting such crimes within state jurisdictions and allowed them to "know nothing" upon federal inquiry. Now with a national civil rights organization to monitor, to collect data, to advocate when there previously was none, this gave Blacks a new method of resistance and a group of new voices to decry the injustices of segregation.

Unconstricted by the conservative influence of Booker T. Washington, who died in 1915-but not before he managed to try to undermine the growth of the NAACP in its early years by hamstringing its financial support with Northern philanthropists, James Weldon Johnson and W.E.B. DuBois were able to make the organization self-sustaining through subscriptions to *The Crisis* magazine and memberships, whereby 1920, the year Johnson was appointed Secretary of the NAACP, 95% of the organizations funding, for the first time, came from black members.[5]

If Johnson, who grew the membership from a few thousand members to well over 100,000 by the time his tenure ended in 1930, was the arms and legs of the NAACP, DuBois was its mind and the voice. As editor of *The Crisis*, whose initial print run was 1,000 copies when it appeared in 1910, DuBois was able to wage the nation's loudest verbal assault against the politics of inequality. The NAACP's voice went far beyond its membership reach. By 1911, *The Crisis* was selling 16,000 a month, and by 1919, at the height of racial conflict, its circulation reached 100,000-a number that was double that of the NAACP's paid membership.[6]

Now, at the forefront of what was being called the "New Negro" movement, DuBois, Johnson, with the likes of Monroe Trotter, A. Phillip Randolph and a Jamaican activist named, Marcus Mossiah Garvey, were preparing to lead a form of resistance to racial inequality that America had never seen, but also brought forth a ferocity of racial hostility, on the part of Whites, unequaled in America's post slavery period. Four different but highly interlinked phenomena led to the rise of an organized advocacy or "black voice," and an accompanying white recalcitrance in the first quarter of the 20th Century.

The first phenomena was the continuing, but more highly volatile, practices of lynching and mob violence, which gave rise to increased occurrences of race riots. Partially in response to black prosperity and black patriotism, both of which gave rise to feelings of black equality, this phenomenon had become so pervasive, that it became a rallying point for Blacks nationwide, from 1915 to 1925. James Weldon Johnson and W.E.B. DuBois led a silent march in conjunction with the Harlem branch of the NAACP, that drew 12,000 people to protest violent acts that were occurring nationwide in the summer of 1917.[7] DuBois called the march to specifically protest what was thought to be the disparate targeting of Blacks in race riots that occurred in East St. Louis, Illinois (May 27-30 and July 1-2, 1917)-the second one, in which it was estimated that as many as two hundred Blacks were killed (though most accounts put the number at forty), eight Whites were killed, 312 buildings and 44 railroad freight cars were destroyed by fire.[8] In the following two years, there would be many more race riots that would injure and kill hundreds of Blacks. So volatile and frequent were the race riots of 1919, that it was deemed "the Red Summer of 1919," because of the twenty six race riots that summer.[9]

160

This nation's most notorious race riot, and many surmise as most egregious-in terms of the complicity of the state and locals government, occurred June 1st, 1921 in Tulsa, Oklahoma when a black delivery boy named Dick Rowland, who was also referred to as "Diamond Dick," was accused of "assaulting" a 17 year old elevator operator-a white girl named Sarah Page two days before. Rowland, who carried messages around Tulsa, stopped in a downtown building to use a toilet located on the top floor, one of the few that was available to "colored" folk. Blacks couldn't catch the regular elevator-racial etiquette prevented it-but they could catch the freight elevator.

Since Blacks were considered "freight," ordinary racial courtesy wasn't required, meaning Rowland could ride alone with a white woman. As Rowland stepped in, Page yanked up the starter, causing him to lose his balance and lurch forward. In an attempt to grab something to catch his balance, he grabbed Page's hand and a part of her dress. Page screamed, which could be heard through the freight cage elevator. Immediately Page claimed Rowland tried to "assault" her, which in the highly racial environment of the time was "sex-speak" codification for a Black trying to rape a white woman.[10] Well, within twenty-four hours, the assault had turned to rape, and Rowland was arrested, though neither allegation could ever be verified.

Newspaper sources conflicted along racial lines. The white paper, *The Tulsa Tribune* reported that Rowland had attacked the girl, scratching her hands and face and tearing her clothes. *The Black Dispatch* reported that the *Tribune* may have incited the riots by publishing false accounts (which the editor of the *Tribune* later admitted), and that Rowland's account that he may have "touched" the girl's hand to steady himself as he stumbled in the elevator she operated was actually closer to the truth, than any assault or malice that the Tribune had implied.[11]

None of it mattered at that point, as Whites had begun to gather at the jailhouse where Rowland was being held. There was talk of lynching him, which got back to the black section of Tulsa-a community called Greenwood. Two variables played central in events leading up to the Tulsa riot; first, Blacks knew that lynching Rowland was a very real possibility for two reasons, 1) "lynch" mentality was very present in Oklahoma, as two persons-a white man in Tulsa and a black man in Oklahoma City (90 miles away) had been lynched eight months earlier. However, in the case of the black man, Claude Chandler-who when accused of killing a white police officer, had been taken from the Oklahoma City jail, and in spite of the fact that nearly a thousand heavily armed black men gathered to stop the lynching, police intervened while white men took Chandler ten miles west of the city, and hung him;[12] 2) Oklahoma was "Klan country" and the resurrection of the Klan (which is the fourth phenomena that will be analyzed as a cause for increased black advocacy during this period) was a very real factor in Tulsa. The Ku Klux Klan had established an ominous presence in Tulsa, to the extent that it considered itself to be the city's real law. Its animosity toward Blacks in the town's "black section was extremely bitter, largely because "separate but equal" segregation had produced an unintended consequence for the black population of Greenwood-equality that produced economic success-a success which Whites termed as "niggers getting ahead of themselves."[13]

Despite efforts to frame Greenwood as a black "ghetto," it drew the envy of Whites in Tulsa, and the wrath of their jealousy was frequently represented in the *Tribune* with references to its black community as "Little Africa," or "Niggertown." The fact of the matter was that the thirty-five block area of black Tulsa was considered one of the wealthiest and most successful business communities in the nation-including Greenwood Avenue, a mile long main street of hotels, hospitals, theaters, doctors offices and various others businesses that served its 15,000 residents, and was proudly and affectionately known nationwide as, "Black Wall Street."[14]

Blacks in Tulsa, Oklahoma, had not only made the best of their societal exclusion, they had succeeded in spite of it. Blacks were not only equal in Tulsa, they were, in many instances, superior, and many of its citizens were of national stature-including Dr. A. C. Jackson, called by a founder of the Mayo Clinic, "the most able Negro surgeon in America."[15] Greenwood was a point of pride for Blacks in Tulsa despite the racial etiquette that dominated the city's black-white interface. Greenwood was proof that equality could be realized.

Moreover, Blacks in Tulsa understood both the racial climate (lynch mentality) and the racial culture (Klan presence) that fueled racial conflict anytime a black/white encounter was called into question. The Rowland/Page incident was one such encounter and fearing for Rowland's life, two dozen armed black men from Greenwood came to help authorities protect "Diamond Dick" (as they had in Oklahoma City), with the intention of preventing what had occurred to Chandler eight months earlier.

The forces of the anti-lynching movement had come face to face with the lynch mentality in Tulsa as the Sheriff tried to get the men to return to Greenwood before word got out on this "show of black solidarity." While returning to their cars, a white man approached an armed black man, asking him, "Nigger, what you doing with that pistol?", to which the black man responded, "I'm going to use it, if I need to."[16] As the white man went to grab his own gun, it went off. Thinking that the white men were shooting at them, the black men shot back at those seeking to disperse them.[17]

As the Blacks retreated back to Greenwood, some 10,000 Whites assembled, looted every gun shop in downtown Tulsa and turned toward Greenwood, supposedly to go after the black men who had shot at them. Instead, they shot every Black they saw, tying corpses to cars and dragging them in the streets, setting homes on fire, and shot Blacks as they ran out of the burning building-sometimes throwing them back into the fire.[18]

Oklahoma's Governor called in the state National Guard, which was suppose to help restore order, who in turn, joined local authorities and the vigilantes looting and burning Greenwood. The mob then followed the National Guard who had turned its anger toward Greenwood Avenue and the destruction of "Black Wall Street," which included the use of airplanes to bomb and level businesses, the only documented use of an armed air assault of U.S. citizens on domestic soil in America's history. Many of the National Guard were assigned to unarming the citizens to bring about peace, but they began unarming just the black citizens and taking them to internment centers-for their own protection. It was estimated that close to half the city's black population, some 6,000 people, under National Guard bayonets, were effectively detained in holding centers, while their community was being destroyed.[19]   However, many Greenwood citizens refused to abandon their homes and businesses, nor would they surrender their weapons, choosing to fight "like tigers" in scattered formation that many had learned from their World War I experience. Instead of protecting the residents of Greenwood who were under war-like assault by two thousand armed white men, the national guard appeared designed to put down "the Negro uprising," as they worked with local authorities to "mop-up" the entire city of Greenwood.[20]

The official casualty count reported by the *Tulsa Tribune* was twenty-four Blacks and ten Whites. However, a Commission on the Tulsa Riot established by the Oklahoma legislature in 1997 indicated that, while the precise number of death was undiscernable, a verifiable estimate put the number at about 300 people, 90% of whom were Black.[21]   More than one thousand families were left homeless, as all thirty five blocks were burned to the ground-in what historians can only describe as a modern day war zone.[22]

The real atrocity of the Tulsa race riot was that a simple race encounter was used as an excuse to disable the most prosperous township, at that time, in America. Twelve hundred buildings were burned, many being looted before set ablaze, and Blacks were never reimbursed by insurance companies, who had anti-riot clauses in their policies, nor did the city of Tulsa ever pay a single cent to any one victim of this tragedy. To add insult to injury, many Greenwood residents saw Whites flaunting their possessions on the city's streets in the days afterward, wearing familiar clothing and jewelry taken from them, their homes and businesses during the riot.[23] The Tulsa Race Riot of 1921 still represents the most egregious violation of black equality, and the most ardent example of the desire to strip Blacks of the benefits and privileges of a free and equal society ever witnessed in the nation's post Civil War era. Tulsa was not an anomaly, by any means.

Many other black townships were burned down out of this

163

same process, something that started out as an individual conflict between a black and a white person, but turned into a racial hysteria waged against Blacks, including a township in Rosewood, Florida in 1922, where another false claim of rape caused the whole town to be burned down. And like Tulsa the year before, to this day, the true number of Blacks who died in this race riot is unknown. It was one of the few that was actually called "a massacre, and was an event that became the subject of a John Singleton movie in 1997, and a case of reparations, for which nine "eligible" Rosewood survivors received an apology from the state legislature and $150,000 each from the state of Florida-some seventy years later in 1994.[24] This lynch mentality phenomena, and the race riot assaults that accompanied it, generated the greatest sense of urgency for the need of black advocacy and a new resistance movement, simply mandating that Blacks be given the right to "just be left alone," given safe haven and the right to be protected equally, under the law.

The second phenomena that helped influence organized black advocacy efforts was emphatically tied to the first. The rise in lynching and race riots, between 1915 and 1925, directly correlates with the second resurrection of the Ku Klux Klan. In fact, the second rise of the Klan, a much more powerful and mainstream product than the original version, was the direct causation of increased lynching and race riot activity. Much of the organized Klan activity of the 19th Century had been eradicated with anti-Klan laws and enforcement legislation targeted at them during the Radical Reconstruction years. After the fall of Reconstruction and the rise of "Redeemers," less emphasis was placed on intimidation, and more emphasis was placed on political trickery. Intimidation, while always present, was a tactic of last resort, usually by small groups of local vigilantes that represented a residual carryover from the Klan's more powerful days, than anything else. For the most part, organized Klan activity had been driven underground, to avoid federal scrutiny and the possibility of federal intervention in state affairs, once Southern Whites regained political control of their state legislatures and local economies. Thus, the Klan, despite its scary reputation, had became more legend than real, a shadow of its former self-though still a very large and looming shadow in the minds of black victims, families and communities who knew its violence firsthand.

However, in 1915, the second Klan's founder, William Joseph Simmons, an Atlanta based organizer for a fraternal benefit society called the Woodman of the World, was unsatisfied with the level of civic involvement of white men in America. Dreaming of the revival of the hooded order that his father belonged to after the Civil War, he pulled together a group of "like-minded" friends, met atop Stone Mountain, an imposing several hundred foot high granite butte outside Atlanta, where they lit a burning cross, opened the Bible to the twelfth chapter of Romans and declared themselves the new Knights of the Ku Klux Klan.[25]

Georgia was the birthplace and national headquarters for this new Klan, and it was seen as an extension of the racial radicalism movement and populist mindset that had returned Whites to power, ushered in *Plessy*, and brought forth a new attitude of new white supremacy empowerment throughout the South. The new Klan was built on the same principle as the old Klan, white supremacy, but it added a few more doctrines, patriotism, conventional mortality, and a new twist-"Old Time Religion," that allowed its member to assert they were on a mission from God, and caused them to pledge "to fend off challenges from any quarter to the rights and privileges of men from the stock of the nation's founders."[26]

Unlike the old Klan who recruited mainly from amongst former Confederate soldiers, their friends and a few local "white only" secular fraternal orders, the new Klan went after a much broader base, espousing a much broader ideology. The new Klan recruited from the two largest bases of organized Whites in the South, with the highest loyalties given to their organizational involvements, national fraternal orders and Protestant churches. America had over six hundred secret societies by the mid-1920s that enlisted over 30 million people, and the church had similar numbers, as white males tended to be involved in both the church and fraternal orders, and used both to cross-recruit. Both organizations appeared very receptive to the new Klan's message, and though recruitment started out slow-only a few thousand members by 1920-once Simmons hired the Southern Publicity Association, whose principles had mastered the art of modern propaganda, by the end of 1921, the new Klan had some one million members.[27]

Most of their base were fraternal orders and church members. By 1923, the Klan boasted a Masonic membership of 500,000 alone. Among the organizations that shared members with the Klan were the Woodmen of the World, the Elks, the Masons, the Odd Fellows, the Knights of Pythias and the Shriners. By 1924, it boasted that it had enrolled 30,000 church ministers, mostly evangelical Protestants from Baptist (including three-quarters of the 6,000 delegates of the

Southeastern Baptist Convention), Methodist, Church of Christ, Disciple of Christ and United Brethren denominations.[28] A third base that the Klan went after, with some limited degree of success, were labor unions. While labor unions sought to resist the influence of the Klan by passing anti-Klan membership policies that excluded workers who identified with the Klan, Klan members still maintained a union presence among the middle and poor working class memberships. In unions where they didn't have a presence-the union lost members. Nationally, union membership fell from over five million in 1920, to under three and a half million in 1923, one of the three "peak years" for Klan membership, to two and a half million by 1930, largely influenced by the Klan anti-labor campaigns that excluded poor Whites during the pre-economic depression years of the early and mid-1920s.[29]

Two other important variables distinguished the old Klan from the new Klan. The former movement wasn't really considered a mass movement, in the populous sense. It was sectional, inasmuch as, it covered ten to twelve states and represented largely fringe elements of society-though some of their members were influential-that did not represent a mainstream society presence. The new Klan movement was a mass movement, and national in scope, that involved chapters in 35 to 40 states. The new Klan's message appealed to white men throughout the nation, because its message of white supremacy, Christianity and male-bonding fraternalism, when targeted at the rise against "the new immigrant movement" that was occurring from 1880 to 1910, particularly focused at Catholics and Jews, as well as, the Great Migration Movement of Blacks from the Southern states into the Northern states that started in 1900 but was peaking in the period from 1915 to 1925.

The loud public articulation of the New Negro movement, the groups of organized Blacks challenging government to uphold equality and equal protection statues, also provided a great incentive for American born white Anglo-Saxon Protestants to ban together. While the Klan targeted all immigrants-the "Klansman's Creed stating, I believe my rights in this country are superior to those of foreigners"-Jews, Catholics and Blacks became easy targets for the Klan, because each conflicted with some segment of white economic, religious or social beliefs.

The Klan held Jews responsible for the crucifixion of Christ, and for controlling the monetary system that aided the capitalist in facilitating industrialism, and causing white jobs and farms to be lost. The Klan held the Catholics responsible for aiding "social equality," by trying to convert Blacks to Catholicism, including the elevating of black priests, and for promoting integrated congregations that, in turn threatened to upend the racial etiquette and cause disruption to the social order-in the same vein as what occurred in Haiti and San Domingo, where religious conversion opened the door to political upheaval, and the full empowerment of Blacks. Lastly, there was no limit to aspersions the Klan cast up on Blacks, including that they were biologically inferior, unfit for democratic participation, criminal and immoral, lazy, oversexed, as well as, Blacks being responsible for competing with Whites for jobs, in the trades and for housing.[30] The subordination of the African American, however, was also tied to the success of the entire Southern economy, as Blacks were the South's "only and best form of domestic and general labor."[31]

The other variable was that the new Klan transcended class lines, where the majority of its members were middle class Whites, who owned businesses, were lower or mid-level white collar managers, and many of whom inherited their home or farms from their parents. This controverts the "poor white trash" moniker that the old Klan had developed. The new Klan was considered "at least, next to the best...the good, solid middle class citizens" largely attributed to its member's Protestant church values and old fashion work ethic.[32] What that meant was the majority of its members weren't the poorest Whites (though a segment of its membership base was poor), nor were they the rich industrialist that represented big business interests (not part of their base).

The face of the new Klan was what would come to represent the core populous of America in the 20th Century, the American "Middle Class," with great dedication to civic responsibility. Many of these people were adherents to fundamentalist Christian principles, reinforced with Social Darwinism, that made them truly believe they were a God risen superior class of people to watch over society and protect the racial hierarchy of society. The birth of white citizens councils, women's leagues and other civic support groups were outbirths of their Christian roots and Klan beliefs, causing W.E.B DuBois to describe the social and political omnipresence of the new Klan in Georgia, as the "Invisible Empire State."[33] The new Klan was so mainstream in Georgia that a Klansman, named Clifford Walker, ran for Governor and won, serving from 1923 to 1927, during which time, he used his official gubernatorial capacity to uphold the Klan's anti-Black terrorist activities throughout the state.[34]

167

As membership in the new Klan grew, so did the membership in the NAACP. In 1914, the NAACP only had three Southern Branches. In the three years following 1916, the launch year for the new Klan, NAACP branches jumped from six to 155, with these new chapters amassing over 42,000, and for the first time, making Southerners the majority of the organization's "rank and file" base.[35] The expansion of the NAACP in the South was also a testament to the fact that the accommodation politics of Booker T. Washington, who had worked hard to suppress the growth of the NAACP in the South (to stagnate DuBois' influence), was truly over. By 1919-the year of the "Red Summer" nationwide race riots, the South accounted for 131 of the NAACP's 310 branches, and in the year 1919 alone, the NAACP gained 85 new branches-most of them in the South-and 35,000 new members.[36]

One piece of popular propaganda that literally became a recruiting tool for the new Klan, and spurned its (and the NAACP's) growth, was D.W. Griffith's "epic classic," *The Birth of a Nation*, released in the same year as the new Klan's creation, but came to symbolize what the Klan stood for, in terms of becoming the ardent defender of white society's "way of life." The movie framed African American freedom as the reason America was in chaos, and showed Klan members coming to the rescue of a white woman under assault by a "big Negro brute," at the end of Griffith's movie, glorifying the Klan as the protector of the virtues of whiteness (i.e. the white woman and American way of life). This was also a factor in many of the racial confrontations of the time. So much so, that the NAACP sought to stop the movie's showing for fear that it would ignite race riots. Those efforts were in vain, more a tribute to the power of the new Klan, but also a sign of resistance to black America's new national voice, the NAACP, giving credence that it was now the most outspoken voice of the New Negro movement-which the new Klan was watching very closely. The Klan wore Griffith's movie as a "badge of honor," and tied the film quickly into its national speaker's bureau portfolio, as its recruiters spoke to large crowds that sympathized with the message. The Klan's recruitment rallies attracted as many as 200,000 people, by the mid-1920s.

Giving credence to the fact that the new Klan was now a national "mass movement" was the fact that the Southeastern or the deeply "Jim Crow" states (the Carolinas, Georgia, Alabama, Mississippi and Louisiana) didn't represent the largest membership base in the new Klan. Georgia, the founding state and headquarters, was second in the

South and eighth in the nation in estimated membership. In 1925, Michigan, a Northern state, boasted the nation's largest Klan membership of 875,000, followed by another Northern state, New Jersey, and a Midwestern state, Nebraska, with its 352,000, which led the nation in terms of the largest percentage of Klan members proportionate to its total state population.[37] The North Central and Southwestern states enrolled the most members, followed by the Southeast, the Midwest, the Far west and the North Atlantic states, causing Klan membership to be estimated by mid decade (1924, 1925, 1926) at five million members and 4,000 local chapters.[38] Though some historical sources cite that the new Klan's membership peaked at only three million members, this did truly represent a populous movement in a nation of 105 million people, 10.4 million of which were African American. This intense minority represented a critical mass of racialized mobilization to which there was little resistance.

The minority of Whites in America, while being indifferent and maybe even despising the Klan, just watched the movement grow and take action. Unlike during the Reconstruction Period, when there was significant white resistance to the politics of the old Klan, America expressed such indifference to the new Klan, that this intense minority was able to impose its social views and political will on a less tense majority of Whites that had no Klan affiliation. The new Klansman did an excellent job of blending the extreme with the mainstream, blending issues of race, class and state power with their conservative views on manhood, womanhood and sexual decorum, where the Klan could be at once-hostile to big business and antagonistic to industrial unions, anti-elitist and hateful to Blacks and immigrants, proponents of "law and order," while still prone to extralegal violence.[39] The new Klan could be anybody, could be anywhere, could see any and everything, and could literally do anything. The new Klan was everywhere and growing at an unprecedented pace.

Black leadership knew they had to organize to protect themselves against it. The bulk of the Black migration into the northern states occurred between 1910 and 1930, with the peak years of flight taking place from 1915 to 1925.[40] While the causation of the migration has been historically attributed to both the personal mistreatment of Blacks, due to segregation and the employment opportunities tied to northern industrialization, it cannot be ignored, nor disregarded that the height of the migration coincides with the rise and growing influence of the new Klan.

169

The third phenomena that influenced organized black advocacy efforts was the heightened practice of economically subjugating African Americans causing them to be hired last (if at all), paid less, given less (or no job) security and fired first. The practice of economic subjugation took full root prior to, and after, World War I in the same periods (1915 to 1925) that the other phenomena occurred. The politics of white supremacy came with a guarantee, or "right to work" in America that put Whites of the lower socio-economic classes at odds with Blacks and immigrants. It particularly affected the relationship of poor Whites and Blacks, who had historically been allies in the fight for jobs and livable wages. The best way to quantify differences in equality was to ensure that Blacks and Whites could not be considered equal. This meant giving preference to white laborers for work, giving white laborers preference in pay deferential and to restricting black labor options, by putting Blacks on unconscionable work contracts, while Whites were free to contract their labor as they saw fit. Impacting the "black tax" on African Americans, particularly when working for, or doing business with Whites, was a way to economically hamstring black wealth and limit black discretionary spending to where Blacks could not economically compete with Whites, in the short run (monthly and annual pay wages), nor in the long run (wealth accumulation).

170

The primary conflicts of the "right to work" competition stemmed essentially from the early stages of the "Great Migration," when Blacks migrated from the rural South to the urban cities in the Northeast and the Midwest, at the turn of century, that caused an upsurge of white-working anxieties about possible displacement by black labor.[41] Competitive race relations in the economic sphere, while always present in the North and the South, were accelerated when hundreds of thousands of southern Blacks went north, between 1900 and 1920, to escape worsening economic conditions and the rising tide of racial persecution. The early part of the migration offered no real threat, largely because Blacks were under-represented in the skilled trades, and were bypassed in the Industrial Revolution. Few, if any, of the factory jobs were open to them. However, as the early 20th century progressed, the combination of white workers organizing to improve their wages and working conditions, and the greater availability of black migrants, who could be used as strike breakers, put working class black and white workers in direct competition for jobs, and in direct conflict over the struggle for unionization.

The East St. Louis race riot in 1917, and the Chicago race riot of 1919 had one common cause, the use of black strikebreakers to replace striking white workers.[42] White workers, in turn, resented black labor as an option to employers, and many refused to open union membership to Blacks. Not only did unionization keep Blacks from competing for "white" jobs, it enabled the Northern white working class the same psychological gratification of "being better off" than African Americans, as did Southern Whites, as well as, Irish immigrants, who had carry-over anti-African American sentiments from a time when free and freed Blacks competed with them at a time when the Irish monopolized the service occupations in the late 19th Century.[43] The employment line, in essence, became "a color line." When Blacks were allowed to work, they worked on very tenuous terms, and, in most instances, for very less pay than white workers, in similar occupations.

Pay equalization, later called comparable worth (equal pay for equal work), during the second phase of the 20th Century women's movement, was never a reality of black compensation, in the 20th Century, and its inequities directly impacted the ability of Blacks to compete with Whites on an equal basis. Black labor contract and job employment opportunities were often composed of the work that Whites didn't want to do-until economic hard times hit in the 1870s-at which time, poor Whites were thrust into direct competition with Blacks, and white employers saw that as an opportunity to either displace Blacks from work, or to pay them less for the same work. In many instances, that pay was sometimes less than a third of what white workers made.

During the period in which the new massive resistance period took hold, the issue of economic subjugation, inequality in compensation (wages), financial resource distribution (grants, loans, subsidies, tax exemptions, and other economic consideration) and wealth accumulation (assets, estates) was the second most important issue (outside of lynching) in the attack on "Separate But Equal." In 1939, the year that the NAACP formed its Legal Defense and Education Fund (then known as NAACP/LDF), black male workers made $450 for every $1,000 white workers made, black female workers made $379 for every $1,000 white workers made; and by 1950 (the year Charles Hamilton Houston died), black male compensation had risen to $613 (three-fifths) of white workers compensation (per $1,000), but black female compensation had actually *dropped* to $369 of what white workers made (per $1,000).[44]

Economic subjugation extended far beyond individual wage

171

disparities. Resources, both from the government, in terms of land grants, farming subsidies and loan guarantees, and from private industry-including banks, were disparately parceled out in unequal rations to white and black farmers, and white and black businessmen. For instance, the federal government, whose programs set up to aid poor farmers-not white poor farmers, but poor farmers-did more to increase disparities between black and white farmers, than equalize them. One of the principle reasons for "the Black Exodus" from the South, as the Great Migration was called, was because of the adverse affect federal agricultural programs had in their lack of support for black farmers and sharecroppers.

In the 1930s, the Agricultural Adjustment Administration, which allowed small farmers to finance the expansion and mechanization of their farms, in order to offset monopolies created by big money industrialists, gave preferential treatment to white applicants of development and mechanizations loans, resulting in an increase in the number of Whites that owned farms, and a *reduction* in the number of Blacks who either owned farms, or worked on them as sharecroppers or cash tenants.[44] This essentially put black farmers and sharecroppers out of work. The number of black farm owners and managers declined from 220,000, in 1920, to less than 174,000 in 1940, while cash and share-cropping tenants declined from 703,555 to 506,638 during that same period.[46]

With nowhere to work, and nowhere to go, many Blacks essentially left the South for more work and less racial violence. Between 1910 and 1920, close to 700,000 Blacks moved north. It was in the following decade (1920-1930) that the combination of Jim Crow social politics, Klan lynching and mob violence, and economic subjugation that drove some 1.25 million Blacks north, literally overwhelming northern cities with their presence. Over five million Blacks migrated north between 1910 and 1960, and many of the "social control" elements of the South made their way North. As the Great Depression came about in 1929, the economic desperation that hit Whites, hit Blacks five fold, as most were the last hired, thus first fired, causing the jobless rate for Blacks throughout the country to average 40%, while the white jobless rate was 25%. In this sense, large urban cities were more cruel than the South, as jobless rates in big cities like Detroit hit 60% for black males, and 75% for black females.[47]

Federal government recovery programs under President Franklin Roosevelt's "New Deal" policies turned out to be the rawest of deals for Blacks, as programs like the Work Progress Administration (WPA), the Civilian Conservation Corps (CCC), the Tennessee Valley Authority (TVA), and the National Recovery Administration (NRA), while espousing racial equality, commonly gave favor to Whites, while overtly discriminating against Blacks. The NRA, which set wage standards, excluded farm workers and domestic servants-roughly three-fourth of the national black workforce (on the insistence of southern conservatives) from receiving governmental assistance benefits, and allowed for traditional (meaning historical) geographic variation in the minimum wage to be set, that allowed for the continuance of economic subjugation in federal programs that were supposed to distribute resources on an equal basis.[48] So discriminatory and disparate was the treatment Blacks received from the NRA, that African Americans no longer could hide their cynicism with respect to so called "government help" programs, and began sarcastically stating that NRA stood for more disingenuous engagements such as, the "Negro Removal Act," or "Negro Ruined Again" or the "Negro Run Around," as relief always seemed to avoid Blacks in need of assistance, from programs that were supposed to benefit everybody.

The Great Migration upset the previously established racial balance that Northern cities had. Many cities had similar racial boundaries to those in the South, only they were more geographic than demographic. Starting with residential racism, the North soon adopted many of the same social disbarments that prevented Blacks from many other facets of social enjoyment-based on a private establishment's ability to refuse service to anyone they pleased.[49] Even cities like New York, Chicago and Boston, which had previously served Blacks, prior to World War I, took on the discriminatory behaviors of the South in barring Blacks from hotels and restaurants after the war, and created separate entrances for "colored" in venues like Harlem's Cotton Club in "South-like" fashion.

Whether it was in the North, or in the South, economic subjugation was a consistent impediment for Blacks, as it represented the clearest demonstration in the un-equalness of the two races. Blacks, who sought to set up businesses in the North, failed in the initial contact with "the urban experience" for principally five reasons; 1) difficulty in procuring capital and credit, 2) difficulty in getting adequate training 3) inability to secure choice locations on main business streets, 4) lack of sufficient patronage to allow them to amass capital and to make improvements, and 5) inability to organize for co-operative effect.[50]

The cultural closeness of the South, that Blacks took for granted, was lost in the expansiveness of Northern cities, though the black population was as close, physically and geographically, as they had ever been, as the birth of "ghettos" created another racially influenced phenomena. Still, the lack of education, the lack of cultural compact and the lack of assets (land) magnified how important cooperative economics was to obtaining equality in the North, something Blacks hadn't really learned in the South. In the face of less money, skewed and unequal economic scenarios, Blacks became unequal very quickly in the North, and inequality was truly a national problem.

Economic subjugation based on race also influenced institutional resource distribution, particularly in education, where in the 1930s forward, nine Southern states spent on average, in excess of three to one, more on children in white schools than on children in black schools, spending $49.30 for each white child and $15.41 for each black one.[51] In the deep South, the spending disparities were much greater. The most "equal" spending disparity was in North Carolina where spending was greater than two to one ($18.08 for Blacks, $41.12 for Whites); almost three to one in Florida ($17.33 for Blacks, $48.71 for Whites); almost four to one in Alabama ($10.72 for Blacks, $40.90 for Whites); more than four to one in Georgia ($9.50 for Blacks, $41.02 for Whites); almost five to one in Louisiana ($12.86 for Blacks, $62.21 for Whites) and almost six to one in South Carolina ($8.08 for Blacks, $53.81 for Whites).[52]

Funding disparities in education created a whole host of residual inequities from teacher's pay, to facility improvement, to textbook and teaching materials, to number of days students received instruction. Economic subjugation created a "matter of fact" circumstance that Blacks would have less than Whites, in those things that represented material incentives and/or of economic benefit, that would assuredly make them less than equal to Whites in the receiving of governmental and private sector financial support, the amassing of individual and collective financial assets, and in the individual amassing of wealth.

The fourth and last phenomena, that influenced organized black advocacy was the treatment of Blacks in the military, at a time when they were trying to prove both their national loyalty and stateside patriotism, during America's short engagement in the "war to end all wars," World War I. As Congress passed the Selective Service Act on May 18, 1917, which required the enlistment of every able bodied

American between the ages of twenty-one and thirty-one, black men out-enlisted Whites, in their desire to serve their country. Of the 2,290,525 Blacks that had registered to serve, 31% (or 367,000) were accepted, versus 26% of Whites who registered being accepted.[53] But more then anything, for Blacks, enlisting in the military for represented nothing more than the painful realization that discrimination was everywhere in American society-including and/or especially in the armed services. Black soldiers soon found out that there was no place they could go where they could be treated equal and enjoy the rights and privileges of full citizenship. None of them were ready, however, for the level of discrimination that Blacks encountered while fighting for their country. Many used the war as a chance to prove their manhood and their patriotism, hoping that if Blacks showed their willingness to protect America and fight for this country's foreign interest, America would show a willingness to accept them as full partners in the "American experience," and protect them in fighting for their societal and constitutional interests, as such. That simply was not to be the case. Black soldiers were forced to endure the same levels, and in some instances-increased levels of hostility and racial subjugation, in the U.S. military, that they suffered in the United States, during so-called peace time.

Even the radical pen of W.E.B. DuBois encouraged national unity, for which DuBois was severely criticized, despite continuing racial conflict at home and pervasive racial prejudice waged by both the French Army and our own American troops-including high army officers. DuBois wrote in a July, 1918 *Crisis* editorial, entitled "Close Ranks," that Black Americans should go to war, that "if this is our country, then this is our war," and that Blacks should stand with Whites in helping to defeat our enemies.[54] DuBois, extorting his newfound influence stated;

> *"Let us not hesitate. Let us, while this war lasts, forget our special grievances and close ranks shoulder to shoulder with our white citizens and the allied nations that are fighting for democracy. "*[55]

The problem, however, was not that black soldiers did not want to fight "shoulder to shoulder" with white soldiers. It was that white soldiers didn't want to fight "shoulder to shoulder" with them, and their hostility toward black soldiers demonstrated that. Other black editors and leaders thought that it was a lot to ask Blacks to put their equality fight on hold, and "forget our present grievances," until after the war, particularly when black soldiers were being segregated and suffering racial abuses everyday. White America hadn't put their war against Blacks "on hold"-so why, they asked DuBois, should Blacks stop talking about it. It turns out that they were right, and DuBois was wrong on this point, as the "Post-War Reconstruction" DuBois hoped would come about was frustrated by the resurrection of the new Klan, and never materialized. Still, black soldiers fought with distinction, to the extent they were allowed to fight.

The biggest and two most degrading factors black soldiers had to endure were segregation and racial exclusion in the respective branches of the armed services. The U.S. army admitted, housed, assigned and dispatched black soldiers on a segregated basis. The U.S. Navy only used black soldiers as menials, such as, cooks and maintenance services. The newly created U.S. Air Force excluded Blacks altogether. Black training bases were hostilely received by communities who didn't want black soldiers interfacing with citizens of their communities, causing frequent conflicts between black soldiers and civilian Whites. Black soldiers who complained were summarily court-marshaled, or subjected to the same kind of racially abusive insults, at the hands of their white military superiors.[56]

When black soldiers were stationed abroad, the treatment they received wasn't much better. French soldiers and citizens were warned not to treat black soldiers as equals, and German soldiers taunted black soldiers that they were fighting for the benefit of "Wall Street Robbers," their term for the industrial capitalists and their monopolizing interest that was challenging America's class construct, and not their own freedom.[57] "Nigger" wasn't an uncommon term directed at black soldiers, and could be heard at any time, in any one of three languages; English, French or German. Black soldiers were frequently harassed and attacked, both, at home while serving military bases in U.S. communities and while abroad in the streets of their allies. Complaints flooded the U.S. War Department, charging that black soldiers were being continuously insulted by white officers, who referred to them as "niggers," "coons" and "darkies," and frequently forces African Americans to work under unhealthy and difficult conditions.[58]

The most notorious act of black soldier provocation came about in Houston, Texas when the community had harassed and goaded men of the 24th Regiment, a "negro" regiment, until the men responded, causing a race riot. When the men's weapon's were taken, in fear that they would be used to defend themselves, the soldiers seized arms from others and went looking for the perpetrators, killing 17 white men and wounding many more. The army held what many saw as a "mock" trial, finding fifty-four men guilty of some role in the riot. No Whites were prosecuted. Thirteen men were hanged and forty-one sentenced to life in prison. Holding up the murdered soldiers as "martyrs," nothing had shaken Blacks faith in federal government as this event. It reminded them of the Brownsville (Texas) event eleven years earlier, when one white merchant's assault on a black soldier (and his regiments' attempts to defend him) caused a local riot and one white man to be killed, which caused President Teddy Roosevelt to suspend three companies of the First Battalion of the 25th Infantry, and discharge them without honor for refusing to cooperate with court and special commission investigation.[59]

It is out of this experience that the principle architect of the New Black Resistance Movement was born. Charles Hamilton Houston, who served in this same U.S. Army during World War I, a highly segregated and volatile U.S. Army, was so affected by the racial indignities of the U.S. military, that he himself became embittered over the treatment of black soldiers. Houston recalled a couple of his own experiences abroad, almost being attacked by a white mob in France, and upon his return to the U.S., on a southbound train from Philadelphia to Washington, D.C., despite being uniform, and despite being an officer (second lieutenant) in the United States, he and another black officer watched as a white person demanded that he be reseated in the dining car, because he didn't want to sit next to black people.[60] These experiences embittered Houston, causing him to say that he was "damned glad" that he hadn't lost his life fighting for this country.[61]

Black soldiers returned from the war, in the midst of a national Klan revival, only to discover that they had helped America win the war, but had not won any semblance of equality, nor any change in treatment for themselves. Within ten months after the close of the war, the Klan made more than 200 appearances in twenty-seven states, to make a statement that America was still "white man's country," and stood for "the preservation of American institutions and the supremacy of the white race."[62] The Klan went on a rampage to demonstrate that nothing had changed, terrorizing the Negro like never before, causing 70 Blacks to be lynched within the very first year of the Post-war period, including ten black soldiers-several of whom were still in

177

their U.S. army uniforms, at the time of their murder.[63]

Houston understood how and why Blacks could be lynched in America, without as much as a peep of public outcry. He knew and concurred, as an editor of a South Carolina black newspaper editor surmised, that Blacks are lynched with the complicity of "a white judge, a white jury, white public sentiment, white officers of the law, [where] it is just as impossible for a Negro to be accused of [a] crime, or even suspected of [a] crime to escape the white man's vengeance or his justice, as it would be for a fawn to escape that wanders accidentally into a den of hungry lions."[64] Houston grew to understand that the law was flawed, and those who practiced and oversaw the law were flawed in their desire to suppress the pride and progress of the African American. He felt that it was an unreasonable expectation for Blacks to expect white America to fight "their fight" for equality. He felt they couldn't depend on in a long protracted battle and that Blacks could only depend on themselves to fight this fight and win this fight. . that when he got out of the army, he would dedicate his whole life to the eradication of racial segregation and pursuit of equality for the African American in the United States, and that he did.

Charles Hamilton Houston was honorably discharged in April, 1919, impatient and embittered about his status in a country that didn't want to recognize his (and other black soldiers) contributions to the war, but wanted to get back to its pre-war capitalism and racial politics. Houston immediately began looking at his options for studying law and committing his life to fighting another war that would define his future career pursuits, shaped by his experience in the politics of war and race. The battleground would be the United States of America. Entering Harvard in September, 1919, Charles Hamilton Houston formerly declared war on "Jim Crow" and the politics of "Separate but Equal" segregation in America. Within three years, Houston became a candidate for the degree of Doctor of Juridical Science, having distinguished himself as an "excellent" or "superior" student, as ranked by his Harvard professors, with an graduate average of 79 (75 was equivalent to an A).[65] Houston was awarded the coveted Sheldon Travelling Fellowship that afforded him the opportunity to study at any university in Europe, of which he chose the University of Madrid in Spain in 1923.

After studying Roman law, civil law and philosophy of law-all offered in Spanish and French, then traveling to Italy, France, Tunisia, and Algeria in countries where his race was rarely noticed, Houston returned to Washington, D.C. to take the bar exam. While studying to take the bar, he was keeping an eye on the new Negro Movement that had multiple voices speaking for various political, social and economic interests, as well as, a spectrum of ideological positions-from cooperatively integrationist to moderately nationalist to radically separatist. In addition, the NAACP and the National Urban League had emerged as a voice to focus on improving employment opportunities and social adjustment of urban Blacks who moved North during the Great Migration.

Founded in 1911, by a group of conservative Blacks, white philanthropists and social workers allied with Booker T. Washington, the Urban League took a more conciliatory approach than the NAACP in seeking to convince urban employers to hire black workers, based on moral suasion and economic sense.[66] William Monroe Trotter, the Boston publisher who helped DuBois organize the Niagara meeting, but opted out of the NAACP organizing meeting because of his distrust of Whites (and the fact that the organizers left he and Ida B. Wells off the initial list of proposed founding board members for the new group), started his own organizing efforts, emerging as a "nationalist voice," even leading a delegation to meet with President Woodrow Wilson at the White House in 1913.

Trotter, DuBois' Harvard classmate-never known for his diplomacy, had delivered 20,000 signatures, protesting "federal Jim Crow."[67] Complaining to Wilson about what appeared to be his sanction of segregation, Trotter and his delegation demanded the President do something about the treatment of Negroes, to which the President said that he saw no solution to "the Negro problem." When Trotter demanded an explanation, Wilson took exception with Trotter's "tone." He promptly ended the meeting and put Trotter and his delegation out of the White House, saying he would not be "blackmailed."[68] Trotter subsequently urged for Blacks to protect their rights as citizens, advocating for them to take up guns and defend themselves as necessary.

Asa Philip Randolph co-founded *The Messenger* newspaper in 1917, and became a loud and volatile voice against America's entry into World War I, and the treatment of Blacks by the government and by labor unions. In a series of editorials during 1917, Randolph stated that "No intelligent Negro is willing to lay down his life for the United States as it now exists." By 1924, Randolph had founded the Brotherhood of Sleeping Car Porters, a voice for 10,000 porters and gained recognition as a certified union by the Pullman Company in 1935. Randolph became the leading advocacy voice for the next 30 years, organizing Marches on Washington for equal rights in 1941 and 1963.

The most significant voice to surface in the pre and post war years was that of Marcus Garvey, who founded the Universal Negro Improvement Association (UNIA) in 1916. There was a segment of the African American population that was bitter over their treatment by Whites, and saw racial equality unachievable as long as there was a fundamental disrespect of Blacks. Garvey's position was that no one would ever respect Blacks, until they respected themselves, owned up to their original heritage and claimed their legacy, at home (in the United States) and abroad (in Africa). Garvey advocated for the separation from white America, called for a "Back to Africa" movement, promoted racial pride in the same way as white supremacist elevated white superiority, and sought to demonstrate economic empowerment to build a black led nation in Africa.

Garvey's "race first" philosophy-while not far-fetched-was alien to anything black Americans had ever heard, and carried a certain appeal among those who were tired of being told that they were nothing. Tired of being treated as worthless in America, "Garveyites" set out to prove the power of black unity. With Garvey shouting a number of mantras focused on blackness including, "One God, One Aim, One Destiny," "Africa for the Africans," "Up you mighty race, Accomplish what you will," and inspired by post war anti-Black sentiments, the UNIA grew at such a phenomena pace, that by 1919, it had more than thirty branches with one million members. By 1923, Garvey claimed six million followers. While many doubted Garvey's numbers, even his staunchest critics-and he had many-had to acknowledge that the UNIA had, at least, 500,000 followers-more than the NAACP had at any time during this period.[69] His *Negro World* newspaper had an even larger circulation than *The Crisis*, and its tone was extremely critical of black leadership-particularly of the NAACP who Garvey termed as an organization "run by white people." He was the first to publicize the intra-race conflicts of African Americans, stating that he had no use for light skinned Blacks, and even called W.E.B. Dubois…"a white negro" and a "rabid mulatto."

This put him in direct confrontation with DuBois, Randolph and others who saw Garvey as "a fool" and a mass distraction from dealing with the real problems affecting African Americans-namely the politics of lynching and segregation. The government, however, saw Garvey's popularity and "nationalist" message as a serious threat, as was the thousands of men Garvey paraded in uniform and sword. The government would use the UNIA business dealings, principally the Black Star Line (BSL), to investigate Garvey. The principle investigator of Garvey was J. Edgar Hoover, who made Garvey the first of what would be many "take downs" of black leaders, including Martin Luther King, Jr. forty years later. He was subsequently arrested for mail fraud, defrauding investors in the BSL using the U.S. mail.

What Garvey actually did was to put a picture of a ship on an investment circular that he was in the process of buying, but had not yet bought. Yet in the photo, the name "Phyllis Wheatley" was on the hull of the ship. The fraud claim involved no money, though the government claimed that Garvey and his wife had taken in over $10 million between 1919 and 1921. That money actually went to the purchase and operation of steamships. The fact that Garvey advertised to his investors that their money was helping to pay off a UNIA owned SS Phyllis Wheatley when the UNIA had no SS Phyllis Wheatley ship in its fleet, was seen as a fraudulent claim by the U.S. government. In reality, the fraud claim was actually a false advertising claim, to which the government could only get one person (out of millions), a man named Bennie Dancy, to say they received the circular in the mail, and that he had been defrauded out of twenty five dollars. Thus, for a ten cent stamp and a $25 response to the solicitation, the most powerful black man in America, and to many-the world, was taken down on a criminal charge of mail fraud. It was enough to get him convicted and sentenced to five years in prison, two of which he served. President Calvin Coolidge, afraid that Garvey's poor health might cause him to die in jail, adding to his martyrdom, causing a mass uprising and a political backlash against the Republicans, pardoned Garvey and deported him to his homeland, Jamaica, in 1927, effectively ending the largest mass movement of African Americans in American history.

While Garvey was effectively discredited in the eyes of the Negro leadership, Charles Houston understood that Garvey was railroaded by an unjust legal system, and saw great value in what Garvey did, stating "understand that it is just a question of reconciling the wants and desires of different human beings, each equally entitled to life, liberty and the pursuit of happiness."[70] It was immaterial that some thought Garvey to be a charlatan and a fool, because Houston felt that Garvey's movement went to the essence of what had kept Blacks in an inferior position in America-the absence of pride and the blight of race prejudice that undermined the self-esteem and dignity of the African

American. Houston noted that Garvey had achieved more, in a short period of time, than any other Negro leader in America and his popularity turned on a very simple point, black pride. Houston publicly stated that "Marcus Garvey, by turning the Negro's attention to the beauty of the color of his own skin has had a profound influence on Negro thought"...that Garvey's movement was "a black man's dream" rooted in a very simple notion, but having long term effects, in that "it made a permanent contribution in the teaching simple dignity of being Black."[71]

Houston knew how racism in America made him feel and every time he encountered it, some of his dignity was taken along with it. This period, from 1915 to 1930, sought to rob African Americans of what little public and personal dignity they had left. In the eyes of Charles Houston, the Garvey movement restored some of that dignity, if just for a moment, something black leaders weren't speaking to in the way Garvey spoke to it. Houston respected that, and in the midst of the failure of that movement, was something he wanted to give back to black people in a future movement. Equality was about being able to lift your head up and look in the eyes of another man, as equals, and with the same degree of personal dignity. Feeling equal, Houston surmised, was essential to being equal, and Garvey made Blacks in America feel equal for the first time in their lives.

Charles Houston wanted to make people "feel equal" by making them "be equal" in the eyes of the law. Thus, he studied and passed the bar exam and was admitted to practice law in the District of Columbia in June, 1924. Joining his father's law firm under the name of "Houston and Houston," Charles Hamilton Houston began perfecting his trade in his trek on the long road to *Brown*.

8

Black Monday:
Houston's Twenty-Five Year Strategy Culminates With The *Brown* Decision

There come times when it is possible to forecast the results of a contest, of a battle, of a lawsuit, long before the final event has taken place. And as far as our struggle for civil rights is concerned, the struggle for civil rights in America is won. What I am more concerned about is the fact that the Negro shall not be content with demanding an equal share in the existing system. It seems to me that his historical challenge is to make sure that the system which shall survive in the United States of America shall be a system that guarantees justice and freedom-for everyone.

- Charles Hamilton Houston (in a 1949 speech)

Why, of all the multitudinous groups of people in this country, [do] you have to single out the Negroes and give them this separate treatment? It can't be because of slavery in the past, because there are very few groups in this country that haven't had slavery some place back in the history of their group. It can't be color, because there are Negroes as white as drifted snow, with blue eyes, and they are just as segregated as the colored man. The only thing it can be is an inherent determination that the people who were formerly in slavery, regardless of anything else, shall be kept as near that state as possible.

- Thurgood Marshall, closing argument
Brown v. Board of Education, et al.

Charles Hamilton Houston's twenty-five year effort to kill Jim Crow began in a subtle and humble fashion, in the confines of his father law firm, helping people. Houston's father, William "Chief" Houston, was a no-nonsense law petitioner, who was "strictly business," in terms of his eye for detail, strict business practices and firm belief that legal services were worthy of the fee rendered-directly put, the senior Houston didn't believe in free legal advice.[1] Whereas the senior Houston saw the law practice as an efficient skill to be regulated, where time and expenses were mitigated when deemed practical-and cases settled to avoid costly and time-consuming litigation, the junior Houston enjoyed the practice of law. Charles Houston found pleasure in advising people of their rights, negotiating settlements-when necessary, but doing battle in court as often as needed. Moreover, case billings weren't as much of a priority for Houston, as it was for his father. The junior partner found satisfaction in pursuing justice, and the fact that the cause was just was fulfilling enough for Charles Houston-while not always exciting or financially rewarding-a pursuit that his father, while admonishing him that he owed it to himself to take care of himself and his family, understood and reluctantly supported. In the third year of practicing full-time law, during the summer of 1924, Houston argued his first case before the U.S. Supreme Court, and demonstrated his future penchant as a court litigator.

In a case called, *Bountiful Brick Company, et al v. Elizabeth Giles, et al*. Enjoining a case with former Harvard classmate, Samuel Horovitz, the two attorneys successfully argued to uphold a lower court's decision to find the brick company negligent of the accidental death of one of its employees, Nephi Giles. Giles had walked into the path of an unmarked crossing, using the shortest path as most of the company's employees did, on the way to work, and was hit by an oncoming train. The brick company was seeking to get the lower court's compensation award set aside, suggesting that it was Giles own negligence, illegal intrusion on the company's property that caused his death, and that Giles casual connection between injury (in this case, death) and employment was insufficient to prove the company liable.[2] The court agreed with Houston that employees commonly used this route-with the company's knowledge-thus making the company complicitous in endangering its employees, by not posting warning signs and advisements. The award was upheld.

This was the first demonstration of Houston's strategy of using "justice" as a legal right, and asserting that the court's role in society was to uphold justice as an essential component of upholding the law. It would prove to be an effective strategy in subtly challenging the integrity of jurisprudence, when the criminal justice system and the court were looking past the rightness of laws, as well as, the rights of citizens, to uphold the politics and practices of America's dominant culture. However, the public suspicions of big business, as corporate raiders of individual wealth and violators of individual equality, gave Houston his crack in the armor to challenge systems and institutions as the principle violators of the equality rights of African Americans. Houston was on his way, but the summer of 1924 would be the last time he would give his full time attention to private practice.

In the fall of 1924, Houston was hired as a part-time law school professor at the Howard Law School, where he began teaching others his social engineering philosophy. It was then that Houston nurtured a true appreciation in his students that the transformation of society only comes about in how the law is interpreted. Houston began to understand that the formal teaching of law was important, because it transformed the interpretation of law beyond confirming precedents, and that if it were not for teachers and scholars, the law might never be more than precedent-judgments confirming the correctness of earlier judgments.[3] It was then that Charles Houston began to understand that the black lawyer had a massive responsibility to not only practice law, but change the law when the law was unjust, and supported by unjust precedents. Houston knew that to change America, he and other black lawyers would have to overturn segregation, and to overturn segregation, he would knew that meant overturning the law that established the basis for segregation. Overturning segregation's legal precedent, *Plessy v. Ferguson*, then had to become the charge of the black lawyer.

185

Houston had his eye on teaching, and had submitted his employment application to the Howard Law School in December, 1923. It was at that time Charles Houston established himself as a legal scholar-not a black legal scholar, but-a legal scholar, period. Testaments to Houston's scholarship were demonstrated in the letters of recommendation received by Howard's Law School Dean, Fenton W. Booth, in support of Houston's faculty application. The Harvard Law School and its faculty of esteemed law professors, including Roscoe Pound and a future U.S. Supreme Court Justice, Felix Frankfurter, who called Houston "one of the best doctoral students he had taught at Harvard Law School," wrote letters of enthusiastic support, deeming it appropriate for the quality of work Houston had demonstrated that caused him to receive "every honor that is possible for a law student to take."[4]

Charles Houston also had a real clear theory as to how black lawyers should view themselves in the context of the overall society. According to his students, Oliver Hill and Thurgood Marshall,

Houston's position on the role of lawyers in society was that, "a lawyer's either a social engineer or…a parasite of society."[5] It wouldn't be long before Charles Houston proved himself to be a standout law professor, at a time when Howard Law School was under some pressure for being a "part-time" day and evening law school, though it had, by the 1920s graduated over 700 men and women-Black and White-and had trained more than three-fourths of approximately to 950 African American attorneys practicing throughout the nation.[6]

However, Houston didn't allow discussion of Howard's part-time status affect the intensity and rigor of the study of law, and how a lawyer must, in effect, evolve the law into a tool for social change, if they were to become first rate lawyers. Houston didn't give his students an option of success. It was these high expectations that "students were sometimes driven to swearing" at Houston, but "also swore by him," in terms of his "aura of extreme competence," whose "very presence in legal dialogue, commanded respect."[7] And it was in this respect that Houston was able to mold his students to be more than just attorneys practicing law.

Houston taught his students that a lawyer who worked as a social engineer had several functions beyond traditional practice; 1) serving as "the mouthpiece of the weak, and the sentinel guarding against wrong," 2) "guiding antagonistic and group forces into channels where they will not clash," 3) ensuring that the "course of change is…orderly with a minimum of human loss and suffering," 4) recogniz[ing] that the written Constitution and inertia against its amendments give lawyers wide room for social experimentation," and 5) engag[ing] in a carefully planned [program of litigation] to ensure decisions, rulings and public opinion on…principle[s], while "arousing and strengthening the local will to struggle." Houston included two additional duties of social engineering, because African American lawyers were members of an oppressed minority group in the United States; 6) being "prepared to anticipate, guide and interpret group advancement," and 7) us[ing] the law as an instrument [for the] minority…to…achieve its place in the community and nation."[8] Houston's philosophy soon became the basis for which Howard Law School advanced its mission, thus becoming the training ground for testing law on social equality, and a principle recruiter for encouraging lawyers to use their trade for the improvement of black quality of life, and in the struggle for justice and equality in America.

Between 1927 and 1929, a number of events impacted, even

changed, the life of both Howard Law School and Charles Hamilton Houston. In 1927, with the approval of the Howard Law School, Houston was appointed to conduct a national study on the status and activities of African-American lawyers. During 1927-1928, he sought to identify the training, skill levels, and activities of black lawyers throughout the nation. Houston traveled to seventeen cities in the North and the South to collect data, and document the impact of black lawyers. With the help of Carter G. Woodson's Association for the Study of Negro Life and History, in whose facilities Houston compiled and analyzed the data, and funded by a grant from the Laura Spelman Rockefeller Memorial, four studies in one were produced.

Under the title, "Status and Activities of the Negro Lawyer," Houston compiled sub-studies that produced data on; 1) Negro Law Schools, 2) the Negro Lawyer, 3) The Negro Lawyer and His Contact with the Administration of Law, and 4) a special "Survey of Howard University Law Students," analyzing the activities and impacts of his own institution's product.[9] Houston's study did more than just analyze where black lawyers were, and what they were doing. The true intent of Houston's study was to analyze how well black lawyers were positioned to take on segregation, and where those fights would most likely occur, in terms of black lawyers' capacity to handle cases, support them in the state court systems and see them through to completion. Houston's thinking was that it was black lawyers, above all, who would advance and defend the equality interests of black America. No one else would "do justice" to it, with the passion and personal understanding of a black lawyer. And he was correct.

187

It took nearly a calendar year for Houston to complete this study. He worked at such a driven pace that he became ill, with what doctors thought was either pneumonia or influenza but eventually turned into tuberculosis. Houston was ordered bed rest, against his will, and forced to take off part of the year because tuberculosis patients, under the laws of the District, couldn't enter any schools, where they would come in contact with students and spread the disease.[10]

While Houston was out on mandatory bed rest, two significant events occurred at Howard University. The first was a change in philosophy about the law school. During this time, Howard hired its first black president, Mordecai Johnson, in 1926. Howard University-the nation's oldest federally funded black university-sought to upgrade the law school, something Houston also wanted to do. Johnson, educated at the University of Chicago, Harvard and Rochester Theological

Seminary, who, like Houston, had been following the discussions of the American Bar Association (ABA) and Association of American Law Schools (AALS) regarding concerns for law schools to maintain higher standards to receive accreditation. He shared Houston's views that it was time for the law school to become a full time day school. Howard Law School, as a part time law school, had experienced some credentialing problems in the past. It was still viewed as suspect, in terms of the quality of its programs-for no other reason than the structure of its program. Johnson and Houston had frequent discussions, during Houston's sick leave, about "professionalizing" the law school, consistent with what was necessary to receive accreditation, turning Howard Law School into a three-year day program.

Both Johnson and Houston were in agreement that it was time to pursue accreditation by the ABA and membership in the AALS (an action the Board had approved in 1928), which meant a conversion of the law school from its current curricula program. Encouraged by Johnson's willingness to advocate for the law school change, Houston completed another study-while still on sick leave-entitled, "Personal Observation on the Summary of Studies in Legal Education as Applied to the Howard University School of Law," which outlined status of the current law school, including faculty, library and research aims, as well as, what should be the goals of the law school's future development.[11] Impressed by this demonstration of scholarship and commitment to the law school, in June of 1929, Howard University's Board of Trustees appointed Charles H. Houston, Resident Vice-Dean in charge of developing the curriculum strategies for implementing the three-year day school, and for building the research capacity of the law library.[12]

The second major event to occur at Howard University was the resignation of the law school's current dean, Fenton Booth, who had been elevated to the position of Chief Justice of the United States Court of Claims. The vacancy couldn't have come at a worse time, with the program in transition, and Charles Houston still out on sick leave. Booth agreed to stay on as acting dean to insure both a smooth administrative transition, and to help implement changes in curricula in the law school's dual program, a three-year day school, and a four year night school. Mordecai Johnson had only one man in mind to replace Booth, Charles Hamilton Houston, Johnson's partner in his push to turn Howard into a first rate law school. In June, 1930, the Board appointed Charles Houston Vice-Dean of the Howard Law School for the upcoming academic year. The board also moved to end the evening program upon graduation of its current class of students.

      Houston served as Vice Dean (and Chief Administrative Officer) of Howard's Law School from 1930 to 1935, several times rejecting the title of Dean for the purpose of showing solidarity for his underpaid faculty and staff, and to direct the money he would have received in promotion increases toward bringing the best qualified professors to Howard's Law School.[13] During Houston's tenure as Vice Dean, he and Johnson came under severe fire for eliminating the evening school program in what many said was them attempting to "Harvardize" Howard's Law School. However, both survived the criticism. Within two years of Houston's appointment, Howard Law School had implemented its three-year day school, built a library of 10,000 volumes, received full accreditation by the ABA, in April of 1931, and membership into the AALS, by December of 1931-with retroactive approval of the work of students currently attending the law school.[14] Houston finally had the type of institution he deemed necessary to train his legal army.

*   *   *

      In the meantime, in the world outside academia, the fight against segregation was heating up, and it did not escape Houston's attention. Houston saw organizational advocacy as a key component to creating the critical mass needed to generate sufficient public interest in overturning segregation. The NAACP had emerged as the leading agitator, on both the question of lynching and segregation, though many, including Marcus Garvey and A. Philip Randolph, saw the NAACP as representing the interests of the black bourgeoisie, rather than the masses. After hearing that the NAACP was looking for someone to head a legal campaign to fight segregation, Houston felt it was an ideal time to take his legal strategy beyond the halls of Howard Law School. Subsequently, Houston was hired to direct a campaign of litigation as part-time NAACP Special Counsel, from October, 1934 to June, 1935, and full-time Special Counsel from July, 1935 to 1940. Houston came to the NAACP during a very volatile period.

      NAACP leadership was at odds on a number of questions, but particularly on the question of segregation. At the center of the conflict was the NAACP's new Executive Secretary, Walter White, who had replaced James Weldon Johnson as acting Executive Secretary, in 1929.

By the time he became the permanent Executive Secretary in 1931, White was committed to some level of continuity, by focusing the NAACP's organizational fight on Johnson's fight, the eradication of lynching through legislation, or what came to be known as "integration" policies. Irrespective of external perspectives, the NAACP, as an organization, had taken a position to fight segregation at every level. By 1934, White was trying to keep the organization on a single-minded focus of segregation and discrimination. On the other hand, W.E.B. DuBois, editor of *The Crisis*, still viewed as the voice of the NAACP, was bidding to attract the appeal of the masses, by speaking to the needs of aggrieved lower income black people-which at that critical point in time, during the midst of the "Great Depression-were largely economic.

DuBois, clearly representative of black intellectual continuity for the NAACP in its first 25 years, was experiencing a shift in thought on the question of segregation. He had come to the more radical position that African Americans had to have economic independence, before they could achieve equality, and that a voluntary segregation from Whites-to build an economic defense against discrimination and inequality-should be considered.[15] Mind you, "Separation" is the same thing that Elijah Muhammad and the Nation of Islam, through his popular national spokesperson, Malcolm X, would espouse 30 years later as a remedy to urban "ghettorization." Yet, it was shocking coming from a man who, just 40 years earlier, publicly chastised black America's leading spokesperson, Booker T. Washington, for suggesting that Blacks accept some measure of segregation by "laying their buckets down where they are," as a means to achieving some other cultural end. DuBois' shift in thought had more to do with a paradigm shift in socio-economic political thought, than a conversion to nationalism-though DuBois called himself a Pan-Africanist.

DuBois' philosophical shift was influenced by comments he had read from Howard University Professor, Ralph Bunche, who suggested that the NAACP was misguided in their efforts to seek political, social and legal equality when he rationalized that any Negro, who thought about it and did not advocate for a major overhaul of America's economic system, simply didn't understand the black's man isolation.[16] Bunche helped DuBois, this period's preeminent black scholar, understand that race discrimination in America had always been economic, and that both its economic and labor systems only survive, as long as, white workers could be kept convinced that their economic stake in America depended on the subjugation of the black worker, whereas, all labor then remains an exploited class.[17] Bunche, who would win the Nobel Peace Prize in 1950, and perceived throughout history as, what Richard Kluger called "every closet racist's Negro-I-wouldn't-mind-living-next-door-to," was seen, in 1934, as a highly militant-decidedly pessimistic scholar, with a strong leftist tilt[18] (though he would shake his mainstream persona for a return to the philosophical militancy, through his involvement of the civil disobedience marches of the 1960s) and wrote;

> *"Extreme faith is placed in the ability of these instruments of democratic government to free the minority from social proscription and civic inequality…the inherent fallacy of this belief rests in the failure to appreciate the fact that the instruments of the state cannot be divorced from its prevailing economic structure, whose servant it must inevitably be."[19]*

Kenneth Clark, who played a significant role in articulating the affects of racial segregation on the African American psyche in the Brown cases, was a student of Bunche, at the time, and viewed his articulation of racism as forceful, and to be understood "not in terms of the black man's deficiencies, but in terms of the white man's."[20] DuBois got Bunche's point, and viewed it as a "new school" of thought that he felt the NAACP should be prepared to embrace, because he embraced it. And the NAACP might have embraced it, had not DuBois couched the economic advocacy position within the separation argument. There were few black leaders that had ever been willing to accept segregation other than Booker T, and now himself.

Still, just as DuBois refused to accept the compromise position, in a prior period, White refused to accept that position in 1934. *The* problem was that DuBois articulated that position in an editorial in the *Crisis* magazine, which White was forced to dispute. Further, DuBois had promised to make segregation the topic of a year-long discussion, given that the association, in DuBois' mind, had never defined segregation with any clarity, and therefore contained some ambiguity that DuBois took the liberty to interpret.[21] This set off a national debate that went way beyond White and DuBois' internal "family fight." It became a battle for the future direction of Black America, in which a flurry of letters flew criticizing DuBois. The most harshly written criticism was by Howard Law Professor, William Hastie, Houston's cousin and law partner, who would become the first black ever appointed to a federal judgeship (five years later in 1939), writing what was essentially and editorial response in a column published by a journal called the *New Negro Opinion*. Hastie wrote the following scathing public editorial on DuBois' stand:

"For fifty years prejudiced white men and abject, boot-licking, gut lacking, knee bending, favor seeking Negroes have been insulting our intelligence with a tale that goes like this:

Segregation is not an evil. Negroes are better off by themselves. They can get equal treatment, and be happier too, if they live and move and have their being off by themselves-except, of course, as they are needed by the white community to do the heavy and dirty work, and why should we object to being set off by ourselves if we are with our own people, who are just as good as anyone else.

But any Negro who uses this theoretical possibility as a justification for segregation is either dumb, or mentally dishonest, or else he has, like Esau, chosen a mess of pottage.

On page 20 of The Crisis for January, 1934, Editor DuBois indulges in all these old sophistries and half-truths. If you don't believe it, read for yourself. I refused to believe until my own eyes had convinced me. DuBois, William Edward Burghart, himself-or not himself-making a puny defense of segregation and hair splitting about the difference between segregation and discrimination! Oh, Mr. DuBois! How could you?

It is a real blow to lose you, Mr. DuBois, and we will not deny that your statement, coming from you, is a powerful weapon in the hands of our enemies.

Oh, Esau![22]

For all the anger and anxiety DuBois' editorial caused, in truth, he was correct about the NAACP's lack of clarity in its position on segregation. The NAACP's top priority issue, in its first 25 years, had been lynching. The NAACP, heretofore, had never taken a national stance on de jure segregation. The NAACP did "study" the impact of segregation, and how it should respond to it-thus, the purpose of the Margold Report-but it had never acted or encouraged any anti-segregation policy, in the way it had acted and encouraged anti-lynching policy. So, DuBois was correct in his position that the NAACP had not done any more than issue a position statement on segregation. But never in the association's wildest dreams did it imagine that its most vocal voice would advance a segregation "compromise" position.

This most certainly would have been a subject for board discussion from the NAACP's white chairman (and principle benefactor), Arthur B. Spingarn, who was shocked of this "separation talk" and insisted that White address it immediately, down to the NAACP's local dues-paying members-many of whom hung on DuBois' every word. *The Crisis* was the bible of the NAACP-read religiously by any and all who followed the nation's social equality fight.

DuBois' apparent willingness to now accept a large degree of voluntary separation seemed to represent a repudiation of the founding principles and goals of the NAACP, stated segregation position or not, and a distinction between forced segregation and voluntary separation was both undiscernable and unacceptable.[23] White was forced to publicly declare in the next edition of *The Crisis* that DuBois was only expressing his opinion, that it was not reflective of the NAACP's position, and that "the N.A.A.C.P. has from the date of its foundation been opposed to segregation in any form, without any reservation whatever."[24] DuBois saw White's repudiation of his statement as another one of White's frequent attempts to censure him.

With this act, DuBois had contradicted the NAACP once too many times, but most saw it as the breaking point for two men that could no longer hide their personal dislike for each other. Both tried to put others in the middle of their fight. White's position was that Blacks must push for integration, and DuBois position was that Blacks must unite and separate, to become an economic force to fight inequality.

William Hastie, Houston's cousin and law partner, as cited earlier, sided with White and the NAACP. James Weldon Johnson, who was liked and respected by both men, remained neutral, saying that either option was acceptable to him as long as Blacks progressed toward one or the other.[25] Houston did the same, though he was being bought to lead the NAACP's "declare war in the courts on segregation" fight, and he was too new to get in the middle of a family fight. Finally, DuBois resigned from his several posts in the NAACP in 1934. The NAACP Board of Directors accepted his resignation with "deepest regrets."

The DuBois conflict with White set the NAACP on its future course, as White was not about to let DuBois criticize him and the association, from outside the organization, as "doing nothing on segregation." By refusing to publish White's response to his editorial (which was published after DuBois' departure), White committed the NAACP in perpetuity to a war against racial segregation in any form.[26] DuBois also literally pushed White into hiring Houston, an ardent and unyield-

193

ing opponent of racial segregation, out of a need to get the legal campaign started with someone who held ending segregation as a high priority. Thus, the DuBois era unceremoniously ended, just as the Houston era began with this "renewed" declaration.

* * *

White was now in firm control of the NAACP, as *the* black voice for the organization. Finally from under the shadow of DuBois, Walter White wasn't interested in sharing the limelight with anyone else. White's interest in Houston's segregation agenda was essentially secondary to his own in challenging lynching in the courts. Though Houston knew he needed a national organization to launch his fight against Jim Crow, and sought out the NAACP as the vehicle to do so, Houston wasn't even White's first choice to lead its legal campaign-though Houston had been recommended and considered as someone with "a very deep interest" in the campaign as early as July, 1933.[27]

A direct challenge to segregation was seen as too risky, because if the NAACP were to lose a challenge to segregation, it would only serve to further affirm *Plessy*, which White wasn't prepared to do. Houston's interest in the NAACP, however, was to challenge de jure segregation in the courts. The first thing Houston did as Special Counsel was to pull out a study that White had shelved on how the NAACP should best go about fighting segregation. Called "the *Margold Report*," named after a white Harvard scholar and expert on constitutional law named Nathan Margold, it was a study to look at how to resolve the policy challenges facing African Americans, caused by legalized segregation. The NAACP emphasized that, though it was funded by the Garland Fund, it was "a NAACP Project," and that Margold was only responsible to the NAACP.

The *Margold Report*, officially called, a "*Preliminary Report for the Joint Committee Supervising the Expenditure of the 1930 Appropriation by the American Fund for Public Service to the NAACP,*"was a 218 page (legal sized) preliminary study analyzing the legal routes, by which segregation could be challenged, in the areas of segregated education and residential segregation, supported by restrictive covenants. The whole basis under which the Garland Fund funded the NAACP to try taxpayer suits was based on the *Margold Report* mentioning education litigation as a suitable basis for examining the legal tenants of equalization-the basis under which taxpayer funds were allotted between white schools and black schools. The report stated that disproportionate school spending, as a matter of law, violated the tenants of "Separate But Equal," and that it was relatively easy for them to prove that. However, finding the proper remedy would be difficult, largely because the states themselves had varying regulatory statues that would require varying legal approaches.

The report categorized the states targeted for violation into three categories; 1) states that required equal expenditures and thus, had no federal remedy, since it would be a matter of filing a compliance order in state courts to bring forth remedy, since noncompliance doesn't bring about a violation of the federal Constitution; 2) states that left expenditures to state officials who violated the tenets of Separate But Equal, by spending more with white schools than black schools, thus bringing about a federal remedy; 3) states that only required officials to provide a "fair and equitable" division of funds, where state and federal remedies were available, but relief would be difficult to obtain due to a number of defenses the states could put up.[28] Margold felt that focusing their energies on using mandamus in state courts to attack segregation was a misplaced strategy, since all the NAACP could do was request for orders to equalize, which could be done at the state's discretionary time tables. Margold argued instead, for the campaign to focus on three simple, easily provable facts; one, that state law required separate schools; two, that expenditures were obviously unequal, and three, that state remedies in practice were unavailable.[29]

This would allow the NAACP to have, in Margold's words, "a case of segregation irremediably coupled with discrimination," requiring simple declarations of unconstitutionality, rather than orders mandating equalized expenditures, and once obtained-state officials would be forced to decide on whether to equalize expenditures or desegregate schools.[30] This was a direct attack on Separate but Equal policies, and an indirect attack on segregation, since Margold himself acknowledged that this strategy "left it open" for the South to engage in some other form of segregation, but reiterated that the NAACP should "attack the practice of segregation, *as now provided for and administered.*[31] Though the final "preliminary" report represented a more aggressive posture than the NAACP represented to its funder, and more confrontational than the NAACP was prepared to engage, *the Margold Report* is seen as a landmark analysis in the duality of laws that were permitted under segregation and the unequal policies that manifested from it cultural practices.

The Margold Report, and the Gunnar Myrdal report called, *An American Dilemma: The Negro Problem and Modern Democracy*, a 1,483 page study on the politics of race in America, started in 1938, completed in 1940-published in 1944, were important policy statements acknowledging that the misapplication and selective application of laws in America were being called into question, as they offered a serious challenge to America's justice system, and a real threat to Constitutional democracy, as defined in the United States. The NAACP was preparing to force the question in the courts and test the validity of this "democracy." Both William Hastie and Thurgood Marshall would later agree that the *Margold Report* became "the bible" of the NAACP legal drive.[32]

Commissioned through a grant that the NAACP had received, in 1930, from the American Fund for Public Service, through a $1 million fund set up by Charles Garland to "benefit mankind"..."the poor as well as the rich"...the "black as much as the white," the report was the first of its kind to study the policy ramifications of race, the effects of de jure segregation, and its legal implications on African Americans.[33] The $294,000 proposal that was initially submitted by the NAACP was for the purpose of funding a program to obtain "black equal rights" through the courts, with emphasis on such tactics as taxpayers' suits, where the use of tax revenue to provide, what was generally viewed as services for the public's benefit, was actually used to discriminate against Blacks. One hundred thousand dollars, almost one third of what was requested, was pledged to the NAACP for the purpose of litigating taxpayer suits to challenge the dual school systems in the South, for the legal protection of black' civil liberties, for litigation seeking an end to segregation, and jury exclusion, but was eventually cut back to $20,000.[34] Margold was paid $10, 000 for the report, and $10,000 was set aside for use in attacking segregated schools and Jim Crow railroads, using all of the actual $20,000 of the $100,000 the Garland fund promised.[35] White, who was acting Executive Secretary at the time, asked James Weldon Johnson-who was on leave-to work with Margold on the original grant proposal, and the two came up with different courses of action.

Johnson explicitly distinguished between pursuing equalization from a direct attack on segregation. Johnson would have used the taxpayer suits to force those states, in three or four areas of the country, including South Carolina, Virginia, Tennessee, and maybe Southern California and New Mexico, to be truly equal in their funding of schools.[36] White felt that the NAACP's best course was to pursue inte-

196

gration through legislation, and litigation-if necessary, but he, in no way, intended litigation and segregation court battles to become the primary focus of the NAACP.

Margold argued for a direct attack on separate schools, which he saw as both legally and politically possible, but Johnson saw as too much of a national challenge, that would include states in the North, like Pennsylvania, and "worst than futile," in the Deep South, given the influence of the Klan on the political and legal systems. Margold, on the other hand, felt it was a waste of time and money for the NAACP to use its small grant to try to litigate within the system of segregation. Margold felt the goal of the NAACP should be to overturn segregation, not seek to uphold it by acknowledging its demerits. Margold's point was that segregation was an illegal system that was not constitutionally sanctioned and the NAACP needed to recognize that, and expend its means and energy fighting the system, not fighting its inequities.

Margold finished his report in May, 1931, in draft form. White sat on the report for two years, because he didn't totally agree with Margold's recommended course of action, which was to challenge segregation head on, by challenging its most formidable legal precedent, *Plessy*. White sided with his mentor, James Weldon Johnson's view. Margold was able to avoid White's conflict with the strategy by declining to direct the NAACP's legal campaign after accepting a federal appointment as Solicitor of the Department of Interior.[37] This put the report on the shelf permanently, while White sought out a replacement for Margold, someone with "equal" qualifications, to direct the legal campaign.

In 1934, White turned to another highly regarded constitutional scholar on the recommendation of Roger Baldwin, ACLU Chair and Garland Fund Board member, Columbia University's Karl Llewellyn, who was also white. Llewellyn wasn't a litigator, and his lack of court experience didn't serve the truest purpose of the campaign, which was to initiate test cases through "in court" challenges. In the meantime, Houston, who had come to the attention of White early in the process, surfaced as a logical choice, because he had developed a reputation as "a brilliant and indefatigable" lawyer and scholar, par excellent, who studied under one of the most clever legal minds of the 20th Century, future Supreme Court Jurist, Felix Frankfurter.[38] Moreover, Houston actively pursued the position, and provided White with letters of glowing support from Margold and Frankfurter. Houston even took on a test case for the NAACP in 1933, a case that involved

197

an indigent black man from Virginia accused of murder. Though Houston lost the case, it proved to be a landmark case for the NAACP, because it demonstrated that a black lawyer could handle delicate, emotion charged race cases in small southern towns, and as in this case, earn the respect and admiration of local lawyers and judges-an attribution to Houston's style, skill and decorum.[39]

With the Harvard "network" definitely working in Houston's favor, though he was White's second choice, and was never the choice of Roger Baldwin (who told Margold to "watch over Houston, because he doubted his academic experience gave him sufficient court experience),[40] Houston was hired in May, 1934 as part-time special counsel, to coordinate the NAACP's legal campaign, which was back on the table as part of a broader community mobilization strategy.[41] Houston was, of course, aware of *the Margold Report* and was also aware of White's trepidation with the report. Still, Houston felt there were some useful ideas in the report that the NAACP should consider.

Houston, understanding the constrictions of the $10,000 grant that left it difficult to put in place a comprehensive litigation strategy, recommended that the entire amount be put in a single campaign against discrimination in education. (Houston offered an alternative recommendation, splitting the money between a school and transportation campaign, just in case, the Joint Committee, a joint board of the Garland Fund board members and NAACP Board members, didn't buy the first one). Houston's memo, though, did offer a variation of strategy and tactics that was different than what Margold had proposed. His philosophy was more consistent with White's, and no doubt brought Houston closer, as he arrested White's concerns about Margold's approach, even though Margold's approach was closer to Houston's ultimate goal of challenging and overturning *Plessy*. He didn't feel that the NAACP needed to go as quickly as Margold had recommended. Houston felt that the NAACP should press equalization, as Johnson had suggested, and seek to "test segregation." Coming from a struggling academic institution, Houston didn't have a problem with forcing state funded institutions to equalize their portions to Blacks, who had been cheated under "Separate But Equal." Houston had a clear desire to see black institutions and students receive more funds and secure enlarged educational opportunities, even within the objectionable and racially discriminatory system that Houston knew they were trying to overturn.[42] It was time to force equality.

It was Houston's desire to bankrupt "Jim Crow," on the way to breaking its illegal standing. What Houston really meant was that if the South wanted to practice "Separate But Equal," the NAACP should make them pay for separate but equal-meaning make the states give equally to Blacks and Whites. Houston felt that Margold was on point that isolated suits meant little in the American legal system, but a collaboration of cases, that the taxpayer suits could prove, would lay a foundation of research, cases, and community involvement in a struggle against racial discrimination, and for equal rights, and that the NAACP should begin fighting segregation under the prevailing "Separate But Equal" system-the pervasive racial discrimination and economic depression segregation creates.[43]

Houston also insisted that this campaign be represented as an NAACP commitment to protracted struggle "for and with black people," meaning that the aims of the campaign-under his direction-would be to, one; arouse and strengthen the will of the local communities to demand and fight for their rights, and two; to work out model procedures through actual tests in court which could be used by local communities in similar cases brought by them on their own initiative and resources.[44] Houston ultimately agreed with Margold that real "Separate But Equal" policies would be too costly to maintain and that segregation states would ultimately be forced to desegregate, and if they didn't, the challenge to *Plessy* would come soon enough.

No one wanted to attack *Plessy* more than Houston, but now with the NAACP willing to support a modified approach, he wanted to make sure it was done slow and done right. Houston wanted to make sure the NAACP understood that black lawyers would be retained to litigate those cases, so that the federal court system could be sensitized to seeing articulate and competent black professionals arguing cases in their own racial interests. Houston had a legal methodology that sought to try segregation cases only in the North or Upper South, and wanted, at all costs, to avoid challenging segregation in the Deep South (limiting legal challenges to equalization cases-forcing "true" equality within segregation), as the political and judicial systems appeared to be too intertwined with local cultures to ensure justice would prevail.

Houston's theory was proven right, when the NAACP came under criticism for not taking the case of the Scottsboro Boys, in 1933. It was something their attorney, Samuel Leibowitz, would have to learn the hard way, when he was never able to get a conviction in Alabama. Houston did file a brief on behalf of two of the Scottsboro boys in the U.S. Supreme Court, that led to reversal of the death penalty conviction of Clarence Norris, and caused Haywood Patterson's case to be remanded back to the Alabama state court, due to the exclusion of Blacks from both their grand and petit juries.[45] Houston marched on their behalf to have all of them freed, but he also understood that Jim Crow would never be whipped in the courts of the deep South, and wouldn't risk his whole campaign trying to do so.

After taking a leave of absence from Howard University, in 1935, Houston's first case before the high court, as the NAACP's full-time "Special Counsel," paid immediate dividends, winning a landmark case that affirmed a very important precedent. In the case of *Hollins v. State of Oklahoma*, Houston successfully defended a black man charged with murdering a white girl, by convincing the U.S. Supreme Court to overturn the conviction on the basis that the man's 14th Amendment equal protection and due process rights were violated, because black people had been excluded from his jury panel. The U.S. Supreme Court had just issued a similar ruling earlier in the year, on the second appeal of one of the Scottsboro Boys, in the case of *Norris v. Alabama*,[46] where it had been proven that Blacks were "habitually prohibited" from serving as jurors. This was a double victory for the stature of the NAACP because it was also the first time in which the NAACP employed exclusively black counsel to represent the organization before the Supreme Court.[47]

*   *   *

Houston's second major victory came in 1936, when he took a case at the request of one of his former Howard Law students. It was a student he took a particular liking to, as he had finished at the top of his class, though he had a gruff but easy personality, and a raw intellect, in which Houston saw great potential. It was in students like these that Houston was hedging his bet on future legal battles on segregation. This one particular student, Houston had soaked with plenty of anti-Jim Crow zeal-so much so, that he graduated from Howard Law School and immediately set out to become a civil rights lawyer. Tall, lanky, and with local roots from Baltimore, Thurgood Marshall was perceived by Houston as a fiery young student with "a good mind that was largely undisciplined and unchallenged," but a young man that had adopted Houston's passion for fighting for equality, thus endearing him to Houston. The "conscience for justice" had been prodded by one of his former classmates, and one of the architects of the Harlem Renaissance,

Langston Hughes, to join a campaign to integrate Lincoln University's faculty that started young Thurgood on his way to advocating for the rights of others. He met Charles Houston, while in Howard's graduate school program, studying to become a dentist, and was convinced he had the moral fortitude and personal conviction to be a good attorney.[48] This was the beginning of a twenty year mentorship that changed America, and the way America viewed the Constitution and the 14th Amendment.

While struggling to build a private practice, Marshall took the case of Donald Murray, who had applied to the University of Maryland law school and was denied, because he was black. Marshall had been looking for a case against the University of Maryland, who he himself passed on, in 1929, because of its segregation policy, which he saw as a futile application process that would have rejected him based on his race. He immediately took the case to his mentor, who had also been looking for a plaintiff to test the University of Maryland's segregation policy. The case fit the NAACP's legal campaign strategy. It was in the upper South. It was a state funded university. It had a segregation policy. Equalization could be demanded, and remedy enforced in the state and federal courts.

While Marshall invited Houston to take the position of lead counsel in the case, Houston opted for the position of co-counsel. He purposely took "second chair" to his former student to give him both the guidance and court experience he needed. The case of *Pearson* (University of Maryland) *v. Murray* (169 Md. 478; 182 A. 590, 1936) was won on a directed verdict to admit Murray on the grounds that the University of Maryland didn't have a "black law school," and didn't have the financial means to build one. The University of Maryland appealed the case, stating that it was a private agency (having been private up until 1914, when the state foreclosed on the mortgage to the university), and that it had provided Murray with the opportunity to receive an "equal" education at Howard Law School.

Out of state scholarships were a common diversion tactic used by segregated universities and colleges to deny black students entry, and uphold the "separateness" of higher education. The Maryland Court of Appeals disagreed, stating that the university was indeed a public institution, and that whatever tuition it had extended to Murray, who was a Baltimore resident, didn't take into account the cost of transportation and/or relocation which Murray would incur, that a student of the University of Maryland would not incur, by their admission standing.

The verdict was upheld and Donald Murray entered the University of Maryland Law School in the fall of 1936, and graduated three years later, in the top third of his class.[49] This case, driven by the passion of Marshall, and the legal wisdom of Houston, became known later as the case of "Marshall's revenge."

A second case that Marshall convinced Houston to take on, was the first of what would be many *Teacher Salaries* cases filed by Marshall. A case filed on behalf of a black principal named William Gibbs. Gibbs was an acting principal for the Board of Education of Montgomery County, Maryland. Gibbs was receiving an average annual salary of $612, while the average salary of a white principal at the time was $1,475.[50] A greater injustice was that white janitors in some Maryland counties, considered school maintenance staff, at $960 annually, received more than they paid their black elementary school teachers, who were considered professional faculty, and received $621 annually.[51] The case was filed in December of 1936. Two years later the Maryland Court of Appeals ordered the equalization of salaries within the county, which established the guideline basis for future NAACP cases to follow. The cumulative pay won for black teachers in nine counties, in the state of Maryland alone, exceeded $100,000.[52] This caused the national NAACP to take notice of Houston's "wunderkind." White and the Board essentially concurred with Houston that "the kid" had "an eye and a gut" for litigating civil rights discrimination.

The *Murray* and *Gibbs* cases showed Houston enough to convince him that he and Marshall worked well together as a team. Houston continued to give Marshall NAACP cases, until he was able to hire Marshall on as Assistant Special Counsel, in 1937. This freed up Houston to move around the country to build a strong legal department for the NAACP, that could work for social change through the law. Houston spoke at meetings, rallies of civic bodies, teacher associations, interracial councils, church congregations, parents groups, sororities, fraternities and student organizations, logging nearly 25,000 miles in urban cities and rural areas of the south, to promote the NAACP's legal campaign for equalization and against segregation.[53] Of greatest interest was the NAACP seeking plaintiffs to file equalization complaints for equality in black and white teacher's salaries. As the *Gibbs* case demonstrated, African American teachers and administrators often earned less than half of what white school employees earned for similar capacities, and often with less facility and material resources.

Between 1936 and 1953, first in Maryland, then in every southern state, except North Carolina and Mississippi, the NAACP went from state to state-county to county-filing equalization petitions on behalf of black teacher associations and individual plaintiffs (when groups were afraid to come forward) to gain equality in teachers salaries.[54] Though many were protracted fights that involved much intimidation, the NAACP's demands that separate be, in fact, equal, benefited black teachers, as most of its remedy claims proved successful in closing the salary gaps in most states, by the end of World War II.[55] In a number of southern and border states, the NAACP won fifty cases dealing with the equalization of teachers salaries, which put over three million dollars into the pockets of Black teachers over a fifteen year period.[56] If nothing else, the equalization fight proved that Whites were willing to pay to uphold segregation. Equalization, up to that point, had done little to break down segregation.

The first serious challenge to segregation, as law, came in the second major education case that Houston and Marshall took on, which was even more landmark than the first. A black law school applicant named Lloyd Gaines had been denied entrance to the University of Missouri Law School, on the basis that he was black. Again, consistent with the NAACP's legal strategy of equalization, the NAACP demanded that the University of Missouri either admit Gaines, or set up a "separate but equal" law school for Blacks.

Houston took the case, solely on its merits, to be able to challenge segregation in the federal courts. Houston saw it as a tactical maneuver in the long range plan to secure a favorable ruling in the U.S. Supreme Court against racial discrimination, that could ultimately serve as one of the "test cases" necessary to strike down the precedent of *Plessy*. With the case of *Missouri ex rel. Gaines v. Canada* (305 U.S. 337, 1938), Houston had *Plessy* in his sights. One thing that Houston could not ignore was the temperament of the courts during this period. The federal courts, in particular, tended to be filled with men who maintained similar ideologies to the men in the Executive and Legislative branches of government that appointed and confirmed them to sit for life.

The NAACP became conscious of their challenges in the Courts at the start of the 1930s, when President Herbert Hoover sought to appoint an outright white supremacist, a circuit court judge by the name of John J. Parker, a southerner from North Carolina to the U.S. Supreme Court. Parker had run for Governor in 1920, and had made a

203

statement opposing black suffrage. Here was a man who was going to be part of the group that were the final interpreters of the U.S. Constitution, having been quoted, on record, in the Greensboro Daily News as saying:

"The participation of the Negro in politics is a source of evil and danger to both races and is not desired by wise men in either race or in the Republican Party of North Carolina."[58]

Quoted directly from his acceptance speech of the Republican nomination for Governor, Parker was exacting in his racial views when he said the following:

"We recognize the fact that he [the Negro] has not yet reached that stage in his development when he can share the burdens and responsibilities of Government...I say it deliberately, there's no more dangerous or contemptible enemy of the State than men who for personal or political advantage will attempt to kindle the flame of racial prejudice or hatred [than to involve the Negro in politics (voting)]..."[59]

Walter White, still acting Secretary of the NAACP, in what he called one of the most important battles of his tenure, saw Parker as a bigot showing contempt for both the Negro and anyone willing to help the Negro, stated that Parker was "not fit to defend the Thirteenth, Fourteenth and Fifteenth Amendments," and spearheaded the Association's campaign to defeat his nomination. There were a host of other issues that affected the Parker nomination, including the distrust of Southern Democrats (who automatically supported Southern judges) who were suspicious of Hoover's attempts to expand southern Republicanism, loss of influence by Hoover due to the stock market crash and the ensuing depression to follow, and Parker's own "anti-union" rulings on the circuit court that contributed to his demise.[60] Race, in and of itself, wasn't viewed as salient enough to block a confirmation, or cause a nomination to be rejected. Still, the NAACP's letter writing campaign and lobbying efforts heightened the salience on Parker's appointment significantly, and probably caused enough damage to it "tip the scales" away from confirmation. Parker's nomination was defeated, 41 to 39.

While most of the Supreme Court jurists of that period showed no apparent "anti-Black" views, and the Chief Justice of the period, Charles Evans Hughes (served from 1930 to 1941) was known to have somewhat "progressive" racial views, the Supreme Court did have its share of racists. Oliver Wendell Holmes, who served until 1932, was considered to be one of the most brilliant legal minds of the first quarter of the 20th Century. He was a Social Darwinist who believed in the prevailing pseudo-scientific race theories on racial differences, as well as, white supremacist theories that showed little humanitarianism toward Blacks-and any one else, for that matter.[61] But clearly the most racially putrid jurist during that period was Associate Justice, James C. McReynolds, who served from 1914 to 1941. An "open and notorious racist," often cited as perhaps "the most bigoted justice to sit on the Supreme Court in this [20th] century," McReynolds openly described Blacks as ignorant, immoral and lazy.[62] Hughes' predecessor as Chief Justice, former U.S. President, William Howard Taft, who himself had closet racial behaviors when he was President, sympathizing with disfranchisement and favoring all-white southern Republican parties,[63] the same views Parker expressed and whose nomination was rejected over, observed that McReynolds was "fuller of prejudice than any man I have ever known."[64] McReynolds once referred to Howard University as a "nigger university" and even snubbed his own colleagues, Justices Louis Brandeis and Benjamin Cardozo, who were the first and second Jewish justices, respectively, ever appointed to the U.S. Supreme Court.[65] So Houston, Marshall and their cadre of staff and local lawyers were not naïve about the federal judicial temperament and court environment in which they sought to litigate and defeat segregation. It was an uphill battle and the first real test was now thrust upon them with the *Gaines* case.

205

Lloyd Gaines, a 25-year old Missouri resident that had graduated from Lincoln University, wanted to attend the University of Missouri, the state's only publicly funded law school. Though Gaines was a qualified applicant, the university's registrar acknowledged that the school admitted white students from other states, Asian American students, foreign students-in fact, everyone except "students of African descent."[66] Gaines went to the St. Louis Chapter of the NAACP and asked that they represent him in a lawsuit. Given the lack of plaintiffs for lawsuits challenging the exclusion of Blacks from public graduate schools, Houston wanted more plaintiffs to insure that they had an "airtight" case. He asked his friend, Sidney Redmond, to investigate the case.

Houston took the case when Redmond, St. Louis' leading black attorney, advised Houston that this was all the case he needed-the test case he was looking for, inasmuch as, the case was a firm case of blatant racial discrimination, since Missouri's segregation statues didn't apply to colleges and the university's admission criteria only stated scholastic ability requirements and made no statement to racial exclusion.[67] The University of Missouri offered Gaines two choices; to accept a scholarship offer to attend an out of state law school, or attend Lincoln University that would, upon demand, create a full-scale law school for black law students. The choices offered to Gaines gave him no immediate satisfactory remedy, which left him no alternative, but to sue the state.

Houston, who considered the university cases his specialty, would personally argue the case on behalf of the plaintiff. He immediately opposed the scholarship option, because it upheld unprincipled "separate" segregation tenets, and created disadvantages for Gaines, because they didn't cover his extra living expenses. Houston also opposed the Lincoln option, because it provided a false "equal" remedy in building a new facility being called the new "black law school," that the NAACP would prove was not equivalent to the quality and prestige of attending the old white law school.[68]

The first trial was brief and uneventful as state courts ruled that the Constitution had not been violated, because the state had fulfilled its responsibility to provide an equivalent option. The NAACP appealed the decision. The Missouri Supreme Court unanimously affirmed the lower court's decision that the state had satisfied its 14th Amendment obligation, by offering Gaines scholarships to several laws schools in Illinois, Iowa, Kansas and Nebraska-none of which excluded Blacks, but each were 300 to 400 miles away from Gaines' home, to which the court said was incidental to abide compliance, but "furnishes no substantial ground for compliant."[69] The NAACP disagreed and appealed again to the U.S. Supreme Court. The Gaines appeal opened arguments on November 9, 1938.

It was during oral arguments of the *Gaines* case that one of the ugliest racial moments in the history of the U.S. Supreme Court occurred. The high Court is the one branch of government that is supposed to be absent of apparent biases, in dispatching justice and equality. As Charles Houston rose to give his oral argument, Associate Justice McReynolds, turned his chair around and faced the wall with his back to Houston, during the entirety of his presentation.[70] While the high court was embarrassed by the antics of its racist colleague, Houston, never the less, gave a stellar presentation of challenging

206

white supremacy as illegal, immoral and inequitable, as simply myths and biased interpretations of *Plessy v. Ferguson* and tied them to the facts in the case, that Gaines had not received equal protection under the law by being excluded from a tax-payer funded university for no other reason than his race; that if white Missourians were entitled to legal education by the state, then black citizens were entitled to an education of the same quality; lastly that the state had failed to prove that an "equal" education (opportunity for legal training) could be obtained, simply be sending black students out of state.[71]

The Court handed down its decision on December 12, 1938. Despite the fact that the University of Missouri tried to fund a "black" law school, and have it ready before the Supreme Court case was heard, that required Houston to argue an extensive comparison on the quality of training within and without the state, Chief Justice Hughes opined that the comparison was "beside the point," and that Gaines' right was a personal one, and that "By operation of the laws of Missouri a privilege has been created for white law students which is denied to negroes by reason of their race."[72] Then came the words Houston and the NAACP had been waiting for,

"That is a denial of the equality of legal right to the enjoyment of the privilege which the State has set up, and the provision for the payment of tuition fees in another State does not remove the discrimination. The equal protection of laws is a pledge of the protection of equal laws. Manifestly, the obligation of the State to give the protection of equal laws can be performed only where its laws operate, that is within its own jurisdiction...It was as an individual that he was entitled to the equal protection of the laws, and the State was bound to furnish him within its borders facilities for legal education substantially equal to those which the State afforded for persons of the white race, whether or not other negroes sought the same opportunity." [73]

207

With these words, the U.S. Supreme Court ruled that the Missouri Supreme Court had erred in its ruling, and that Gaines had been denied his federal rights. The state must either provide a law school for Blacks within the state, or allow Gaines to attend the University of Missouri. It reversed the decision of the state court and remanded it for further opinion. This was a landmark victory for the NAACP on several accounts; first, *Gaines* was the first Supreme Court decision to invalidate a state's school-segregation practices; second, it outlawed out-of-state scholarships and regional university programs for

Blacks as a means by which states might maintain segregation and shirk constitutional duties within their borders; third, it redefined "equality," eroding the principle of "separate but equal," by acknowledging that separate facilities doesn't necessarily mean equal facilities, and mandated states to set up truly equal facilities; fourthly, southern states could be brought to court for failing to provide truly equal rights and enjoyments, and last, and most importantly, *Gaines* gave Blacks equal protection under the law within a state. *Gaines* established an "actual equality" test that removed the court's deferential standard of review that upheld *Plessy* for over 40 years. Securing the first Supreme Court decision eroding the principle of "separate but equal" in a way that even the *New York Times* suggested "severely jolted" southern educational systems, to the point where they were forced to make "far-reaching readjustments," Houston knew that Jim Crow policy had taken a serious hit at its most vulnerable point, public education.[74]

With the *Gaines* decision in hand , Charles Houston was ready for his assault on *Plessy*, making education the focus, larely due to the fact that, the NAACP could now litigate the question of equality, in fact, not in theory, and force courts to take seriously the question of the equality provided by separate facilities, a question Houston knew they could win on.[75] Why? Because public education was where the most quantifiable disparities existed, and where tangible inequalities could be most easily proved. The first step toward ending Jim Crow had been won.

With the attack on *Plessy* well on its way, in light of the *Gaines* victory, Charles Houston had proven the worth of the NAACP, focusing on legal campaigns in the judicial branch of government, as a foremost strategy for fighting segregation and discrimination. Houston and Thurgood Marshall, who had proven himself to be such a worthy litigator and administrator, that he had been promoted to co-Special Counsel in 1938, had justified the need for the permanent existence of a separate litigation unit in the NAACP. White saw it as a way to enhance the organization's fund-raising capacity.

Though Houston would retain the title of Special Counsel, and continue to "quarterback" the legal strategy on segregation, he reduced his role to a part-time one, as he returned to Washington, D.C. in July of 1938, to serve the family law practice. His father was then serving as Special Assistant to the U.S. Attorney General, and his law partner, William Hastie was appointed by President Franklin D. Roosevelt to a federal judgeship in the Virgin Islands. Houston left Marshall to run the

New York office on a full-time basis, and would handle his reduced role from Washington-appearing in court at crucial times. Houston believed he had served his purpose in the NAACP, and had grown tired of the politics of the organization, as well as, the constant fights over money. He told his father that he felt it was time to move on, assessing that he could do more outside the NAACP, than within the organization, stating, "I have had the feeling all along that I am much more of an outside man than an inside man...Certainly, for the present, I will grow much faster, and be of much more service, if I keep free to hit and fight wherever the circumstances call for action."[76]

In October, 1939, the NAACP Defense and Educational Fund, an organization separate and apart from the NAACP itself-but whose board of directors were intertwined to maintain a large degree of oversight and control-was incorporated. The NAACP/LDF, or "the Inc. Fund," as it was called through most of its early "heyday," became fully functional in 1940 to focus on education litigation, while the NAACP's own staff lawyers would handled other civil rights discrimination cases, most notably-the Restrictive Covenant Cases that barred Blacks from living in certain neighborhood by virtue that property owners were restricted to selling their properties to "Whites only." However, the core of the NAACP's legal thrust was against segregation.

209

The NAACP, the organization, would never reach the high visibility and level of success in the courts that the Inc. Fund enjoyed. The Inc. Fund was the NAACP, as far as most were concerned (an issue that became a point of contention in the mid-1950s and again in the 1970s). Thurgood Marshall was hired as its first head, under the title, Director-Counsel, but it was well known that Marshall never made a move without first talking to either Charles Houston or William Hastie, as Houston continued his involvement with the NAACP, through a resumed role on the organization's National Legal Committee.

*   *   *

In 1939, the NAACP won its second major victory in the federal courts, this time on the first teachers salaries equalization to reach a favorable federal ruling, after a black teacher in Anne Arundel County, Maryland, sued the local school board.[77] The federal judge

ruled that the lower salaries received by black teachers were not related to differences in qualifications or competence, as the school board
tried to assert, but to racial discrimination-again re-affirming Gaines,
that while "separate but equal" was truly separate, it was not truly equal.

In 1944, under the full direction of Thurgood Marshall, the
NAACP won its third major landmark case, in what many hailed as
"the Second Emancipation Proclamation," when it argued the case of
Smith v. Allwright, in which a black dentist, by the name of Lonnie
Smith, sued a Texas election official who refused to let him vote in the
state's Democratic Primary. "White Primaries" came into existence during the disfranchisement period of the Post Reconstruction era, where,
in order to marginalize the black vote, a host of discriminating barriers
were set up to discourage Blacks from voting. While some county
Democrats in the South began excluding Blacks, as a matter of rule or
custom, during the redemption periods of the late 1870s and early
1880s, state parties adopted the first rules barring Blacks in the 1890s,
and the first legal statutes regulating primaries around 1900.[78] Most
restrictions were extralegal in nature, as manipulations of existing law
(like literacy tests and poll taxes). However, restrictions on Blacks voting in primaries, which literally nullified black political influence,
became a popular legal method, born out of the de jure segregation
policies of the post-*Plessy* era.

Whites primaries had been challenged three times previously,
all in Texas (*Nixon v. Herndon in 1927, Nixon v. Condon in 1932 and
Grover v. Townsend in 1935*), where each time the Supreme Court
struck down a measure, the state party re-legislated around the ruling.
What made the outcome of the fourth case in Texas different was that,
in 1940, a precedent case outside of Texas was established, when in a
Louisiana case involving vote stealing, the U.S. Supreme Court ruled
that the Democratic primary was "an integral part of the state's electoral machinery, and therefore, subject to relevant federal safeguards."[79]
Thus, in the case of Smith, the Supreme Court viewed the latest Texas
vote challenge in the context of violating Blacks' rights under 14th
Amendment equal protection laws and ruled that the "white primary"
was a discrimination tool that prevented Blacks from being treated as
any other voter, constituting what amounted to "illegal racial discrimination."[80]

The U.S. Supreme Court had not only defined "equality," but
it now had defined "equal treatment" and equal protection under the
law, as well. This was probably the NAACP's most significant ruling,

Cripus Attacks was the first to "equally" die for freedom, in what later became, the United States of America; a nation that subsequently deemed enslaved Blacks as "three-fifths" a person, for representation purposes, and devoid of the socio-political rights and privileges that were conferred on Whites. Photo courtesy of the Mamye Clayton Library Collection

Early America's society viewed slavery as a "necessary evil" of a developing nation, and an acceptable form of commerce. Enslaved blacks were considered chattel property to be traded and sold, inferior to whites and expendable.
Photo courtesy of the Mayme Clayton Library Collection

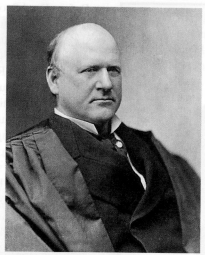

Justice John Marshall Harlan, who was the lone dissenter in the case of *Plessy v. Ferguson* in 1896, wrote, "there is in this country no superior, dominent, ruling class of citizens. There is no caste here. Our Constitution is color-blind, and neither knows nor tolerates classes among citizens." Photo courtesy of the Mayme Clayton Library Collection

Booker T. Washington, founder of Tuskegee Institute, also known for the "Tuskegee Machine" for its connection to Northern philanthropists, succeeded Frederick Douglass, as the spokesperson for Blacks at the turn of the 20th Century. Washington called Blacks pursuit of social equality, "extremest folly" in 1895. Photo courtesy of the Mayme Clayton Library Collection

W.E.B. DuBois, the first black to receive a Ph.D. from Harvard University, and considered the foremost black thinker of the 20th Century, saw social equality as achievable, via a "talented tenth," who would lead the race to equality. DuBois criticized Washington for his willingness to compromise on black equality in his 1903 book, *The Souls of Black Folk*. Photo courtesy of the Mayme Clayton Library Collection

The rise in the number of black men lynched at the turn of the Twentieth Century caused Dubois, center in white hat, and Boston black newspaper publisher, Monroe Trotter, convene a meeting of black activists and intellectuals, from fourteen states, to discuss the plight of Negro equality in Niagara Falls, Canada, July11-13, 1905. The delegates resolved to demand the abolition of all distinctions, based on race, and the need to form an organization to protect the equality rights of Blacks in America. Called the "Niagara Movement," it is largely acknowledged as the organizing genesis for the formation of the NAACP in 1909. Photo courtesy of the Mayme Clayton Library Collection

Seeing the integrated NAACP as a non-viable option to achieve racial equality for Blacks, Marcus Mossiah Garvey founded the Universal Negro Improvement Association and led the greatest mass movement of Blacks in American history. Garvey asserted that racial pride was essential to the achievement of racial equality. Garvey was jailed and deported when the U.S. Government viewed his movement as a threat to the U.S. racial status quo. Photo courtesy of the Mayme Clayton Library Collection

Asa Phillip Randolph, right, was black America's first national spokesman for organized black workers, and started the first AFL-CIO endorsed black labor union, The Brotherhood of Sleeping Car Porters, which organized the right to work and job benefits for 10,000 sleeping car porters. Randolph organized "the March on Washington in 1963. His Messenger Newspaper was an early critic of America's "racial politics" and early advocate for "social equality" that led to Franklin D. Roosevelt's efforts to desegregate the federal government in 1941.
Photo courtesy of the Mayme Clayton Library Collection

James Weldon Johnson, as field secretary of the NAACP, from 1916 to 1920, was responsible for its massive growth in membership. Johnson was the NAACP's first black Executive Secretary from 1920 to 1930.
Photo courtesy of the Mayme Clayton Library Collection

Walter White succeeded Johnson as Executive Secretary and was responsible for commissioning the Margold Report, considered the first study on racial inequality in America. It led to the hiring of Charles Houston and the NAACP launching a 20 year legal campaign to end segregation. Photo courtesy of the Mayme Clayton Library Collection

William H. Hastie, Jr., was the first cousin of Charles Houston, and like Houston, a graduate of Harvard Law School and followed Houston as Dean of the Howard Law School. He was Marshall's closest advisor on the *Brown* case, after the death of Houston. Hastie was the first black appointed to a federal judgeship in 1939, and was considered the hands on favorite to become the first black Supreme Court Justice. Kennedy passed over him, when a vacancy opened in 1962, because his advisors called him "too conservative." Hastie was also one of the first to compare the condition of Blacks in America to those in South Africa, stating, "Apartheid seemed as irradicable and almost as pervasive a feature of the American legal order as it appears to be in South Africa."
Photo courtesy of the Mayme Clayton Library Collection

The first thirty years of the NAACP was spent on the first civil rights challenge of the Twentieth Century, the lynching of black citizens in the United States. From 1883 to 1941, 3,811 black citizens were lynched. Every time a lynching occurred in America, the NAACP hung a black flag outside its New York office window (above). Both James Weldon Johnson and Walter White set Anti-Lynching legislation in Congress as the organization's highest priority from 1920 to 1940, until the organization shifted its priority to concentrate its efforts on a legal campaign to end segregation. Anti-lynching bills were proposed in 1922, 1937 and 1940 but never made it out of Congress. In spite of the advocations of two U.S. Presidents (FDR and Truman), the federal government of the United States of America never, in its history, passed a stand alone anti-lynching bill, to give protection to black citizens against this racial crime.

Photos courtesy of the Mayme Clayton Library Collection

Race riots spread throughout the United States from 1916 to 1921. Most occurred in the "Red Summer" of 1919, when 70 Blacks were lynched, including ten World War I black veterans, soldiers returning from war, hung while still in uniform. Above, a black man is burned alive in Omaha, Nebraska in 1921. Below, the most notorious race riot of the period, one that was covered up for over 60 years, the 1921 Tulsa riot race in the Greenwood section of Tulsa, Oklahoma. Called "Black Wall Street," because of its thriving economy and sucessful black businesses, thirty city blocks were burned to the ground for a black man touching a woman's hand when an elevator suddenly stopped. There were reports of police involvement, military fire and air bombings. The Oklahoma City Black Dispatch offered this panorama portait of the event to subscribers of their papers. Photos courtesy of the Mayme Clayton Library Collection

The resurrection of the Ku Klux Klan, above, after World War I led to increased social and political intimidation of Blacks in America, fostering a racial polorization in the United States for the next fifty years. Below, the NAACP wages a silent march in the streets of Harlem against lynching.

Photos courtesy of the Mayme Clayton Library Collection

The 20th Century DeJure segregation ("Jim Crow") era of America (1896-1964) was the most socially debilitating era for African Americans in the history of America, outside of the three centuries of legalized slavery. The legal philosophy of its practice was established in the *Plessy v. Ferguson* decision when the U.S. Supreme Court ruled that it wasn't illegal to separate white and black passengers on a Louisiana Rail Car as long as the accommodations were equal. This doctrine soon spread to every form of social interface in the American South, and immediately became the basis for racially discriminating practices that prohibited "social equality" to African Americans. The staple of segregation era politics was its "Separate But Equal" racial etiquette that required black subordination to all white citizens, and required a separation of the races that legally prohibited black citizens from socializing with Whites, in private establishments and public areas of enjoyment, including restaurants, theaters, hotels, waiting rooms, lunch counters and public schools. The "Separate But Equal" era was enforced by social attitudinal and normative behaviors, legal and extralegal means. Though Separate But Equal or "Jim Crow" laws were deemed unconstitutional in the *Brown* decision in May of 1954, most remained in effect until the passing of the Civil Rights Act of 1964, ten years later. Photos courtesy of the Mamye Clayton Library Collection.

Charles Hamilton Houston was the chief artchitect of a 25 year legal campaign to eliminate segregation that started in 1929, when he took over as Vice Dean of the Howard Law School, transforming it from a part-time evening school to a full time accredited law school that became the incubator for a new generation of civil rights lawyers, including Thurgood Marshall. Houston then was hired to lead the legal strategy for the NAACP, and won the *Gaines* case that paved the road to *Brown*. It was Houston that hired Marshall, who took over the newly formed Legal Defense Fund in 1940. Photo Courtesy of the Mayme Clayton Library Collection

Thurgood Marshall, Houston's mentee, and the first chief counsel of the NAACP Legal Defense and Education Fund, was known as "Mr. Civil Rights," for his tireless work in the early legal battles against segregation. Marshall didn't anticipate the success of *Brown*, but promised that blacks would be "free by '63," 100 years after slavery ended. Photo courtesy of the Mayme Clayton Library Collection

George Nabrit took over the Washington, D.C. desegregation case, at the request of Charles Houston, just before his death in 1950. *Bolling v. Sharpe* was a companion case decided the same day as the *Brown* decision. Nabrit would later become President of Howard University.Photo courtesy of the Mayme Clayton Library Collection

Robert L. Carter, right, was the NAACP/LDF's lead attorney for the Topeka, KS school desgregation case that became the namesake for the most famous case in the 20th Century, *Brown v. Board of Education*. On the 50th Anniversary of *Brown*, Carter stated that segregation was simply "a symptom of a greater problem in America, white supremacy."
Photo courtesy of the Mayme Clayton Library Collection

12 year old Linda Brown and her sister, Terry, left, walk along active railroad tracks to get to their bus stop for a six mile ride to their segregated school. Her father, the Rev. Oliver Brown, filed suit against the Topeka School District, and the most famous judical case of the 20th Century would bear her name. Photo courtesy of the Mayme Clayton Library Collection

Thurgood Marshall and the some of the *Brown* attorneys prepare for oral arguments in the biggest legal fight for equality in the 20th Century. The case Charles Houston said "would one day kill Jim Crow." Photo courtesy of the Mayme Clayton Library Collection

The most remarkable protest against educational inequality was a totally led student strike for better schools by the youth of Moton High School in Prince Edward County, Virginia. Its leader was a young woman by the name of Barbara Johns, who was subsequently forced to move to Alabama to complete her high school education. Their claim of inferior schools ended up being one of the *Brown* cases. Photo courtesy of the Mayme Clayton Library Collection

The Attorneys for the Prince Edward County students filed suit to obtain an equal education on par with white students that would bring about the most protracted desegregation fight of the *Brown* cases. The Virginia legislature would adopt "massive resistance" policies that would close public schools, and reopen them as "private academies" to get around the desegregation orders. It would be well into the 1960s before some Virginia school districts would comply with the *Brown* decision. Photo courtesy of the Mayme Clayton Library Collection

Jack Greenberg (left) was the LDF attorney for the Delaware case, and succeeded Thurgood Marshall as Chief Counsel of the NAACP Legal Defense Fund. Photo courtesy of the Mayme Clayton Library Collection

In the year that the Supreme Court took the *Brown* case under submission, its Chief Justice, Fred M. Vinson died. President Eisenhower appointed former California Governor Earl Warren, who joined a court divided. Warren brought together a united court, in favor of declaring segregation unconstitutional. Thus, a new legal era came into existence and the activism of the Warren Court changed how the nation viewed equality and the 14th Amendment.
Photo courtesy of the Mayme Clayton Library Collection

The *Brown* Attorneys celebrate their victory on the steps of the Supreme Court but show apprehension over the lack of immediate relief. Their concern was justified a year later when the Court announced the enforement would take place "with all deliberate speed." Photo courtesy of the Mayme Clayton Library Collection

Southern Senators issued a "Southern Manifesto" that called for the repeal of the *Brown* decision and the impeachment of Supreme Court Chief Justice, Earl Warren. Claiming he allowed the use of "psuedo science" (sociological arguments) to outlaw segregation in the *Brown* decision, the Congress led Southern Manifesto ignited what was a decade long "massive resistance movement" against racial equality that didn't end until the passing of the 1964 Civil Rights Act. Photo courtesy of the Mayme Clayton Library Collection

WANTED
for Impeachment

EARL WARREN

OCCUPATION: Chief Justice of U.S. Supreme Court. PREVIOUS JUDICIAL EXPERIENCE: None. Warren reportedly leans heavily upon the writings of alien sociologists as authority for many of his court decrees.

DESCRIPTION

WARREN IS CONSIDERED TO BE A DANGEROUS AND SUBVERSIVE CHARACTER. HE IS AN APPARENT SYMPATHIZER OF THE COMMUNIST PARTY AND HAS RENDERED NUMEROUS DECISIONS FAVORABLE TO IT. HIS ACCOMPLICES INCLUDE JUSTICE FELIX FRANKFURTER, WHO IS A FORMER DEFENSE ATTORNEY FOR COMMUNISTS, AND JUSTICE HUGO BLACK, WHOSE SISTER-IN-LAW IS A REGISTERED COMMUNIST.

WARREN IS A RABID AGITATOR FOR COMPULSORY RACIAL MONGRELIZATION AND HAS HANDED DOWN VARIOUS DECISIONS COMPELLING WHITES TO MIX WITH NEGROES IN THE SCHOOLS, IN PUBLIC HOUSING, IN RESTAURANTS AND IN PUBLIC BATHING FACILITIES. HE IS KNOWN TO WORK CLOSELY WITH THE N.A.A.C.P. AND FAVORS THE USE OF FORCE AND COERCION TO COMPEL WHITE SCHOOL CHILDREN TO MINGLE INTIMATELY WITH NEGROES.

CRIMINAL RECORD

WARREN HAS BEEN ACCUSED OF GIVING AID AND COMFORT TO THE COMMUNIST PARTY ON FREQUENT OCCASIONS. HE IS GUILTY OF PROMOTING AND INCITING RIOT, DISORDER AND ANARCHY IN LITTLE ROCK AND ELSEWHERE IN THE SOUTH THROUGH HIS ATTEMPTS TO IMPOSE JUDICIAL TYRANNY UPON WHITE SOUTHERNERS. HE HAS ILLEGALLY TRANSFORMED THE SUPREME COURT INTO A SOVIET-TYPE POLITBURO WITH POWER OVER THE CONGRESS AND OVER THE VARIOUS STATE GOVERNMENTS. AT HIS INSTIGATION FEDERAL MARSHALS AND BAYONET-EQUIPPED FEDERAL TROOPS HAVE BEEN EMPLOYED TO TERRORIZE AND INTIMIDATE WHITE CITIZENS OPPOSED TO HIS INTEGRATION DECREES.

CAUTION

EARL WARREN IS A FANATIC WHO WILL STOP AT NOTHING TO ACHIEVE HIS GOALS. HE SHOULD BE HANDLED WITH EXTREME CAUTION, AND ALL DECREES AND DECISIONS HANDED DOWN BY HIM SHOULD BE REGARDED AS SUSPECT. PERSONS WISHING TO AID IN BRINGING HIM TO JUSTICE SHOULD CONTACT THEIR CONGRESSMEN TO URGE HIS IMPEACHMENT FOR TREASON.

In December of 1955, a new phase of the civil rights movement began when a streamtress refused to give up her seat on a public bus to a white man. Rosa Parks was arrested and the community, appaulled over the incident, refused to ride Montgomery buses for 381 days. At right, Rosa Parks, accompanied by the arresting officer and her attorney, is on her way to the Montgomery Courthouse to be arraigned. Photo courtesy of the Mayme Clayton Library Collection

A new voice emerged from the Montgomery Bus Boycott, Dr. Martin Luther King. Jr., who was elected to head the Montgomery Improvement Association. At left, King is arrested in Montgomery during a protest outside the city's courthouse.
In 1957, King would found the Southern Christian Leadership Conference that would lead non-violent protest throughout Alabama, which would become its base, after the forced departure of the NAACP. SCLC also led protest throughout the South. Photo courtesy of the Mayme Clayton Library Collection

At right, King, his wife, Coretta, and the community celebrate the NAACP filed federal court order that mandated Montgomery Public Transit System to operate on a non-segregated basis, ending the 381 day bus boycott. Photo courtesy of the Mayme Clayton Library CollectionPhoto courtesy of the Mayme Clayton Library Collection

Above, Little Rock NAACP Branch President, Daisy Bates, prepare nine blacks students for their first day of school, after a federal court order mandated integration in Little Rock, Arkansas. At left, crowds gather in anticipation of the arrival of the black students selected to attend the newly integrated Central High School in Little Rock Arkansas. Federalized National Guard forces await at the school's doors. Below, the "Little Rock Nine" are escorted away from Central High School under federal protection on the first day of school in fall, 1957. President Dwight Eisenhower ordered the protection when the Governor of Arkansas called him to advise him that he could not insure the students safety. Photos courtesy of the Mayme Clayton Library Collection

In 1960, the Congress of Racial Equality organized "freedom rides" in the South to desegregate interstate bus transportation, and to intergrate waiting rooms. The strategy was for northern travelers, above, to go into southern states, violate local public segregation laws, and force local law enforcement to arrest violators in order to get "equal rights" challenges into the courts. The freedom rides represented the first time activists from the North, en mass, joined the civil rights movement. Labeled "Yankee agitators" and "troublemakers," the freedom riders were soon targeted for violence (below), but were successful in gaining equality in interstate transportation.

Photos courtesy of the Mayme Clayton Library Collection

James Meredith became the first black student to be admitted to the University of Mississippi in 1962. After two failed attempts at a admission, and a campus riot, President John F. Kennedy sent federal troops to escort Meredith for the entire time he attended "Ole Miss."
Photo courtesy of the Mayme Clayton Library Collection

Alamaba Governor, George Wallace came to symbolize the Massive Resistance Movement, proclaiming "Segregation Yesterday, Segregation Today, Segregation Forever." Wallace stands of the doorway to the admissions building at the University of Alabama before U.S. Army Commading Brigadier General, Henry C. Graham, escorting two black students, asks him to "step aside" June 11, 1963.
Photo courtesy of the Mayme Clayton Library Collection

The Civil Rights Movement and the fight for equal rights was influenced significantly by the presence of the church, in what became popularized by the Rev. Dr. Martin Luther King, Jr. as the "politics of moral suasion." Photo courtesy of the Mayme Clayton Library Collection

The spree of assassinations in the 1960s began with the murder of NAACP Mississippi State President, Medgar Evers, who was shot in the back by a sniper in the bushes across from home, while getting out of his car in his driveway. Evers crawled to his front door, and died in front of his family, as the trail of blood in this crime scene photo depicts (below). Photo courtesy of the Mayme Clayton Library Collection

When the NAACP was shut down in Alabama, after it refused a federal court to surrender its membership lists, Mississippi became an active base for the organization to address southern racial discrimination. No state came to symbolize the debilitating racial effects of segregation and the hostility toward social change as Mississippi, who like its neighboring state, Alabama, resisted segregation to the very end, first with the murder of NAACP State President, Medgar Evers, above, the major force behind getting James Meredith admitted to the University of Mississippi. This act was followed up a year later with the murder of three civil rights workers, Goodman, Chaney and Schwerner. Photo courtesy of the Mayme Clayton Library Collection

At left, students take abuse from a hostile crowd in Jackson, Mississippi, as they sit in at an segregated lunch counter during the summer of 1963. Lunch counter sit-ins were started in 1961 by students in Greensboro, North Carolina. By 1963, there were literally thousands of sit-ins in cities nationwide, as the direct action activity of the Civil Rights Movement became a strategic ploy of the non-violence protest. Photos courtesy of the Mayme Clayton Library Collection

The home of Rev. Fred Shuttlesworth was bombed in Birmingham after it was announced Dr. Martin Luther King, Jr. and SCLC would be coming to lead mass direct action protests against segregation policies in the city.
Photo courtesy of the Mayme Clayton Library Collection

Birmingham gave rise to a new tactic in the Massive Resistance movement, the bombing of gathering places where Blacks congregated and organized during the Civil Rights Movement. The photo above was the site of the Gaston Motel. The photo, at left, was this period most shockingly outragous bombing, the Sixteenth Street Baptist Church, where little girls were killed September 15th, 1963. Racial extremists in Birmingham gained a reputation of being so violently ruthless that civil rights workers called it, "Bombingham."
Photo courtesy of the Mayme Clayton Library Collection

The Birmingham Protests of April and May of 1963 reinvigorated the Civil Rights Movement, as the "eyes of the nation" watched the brutal treatment of the protesters. Over 1,200 youth were jailed in an attempt to bust down the walls of segregation. Martin Luther King said that "nothing had inspired the movement like the youth of Birmingham," and he'd never seen anything like it in all his days in the movement.
Photo courtesy of the Mayme Clayton Library Collection

The violence and brutality that occurred in the Brimingham protests focused the nation's attention on the racial equality question. The nation was shocked by what they saw as aggression against people simply protecting for "equal rights." The media played an important role in sensitizing the nation to what was happening to Blacks in the South.
Photo courtesy of the Mayme Clayton Library Collection

The strategy of the Birmingham movement was for protesters to engage in civil disobedience, then volunteer to be arrested, so that the jails would be so filled that there would be no choice but for city officials to sit down and negotiate. The strategy worked as 2,500 persons were arrested, including King himself, where wrote the most prophetic insight of the movement, "Letter from a Birmingham Jail." Some 1,200 teengers were also arrested as King was criticized for putting children in harm's way. By June of 1963, Birmingham was the first southern city in the deep South to voluntarily desegregate on a "go slow" basis, that removed the signs, symbols and racial barriers in public facilities, lunch-counters and waiting rooms.
Photo courtesy of the Mayme Clayton Library Collection

The NAACP awards Ms. Myrie Evers, the widow of slain civil rights lea-ger, Medgar Evers, the organization's highest award, the Spingarn Medal, at its national convention following Evers' murder in 1963. Ms. Evers never stopped pursuing her husband's killer and in 1994, thirty years after the murder and three trials later, Byron de la Beckwith, was convicted of the murder. Ms. Evers, in 1995 became Chairperson of the NAACP at a time when the organization was on the brink of collapse. Her leadership re-stored both the NAACP's solvency and credibility. Photo courtesy of the Mayme Clayton Library Collection

Senator John F. Kennedy and Senate House Majority Leader Lyndon Johnson meet in 1960 to discuss the future of the Democratic Party. These two men, each in their own right as President, would do more for black equality than anyone in American history; Kennedy introduced the first meaningful civil rights bill of the 20th Century and issued Executive Order 10925 forbidding discrimination in fed-eral contracting. Johnson passed the 1964 Civil Rights Act, 1965 Voting Rights Act, put Thurgood Marshall on the U.S. Supreme Court and issued Executive Order 11246, considered the first affirmative action order in 1965.
Photo courtesy of the Mayme Clayton Library Collection

and important achieving in the orchestration of the "in-direct" attack on *Plessy* and the deconstruction "separate but equal" precedents. It also put political equality back on the nation's mind, in a way that it hadn't been in the 20th Century. *Smith v. Allwright*, juxtaposed against social and political conditions launched a racial revolution in Southern politics-but could not remove the obstacles to black voting in the rural Deep South (which would not come about until the 1960s civil rights movement).[81]

Also in 1944, Charles Houston, as a private attorney for black locomotive firemen in Alabama, won a landmark case for "economic equality." In a case named *Steele v. Louis & Nashville Railroad*, the U.S. Supreme Court ruled that the Brotherhood of Locomotive Fireman and Enginemen, the union for railroad workers, could not exclude black workers from its bargaining agreements. While the union was not required to accept black workers as members of its union, it had a duty under the Railway Labor Act, which made the union the sole bargaining agent for all railroad workers, to represent Blacks-members or not-fairly and impartially, in their bargaining for the railroad unit.[82] This decision created the rise of a new black middle class, by equalizing black workers wages with unionized worker wage gains in the rising era of collective bargaining. Still, the principle advocacy focus of the 20th Century had been, and would continue to be, on "social equality," and the absence of such.

211

Now, both social equality and political equality were at the forefront of America's national policy agenda, and it presented a serious problem for a vast many white people. The strategic advocacy that the New Negro movement had produced, in speaking through organizations, in advancing culturally centered ideology, in engineering and implementing integrationist philosophy, and in using the Constitution and the courts to demand "equality" was being framed in the dominant culture's public discourse as, quite curiously, "a problem." Particularly, since much of this "problem" was being influenced by a number of factors. One of which was the rise of Communism in America-which had targeted African Americans as a vulnerable population that had become frustrated with "democracy" as practiced toward them.

Many, including DuBois, were prepared to extend an ear to socialist views. Secondly, the beginning and advancement of World War II, in which African Americans, tired of defending democracy abroad, and being treated as second class citizens at home, politicized the war with the now famous "Double V" campaign (Victory against fascism abroad, and victory against "Jim Crow" racism at home). Third, African Americans were in the midst of a political shift, in which they had grown tired of Republican party rhetoric in their failure to address anti-Jim Crow and anti-lynching legislation, and were beginning to leave the "Party of Lincoln." Finally, the migration of Blacks into the Northern States was reaching monumental proportions, and though the majority of Blacks still lived in the South, the tension that the "Great Migration" had created on the racial geographies of the North now made Black/White relations troublesome, in both the North and the South.

The 1940s brought forth the national realization that African Americans weren't going anywhere, and that it was time for the nation to deal with their presence, or this "problem" as it was framed, in the context of their impact on America's national landscape. In fact, in the same year that the *Smith* decision came down, America's first national study on race was published. It was entitled, appropriately enough, *An American Dilemma: The Negro Problem and Modern Democracy.* Thus, race was finally acknowledged in the country's academic discourse, and American racism was finally recognized as a problem to the promotion of egalitarian values in America. Though framed as the "Negro problem," the Myrdal study officially chronologized the presence, influences and problems of the African American as part and parcel to the social, political and economic changes that were taking place in American society.

Commissioned by the Carnegie Corporation, in 1937, a Swedish social economist and international scholar named Gunnar Myrdal was hired to lead a "comprehensive study on the Negro in the United States, to be undertaken in a wholly objective and dispassionate way as a social phenomenon."[83] The selection of Myrdal was widely questioned by both Blacks and Whites, who thought an American scholar should lead the study. The most frequently mentioned candidate was, of course, W.E.B. DuBois, who had written extensively on the subjects of race, democracy and social construction over the prior 50 years. DuBois' writings were largely influenced by the shift in political and social policy brought on by the *Plessy* decision, so he was "on record" as having already studied much of what Myrdal was being asked to study. DuBois, however, was seen as too much of a "racial" radical, whose recent shifts in political ideology called into question his ability to be objective in his analysis. In fact, the Carnegie Corporation didn't think there was anybody born and socialized in the United States who could provide an objective, unbiased study on race relations in America. The Carnegie Corporation wanted not only an "outside perspective," but wanted to assess how America's treatment of the Negro was perceived in the global community, and they gave him a free hand in selecting whatever resources he needed in completing the study. Myrdal did enlist DuBois and many other American scholars to help him in his research, and his study had a very heavy slant on the politics of "social equality" in America.

Myrdal's study was highly celebrated when it was released, though NAACP officials stated that Myrdal didn't tell them anything that they didn't already know-other than, the country needed to pay attention to what the NAACP had been saying on the question of social inequality, and that sociological arguments on "the effects of race discrimination" were relevant to both the public and legal discourse.[84] Myrdal's study reinforced several themes on the practice of "social inequality" in America-principally, that there was an absence of social equality for the Negro in America, mainly because social relations, as it related to the freedom to pursue personal relations-and the liberty to chose which relations one could pursue, were essentially denied to American Negroes.[85]

Advancing what he called the "No Social Equality" Theory, Myrdal identified social equality as an opportunity precept that Whites held exclusive to themselves, establishing a color caste centering around the aversion to the "amalgamation of the races," whereby Whites identify, in rank order, a set of segregation and discriminatory measures (that Myrdal was able to identify) against Negroes that included: 1) the ban on intermarriage and other sex relations involving white women and colored men takes precedence before everything else; 2) all sorts of taboos and etiquettes in personal contacts; 3) segregation in schools and churches; 4) segregation in hotels, restaurants, and theaters, and other public places where people meet socially; 5) segregation in public conveyances; 6) discrimination in public services; and, finally, inequality in, 7) politics, 8) justice, and 9) breadwinning and relief (economic subjugation).[86] Myrdal called out three points, in particular, as to how social inequality was promoted and survived in America.

First, there was a "one-sidedness" in the practice of segregation, that allowed Whites total liberty to socialize in any way that they saw fit, including socializing among Blacks-if they chose to (black churches, black theatres, black restaurants) and to be welcomed by Blacks.

213

However, Blacks did not have the same liberty to socialize with Whites and in white establishments. Myrdal's point was that segregation was a "system of deprivations forced upon the Negro group by the white group" and as such, represented a one-sided legal arrangement, written under the pre-text of equality, but only applied, and enforced, against Negroes that went against the basic premise of egalitarian democracy.[87]

Second, Myrdal noted that the rules of segregation were often enforced beyond what the law allowed, pointing out that the police and the courts "are active" in enforcing not just law, but also customs far outside those set down in legal statutes, and that the various "enforcements" (threats, intimidations, and open violence) were to be applied by Whites on Blacks, but never by Blacks on Whites. On occasion, enforcement were not just directed at Negroes, but at "nigger-loving casteless Whites," who chose not to recognize and uphold the custom of an enforced racial caste system.[88]

Third and most importantly, Myrdal noted that Whites understood very clearly what they were doing, and that they understood that in setting up a system to serve Whites, that the social rules, rituals and etiquettes also sought to protect Whites, and while an individual white could waive most of the customs, in terms of his individual practice, one individual could not waive away the societal customs that benefited the total white society-lest they run the of risk bringing on volatile reactions on the part of the collective white populous, of being labeled a "nigger lover," and, in a sense, forfeiting their whiteness, to suffer the same fates exacted on the Negro.[89]

The Myrdal Study crystallized race and sociological arguments, that the NAACP had contemplated using in legal cases, in a way that the NAACP couldn't do by validating "separate but equal" policy in an academic qualitative study of American human and social behaviors, that Whites couldn't discount as reason-laden advocacy, on the part of the afflicted masses. Myrdal's "outside perspective" provided a different kind of credibility about 20th Century American society that no American could offer in a "self-critique," just as Alex De Tocqueville, the French sociologist offered earlier outside "observations" on democracy and American culture in the early 19th Century-absent the race critique due to slavery prohibiting most Blacks from having any social standing among Whites. The study's impact was immediately felt, as the courts began to allow sociological study in as evidence to offer reasonable analysis of the injury and impact of certain laws. The NAACP was contemplating a direct attack on segregation, but didn't know how sociological arguments would be viewed by the court.

      The NAACP had chance to test the theory in 1946, when a lower court case, out of California, provided them some insights in to how the courts would be predisposed to the issue. The parents of a Mexican American had filed a segregation lawsuit in 1945, unbeknownst to the NAACP, against an Orange County school board who sought to segregate their children from white children, in a case called *Mendez v. Westminster School District of Orange County*. The trial judge found that segregating children on the basis of race was unconstitutional, using "equivocally strong" language that was, in the words of federal judge, Constance Baker Motley (then a clerk on the NAACP/LDF legal staff) in her 1998 autobiography, "totally unrestrained by prior legal reasoning" and "radically new at the time," as it related to prior legal reasoning courts had advanced in the past in cases "involving the segregation of Blacks."[90] The school board, of course, appealed and the NAACP and other organizations filed briefs in support of the lower court decision. It was in this brief that the NAACP, not being a party to the case, and thus having nothing to lose, advanced its first sociological argument detailing the harms of segregation with support of published materials (including *the Myrdal Study*).[91] The appeals court affirmed the decision, but neither accepted, nor rejected the sociological argument, which the NAACP did not view as a good thing. The victory was in that the decision was upheld, giving the NAACP a new precedent to include on its direct attack legal campaign on segregation.

      Mendez was a heralded decision, even though it was not tried in the Supreme Court, and was tried outside of the de jure segregation politics of the South. It "amazed" everyone in the civil rights community, largely due to that, as Judge Baker-Motley stated, "a sitting judge would have the courage to throw down the gauntlet" on segregation.[92] Later that year, the NAACP filed a lawsuit against the University of Oklahoma, when a black women by the name of Ada Lois Sipuel decided to apply to its law school, even though Oklahoma had a state supported college that she could have attended. The university's Board of Regents went on record, adopting a resolution directing that Blacks be denied admission. The university's president, after meeting with Sipuel and the a local attorney (who owned one of Oklahoma's leading newspapers), defiantly hand carried her application over to admissions, promising that she would be denied on the grounds of race, and for no other reason. [93]

The NAACP took the case and sued on behalf of Sipuel, and the case was dismissed, and upheld in the Oklahoma Supreme Court, because Ms. Sipuel did not offer the state the opportunity to remedy the situation, meaning she didn't demand that Oklahoma build a law school for Blacks. When the Supreme Court agreed to hear the case in January, 1948, it was a case that Thurgood Marshall felt had a chance to lose, and re-affirm "separate but equal" in the process, if the Supreme Court viewed the "thin record" as a weakness of the Sipuel case. They could then rely on mythical definitions of segregation, in the absence of evidence-which then caused Marshall to flush out his sociological argument much sooner than he wanted to, mounting a direct attack on *Plessy.*[94]

In *Sipuel*, Marshall cited Myrdal's *American Dilemma* and several dozen other works of social science research denouncing "Jim Crow" policies.[95] It was enough to bring about a unanimous decision. Giving little credence to the state's defense, the Supreme Court, saw the Oklahoma Supreme Court's dismissal on the grounds of the absence of a "demand to establish separate facilities" as "shadow boxing," and within four days of oral arguments, brought forth an order to provide Sipuel with legal instruction, "as soon as it does for applicants of other groups.[96] The Supreme Court specifically mentioned that the state must do so "in conformity with the equal protection clause of the Fourteenth Amendment." This time the public was shocked with the relative ease in which the courts were now attacking segregation policy. So appalled that the high court overturned the state court, that public opinion began criticizing the U.S. Supreme Court. Though segregation had been upheld for 50 years based on one case, *Plessy*, the *New York Times* called the *Sipuel* decision "a move of startling sadness," because it had relied almost solely on the precedent of *Gaines*.

Having won another precedent-setting victory, and dodging a bullet at the same time, the NAACP was now positioned for a direct attack on segregation. The question was whether or not they were willing to press it. Marshall's deputy counsel, Robert L. Carter had been reviewing some cases at the elementary and high school levels, and thought that the NAACP was now ready to move past equalization. He conferred with other NAACP attorneys like Spotswood Robinson in Virginia. They both concluded that equalization was becoming an acceptable remedy for schools, because it allowed them to "take minor steps" toward equalization, without making any further obligation toward equality. Carter, in a letter, suggested that unless the NAACP "attack these cases on the ground that segregation itself is unlawful-and unless you refuse to accept any settlement short of that-you are taking steps in these cases which...are short of the goals which you have set..."[97] Carter was the most aggressive of the NAACP staff in pushing for the direct attack campaign, and even Marshall's mentor, Charles Houston, felt that it was time to push forward, if the NAACP was going to achieve, what Houston called, "a foundation of precedents" against *Plessy*. Marshall and Houston were working together for, unbeknownst to both of them, one last hooray in assisting the association (the name for NAACP legal cases, versus "Inc. Fund" cases) for oral arguments in the NAACP restrictive covenant cases, which were also being heard, in January of 1948. The post war migration of Blacks to northern cities was impacted by residential restriction laws that prohibited the renting or selling of property to Blacks in certain areas.

These "racial covenants," by the 1940s, covered huge tracts of land in northern and western cities, perhaps, as much as, 80 or 90 percent of white owned housing in Chicago, Detroit and Los Angeles that were instrumental in creating boundaries that confined Blacks to highly concentrated areas that could hardly accommodate the population influx, creating a phenomena, in what became known, as America's "urban ghettos."[98] Racial covenants were not only imposed by the cultural behaviors of individual Whites, but enforced by institutional norms and governmental policies that included bank lending practices, federal government underwriting practices, real estate industry practices, public housing and urban redevelopment decisions of local governments, and collusion among white homeowners that resisted residential integration.[99] If education was the first battleground of segregation, and segregation in wages and employment was the second, housing segregation was the third. "Keep[ing] Blacks out" was more pervasive in Northern cities, than in the segregated south, causing the North to become known for its "up south" Jim Crow practices.

The preparation for the racial covenants cases was particularly highlighted by frequent trips to Washington by NAACP and Inc., Fund attorneys to Howard University Law School, to practice their famous "dry runs" of the trial, on Howard law students, before each appearance before the Supreme Court, since only Houston, Marshall and Loren Miller had experience in arguing before the high court.[100] Challenging segregation in all forms was coming to a head, and preparation was critical. The law school's moot court served as a fertile testing ground to argue the merits and demerits of segregation law, with the students serv-

217

ing as a vital backdrop to research and critique the best black lawyers in the nation, as they sought to evolve the law through re-interpretation and revolutionary law arguments. It turned out that a possible flaw in the NAACP's argument was observed and raised by a second year law student-that was later raised in the Court by Associate Justice Frankfurter-giving the lawyers advance warning of the flaw, and ample time to work out a response to the anticipated question.[101] This was exactly what Charles Houston had envisioned for the law school, and it had become reality, as the school had the become the incubator, the training camp, where black lawyers came to get in shape for the ultimate fight in the restrictive covenant cases, as well as, in the upcoming education cases leading up to *Brown*.

Oral arguments for the covenant cases opened on January 15, 1948, with attorneys George Vaughn and Herman Willer arguing for the St. Louis appellants (*Shelly v. Kraemer*), Charles Houston and Phineas Indritz arguing for the District of Columbia appellants (*Hurd v. Hodge* and *Urciolo v. Hodge*, a consolidated case), and Thurgood Marshall and Loren Miller arguing for the Detroit appellants (*Sipes v. McGhee*).[102] On May 3, 1948, the U.S. Supreme Court ruled, in a 6-0 unanimous decision that judicial enforcement of racially restrictive covenants, in one case, violated equal protection rights guaranteed under the Fourteenth Amendment, and local and state sanctioned racial restrictive covenants, in the two other cases, limiting Negroes to certain neighborhoods, violated their rights to "acquire, enjoy, own, and dispose of property" established by the Civil Right Act of 1866 that was upheld and "vindicated" by Fourteenth Amendment in 1868.[103]

218

With a major victory in housing discrimination cases under their belts, Marshall and his attorneys turned their attention back to the education cases, in particular, a case the NAACP had filed in Texas, where the university was fully prepared to fulfill its "separate but equal" obligation to up hold segregation. It was in this case where the sociological arguments advanced in the *Sipuel* case would be fully tested. A mail carrier by the name of Heman Sweat applied to the all-white University of Texas Law School, at Austin, in February, 1946, a few weeks before Ada Sipuel had applied to the University of Oklahoma. Sweat was similarly rejected, on the basis of race, and he, of course, sued for admission. Whereas Sipuel's case took four day's, Sweat's case would take four years. Filed under the court name of *Sweat v. Painter* (339 U.S. 629, 1950), the first hearing was June of 1946. At that time, the district court gave the University of Texas six months to build a law school at Prairie View University, which was really a vocational school formerly named Prairie View State Normal and Industrial Colleges for Negroes. The state rented a few rooms in Houston-forty miles southeast of the actual campus-hired two black lawyers as "faculty," and called the site Prairie View Law School.[104] When the second hearing came up in December of 1946, the district court found that the state had satisfactorily met its remedy requirements, even though the "law school" had no trained faculty, no library, and no students. It was done solely for the purpose of accommodating Sweat. The NAACP appealed the district court's ruling.

Before the case could be heard before the Court of Civil Appeals in March of 1947, the Texas legislature shelved the Prairie View idea, by appropriating three million dollars to create a new, "first class" Texas State University for Negroes.[105] The state set up another temporary site, this time in downtown Austin-eight blocks away from the university-and this site, in the basement of an office building, came complete with three rooms, three faculty (part-time, first year instructors at the law school), a library of 10,000 books, plus access to the state capitol law library. Again, to accommodate *one student*. The "law school" was to open for Sweat to start classes on March 10, 1947, if he accepted his admission invitation. He didn't, instead choosing to go back to court, with Marshall preparing an equalization argument as to whether or not a one- student law school could be considered truly "equal" to the white law school at the University of Texas. Everyone around the case could see the asinine-ness of this folly of a law school, including the students themselves who showed up at a mass rally, 2,000 persons strong, to show support for Sweat and the NAACP-even taking out 200 memberships in the NAACP, and organizing the first "all-white" branch in the country.[106]

219

The state challenged the NAACP aggressively on the motives behind the case, whether or not Sweat wanted to go to law school, or serve as an *agent provocateur* for the NAACP to gain "social equality." Marshall knew that he was in a different setting deep in the heart of Texas, and expressed concerns that it was going to "be a real showdown fight against Jim Crow in education," and it was, as the hearing represented a five day trial in which the court rendered no immediate decision. A *month* later, the court upheld the lower court's decision, after which time, it would be three years before Sweat's appeal would be heard in the U.S. Supreme Court.

While the appeal on the *Sweat* case was pending, Marshall took a second case against the University of Oklahoma that was different from the *Sipuel* case. George McLaurin was a sixty-eight year old professor, who had earned a master's degree and now wanted to pursue a Ph.D. in education. The university rejected him. The NAACP picked him out of eight other possible plaintiffs, because he was the least likely candidate to pursue "social equality" in the context Whites most feared (inter-racial marriage). While McLaurin was denied admission based on his race, his case didn't require the university to equalize, as did the law school cases. McLaurin could attend other schools in Oklahoma that admitted Blacks, and would allow him to pursue a doctorate in education.

The NAACP filed the suit under *McLaurin v. Oklahoma State Regents* (339 U.S. 637, 1950), and took the *McLaurin* case around the regular three step trial-appellate-Supreme court process, whereby the case could be heard by a special three-judge federal District Court, in instances where an injunction is sought against enforcement of a federal, state or local law, on the ground that it is in conflict with the Constitution.[107] The U.S. Supreme Court had just ruled against the University of Oklahoma, in January, forcing them to admit Ada Sipuel. The NAACP felt that, because of McLaurin's age, and the university's decision violated the Constitution under the *Sipuel* decision, that this was the quickest way to a Supreme Court appeal, if the special district court ruled against them. The *McLaurin* case was heard by the special district court in August of 1948, and the three-judge panel ruled the next month in the same way the high court had ruled in the *Sipuel* decision, ordering the state "to provide the plaintiff with the education he seeks, as soon as it does for application of any other group."[108]

The University of Oklahoma complied, only instead of allowing McLaurin to pursue his studies among the general student population, they sought to isolate him within the school, by requiring that he conform to segregation policies created especially for "colored students" under the state's "hurry-up" revisions. This meant that McLaurin had to; sit outside the classroom door in the hallway to receive his instruction, study at a segregated table in the mezzanine of the library-behind newspaper stacks where he couldn't be seen in plain view, and eat in the cafeteria in an alcove away from the other students, or at different times than white students. Marshall went back before the three-panel court to demand that the segregation stipulations on McLaurin be eradicated. At that hearing, he presented his sociological arguments that the university was punishing McLaurin for having to honor his rights, and that his "required isolation from all other students, solely because of accident of birth, creates a mental discomfiture, which makes concentration and study difficult if not impossible..." and that these regulations scarred McLaurin with "a badge of inferiority which affects his relationship, both to his fellow students and to his professors" that McLaurin himself testified as being "quite strange and humiliating to be placed in that position."[109] The special district court district didn't buy Marshall's argument, and declined McLaurin's request to attend the university on a non-segregated basis. Marshall appealed to the U.S. Supreme Court. The stage was set, for all the marbles, in both the *Sweat* and *McLaurin* cases, and as fate would have it, the Supreme Court would take them both under consideration in the same session, as Marshall would present oral arguments, for both cases, in April of 1950.

*   *   *

April of 1950, was a significant turning point for the fight against segregation. Its principle architect, Charles Houston, had been hospitalized the month before, with what had been a steadily weakening heart. Having had two heart attacks in the prior two years, Houston had already begun to forecast the change in strategy in the fight against segregation and he knew where the next phase of that fight would take place, because he had already begun to engage it three years earlier. Charles Houston was always ahead of the legal curve.

In 1947, in his weekly editorial column for the *Afro-American*, essentially demonstrating his role as "shot caller" in the orchestration of the legal campaign against Jim Crow, Houston wrote: "NAACP lawyers in order to get the campaign underway accepted the doctrine that the state could segregate...provided equal accommodations were afforded...Now the NAACP is making a direct, open, all-out fight against segregation...There is no such thing as 'separate but equal.' Segregation itself imports inequality."[110] In that article, Houston declared that de jure segregation was a charade, and that in the 15 preceding years that he had handled cases for the NAACP, he and the lawyers he had trained, both at Howard and in the NAACP, had gone along with the masquerade for the purpose of tipping up on, and chipping away at segregation's most holiest of precedents, *Plessy v. Ferguson*. Now Houston was declaring that there was no such foolishness as "separate but equal," under a just legal system, and that it was time to stop

221

the charade. With the cases of *Sweat* and *McLaurin* pending, Houston's "Trojan Horse" had rolled right up on *Plessy*, and as the states and the courts were making minor adjustments to the subtleties of equalization, the NAACP was preparing to take a major leap on the neck of Jim Crow. Houston knew it was time to change the subtle attack into a direct attack on white supremacy's figment of equality law, which was in fact-racial separation for the purpose of denying African American's social equality. The direct attack would go to the core of where the impact was psychologically and sociologically greatest, school children. This was the fight Houston had waited for all of his adult life and he would lead the second part of the fight as he had led the first-challenging segregation and discrimination against black children in the elementary and secondary public school system of his native city, the nation's capital, Washington, D.C.

The same year Houston "declared war" on segregation, black parents in the District of Columbia declared war on the poor and disparate inequalities of segregated schools. They waged a protest strike in December, 1947, pulling their children out of what they called "part-time education," in Browne Junior High School, a school built for 800 students-but housed 1,800 students-while nearby junior high schools that Whites attended had empty seats in many of their classrooms. Though these parents were low income parents, they were sophisticated enough to understand that the policies under which their schools were run were discriminatory, and they also saw "well to do" middle class Blacks as part of the problem.

They organized a formal organization called, the Consolidated Parent Group, Inc., and despite their suspicion of "upperclass" Blacks, took a vote to approach Charles Houston, who they knew was "one of the 'big people' who as a class, in general, had 'hurt' the 'little people'," to represent their children's interests.[112] After meeting with the parents, and despite the apparent symptoms of failing health, Houston agreed to represent the Consolidated Parent Group, Inc., telling the parents, "I want nothing for my services and I'm in it to the end."[113] Charles Houston, now considered by most at that stage of his life, as recalled by federal Judge, Constance Baker Motley, as-the "best trial lawyer in America-black or white,"[114] was concluding his legal career, just as he had began it in his father's law firm, helping people whether they could pay or not. Over the next few years, Houston would file several cases on behalf of parents in Consolidated Parent Group, Inc., including one for the 14 year old daughter of the president of the group and the man responsible for convincing Houston to take up their cause, and who befriended him in the last years of his life, Gardner L. Bishop, in the U.S. District Court for the District of Columbia.

These cases, *Bishop et al. v. Doyle et al., Gregg et al. v. Sharpe et al.* and *Haley et. Al. v. Sharpe et al.* were later consolidated under the name of *Bolling v. Sharpe* and included, as a companion case, to the four state cases that later made up *Brown v. Board of Education, Topeka, KS, et al.* Unbeknownst to the NAACP, who had not yet begun to take on elementary and high school cases, Charles Houston had already gotten the ball rolling on the "next phase" of the fight, public school desegregation cases. He wouldn't be there to stand with the NAACP when these, and the other, cases would be heard. A week before the end of his life, Charles Houston won his last case with Marshall, as he started his first, with a case against the University of Maryland.

Houston was back in the hospital, after a recovery relapse from a heart attack he suffered, in October of 1949. Unable to practice law, he asked Marshall, who was preparing for oral arguments for *Sweat* and *McLaurin*, to take over as lead counsel in the case of *McCready v. Byrd*, involving the denial of admission of a black woman to the nursing school. The University of Maryland, whom Houston and Marshall together-defeated-in the *Murray* case, argued that this case involved a "different principle," and that there were plenty of colored nursing schools that would accept black students. Marshall, had a young law clerk named Constance Motley track the case-her first. He was able to stand right in, and proved that there wasn't a different principle involved, based on the fact that Houston had so adequately prepared the case, that Marshall, or any of the other black lawyers, could handle any of the "racist chicanery" anti-segregation attorneys commonly received from opposing counsel.[115]

Marshall had helped Charles Houston win his last case, as Houston had helped Marshall win his first. On April 22, 1950, the week after his most successful protégé, Thurgood Marshall, gave, before a packed courtroom, the most furious oral arguments against segregation to date, and two months before the Supreme Court would render its decisions on the cases of *Sweat* and *McLaurin*, Charles Hamilton Houston, at 2:15 p.m., died of acute coronary thrombosis. He was 54 years old. His legacy, an impassioned battle to destroy segregation-to kill "Jim Crow"-was well on its way. His place in history, though largely forgotten outside legal and civil right historian circles, was firmly cemented, in the fact that, it was "Houston's army" carrying forth the fight.

223

*   *   *

By the time the U.S. Supreme Court was ready to render its decision on *Sweat v. Painter* in June of 1950, there had been some dramatic changes in the environment of both the Supreme Court and the NAACP. Two left leaning judicial activists on the Vinson court, Associate Justice, Frank Murphy, and Associate Justice, Wiley Rutledge, died in the summer of 1949. President Harry Truman replaced them with two southerners from border states, his Attorney General, Tom Clark, from Texas (the first Texan on the Court), and Sherman "Shay" Minson, not considered one of the sharpest justices to ever sit on the court. Neither appeared too friendly to civil rights, but didn't appear outwardly hostile either. While it made Marshall feel somewhat unsure where the Vinson court stood on segregation, he did know that Truman had proven to be a friend to Blacks, having withstood a challenge within his own party, when a Southern congressmen, upset over Truman's positions in advocating black voting in the 1948 election, and urging non-discriminatory hiring in the federal government, left the party to start "the States Rights" party. It didn't appear that Truman would put anybody on the high court that would give any credence to the divisiveness of "Dixiecrat" policies, given the hostility Southern democrats or Dixiecrats had shown toward him. Still, the change in the judicial temperament of the U.S. Supreme Court environment was unsettling, at a time when the stakes were so high.

On the NAACP front, the legal dominance of the Inc. Fund and its string of monumental successes had clearly established Thurgood Marshall as the focus of the organization's national persona. Commonly recognized as the braintrust of the NAACP's legal thrust, Thurgood Marshall had become the largest single personality since the departure of W.E.B. DuBois. And in much the same way DuBois' views became that of the organization, Marshall's views on civil rights became those of the organization. So large had Marshall's aura become, that his very name became synonomous with civil rights. By 1950, Marshall was frequently summoned to speak around the nation and often called-even billed in public appearances as "Mr. Civil Rights," a tribute to his courage, tenacity, his legal expertise and his "common touch" among the poor black masses he represented, on behalf of the NAACP.[116]

This brought an increasing amount of scrutiny and even antagonism from Walter White, who worked diligently to keep the organization's focus on himself. Because the Inc., Fund's budget was funded directly from the NAACP, White would commit the Legal Defense Fund's help to an office already overworked and understaffed, and often send out press releases commenting on work that the Inc. Fund, not the NAACP, had accomplished.[117] The more successes the Inc. Fund achieved, the more demands they received-sometimes from small rural communities who sent barely literate letters asking for the NAACP's help. This required Marshall to spend endless days on the road, either investigating cases, or fundraising, so that the fund was not completely under the control of White. Marshall began to rely more on his first lieutenant and key assistant, Robert Lee Carter, who had come to the Inc. Fund in 1944 at the age of twenty-seven, and soon became the work horse of the staff-carrying the heaviest load of churning out briefs on time, that kept the Inc. Fund's ship afloat. Understanding that the courts and their opponents were looking for any technicality to have a NAACP case thrown out, Carter's results-oriented self-discipline played vital in the Inc. Fund's legal machine. If the Marshall was wind that blew the NAACP's sails, Carter was the keel that kept the ship steadily on course.[118] Carter was an "action man" who was ready to challenge the system of segregation, while Marshall was much more cautious.

225

As Carter prepared the briefs for both the *Sweat* and the *McLaurin* cases, it became clear that equalization was no longer the core of the arguments. The NAACP had advanced its first true test, using sociological rationalization as their primary argument-not a secondary argument as it was in the *Sipuel* case. However, the case would still be argued in support of *Plessy*, and within "separate but equal," instead of attacking *Plessy* and arguing outside of "separate but equal" policy. Marshall's caution, hastened by William Hastie-whose mentor role now filled the void Houston had held-was well founded. No one had been bold enough to antagonize the courts, or white court watchers, by taking *Plessy* head on, until the *Henderson v. United States* case, where the Southern Railway violated its dining car regulations approved by the Interstate Commerce Commission, when it segregated dining tables in its dining car.

Elmer Henderson was a federal government employee, Traveling on government business on his way from Washington to Georgia, a federal government employee named Elmer Henderson went unfed, when tables set aside for black passengers went unserved. Henderson hired an attorney named Belford Lawson, and, with the

financial backing of Alpha Phi Alpha Fraternity, sued the federal government, filing one of the few civil rights lawsuits outside the NAACP
controlled organizations in 1940.[119] In the ten years it took for
Henderson to reach the Supreme Court, the antitrust division of the
Justice Department had grown tired of defending the illusion of equality under separate but equal.

Losses in the *Steele, Sipuel* and *Restrictive Covenant* cases, and
with the Solicitor General's office preparing to defend state sanctioned
"separate but equal," in the *Sweat* and *McLaurin* cases, Solicitor
General Philip Perlman, a lieutenant of newly appointed Supreme
Court Justice, Tom Clark, took charge of the *Henderson* case, arguing
for the first time that *Plessy* was wrong.[120] In his oral arguments,
Perlman suggested that it was disingenuous for the government of the
United States to continue to, in good conscience, "defend the degradation of black Americans," and that it was time for the Court to over-
rule *Plessy*.[121] He not only stated so in his case, Perlman willingly filed
amicus briefs saying the same in the *Sweat* and *McLaurin* cases.[122] On
June 5, 1950, Marshall's caution came to an end.

In what many consider as the greatest day for the civil rights
legal campaign that preceded *Brown*, the U.S. Supreme Court, with
Chief Justice Vinson writing the opinion for a unanimous majority,
ruled on both *Sweat* and *McLaurin*, which he said "presented different
aspects of the same general question," to what extent the equal-protec-
tion clause of the Fourteenth Amendment limited the power of a state
to distinguish between students of different races in professional and
graduate education in a state university?[123] Since the NAACP had
framed its question within the context of demanding equal facilities in
the University of Texas case, Vinson ruled-at the caution of Justice
Frankfurter, not to go beyond what the case had requested, or what the
precedent of *Gaines* had established-that the University of Texas had-
n't met the equalization standard in trying to set up a law school for one
student (subsequently 23 students). Vinson stated that when one
looked at the physical comparison of the two "law schools," the differences in comparison was very noticeable. Vinson, however, noted that
the University of Texas possessed "qualities" that make for the greatness
of the law school, that couldn't be objectively measured in bricks and
mortar, including "the reputation of the faculty, experience of the
administration, position and influence of the alumni, standing in the
community, traditions and prestige," all of which made the University
of Texas obviously superior to "one who had a free choice."[124]

The Court surmised that the "equal alternative" offered to Negro students wasn't an equal alternative, and ordered the University of Texas to admit Heman Sweat to its law school. However, Vinson, in the case of *McLaurin*, an obvious "segregation case" the NAACP thought would hit directly at *Plessy*, avoided the question-even the word, segregation, all together, following the sociological arguments of the NAACP, but not its conclusion. The Court called "the restrictions" placed on McLaurin within the institution provided, an unequal education, because it impaired and inhibited his ability to study, engage in discussions and exchange of views with other students, and an impairment, in general, to McLaurin's ability to learn his profession. Vinson viewed McLaurin's education as "unequal to his classmates," thus ruling that "state-imposed restrictions which produce such inequalities cannot be sustained.[125]

The Supreme Court essentially said-without saying it-that separate but equal had no place in the institution, once the university accepted the student. Once admitted, students had to be taught equally, without "restrictions," or segregation policies in the school. So Vinson avoided *Plessy* in both of the NAACP cases.

The high Court danced around a third decision, in the case of *Henderson v. the United States*, ruling that same day, that a ticketholder entitled to use the diner must be equally free to do so. Also a unanimous decision that was seen as an extension of *McLaurin*, *Henderson* tapped at the root of *Plessy*, that once said, once admitted, you could segregate. Now, the Court was saying, in *McLaurin* and *Henderson*, "Once admitted-you could no longer segregate"-a change in the basic tenet of *Plessy*. Like *Plessy*, *Henderson* focused on segregation in transportation, and went to the core of what equal treatment for "equal" fare paying passengers was supposed to represent, which was why Homer Plessy filed his case in the first place. Elmer Henderson received the outcome that Homer Plessy desired, and might have received-had he had this Court.

Times were changing and the Supreme Court knew it. The Vinson Court just couldn't bring itself to say it, but they did what the Fuller Court couldn't bring itself to do. Clearly, the Supreme Court had finally got it, and in three decisions asserted that, for the first time, "separate but equal" could not be an empty promise of separation and nothing else, or it wouldn't be constitutionally sanctioned.

Even though the Supreme Court was able to intentionally avoid the question of overturning *Plessy*, it would be the last time they would be able to do so. Marshall finally had the "foundation of cases" that Houston had predicted they would need to overturn *Plessy*. *Sipuel v. Board of Regents* and *Sweat v. Painter* were the cases most instrumental in opening the door for the *Brown* Decision, by desegregating higher education in the border states, and the peripheral, forcing the southern states to "equalize" or admit black students.[126] Most admitted black students, but only if the state's black colleges didn't offer the courses. Now the question of "separate but equal" had been severely diminished, because the courts had upheld the rights of black students to enter Jim Crow institutions in the absence of suitable equivalents, which was the case most of the time. The NAACP had proven "separate but equal" was a sham. Marshall knew it was time to directly challenge *Plessy*. Three weeks after the *Sweat* and *McLaurin* decisions, Marshall called a conference of lawyers to map out the legal strategy to the direct challenge, the "all-out attack" on segregation, and announced that "we are going to insist on non-segregation in American public education from top to bottom-from law school to kindergarten."[127]

*   *   *

228

The Supreme Court's toleration of *Plessy* probably did more than any one event to bring on the direct attack on segregation. In case after case, the NAACP (and other groups) demonstrated that "Jim Crow" policy had nothing to do with equality, and everything to do with limiting the progress of the Negro. "Separate But Equal" was, in fact, a special sanction on the Negro that hardly impacted other people of color. "Jim Crow" law was the re-invention of black codes that no black man, or woman, could escape without legal protection. If the Supreme Court tolerated it, the rest of society would also. Marshall knew this, but rationalized that the Vinson Court, as many times as it had a chance to overturn *Plessy*-didn't.

For some reason, the Supreme Court avoided the question of overturning *Plessy*, because it represented a confrontation of racial feelings inbred in white America that were firmly entrenched throughout the South, and in many parts of the nation. The Supreme Court's tolerance to *Plessy* was reflective of the nation's tolerance of racial discrimination, and the Court had to show judicial restraint consistent with that. As long as the NAACP never asked the question on the constitutional legality of segregation, the Supreme Court would never assume a question was being asked, and thus, never give a direct answer.

The NAACP was now prepared to ask the question, "Is segregation legal?" It would be asked in four separate cases (a fifth case would be added by the courts).

The first case for the all-out attack that Marshall turned to was in Clarendon County, South Carolina in 1949. In what became known as *Briggs v. Elliott*, Marshall took this case as an equalization case, and filed on November 11, prior to the *Sweat* and *McLaurin* decisions. The NAACP's change in strategy shifted both the tactic and the emphasis on this case. Clarendon County was a rural community that had the highest percentage of black citizens (70%) of any county in the state. In the district in which the suit was filed, there were 870 black pupil and 276 white ones, yet the disparities between the two races were glaring.

District 22 had maintained three black schools, two elementary schools and an elementary-high school combination, as well as, an elementary school and a high school for white students in the district. The cost to maintain all three black schools was $10,900. Furniture and fixtures at the three schools totaled $1,800. There were no water fountains, no inside toilets, and one of the schools had *no desks*. The cost to maintain the white elementary school alone was $40,000. Furniture and fixtures at the white schools were $12,000. The white schools had water fountains, indoor restrooms, and newer buildings made of brick and mortar, while the black schools were literally shanty houses.[128] Moreover, the student- teacher ratios for the white schools were 28 students for every teacher, 47 students for every teacher for the black schools.

The problems were just as pervasive throughout Clarendon County, where in the 1949-50 school year, the county spent $149 for every white child, while spending $43 for each black child, totaling $194,575 for 61 black schools that taught 6,531 black students, while white schools assessed $673,850 to divide amongst twelve schools that taught 2,375 white students.[129] There were other disparities, such as, class offerings at white schools that weren't made available at the black schools, and accommodations, such as school buses, which the black schools had none. In documenting the disparities, Marshall discovered that two Clarendon County black first graders, each six years old, walked five miles to school each day-each way, a total of ten miles unescorted.[130]

The first person to bring to light these disparities was a teacher in the district named Rev. Joseph S. DeLaine, who was fired for organizing black parents to demand improvements in the conditions of their schools. The district proceeded to fire his wife, also a teacher in the district, then offered him a principal's position, if he helped squash the protests.[131] He refused. Twenty black families came forth on behalf of their children. Harry Briggs, who was also fired from his job as a gas station attendant, and had his bank credit cut off, was the first plaintiff, because the South Carolina plaintiffs were listed in alphabetical order, in the first of the cases that would come to be known as *Brown*. This case went to trial in the spring of 1951.

The second case was filed on February 28, 1951, in Topeka, Kansas. One of the biggest misnomers in the legacy of what became the lead case of the school desegregation cases, was that Thurgood Marshall tried this famed case. The truth is that Marshall's commitment to the *Briggs* case, in South Carolina made, it impossible for him to participate in the *Topeka* case, which was actually directed and tried by Robert Carter, with assistance from local attorneys, John and Charles Scott, and Charles Bledsoe.[132] The *Topeka* case stemmed from an 1868 state statute that gave communities of 15,000 or more the local option of requiring segregated elementary schools, if they wished. Because Blacks represented less than four percent of the Kansas' statewide population, they were literally held captive to the wishes of the white electorate.

In Topeka, a city of approximately 100,000 people, there were 8,000 black residents, 7.5 % of the total population of the city. However, nine of its twelve communities, whose populations qualified them to institute segregation, did so, putting 658 black elementary school pupils in four schools, while 6,019 white pupils attended eighteen white schools.[133] Other than the black schools housing almost twice the number of students that white schools housed, facilities in Topeka were pretty equal. The problem in Topeka was that black students could not attend schools in their local neighborhoods, requiring them to often walk past their local neighborhood to catch a school bus to a segregated school. Black schools in Topeka, unlike those in Clarendon County, had school buses to take their children to school, while the white children didn't.[134] White children mostly walked to schools in their neighborhoods, and though some were required to walk anywhere from six to thirty blocks, the district didn't see the need to provide white children transportation, because they weren't needed in sufficient numbers.

The *Topeka* case represented the ideal case to test the legality of segregation because equalization wasn't really the issue. Access to neighborhood schools, and the fundamental right to attend the school of their choice that excluded simply on the basis of race were the issues. Clearly, Topeka was a "Jim Crow" town, and while it didn't have separate waiting rooms in train and bus stations, or require Blacks to ride in the rear of the bus, it maintained separation in many other facets of life, both by law and by custom.[135] There were segregated theaters, restaurants and other private establishments.

However, Topeka had mixed race neighborhoods, and therein lied the problem. Children who played together on weekends, couldn't go to school together on weekdays. Black children had to walk past neighborhood friends playing on school yards, on their way to bus stops, to be taken to 'their schools." This was problematic for many black parents, particularly, Oliver Brown, whose seven year old daughter, Linda, had to leave home at 7:40 a.m., walk six blocks through dangerous railroad switching yards, and across the city's busiest commercial street to catch a bus, that then took her a mile away to "her school," that started at 9:00 a.m.[136] Thirteen parents came forward on behalf of their 20 children approached the local NAACP branch to request that a suit be filed against the state's segregation statute.

The lead plaintiff, Rev. Oliver Brown, a lifelong Topeka resident, and a World War II veteran, was not an NAACP member, but he had other qualifications that made him ideal to be out front. As a welder for several years in the Santa Fe shops, he had union membership that protected him from the economic threats of unjustified firing. Secondly, he was a black Methodist who was considered the "black establishment" in Topeka-few of whom had anything to do with the NAACP-and served as an assistant pastor of St John AME Church.[137] In essence, he lent credibility, because of his non-militant demeanor, and more importantly, he lent urgency to the case that even non-threatening Blacks in Topeka were tired of "being second class citizens."

The case was filed in the federal district court. The local NAACP branch had trouble filling the courtroom when the case was heard June 25, 1951, largely because the community was divided over the case. One issue that complicated the Topeka case was that it did not have the support of the black teachers of the Topeka school district, who thought the case would lead to integrated schools, which, in turn, would lead to the displacement of black teachers, since the school system would not displace any white teachers, nor would white parents submit to allowing Blacks to teach their children.[138] This didn't discourage Robert Carter, who wrote Thurgood Marshall, before trial, that

231

"our possibilities of winning here seem better than they are in South Carolina."[139]

What made the *Topeka* case the center of attention was that Robert Carter, not having the equalization argument to fall back on, relied on sociological arguments to win the case, and introduced social science analysis into the court record to demonstrate the psychological impact the debilitating effects of segregation had on black children. The introduction of sociologists, Dr. Kenneth Clark, Professor of Sociology at the City College of New York, and his wife, Dr. Mamie Clark, who performed what was called, "the doll tests," sought to demonstrate to the Court how children could discern the differences of race (black and white), the differences in social equality, and the differences in perceived social status, whereby they could internalize these differences in ways that affected their self-esteem and perception of themselves.

Though Dr. Clark would testify in every case, except the Kansas case (because racial disparities were more exaggerated in all of the other cases), the Kansas case presented the basis for the dilemma, that segregation had a stigmatizing effect on black children, who couldn't understand why they couldn't go to their neighborhood school-solely because they were black. Did that mean black was bad, and white was good? In a period where social science was perceived as pseudo-science, meaning it wasn't subject to definitive outcomes every time tested, and was largely interpretive, or subjective (versus objective) in its analysis. Yet, Dr. Kenneth Clark, one of the researchers involved in the *Myrdal Study*, was able to compile a body of work in several states in the North, and the South, that produced consistently credible results.

The most controversial of the doll tests was a two-doll test administered to sample groups of black children from the ages of six to nine. The dolls were identical in every way, except for their color. One was brown, and the other was pink. Children were asked a set of question as to how they perceived the dolls, in relation to themselves. Dr. Clark asked the children, individually, which doll did they perceive to be the "nice doll," and the child, invariably, in the overwhelming number of the cases, picked the white doll. If Dr. Clark asked them which they perceive to be the "bad doll," the same child would pick the black doll-a perception that Dr. Clark analyzed as negative. When Dr. Clark asked why the doll was bad, children couldn't really verbalize it, but they understood that there was something associated with its color that made it bad. When Dr. Clark concluded his questioning of the child by

asking them to pick the doll that was most like themselves, black children in sample groups, either in consensus or in unanimous fashion,
chose the white doll, as most like themselves, a telling analysis of how
children could discern race, and had an innate desire to associate with
something good, and disassociate with something negative.

In testing over 300 children in various locations, with similar
results, Dr. Clark was able to interpret that black children accepted, as
early as six years old, negative stereotypes about themselves.[140] The doll
tests, which history has represented as the turning point in the case,
was then, and is now, still the most controversial aspect of this historical decision, and has withstood years of critique, both positive and negative.

The third case filed was in Prince Edward County Virginia, and
is probably the most fascinating of the desegregation cases, because it
was the only one of the cases that was totally student led. The Prince
Edward County Case stemmed from a massive inequity in school
resource distribution between white and black children, despite the fact
that Blacks represented 59% of the county's population. The debilitating conditions at the only black high school in the county were the
epitome of the mockery "separate but equal" represented in the South.
Moton High School was built for 180 pupils, but housed 450 students
who were accommodated by three shacks covered with tarpaper, and
heated by stoves. The school had no cafeteria, no gymnasium, no show-
ers, no dressing rooms, and didn't offer courses in physics, world history, advanced typing and stenography. The 384 white students of Prince
Edward County had two high schools to attend, both of which, had all
of the aforementioned amenities and coursework. The "black" high
school cost $131,000, while one of the "white" high schools alone cost
$500,000. Prince Edward County spent 18 cents per black student, for
every dollar it spent on white students.[141] Many attempts to get a new
high school for black students, by both the Moton PTA and the local
NAACP chapter, went unheeded.

Then, a 16 year old student by the name of Barbara Rose Johns
took matters into her own hands. Unbeknownst to the parents of the
Moton High students, she organized and mobilized 450 students to
walk out of Moton High School, until the district provided black students with a new school. On April 23, 1951, Johns electrified the
whole community when the *entire* student body went out on strike.
Fearing the retaliation of Whites, the local NAACP branch was at first
reluctant to back the strike. The students called the national office two

233

weeks later, convincing two of the Inc. Fund lawyers, Oliver Hill, already a well known attorney in Virginia and Spottswood Robinson, who along with Hill was a graduate of Howard Law School, to come to Prince Edward County to hear their case.[142] Hill and Robinson, reluctant to take on another desegregation case, in a majority black area, went to Virginia with the intention of convincing the students to go back to school, but once hearing their suffering, warned them that lawsuits were no longer about equalization-that they'd have to push for desegregation.[143]

Once the parents agreed to back the students, Hill and Robinson filed *Davis v. County School Board of Prince Edward County*, on May 23, 1951, in the Federal District Court for the Eastern District of Virginia, representing 117 black students. The student most responsible for the strike, and subsequently the desegregation lawsuit, Barbara Rose Johns, was sent away to finish her senior year of high school, by her family who was fearful of her safety. She went to live with her uncle, Reverend Vernon Johns, a vigorous and uncompromising opponent of white supremacy practices, who profoundly influenced the advocacy of his niece in the Moton High strike. Rev. Johns preceded Dr. Martin Luther King, Jr., as pastor of the Dexter Avenue Baptist Church in Montgomery, Alabama.[144]

234

The fourth and final case filed by the NAACP was two cases consolidated into one, where, in each case, black students were prohibited from attending schools reserved for white students, the truest reflection of Jim Crow practices in a border state that promoted segregation every bit as the Deep South. The city of Claymont barred black students from attending the local "state of the art" high school, instead, bussing them nine miles away to an older, ill equipped school, Howard High in Wilmington. Ethel Belton, who became the lead plaintiff in the case, asserted that her daughter lost 30 minutes a day being bussed, that could be used for study or piano lessons, but moreover, "I and others are made to feel ashamed and embarrassed, because such separations humiliate us and make us feel that we are not as good Americans as other Americans."[145] Black parents of eight students of Claymont filed suit to desegregate the Claymont school system.

The second case involved a rural school system in Hockessin, Delaware, that excluded black children from attending the local elementary school, and were forced to attend a one room school house on the outskirts of town, where two teachers taught 43 students. The school district provided transportation for white children to get to school, but made no provision for black children to get to segregated schools miles from their homes. One child, Shirley Barbara Bulah, was not allowed to board a school bus that passed right in front of her house each day, and thus was only able to get to school two miles away by car, driven by her mother, Sarah.[146] Mrs. Bulah, after writing the state on several occasions, contacted celebrated Wilmington civil rights attorney, Louis Redding, to ask him if he'd help Hockessin's black children get a school bus. Redding responded that if Mrs. Bulah was interested in getting a segregated bus to take her daughter to a segregated school, he wasn't interested-but if she was interested in sending her daughter to an integrated school, "then, maybe he'd help."[147] Sarah Bulah and ten other parents filed a lawsuit on behalf of their children to desegregate the local elementary school.

Delaware represented an interesting case, because it was the one case in which the door to desegregation had already been cracked open. A year earlier, the NAACP had fought and won a case that called on the state of Delaware to desegregate its state funded higher education institution, University of Delaware, the first time anywhere in the United States that a court order forced a white state institution to open its doors to Blacks.[148] The judge who decided the higher education case was Chancellor Collins Seitz, who was only thirty-seven years old, and the first (only) Catholic judge involved in the school desegregation cases, who thought that segregation created "a mental health problem in many Negro children, with resulting impediment to their educational progress," and that 'separate but equal' should be rejected as an impossible contradiction of terms.[149]

This fed right into the NAACP's sociological argument and was tailor-made for the all-out attack on segregation, plus, they had a recent precedent within the state. Redding and NAACP Inc. Fund's attorney assigned to the case, Jack Greenberg, who had worked together on the University of Delaware case a year earlier, filed both cases in October of 1951. Chancellor Seitz also handled this trial, and consolidated the two cases under the title, *Belton v. Gebhart* (*Bulah v. Gebhart*), which involved challenges at both the elementary and high school levels.

In the meantime, a fifth case was working its way through the court system. Cases filed by the late Charles Hamilton Houston, in 1948 and 1949, for the Consolidated Parents Group, Inc. were still on the court dockets. When Houston was hospitalized for the last time, and put under strict order not to do anything strenuous, like practice

235

law, meet with clients or any such thing, he disobeyed his doctors order, on one occasion, when he called in Gardner Bishop, who was then a friend, to discuss the future of the school equalization cases. While Houston had some idea of how ill he was, he could not have foreseen that his instructions to Gardner would essentially become a deathbed wish. Few matters were of greater concern to Gardner, and now to Houston, as the future of children in the District of Columbia. Houston wanted to put Bishop's concerns to rest by instructing him how to move the cases forward, and specifically, who could do as good a job as Houston himself, another concern of Bishop's-who still retained his disdain and distrust for black elites. Houston told him, "Ask [George E.C.] Hayes to take full charge...and ask [James M.] Nabrit [Jr.] to help him"...go tell "Hayes and Jim Nabrit [that] they owe me and take your case."[150] Charles Houston called in a favor for the children in D.C., and George Hayes and James Nabrit, Jr. honored the request, taking over these cases.

Nabrit, a Howard law school professor who was seen as "an outspokenly militant member" of the Inc. Fund's "inner circle" of advisers, took the lead in case-but not as part of the NAACP cases. Nabrit met with Bishop and the Consolidated Parent Group, Inc. to advise them that the strategy had changed, and that amended lawsuits would have to be filed to ask for desegregation, instead of equalization. The parents agreed, and decided to focus their effort on the newly opened Sousa Junior High, by having a taxicab take eight students to the school on admission day (September 11, 1950) to enroll in the new school. They were denied admission on the basis of their race.

Consolidating the plaintiff's from Houston's old cases, Nabrit filed a new case in early 1951, abandoning the prior strategy-making no mention of equalization, requesting that the district's school system be desegregated in the case that became known as *Bolling v. Sharpe*.[152] The plaintiffs were listed alphabetically, thus making 12-year old Spottswood T. Bolling the lead plaintiff. Because the District of Columbia was a federal territory, Nabrit could not claim violation of the Fourteenth Amendment, since the language of the equal protection clause was seen as only applying to the states.[152] Instead, Nabrit claimed that D.C. black students' rights were violated under the due process clause of the Fifth Amendment, which guaranteed equal protection, in the same manner as the equal protection did under the Fourteenth Amendment.[153]

The first of the school desegregation cases, *Briggs*, reached the

Supreme Court in May, 1952, where the NAACP filed a new statement of jurisdiction and the Court responded affirmatively, setting *Briggs* and *Brown* for the fall court calendar, starting in October. The *Davis* appeal was filed on July 12, and the Delaware Supreme Court upheld the lower court's decision in favor of the state, in the cases of *Belton* and *Bulah*. The NAACP appealed to the Supreme Court. Then the Supreme Court rescheduled *Briggs* and *Brown* for December 8th. The clerk of the Supreme Court then took the extraordinary step of calling James Nabrit, asking him to petition the Court to hear *Bolling*, which was still in court of appeals.[154] The petition was accepted. In November, the Delaware attorney general requested a writ of certiorari on the two Delaware cases. The Court accepted the writ. It appeared that the Supreme Court was ready to settle the issue of school desegregation and its direct attack on *Plessy*, once and for all. The four NAACP cases, and the *Bolling* case, considered by the Court as a companion case, were scheduled for arguments in December, 1952.

On December 9th, 1952, all five school desegregation cases were argued concurrently under the title, *Brown et al. v. Board of Education of Topeka, Shawnee County, KS et. al.*, for three days. The NAACP Legal Defense Fund, Inc. assembled what many historians believe to be the most brilliant cadre of legal minds the black community had ever witnessed for the greatest fight of the 20th Century. The career accomplishments of the *Brown* attorneys have never been equaled. Thurgood Marshall, the first director-counsel of Inc. Fund went on to become a federal district court judge, the first black U.S. Solicitor General, and the first black U.S. Supreme Court Justice. James Nabrit, Jr. headed the Howard Law School, then became President of Howard University. Oliver Hill, who finished second in his 1933 Howard law school class (to Marshall), became the first black to serve on the Richmond (VA) City Council. Spottswood Robinson became the dean of Howard Law School, and later a federal appeals judge. Robert Carter became General Counsel for the NAACP (the organization), and a federal judge. Constance Baker Motley (who prepared many of the *Brown* cases) became a federal judge. Jack Greenberg succeeded Thurgood Marshall as director-counsel of the NAACP/LDF, Inc.

Another dozen local attorneys, John and Charles Scott, Charles Bledsoe in the Kansas case, Louis Redding in the Delaware case, George E.C. Hayes, Frank Reeves, Harry B. Merican, George Johnson, Julian R. Dugas, Herbert D. Reid, Sr. and James A.

Washington, Jr. in the District of Columbia cases, were the best of their profession and deeply committed to the desegregation cause.

They needed such an expert group of men for the challenge they were up against. Not only were they looking the legal policy defense of America race caste system (*Plessy*) in one eye, they were looking at the historical defenders of the system, the U.S. Supreme Court, in the other eye. Marshall was not optimistic about their chances. The Court had hoped not to be forced to confront the issue of desegregation so quickly, after deliberately avoiding the issue in the *Sweat* and *Mclaurin* cases, and the NAACP had not planned to force the issue this soon.[155] Marshall, in many of his speaking engagements, saw the fight to overturn *Plessy* as a protracted fight, still as much as ten years (or more) away. Marshall surmised that it would take the Negro 100 years to overcome racial segregation in America, but he had a saying that he often used to conclude his speeches, in a spirit of optimism. Marshall promised that Blacks would "Be free by '63," meaning 1963, 100 years after the Emancipation Proclamation took effect.

Marshall knew he was dealing with, what Carl T. Rowan called "nine very troubled men:"[156] Chief Justice, Fred M. Vinson (age 62) from Kentucky, who was viewed as a defender of segregation, but willing to hold "separate but equal" accountable to protect the system; Stanley F. Reed (age 68), also from Kentucky, whom Marshall saw as a closet supremacist, when he ruled against him in the *Lyons* murder case; Felix Frankfurter (age 70), who was seen as sympathetic to the civil rights cause, but practiced judicial restraint and discouraged judicial activism amongst his colleagues; Robert H. Jackson (age 60), who was the former chief counsel for the United States at the Nuremberg trials; Harold H. Burton (age 64), who was a former mayor of Cleveland, Ohio; Tom C. Clark of Texas (age 53) was a former U.S. Attorney General, who for years upheld *Plessy*, in the courts; Sherman Minto (age 62), a former Senator from Indiana, viewed as conservative; Hugo Black (age 66) a former Klan member from Alabama, who became liberal in his views and an ardent defender of civil liberties, and William O. Douglas (age 54), African Americans biggest advocate for equality on the court.[157] In taking *Brown* under submission in 1952, the Court saw the cases as "difficult," and many of the Court's longstanding feud's amongst the justices came to fore.

Vinson saw the law as clear, and felt that, until Congress declared that there shall be no segregation, the Court had a body of law to back them on "separate but equal." Hugo Black, the only justice from the deep South, predicted violence, if the Court held segregation as unlawful, and warned that the states would probably take evasive measures, while "purporting to obey"-but stated he would vote to abolish segregation, though he expressed concerned as to whether his colleagues would.[158] Reed, the justice most disposed to uphold segregation, both in policy and in constitutionality, saw it as a problem for the states to work out, given that the state legislatures, in his opinion, had "informed views" on the matter, but felt in the Deep South "separate but equal" schools must be allowed.[159]

Frankfurter, considered the court's "expert" on the Fourteenth Amendment, had feuded with Black over interpretations, loathed segregation, but couldn't find anywhere that the Constitution said abolishing segregation and treating Blacks differently under separate but equal were unconstitutional. He found the moral argument of the D.C. case compelling but felt the case should be re-argued to give the Executive Branch (the Eisenhower Administration) time to fulfill a campaign promise to end racial segregation in areas under federal control, that would greater social gains than through judicial intervention.[160] Douglas saw segregation as an easy problem to solve, simply by abolishing it-which he backed with both the Fourteenth and Fifth Amendments. Jackson was conflicted because he also disdained segregation, but didn't see it as unconstitutional, ridiculing the NAACP's brief, as sociology and not law, and felt the case should be reargued with House and Senate Judiciary Committees, involved so that Congress might be "stirred up" to abolish segregation.[161]

239

Burton, being from Ohio-a state long in support of racial egalitarianism-saw segregation as a violation of the equal protection clause of the 14th Amendment, that the states had no choice in upholding. He favored invalidating segregation in public education on a "go slow" basis.[162]

Clark was in favor of remanding the cases back to the lower courts to let them work it out, feeling that a delay would be helpful, and thus was undecided. Minton saw "separate but equal" as a law, whose standing had been eroded by recent decisions, and was a way of life that was on its way out. He saw segregation as an illegal extension of slavery, and was in favor of voting to end segregation. Clearly this was a Supreme Court highly divided on the question of segregation.

This confliction caused the Supreme Court to deliberate almost six months. There was no clear majority, in favor of invalidating segregation, or against ending "separate but equal." An informal vote of the justices indicated that there were four justices in favor of ending segregation, two justices against ending segregation and three justices undecided. As best historians can definitely conclude, the 4-3-2 split broke down as follows; Black, Douglas, Burton and Minton-for ending segregation, Vinson and Reed-for reaffirming *Plessy*, and Frankfurter, Jackson and Clark-undecided.[163] On June 8, 1953, after five justices (Black, Frankfurter, Jackson, Burton and Minton) voted for reargument, an order was issued for the cases to be reargued in the next term-October 12, 1953, a rare occurrence for the high Court. The Court directed the parties to submit briefs to address the following questions:

1.   What evidence is there that the Congress which submitted, and the State legislatures and conventions, which ratified the Fourteenth Amendment, contemplated or did not contem plate, understood or did not understand, that it would abolish segregation in public schools?

2.   If neither the Congress in submitting, nor the States in ratify ing the Fourteenth Amendment, understood that compliance with it would require the immediate abolition of segregation in public schools, was it nevertheless the understanding of the framers of the Amendment:

        a)   that future Congresses might, in the exercise of their power under section 5 of the Amendment, abolish such segregation, or

        b)   that it would be within the judicial power, in light of future conditions, to construe the Amendment as abol ishing such segregation of its own force.

3.   On the assumption that the answers to questions 2 (a) and (b) do not dispose of the issue, is it within the judicial power, in construing the Amendment, to abolish segregation in public schools?

4.   Assuming it is decided that segregation in public schools vio lates the Fourteenth Amendment:

        a)   would a decree necessarily follow providing that, with in the limits set by normal geographical school dis tricting, Negro children should forthwith be admitted to schools of their choice, or

        b)   may this Court, in the exercise of its equity powers, permit an effective gradual adjustment to be brought bout from existing segregated systems to a system not based on color distinctions?

5.   On the assumption on which questions 4 (a) and (b) are based, and assuming further that this Court will exercise its equity powers to the end described in question 4 (b),

    a)   should this Court formulate detailed decrees in these cases;

    b)   if so, what specific issues should the decrees reach;

    c)   should this Court appoint a special master to hear evidence with a view to recommending specific terms for such decrees;

    d)   should this Court remand to the courts of first instance with directions to frame decrees in theses cases, and if so what general directions should the decrees of this Court include and what procedures should the courts of first instance follow in arriving at the specific terms of more detailed decrees?[164]

The NAACP saw the order as a "positive sign," because the court didn't rule against them. However, it also increased the pressure of what was at stake. Their sociological arguments were being scrutinized by the highest Court in the land, and their response was such that it was going to the very essence of the race caste in America. In responding to the court's original intent question, the NAACP engaged some of the nation's top lawyers, scholars, historians, including John A. Davis, John Hope Franklin, C. Vann Woodward and a young black lawyer named William Coleman, who finished first in his class at Harvard, and had clerked for Justice Frankfurter, who agreed to coordinate research in the various states.[165] The core of the NAACP's response to the Court would rest on their assertion that *Plessy* was based on a false premise, that segregation was "convenient legal fiction" intended, from the outset, to stigmatize Blacks, and thus establish a doctrine called "separate but equal," that would be used to maintain a racial hierarchy, and lastly, that the Fourteenth Amendment was intended to prohibit state sponsored segregation.[166] Fate would impact the case another way.

On September 8, 1953, while awaiting rearguments in the *Brown* case, the Supreme Court's Chief Justice, Fred Vinson, died. This put the court in a state of flux with the century's most important case hanging in the balance. A comment by Associate Justice Frankfurter

241

may have been indicative that the justices were feeling the pressure of the case also. Knowing that the Court may have had the crucial fifth vote it needed to overturn *Plessy* (historians assert that Frankfurter may have been leaning in support of invalidating segregation though some of his own comments of having filibustered the decision in 1952-53 controvert that fact),[167] but not the kind of consensus building leadership necessary to show the Court as united on the century's most controversial ruling, Frankfurter said upon hearing of Vinson's death, that it was "the first indication I have ever had that there was a God. "[168]

President Eisenhower, anxious not to cause a long delay and knowing that he needed a consensus builder, appointed former California Governor, Earl Warren, to a recess appointment on October 2, 1953. Warren played a key role in helping Eisenhower win the Republican nomination for president, and the appointment was viewed as a just reward. Warren was viewed as an ideological twin of Eisenhower, a moderate conservative, with unclear views on race, though he had advocated, while serving as California's Attorney General, for the evacuation of 110,000 Japanese and Japanese Americans from the West Coast, in April of 1942.[169] Less than thirty days later Vinson's death, on October 5, 1953, Earl Warren took the oath of office as the 14th Chief Justice of the Supreme Court of the United States of America. The irony of Warren's appointment was that he was the 14th Chief Justice over a Court that had the responsibility of reinterpreting the Court's longstanding view of the Fourteenth Amendment.

On December 7, 1953, the *Brown* case commenced three days of rearguments before the newly constituted Warren Court. This Court had a Chief Justice that maintained a totally different mindset about segregation than its predecessor. The first thing that Warren did, that Vinson was reluctant to do, was to eliminate the essential premise for which segregation was based, the premise that African Americans were "an inferior race," and it was the only way to sustain *Plessy*.

Opening the arguments, with an informal discussion on the appropriateness of the premise of "separate but equal," was famed lawyer and former presidential candidate, John Davis. Davis, who had argued and won more cases before the Supreme Court than any attorney before this case, and himself nominated for the U.S. Supreme Court in the 1920s (he declined, it would've been too big of a cut in pay),[170] stated the premise under which the NAACP was arguing this case was totally inappropriate. However, Warren saw it as a false premise-saying the 13th, 14th, and 15th Amendments "intended to make equal those who once were slaves."[172]   Warren continued that, "We can't set one group apart from the rest of us and say that they are not entitlted to same treatment as all others." Warren's concluding statement left no doubt which way the Court was going to rule. Warren stated, "We must act, but we should do it, in a tolerate way." The only question now was whether in would be a unanimous or a divided Supreme Court. The Court recessed on the case of *Brown v. Board of Education*, on December 9, 1953 at 2:53 p.m., deliberating for the next six months on how it would make equality for Blacks legal.

On May 17, 1954, the United States Supreme Court would culminate Charles Hamilton Houston's twenty-five battle to overturn the South's fifty-eight year tradition of illegal racial separation. It handed down an expected decision, in an unexpected manner, a unanimous and very non-dramatic fashion, as was customary for the court to issue its ruling-on a Monday, the first day of the work week. For ten million black Southerners, and other Americans, who had long fought for equality and equal protection under the Constitution, it was a day of hope long overdue and a promise fulfilled. For millions of Whites, North and South, who were supporters and sympathizers of a system of white supremacy, and a publicly mandated race caste, it was a dark and despondent day. Their beloved "Jim Crow," and its system of "separate but equal," was declared, at least, legally, dead. To them, May 17, 1954, would forever become known as, *Black Monday.*[173]

243

9

In Defense of White Privilege:
The Massive Resistance Movement

Having fought the issue in the highest court in the land and seen the decision given in their favor, Negroes experienced the most shameless perversion of justice. In state after state, and school district after school district, human ingenuity was employed to defy the clear statement of the court. And where elusive action failed to nullify the court decision, violence, intimidation, legislative evasion and even assassination were employed.

Whitney Young, the late Urban League CEO,
in his book entitled, *To Be Equal*

Newly appointed, not yet confirmed, but clearly in the midst of a historical moment, Chief Justice, Earl Warren, read the Court's opinion in the school desegregation cases in a somewhat plainly mundane orderly manner-barely above a whisper. The political significance of the case, muted by the simplicity of the Court's Constitutional interpretation, and sealed by the dignity accorded the highest Court in the land, the Court first handled an antitrust opinion read by Justice Clark. Then two opinions were read by Justice Douglas. Then Chief Justice Warren unceremoniously announced, I am authorizing to report the decisions of the Court in cases Numbers 1,2,4 and 10 on the docket..."[1] Reading the opinions of the NAACP filed desegregation cases of *Briggs v. Elliott, Brown v. the Brown of Topeka, KS, Davis v. County School Board of Prince Edward County* and *Belton v. Gebhart*, Warren recounted the points of re-argument centered around how each side viewed the Fourteenth Amendment, and the courts role in its reinterpretation. Giving no hint as to how the Court had ruled, Warren outlined the legacy of *Plessy*, and the segregation policy in public schools, serving as the primary vehicle for socialization in young children. Warren stated that policy was being inconsistent with equal protection under the law, then analyzed recent decisions that had sought to address the inequities of "separate but equal." Finally, Warren came to the question of segregation and its effects on black children. Warren read, "Does segregation of children in public schools solely on the basis of race, even though the physical facilities and other tangible factors may be equal be equal, deprive the children of the minority group of equal educational opportunities?" With barely a pause stated, "We unanimously believe that it does," bringing forth what Warren recalled as, essentially a sense of collective gasp from the people in the courtroom, "a wave of emotion," without sound or movement, "yet a distinct emotional manifestation that defies description."[2] Without changing his tone of voice, Warren said the words Marshall and the NAACP lawyers had been waiting to hear for the nearly two decades, since Charles Houston took up the legal campaign against segregation;

We conclude, that in the field of public education the doctrine of "separate but equal" has no place. Separate educational facilities are inherently unequal. Therefore, we hold that the plaintiffs, and others similarly for whom the actions have been brought are, by reason of the segregation complained of, deprived of the equal protection of the laws, guaranteed by the Fourteenth Amendment. This disposition makes necessary any discussion, whether such segregation also violates the Due Process Clause of the Fourteenth Amendment.[3]

The Court was quiet with a stunned silence. The Chief Justice then read the Court's decision in the case of *Bolling v. Sharpe*. Laying out the basis, under which the case was summoned, Warren cited the importance of the constitutional question presented in docket 344 U.S. 873 (*Brown et al*), then stated that the Court now had a new precedent, having "this day held that the Equal Protection Clause of the Fourteenth Amendment prohibit the states from maintaining racially segregated schools."[4] Then Warren reinforced what the Court had decided earlier in *Brown*, stating:

Segregation, in public education, is not reasonably related to any proper governmental objective, and, thus, it imposes on Negro children of the District of Columbia a burden that constitutes an arbitrary deprivation of their liberty in violation of the Due Process Clause.

245

In view of our decision that the Constitution prohibits the states from maintaining racially segregated public schools, it would be unthinkable that the same Constitution would impose a lesser duty on the Federal Government. We hold that racial segregation in the public schools of the District of Columbia is a denial of the due process of law guaranteed by the Fifth Amendment to the Constitution.[5]

Warren ordered both the *Brown et al.* and *Bolling* cases to petition the Court for further arguments, on what decrees the Court should consider in carrying out these decisions. And with that, the Warren Court, went down in history as the Court that overturned Jim Crow. Warren did what many considered to be the impossible; invalidated "separate but equal," which the Chief Justice said in later years, was a comparatively simple case, given that the Court had chipped away at the doctrine for years, and that only the fact of segregation itself, had been unconsidered. Warren reflected that based on the merits, the natural, the logical and the practical, "the only way the case could be decided, was clear."[6]

Thurgood Marshall, while elated with the decision, was highly skeptical of the "next steps." He stated, later in his career, while serving with Warren on the Supreme Court, that Warren was "the greatest leader I've ever run across in my life," having pulled off a political judicial miracle, in getting a unanimous vote of the Court, dealing with justices highly sensitive to the attack on the traditions of *Plessy,* and profoundly affected by the arguments made by the NAACP with their social and educational psychiatric experts, that essentially made the case for the damage that state imposed segregation had on black children. Yet, Warren was cautious, even protective of the social order, in terms of how the *Brown* decision would change southern life.[7]

On the other hand, many were outraged at the decision. While not unanimous in their condemnation of the *Brown* decision, various parts of the country reacted differently. Between the time the decision came down, and the time in which the Court would consider an implementation decree, the various states would be rife with indecision, attempted progress and untempered reaction-that became known as, massive resistance. The border states used the time to make constructive preparations for compliance. The Deep South used the time to prepare for confrontation, by entrenching itself further in the cloak of segregationist views. The states of the peripheral South, in varying degrees, hesitated, watched, waited and searched for leadership, while

Congress debated, and the President equivocated.[8]

There was no more volatile response than came from the leaders of the "southern bloc," the states of the Deep South, who were impacted by the elimination of racial segregation. Senator James O. Eastland, an arch-segregationist from Mississippi, quickly charged that the Supreme Court had been "indoctrinated and brainwashed" by left-wing pressure groups.[9] Eastland began to organize other members of Congress in the South, to respond to the Supreme Court's decision. The Governors of the states, most impacted by the opinion, were varied in their responses to the decision, according to how they felt their constituents were most inclined to respond to the decision. With some exceptions, governors from the Deep South (Louisiana, Mississippi, Alabama, Georgia and South Carolina) were strongly critical of *Brown*. Those from the upper South (Arkansas, Tennessee, North Carolina, and Virginia) were critical, but more restrained. Only the governors from the border states (Delaware, Maryland, Kentucky, Missouri, Oklahoma and West Virginia), all states where segregation was required by law, felt secure enough that their constituents would not rebel against the decision to offer more constructive responses to the opinion.[10]

In the months following the decision, several Southern states did begin to integrate their schools. In seeking to comply with the Court's directive, sooner rather than later, 350 school districts in Oklahoma, Texas, Kentucky, West Virginia, Maryland, Tennessee, Arkansas and Delaware decided to obey the court, though none could ascertain when full integration would be achieved, and in most instances, the degree of compliance could best be viewed as token efforts.[11]

However, a large majority of those living in the Southeast, continued to view school integration as very much an open matter, supported by their elected representatives at every level of government.[12] Other states were taking a "wait and see" approach to the *Brown* decision and the Court's reinterpretation. The deep South was organizing meetings to find ways to work around the *Brown* decision, including the possibility of maintaining segregation on a voluntary basis-*with the cooperation* of Southern Blacks.

Several states were pursuing "local options" (the catchword for enforcing state's rights), to address remedies before racial hysteria came about. To avoid racial hysteria, the reigning governors of the South, met in Richmond, Virginia (a month after the decision in June, 1954),

247

and voted unanimously to do nothing, vowing "not to comply voluntarily with the Supreme Court's decision against racial segregation in
the public schools."[13] The implied power of the states, to pursue local
remedies in possibly resisting *Brown*, were further imbued when
President Eisenhower expressed his view, of what he thought the
Courts would do when the decree hearings came to pass.

In a rare statement about the *Brown* decision, being careful not
to give support to or detract from the Supreme Court's holding, the
President stated that he expected the court to decentralize the implementation of desegregation, given the difficult problems involved.[14]
Decentralization would allow states to pursue local options and put
desegregation at risk. In the weeks prior to Eisenhower's statement, the
Southern Governors Conference had met in Boca Raton, Florida, and
issued their most defiant statement to date, moving past "wait (on the
Court) and see," pledging to engage every legal effort "to preserve the
right of the states, to administer their public school systems to the best
interest of all the people."[15]

This was the most direct signal yet sent, by the states, that
resistance was on the horizon. Louisiana had passed the first "resistance" amendment that upheld the state's police power to provide for
the health, safety and welfare of its citizens. The early months of 1955
produced pro-segregation legislation, popularly becoming known as
"Resistance legislation," in Mississippi, North Carolina, South
Carolina, while such legislation failed in Arkansas and Tennessee,
demonstrating that some of the upper states were still in a "wait and
see" posture.[16] But such laid back posture wouldn't last long.

On May 31st, 1955, the United States Supreme Court
announced its now (and forever) famous enforcement decree, instructing the states to proceed on the desegregation of public schools, *"With
All Deliberate Speed."* The Court remanded the cases back to the lower
courts, directing them "to take such proceedings, and enter such orders
and decrees consistent with this opinion as are necessary and proper, to
admit to public schools on a racially nondiscriminatory basis with all
deliberate speed, the parties to these cases."[17] This continuation case
would effectively put an end to legally sanctioned racial "apartheid" in
publicly funded institutions, within the United States, and began the
ambiguous, confusing and stagnating career of "all deliberate speed,"
seen as the bridge by which the massive movement crossed, to forestall
the truest intent of *Brown*. Obtaining equality, within public schools
first, then, throughout society later, would be a painfully deliberate

engagement. By most accounts, fifty years later, the promise of *Brown*, and, to a large degree, the failures of *Brown*, are attributed to the vast, and conflicting, interpretations of those three words.

Historians have analyzed the Court's non-specific, no deadline or timeline, no further instructions decree, as a wink to the Southern states, in implementing plans most comfortable to them. The Court did not provide immediate relief, as most decrees do, for black students to enter integrated schools. The Supreme Court did not order the immediate end of segregated schools. They, instead accepted the Southern states worse case scenario, where if they had to go at all (move toward desegregation), then to "go slow." Of course, the best case scenario would have been to allow those states that wanted to keep segregation-to do so. The Court didn't offer that option, but they did offer the South the opportunity to gradually phase out school segregation, denying that black plaintiffs had a personal and immediate right to an integrated education.

The second *Brown* opinion, that came to be known as *Brown II*, was the first case in anybody's memory, outside of nuisance or antitrust cases, where delayed relief is an occasional occurrence, to hold that the vindication of one's constitutional rights was deferred, when it was deemed essential to the protection of other legitimate interests.[18] The Court gave the state's legal sanction to take their time in complying, and most did, until 1969, when the Supreme Court, with Thurgood Marshall now on the Court, recognized the South's lack of compliance for what it was, purposeful foot-dragging, and in an act of lost patience, ordered all school districts to "operate now and hereafter only unitary schools," 15 years after *Brown I*.[19] Southern Blacks viewed Brown II as a function of the legal process. Southern Whites viewed Brown II as an opportunity to take control of the process, under "states rights" declarations. The battle had now begun, and the massive resistance movement was now in full effect.

In the wake of the *Brown II* announcement, the South's public officials, for the most part, discarded their "wait and see" posture, and began evolving a state policy of in-depth resistance and legal challenge, mainly, by defiance of federal authorities expressed through political maneuvering, legal challenges and propaganda campaigns-not the overt forms of violence for which the resistance movement would later become known.[20]

The Massive Resistance Movement, as a stonewalling barrier to policy compliance and social engineering engagement, is one of the

249

most understudied phenomena in 20th Century behavioral sciences. Very rarely, is the massive resistance movement given attribution, except in an abbreviated measure, to the policy failures created out of the *Brown* decisions. The Massive Resistance Movement effectively stonewalled the implementation of school desegregation plans in, at least, half the cities (if not most of the cities) in this nation, as well as, public accommodations and private venues (membership clubs, golf clubs, etc.). While the Massive Resistance Movement has long been view as analogous with *Brown* and subsequent Civil Rights Movement, ending in the 1960s, major vestiges of massive resistance were present throughout society in the 1980s and 1990s, and to some degree, are still present in American society today. The resistance levels and degrees of intensity associated with massive resistance, were greatly under-estimated then-as it is today. The potential for massive resistance is always present in American society, and the 1950s offered the first hint what society tolerated resistance could produce, namely, confusion, confliction and fear. All of which, adds up to, an inability to achieve the optimum goal, total integration.

The ideology of Massive Resistance has been viewed in the context of counterrevolutionary activity, rationalized in its movements. The white backlash to the *Brown* decisions were part of that analysis. It was a rational choice on the part of Whites, and it was a movement in its unanimity. Whether the Massive Resistance Movement was counterrevolutionary is questionable? If Blacks' twenty-five year fight to overturn segregation could be considered a revolution, of sorts, then massive resistance did work counter to that. But if you look at segregation, and the right to maintain segregation, as an extension of the American Revolution, where colonists rebelled against the British in pursuit of rights and freedoms-to the exclusion of the rights of Blacks, as an extension of the Civil War, where the Southern states rebelled against the Union. In pursuit of their right to maintain and expand slavery-to the exclusion of the rights of Blacks, the South's rebellion against the *Brown* decision to uphold and maintain segregation-again to the exclusion of the rights of Blacks, caused massive resistance to be a phase of a constant exclusion process where the current activities of white opposition only represented a continuation of one long on-going "white only" revolution, advancing inequalities and injustices that Blacks were trying-and are still trying-to counter.

As will be asserted in the next chapter, the Civil Rights movement and its principle strategy of civil disobedience was engaged to counter the "white privilege" revolution in America that was now ignoring the law. Segregation was once legal, but never moral. Yet, the law was on their side. Massive resistance, it could be argued as part of American tradition, and for as long as the law is acceptable to the masses, no matter how just (or unjust), they are part of the social fabric.

When laws are no longer acceptable, even if they are just, they bring about resistance, and in some instances, rebellion on the part of the masses. This particular movement represented a kind of a regional nationalism that, in spite of all itself bravado, revealed a deep uncertainly and angst about key aspects of Southern life.[21] Whether you view the Massive resistance movement as revolutionary, or counterrevolutionary, ideological movements like it serve four basic functions; 1) it legitimates a given social system, 2) it promotes group cohesion, 3) it provides its adherents with propaganda ammunition for psychological and political warfare against its opponents, and 4) describes both a special view of reality, and prescribes what that reality ought to be.[22] One can observe, by these definitions, how ideology creates the confines of thought that define one's political reality.

This methodology, in the 1980s and 1990s, would be termed, Relativism, and no matter what validate and legal justifications one gives, if it's outside the relativist's "confines of thought," it's outside their political reality, and they can't accept it as part of their reality. According to relativists, their position is just as valid as anyone else's, because of their freedom of thought and entitlement to believe what they choose to believe. Like most opinions, one's right to believe should not be construed that that belief is valid. Most ideologues can't, or choose not to separate ideology from objective arguments. True facts, or not, for every fact you have, relativists have one to which they assert-both are valid. Relativists don't make distinctions in validity, causing them to support false arguments, and more critically, rest their arguments on, largely, false facts.

For white segregationists, integration with black people was outside the confines of their thought, and thus, outside their political reality-a political reality that was based on false arguments and false facts. Those old arguments and facts had been replaced with a new set of objective legal arguments, and a new set of court ordered "facts," which segregationists could not bring themselves to accept. These Whites thought their views of Blacks were still correct, and they saw their position as relatively correct, or just as right under states rights, as the federal government asserted under federal rights. So, they prepared

251

to resist.

One key component necessary for a successful massive resistance movement were people prepared to inspire the movement. Demagogues are people, who have the ability to appeal to the emotions, and prejudices of the people, and mobilizes opinion, valid or invalid, in order to gain political power. Demagoguery was at the center of the resistance to the *Brown* decision, from the very start. After 1954, the South was blessed (or one could say cursed) with a host of charismatic demagogues, all deeply committed to the myths of Massive Resistance. Most were leaders in state government, and most all of them made history, in taking their respective stands, which included the likes of "Bull" Connor, Ross Barnett, Herman Talmadge, Orval Faubus, George Wallace and Lester Maddox.[23]

With charismatic leaders edging them on, the other key component to massive resistance was mass organization, and it was during the massive resistance movement twhen the rise of resistance groups appeared. The most common name for them was "Citizens Councils," though they were most commonly acknowledged-and referred to-as, "White" Citizen Councils. White Citizens Council's were viewed as "upscale" versions of the Ku Klux Klan, because their open, yet hidden, motives promoted white supremacy, all under the guise of states rights.[24] The Citizens Council's recruited local businessmen, bankers, state legislators, industrialists, professionals, farmers, and other hard-line segregationists committed to maintaining their old way of life. Their primary tactic was to use economic pressures, and economic reprisals against local Blacks, who worked with the NAACP. After 1956, more direct action oriented civil rights groups like the Southern Christian Leadership Conference (SCLC) founded by Dr. Martin Luther King, Jr. in 1957, responded to attempts to reinforce the old status quo.[25]

The first Citizen Council was organized in July, 1954 in Indianola, Mississippi, down in Sunflower County, near the heart of the Mississippi Delta. Its founder was a plantation manager named Robert B. Patterson, who organized other area businessmen, and local political officials, by pointing out the need to advance a resistance strategy, which he formulized in a handout pamphlet called *Black Monday*.[26] The Indianola Council devised the organizational structure that became the model for future local groups and the *Black Monday* pamphlet, became the handbook-essentially the proselytizing "playbook" that spread the message-for the Massive Resistance movement. Pretty soon, the ideology of resistance to integrated schools soon became intermixed with the protection and promotion of white supremacy, as men, like Patterson, carried over their lifelong racial biases into the councils. The Councils, in Mississippi, and in several other states, represented a true grass roots movement, serving as the militant reflex of black belt towns and rural communities, to whom the county seat elite reacted. The councils drove the movement that soon became an influence on state legislatures.

By October, 1954, Mississippi had some twenty counties organized, and Citizen Council leaders formed a state association to coordinate Council activity, that served as an information network that strove to "organize every town and county in the state."[27] The resistance movement had outposts in every southern state. Citizens Councils existed in Mississippi, Alabama, Louisiana, South Carolina, Texas, Florida, Arkansas, Tennessee, and Virginia, with allied organizations that included the Defender of State Sovereignty and Individual Liberties in Virginia, the Patriots of North Carolina, the States Rights Council of Georgia, and the Tennessee and Florida Federations for Constitutional Government.[28]

In June of 1955, the NAACP asked all of it branches to file a petition with each school board, requesting that the school board act in accordance with the May 31st decision, and they received 60 petitions in the summer of 1955 alone.[29] Reaction to the petitions, in the white community, was "swift and vindictive," as Blacks, whose names appeared on the petitions, were retaliated against-frequently finding themselves without jobs, credit, and even the small doses of paternalism that gave warnings to Blacks.

253

The sentiment in the white community crystallized into a "stone-like unanimity" that demanded the racial orthodoxy of the Southern traditions they had come to know, and expect.[30] Terms like "defiance" and "resistance" and "refuse to obey" were being used in disobedience to desegregation orders compliance. Even terms like nullification and secession, terms that hadn't been used since before the Civil War, were being thrown around to show the level of distain these Southerners had for the prospect of desegregation. One thing was for sure, any Southern Blacks who sought to facilitate desgregation would be the target of resistance activities. As one council organizer proclaimed, "We intend to see that no Negro who believes in equality has a job, gets credit, or is able to exist in our communities.[31]

By August of 1955, the Mississippi Citizen Councils state association claimed 60,000 members. By the end of 1956, the association claimed 85,000 members with chapters in sixty-five of Mississippi's eight-two counties.[32] Mississippi was described as the biggest, most powerful, most tightly organized of all the Citizen Council organizations, and the only one to rival it was its neighboring state Alabama, whose membership was estimated at 60,000 by the middle of 1956. Louisiana, whose Councils were organized from the top down, as opposed to from the bottom up, claimed 100,000 members, a figure that was known to be exaggerated, bringing estimates closer to 8,000 members, in thirteen parishes, by January of 1956.[33] South Carolina had 30 Councils, a state association, and had some 40,000 members, at the height of its movement. In Virginia, the Defenders never numbering more than 15,000, but influenced legislation, to prohibit any public expenditures for mixed race schools.

Prince Edward County, Virginia, one of the *Brown* case litigants, became one of the more extreme demonstrations of the effectiveness of massive resistance. This county legally stalled desegregation in the courts for five years. Then, in 1959, closed the public school system down for another five years, avoiding desegregation, for a total of ten years, until the federal courts ordered schools to open "without further delay," and fixed a start date as the beginning of the school year of 1965.[34] These five states, Mississippi, Alabama, Louisiana, South Carolina and Virginia, represented the bulk of the white supremacy organizational strength achieving membership and political influence far beyond the other states. Though supremacists in the other states were organized enough to exert timing political pressure and influence within the course of events of their respective states.[35] The rise of White Citizen Councils, which numbered 127 branches in the Deep South by 1956, also had a dramatic effect on NAACP membership. In states like Mississippi, where there were 5,000 NAACP members, at the time of the second *Brown* decision, but fell to 1,700 in the three years to follow.[36] It was in the months prior to the second decision that extralegal means began to become an issue in desegregation efforts.

Acts of violence became more frequent. Between January 1, 1955 and January 1, 1959, the eleven states of the old Confederacy experienced 210 recorded incidents of intimidation, which ranged from Klan rallies and cross burning to death threats, attributable to the increased racial tensions generated by the *Brown* decision.[37] In 1955, Segregationists killed four Blacks in Mississippi, and no convictions were gained for any of the four "assassinations," including one that occurred in broad daylight on the lawn of the Lincoln County court-

254

house, and the other that become the most publicized event that marked the degree viciousness that massive resistance was prepared to exact-the murder of 14 year old Emmitt Till.[38] Till, down from Chicago living with relatives, was found floating face down in the Tallahatchie River after he allegedly whistled, and saying "Bye Baby" at a Mississippi white woman. An all white jury found the two men, who admitted abducting Till on the night of the killing, "not guilty." The Till murder made the national news. Till's mother held an open casket funeral to "show the world," how her son was tortured, his face badly disfigured, his head swelled to twice its size.

Between 1955 and 1957, southern juries freed white defendants in all but one of fourteen widely publicized cases involving the rights of Blacks.[39] Blacks, who attempted to exercise the right to vote, also became targets of the sort of "terrorism," which grew increasingly common after the *Brown* decision, including the 1955 murder of Reverend George Lee in Humphreys County, Mississippi, the first black to register to vote there.[40] The same year, the local president of the local NAACP branch, George Counts, was shot and wounded.

The most volatile of the Massive Resistance Movement's activities were bombings, which first became of serious concern during an economic boycott of a segregated bus system in Montgomery, Alabama. On January 30, 1956, the home of a young Baptist minister named, Dr. Martin Luther King, Jr., who had recently moved to the city, and was serving as head of the Montgomery Improvement Association, was bombed. The homes of desegregation leaders became targets of dynamite bombers. Public schools became another favorite target of racist bombers when between 1956 and January of 1959, nine educational institutions in Tennessee, Florida, North Carolina, Louisiana and Virginia were bombed.[41] This practice would only escalate in the 1960s, but it found its roots in the heightened racial hostilities stemming from the *Brown* decision, where white "extremists" found their role in the Massive Resistance Movement was to keep the races separated "at any cost," and "by any means necessary."

In January, 1955, government officials and private individuals from eleven states of the Old Confederacy met in Jackson, Mississippi, to organize a regional anti-desegregation group called the Federation of Constitutional Government. The group's specific goal was to organize resistance to "fight racial integration, and other efforts to destroy the Constitution that had been created, or reborn since the Court's May 17, 1954 desegregation decision.[42] This organization with a governing board that included U.S. Senators Eastland and Thurmond, six U.S. representatives and four state Governors, sought to heighten the opposition to *Brown*, and brought forth the most blatant challenge, to *Brown*.

In March of 1956, the Massive Resistance Movement officially moved beyond the local and state level to the national stage, when Southern congress members introduced "a Declaration of Constitutional Principles" on the floor of Congress, called the *Southern Manifesto*. This declaration labeled the school desegregation decisions as judicial activist gone awry, and asserted that the Supreme Court had overstepped its bounds, in seeking to legislate social equality. It was seen as a blatant challenge to the legitimacy of *Brown*, and a political declaration against the Court, and its decision.[43] But what the declaration really did was rally the forces of defiance in the South, at a time when it appeared that more moderate leadership might prevail.[44]

Originally conceived by South Carolina Senator (former Governor and State's Rights Party Presidential Candidate in 1948), Strom Thurmond, as an endorsement of interposition. Thurmond advanced his declaration to influential Virginia Senator, Harry Byrd, the man credited with coining the term, "massive resistance." The manifesto soon became a banner for unified Southern protest when the document was modified (six times), under threat of division, to exclude passages specifically approving interposition, and branding the Court's decision as unconstitutional and illegal, was approved by a committee of five senators and advanced to the full body.[45] The document, a historic break of legislative protocols, was read into the Congressional record on March 12, 1956, as follows;

THE UNWARRENTED DECISION of the Supreme Court in the public school cases is now bearing the fruit always produced when men substitute naked power for established law.

The Founding Fathers gave us a Constitution of checks and balances because they realized the inescapable lesson of history that no man or group of men can be safely entrusted with unlimited power. They framed this Constitution with its provisions for change by amendment in order to secure the fundamentals of government against the dangers of temporary popular passion or the personal predilections of public officeholders.

We regard the decision of the Supreme Court in the school cases as a clear abuse of judicial power. It climaxes a trend in the Federal judiciary undertaking to legislate in derogation of the authority of Congress, and to encroach upon the reserved rights of the States and the people.

The original Constitution does not mention education. Neither does the 14th amendment nor any other amendment. The debates preceding the submission of the 14th amendment clearly show that there was no intent that it should affect the systems of education maintained by the States.

The very Congress which proposed the amendment subsequently provided for segregated schools in the District of Columbia. When the amendment was adopted, in 1868, there were 37 States of the Union. Every one of the 26 States that had any substantial racial differences among its people either approved the operation of segregated schools already in existence or subsequently established such schools by action of the same lawmaking body which considered the 14th amendment.

As admitted by the Supreme Court in the public school case (Brown v. Board of Education), the doctrine of separate but equal schools "apparently originated in Roberts v. City of Boston...(1849), upholding school segregation against attack as being violative of a State constitutional guarantee of equality." This constitutional doctrine began in the North, not in the South, and it was followed not only in Massachusetts, but in Connecticut, New York, Illinois, Indiana, Michigan, Minnesota, New Jersey, Ohio, Pennsylvania, and other northern States until they, exercising their rights as States through the constitutional processes of local self-government, changed their school systems.

In the case of Plessy v. Ferguson in 1896 the Supreme Court expressly declared that under the 14th amendment no person was denied any of his rights if the States provided separate but equal public facilities. This decision has been followed in many other cases. It is notable that the Supreme Court, speaking through Chief Justice Taft, a former President of the United States, unanimously declared in 1927 in Lum v. Rice that the "separate but equal" principle is "within the discretion of the State in regulating its public schools and does not conflict with the 14th amendment."

This interpretation, restated time and again, became a part of the life of the people of many of the States and confirmed their habits, customs, traditions, and way of life. It is founded on elemental humanity and commonsense, for parents should not be deprived by Government of the right to direct the lives and education of their own children.

Though there has been no constitutional amendment or act of Congress, changing this established legal principle almost a century old, the Supreme Court of the United States, with no legal basis for such action, undertook to exercise their naked judicial power and substituted their personal political and social ideas for the established law of the land.

This unwarranted exercise of power by the Court, contrary to the Constitution, is creating chaos and confusion in the States principally affected. It is destroying the amicable relations between the white and Negro races that have been created through 90 years of patient effort by the good people of both races. It has planted hatred and suspicion where there has been heretofore friendship and understanding. Without regard to the consent of the governed, outside agitators are threatening immediate and revolutionary changes in our public-school systems. If done, this is certain to destroy the system of public education in some of the States.

With the gravest concern for the explosive and dangerous conditions created by this decision and inflamed by outside meddlers;
We reaffirm our reliance on the Constitution as the fundamental law of the land.

We decry the Supreme Court's encroachments on rights reserved to the States and to the people, contrary to established law and to the Constitution.

We commend the motives of those States which have declared the intention to resist forced integration by any lawful means.
We appeal to the States and people who are not directly affected by these decisions to consider the constitutional principles involved against the time when they, too, on issues vital to them, may be the victims of judicial encroachment.

Even though we constitute a minority in the present Congress, we have full faith that a majority of the American people believe in the dual system of Government which had enabled us to achieve our greatness and will in time demand that the reserved rights of the States and of the people be made secure against judicial usurpation. We pledge ourselves to use all lawful means to bring about a reversal of this decision which is contrary to the Constitution and to prevent the use of force in its implementation.

In this trying period, as we all seek to right this wrong, we appeal to our people not to be provoked by the agitators and troublemakers invading our States and to scrupulously refrain from disorders and lawless acts.[46]

Affixed to the document were the 96 original signatures of the members that supported this statement. Five additional signatures would be added later. Of the 128 men representing the South in Congress, 101 members, 19 Senators and 82 House members, signed the "Southern Manifesto," attacking *Brown*, and urging their states to ignore the U.S. Supreme Court's decision.[47] This was essentially the "green light" for the Massive Resistance movement, which appeared to

258

be working in those states most populated by Blacks, and most deeply engulfed in the jaws of Jim Crow. From the outside looking in, resistance in those areas appeared to be working. In September, 1955, *Time Magazine* reported that segregation seemed to be ending in those county and city school districts where the African American was less than 10 percent; where the population was between 10 and 25 percent, "the fight may not be too hard," *Time* reported; Where it approached or exceeds 50 percent, "the end can hardly be imagined," *Time* concluded.[48]

In 1956, a year after the *Brown II* decree was pushed down to the federal district courts, soon labeled the "58 Lonely Men," because of their difficulties in implementing desegregation without guidelines or timelines, *Time Magazine* asked NAACP Chief Counsel, Thurgood Marshall to grade each state's progress toward ending segregation. Publishing Marshall's "report card," it showed where the critical "war zones" were located, and was a testament to the demonstrated effectiveness of the Massive Resistance Movement. Marshall graded the legal compliance behavior of the seventeen southern states as follows; only one state, Missouri, received an A grade for its immediate desegregation of its public schools; one other state, West Virginia, received an A-minus because more than half of its school districts had desegregated in time for the start of school in September, 1955; Three states, Kentucky, Maryland, and Oklahoma received from a B+ plus to a B-minus for their desegregation activities; Five states, Arkansas, Delaware, North Carolina, Tennessee, and Texas were given grades in the C range for their efforts; Two states, Florida and Virginia, received Ds because there was hardly any movement toward desegregation; and five states, Alabama, Georgia, Louisiana, Mississippi and South Carolina all received F grades by Marshall, because there was absolutely no movement toward desegregation, confirming for Marshall that the real fight for achieving an end to segregation was in the Deep South.[49]

President Eisenhower didn't know how to respond to the massive resistance of the Southern states. Though he resisted concerns many had about Chief Justice Warren's lack of judicial experience when he appointed him, Eisenhower appointed Warren, because, in his own words, "we need statesmanship on the Supreme Court...he (Warren) represents the kind of political, economic, and social thinking that I believe we need on the Supreme Court...Finally, he has a national name for integrity, uprightness, and courage that, again, I

259

believe we need on the Court."[50] After the *Brown* decision came to pass, and the confusion over how desegregation would be carried out that ensued, Eisenhower was obviously rethinking that position. He actually reversed himself, saying that appointing Earl Warren was "the biggest damn fool mistake" he ever made.[51] However, the President knew the law had to be obeyed and he ordered the immediate integration of every school in the District of Columbia, and all remaining vestiges of segregation in the armed forces. What Eisenhower wouldn't do was personally urge the South to comply with *Brown*, showing sympathy to the sudden shock Southerners were experiencing, but also giving caution to the "extremists on both sides of the issue," comparing Blacks seeking equality to go to decent schools in their communities, to the die hard segregationists trying to keep them out.[52]

By 1960, there had been well over 200 pro-segregation statutes, resolutions and constitutional amendments adopted by Southern states, in hopes of delaying as long as possible the full implementation of *Brown*.[53] Despite this almost fanatical mass resistance and questions about its legitimacy, the value of *Brown* did not go ignored in the legal system. The principle announced in Brown was quickly used to desegregate other public facilities and public operated recreational facilities in the South, as the Court in the years immediately following the decision extended the case's constitutional reach beyond public school desegregation, by issuing very short unsigned *per curiam* opinions that essentially directed their legal reasoning for their decisions in two words, See *Brown*.[54]

The Court went right down the line ending segregation in a variety of public and state-connected places; in the case of Municipally owned parking-lot restaurants (*Burton v. Wilmington, Delaware, Parking Authority*) the Court said, See *Brown*; in the case of segregated courthouses (*Johnson v. Virginia*) the Court said, See *Brown*; in the case of segregated cemeteries (*Rice v. Sioux City Memorial Park Association*) the Court said, See *Brown*; in the case of segregated hospitals (*Simkins v. Cone Memorial Hospital*) the Court said, See *Brown*; in the case of public parks and playgrounds (*Watson v. City of Memphis*); in the case of public golf courses (*Holmes v. City of Atlanta*) the Court said, See *Brown*; in the case of public buses (*Gayle v. Browder*) the Court said, See *Brown*; in the case of public beaches (*Dawson v. City of Baltimore*) the Court said, See *Brown*; and in the case of city-owned amphitheaters (*Muir v. Louisville, Kentucky, Park Theatrical Association*) the Court said, See *Brown*.[55]

When future historians and revisionists look at what *Brown* did, or didn't do, what is hardly ever taken into consideration is that *Brown*, and subsequent desegregation measures, were never implemented in an environment of acceptance or cooperation. Nor was desegregation policy outcomes ever truly measured, in the context of the constraints and barriers that prohibited fair implementation and evaluated in the truest context of ever being afforded the opportunity to succeed. Lastly, the success or failures of *Brown* is hardly ever measured in consideration of the largely underestimated impact of the massive resistance movement. *Brown* succeeded, in some regards, in spite of massive resistance, but its success was largely marginalized and its policy effects, if they failed-failure, can be largely attributed to the ferocity of the massive resistance movement that challenged attempts at achieving black equality in public education, and that just didn't stop at *Brown*, but would continue throughout the Civil Rights movement, and beyond.

261

10

"I AM A MAN:"
The Civil Rights Counter Movement and the Politics of Moral Suasion

Slowly we have lifted ourselves by our own bootstraps. Step by halting step, we have beat our way back. It has been a long and tortuous road since the Dred Scott Decision of 1857, which branded us as non-citizens, and by the Plessy Decision, which gave the nation the green light to treat us as they pleased.

- The late NAACP Executive Secretary, Roy Wilkins

The Black civil rights struggle against American racial segregation has the same spirit that led the Africans and Asians to overthrow European colonialism. Both are denials of human dignity.

- Rev. Dr. Martin Luther King, Jr.

Brown v. the Board of Education, as the new legal precedent for interpreting the Fourteenth Amendment, ushered in such an unanticipated reaction in the South, that nation really didn't know how to address it. So, it just waited to see how the Court, over a year later, would sort it out. One thing was for sure, southern Whites were not going to take legalizing equality for Blacks, and the decision that brought it about, sitting down. Except for secession from the Union preceding the Civil War, segregationists organized such an unprecedented and unequaled resistance strategy, that it created a predicament that Blacks had to counter. The predicament was, how could they *force* white people to recognize their equality, *honor* their humanity, and, at the same time, *make* them obey the law. For the first time in America, since Reconstruction, black Americans could assert, with some backing of authority-in fact, the highest legal authority in the land, Supreme Court, that they were constitutionally in the right-and that the law was on their side. After the *Brown II* declaration to proceed desegregating schools *with all deliberate speed*, the will of white supremacists to stall integration would have to be matched by a determination on the part of Blacks, who were now being termed as integrationist, in their pursuit of *civil rights*. Notice the transition in terms.

Prior to the *Brown* decision, Blacks were in pursuit of equal rights-civil rights that were present under segregation, just not in evidence. They were just denied in the previous interpretation of the 14th Amendment under the *Plessy* precedent. Now under the *Brown* precedent, with equal rights was no longer in question, the demand turned to civil rights, an affirmation of rights that Blacks were not guaranteed previously-but were guaranteed now, and not being recognized as legitimate. The call began to be heard, "We want our civil rights!" When do we want 'em?" We want 'em, NOW!" The demand for recognition of civil rights brought on by *Brown*, in a very direct and fundamental way, gave birth to a "counter" movement to the Massive Resistance movement. In the same way the Massive Resistance movement organized proactively to defy *Brown's* enforcement, the counter movement, which would become the signature component of the greatest social change movement America had ever known-called the Civil Rights Movement, would organize in reaction to what obviously had become attempts on the part of state and local governments to ignore desegregation edicts. Within six months of the *Brown II* decision, black communities had become fed up with waiting for governments to comply with desegregation orders.

On December 1, 1955, one event gave rise to a new and massive "civil rights" movement that began in the shadow of *Brown* but would soon cast a looming shadow over the South, the nation and the world as America's race politics would take centerstage. Thurgood Marshall stated, that *Brown* "probably did more than anything else to awaken the Negro from his apathy to demanding his right to equality."[1] Marshall was correct in this analysis. Prior to *Brown*, Blacks, in order to demand equality, in a similar massive resistance fashion, risked violence by race riots, in the collective, and risked arrest, as individuals, for breaking the law. What law did Blacks break? Nothing more than violating the racial etiquette of segregation, which could be something as

263

simple as not surrendering a seat on a bus. In the aftermath of *Brown*, there no longer was a racial etiquette-though Whites tried to hold on to one, as long as they could (and did for another 10 years after *Brown I*)-and, Blacks could assert their equal rights. Even though many were arrested for ignoring laws that were now out of compliance with federal laws, for southern states-nullification of the *Brown* decision was in full effect. It was business as usual in trying to keep Blacks "in their place," which was beneath them in their social equality rights. There was nothing "civil" about asserting civil rights, which almost always led to arrest, confrontation and public humiliation, but one thing that Whites could no longer say, was that black people were breaking the law by simply trying to be equal.

This was the case on the first day of December, when a black seamstress from Detroit left work one day, caught a public bus paid her dime and took a seat. Rosa Parks, in her quiet and unassuming demeanor, was an activist who had studied at the highly regarded Highlander Folk School where black and white students studied together in the 1930s, in violation of the state's segregation laws, to learn how to overcome barriers of "separate but equal," in preparation of advocating for equal rights.[2] With an upstanding reputation among black and white progressives, and the least likely person to initiate a confrontation, Rosa Parks seemed to be the perfect person to challenge Montgomery's system of segregation in public transportation.

The circumstances were not planned, like in the test cases of *Dred Scott* and *Homer Plessy*, but the principle was the same, as Rosa Parks took a seat in the fifth row of the bus-the first row available to Blacks (the first five rows were "white only")-equal treatment for the same fare paid. Blacks could not sit next to Whites, nor could they sit in the same rows abreast from each other (though they were separated by the aisle). Mrs. Parks boarded at Dexter Avenue, and by the third stop, a white man boarded, and there were no seats left in the first five rows. The bus driver told four black passengers in the fifth row to give up their seats in a manner that reflected the racial etiquette, where Whites, with little power, spoke to Blacks, with no power, most condescendingly. Three of the passengers moved. One passenger "sat tight." It was Mrs. Rosa Parks, who not only didn't get up, but told the bus driver that she would not get up. The driver warned Mrs. Parks that if he had to stop the bus, and call the police, that she would be arrested. Mrs. Parks ignored his request. He pulled the bus over, got out, and called the police. Within minutes, Mrs. Parks was arrested, put into a police car, taken to city hall, then to the city jail, fingerprinted, and had her "mugshot" taken. Parks was given the whole criminal treatment, as a violator of Montgomery's racial etiquette.

After being bailed out by her husband, Raymond, and a white couple, Atty. Clifford and Virginia Durr, the four of them met that same night with Rev. E.D. Nixon, the President of the local NAACP Chapter. Rev Nixon saw Mrs. Parks arrest as a prime opportunity to test Montgomery segregation law. Mrs. Parks agreed to be the test case against her husband's wishes, given Montgomery's violence prone nature, when race was involved. The community, however, was already in motion over the Parks arrest. The next evening, a meeting was held at Dexter Avenue Baptist Church which was across form the State Capitol. The church had recently brought in a new pastor, a 26 year old Minister from Atlanta. An unknown young Minister named, Martin Luther King, Jr., had been contacted by another Montgomery native, a minister by the name of Ralph Abernathy, who asked King to host the meeting. By the end of the meeting, the group had formed an association, called the Montgomery Improvement Association, elected Rev. King as chairman, and decided that it would engage in a one-day protest on the day of Mrs. Parks court hearing. A black college professor named, Jo Ann Robinson, mimeographed enough handouts to have her students cover 52,000 African American households.[3] The handout flyer said the following:

265

This is for Monday, December 5, 1955. Another Negro woman has been arrested and thrown into jail because she refused to get up out of her seat on the bus for a white person to sit down. It is the second time since the Claudette Colvin case that a Negro woman has been arrested for the same thing. This has to be stopped. Negroes have rights, too, for if Negroes did not ride the buses, they could not operate. Three-fourths of the riders are Negroes, yet we are arrested, or have to stand over empty seats. If we do not do something to stop these arrests, they will continue. The next time it may be you, or your daughter, or mother. This woman's case will come up on Monday. We are, therefore, asking every Negro to stay off the buses Monday in protest of the arrest and trial. Don't ride the buses to work, to town, to school, or anywhere on Monday. You can afford to stay out of town for one day. If you work, take a cab, or walk. But please, children and grown-ups, don't ride the bus at all on Monday. Please stay off of all buses Monday.[4]

By all accounts, the organizers of the boycotts had hoped for 60 percent compliance, enough to send a message to public officials that they needed to meet a very basic demand, to treat black bus riders with dignity and respect. However, with close to what King considered a miracle, there was almost 100% compliance by black riders to the boycott request. King, and the other ministers, decided to continue the boycott on a permanent basis, until two modest demands were met; 1) that drivers treat Blacks with courtesy, 2) that black sections of the buses be reserved for Blacks even if Whites completely filled their own seats.[5]

Even in the midst of the new legal precedent that said "separate but equal" was no longer constitutional, Blacks in Montgomery didn't ask for an end to segregation-they asked for equalization on the buses, and for respect, in exchange for their deference. The bus company refused even these subtle changes in racial etiquette. The bus boycott continued, for 381 days-until the bus company relented to desegregate the buses. This was more than the group had asked for, but in their effort, discovered a new form of empowerment-direct action protest, in the form of non-violent civil disobedience. Lost in the celebrity of its new hero, Martin Luther King, Jr. who became the first passenger to ride an integrated city bus in Montgomery, Alabama, was that fact the it was Thurgood Marshall, Robert Carter and the NAACP that wrote the petition to the Supreme Court, asking that a lower court's ruling striking down bus segregation be allowed to stand, and the Court responded ruling in favor of the NAACP's request and in support of King's boycott.[6] As King took the bows in the media, in what started a generational conflict between King, who was 27 years old, (and thought he had found a new activism to bring about desegregation) and, Marshall, now 48 years old, who took the high ground but chided King's irreverence to their contribution, noting that King would still be marching and protesting, if not for the NAACP's victory in the courts.[7]

The Montgomery Bus Boycott was the first, and most prominent demonstration of how legal authority had shifted in favor of Blacks. The enforcement of civil rights was the moral responsibility of government, meaning it was the right thing to do-if they where truly honoring the laws of the nation, and its revered Constitution. However, the local government authorities of Montgomery, in the midst of organizing their Massive Resistance strategies, ignored the legal precedent, claiming nullification (federal law didn't apply) and arrested Rosa Parks, though she now had the right to retain her seat.

Whereas, in the past, Whites could question the rightness of Black's equality assertions-though they were always morally correct. Before *Brown*, the law was against Blacks. However, in the Post *Brown* era, Whites could no longer question the legal, or moral, rightness of Black's equality assertions, because law was no longer against Blacks. The law was now against what Whites in the South had practiced, and it was their (white America's) Supreme Court that said "'separate but equal' has no place in our society." African Americans now had a right to socialize as they pleased, as society could no longer take that away from them. The law was now on their side.

What was not on their side, however, was how many Whites ignored recognition of the law, as it applied to the civil rights of Blacks, to which black leaders asserted was morally wrong and ethically bankrupt. The organization of the Montgomery Bus Boycott sought to counter the City of Montgomery's resistance to the new law of the land. White Montgomery residents reacted in the only way they could, in recalcitrance, because they saw the boycott as an infringement-not on their rights but-on their culture, or "way of life." As Whites responded in the only way one would expect the first capital of the former Confederacy to respond-in a city that helped establish racial etiquette, by taking up membership in the Montgomery White Citizen's Council, they posited themselves to attack *Brown*, en masse. White Citizen's Councils increased its membership "handsomely," in retaliation against giving in to "negro demands."[8] They rejected any disobedience to segregation law. They saw these acts as criminal, and saw no fault in trying to enforce laws that were now considered illegal in the courts. King, and the new black leadership, would soon feel the force of the massive resistance movement, in a way nobody could have ever anticipated, as the conflict between "what was right" and "what was just," would be the struggle for the mind, and soul, of America. America's conscience would be tested over equality for Blacks.

America has always been conflicted over its treatment of Blacks, as fair minded and right minded Whites had always sought to be moral, and upright, in their application of freedom, liberty and equality. The sectional split of this country was not just directional, as in North and South. It was philosophical, and it was cultural, in its tolerance of what it would accept versus what it wouldn't accept on the racial front. While both the North and South impaired the rights of Blacks, on some level, one took it to a more extreme measure than the other, and the other was viewed as hypocritical in turning its head, as

267

if it didn't see the compromise, or do the same thing, when it was con-venient or necessary. However, there has always been a segment of the "attentive public" that would be absolutely shocked at the level of treatment Blacks received, if it was presented in a way that they could-n't turn away from. The Civil Rights Movement became "that way" that America was forced to look in the mirror, see itself, and no matter which way they turned to run away from the ugliness of massive resist-ance, they couldn't turn away. And every time America turned away, black leadership was there to remind them of their lack of moral stand-ing, and lack of ethical integrity, in ignoring laws that they lived by when the laws applied to them, but were denied when they applied to Blacks.

This engagement of what Greg Moses called the "revolution of conscience" became known as the politics of moral suasion. And its leader would come out of the most unlikely of events-not a law school formulation, like Charles Hamilton Houston did it-not a Supreme Court challenge, like Thurgood Marshall did it, but out of a local woman-countering massive resistance with her own form of resistance, and a local community taking a stand countering continuing segrega-tion with their own form of resistance, and a local minister confronting massive resistance with a simple question, "Did Blacks have the moral right to stand for right when the law was on their side?" A second ques-tion asked was, "Did the government have the moral right to protect Blacks in their 'legal right' to be treated as equals?" These were ques-tions that couldn't be asked, less than two years earlier. But it was being asked now, thanks to *Brown*.

A whole new set of questions were about to be asked after *Brown*, and they would come with an immediacy that the legal cam-paign couldn't bring. This was the whole premise under which King founded the Southern Christian Leadership Conference (SCLC), in 1957. There were facets of the equality struggle that changed with the advent of SCLC. First and foremost, SCLC was truly a southern move-ment, started by a small group of Baptist ministers, not representative of the Baptist Minister mindset-which was to avoid politics. It was unique in that sense.

Secondly, SCLC filled a void in advocacy, in the South, that was created as a result of the Massive Resistance Movement's clamp-down on the NAACP. In fact, most of SCLC's early (and most noted) activity was centered in Alabama (Montgomery, Birmingham, Selma) due to the fact that all operations of the NAACP had ceased, because

268

White Citizens Councils had successfully linked the organization to communist influences, during the post-WW II 'red scare" investigation activity of McCarthyism, and went to court to demand the NAACP to turn over its membership lists. The state courts ordered the NAACP to turn over its lists, and rather than do so-the national office closed all of its Alabama branches. Thus, SCLC replaced the NAACP in Alabama, where the state served as its principal base of operations, and its loose structure-absent of individual members-afforded it another layer of protection against the undermining tactics of massive resistance of intimidating members by demanding lists.[9] SCLC had no members so it was afforded the ability to operate under a "mass action" banner, which the NAACP avoided.

Thirdly, SCLC provided something new and different (in terms of socio-political advocacy), in that it established its advocacy based on Christian principles (an evolution of Lockean "Natural Law" theory) that sought to situate the organization "above politics," by appealing to the most cherished values of American social ideology, Christianity.[10]

Lastly, SCLC represented the reengagement of "personality leadership" that had been stymied, and put to sleep with the imprisonment, and deportation of the central figure of African Americans last "personality cult" movement, Marcus Garvey. The excitement of a single voice rising from amongst the masses to "speak truth to power," with the legal backing of the law, and the moral authority of the church, made SCLC synonymous with King that changed the movement in a way that Adam Fairclough concluded, "promoted a personality cult that grew to excessive proportions."[11]

The politics of moral suasion refocused the fight for racial equality. It moved from one that had been largely based on racial entitlement, white versus black, black versus white, a bifocal engagement in what Blacks wanted, in terms of equal treatment, versus what Whites didn't want them to have, in terms of racial subordination, to one based on social justice. Rightness of either side's position was a convoluted argument that could never be advanced because, in a very twisted sense, both were right. Blacks were correct to demand equality on a moral high ground, in a "Lockean" sense, where, according to Natural Law theory, no man was entitled to own another, and all were equally entitled to natural rights of liberty, equality and justice in a society of equals.

However, Whites had their man-made law on their side, and could assert that they were "right" according to their laws-even from time to time using God, and religion, to assert that somehow their man-made laws were affirmed in scripture-even though, on its face all could see the inequities in the law. Whites could claim their rightness on legal ground, but never on the moral high ground. The laws that created a race caste in America stemmed from racial tyranny backed by popular sovereignty where majority will is majority rule. Just because laws were affirmed by the majority of society as "legal," didn't make them right, or more importantly, didn't make them just. The twenty-five year fight that preceded the *Brown* decision was a battle over what was right, what was just and what was legal.

The Supreme Court found that segregation was not legal, but in the minds of many Whites, segregation relative to their personal racial preferences, was still right. But Whites could never argue, before the *Brown* decision, and after, that segregation was just, and in resisting the change of the law, Whites had neither, law or justice, on their side. Blacks could never win an argument with Whites on what was right, with respect to equality, because, after living in a society where a racial hierarchy existed in one form or another (be it slavery or segregation), it was obvious, in their insistence on maintaining the racial status quo, that they didn't know what was morally right. Now, through the Massive Resistance Movement, many were controverting what was legally right. The Massive Resistance Movement, and a countering Civil Right Movement positioned the battle for racial equality to be viewed in terms of, "who was right?" Blacks or Whites? Rightness was a relative argument, as far as Whites were concerned-a false argument-but right in terms of the goals of their cause, which was maintaining white supremacy, at best, and white privilege, at worse. Thus, they were right, in their own relative opinion, and what makes opinion different from fact is, opinion can't be proven false.

Dr. Martin Luther King, Jr., who would inherit and lead the next phase of the equality movement, understood this, and chose not to pursue a battle on the basis of the rightness of one group's racial views. He suggested that the only way to win a battle of relative rights with Whites, who had the authority and the wealth-but whose motives and ethics on race was highly tainted-was to appeal to an argument of moral integrity. Charles Hamilton Houston and Thurgood Marshall started the argument by asking, what is right and what is equitable? They were able to prove, through a "foundation of precedents," that segregation was neither, right nor equitable. That didn't end the argument.

What Dr. King did was take the question of equality to another level by asking, "What is just, and what does your conscience tell you?" In Houston's and Marshall's battles for equality, Whites knew in their heart of hearts that the black lawyers and activists were right, and the "separate but equal" was neither right, or ethically moral. The argument at that point, however, wasn't about what was right and what was moral. It was about what was legal, so rightness and morally, the correct answer, would never be admitted. Now that legality was no longer a point of contention, at least according to the Courts, and what was right was a matter of who asked the question, black or white, what was just became a very important turning point.

King forced segregationists to address the "justice" question, and the moral correctness of their position, by appealing, not to their ideology or logic, but to their conscience. Not just white people's conscience, but also black people's conscience. King's persona, as a leader was not singularly attributed to his ability to lead great protests, but in his intelligence with which he chose the grounds, timing, means, or issues that the protest would address, for which he is less appreciated. As King's influence on the fight for equality grew, so did the process of developing a general theory that would guide these considerations toward justice.[12]

The flaw in the segregationist's argument played to Dr. King's "revolution of conscience," in a way that the NAACP's legal campaign did not. For years, segregation was upheld as right, though it wasn't just. King's argument was that everything that appears right or fair seeming isn't just-but everything that is just will be right. Moral suasion shifted the discourse from what was right to what was just, and held all involved to be just in their actions, and to not only pursue what is right, but what is just. What panicked segregationists more than the legal activity of the NAACP was King's emphasis on direct action protest.

The NAACP has never been heavily involved in direct action (boycott) protest. In its near 100-year history, while often threatening to boycott companies, the NAACP, as a national organization, has been involved in less than a dozen direct action protests. The Southern Christian Leadership Conference, founded by King in 1957, was involved in more than a dozen direct action campaigns in its first six years of existence. Direct action, in the form of non-violent civil disobedience, to force desegregation, was a principle strategy in King's revolution of conscience. By making "White's do, what they knew in good conscience, was the moral and just thing to do," direct action tactics, in Montgomery (a campaign King did not initiate), in Birmingham and Selma (campaigns King did initiate) that created structural problems in discriminatory systems, that would bring about the collapse of either, segregation policies, or, the institutions that advanced them. In Montgomery, in was the bus system. In Birmingham, it was the Jim Crow structure. In Selma, it was the voting rolls.

In each instance, King operated within a general theory aimed toward justice, and in each instance, the targets of racially discriminatory behavior gave way to revolutionary structural change.[13] King had to often remind those in the movement that the fight wasn't about race, it was about justice. When four black students sat down at a Greensboro, North Carolina, Woolworth's segregated lunch counter in February of 1960, those four students "revolution of conscience," at one location, turned in a national movement throughout the South where students, black and white, joined, because Blacks right to eat at public lunch-counters was morally correct posture, and just.

The action of the four Greensboro brought another generation to the equality movement, as students were assaulted and arrested. Many of the white students were heckled worse than the black students. However, as the beginning of the modern "sit-in" movement began, some black students became anxious over what they saw as an increasing number of white student involvement. Conflicts around racial philosophies arose, as was the case during the freedom rides into the South to desegregate interstate travel, and during trips South to educate Southern Blacks on voting. The struggle was viewed, in very narrow terms, by some, in what was then seen as a fundamental black versus white, "Negro rights (later framed as "Black Power") against 'Whitey'," struggle. King admonished black student leaders "not to forget that the struggle was for justice versus injustice, not black versus white."[14]   This helped transition the fight for equality into a multiracial movement, because it allowed non-Blacks of goodwill and moral conscience to join the fight, in more than the advisory capacities that they had served in the NAACP's legal campaigns.

Another thing King did was take the focus off the biological and psychological differences between Blacks and Whites-whether one was human and the other was sub-human-and focused the argument the tenets that everyone was entitled to basic a human dignity. The humanity of the African American, while always implied, had never been the center of the argument for equality. King put the question to Whites, succinctly, "Aren't Negroes human?" "Doesn't the Negro deserve to receive the basic dignities afforded all throughout humanity?" Heretofore, Blacks had been allowed to be viewed outside the realms of humanity. King's revolution of conscience, and his politics of moral suasion, focused on the vilification of the African American through segregation's racial etiquette, and how that racial etiquette sought to demean the morale and self-esteem of Blacks in some very inhuman ways.

Moral suasion allowed King, and others, to reject the etiquette on the basis of Christian love, and non-violence, whereby, he was able to equate even "the least of God's children" as deserving of being treated with dignity and respect, and bring the humanity piece in a way that even the legal campaign for equality largely ignored until the very last days of its sociological arguments (that segregation cast a "long shadow of shame" on Blacks). King brought to fore the humanity of African Americans, as essential to viewing them as equals, his position being that one can't see Blacks as equal, if they can't see Blacks as human. The social status of Blacks, and the humanity of Blacks, were not separate propositions. They were one and the same. This was a basic value that King held all the way to his death.

The last campaign he was involved in was a labor strike over the treatment of Sanitation workers in Memphis, Tennessee, who were being treated as less than human, and being forced to work under less than human conditions. The one message that these mostly black men wanted to communicate to management, and with King's involvement-to the world, that they were, in fact, human. Each man walked the picket line with signs around their neck, not demanding equal wages, or unfair treatment, or poor working conditions. The signs, in four simple words, asserted humanity for 1,300 men. They simply read , "I AM A MAN."

That message, in and of itself, went to the very psychology of the equality movement. The Courts could equalize Blacks all they wanted. Congress could (and would) legislate equality all they wanted. Blacks could demand equality all they wanted, but if Whites, as individuals and in the collective, as institutions, as systems, as politic, as a dominate cultural society, didn't see Blacks as equal, and didn't treat them any differently before the law had changed-what would be the gain to Blacks to have every benefit that Whites had, and still be treated inhumanly? It became obvious to King that Whites were not just resisting the change in law-they were resisting the change in the racial etiquette that allowed them to treat African Americans any kind of way they wanted to treat them. The hatred that was spewed at black children, at black teachers, at Blacks, who now engaged Whites on a desegregated basis, clearly stated that desegregation was more than about Blacks intermixing in their societies. Whites, in segregated communities, had come to despise Blacks, in ways that the racial etiquette had allowed them to indiscriminately revile them. Changing that mindset would take more than a court order, or public policy legislation. It would take changing the moral composition of the white mind that inherently believed that the years of black servitude, and subordination, that de jure segregation forced upon Blacks for their benefits, was not an error in legal judgment, but an error in spiritual judgment.

James Weldon Johnson, and later Roy Wilkins, used to say that they were in the business of "saving black folks' hides and white folks' soul." Well, Dr. Martin Luther King, Jr., in attacking the conscience of the moral and spiritual judgment of the backers and sympathizers of white supremacy, went after the souls of white folk. The politics of moral suasion was the most valiant effort, to date, to appeal to the moral conscience of the mass indifference of the majority of white Americans that turned their heads as Blacks were inhumanly denied equality, and received massive privileges and benefits from their societal subjugation.

274

On a couple of occasions, King extended himself beyond the social justice question, to expound deeply and profoundly on the humanity question. Some of King's most articulate engagements in the politics of moral suasion centered around challenging the conscience of the white majority to look, beyond the racial constrictions of societal perspectives of the Negro in the South, into the deeper rationalization of why Blacks needed to be supported, in the attainment of their equality rights as viewed on a very basic humanity level. While King was jailed in desegregation protests in Birmingham, Alabama in April of 1963, he wrote a letter to the clergy who suggested that King was an outside agitator who was moving "too fast" on the question of segregation. In "Letter from a Birmingham Jail," King addressed the conditions Blacks faced in society as an indictment on America, calling into question both the conscience and moral judgment of his fellow clergy essentially in two paragraphs;

We know through painful experience that freedom is never voluntarily given by the oppressor; it must be demanded by the oppressed. Frankly, I have never yet engaged in a direct action movement that was "well-timed," according to the timetable of those who have not suffered unduly from the disease of segregation.

For years now I have heard the word, "Wait!" It rings in the ear of every Negro with a piercing familiarity. This "Wait" had almost always meant "Never." It has been a tranquilizing thalidomide, relieving the emotional stress for a moment, only to give birth to an ill-formed infant of frustration. We must come to see with the distinguished jurist of yesterday that "justice too long delayed is justice denied." We have waited for more than 340 years for our constitutional and God-given rights.

The nations of Asia and Africa are moving with jetlike speed tpward the goal of political independence, and we still creep at horse and buggy pace toward the gaining of a cup of coffee at a lunch counter. I guess it is easy for those who have never felt the stinging darts of segregation to say, "Wait."

But when you have seen vicious mobs lynch your mothers and fathers at will, and drown your sisters and brothers at whim; when you have seen hated filled policeman curse, kick, brutalize and even kill your black brothers and sisters with impunity; when you see the vast majority of your twenty million Negro brothers smothering in an airtight cage of poverty in the midst of an affluent society; when you suddenly find your tongue twisted and your speech stammering as you seek to explain to your six-year-old daughter why she can't go to the public amusement park that has just been advertised on television, and see tears welling up in her little eyes when she is told that Funtown is closed to colored children, and see the depressing clouds of inferiority begin to form in her little mental sky, and see her begin to distort her little personality by unconsciously developing a bitterness toward white people; when you have to concoct an answer for a five-year old son asking in agonizing pathos: "Daddy, why do white people treat colored people so mean?"; when you take a cross-country drive and find it necessary to sleep night after night in the uncomfortable corners of your automobile because no motel will accept you; when you are humiliated day in and day out by nagging signs reading "white" and "colored"; when your first name becomes "nigger" and your middle name becomes "boy" (however old you are) and your last name becomes "John," and when your wife and mother are never given the respected title of "Mrs."; when you are harried by day and haunted by night by the fact that you are a Negro, living constantly at tiptoe stance never quite knowing what to expect next, and plagued with inner fears and outer resentments; when you are forever fighting a degenerating sense of "nobodiness"; then you will understand why we find it difficult to wait. There comes a time when the cup of endurance runs over, and men are no longer willing to be plunged into an abyss of injustice where they experience the blackness of corroding despair.

I hope, sirs, you can understand our legitimate and unavoidable impatience.
You express a great deal of anxiety over our willingness to break laws. This is certainly a legitimate concern. Since we so diligently urge people to obey the Supreme Court's decision of 1954 outlawing segregation in the public schools, it is rather strange and paradoxical to find us consciously breaking laws. One may well ask, "How can you advocate breaking some laws and obeying others?" The answer is found in the fact that there are two types of laws: there are just laws and there are unjust laws. I would agree with Saint Augustine that "An unjust law is no law at all."[15]

King was able to articulate the inhumane conditions of "being black" in America, in ways that the decorum of the courts didn't afford, and the sanctity of church accommodated. In announcing the Birmingham protests were successful, in desegregating all public facilities from rest rooms, lunch counters to fitting rooms to drinking fountains, King remarked that "Nothing has so stirred the conscience of this nation as this Birmingham movement. I can think of nothing, and I say this as one who has been in several struggles for freedom over the past few years. And I have never seen people as aroused over any struggle that we have had... " These "separate but equal" conditions had sustained for 67 years after America had re-slaved Blacks with the *Plessy* decision, and King would go back even farther than that to articulate again, before 250,000 marchers, and a nationally televised audience, how America had avoided the question of equality for Blacks. King stated that freedom and equality in America had amounted to little more than a broken promise. Nobody ever remembers that he said that-all, instead choosing to remember that he said, he "had a dream," and America was prepared to deal with King as long as his call for equality remained just a dream. As he delivered, what will forever be known as, the "*I Have A Dream*" speech, Dr. King was actually laying out for America the litany of failed promises made to Blacks.

The thought behind the "*Broken Promise*" (*I Have A Dream*) speech was that America had not taken seriously the conditions and circumstances that it had placed on African Americans, and was still resisting the guarantees of freedom, justice and equality that it had promised 100 years earlier. Again, King calls into question the conscience and moral judgment of America, only this time he also calls into question America character, stating that he "dreamed" that one day America would live up to "the true meaning of its creed." Still, the first five paragraphs of the speech is a factual study in admonition and caution. Introduced by march organizer, Asa Philip Randolph, as "the moral leader of our nation," Dr. Martin Luther King, JR (Randolph's emphasis) began his speech calling their assembly the "greatest demonstration for freedom in the history of our nation," then exacted his critic on America's continuing assault on Negro rights, stating;

Five score years ago, a great American, in whose symbolic shadow we stand today, signed the Emancipation Proclamation. This momentous decree came as a great beacon light of hope to million of Negro slaves who had been seared in the flames of withering injustice. It came as a joyous daybreak to end the long night of captivity.

But one hundred years later, we must face the tragic fact that the Negro is still not free. One hundred years later, the life of the Negro is still sadly crippled by the manacles of segregation and the chains of discrimination. One hundred years later, the Negro lives on a lonely island of poverty in the midst of a vast ocean of material prosperity. One hundred years later, the Negro is still languishing in the corners of American society and finds himself an exile in his own land. So we have come here today to dramatize an appalling condition.

In a sense we have come to our nation's capital to cash a check. When the architects of our republic wrote the magnificent words of the Constitution and the Declaration of Independence, they were signing a promissory note to which every American was to fall heir. This note was a promise that all men would be guaranteed the inalienable rights of life, liberty, and the pursuit of happiness.

It is obvious today that America has defaulted on this promissory note insofar as her citizens of color are concerned. Instead of honoring this sacred obligation, America has given the Negro people a bad check which has come back marked "insufficient funds." But we refuse to believe that the bank of justice is bankrupt. We refuse to believe that there are insufficient funds in the great vaults of opportunity of this nation. So we have come to cash this check-a check that will give us upon demand the riches of freedom and the security of justice. We have also come to this hallowed spot to remind America of the fierce urgency of now. This is no time to engage in the luxury of cooling off or to take the tranquilizing drug of gradualism. Now is the time to open the doors of opportunity to all of God's children. Now is the time to lift our nation from the quicksands of racial injustice to the solid rock of brotherhood.

It would be fatal for the nation to overlook the urgency of the moment and to underestimate the determination of the Negro. This swelter-

ing summer of the Negro's legitimate discontent will not pass until there is an invigorating autumn of freedom and equality. Nineteen sixty-three is not an end, but a beginning. Those who hope that the Negro needed to blow off steam and will now be content will have a rude awakening if the nation returns to business as usual. There will be neither rest nor tranquility in America until the Negro is granted his citizenship rights. The whirlwinds of revolt will continue to shake the foundations of our nation until the bright day of justice emerges.[16]

Nowhere, in the first two-thirds of King's speech, did he mention anything about a dream. Not until the eleventh paragraph of the speech, did King back off, and suggest that he still held out hope that America would change its resistance posture, and he had to frame it in the context of 'eyes closed," not eyes wide open.

King's politics of moral suasion had a profound impact on the public discourse in 1963. The year of the March on Washington, questionably, was the most volatile year of the Civil Rights Movement. After his speech on the March on Washington, King had clearly pricked the conscience of America. President John F. Kennedy had remained quiet on the issues of civil rights, for the first two years of his administration, after hinting that he, somehow, had a greater sensitivity to the plight of Blacks, than Nixon in the 1960 Presidential elections, when he called King's wife, Coretta, after Dr. King had been jailed in Atlanta while participating in lunch counter sit-ins.

Yet it wasn't until February 28th, 1963 that Kennedy sent to Congress his first message devoted exclusively to civil rights, in which he gave credence to King's politics of moral suasion in the part of his message devoted to education. Kennedy said, "Nearly nine years have elapsed since the Supreme Court ruled that state laws requiring or permitting segregated schools violate the Constitution. That decision represented both good law and good judgment-it was both legally and morally right..."[17] Kennedy sent the first serious civil rights bill in the 20th Century, one with federal enforcement powers, to Capitol Hill on June 19, 1963 that, in addition to the voting rights he had called for in February, called for equal accommodations in public facilities, the grant of authority to the Attorney General to initiate school desegregation suits, new programs to assure fair employment (including support for the Fair Employment Practices Commission), the establishment of a Community Relations Service, and a provision authorizing the federal government to withhold funds for programs or activities in which discrimination occurred.[18]

President Kennedy then exhorted "moral leadership" on the race issue, by going on television and challenging the American people to live up to the promise of "American ideals" by posing the following questions; "If an American, because his skin is dark, cannot eat lunch in a restaurant open to the public, if he cannot send his children to the best public school available, if he cannot vote for the public officials who represent him, if in short, he cannot enjoy the full and free life which all of us want, then who among us would be content to have the color of his skin changed, and stand in his place? Who among us would then be content with the counsels of patience and delay?" Kennedy concluded, "We preach freedom around the world, and we mean it, and we cherish our freedom here at home; but are we to say to the world and, much more importantly, to each other that this is a land of the free except for the Negroes; that we have no class or caste system, no ghettos, no master race, except with respect to Negroes?"[19] King directly influenced Kennedy's mindset by challenging him to bring a moral authority to the government's position on the question of racial equality. Though he would never live to see it accomplished, Kennedy used his position as President, as no President ever had, to "establish a moral leadership to provide equality of education in all sections of the United States."[20] King had shifted the whole nation's thought, from just focusing on the "legal" obligation, to focusing on the nation's legal *and* moral obligations.

Vice President Lyndon Johnson, a Southerner who had never voted for a civil rights bill before 1957, when in his role as Senate majority Leader-he facilitated watered down bills in 1957 and in 1960-began to change his views, while in the Kennedy administration, giving an indication of what type of President he would be on civil rights. In the spring of 1963, at Gettysburg, Pennsylvania, Johnson gave a speech that many called "the second Gettysburg Address" in which he expressed dissatisfaction with the slow pace of the Negro's struggle against "injustice and inequality" stating, "Until justice is blind to color, until education is unaware of race, until opportunity is unconcerned with the color of men's skins, emancipation will be a proclamation, but not a fact...The Negro today asks justice; We do not answer him-we do not answer those who lie beneath this soil-when we reply to the Negro by asking, 'Patience.'"[21] Johnson obviously had been paying attention to the public discourse, in which the most compelling moral arguments for equality and justice were being made by this "revolution of conscience." Lyndon Johnson, as had many Whites during this heightened period of massive resistance, knew that resisting equality wasn't the right and moral thing to do. He could see segregationists' mouths moving, but Johnson was listening to his conscience.

Even former President Dwight Eisenhower, who had never given an endorsement to the *Brown* decision while he was in office, in October of 1963, for the first time gave his personal endorsement to the *Brown* decision three years after he left office based on King's moral suasion argument, stating, "I believe the decision expressed the intentions of our Constitution, and therefore is morally and legally correct."[22] King had gotten to the core of what he called, " this nation's 'schizophrenia,'" the duality of conduct that allowed America to separate people on superior, and inferior qualities, while evoking the democratic spirit of "equality," which caused the country to go back and forth, on the question of racial justice.[23] This was a period in which the politics of equality, its rationale and reasoning, went beyond the courts, beyond the halls of the Congress, and beyond the confines of the Oval Office. The politics of equality were no longer being discussed on legal grounds. The politics of equality were being discussed on moral grounds.

A new black leadership emerged that went beyond trying to intellectualize equality on the basis of subjective merits and demerits. The focus changed from the legality of policies to the ethics of methodologies, and the people behind the methodologies, that sought to cheat African Americans out of equality, despite the fact that the law was now on their side. The emphasis changed from freedom to justice, as it because obvious that white supremacists were not prepared to let Blacks go free to pursue opportunities on a desegregated basis. As the resistance became more violent, the moral arguments became louder, just as the more wrong one does, the louder their conscience speaks out to them-and the harder it becomes to ignore that voice in one's head. The politics of moral suasion had become America's conscience. Martin Luther King, Jr. had become the voice in America's head that became louder and louder, as massive resistance became more stubborn and violent. The more violent massive resistance became, the louder protestation became, and the harder it became to get King's voice out of America's head. King had become synonymous with moral suasion, and his direct action campaigns had become a nagging reminder of the law-breaking that was taking place in the South. The very presence of the marches, and the sit-ins, and the freedom rides represented America's conscience sitting on its shoulder, getting louder and louder and louder and louder, until America couldn't take it anymore.

Some parts of America would give in to the politics of moral suasion, while other parts of America would continue to resist. This revolution of conscience, this moral struggle with rightness and justice would continue over the next few years, in the face of greater social unrest. And the voices of conscience would only multiply. In a last desperate attempt to silence the voices in its head, America would commit the ultimate sin and try to eliminate, one by one, the voices of change. The assassinations wouldn't stop until, at last, it killed the voice of moral suasion and the leader of the greatest social change movement in its history. On April 4, 1968, America killed its conscience, just as he was preparing a march for basic dignity of sanitation workers. The mantra of the march…*I AM A MAN.*

The politics of moral suasion, while occasionally invoked, died soon thereafter, but before it died-it gave rise to federal legislation, discussed in the next chapter, that brought forth the full and complete death of segregation.

281

11

Legislating Change:
Federal Acts and the Politics of Forced Integration

"It should be clear by now that a nation can be no stronger abroad than she is at home. Only an America which practices what it preaches about equal rights and social justice will be respected by those whose choice affects our future."

-President John F. Kennedy, Undelivered luncheon
speech, Dallas, Texas, November 22, 1963

"You can't legislate integration, but you can certainly legislate desegregation. You can't legislate morality, but you can regulate behavior. You can't make a man love me, but the law can restrain him from lynching me."

- Martin Luther King, Jr.

Moral suasion had first began to see its decline, in the summer of 1963, after President John F. Kennedy introduced a civil rights bill, to facilitate desegregation plans in the South, and to give authority to the federal government, in instances when the states and local governments resisted the law. The bill was the result of recommendations that came from all six members of the Commission on Civil Rights, appointed during the Eisenhower administration, who urged Kennedy, in April of 1963, to "explore his legal authority" to withhold all federal funds -not just federal funds to segregated schools, but to the states that continue to resist desegregation, and subvert the Constitution.[1] While the Commission had recommended, on a previous occasion, to withhold federal grants, and aid to colleges and universities practicing

Leader of the Nation of Islam, The Honorable Elijah Muhammad, lifted the urban disenfranchised with a cultural spirituality that changed the black church forever. Abandoning the notion of a white god, heaven after death and deference to white people, Muhammad's spiritual message included a black pride message of "know thy self," "love your own and be yourself," and an economic message of "do for self" produced a "black nation. The Nation of Islam became black America's leading reformer of incarcerated black men and the drug afflicted. Photo courtesy of the Mayme Clayton Library Collection

The fiery oratory of Malcolm X, right, took America by storm, gaining national attention for his critiques of both white ambivalence and civil rights resistance to violence. Malcolm warned that the conditions of the inner cities would produce riots, and "prophets of rage" that would force the nation to take notice and that Blacks should protect themselves against white aggression "By any means necessary."
Photo courtesy of the Mayme Clayton Library Collection

Elijah Muhammad's national spokespersons, Malcolm X and later, Louis X (later known as Louis Farrakhan) offered the most critical assessments of black inequality in the fifty years since *Brown*. Farrakhan succeeded Malcolm as the Nation's national representative, and became a global voice for the oppressed in his own right when he resurrected the Nation of Islam in 1976.
Photo courtesy of the Mayme Clayton Library Collection

John F. Kennedy arrives in Dallas, Texas on the morning of November 22, 1963, telling the city greeters that it was time for the nation to consider equal rights for the Negro. Later that morning, Kennedy, while waving to the crowd on a parade route, would be assassinated.

Photo courtesy of the Mayme Clayton Library Collection

In his first public speech to the nation, as President of the United States, Lyndon Johnson seeks to calm a grieving nation by telling a joint session of Congress that "No memorial oration or eulogy could more eloquently honor President Kennedy's memory than the earliest possible passage of the civil rights bill for which he fought so long. We have talked long enough in this country about equal rights. We have talked for one hundred years, or more. It is now time to write the next chapter--and to write it in the books of law."

Photo courtesy of the Mayme Clayton Library Collection

Senator Hubert Humphrey was credited with steering the 1964 Civil Rights bill through a Senate, armed with the filibuster in one hand, and a Southern Manifesto in the other. His success carried favor with President Johnson, who was set to reward him with the Vice Presidential at the 1964 Atlantic City Democratic. However, Johnson threatened to take it away if Humphrey didn't resolve a floor fight between white Mississippi party delegates and the black delegates of the Mississippi Democratic Freedom Party led by Fannie Lou Hamer. While no compromise was reached, Humphrey did become Vice President. Photo courtesy of the Mayme Clayton Library Collection

By August of 1963 , the nation was now aware that social change was in full swing. "Equal Rights" was, at last, on the national domestic agenda. Key in rising the public debate of what Blacks in America were experiencing was black America's first international literary figure, James Baldwin, center right, whose book *The Fire Next Time*, released in 1963, was called the most important literary work of the period. The celebrity support for the cause was well documented as Charleston Heston, Harry Belafonte and Marlon Brando join Baldwin at the March on Washington. Many other celebrities also present included Sammy Davis, Jr., Sidney Portier, Diane Carroll and Mahalia Jackson.

Photo courtesy of the Mayme Clayton Library

The "Mighty March" also drew nationwide support of persons from every walk of life. At left, 14 year old, William Tyrone Pugh (Chinn), and co-activist, Florese Harris, traveled from Jackson, Mississippi to join the nation's largest civil rights demonstration. *Life Magazine* analogized Pugh's overalled presence in this photo, as reflecting a "Negro Gothic," reminiscent of the famous Grant Wood painting, representative of the agrarian populism that speaks to being equals in American society. Photo courtesy of personal collection of Inetta Elmore Chinn.

A. Philip Randolph, left, and Bayard Rustin, far left, organized what was considered the defining moment of the Civil Rights Era, the March on Washington in August of 1963. Randolph pulled this 20 year plan off the shelf. A similar march to protest job discrimination in the federal government had been planned for June, 1941. A week before march, President Roosevelt issued Executive Order 8802, the nation's first anti-discrimination bill and Randolph called off the march. Photo courtesy of the Mayme Clayton Library Collection

Martin Luther King, Jr. was the keynote speaker for 1963 march, and this moment in time propelled him into immortality, as the curator of America's modern social change movement. King became the only third person in American history, and the only person in the 20th Century to have a national holiday named in his honor. Photo courtesy of the Mayme Clayton Library Collection

Fannie Lou Hamer demands equality for the black delegates of the Mississippi Democratic Freedom Party (MDFP), as they storm the floor of the 1964 Democratic National Convention. Twenty-two delegates sat in the vacated seats of the white Mississippi delegation after white delegates left the Convention, when President Johnson demanded they sign a loyalty pledge to support him. The convention's Sergent-at-Arms had the members of the MDFP physically removed but not before the national media heard their concerns. Photo courtesy of the Mayme Clayton Library Collection

The third Selma March to Montgomery, after two attempts, in March, 1965, was, by and large, viewed as the "Last Hurrah" for the King led Civil Rights Movement. Selma focused the on voter disfranchisement in the South, and led to what President Johnson called his proudest achievment, the 1965 Voting Rights Act. Photo courtesy of the Mayme Clayton Library Collection.

Floyd McKissick, head of the Congress of Racial Equality, Dr. Martin Luther King, Jr., head of the Southern Christian Leadership Conference, and Stokely Carmichael, head of the Student Non-Violent Coordinating Committee hold a press conference on the news that James Meredith holding a one man march in Mississippi had been shot in June of 1966. The movement had taken a more militant tone when the volatile McKissick took over for the moderate James Farmer, and the fiery Carmichael replaced John Lewis, as president of SNCC. Carmichael's call for "Black Power" agitated King, who said the term was a precipatant to violence. Photo courtesy of the Mayme Clayton Library Collection

Watts, California explodes after a police assault on motorist Marquette Frye at 116th and Avalon (in the city of Los Angeles) caused an estimated 35,000 "active" rioters to take to the streets. 34 people died, 1,000 were injured, 4,000 were arrested. Watts was the first major city revolt of over 150 urban riots that would occur between 1965 and 1968. Photo courtesy of the Mayme Clayton Library Collection

The National Guard's 40th armored division was called in with "live ammunition" on the fourth day of the riot to confront rioters. The rioting took place from August 11 to 18th, 1965, most of it under state order curfews. Photo courtesy of the Mayme Clayton Library Collection

The Watts Riots covered a 46.5 square mile area and destroyed 261 building causing an estimated $200 million in damages. Few homes, churches and libraries were damaged supporting the contention that the Watts Uprising was conscious insurrection. Photo courtesy of the Mayme Clayton Library Collection

The Watts Revolt was caused by years of social and economic neglect. Looting was widespread as many rioters sought to vandelize local merchants of materials that they couldn't afford or simply had been denied by virtue of their economic circumstances. The overhead shot above reflects the chaos in the streets while the shot on the right shows looters escaping with stolen goods. Photos courtesy of the Mayme Clayton Library Collection

Dr. Martin Luther King, Jr. and Bayard Rustin have a heated exchange with the frustrated residents of Watts, where angry speakers shouted him down when he couldn't provide anwers to their questions. King left Watts committed to change the conditions in the urban cities. Photo courtesy of the Mayme Clayton Library Collection

By 1966, the "Pro-black Radical Movement" was in full effect as Stokely Carmichael began to tie black empowerment philosophy to the more global issues of Pan Africanism. Carmichael eventually left SNCC, changed his name to Kwame Ture', and formed the All African People's Revoluntary Party, where the cry shifted from "Black Power" to "Power to the People" and "Ready for the Revolution." Seated is poet/playright, Leroi Jones, who became Amiri Baraka. Photo courtesy of the Mayme Clayton Library Collection

West Coast radicalism was split between the "revolutionary militants" (the Black Panthers), who demanded control of black neighborhoods (social, economic and political realities) and "cultural militants" (the US Organization), who demanded cultural centered beliefs that rejected eurocentric influences responsible for corrupting and oppressing Africans in America. At right, UCLA Professor Angela Davis leds a protest on the steps of the Marin County Courthouse in defense of Soledad Brothers. Below, Maulana "Ron" Karenga, Chairman of the US Organization, hold a press conference with East Coast Activist, H. Rap Brown and Comedian/Activist, Dick Gregory.

Photos courtesy of the Mayme Clayton Library Collection

In April, 1967, Elijah Muhammad advises his most famous convert, heavyweight world boxing champion, Muhammad Ali. Ali had refused indiction into the U.S. armed services on the basis that he was a consciencious objecter to the Viet Nam War on religoius grounds. Ali became the symbol of black defience, anti-conformity and cultural pride for a new generation that became known as the "Black Power" movement. His subsequent vindication endeared him to millions, as Ali twice regained his heavyweight tile. Ali became the most recognizable person in the world, and by the end of the 20th Century, had gained icon status. Muhammad Ali was selected by several polls and magazines as the most significant sports figure of the last 100 years. Photo courtesy of the Mayme Clayton Library Collection

Thurgood Marshall, as Solicitor General, gave the go ahead for the government to prosecute Ali the same spring he was nominated for the Supreme Court. President Johnson later told Marshall that putting him on the high Court "lost him the South," and caused him a chance at re-election. Marshall's 24 years on the U.S. Supreme Court was a distinguished career that earned him the title as "the Court's conscience." Photo courtesy of the Mayme Clayton Library Collection

NAACP Executive Secretary, Roy Wilkins opposed the direct action mass protest of Martin Luther King and SCLC. After King's death, Wilkins lost control of the movement as the focus of the equality struggle shifted toward the younger activists. This began the decline of the influence of the NAACP as prime mover in the civil rights arena.Photo courtesy of the Mayme Clayton Library Collection

Congressman Adam Clayton Powell, Jr. became a symbol of "black power" within America's political system, as chairmen of the powerful House Education and Labor Committee. On January 9, 1967, the House Democratic Causus voted to strip Powell of his committeeship, cencure him and deny him his seat in Congress, on misappropriate charges. Powell said his colleagues' charges were racially motivated, and that many of them had done what he was accused of, and he sued the Congress. The Supreme Court restored his seat two years later but not his chairmanship, senority and back pay. Photo courtesy of the Mayme Clayton Library Collection

The Warren Supreme Court, here with Thurgood Marshall, is credited as being the most activist court in the 20th Century, redefining individual Constitutional rights for minorities, women, the accused, workers, and institutional rights for corporations, schools and government.

Photo courtesy of the Mayme Clayton Library Collection

In 1966, the Southern Christian Leadership Conference rolled out its urban economic development initiative called "Operation Breadbasket." King felt that the urban equality problem was a function of years of economic subjugation, and that jobs was the only solution to the urban crisis. The program's first director was a young Chicago based activist named the Reverend Jesse Jackson, Sr. Jackson ran the SCLC Operation for three and a half years after King's death, before leaving to start his own organization, People United to Save Humanity, or what became known as Operation PUSH.

Photo courtesy of the Mayme Clayton Library Collection

Dr. Martin Luther King, left, arrives to lead a march for the dignity of sanitation workers in Memphis, Tennessee on March 28th, 1968. The march was discontinued when violence broke out. When King returned to lead a second march a week later, he was assasinated. His wife, Coretta Scott King, and a national delegation of activists and dignitaries, below, returned to Memphis to lead King's last march, a peaceful march on April 8th, the day before King took his final march in a mule drawn wagon to be laid to rest in Atlanta. Photos courtesy of the Mayme Clayton Library Collection

Angela Davis heightened the Pro-Black Radical Movement's socio-political activities by becoming an international fugutive, after being charged with aiding a prison break that killed four people at the Marin County (CA) Courthouse. Davis, then America's most vocal advocate for political prisoners, befriended Soladad Brother, Jonathan Jackson, who attempted to escape and free another prisoner while in court. The guns used in the jail break attempt were registered to Davis. Davis, charged with murder, kidnapping and conspiracy, went underground in 1970 and immediately became one of the FBI's 10 Most Wanted Fugitives. When she captured in a motel room in New York (above), it set off nationwide protests to "Free Angela" on college campuses around the nation. Photo courtesy of the Mayme Clayton Library Collection

Davis was imprisoned for 18 months while she stood trial, at times defending herself. Though Davis wasn't at the courthouse, the government claimed that Davis had muggled the guns to Jackson during visits, hiding the weapons in her famous "Afro" hairdo (left). Davis was eventually acquitted of all charges. Photo courtesy of the Mayme Clayton Library Collection

King's death brought on an intensified national debate as to whether non-violence was still the most appropriate remedy to achieve racial equality in America. At right, Huey P. Newton, Chairman of the Black Panther Party for Self Defense, makes his point in an interview British broadcaster, David Frost.
Photo courtesy of the Mayme Clayton Library Collection

The Civil Rights Movement, as volatile as it was, brought about black power of a different type, as Edward W. Brooke, in November of 1966, became the first black to serve in the United States Senate since Reconstruction. Brooke was also the first Black to be popularly elected to the Senate in U.S. history. Though Massachusetts was only six percent black, Brooke election was viewed as a changing of the tide in America's political landscape as whites chose Brooke over a white incumbent. Photo courtesy of the Mayme Clayton Library Collection

Barbara Jordan of Texas, along with Andrew Young of Georgia, in 1972, became the first blacks elected to the Congress from the deep South since late Reconstruction. Jordan was the first black woman ever to serve in the U.S. Congress, as well as the first woman ever to serve in the Texas State Senate. Jordan keynoted the 1976 Democratic Convention. Photo courtesy of the Mayme Clayton Library Collection

Tommie Smith, left and John Carlos, right, put the United States' politics of inequality on the world's stage, during the national anthem, while accepting their gold and silver medals at the 1968 Olympic Games in Mexico City. This stand against racial oppression, in the aftermath of the King assassination, was seen as a "political act" by Olympic officials that caused both Smith and Carlos to be banned for life from the Olympic Games. However, it represented a signal that the freedom struggle was still alive in America. Smith and Carlos' act of defiance was a statement seen worldwide, and is now considered one of the Olympic Games "Most Memorable Moments."
Photo courtesy of the Mayme Clayton Library Collection

In 1969, St. Louis Cardinal All-Star, Curt Flood, right, fought for wage equality in sports when he challenged Major League Baseball's Reserve Clause, also called "the Slave Clause" because it allowed team owners to own players for life. Flood was blackballed but his stand led to players being free to play for whomever, and for however much, they wanted, owning their own services. Flood is considered the father of Free Agency.
Photo courtesy of the Judy Pace Flood Collection

Rev. Jesse Jackson, head of the newly formed People United to Save Humanity (Operation PUSH) is arrested in a Chicago protest march, in late 1971, as the pro-black radical demonstrations, and racial equality protests dominated the civil rights movement in early 1970s. Photo courtesy of the Mayme Clayton Library Collection

President Richard Nixon, shown here at a White House Gala featuring Duke Ellington, often "zigged" with Blacks, in pretending to support black equality, while he zagged with conservatives to marginalize federal programs and stigmatize "black protesters" as "criminals." Though Nixon resigned in disgrace, his policies as President started the demise of affirmative action. Photo courtesy of the Mayme Clayton Library Collection

James Forman, a SNCC activist, appeared before the general assembly of United Presbyterian Church's national convention in San Antonio, Texas, to demand reparations for Blacks from the nation's religions in May of 1969. Called the "Black Manifesto," the demand called for white Christian Churches and Jewish Synagogues to "reimburse" the black community $500 million, for past racial justices. While reparations was denied, many churches gave thousands of dollars to the National Black Economic Development Conference to rectify the social ills of the inner cities of America, including $200,000 from the Episcopal Church's House of Deputies and $15,000 from the Washington Square United Methodist Church. Photo courtesy of the Mayme Clayton Library Collection

One of Nixon's favorite domestic "self help" programs was Rev. Leon Sullivan's "Philadelphia Plan" that called for training of urban unemployed and youth, then giving them jobs. Founded as the Opportunities Industrialization Centers (OIC), Nixon supported it because of its "bootstrap" philosophy. Sullivan later developed corporate guidelines for doing business in South Africa. Photo courtesy of the Mayme Clayton Library Collection

The Poor People's March was King's effort to focus the nation on the sheer effects of poverty in America. Scheduled to launch on May 1, 1968, King didn't live to see this effort come to reality. The campaign went off as planned, and set up a shanty town on the Capitol Mall. The town was called Resurrection City and it represented a protest site for the poor and oppressed for several days before President Lyndon Johnson had it shut down Photo courtesy of the Mayme Clayton Library Collection

The Civil Right Era ended in racial strife in the early 1970s, as the U.S. Supreme Court permitted forced integration to put an end to the last remnants of Massive Resistance. Busing led to large protests and racially inspired confrontations, even in Northern cities, such as this attack in the city of Boston in 1976. Photo courtesy of the Mayme Clayton Library Collection

The election of Jimmy Carter was largely attributed to the work of former King aide, Andrew Young, who was the first black from Georgia elected to Congress since Reconstruction in 1972. Young rallied a battleworn and distrusting black electorate behind Carter and was rewarded with an appointment as U.S. Ambassador to the U.N. Young was later forced to resign after it was disclosed that he had met with PLO leader, Yasser Arafat. Young went on to become Mayor of Atlanta. Photo courtesy of the Mayme Clayton Library Collection

President Ronald Reagan was the first President to actively deconstruct the gains of the Civil Rights Movement, by defunding and dismantling social programs, attempting to give tax credits to Bob Jones University for abandoning its affirmative action program, and putting three conservative justices on the U.S. Supreme Court. Reagan did sign the Martin Luther King Holiday Day bill in 1983, but black unemployment was higher under Reagan than under any President since the Great Depression. The policy agenda had such an adverse effect on the black community that it produced the first serious challenge by an African American for President of the United States in the Rev. Jesse Jackson in 1984. Although Reagan won all 50 States, Jackson electrified the nation by raising issues for the poor and disenfranchised, and registered over one million new voters. In 1988, Jackson ran again under a "Rainbow Coalition" banner, won several state primaries, gained over 1,200 delegates and registered over two million voters. Despite demands to put Jackson on the presidential ticket as second place finisher, Presidential nominee, Michael Dukakis selected Senator Lloyd Benson. Photo courtesy of the Mayme Clayton Library

Former Massachusetts Governor Michael Dukakis attended a 1988 summit with Rev. Jackson, but continued to ignore Jackson, as a serious running mate. Dukakis was subsequently defeated by George H.W. Bush when the Bush Campaign engaged in racial symbolism, running the infamous Willie Horton campaign that made an issue over a Dukakis prisoner release program. Photo courtesy of the Mayme Clayton Library

Clarence Thomas became the second African American to sit on the U.S. Supreme Court, when he replaced Thurgood Marshall in 1991. Viewed as part of the new Conservatives' "Color-blind" philosophy, Thomas' race-neutral perspective has contributed to the demise of many of the legal victories of the Civil Rights Movement. Justice Thomas, whose confirmation hearings gained national attention, due to sexual harass-ment allegations, escaped what he called a "high tech lynching," with the closest Senate confirmation vote in U.S. history. He has consistently been the fifth vote of the Court's conservative majority over the course of his 13 year tenure. Photo cour-tesy of the Mayme Clayton Library Collection

Carol Moseley-Braun was elected ithe fourth Black in history, and the first African American woman to serve in the U.S. Senate in November, 1992, a year called the "Year of the Woman." An unprecedented number of women were elected to the U.S. House and Senate after the nation watched an all male Senate Judiciary Committee cross-ex-amine Anita Hill during the Clarence Thomas confirmation hearings. Moseley-Braun ran against and defeated two-tern Democratic Senator, Alan Dixon, who voted to confirm Thomas and thus was targeted by women for defeat. She was defeated in November, 1998 by conser-vative Republican Peter Fitzgerald, and resurfaced for a brief run for President in early 2004. Photo courtesy of the Mayme Clayton Library Collection

One era begins as another era ends. Above, Clarence Thomas confirms his investiture as Marshall's successor, under the watchful eye of Chief Justice William Rehnquist (far right). Rehnquist, now one of the nation's longest sitting Chief Justices, resides over a divided Court with more 5-4 votes in history.The Rehnquist Court, after the Thomas appointment, shifted the Supreme Court firmly to the right and became the legal defender of the conservative's individual rights movement. Below, Thurgood Marshall makes one of his last public speeches at Independence Hall on July 4, 1992 in which he asked the audience to "Knock down the fences that divide...Tear apart the walls that imprison...Reach out; freedom lies just on the other side." In the background is federal judge A. Leon Higginbotham, Jr., who became the voice of black America legal rights after Marshall's death. Judge Higginbotham writings on racial politics and the legal system in the 1990s included *An Open Letter To Clarence Thomas from a Federal Judicial Colleague (1991)* that was a lesson on judicial scholarship, judicial fairness and race responsibility. He also headed the national search committee to find a new Executive Director for the NAACP in 1996. Photos courtesy of the Mayme Clayton Library Collection

AMATEUR VIDEO
MAR. 3 1991

Just when America felt that racial turmoil had subsided, the Rodney King beating shocked the nation, and brought attention to the type of hidden abuses black America were now experiencing. The beating exposed a new trend of police abuse, and misconduct that had surfaced in urban cities during the 1980s and 1990s, and a new debate as to whether black Americans could receive equal protection under law in the Post Civil Rights Era. Photo courtesy of the Mayme Clayton Library Collection

Four of the twenty eight officers present at the above scene were charged with using excessive abuse under the collar of authority against Rodney King, left. A highly racialized criminal trial took place in the nearly all white suburb of Simi Valley. The four officers were found not guilty, causing riots in Los Angeles for the second time in 26 years. King was brought out to calm the masses, in which he spoke his famous line, "Can't we all just get along." Two of the officers were later found guilty, and sent to jail in a federal trial, on violation of civil rights charges. Photo courtesy of the Mayme Clayton Library Collection

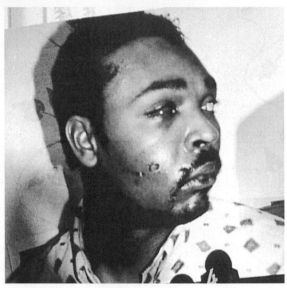

President Bill Clinton got elected on a combination of black support, and racial symbolism, when he attacked Sista Souljah to show Southern whites he could stand up to Jesse Jackson, and wouldn't be a rubber stamp for black equality programs. Black community developed a great affinity for Clinton, and the President showed a natural comfortability around Blacks that no President had previously shown. The first President to appoint four Blacks to cabinet posts in his first term, all whom served simultaneously. So familiar was Clinton in relating to Blacks that Nobel Laureate, Toni Morrison called him "the first Black President."
Photo courtesy of the Mayme Clayton Library Collection

The 1994 O.J. Simpson trial, with all its major players, Simpson, above, Mark Fuhrman, right, and Johnnie Cochran, below, was the most racially polarizing event of the 1990s, and was considered one of the primary reasons for the "Angry White Male" takeover of Congress in November, 1994. The Republican takeover of a Democratic Congress was the first in 40 years, and introduced an equally racially polarizing policy agenda called, "Contract With America" that brought a direct attack on affirmative action,   and social welfare programs. Photo courtesy of the Mayme Clayton Library Collection

1995 served as a year of contempletion for the racial equality struggle. Above, the US Organization celebrates the 30th anniversity of its founding with a "Critical Issues" Conference to assess the status of black struggle in America. Panel includes Professor/Author, Haki Madhubuti, Author/ Economist, Dr. Julianne Malveaux, Columnist/Author, Anthony Asadullah Samad, and Reparations Activist, Conrad Worrill. At right, the Honorable Louis Farrakhan call for a day of atonement drew estimates from 700,000 to 1.8 million black men seeking to change the conditions of their lives and communities (photo below). Farrakhan's influence grew dramatically in the 1990s, as he was viewed globally as the voice for the oppressed in America.
Photos courtesy of Malcolm Ali

The Million Man March served as a time of reconciliation for living participants both the Civil Rights and Black Nationalists movements. Above is Rev. Jesse L. Jackson, Mother Betty Shabazz and her daughter, Ilyasah, Mother Rosa Parks, Mother Khadijah Farrakhan and C. Deloris Tucker. The nation's two largest black organizations, the NAACP and the National Baptist Convention chose not to participate in the march, though many of their members attended.

Photo courtesy of Malcolm Ali

Author/Columnist Anthony Asadullah Samad, during the 1995 Million Man March, served as stage protocol director for the march. Called "the Day of Atonement," the march represented the most significant demonstration of black advocacy since the 1960s. The expectations after the march were as great as those created by the march itself. Not a single act of violence was committed that day and black on black violence fell in urban cities nationwide in the year following the march, as well as thousands of black children were adopted by families all over America as part of the march's respect pledge and "call to action."

Photo courtesy of Malcolm Ali

Current NAACP President and CEO and former Maryland Congressman, Kweisi Mfume, above left, and civil rights veteran, Julian Bond, above right, who succeeded Myrlie Evers-Williams as NAACP Board Chairman, have brought the NAACP back from the brink of financial collaspe and organizational irrelevancy in the fight for equality as they brought to light continuing disparities in television hiring, home and business lending, and "report-carded" the hotel industry for their racially discriminating treatment of Blacks in America's turn of the century "Colorblind Society" era. The organization called non-responsive to the issues facing African Americans and was labeled as "hostile" by the Bush II Administration in face of historic appointments of Colin Powell, below left center, as the first black Secretary of State and Condelezza Rice, far right, as the first black National Security Advisor.

Photos above courtesy of the NAACP. Photo below courtesy of the Mamye Clayton Library Collection.

racial discrimination (in January, 1961), they had expanded their recommendation to target the obstinacy of the state of Mississippi, the nation's poorest state, but most reliant on federal funds (Mississippi received $650 million in federal grants in 1962, while only paying $270 million in federal income tax), and the state that was the most unyielding on the question of segregation.

Kennedy, at the time of the request, didn't think the Executive branch had the power to withhold federal aid to the states, "in a general way," and thought that it would "probably be unwise to give the President of the United States that kind of power."[2]   However, Mississippi was out of control. Kennedy felt that he had to empower the federal government, in some way, to punish states that ignored federal edits. As a result, he included both withholding power, and greater intervention power, in the civil rights bill. The federal government was essentially powerless to make the states do anything beyond giving equal protection to all of its citizens. It was on this premise alone that the federal government had the basis to intervene in state affairs.

Prior to the passing of, what would become, the Civil Rights Act of 1964, the U.S. Attorney General lacked the authority to intervene in the police powers of the states. And though he proposed, and drafted, civil rights legislation, and next to the President, was the federal government's principle spokesperson on civil rights, the Attorney General and the Justice Department could only intervene in legal civil rights challenges, as a "friend of the court."[3] The executive branch relied on, and gave support to, the courts on the enforcement of the law. The states, however, saw that only relative to the enforcement of federal law, and not applying to the state laws.

Officials of the state of Mississippi, namely Governor Ross Barnett, and Lieutenant Governor, Paul Johnson, had thoroughly embarrassed the Kennedy administration in 1962, when they had agreed to allow James Meredith to register at the University of Mississippi (Ole Miss), after the federal courts threatened hold them in contempt if they did not admit him. It took three attempts to register Meredith. The first time, at night, where he was turned away by the Lieutenant Governor Johnson. The second time, again at night, the state had guaranteed Attorney General, Robert Kennedy, protection for Meredith, and instead, was met by a mob that caused a riot, killing two people.[4] The next day, under Presidential order, and escorted by sixteen thousand federal troops, Meredith was successfully registered. However, the hostility was so intense that the threats on his life confined him to his dor-

283

mitory. Federal troops had to sleep in his room, and escort him everywhere on campus, until he graduated the following June.[5] Mississippi was just the latest of the top down massive resistance strategies that Southern states had employed, since the Southern Manifesto had been issued, but represented a set of circumstances in which, both, Kennedy, and Barnett, had hoped to avoid, given that these same set of circumstances had played out five years earlier, in Little Rock, Arkansas. The University of Mississippi, at Oxford, was the scene of the most severe violence that the desegregation period had witnessed during this decade, where, as many as, twenty thousand federal troops were used over the course of the conflict.[6] While this was Kennedy's first challenge from the states, where he had to impose federal authority, it wasn't the nation's.

The first, and most memorable challenges to federal authority came in the Eisenhower administration, when President Eisenhower was asked to use federal authority in Alabama, Arkansas and Louisiana to escort black students to newly integrated schools. Eisenhower would send federal protection in the cases of Arkansas and Louisiana. In the case of Alabama, he would not-which probably influenced what he would have to do in future instances.

After three years of litigation, a young black woman named Autherine Lucy, secured a federal court order to attend the University of Alabama, in February of 1956. Lucy was admitted, and showed up for the first day of class, with minimal incident. However, on the second day of class, she was met with a major demonstration, and a cross-burning, on campus, as nearly 1,000 students-mostly men protested her attendance, while a similar demonstration of another 500 people was held in downtown Tuscaloosa, where the demonstrators sang, "Dixie,"[7] and chanted, "Keep Bama White," and "To Hell with Autherine." When Lucy showed up on the third day, the crowd turned even more hostile, pelting her with rotten eggs, as members of the Klan, along with her fellow students, shouted, "Lynch the Nigger," "Hit the Nigger Whore," and "Kill Her, Kill Her!" The University's Board of Trustees voted unanimously not to let Lucy return to campus, but for several days thereafter, mobs roamed Tuscaloosa, burning crosses, waving Confederate flags and attacking cars driven by local Blacks.[8] Lucy was later expelled. However, mobs in Texas and North Carolina kept black students from attending high schools and junior colleges, in 1956 and 1957. Desegregation, without federal protection, was an endangering risk in the South, and it never became more evident than when

President Eisenhower had to intervene when nine students, six boys and three girls, sought to attend the newly integrated in Little Rock, Arkansas, in September, 1957. The Little Rock desegregation case gained the most notoriety, because it was the case that invoked the most violence, and the case in which Eisenhower was forced to intervene, and give federal protection to the students, after the state failed to uphold the federal order.

At the center of the Little Rock debacle was the state's Governor, Orval Faubus, considered a racial moderate-even though he was behind the scenes urging Tennessee Senators to sign the Southern Manifesto, and assured the President that it was his intent on carrying out court ordered desegregation. Only Faubus operated under the guise that he wanted to ensure that there was no violence, though there was no evidence of a threat of violence, before he called the Justice Department requesting federal protection. The Justice department stated that there was nothing they could do, so Faubus went to the state court seeking an injunction to stop the school board from implementing its gradual desegregation plan, on the grounds of potential violence. The federal court nullified the injunction.

Then Faubus ordered the state national guard to active duty, and on opening day, September 3rd, turned back the nine black students seeking to enter Central High, though there were no mobs present, on the grounds that he as "the head of a sovereign state could exercise constitutional power, and discretion, in maintaining peace and order."[9] On the second day of school, irate Whites showed up, and began shouting obscenities at the students, thus, justifying the idle troops presence. It had become obvious to the federal courts, however, that Faubus was using the state's police power to deny the constitutional rights of black students, in order to maintain segregation, in defiance of the federal courts. Still, the National Guard, on Faubus' instruction, kept the black students out of the school for three weeks, until the federal courts enjoined Faubus from preventing the "Little Rock Nine" from entering the school.

Instead of leaving the protection in place, Faubus withdrew the troops on September 23rd, allowing the hostile crowds to "have at" the black students, who had entered the school. Once in, some students yelled, "The niggers are in our school," and violence broke out. Local Blacks, as well as, "yankee" reporters, and news photographers came under attack.[10] This put the incident in the national news, and the advent of television brought the Little Rock race conflict into millions

285

of American homes, creating a national crisis for Eisenhower. The President had resisted intervention up to this point, and really hesitated using federal authority, but he viewed Faubus' action as an affront to his responsibility that was too blatant to ignore. Eisenhower saw this as an assault on his honor to uphold his oath to defend the Constitution, and considered himself bound to how the Supreme Court interpreted it.[11] Eisenhower then federalized the Arkansas National Guard, and supplemented them with the federal military-parts of the 101st Airbourne Division-a true show of federal authority that Eisenhower really didn't believe was necessary to preserve law and order, but was necessary to remove obstructions to the authority of the United States, and to put down violence which hindered the execution of federal law. For those reasons, the army was called in.[12]

In a show of Southern solidarity against what appeared to be federal subversion of a state, the four Southern Governors met with Eisenhower, to find a compromise on how to get the army out of Arkansas. All Eisenhower wanted was a public declaration on the part of Faubus that he would not obstruct the federal courts, and take full responsibility in maintaining law and order in Little Rock for all citizens, all of which Faubus agreed to do. But Faubus continued his trickery, publicly declaring that he, himself as Governor, would not obstruct any federal laws, but he couldn't be responsible for anyone else who did. Thus he claimed he couldn't guarantee the safety of the black students at Central High, so the federal troops remained.[13] Eisenhower wouldn't be tricked again by the semantics of state and local rhetoric. One of his last acts in office was to give federal protection to a federal court order for a desegregation plan in the Deep South, where no desegregation of any public elementary, or secondary, school had occurred, to this point. New Orleans was targeted, because of the desegregation actions that it had taken on buses and parks in 1958, and the judge that issued the school order

In 1960, when New Orleans was forced to comply with a federal court order, he would sent federal marshals to escort six year old, Ruby Bridges, to her first grade school, where from angry Whites threw tomatoes, rotten eggs, and spat on her while chanting, "Two, four, six eight-we don't want to integrate; Eight, six, four, two-We don't want a chiggeroo."[14] White parents pulled all of their children out of Ruby's class, where she studied alone, was given instruction on a one on one basis by a teacher brought from Massachusetts (because no New Orleans teacher would accept the job), while white children were placed in private schools paid for by public funds.[15]

The school, however, remained open in compliance with the federal court order. While surrounded, by what must have seemed like monstrous, federal officials to a six year old, in the most hostile environment imaginable, Ruby Bridges demonstrated the courage and maturity that was, by most accounts, unimaginable. Her experience went largely unnoticed in the midst of the frenzy of the last weeks of the Kennedy-Nixon campain in what would be the closest Presidential election in American History (until November, 2000). The brutal viciousness, indignant pain, and the blunt candor of the American race politic that stemmed from the treatment of Ruby Bridges was memorialized in a 1964 painting by iconic American culturalist, painter Norman Rockwell, who in an artistic cultural expression entitled, *The Problem We Live With*, gave public recognition to what had long been the nation's dirtiest little secret, but had now become America's biggest public problem-its race problem.

Kennedy was elected, in the midst of increasing civil rights conflict that was being fueled by the court orders, sit-ins, freedom rides, and mass demonstrations (on the part of both the obstructionist resisters and civil disobedient protesters). Kennedy, like Eisenhower, knew he had to uphold the law, and the Meredith event in Mississippi was only his first test. Alabama Governor, George Wallace, inaugurated in January of 1963, who coined the segregationist mantra, "Segregation today, Segregation tomorrow, Segregation forever," had promised to uphold segregation in Alabama, if he had to stand in the school house doorway himself.[16]

287

By 1963, Wallace, like most Southern Governors and Senators, felt that their resistance measures would somehow cause the federal courts to reverse course, and repeal the *Brown* decision, either by showing judicial restraint on segregation, in some new case, or affirming segregation through some act of Congress. There was no such judicial reversal, or act of Congress forthcoming, and the Kennedy administration was now making it known. Attorney General, Robert "Bobby" Kennedy, who had drawn the ire of southern segregationists-and were now openly disrespecting him by calling the nation's top law enforcement officer, "Bobby-Socks," an indirect reference to his age (38 years old, at the time), inexperience and unfamiliarity with Southern culture-was publicly criticizing the South's false hopes, and advocating for the South to get with the desegregation program, or face federal intervention.

In a speech to the Missouri Bar Association, Kennedy stated the following about those lawyers and officials, who sought to obstruct the enforcement of laws and court order;

"With regard to the Brown decision, I think we can all agree that the probability of its permanence is so overwhelming as to counsel the abandonment of anyone's hope for the contrary. The decision was, after all, a[n] unanimous one. Since 1954 there have been six vacancies in the Supreme Court, which means that by now a total of 15 Justices have endorsed it...To suggest, at this point in history, that there is any real likelihood of the Brown decision's being reversed is irresponsible to the point of absurdity. No lawyer would advise a private client to contest the validity of a decision as solidly established and as often reiterated as this one; he would not want to victimize his client by raising frivolous questions. Yet a client is being victimized every time this frivolous question is raised today-and the client is the American public itself."[17]

The fact the Kennedy administration had begun to see the massive resistance movement for what it really was, an attempt to frustrate the American judicial system, while it worked out what Bobby Kennedy called "a crisis in the legal profession," in hopes that the courts would relent, and reverse itself. This didn't stop Southerners from becoming more adamant in their position, even though it was one based on false hope, and a danger to the stability of America's democratic system.

Following a federal court order issued on May 21, 1963, two black students, Vivian Malone and James Hood, were ordered to be admitted to the University of Alabama, one at Tuscaloosa campus on June 11th, and the other to the University's center at Huntsville on June 13. Governor Wallace poised for confrontation with the federal government, asking the people of Alabama to stay out of it, while he ordered a 500 man unit of the Alabama National Guard, and a 150 man force of Alabama highway patrolman, and other state police, to meet him in Tuscaloosa on June 11th.

President Kennedy put 2,000 federal troops on alert, as Wallace honored his pledge, and when Malone and Hood showed up with Justice Dept. officials to register, at the Foster Auditorium on the Tuscaloosa campus, Wallace in the doorway, as promised, and read a five page statement that concluded with the words, "I denounce and forbid this illegal act," turning around both students and the federal officials.[18] Within an hour, Kennedy federalized the National Guard, who returned the students to the campus. Commanding Brigadier General Henry C. Graham walked up to Wallace, with the students, and instructed the Governor that he represented "the Government of the United States of America, and on order of the President of the United States, I've been ordered to ask you to step aside." Wallace did so, and two days later, the first black student in the history of the University of Alabama was admitted, without incident. This confrontation represented the last straw for Kennedy, as he went on television the next day to speak on events that had occurred at Tuscaloosa, stating that the nation was founded on the principle that "all men were created equal, and that the rights of every man are diminished when the rights of one man are threatened." In specific reference to the Tuscaloosa incident, Kennedy stated:

"It ought to be possible for American students of any color to attend any public institution without having to be backed by troops. It ought to possible for American consumers of any color to receive equal service in places of public accommodation, such as hotels and restaurants and theaters and retail stores, without being forced to resort to demonstrations in the street, and it ought to be possible for American citizens of any color to register and to vote in a free election without interference or fear of reprisal...In short, every American ought to have the right to be treated as he would wish to be treated, as one would wish his children to be treated. But this is not the case." [19]

289

Kennedy had clearly made up his mind to do something on civil rights. This did not deter the obstructionists, however, and Kennedy was sent a clear signal of the type of opposition he would encounter over the next six months. On the night he gave this speech, Medgar Evers, State Director of the Mississippi NAACP, friend and advisor to James Meredith-the man Kennedy gave federal protection at the University of Mississippi, was shot in the back by a sniper in Jackson, Mississippi, and killed in his driveway, while getting out of his car.[20] A week later, on June 19th, while Robert Kennedy attended Evers funeral service, at Arlington National Cemetery, the President submitted his civil rights bill to Congress. Thus, began the summer of 1963, which, along with 1964, would be the Civil Rights Movements most violent years to date.

1963 represented a focal point for both movements (Massive

Resistance and Civil Rights), due to the fact that each movement had reached its ideological crescendo, and raised its political, philosophical, legal and extralegal activities to a fever pitch. As both sides dug in, demagoguery heightened, and varying degrees of antagonism, and even insanity, began to assert itself into the public discourse on racial equality politics. 1963 was the year of confrontation, where the passive resistance of civil disobedience insisting on change of outdated laws, met the massive resistance of cultural disobedience, insisting on the invalidity of new laws.

1963 was the year that Dr. King said, "the non-violent struggle came of age," where "physical force" was met with "soul force" and one movement's "capacity to inflict pain" was met with the other movement's "capacity to endure pain," each in reinforcement of their respective bipolar positions on racial equality. The politics of integration, and the conflicts that ensured from the clash of these movements, became very real to the nation in 1963, because the most visible and long lasting images of this time period manifested itself in the events of 1963. Civil rights, as a national issue, became the fodder for both public support and public critique largely because of the use of mass public protests. One, of which, took its genesis in the lunch counter sit-in demonstrations of 1960, and in that year alone had moved to over one hundred cities, and brought over 100,000 black and white protesters into the Southern and border states, demonstrating against every form of segregation, including hotels, restaurants, beaches, libraries, parks, playgrounds, swimming pools and theaters.[21] Protest grew intensely, in nature and scope, by 1963.

By 1963, the world was changing, and freedom, equality and justice were the focus of oppressed people everywhere. Thirty four African nations had freed themselves from colonial bondage by 1963, but in America-more than two thousand school districts remained segregated in the South, and at the current rate of progress, civil rights leaders observed, it would be 2054 before school desegregation became a reality, and 2094 before Blacks would secure equality, in job training and employment.[22]   Though Blacks in the North were becoming increasing vocal about conditions in American urban "ghettos," and had an increasingly radical spin to its protest, in the voice of Nation of Islam national spokesperson, Malcolm X (who was getting as much attention in the national media as King, providing a contrasting alternative in the eyes and minds of Whites), 1963 demonstrations were largely regional in scope, in that they spread throughout the South, involved much larger numbers, and attracted people of all ages, and backgrounds.

Literally every city, and every town in the South, had some sort of non-violent protest against segregation; some 115 communities engaged some 930 demonstrations-the largest mass protestations since the sit-in movement of 1960-where over 20,000 people were arrested for civil disobedience (four times the number arrested in 1960).[23] By the end of 1963 (as well as summer of 1964), the Southern Regional Council estimated that nearly 24,000 civil rights demonstrators had been arrested by police, including thousands of college students and school-age children.[24]

For this reason, the summer of 1963 was dubbed "Freedom Summer," and the most visceral images that came out of the months leading up to this summer defined the truest contexts of the equality struggle, as well as demonstrated the ferocity and intensity of both movements. Most of the intensity came out of the twin capitols of 20th Century segregation, Alabama and Mississippi. It was these years, from 1960 to 1963, that television and newspapers, throughout the nation, as well as much of the world's press, sent reporters South-who in turn, sent back pictures and reported daily clashes between civil rights workers and hostile white resisters.[25] But it was one city, and one city alone, that captured, and held, the nation's attention, in terms the extent of violent measures massive resistance would engage. It was this city that transformed the Civil Rights movement more than any other, due to its hostile and volatile acts against racial equality. So violent, the city came to be known in the South as "Bombmingham." The nation knew this city as, Birmingham, Alabama.

Before the assassination of Medgar Evers, no other aspect of the equality struggle defined the crisis of civil rights in America, and created more negative images that most distressed that nation-fire hoses being turned on peaceful marches that included women, children and teens filling jails, police dogs turned on crowds, the beatings and the bombings-than in Birmingham, Alabama between April 3rd and May 8th of 1963.[26] It was Birmingham, and the daily images of violence televised to the nation, that made civil rights a matter of high priority for the Kennedy administration. The politics of segregation, and massive resistance, were no longer being hidden within the confines of the states below the Mason-Dixon line. During a single three week period, after the images of Birmingham were spread across the nation, the Justice Department noted that 143 cities had acceded to some degree

291

of integration. Because many cities wanted to avoid "a Birmingham," they had set up biracial committees that enabled Blacks to press for further desegregation. As a result, the number of cities consenting to integration policies rose significantly, and exceeded 300 by the year's end.[27]

The non-violence movement was in full force, and Birmingham was the eye of the storm. Violence among the young marchers was of concern to King, at this point in time. Many were listening to that firebrand up North, Malcolm X, who was critical of Southern Blacks passive strategy. Malcolm X, and author, James Baldwin, a protégé of both King and Malcolm, publicly warned of the growing unrest in the North, and the unlikelihood that doctrines of non-violence would be followed up there. As more white clergy and college students from the North came south, King made sure they understood where they were, and trained them in the ways of the non-violent protest movement. King considered the training mass action protesters received, including verbal abuse, slapping and hitting, essential to building a non-reactionary tolerance-a refusal to hit back-to the abuse they would receive in the South. Protesters, in their willingness to go to jail for acts of civil disobedience, were asked to commit themselves to non-violence, under any circumstance. Their "pledge" was considered the equivalent to a civil rights "ten commandments," where they signed and carried a pledge card that read:

292

I hereby pledge myself-my person and my body-to the nonviolent movement. Therefore, I will keep the following ten commandments:

1.   *Meditate daily on the teaching and life of Jesus.*
2.   *Remember always that the nonviolent movement in Birmingham seeks justice and reconciliation-not victory.*
3.   *Walk and talk in the manner of love; for God is love*
4.   *Pray daily to be used by God in order that all men might be free.*
5.   *Sacrifice personal wishes so that all men might be free.*
6.   *Observe with both friend and foe the ordinary rules of courtesy.*
7.   *Seek to perform regular service for others and for the world.*
8.   *Refrain from the violence of fist, tongue, and heart.*
9.   *Strive to be in good spiritual and bodily health.*
10. *Follow the directions of the movement and of the captains on a demonstration.*

King feared that if the non-violent movement, now reinvigorated by the magnetic energies of the Birmingham youth, failed to hold against violence, young Blacks would turn to leaders, like Malcolm X. Malcolm, early on, had mocked non-violence strategy, which he saw as a tactic in a larger strategy-not the total encompassing strategy, and had nothing but disdain for integration-a word Malcolm stated, was "invented by a Northern liberal."[29]

Later, after the beating of the Selma marchers in 1965, SNCC students leaders took up Malcolm's mantra, in the shadow of his assassination, and King's "prophets of peace," later became the movement's "prophets of rage," building a movement within King's movement, and coining their own term, in demanding what they wanted out of the equality movement. The term was, "Black Power."

While King continued to emphasize moral suasion as the force behind the equality struggle, historians, like Clayborne Carson, saw Malcolm X as "the key individual in the transformation of African-American political thought" between 1964 and 1966, as every element in the evolving "Black Power" philosophy, that SNCC players would adopt in 1966, were frequent staples of Malcolm's speeches.[30] Still in 1963, King was still in control of the movement, and its young cohorts, despite the elevation of massive resistance violence taking place in the South. The viciousness of America's race politics was now being presented on the national and international stage and was being broadcast throughout the world. Kennedy had little choice but to submit a bill to Congress, that would end de jure racial segregation in America, once and for all.[31] This would make President Kennedy reviled in the South, and only increased the determination of obstructionists to defy the courts-and now, the President of the United States-in protection and defense of the southern cultural tradition of segregation.

At a White House conference, on the proposed civil rights bill, President Kennedy told Martin Luther King, Jr. that "Bull Conner (Birmingham's vicious Public Safety Commissioner, what the police chief was called) has done as much for civil rights as Abraham Lincoln."[32] During 1963, ten persons died in circumstances directly related to racial protests, and there were at least thirty-five bombings in the South-largely targeting headquarters of civil rights groups (SCLC, SNCC, CORE, and NAACP offices) and the homes of organizers of voter registration and desegregation campaigns.[33] Yet, people were still questioning the need for a civil rights bill, including Kennedy's own Vice President, Lyndon Johnson. New York Senator, Jacob Javits, cap-

293

sulized the need for a strong civil rights bill in committee testimony during congressional debates in July, 1963 when he pointed out the lack of progress on desegregation in citing the racial integration status of the fifteen Southern and border states. Javits stated;

"Of some 275 cities with populations of over 10,000 in 65% [of them], all or parts of the hotels and motels, were still segregated, and so were nearly 60% of, all or part of, the restaurants and theaters. In ninety-eight cities with under 10,000 population, 85% to 90% of all or part of these types of establishments remained segregated. On a trip from Washington, D.C. to Miami, the average distance between hotel-motel accommodations of 'reasonable quality' available to Negroes was estimated to be 141 miles. Traveling from Washington, D.C. to new Orleans, the average between "locations" amounted to 174 miles."[34]

Javits' point was that the Southern states were not complying with the *Brown* decision, due to the fact that, between 1960 and 1964, another 79 federal court actions had to be filed to facilitate equal access to public accommodations.[35] Even the U.S. Supreme Court was beginning to understand what was going on, in terms of the massive resistance efforts, and recognized that it was the ambiguity of its *"All deliberate speed"* instruction that compliance was being manipulated, in ways they hadn't intended. In a case handed down at the end of the 1962-1963 term, *Watson v. City of Memphis*, a case where the city of Memphis sought a court injunction to prohibit the desegregation of parks and recreational facilities owned and operated by the city, where the black petitioners had called for "immediate and complete" desegregation action, the Supreme Court unanimously overturned the lower courts injunction, and admitted the errors of its ways, noting that nine years had already passed since *Brown*, and "the context in which we must interpret and apply its language to plans for desegregation has been significantly altered." Speaking directly to the massive resistance tactics, Justice Goldberg wrote;

"Brown never contemplated that the concept of "deliberate speed" would countenance indefinite delay, in eliminating racial barriers in the schools, let alone other public facilities not involving the same physical problems, or comparable conditions; (2) the rights here asserted are, like all such rights, present rights...not merely hopes for some future enjoyment of some formalistic constitutional promise; (3) ...neither the asserted fears of vio-

294

lence, and tumult, nor the asserted inability to preserve the peace were demonstrated at trial to be anything more than personal speculations, or vague disquietudes of city officials."[36]

The Warren Court, still leading a constitutional revolution, unlike one America had ever seen, had pulled the cover off "all deliberate speed," and was demanding that segregation take place with "all immediate speed," eight years after giving the South a chance to warm up to the idea of desegregation, in 1955. The Supreme Court would not only pull the cover off the manipulation of its nonspecific enforcement mandate in 1963, it would pull the bed sheets off the technicalities of the practices of discrimination, that limited Fourteenth Amendment protections to "state action." Discrimination violation were limited to what was called, "state action," in two landmark cases, the *Civil Rights Cases* (1883) and *Shelly v. Kramer* (1948), where prior Supreme Court held that the Fourteenth Amendment was restricted, in its applications, to only those activities which involved state governmental actions, and sanctions, and excluded private action, stating the Amendment "erects no shield against merely private conduct, however discriminatory or wrongful."[37]

The Supreme Court established new precedents on this legal interpretation, by reversing two cases, on May 21, 1963, *City of Greenville v. Peterson* and *Lombard v. Louisiana*. Both were lunch counter sit-in cases in which employees of private businesses called law enforcement in to remove protesters, giving sanction to private acts of discrimination. In each instance, law enforcement, in advising protestors why they were being arrested, told them they were in violation of local and state segregation laws (even though New Orleans had no such city ordinance, and Louisiana had no such state law). The Supreme Court stated that both state governments and state courts sought to preserve private acts of business discrimination, in the absence of law, and state action, and private acts were carried out under "the voice of the state," and thus unconstitutional.[38]

Justice Douglas, in his concurring opinion, stated "when doors of a business are open to the public, they must be open to all regardless of race if apartheid is not to become engrained in our public places."[39] Justice Douglas (and Judge William Hastie) were two of the first in government to publicly acknowledge and equate America's race caste system, as an apartheid system, and his point was-which his Court colleagues did not agree-that discrimination in public accommodation was

295

unconstitutional, even in the absenceof state action. Still, these decisions shattered most of the legal immunities the South had put in place, to protect segregation and maneuver around demands for integration. This provided further support for Kennedy's bill, and set the stage for "Freedom Summer" and its season of confrontation-and violence.

As pro-desegregation activists heightened their activities, anti-civil rights resisters heightened their outrage-which in most instances, caused a very public demonstration of violence-to send a message that segregationists were not being moved by the emotion of the times. The largest pro-desegregation protest in American history was held on August 28, 1963, in Washington, D.C. Called a March for Jobs and Freedom, Dr. King, during his keynote address, specifically called out Mississippi and Alabama, as the nation's symbols of the resistance, their lips "dripping with words of interposition and nullification," publicly calling their obstructionist government officials, "racists." A little over two weeks later, in the most indiscriminately heinous act of the movement, segregationtists demonstrated that they were not moved by the biracial support of the march, nor the emotional appeal of King's public admonition.

On September 15th, 1963, one of the pillars of the Birmingham black community, the 16th Street Baptist Church, was bombed right before its Sunday church service, just as a Sunday school class was concluding. The church had been the meeting place where the Civil Rights movement, waning of energy, had a reinvigoration, after 1,000 children ages six to sixteen met with Dr. King on May 2nd (called D-Day), and proceeded to go on a protest march against segregation. Nine hundred fifty-nine of them were arrested that day.[40] The next day, 1,000 more skipped school to join the protest, and they were arrested also. This occurred until the Birmingham jails were filled with some 3,300 people, and could no longer hold any more protesters. That is when the fire hoses, and the dogs were brought out, thus representing a significant turning point in the movement. The day the church was bombed, four little girls were killed, in an act viewed as despicable, incomprehensible and indefensible-no matter how much of a segregation supporter one was.

From the beginning of the sit-in demonstrations in 1960, through the spring of 1965, at least twenty-six black and white civil rights workers died at the hands of southern racial violence-of which, only one killer went to prison. All of the others avoided punishment, due to not being arrested, not being indicted or not being convicted.[41]

Despite white citizens beingbdisturbed by the bombing, and creating a $100,000 reward fund, the FBI assigned 231 agents to the case, investigated more than eight thousand suspects and suspected white hate groups. Those responsible for the killing of 11 year old, Denise McNair, as well as, Cynthia Wesley, Carole Robinson, Addie Mae Collins, all 14 years of age at the time of this atrocity, were never arrested.

The movement had finally reached what many saw as, the brink of insanity-where few in the nation would not be affected. The insanity even reached into highest levels of the federal government. Not even the President of the United States was isolated from the madness surrounding the resistance to racial equality. During his first re-election campaign stop in the South, President John F. Kennedy, was assassinated, on November 22, 1963. Though a commission headed by Supreme Court Chief Justice, Earl Warren, concluded that a lone gunmen, Lee Harvey Oswald, carried out that assassination, several more plausible conclusions were reached after 40 years of asking the question, "Who killed JFK?"

On the 40th Anniversary of the assassination, several documentaries concluded that the most logical motives behind all of the conspiracy theories stemmed from three sources; 1) "the mob" in retaliation for Robert Kennedy's war against organized crime, 2) a Cuban retaliation hit for the United States persistent attempts to kill Castro (up to 1963, the CIA had tried eight assassination attempts), and 3) retaliation by Southern Segregationists for Kennedy's push for a civil rights bill. In any instance, the lone gun theory went out the window. But many scholars, civil rights historians and political observers, to this day, think that massive resistance started an assassination spree with Evers and Kennedy, that changed the course of this nation's history.

The death of Kennedy put Lyndon Baines Johnson, from Texas-ironically, the very state in which Kennedy was killed, and someone who wasn't totally supportive of the late President's civil rights initiatives-in the White House and directly in the middle of the equality fight. However, the policy initiatives and federal intervention efforts of Kennedy weren't easily forgotten. Whether one agreed or disagreed with his policies, he was a popular president that brought a youth, vitality and excitement to the Presidency that the nation hadn't seen since FDR. His supporters, and critics alike, were in agreement that President Kennedy did not deserve such a tragic end to such a bright beginning.

A poll in 1964 stated that, behind Abraham Lincoln and Thurgood Marshall, no single individual had done more to obtain equality for black people, than John F. Kennedy.

President Johnson went before the Congress, five days after Kennedy's assassination, and after offering condolences to Kennedy's widow and children, stated, "No memorial or eulogy could more honor President Kennedy's memory than the earliest possible passage of the civil rights bill for which he fought so long."[42] Johnson had thrown down the gauntlet at the feet of the massive resistance movement and its persistent delays as being the reason equality has taken so long. Johnson concluded, "We have talked long enough in this country about equal rights. We have talked for 100 years or more. It is time now to write the next chapter-and to write it into the books of law.[43]

It was Kennedy's civil rights bill had been stalled in the Congress for months. Southern members took little comfort in having to challenge another southerner in the White House, the first southern president in 100 years (since Andrew Johnson succeeded another assassinated President in Abraham Lincoln). Southern resisters in Congress were confident that they could defeat Kennedy, but saw defeating Johnson as three times harder. As Georgia Senator, Richard Russell stated, "Lyndon Johnson knows more about the uses of power than any man...Now he's President, with the greatest power in the world at his disposal...President Kennedy didn't have to pass a strong bill to prove anything on civil rights, President Johnson does."[44]

The nation went into shock, then a year of mourning, accompanied by period of battle fatigue, over the issue of racial equality. But Southerners in Congress didn't relent, and promised to filibuster the bill. Civil rights bills were no stranger to filibustering tactics in the 20th Century. Civil rights bills were passed in the 19th Century, within two years after the end of the Civil War. It took almost two-thirds of the 20th Century to pass one. In 1957, a civil right bill was introduced into Congress that sought to create an investigative commission with subpoena powers to examine civil rights problems, as well as sought to expand the Civil Rights Section of the Justice Department into its own division, extend conspiracy prosecutions to individuals as well as groups, allow citizens to sue for redress when denied the right to vote and empower the attorney general to seek injunctive relief for civil rights violations.[45] It came close to passing.

However, Senator Strom Thurmond, in the longest speech on congressional record, filibustered the bill for a full 24 hours, and had several other southern Senators prepared to do the same, until the bill was withdrawn. The bill was passed only after all of the enforcement provisions were deleted and a jury trial provision was added, that allowed civil rights violators to be tried by members of their own community.[46] The 1957 Civil Rights Bill was essentially a powerless commission. The 1960 Civil Rights Act provided for federal sanctions against local officials obstructing the registration, and voting rights, of Blacks. It also gave the Civil Rights Commission the power to give oaths to federal referees, and take sworn statements from Blacks denied the right to vote, and the power to preserve registration and voting records in federal elections. But the 1960 Act gave voting referees no authority to arrest or prosecute, only to observe, and report back to the Justice Department, after the fact of the impacted elections-again rendering the federal government powerless to change local election outcomes due to black disfranchisement. It quickly became apparent that the 1960 Civil Rights Act could accomplish little, without enforcement power, in the mounting confrontations that stemmed from the gaps in ideological positions of the Civil Rights movement, and the resistance to it by powerful interests in Southern communities between 1960 and 1963.[47] Johnson intended the 1964 bill to have plenty of enforcement.

The 1964 civil rights bill was a revised bill that was stronger than its original (Kennedy's) version, attacking racial discrimination in employment, banishing Jim Crow policies in public accommodations, gave the Attorney General authority to bring suits against resisting school administrators (taking the burden off black litigants) and threatened segregating schools with cutoff of federal funds, if they continued the practice.[48]

Clearly, the most discussed provision of the 28 page law was Title II (one of ten titles), that declared that all persons were entitled to the full and equal enjoyment in places of public accommodation, such as hotels, motels, restaurants, and movie theaters, "without segregation on the ground of race, color, religion or national origin."[49] It was this provision that southerners feared most. By enumerating the practices that would be outlawed, every facet of Jim Crow would be eliminated.

Coming out of committee in the house on January 31, the bill passed on February 10th, by a vote of 290 to 130, with only seven of 95 southern representatives voting for it.[50] Sponsored by Minnesota Senator, Hubert Humphrey, in the Senate, the Senate debated the civil rights bill for seventy five days, until cloture was invoked, on June 10th, by a 71 to 29 vote, with only one Senator, Ralph Yarborough from

299

Texas voting in favor of ending the filibuster.[51] On June 19th, one year after Kennedy had sent the bill to Congress, the 1964 Civil Rights Act passed the Senate, enduring the longest filibuster in American history.[52] Johnson had an advantage that Kennedy didn't have, in that he was a Southerner who knew where a lot of the bodies were buried in the Senate. He knew where a lot of his colleague's skeletons were, and in what closets, and had a lot of IOUs outstanding from his days as Senate majority leader. Johnson also had a greater determination to prove that he was more than just "a country boy from Texas, seeking to be a more effective President than Kennedy, in his ability to get legislation, past what he knew to be, Southern racists in Congress.[53]

Johnson not only was determined to pass Kennedy's civil rights bill, he intended to build upon it, and also do something that no other President dared to do-put a black man on the United States Supreme Court. On July 2nd, 1964, President Lyndon Johnson signed into law the first meaningful Civil Rights Act of the 20th Century, and the most sweeping civil rights law in the nation's history. Johnson had become the African American's champion of the equality struggle.

Moreover, after leading the Constitutional revolution, in the fight for equality of the 19th Century against obstructionist Supreme Courts, the United States Congress had finally joined the 20th Century Constitutional revolution started by the U.S. Supreme Court ten years earlier. The Civil Rights Act of 1964, passed a full ten years later, gave legislative authority, and executive enforcement, to the *Brown* decision. But it was the legislative act itself that gave force to the *Brown* decision, and provided the proper context for the Fourteenth Amendment, and served a mortal wound to segregation policies, making Jim Crow "all but dead" in every area. Every area that is, except for one, the right to vote.

Senator Humphrey, as the majority Whip that delivered the bill to Johnson, was rewarded for his persistence, in getting the Kennedy-Johnson civil rights bill through the Congress. As the surprise pick over Robert Kennedy, at the 1964 Democratic Convention, Humphrey was given a position on the party's ticket in the 1964 Presidential election. He would become Johnson's Vice President. The biggest tribute of the convention was given to the late president, John F. Kennedy. The biggest controversy of the convention was the removal of black delegates from Mississippi, including the physical removal (picked up, kicking and screaming) of Fannie Lou Hamer, co-founder of the Mississippi Freedom Democratic Party (MFDP), who protested

300

on the convention floor, their exclusion for the state party's delegate selection process.

The MFDP saw its role as launching excluded black residents on the road of political organization, and in pursuit of their own political interest. Given the fact that the regular Mississippi Democratic Party had not only excluded Blacks-who represented almost half of Mississippi residents-from becoming party members, but had already made it clear that it would not support President Johnson, opting for the Republican candidate, Arizona Governor, Barry Goldwater, in the 1964 Presidential election. Black delegates went to the convention to represent their own political interests.[54]

Hamer, who coined the term, "I sick and tired of being sick and tired," was at the center of the movement, and was quite aware of the dangers of trying to register Blacks, and pursue black suffrage in Mississippi. The disappearance of three civil rights workers of the Mississippi Summer Project, a voter education project, funded by the Congress Of Racial Equality, less than two weeks before the civil rights bill was signed, had shocked the nation.

James Chaney, age 21, Andrew Goodman, age 20, and Michael Schwerner, age 26, disappeared June 21st, 1964, on a lonely road in Neshoba County, Mississippi after being stopped for speeding. After being taken to the county jail and posting bond, they left on their way to Meridian, Mississippi. The last person to see them was Neshoba County Sheriff, Ray Price, who said they were alive when he last saw them. Attorney General, Bobby Kennedy, federalized the investigation the next day, and literally had to make J. Edgar Hoover send 150 FBI agents to Mississippi, to aid in the search. It wasn't until August 4th, almost six weeks later, after a tip from a paid FBI informant, that the decomposed bodies of Chaney, Goodman and Schwerner were found under a dam on a private farm-all three had been beaten and shot.[55]

The state of Mississippi alone reported 35 shootings, 30 bombings, 35 church burnings, 80 beatings and, at least, six murders during the summer of 1964.[56] If the summer of 1963 was "Freedom Summer," 1964 was its continuation, only more violent, or as historian Michael Belknap referred to it, "Bloody Freedom Summer."

Fannie Lou Hamer, and the folk of the MFDP, were under no misconceptions of the danger they faced. But in their resolve to vote, "to tell the truth" about the denial of voting rights in Mississippi and be represented in the state parties, Hamer plainly stated, "Sometimes, it seems like to tell the truth today, is to run the risk of being killed, but if I fall-I'll fall five feet four inches forward in the fight for freedom."[57] By "freedom," Hamer and others meant the freedom to vote.

Robert Moses, an SCLC organizer, had conceived the idea of the "freedom vote" in the fall of 1963 as an idea to register Blacks, when white folks in Mississippi would refuse to do so. When the MFDP was founded in April of 1964, as a party open to all but specific for Blacks to be represented in the delegate process, and to run Blacks for office, it enrolled almost 80,000 African Americans, and they elected forty-four delegates and twenty-two alternatives to represent the disfranchised voters of Mississippi.[58]

Sixty-eight members of the MFDP arrived at the Democratic National Convention in Atlantic City, New Jersey on August 21st to fight for all of its delegates to be seated with the Mississippi Democratic Party delegation. After lobbying the members of the convention, the delegation selected Hamer to testify before 110 members of the party's Credentials Committee on August 22nd to make the case for the humiliation, fear and violent abuse poor black Mississippians endured while trying to vote.

The committee meeting was nationally televised, and before a national audience, Fannie Lou Hamer, perspiring from the television lights, eyes swelled with tears, spoke of the death threats, beatings and burnings she, and the other members, had experienced, was all "on account we want to register to become first class citizens," and she concluded saying, that "If the Freedom Democratic Party is not seated now, I question America…," and choked with emotion, she then asked the committee members (a number of whom also now had tears in their eyes), "Is this America-the land of the free and the home of the brave?"[59]

President Johnson, who thought that Bobby Kennedy was trying to steal the nomination from him, and was behind the MFDP refusal of his compromise, was enraged by Hamer's testimony, and told Hubert Humphrey, to whom he was assuredly going to reward the Vice Presidency, for his handling of the passage of the 1964 Civil Rights Act, that he would never be Vice President if he didn't avoid a floor fight, by getting the MFDP to accept of compromise of seating two black delegates-and neither of them could, on any account, be Fannie Lou Hamer.

Johnson, and Humphrey soon found out that the men in the delegation, including chairman of the delegation, Aaron Henry, who considered and made an argument for accepting the compromise, were powerless against Hamer, Victoria Gray, Annie Devine, and the other women of the delegation. These women caused the proposal to be soundly defeated. Then Hamer, and some twenty delegates, charged into the convention hall that night singing, "We Shall Overcome," and took the empty seats that were occupied by the white Mississippi party delegation-most of whom had left, because they had refused to take the Democratic Party's loyalty oath to back the Party's choice to head the party. When ordered to vacate the seats by the convention's sergeant at arms, they denounced the President, again on national television, blasted the Democratic Party for its hypocrisy in claiming to favor civil rights, but refusing to seat an integrated delegation that was fully supportive of the Democratic Party's policies.[60]

The Mississippi Freedom Democratic Party was physically removed from the convention hall, and never seated, but their stand would be the basis for full inclusion of segments of the party's constituents in future Democratic Conventions, including 50% of the delegates being women-which can be directly traced back to the repercussions of keeping the MFDP and its representation claim out of the 1964 convention.[61]

Lyndon Johnson did get the nomination without a challenge. Humphrey did get the Vice Presidential slot, and the Johnson-Humphrey ticket won the November election by the biggest landslide in history. But the convention proved that the 1964 Civil Rights Act, for what President Johnson felt every black person-including those in Mississippi-should be grateful, didn't solve all of African American's equality problems. Johnson came into the 1964 Convention riding high on civil rights, and left the Convention, riding low on the politics around voting. This made the issue of black voting disfranchisement a high priority for the Johnson administration, and it would be taken up by Johnson, post haste after his inauguration in 1965.

While some progress, in registering voters, had been made in the North, progress in the South was abysmal. Compared to the 60 to 70 percent of northern Blacks who were registered in 1964, just over one-third of eligible Blacks were registered in the South, and as always-Alabama, who had registered only 22% of eligible Blacks, and Mississippi, who'd only registered seven percent of its eligible black voters, lead the way in the South's continuing resistance to black enfranchisement.[62]

Martin Luther King, who had just returned from Oslo, Norway, from receiving the Noble Peace Prize, had now turned his attention

303

from social equality to political equality, and, again, returned his attention to Alabama-but this time included Mississippi, in devising a strategy to register black voters. In January and February of 1965, King led
mass meetings in Selma, Alabama and Marion, Mississippi, both considered "black belts" for their densely populated black constituencies.
In both of these cities, Blacks were a considerable portion of the city's
population-actually a majority in Marion-but were essentially powerless
because they were prevented from voting. Blacks were escorted by civil
rights workers to each county courthouse, to attempt to register to vote,
only to be denied or turned away by police.

The first casualty of the 1965 voter registration campaign came
about on February 18th, 1965 when, after several people had been
arrested for attempting to vote, a protest march turned violent, after
city officials turned out the streetlights as police and white supremacists
charged the marchers and began beating them with clubs.[63] Jimmie Lee
Jackson was shot that night, and died eight days later. He was martyred
at his funeral, buried in blue denim overalls, and eulogized by King, in
a sign of things to come.

The day Jackson died was the day after Malcolm X was assassinated in Harlem. Malcolm had gone to the South earlier that month to
give support to the movement, while Dr. King had been jailed the first
week of February. A group of two hundred and fifty peaceful protesters
marched on the Selma Courthouse, to protest the refusal of city officials to register black voters. They were all arrested and jailed for five
days, including King, during which time Malcolm came to town unan-
nounced to speak at a mass meeting.

Malcolm told the crowd to help Dr. King, and told southern
Whites that they had better listen to Dr. King's warning, because all
Blacks were not necessarily committed to this doctrine of non-violence, and there was an alternative. Malcolm was no doubt talking
about militant NACCP President, Roberts Williams, who had advocated for Blacks in Monroe, North Carolina, to arm themselves in
1959, published a book called *Negroes With Guns* in 1962, a newsletter
called *The Crusader* (that had a southern black readership of 40,000)
and was then broadcasting for Havana, Cuba, a radio program called
"Radio Free Dixie." Williams continued to advocate armed self-reliance,
as well as, other black vigilante groups being organized in Alabama.

One such group of armed black men became legendary, in their
defense of black rights. They were called "the Deacons For Defense."
King's non-violent philosophy became seriously tested after the Jimmie

Lee Jackson murder, as the tension of the movement rose intensely. After his speech in Selma, Malcolm had to immediately leave for a trip to London to speak at an African Students' Conference, but he met Ms. King, on his departure, and told her to tell Dr. King that he had planned to visit him in jail, but to convey, "That I didn't come down here to make his job more difficult; I really did come thinking I could make it easier. If white people realize what the alternative is, perhaps they will be more willing to hear Dr. King."[64]

Three weeks later, Malcolm X was dead and his death dramatically affected the young people of the movement, who had begun to insert such of his "Northern philosophies" of freedom "by any means necessary" (a term which Malcolm actually got from Southern Senators and their Southern Manifesto) into this Southern Movement. Selma would become the focus of the South's new political rights movement from this point on.

Selma became significant, because it was there that Southern massive resistance, as the nation had come to know it in its initial form, made its last stand. King had a two and a half hour meeting with President Johnson on March 5th, to discuss the need for the President to urge Congress to pass a voting rights bill that included federal registrars of voting applicants, to eliminate obstructionist interference that was paralyzing voter registration efforts, in Alabama and Mississippi. Despite all the time King had spent in Selma over the prior two months--the speeches, the meetings, singing and local protest marches, the Selma movement was stalling, and the confrontations were only escalating.

In the two and a half months since King had arrived in Selma, right after New Year's Day in 1965, there had been two murders, nearly 3,800 arrests, including King himself, and despite all the activity, and nationwide attention given to Selma-only about fifty people had been registered to vote.[65] Selma was upholding its reputation, as a symbol of black oppression, in the "Cradle of the Confederacy."

King announced that there would be a march from Selma, to the state's capitol fifty four miles away in Montgomery to confront Alabama Governor, George Wallace, on the state's benign disenfranchisement policies that allowed its counties to prohibit Blacks from voting. It would take King three attempts to march from Selma to Montgomery. The first march was announced to take place on March 7th, however Wallace issued an order prohibiting the march, and in anticipation of a confrontation, SCLC strategists convinced King, at the last minute, not to start with the marchers, as it was the organizations strategy not to have leaders of campaigns arrested in its opening stages, because it would "leave the army with no generals."[66] Campaign organizer, Hosea Williams, and SNCC President, John Lewis, were asked to lead the first march attempt.

The first march had 600 black marchers with a few white people intermixed. As the marchers reached the four lane highway of Interstate 80, they had to cross the Edmund Pettis Bridge, where they were met by Selma County Sheriff, Jim Clark (Selma's version of Bull Connor) and Alabama Highway Patrol Officer, Colonel Al Lingo, who, along with 60 state troopers, asked the marchers to "halt," and gave them two minutes to turn back. But before any of the marchers could react, they heard Sheriff Clark yell, "Get those goddamn Niggers!! Get those goddamn White Niggers (the term used for Whites who supported the civil rights movement)!!"

From that point, tear-gas grenades were thrown in the crowd, the troopers moved forward with batons-flattening about twenty marchers, as the rest knelt to pray-and officers on horse starting beating, clubbing and trampling men, women and children.[67] The confrontation was documented in the national news (and in history) as "Bloody Sunday," and the nation hadn't seen such appalling images since Birmingham a couple of years earlier.

Undaunted, King set a second march for the following Tuesday. This time Alabama secured a federal injunction against the march. King put out a national call to clergy nationwide to join him in Selma on March 9th, and 1,500 showed up-including 450 clergy. King led this march, and this time the marchers made it across the Edmund Pettis Bridge before they met National Guardsmen. To avoid unnecessary violence, King turned the marchers around, but that night a white Unitarian from Boston out to dinner with two other clergymen was attacked by four Klansman. Rev. James Reeb had his skull crushed in, and died two days later, never regaining consciousness.

This act appalled President Johnson, who went on national television on March 15th, the evening of James Reeb's memorial service, announcing that it was his intention to introduce a voting rights bill to Congress, and that it would be the first priority of his proposed legislation. It was in this speech that Johnson termed Selma the spot, where "history and fate meet at a single time, in a single place to shape a turning point in man's unending search for freedom," comparing Selma to Lexington and Concord, as turning points in the Revolutionary War-

Appomattox, in the turning point of the Civil War one hundred years earlier. The President stated;

"What happened in Selma is part of a far larger movement which reaches into every section and state of America. It is the effort of American Negroes to secure for themselves the full blessings of American life.

Our mission is at once the oldest and the most basic of this country- to right wrong, to do justice, to serve man.

Their cause must be our cause, too. Because it is not just Negroes, but really all of us, who must overcome the crippling legacy of bigotry and injustice.

And we shall overcome!"

As unbelievable as it was, the President of the United States-a southerner from Texas, using the word "we"-had just picked up the mantra of the civil rights movement and declared it his own. When President Lyndon Johnson said "And we shall overcome," the marching chant of the cause for all of the 1950s and 1960s (and the 1970s, 1980s and 1990s, as well), King and the others in the movement knew their message had finally gotten through, and that the President was now "a believer" in the cause for equality and justice.

At the same time, Johnson had just made others a believer in him. Johnson's "We Shall Overcome" speech represented a significant moment in American history-not black American history, but American History. No other President of the United States had said what Johnson had said, and, as history proved, done what Johnson had done to advance the cause of equality for the African American. Many historians had seen Johnson's signing of the 1964 Civil Rights Act as finishing Kennedy's legacy. The next two civil rights acts, starting with the Voting Rights Act of 1965, would be all a part of Johnson's legacy.

Now with the authority (both moral and legal) of the President, King called for a third attempt to march, from Selma to Montgomery, on March 21st, two weeks after Bloody Sunday, and under the protection of the federal government. President Johnson federalized the Alabama National Guard, and supplied an additional 4,000 regular army troops. Five thousand marchers reached Montgomery, where the mass protest movement started ten years earlier, without incident-and in the midst of the first widely acknowledged pronouncements of assassination threats against King's life.

President Johnson signed the Voting Rights Act of 1965 into

307

law on August 6th, 1965, which outlawed poll taxes, literacy tests and other forms of extralegal manipulations, that prevented Blacks from voting in areas where voting age adults represented, at least, 50% voting age population, or less than 50% had voted in the 1964 presidential election. It gave federal election examiners the authority to take over registration procedures, and elections where voting abuses were found, and it provided stiffer penalties for those found intimidating voters. The voting rights act ushered in a new era of political empowerment for African Americans that provided huge dividends, including the election of thousands of African American elected officials. There was no place that the Voting Rights Act made a bigger difference than in Mississippi, where in 1960-only 22,000 black voters had registered. By the end of 1965, mostly accomplished in the four months since the law had taken effect, Mississippi had 175,000 registered black voters.

King had thought his work in the movement was finished, but 1965 had taken its toll on his non-violent struggle. After the Selma to Montgomery march, a civil rights worker from Detroit, Viola Liuzzo, was shot and killed on the highway, taking marchers back to Selma. Another civil rights worker, Jonathan Daniels, was murdered and his accused killer, Collie Wilkins, was acquitted, causing King to cut a European trip short, to come back to advocate for legislation, making it a federal crime to commit violence on any one in pursuit of equal rights or equal justice.[68]

By April of 1965, the Justice Department was proceeding rapidly to design a bill for that purpose, and assembled a "Klan task force" to study the problem of racist violence in the South. Both the Civil Rights Commission, and the Leadership Conference on Civil Rights, made specific suggestions for legislation against racial violence, and an inter-agency task force unanimously concluded that such legislation was needed.[69] Johnson introduced such a bill in 1966, but it met a two year stall in Congress, and met a very unceremonious, anti-climatic conclusion.

Still, the significance of this time shouldn't be lost on the violence that permeated it. 1964 and 1965 had produced equality gains that were unequaled in the 20th Century, and unequaled in the history of this country, except for the first five years of the Reconstruction Period, where the 13th, 14th and 15th Amendments were passed. Slavery, the basis for the 13th Amendment, and its principle vestige-de jure segregation, had been eradicated by both the courts in *Brown* and the Congress' passing of the Civil Rights Act of 1964. Citizenship for

308

Blacks (equality), due process and equal protection of the law, the basis for the 14th Amendment, had been reinterpreted in *Brown*, and reinforced by the Civil Rights Act of 1964. Equal Suffrage, the basis of the 15th Amendment, had been reaffirmed by the Voting rights Act of 1965.

It seemed that Blacks were finally "legally" equal in American society, and moral suasion had convinced a great number in America that it was not only time, not only the right thing to do, but the just thing to do. African Americans were now prepared to advance themselves, 100 years after Reconstruction began, as social and political equals, in a society of social and political equals.

Or, so they thought...

12

Affirmative Action as Reparation for Past Discrimination:
Making Up Ground or Making Grounds Worse?

Freedom is the right to share, share fully and equally, in American society-to vote, to hold a job, to enter a public place, to go to school. It is the right to be treated in every part of our national life as a person equal in dignity and promise to all other.

But freedom is not enough. You do not wipe away the scars of centuries by saying: now you are free to go where you want and do as you desire, and choose the leaders you please.

You do not take a person who, for years, has been hobbled by chains and liberate him, bring him up to the starting line of a race and then say, "You are free to compete with all the others," and still justly believe that you have been completely fair.

Thus it is not enough just to open the gates of opportunity. All our citizens must have the ability to walk through those gates.

This is the next and the more profound stage of the battle for civil rights. We seek not just freedom but opportunity. We seek not just legal equity but human ability, not just equality as a right and a theory but equality as a fact and equality as a result.

-   President Lyndon Johnson,
    speech at Howard University, 1965

Segregation, as law, had not given way to the forms of segregation that Malcolm X had long criticized, in the North, but gained little attention, because of his perceived militancy, coupled with the stature of King's involvement in the more overtly violent activity of the South. De jure segregation was a southern phenomenon that was truly contradictory to the tenets of the Constitution, simply because it created separate laws for separate groups of people, facilitating racial inequality. It was de Facto segregation, however, that was truly the "American Way," in terms of using societal cultural norms to create racial inequality throughout the country. The simple, yet complex, dynamic of how Whites dealt with Blacks regionally, was never more poignant than as described by Andrew Young, former SCLC aide to Dr. King, who went on to become Congressman, Ambassador to the United Nations, and the second black Mayor of Atlanta. He once said, "In the South, Whites didn't care how close Blacks got, as long as, they didn't get too big; but in the North, Whites didn't care how big Blacks got, as long as, they didn't get too close."

Closeness, defined as geographical proximity, was a socio-political barrier that defined economic reality in the North. It reinforced some of the same psychological boundaries that dictated how Blacks and Whites interfaced in the South, but with the added constrictions of geographical "redlines" that hid the contrasts of the social inequities that existed between the two races. The population density of Northern Blacks was a function of discriminatory redlining that restricted their movement within certain geographical boundaries. The absence of industry and commerce in black communities, combined with the high unemployment, and poor education, as a result of de facto separation, caused a different type of pain and frustration, and produced a different indignity in the North, than the pain and frustration of the "White Only" and "Colored Only" signs that humiliated Blacks in the South.

What King, and the other civil rights leaders like Roy Wilkins and Whitney Young, had discovered, and they, as other Northern leaders chose to ignore, was that the deeply entrenched poverty of urban Blacks resulted from years of benign economic neglect. However, as Malcolm had pointed out, the conditions of the urban "ghetto" were always economic, and the equality state of the African American was a political reality that Whites had consigned to Blacks.

The appeal of Malcolm's message in the North was, that it was absent of the emasculating posturing of "bowing" and "knelling" in the face of hateful oppression, for rights that were God-given rights. The volatility of the Northern and Western urban cities, that would be evidenced in the second half of the 1960s, stemmed from a voiceless frustration that did not manifest itself, until Malcolm X brought it forward, in the rawest of terms. Despite the fact that both the NAACP, and the National Urban League, were based in the North, Malcolm X was the only voice in the North that resonated the truest sentiments of injustice for the northern Black. The bluntness with which Malcolm X, and the Nation of Islam, viewed race in America wasn't totally antithetical to the moral suasion invoked in the civil rights agenda.

Justice was an operational principle in the moral suasion argument, and in the nationalism argument. Only the nationalist perspective didn't appeal to the sensibilities, or the conscience, of Whites, to see the black point of view. It appealed for Blacks to define themselves, and cause others to see them, as they see, and define, themselves. The genesis of the "Pro-Black" movement was shaped by the Nation of Islam's paradigm that viewed America as immoral, irrational and unworthy of intellectual discourse on the question of race, and used the documented behaviors of lynchings, shootings, bombings, and beatings as justification that Whites, as a race caste, were inhuman and inhumane-and they were not totally incorrect in that regard.

What most who heard the doctrine had a problem with, was what the NAACP's Roy Wilkins called, a "hate white" message, that was as dangerous as white racism, which caused people in the social change movement and the American social mainstream to ignore the Nation's views, as a legitimate force in the movement.[1] Only, many Blacks in the North were listening to the Nation of Islam, because they didn't view King's doctrine of non-violence, in the midst of hostile racial confrontation that used fire hoses, mad biting dogs, and the beating of women and children, as a plausible strategy for achieving equality. There was no one more appalled at the bombing of the 16th Street Baptist Church than Malcolm X, who framed it as an "act of cowardice," deserving of a response. Through the voice of Malcolm, Elijah Muhammad, the spiritual leader of the Nation of Islam, crystallized the treatment of the "so-called Negro" in America, as anti-Christian, and framed all Whites as "devils" or doers of evil, for how they practiced or condoned racism in America.

Elijah Muhammad was essentially the first since Marcus Garvey to reintroduce black nationalism into the equality equation, by telling Blacks to "Love your own," "Be your self," "Do for self," and "Be not the aggressor, but fight with those who fight with you." Self-love, black pride, self-sufficiency and self-defense doctrine of what society then called, "Black Muslims," was a mass contradiction to what Martin preached in the South, that Blacks had "a right to stand for right," that they must "suffer in the face of oppression," "turn the other cheek to violence," "meet hate with love," and justice will prevail. Black Muslims called for the separation of Blacks from Whites, controversial, given the push for integration, and a position consistent with the massive resisters, but rationalized it from a different vantage point.

Malcolm articulated the Nation of Islam's position as black America being "in exile" in their own country, seeing America through the eyes of those being victimized. Malcolm saw a different conclusion to black America's social realities. The "American Dream," that King envisioned, Malcolm saw as "an American Nightmare."[2] This put the Civil Rights movement of the South at odds with the Pro-Black Radical Movement of the North, because they had the same goals in mind, namely, Freedom, Justice and Equality. They just had different aims of attaining them.

Many historians try to differentiate the ideological stances of the "Nation Malcolm," versus the "Post-Nation Malcolm," in trying to determine how his spiritual enlightenment affected his "Pre-Mecca," and his "Post-Mecca," (the 1964 Mecca, because Malcolm had visited Mecca in 1959 while still in the Nation) racial views. Much of this was done to ascertain how Malcolm X fit in the scheme of revolutionary societal change, during this time. In less than a year, Malcolm had shifted from black nationalism to "Afro-American" internationalism, which caused two changes of ideological position; the first change, being racial-religious, the second being political-cultural, whereby it could be argued that-if Malcolm changed-he changed from a racial militant to a political radical, fostering a broader self-conscious racial militancy that sought to bring a greater unity among all Blacks of various ideologies, on the grounds of black cultural identity, and an enlarged field of political activity.[3]

In the founding of the Organization of Afro-American Unity, Malcolm saw his mission of being wherever black people needed help, whether it was in being the only American delegate to speak at a meeting of the Organization of African Unity in Cairo, Egypt, going to Selma, Alabama or Jackson, Mississippi to support the southern Blacks, flying to Paris, France to speak to an African Student Conference (the French government didn't let him into the country) or being scheduled to speak before the United Nations to bring human rights violation charges against the United States (in the days following his assassina-

313

tion). Aside from a theological shift to orthodox Islam, there is no valid basis for asserting that Malcolm had "changed his views" about race in America. On the issue of equality, a post-nation perspective (his purported less militant phase) during his "Ballot or the Bullet" speech offered a clear position on how Malcolm saw violent racial conflict and the need for a broader struggle, stating;

> *I don't mean go out and get violent; but at the same time you should never be non-violent unless you run into some nonviolence. I'm nonviolent with those who are nonviolent with me. But when you drop that violence on me, then you've made me go insane, and I'm not responsible for what I do. And that's the way every Negro should get. Any time you know you're within the law, within your legal rights, within your moral rights, in accord with justice, then die for what you believe in. But don't die alone. Let your dying be reciprocal. This is what is meant by equality. What is good for the goose is good for the gander.*
>
> *When we begin to get in this area, we need new friends, we need new allies. We need to expand the civil rights struggle to a higher level-to the level of human rights....No one from the outside world can speak out on your behalf as long as your struggle is a civil rights struggle. Civil rights comes within the domestic affairs of this country...You may wonder why all of the atrocities that have been committed in Africa and in Hungary and in Asia and in Latin America are brought before the U.N. and the Negro problem is never brought before the U.N....This old, tricky, blue-eyed liberal who is supposed to be your friend and my friend, supposed to be in our corner, supposed to be subsidizing our struggle, and supposed to be acting in the capacity of an adviser, never tells you anything about human rights...When you expand the civil rights struggle to the level of human rights, you can then take the case of the black man in this country before the nations of the U.N.*[4]

These comments were not indicative of a philosophical change toward American racism. Malcolm's fanatic commitment to the liberation of poor black people alienated him, not only from most Whites, and many persons in the black middle class, but also from his own religious community, and from Elijah Muhammad, as well.[5] What separated Malcolm X from Martin King, and subsequently his mentor, was that the former two, though polar opposites on the question of integration, operated from a spiritual perspective in their analysis of America's race relations that didn't allow them to dismiss one's humanity, and excuse injustice. Both espoused that the fate of unjust Whites would come by

314

the punishment of God's hand. Malcolm was a spiritual man that operated out of a very political nature, and many of his speeches articulated the political and economic realities of being Black in America, espousing that the conditions of Blacks would not change until Blacks, themselves changed them, and defended themselves by their own hand. Malcolm expressed the right of Blacks to do everything that Whites could do, including protect and defend themselves-including represent themselves in positions of political power-including building economic realities for themselves, all functions of equality that had been denied to Blacks in the North, as well as, in the South. Spiritual men engage in spiritual acts, and political men engage in political acts.

Malcolm framed the "politics" of the black power paradigm for another generation long before Kwame Ture (then Stokely Carmichael) made it the slogan for the black youth joining the movement, as calls for "Black Power" replaced "We shall Overcome" amongst the youth. America's black youth were listening to Malcolm, while he was in "the Black Muslims," and didn't stop listening to him, when he left. Moderation of Malcolm's view was what Whites, and moderate Negroes, were seeking. The youth sought, and continued to seek, the truth Malcolm spoke, and the rage in which he spoke it. The "fire-breathing" Malcolm X, AKA, Hajj "El Malik Shabazz," got America's attention, every bit as much as the "bible-thumping" Right Reverend, "Dr." Martin King.

315

In talking about the implications of dire black poverty, and its effect on the black psyche, when everybody else was talking about anti-segregation and voting rights, Malcolm X was the center of the universe for those who wanted to "act in a political nature," and strike back at all forms of racial oppression, in a non-spiritual, non-passive way. It was difficult for Malcolm to stay strictly in the context of spiritual discourse, when the nation was ignoring the conditions of poverty, economic deprivation and voluntary segregation.

De facto segregation was hardly ever discussed, while de jure segregation was in existence. But in the absence of de jure segregation, the depth and impact of de facto segregation, and what it produced, became clear. De facto segregation produced poverty, and it was a socio-economic reality the nation was not unacquainted with. Malcolm X's voice, though the mainstream discourse tried to ignore it, was not irrelevant, in its articulation of the political and economic circumstances of Blacks in the North-and the South. Thus, the reason for his trip to Selma-in the last month of his life.

The 1960s produced a "rediscovery of poverty" that was, by and large, restricted to the elite of high power politics, where Presidents Kennedy and Johnson, and their advisers analyzed how to be serve this population. Yet, the impact of poverty was largely misunderstood by the great masses of people.[6] In 1960, 55% of African Americans lived in poverty, and yet nobody in the nation really noticed. Poverty was invisible to those who didn't want to see it, because it was a by-product of the racial separation that permeated the Northern and Western parts of the country.

Further, there was a realization that racial biases, that permeated society in residential and public enjoyment patterns, had made their way into employment hiring patterns, producing an employment discrimination that dramatically effected the economic standing of Blacks, and the communities in which they lived. One of Kennedy's legacies, for which he has received little credit, was that he was the first to use the term "affirmative action" in his Executive Order 10925, in 1961, that forbade government contractors from employment discrimination hiring based on race, creed, color and national origin. While not inventing affirmative action, he set a precedent for "affirmative action" programs, in the public and private employment sectors, by initiating a watchdog agency, the President's Committee on Equal Employment Opportunity (PCEEO).[7]

It was President Johnson, however, who is credited with inventing the premise of "affirmative" hiring policies, as a necessary policy tool, to disengage continuing discriminatory hiring practices. Johnson issued Executive Order 11246, in 1965, to give force to Title VII of the 1964 Civil Rights Act, which outlawed all employment discrimination, private and public sector, and established the Equal Employment Opportunity Commission (EEOC) to receive, hear, and monitor employment discrimination complaints. President Johnson's order made the Secretary of Labor responsible for formulating a specific plan of implementation, which the Labor Department focused on companies and agencies that had government contracts like construction companies, unions, civil service employers, and later included banks, trucking companies, steel mills, aircraft manufacturers, where it could establish and impose specific timetables to meet government-imposed hiring goals.[8]

Executive Order 11246 surpassed Kennedy's order, in that it required federal contractors to ensure that racial equity would be achieved, based on race, and that equal employment opportunity would

316

be given to Blacks-and later others. This included women (ultimately the biggest beneficiary of affirmative action), as well as, the other "protected classes" that included other people of color, veterans and disabled-which resurrected cries raised during the 1963-64 Civil Rights Bill filibuster that such policies would create a "black quota system."[9] Johnson, being a Southerner, knew mandating compliance was the only way to bring about results. Affirmative action was simply a policy measure to make up ground on historical employment discrimination.

However, Affirmative action came to signify a form of positive discrimination, in favor of African Americans, to catch up on missed opportunities, particularly in the areas of employment and education-areas that tended to receive, directly or indirectly, a modicum of public, or federal funds, on the grounds that, only by way of such race-conscious selection of Blacks, could the crippling legacy of centuries of institutional racism be overcome.

Of course, Whites didn't see it as necessary and, viewed affirmative action as another government imposed policy, to infringe upon their social and personal choices, which produced the very separation, and inequalities, that had brought America to this point. The racial disparities between black and white in America had become too large to ignore, though for years-the country had successfully done so. For decades, separate defined equal. Now in the mid-1960s, equal defined equal, and the economic realities of both white and black America was the measuring stick. By this time, society understood that "separate but equal" couldn't have been equal, given the gross inequalities of black/white life standards in the mid-1960s. What nobody had talked about, in terms of the inequities in wealth and income between Blacks and Whites, was most telling reality in what the state of black equality in America was, at this conjuncture.

No one really talked about the economic conditions that Blacks lived under, until Malcolm offered his critique of how Whites in the South were essentially resisting equality on a false premise that was both heinous and inhumane, and while it fit the Nation's ideological slant to cast Whites, in the collective, in a demonic light, for what had obviously become social reality of a second nature-in terms of racial practices-Malcolm X's insights offered a very factual analysis of how America had dehumanized the African beyond recognition, and had literally made it impossible to be self-sustaining in America. Malcolm was one of the first national black leaders, to raise the issue of reparations for black Americans, based on past discrimination and past humiliation. America, black or white, wasn't ready for that conversation in 1964 and 1965. Yet, even President Johnson understood that corrective measures were necessary to change the economic reality of African Americans, after years of racial discrimination and economic subjugation robbed Blacks of equal opportunities to compete, and benefit materially, in America's free market enterprise system.

Johnson declared a "War on Poverty," and attempted to create economic reform, through what he called his "Great Society" programs, one of which was specifically targeted at the African American community. Through the Economic Opportunity Act of 1964, Johnson hoped to create jobs by community action through the Office of Economic Opportunity, funding the program to the tune of $1.7 billion a year, to eradicate poverty. But most of the money was spent on bureaucracy, and from 1965 to 1970, the number of poor people in America actually rose from twenty-five million to thirty-three million.[10] The "War on Poverty" barely scratched the surface, representing another broken promise, and another level of frustration, for the overly deprived inhabitants of the urban core.

It was during this period of failed government programs that many of the black "underclass" began taking matters into their hands, to change their quality of life. With Malcolm's voice silenced, but his influence magnified by martyrdom, in the North, and among young people-many of whom were in King's SNCC ranks-the roots of "black power" methodology, of political empowerment and economic self-sufficiency, that redefined cultural thought, began to take shape. It dictated a new advocacy framework that would make up the next phase of the movement. King recognized that this next phase would include fighting the subtle race politic of de facto segregation, and the economic discrimination born out of it.

The new advocacy framework of "Black Power," however, caused King to lose control of his tightly knit non-violence approach that he had planned to take nationwide, in Philadelphia, Baltimore, Chicago, Detroit and Los Angeles.[11] Two weeks after the 1965 Voting Rights Act was signed, riots broke out in the section of Los Angeles known as Watts. The issues in this most violent revolt were the conditions that stemmed out of two factors, police abuse and economic subjugation.

When King went to Los Angeles to talk non-violence, he came away with a real sense that issues in the North and the West, were quite different than the enforcement of legal issues in the South. Blacks had rights in the North and the West; they didn't have anything else.

After the Watts revolt in 1965, California Governor, Edmund "Pat" Brown engaged the McCone Commission, headed by former CIA director, John McCone, to investigate the cause of the uprising. The McCone Commission reported back that the uprisings were a result of "despair in the ghetto" that was caused by a vicious spiral of economic failure and feelings of lassitude and helplessness that Blacks had felt as early as 1945-the beginning of a mass western migration of African Americans after World War II.[12]

The McCone Commission also offered an unique observation on the effects of de facto segregation that went to the center of what Whites knew (or didn't know) about the living conditions of urban Blacks. McCone's commission was critical of white ignorance of, and complacency toward, the living conditions of Blacks, surmising that riots stemmed from an absence of ownership in the community (both home and business), whereby "ghetto dwellers" could take no pride of ownership in their community, and see destruction (principally arson) as a way of lashing out at society. The McCone report viewed urban riots as "opportunistic warfare" against the ghetto "interment camps" in which Blacks had been interred by a racially hostile society.[13]

When the nation urban cities, including Chicago, broke out in riots in the summer of 1966, then repeated the occurrences of the summer of 1967, including the worst riot in American history occurring in Detroit, as well as, in Newark, New Jersey, and seventy-five other cities, President Johnson replicated Brown's California model, two years later in 1967, to investigate the causes of urban riots throughout the nation. He appointed Illinois Governor Otto Kerner to head the commission. America's most significant study on race, since the *Myrdal Report* almost twenty five years earlier, in 1944, was published on March 3, 1968.

Whereas Myrdal's report, *An American Dilemma*, was privately funded by a research foundation, published for public consumption in relative anonymity, the *Kerner Report* was a 426 page study that was government funded, much awaited, and when published-sold over *two million copies*. Race was now the issue in America and the Commission, with the possible exception of the urban crisis component, really didn't reveal anything more than Myrdal had revealed 25 years earlier, as it related to racial attitudes. America had become sensitized to race by *Brown*, the Civil Rights and Voting Rights Acts, and two violent summers (1963-1964) of televised mass protest, and racial confrontation.

America was just more ready to listen by 1968.

What came to be known as "*the Kerner Report*," the President's Report of the National Advisory Commission on Civil Disorders, responded to three very basic questions with respect to the nation's "riot" crisis; 1) What happened?, 2) Why did it happen?, and 3) What can be done to prevent it from happening again? *The Kerner Report* confirmed what the *McCone Report* had concluded a year earlier, that the riots were rooted in segregation, that remained a reality even after the 1964 Civil Rights Act, and economic inequality and that the condition wasn't just a "Watts" or California reality, but a nationwide reality. The Watts riot just represented "the front end" of a pattern of socio-economic frustration, turned national crisis, that the *Kerner Report* concretized in one simple contrasting conclusion; "America is a nation moving toward two societies, one black, one white, separate and unequal."

Then the report proceeded to analyze urban conditions with a candor that couldn't be mistaken. After outlining their analysis of the causes in several cities, the commission saw the riot phenomenon of 1967 as "unusual, irregular, complex and unpredictable social processes...like most human events, they did not unfold in an orderly sequence...acting against local symbols of white American societal authority and property in Negro neighborhoods-rather than against white persons.[14] The commission saw discrimination and segregation as long permeating much of American life, now threatening the very "future of every American," because segregation and poverty had created in the racial ghetto "a destructive environment totally unknown to most white Americans."[15] While the commission disavowed the violence and disorder that stemmed from the riots, it brought forth a concise rationalization that went to the center of the issue in helping Whites understand the intensity of black hostility and the "permanent apartheid" that poverty was creating, stating;

What white Americans have never fully understood-but what the Negro can never forget-is that white society is deeply implicated in the ghetto. White institutions created it, white institutions maintain it, and white society condones it.[16]

A statement framed, as hateful, when Malcolm X said it, but framed, as factual, when the Kerner Commission said it. The commission proceeded to list and rank twelve deeply held grievances that were identified in each of the 24 disorders surveyed in 23 cities (there were 164 disorders in the first nine months of 1967) prone to cause riots. The first level of intensity were three factors; 1) Police Practices, 2) Unemployment and underemployment, 3) Inadequate housing; the second level of intensity was composed of three factors; 4) Inadequate education, 5) Poor recreation facilities and programs, 6) Ineffectiveness of the political structure and grievance mechanisms; the third level of intensity involved another six factors; 7) Disrespectful white attitudes, 8) Discriminatory administration of justice, 9) Inadequacy of federal programs, 10) Inadequacy of municipal services, 11) Discriminatory consumer and credit practices, 12) Inadequate welfare programs.

In further responding to the question of "Why Did It Happens?" the committee listed as "ingredients;" Pervasive discrimination and segregation in employment, education and housing...Black in-migration and white exodus...Crime and poverty-ridden "Ghettos" that breed bitterness and resentment against society in general and white in particular...Frustrated hopes from unfulfilled expectations aroused by recent judicial and legislative victories of the Civil Rights Movement...A Climate of approval and encouragement of violence as a form of protest...frustrations of powerlessness that see violence as the only means of achieving redress..."A new mood" among young Negroes where self-esteem and enhanced racial pride replaced apathy and submission to 'the system"... and finally, Police as "a spark factor" in their symbolism of white racism and white repression.[17] The *Kerner Report* picked up on several important cultural shifts within black America. Most importantly, the absence of high paying jobs, and an attitudinal shift in the Civil Rights Movement, as well as, a need to acknowledge black youth's impatient, and intolerant, "call for action."

Joblessness had long been a problem for migrating Blacks. By the mid-1960s, almost 50% of the nation's African American population lived in the Northern, and West parts of the United States. However, Blacks were still suffering some of the same forms of discrimination, as they had in the South-relegating Blacks to lower paying, less desired jobs, and employing Blacks in positions with the least job security. The politic of "last hired, first fired" didn't start in the South, it started in the North, as Blacks were excluded from union jobs that had guaranteed pay wage scales, and no firing "without cause" status. The "right to work," and earn a living had always been subjugated to issues of societal access and voting.

Now that access and voting were no longer legal issues, eco-

321

nomic deprivation was an issue that was blatantly evident. So much in
evidence, King turned his attention North and West. Only King found
a different mentality, in both Whites and Blacks, when he went North.
King's attempt to bring attention to the economic discriminations of
the urban core, by staying in a housing project in Chicago and in
attempting to lead a march through all-white Cicero (a Chicago suburb), caused him to say that he'd never seen poverty like this in the
South, and he'd never seen hatred in Alabama and Mississippi like he'd
seen in Chicago.

This produced a different level of frustration (intensity of frustration as the Kerner Commission measured it) that led to confronting
the system, in a different way that the nation had seen in the South.
Malcolm had prophesied the anger and the rage. James Baldwin had
prophesied "the fire" next time. What America had basically written
off, in terms of these warnings, as demagoguery, and literary rhetoric,
came up on the nation rather quickly. All the warning signs were
ignored.

Black Power movement had its roots in the political and economic subjugation that Malcolm X had spoken of, like cries in the
wilderness, for eight long years. White America had tried to ignore
King, and the Southern movement, but the protest and resistance was
too great. They did ignore Malcolm, and the Northern movement, during this period, until the nation's "big cities" went up in smoke and violence. The Kerner Commission called it for what it was, and also
offered concrete recommendations, which can only be termed as the
closest to a reparations statement since Thaddeus Stevens proposed "40
acres and a mule" in a congressional bill (that never made it to the
floor).

The highlights of the commission's recommendations included; the construction of six million decent homes, in urban cities, over
five years, the establishment of two million jobs-one million in the private sector, and one million in the public sector-within three years, the
creation of a nationwide public relief to establish a minimum standard
of living-the poverty threshold-where the government will pay 90% of
a minimum income stipend of $3,335, provide "on the job" training by
both public and private employers, with reimbursement to private
employers with extra reimbursable costs of training the hard to employ
(now called the unemployable), remove artificial barriers to employment and promotion-including arrest records and lack of a high school
diploma, and the elimination of racial discrimination in Northern, as

well as, Southern schools, by vigorous application of Title VI of the Civil Rights Act of 1964.[18]

In total, the Kerner Commission offered a total of 37 ground-breaking, and far reaching, recommendations in the areas of employment, housing, education, and social welfare. The commission went to the core of the social and economic problems in America, and in almost every instance, race and race bias was an underlining factor in the condition that the Kerner commission called out. With each condition, the commission offered a recommendation to correct the condition.

Just as the legal advocacy, and non-violence protest of the South, had brought out the race problems of the South, the urban riots brought clear the race problems of the North. President Johnson, as best he could, tried to deal with the problems of two different regions, with two different cultures, both polarized, and now paralyzed, by the same issue, race. And there still the issue of the "white backlash," the remnants of massive resistance, of which neither court decisions, congressional legislation, nor presidential executive action could arrest. As the civil rights movement turned to eliminate employment and economic discrimination, white resistance became a nationwide endeavor, which took various different forms, and got only worse.

One month after the release of the Kerner Report, the conscience of America-its moral compass on the integrity of race relations in the United States for the past 13 years, the Rev. Dr. Martin Luther King, Jr., was killed by a sniper's bullet in Memphis, Tennessee. The assassination of King, on April 4, 1968, ignited another 125 riots nationwide. The murder of King was seen as the ultimate affront on Black America's pursuit of racial equality. If America could not tolerate King, who called for non-violence in the midst of the nation's most hostile times, it certainly wouldn't be able to tolerate a new generation of "pro-Black radicals," who were a lot less tolerant than King's movement was. The influence of the "children of Malcolm" had moved King's ideological stance, from the mainstream center to the "radical left," as King began to see that civil rights wasn't enough to address the overwhelming problems associated with economic deprivation and high unemployment, among Blacks.

323

In King's last years, he became a real-not imaginery-threat to the establishment, as his public criticisms of the Vietnam War, and his comments that he saw his "dream turning into a nightmare" (the realization of Malcolm's perspective-and words-coming out of Martin's mouth). King stated in 1967, after his Chicago experiment, that "people expect me to have answers, and I don't have any answers." King began to realize that full citizenship rights for Blacks went beyond the grounds of moral suasion, into some economic realities that he had never acknowledged. His assessments of America greed, and unwillingness to equitably distribute wealth and resources, turned King from an optimistic crusader of civil rights to a pessimistic, controversial politician, becoming so radical in his views that he became a somewhat revolutionary figure in his own right, propelling his legacy into a martyrdom that even Whites felt compelled to honor, when he became one of only three persons in American history to have his birthday recognized as a national holiday.[19] Essentially, the equivalent of being "canonized" in America.

Johnson realized more than anybody the magnitude of the King assassination, and the statement that it made in the equality struggle, that the intolerance of a peacemaker like King, was the ultimate demonstration of resistance to racial equality. The spirit of non-violence seemed to die with Dr. King, as Chicago Mayor, Richard Daley (Sr.) ordered his police to "shoot to kill," if necessary to restore order in his city, from rioting that occurred in the King assassination aftermath.[20] President Johnson rushed to sign another civil rights bill that was actually introduced in 1966, and had been stalled in Congress for the better part of two years, three days after King's murder in hopes of putting an end to the rioting.

The Civil Rights Act of 1968 was represented as an act to outlaw discrimination in the sale and rental of housing, but was amended to include the very legislation that King, and other civil rights workers, had hoped would protect their lives. It didn't save King's life but future activists would receive federal protection that would make it a crime to commit violence against civil rights workers, or cross state lines to commit mob violence and invoked stiffer penalties for civil rights violations. One tribute to the work of Dr. King that came too late.

Without King-his wisdom and maturity-in the mix, the Civil Rights Movement was subsequently overtaken by the more vocal young "radicals" of the Pro-Black Radical movement, who was determined to bring about equality and justice in their way-in defense of their rights, and in defense of themselves. Termed the "Prophets of Rage," Stokely Carmichael and H. Rap Brown on the east coast, and Huey P. Newton and Bobby Seale on the west coast, offered white America a two-edged sword that didn't offer the clear alternative that the Martin-Malcolm contract offered. In the two years prior to King's death, it had been said that he was losing his grip on the non-violence movement, as more and more youth joined the cause. Malcolm had predicted riots were coming before his death in 1965, and when Watts erupted, it hastened King's loss of power and the ascendancy of Malcolm's angry heirs within the movement, as strategies for social change was replaced by pure rage.[21] Anything "Black" was in, anything "Negro" was out, and there was no "in-between." You were either with the movement or with "the man."

By the end of 1968, police estimate that there had been fifty thousand arrests, and 8,000 casualties, in some 300 race riots, since 1965, while some 500,000 Blacks had participated in burning, and looting, and another half million were drafted to fight in "the white man's war"-the draft also seen as a tool of racial subjugation.[22] It was at this juncture, that the civil rights movement became irrelevant, as integration only represented compromise, to those whose only interest was "black power."

Thus, economic remedies became the policy priority for the nation to arrest, and pre-empt, urban riots never had a chance to work in the immediate days following their implementation. Social unrest over racial strife, and opposition to the war was just too great. This caused Johnson, Blacks' greatest equality advocate, to date, to shorten his administration. In choosing not to run for re-election, Johnson left the implementation of the *Kerner Report* recommendations to the next president. Blacks had hoped that would be Robert Kennedy, but he was assassinated two months after King in June, 1968. Subsequently, the Democrats were not able to hold the White House, and the Nixon administration, who played to a "white backlash," started latently enough by then California Governor, Ronald Reagan, who vocalized the riots as started by "criminals" and "mad dogs" that manipulated white resentment on a number of fronts, including mandatory minority hiring policies, and the violence of the urban riots.[23]

Reagan, who challenged Nixon for the nomination, in 1968 and 1972, would become the voice for racial resisters, who saw affirmative action as taking jobs from white people. Attempts to make up ground in the battle for equality made grounds worse. Any hopes that equality would become a cooperative process evaporated, as Whites, in 1968, voted their worst racial fears, and best hopes for relief from racial issues. Richard Nixon was elected, on a "Southern strategy" that promised to repeal some of the recent judicial decisions that had forced integration to proceed in the South.[24] The strategy was aided by

325

Alabama Governor, George Wallace's independent candidacy, that took 11 states that probably would have went to Nixon anyway, but Nixon's campaign definitely had a "racial edge" to it.

Nixon was left with little incentive to examine the causes of black economic deprivation, particularly employment, discrimination, causing him to deflect race issues, in exchange for racially codified policies that cued Whites, like "law and order" which meant safety and protection from riots (Nixon signed three crime bills). The recommendations of the Kerner Commission were never implemented. Nixon rejected the report, as making everybody responsible for the nation's civil disorders, except the Perpetrators and planners" who created them. Nixon ignored the Kerner recommendation, but promised to deal with the urban cities, by force, if he had to.

Thus, this policy stance was the impetus for his "tough on crime" position, and the crime bills he would later sign, that created the modern day Republican diversionary tactic, of dealing with the effects of social ills rather than its causes. Instead of pursuing affirmative action, Nixon used the economic conditions of Blacks to promote "black capitalism," a "bootstrap strategy" that became popular in the 1980s, as Republicans sought Blacks that were more interested in business than government facilitated employment. This was so Nixon wouldn't alienate his white blue-collar worker base, over the issue of racial "quotas" in the workplace. Employment gain was the source of real tension between Blacks and Whites, as affirmative action policies caused faster progress of Blacks than Whites, in income, and employment, during the decade of the1960s. Measured in constant dollars, annual income blue-collar black families, aged 25 to 34, increased from $5,785 in 1960 to $9,494 in 1970-a gain of 64%, compared to a 46% increase for white blue collar workers and increased the number of blue collar jobs held by Blacks, in the prior decade, by 42%, while Whites had only increased 7%.[25]

Despite closing the gap in employment among blue collar workers because the number of poor people grew (of which Blacks families disproportionately represented), the total dollar gap in income between Blacks and Whites actually widened. In 1950, the median income for nonwhite families was $3,014 as compared to $5,601 for white families-a gap of $2,387; by 1970, median income for Blacks were $6,516 while median income was $10,236-an income gap of $3,720, increasing the income gap differential by $1,133.[26] Whites still held the overwhelming number of blue collar jobs (what the 1970 Census called "operative and craftmen"), 14.3 million for Whites to 1.4 million for non-Whites.[27] Much of the hiring was a function of the riots, and attempts on the part of employers fearful of the economic consequences of future outbreaks, to mitigate their losses should riots re-occur.

For instance Detroit business executives hired over 50,000 unskilled workers for six months, from August 1, 1967 to February 1, 1968.[28] However, the jobs weren't permanent, low wage, non-union (in a union town), and viewed as largely tokenistic, and patronizing, as auto industry jobs previously denied to black workers suddenly became available-and although they were the worst jobs available-were seen as the next generation of "Niggermation."

Niggermation was a term Blacks coined earlier in the 20th Century, and it represented labor exploitation, when a black man did the job previously done by three Whites in the auto industry's pre-automation days, to keep labor costs down, while allowing equipment to deteriorate, causing unsafe working conditions for the black employee.[29] This usually led to black worker rebellions in the workplace.

Still, Whites were upset over the presence of Blacks, in "their" work environment, and appearance was everything to Nixon, who was anxious to generate some level of optimism that he was doing something about the "race problem" among his "Silent Majority (another code word)" base. The patronage of dissatisfied white voters reflected the early rise of what later became "Reagan Republicanism."

327

While Nixon's assistant secretary of labor for employment standards, Arthur Fletcher (who later was called "the Father of Affirmative Action"), was explicitly pushing for the need for "quotas and timetables" to correct for past and present discrimination, Nixon saw Blacks "making their own jobs" as a strategy to calm militant protest against job and wage discrimination. He searched feverishly to find a new "Booker T. Washington" to carry out this message.[30] Fletcher would temporarily serve that role as he convinced the Nixon administration that, rather than writing new civil rights law, the administration could use "existing government regulations (procurement laws)," and the "ingrained bureaucracy" to include Blacks in the economy and give them a "piece of the American pie" (business enterprise).[31]

The Pro-Black Radical Movement, which questioned the "good intentions" of Nixon, and the rest of White America, put the moral authorities-the church-to the equality test in Nixon's first six months of office. At a National Black Economic Development

Conference in Detroit in April of 1969, a "Black Manifesto" was issued calling upon "White Christian Churches," and "Jewish Synagogues," in the United States, and "all other racist institutions," to pay $500 million in reparations, and to surrender 60 percent of their assets to the conference, to be used for the economic, social, and cultural rehabilitation of the black community.[32] Calling for the same recommendations the Kerner Commission had called for a year earlier, the conference engaged the first large scale call for reparations, for the 300 years of economic deprivation inflicted on Blacks. Though short of the $500 million they asked for, churches gave millions of dollars of support to individual communities.[33]

Three years later, at the 1972 National Black Political Convention, held in Gary, Indiana, the body tied the economic impoverishment of the black community to both "historical enslavement," and "racist discrimination...subjected since 'emancipation,'" producing "an incalculable social indebtedness...owed to Black people by the general American society."[34] The Gary Convention called for a Presidential commission to be established, "to determine a procedure for calculating an appropriate reparation payment in terms of land, capital and cash..."[35]

It was highly questionable as to whether affirmative action would be fully implemented, and whether Blacks would ever be equitably compensated, under affirmative action strategies. As discussed in the next chapter, affirmative action started to be dismantled, legally and legislatively, and significantly weakened, within ten years after it was first launched. However, the call for reparations, in various forms, would only gain momentum over the next 30 years.

328

13

Bakke, Meritocracy and the Premise of "Reverse Discrimination"

"They did not bring us here to be educated! They brought us here to be enslaved! They did not bring us here to do for us! They brought us here to do us in!

Dr. Anyim Palmer, Founder of the Marcus Garvey School and Author of, *The Failure of Public Education in the Black Community*

329

Affirmative action, arguably the most sincere attempt to rectify past discrimination, and, at the same time, the most disingenuous effort to address past discrimination, became America's most attacked piece of public policy, in the last thirty years of the 20th Century. Equality resisters and civil rights obstructionists, who were singularly focused on the repeal of the *Brown* decision, shifted their focus to reverse a policy that threatened the economic standing of Whites in America, in a way that pursuit of equal rights had not. While integration was, by no means, forgotten-as documented by the very volatile busing battles of the 1970s, it was put on the back burner, as it related to the most pressing priority of white America, affirmative action policies. Affirmative action was something to be dealt with, and dealt with immediately, as far as Whites were concerned. Economic equality had never been a reality in America-and it's still not a reality, as will be discussed in later chapters. The accelerated hiring of African Americans threatened to overturn the inner core of racial inequality, the system of economic subjugation that undermined Blacks societal standard of living, quality of life, and ability to acquire wealth as "equals" in this society. The two most unstable rights of the African American were "the right to work," and "the right to earn equitably."

Affirmative action, as an enforcement policy, went directly at the integrity of both. While social and political equality were both functions of an egalitarian society, the practice of free market capitalism offered the most independence for those who practiced true democracy. America's economy has always been a political economy, where the production and consumption behaviors of society dictates policies that drive the economy, and the political and social benefits derived from that economy, in a way Harold Laswell termed, "Who gets what, when and how." Affirmative action was a policy shift that was not consistent with the beliefs and behavioral practices of America's dominant culture. It was also a policy didn't reinforce the myths of America's racial hegemony, that the economic interests of Blacks were always to be subordinated to the economic interests of Whites.

America practiced cultural hegemony that operated out of a group system whose principle stratification was a hierarchy based on race-to hide economic class differences. Euro-centric Americanism had engrained a set of ideas and values, on the privileges of whiteness, and socializes its dominant group, Whites, that there are benefits to their "top" status in society, one of them, of which, was the right to work. Just as Whites had socialized themselves to value the privileges of whiteness, they also socialized themselves to learn, and develop, anti-Black impulses that, consciously and unconsciously, frame blackness as dirt, excrement, danger, ignorance and other unknowns that, in essence, differentiate Blacks from themselves and cast them outside their own self-perceptions as American society's "in group."[1]

As human social systems are predisposed to form group based social hierarchies, as Karl Marx observed, group systems don't usually emerge until societies become more technologically sophisticated, and begin to amass economic surpluses.[2] America's economic surplus began amassing in 1619 (some suggest 64 years earlier, when slave trader, John Hawkins, captained the first slave ship to come to America a dozen years after Columbus came in 1555), when colonists understood what profits an out group, matched to the labor needs of an agricultural society, could produce. Africans soon became the engine of a slave labor economy-the fundamental reason the Transatlantic slave trade became as large as it did. As output (and profits) became tied to the economies of scale, more and more slaves were imported, that produced more and more profits.

Even after America became a nation of "equals," even after slavery was abolished, and even though segregation was legally dead, Africans in America-Colored, Blacks, Afro-Americans (later to be African Americans)-were never invited to be, nor accepted as, part of the in-group. As the "out group," or the negative reference group, Blacks, individually and collectively," became referred to by Whites as, "them," or "you people," and because of their historically subordinated relationship, became the recipient of a racism that made them "objects of hostility," versus "subjects of humanity" that produces an outpouring of empathy required to view society from the outgroup's perspective.[3] Well, in the 1970s, for the first time in American history, Whites got to view society from the outgroups' perspective, as affirmative action made Blacks-and later, anybody but Whites, the in-group in America's competitive political economy of jobs, wages and education.

Affirmative action, and the pursuit of economic equality, clearly threatened the "in-group" status of white Americans, that affected their emotional state, in a way that pursuits of social and political equality had not. Whites had been socialized to be the "in" group in the United States, the preferred group, the privileged group in a society, where the hegemonic group on top, gets the benefits, and, at least, one negative reference group, is on the bottom, and receives little, or no benefits.[4] The same hostility that manifests racism was now a tool to express dissatisfaction as Whites became angry "subjects" of a policy that went against two types of social hierarchies (achieved and ascribed) that defined their position in the American social system.

Achieved hierarchy represents a social preference, or status structure, based on socially useful and/or desirable characteristics, possessed by a given individual, while ascribed hierarchies are based on one's membership on a particular primordial group.[5] Ascribed hierarchies are group based, while achieved hierarchies are viewed as "ability based." When one's place in society's pecking order is based on abilities, or merit-as this hierarchy comes closest to what is referred to as, "meritocracy." Whites, who perceive themselves above Blacks, as a group, and in ability, internalized affirmative action as an affront on their group (whiteness), and their abilities (merit), as well as their anger, and their anti-Black feelings. White emotions affected their imaginative fantasies and social perceptions that caused Whites to subjectively represent affirmative action in more dramatic terms than had actually occurred. White subjects affected, and angered, by affirmative

331

action tended to tell hostile stories, find fault with others, and generate angry associates, as actions by employers to recruit, hire and promote from the "out-group" played an important function in the framing hostile racial attitudes among white workers. Black employment, or the presence of black workers, often serve as a gauge, of where the white group status barometer is, in Whites being able to feel better about themselves. Racial hegemony in America dictates that no matter how poorly white workers may be fairing in the society, they accept their status, and in many instances, their economic fates-as long as they're doing better than black workers.[6]

Whites, in America's existing social construct, also tended to feel better about themselves, as society upheld public policy decisions, individual acts of discrimination, and the behavioral asymmetry that legitimized mythical attitudes, values, beliefs or ideologies that provided moral and intellectual support to, and justification for, group based hierarchical social structures that promoted unequal distribution of value in social systems.[7] What James Sidanius termed as, "Legitimizing myths," come in three broad definitions; 1) Paternalistic myths, that justify social hierarchy, and inequality, by asserting that hegemonic groups (in this case, American Whites) are actually serving the interests of the entire society, including negative reference groups (in this case, American Blacks). Slavery was a considered a paternalistic myth, because it was argued that it was benevolent, and in the interest of Blacks who were incapable of taking care of themselves; 2) Reciprocal myths, that justify the "status quo" social hierarchy, as an equitable arrangement, between the hegemony's elites, and others in the population. Egalitarianism, in the midst massive economic inequalities, among industrialist and populist Whites, during the industrial revolution was a reciprocal myth, because Whites were assured that a class caste would never come about, as long as race mattered, and Blacks were assured to be at the bottom of the race caste-despite the fact that an economic class caste did exist; 3) Sacred myths, that justify the hegemonic structure by arguing that God gave the ruling elites their position in society, and these myths tend to be guided by ideological slants.[8]

A left wing sacred myth would be Lenin's theory that only communists understand the "real interest" of the working class, while a right-wing myth promotes beliefs that Manifest destiny was the burden of Whites to advance society, and the nation. Centrist/liberal myths would include such things as, the theory of meritocracy, the American

Protestant work ethic, and the myth of individual achievement.[9] Legitimizing myths are potent, or robust, and embraced by all major segments of the social system (including members of the negative reference group) to the extent they; a) help promote and maintain a given group-based hierarchy, and b) are well-engrained within, and consistent with, other central concepts of what's "moral" and "true" within the social system.

Two such powerfully robust legitimizing myths were the inherent belief of white superiority, and the Western beliefs of meritocracy, and individual achievement. The meritocracy myth is extremely powerful, because it is so well-anchored, and consistent with Americans' general notions of morality and fairness, that the idea of advancement, by merit, takes on the appearance of a self-evident truth.[10] True, except when it came to what could be achieved, and merited, by Blacks. This is because, in America's race caste, the notion of "black" meritocracy wasn't seen as true, within the American social system, and actually conflicted with another powerful legitimizing myth, that Whites were superior to Blacks. This meant that Blacks could not achieve, or merit, anything equivalent to what Whites achieved or merited. White supremacy, however, gave Whites the same "protected class" status, and denied Blacks rights that they both achieved and merited, in the same ways affirmative action defined individual Whites for group-based discrimination.

333

Whites could not equate the analogies when they received the privileges and benefits of race discrimination. Yet, when others became protected and began receiving benefits and privileges in the society that Whites had always received, Whites could equate such analogies of, say, achievement of others, based on infringement of their rights, caused by their racial exclusion, and suddenly, "merit" based achievement was being touted as "the American way."

American meritocracy has always been viewed as cloudy as egalitarianism, in terms of how both privileges and resources (principally wealth) has been redistributed amongst the American population. It never has been truly equal, and access has never been truly merited, as nepotism and cronyism has persisted since John Adams delivered the presidency to his son, John Quincy Adams, in 1824 to defeat Andrew Jackson, and Jackson got his revenge, when he became president in 1828 and introduced a crony "spoils" system in government that, while modified after the assassination of James A. Garfield in 1881, still permeates society today. Merit has been a selectively subjective inversion on American societal practice, but seen as a commonly held derivative of what is expected to hold true when "equals" compete for positions of privilege.

The definition of Meritocracy, as a political system, was first used in British sociologist, Michael Yong's book, *Rise of the Meritocracy*, where a social system would be lead by social revolutions, where one's intellectual quotient (IQ) plus one's effort that would produce a level of achievement that determines one's place in the society, after the masses overthrow elites, who lose touch with mass public sentiment. Proponents of meritocracies are better for the overall society, because it is more just, more productive, and allows for the end of distinctions based on social class or race. However, these ascertains can't be proved, because nowhere in the world do meritocracies run countries, nor practice the system in its totality.

Many countries practice some elements of meritocracy, such as representative democracies, like the United States, who choose candidates, based on how they've performed in the past, or how they campaign, and develop voter appeal. A voter will, many times, use merit as a principal consideration, based on who he or she perceives the candidate "earned their vote" or "deserved to win." Merit in employment became the primary consideration after Congress passed the Pendleton Act of 1883, that changed government hiring from the spoils system to the "merit" system, and established the Civil Service Commission that protected against unjustified firings. But private employment was, by and large, excluded from such regulation. Blacks and other minorities have historically sought government employment largely due to the civil service protection.

However, merit was, figuratively, an agreement among Whites as to how they would compete, and make social "fair and just" choices among themselves. Even prior to affirmative action, many Whites resented Blacks being chosen over them, in arenas where they both were allowed to compete. Particularly, in the case of prized benefits or rare opportunities, where the selection of a Black is viewed as more political than ability based. Never was this better articulated when Thurgood Marshall, in 1987, recounted a discussion with President Lyndon Johnson-who Marshall loved, for obvious reasons, not withstanding the fact that Johnson had done more for Blacks, in the areas of civil rights, than any other President in history, before or since-as to why he was considering not running for re-election in 1968.

Keynoting the annual Leadership Conference for Civil Rights

Conference dinner, Marshall told the crowd that Johnson told him in 1967, "It was not the Vietnam War that ruined me. I could lose the North (where most of the war protest was occurring), but not the South; it was my role in civil rights-especially your nomination, that lost me the South."[11] If Johnson made the ultimate sacrifice-his presidency-in doing the most for Blacks, his successor, Richard Nixon did the most to stymie the progress of Blacks created by the momentum of the Johnson administration. According to the first black cabinet member, and distinguished journalist, Carl Rowan, who wrote, "historical records make it clear that no single American did more to stunt the movement toward racial and ethnic equality in America than Richard Milhous Nixon," who Rowan called "a stealth bigot," and the country's most prominent mouthpiece for those who argued that "you can't legislate morality," and that "civil rights laws will do more harm than good."[12]

Nobody played racial politics like Nixon, who was on record as in support of civil rights, but used codified race language to undermine what he (and later Reagan) termed as "race policy." Nixon clearly double-talked the equality movement, by continually asserting that his administration was reaching out to black America, while advancing policies on civil rights to maximize a political payoff or as Nixon's insiders termed it, "contradictory policies for short term tactical gains," what Oval Office advisers called, the "zig-zag."[13] Nixon felt that making the Democrats pay attention to civil rights would ultimately benefit the Republican party, so he would throw the proverbial "bone" to Blacks and liberals, to preserve the peace-and the Union, while feeding the southern strategy goal of hyping the "Negro-Democratic Party" connection that ingrained hostilities of southern Whites toward the party, and permanently breaking up the solid south enmity toward the "party of Lincoln"-playing the racial-justice "zigs," in a way that also accompanied the southern strategy "zags."[14] Busing policy was one way Nixon played to the equality call, while fueling the ire of white fears-in the North, and the South.

In discussing court order busing in the period that shifted from "all deliberate speed" to "immediate speed," Nixon shrewdly played to anti-black propagandists, by adding "forced" to the word "busing," and tacked on "to achieve racial balance, that made the term "busing" so inflammatory that most Whites, and many Blacks, decried the policy, as against the will of local communities and parental choice.[15] Nixon was essentially using what his predecessors had left him, both in the

335

civil rights laws, and the enmity Southern Whites had for the men who had unraveled their southern culture. While Truman and Eisenhower had angered southern men, with their subtle enforcement measures that constituted marginal threats to the segregation system, Kennedy and Johnson, totally dismantled "the system," and became the first 20th Century Presidents to make southern bigots question their loyalty to the Democratic Party.[16]   By the time, Johnson left office, the Labor Department had set up a two pronged attack on employment discrimination, primarily, the Equal Employment Opportunity Commission, which became the investigation center for discrimination complaints where they attempted to use conciliatory mediation to resolve complaints; secondarily, the Office of Federal Compliance Program that tracked and monitored compliance. Though, many were now calling affirmative action compliance programs, "quota" enforcement programs, one thing can't be refuted-that there was a clear backlash mounting, against any equality program that resisted white hirings.

Nixon "talked their talk," and he knew it. While Nixon offered a cautious lip service to affirmative action, Congress was offering substance that was seen as fueling the fire for raced based preferences, by passing the Employment Act of 1972, that required state and local governments to set equal employment opportunity compliance programs, to collect employment records by race, to evaluate governmental hiring practices below the federal level, and required contractors who received government contracts, to demonstrate that they had met affirmative action requirements. However, most agencies failed to monitor the contracts, or understaffed monitoring offices, where it could not be adequately demonstrated that contracts were in compliance with affirmative action goals.

Nixon surrounded himself with advisors, who had skewed-even race-baiting-views, that helped frame "the quota system" arguments, in a way which made affirmative action a wedge issue, including one ideologue who endeared himself to Nixon, as a speechwriter with "catchy phrases," named, Pat Buchanan. Buchanan later became such a conservative demagogue that his views scared off moderates, and contributed to the party's loss of the White House in the 1990s, to a more centrist, Bill Clinton. Buchanan, who left the party in 2000 for a reform party started by Ross Perot, was Nixon's primary communicator. His words became Nixon's words, as he was able to convince that President that "the race issue" was the "dividing line," which would pry apart "the old Roosevelt Coalition (of Blacks, labor unions and white liberals)," and set one member group against another.[17] Contrary to popular belief, much of the codified language like "law and order" as a phase for controlling militant urban populations, and "tax and spend liberals" for opposition to those who support income redistribution, or sensitivity to social welfare policy, "the wealth state" for social conditions that required government assistance, and, of course, "racial quotas" for remedies of past discrimination, found its genesis among the operatives within the Nixon Administration. Affirmative action, Buchanan surmised, was the policy that would achieve that reality.

Nixon embraced affirmative action, as a neo-conservative "zig," calling quotas, "totally alien to the American tradition," beseeched America, during his 1972 party nomination acceptance speech in Miami, to "reject a philosophy that would make us the divided people of America," while "zagging" with civil rights groups in support of the "8-A" set-a-side program, that reserved fixed percentages of federal contracts for minority- owned businesses, and sung the praises of the "Philadelphia Plan," a program that increased black access to union jobs in the construction trades that required thousands of businesses to meet "goals and timetables." This drove a wedge between Blacks and labor, who accused Nixon of making labor "the whipping boy of affirmative action," and trying to "score 'brownie points' with civil rights groups."[18] Nixon's strategy worked, as the Philadelphia Plan, in particular, viewed as anti-labor and pro-black, drove a wedge between the Democratic Party and labor, as labor withheld their resources, in 1972 causing the President to win 61% of the popular vote. His Democratic opponent, George McGovern, took only one state (Maine), and the District of Columbia, as union membership abandoned him, leaving only the hardcore anti-war activists, and liberals, the impoverished (poor), and Blacks.[19] Affirmative action had become the political albatross of the Democrats that Richard Nixon effectively hung around their collective necks.

Nixon would soon become embroiled in the controversy that would force him to resign the presidency, but he had done his part to make a mockery of the policies that were intended to help Blacks, in their equality efforts. He did little, however, to dismantle affirmative action, as most of the policies he inherited, were left in place after his resignation. His use of affirmative action policies was solely political, as Nixon used it to mobilize new Republican voter bases, and alienate traditional Democratic voting bases. Nixon did little to push civil rights beyond what political use he had for it.

337

Meanwhile, the first U.S. Supreme Court decision relevant to affirmative action actually upheld the policy. With Thurgood Marshall now firmly entrenched in an ideologically shifting court, influenced by Nixon who had appointed a new Chief Justice, Warren Burger, and the first of the Associate Justices, Harry Blackmun (Nixon would have four Supreme Court appointments, as many as any President in the 20th Century, except FDR, who was elected for four terms), shifting the Court's ideology from left of center firmly to the right, the Supreme Court heard the case of *Griggs v. Duke Power Company* (1971).

In *Griggs*, African American petitioners argued that their rights had been violated, under Title VII of the 1964 Civil Rights Act, because Duke Power Company used criteria unrelated to job performance, in hiring and promotion considerations, that adversely affected decisions in their not being hired, or promoted.[20] The Burger Court, in the one, and only, unanimous decision by a Supreme Court on affirmative action, found in favor of the petitioners 8 to 0, though a Supreme Court, of a different composition would overturn this decision later on a five to four vote.[21]

The first higher education case filed to challenge affirmative action to reach the Supreme Court, was the case of *DeFunis v. Odegaard* in 1974. Marco DeFunis, Jr., was a white Jewish male of Spanish-Portuguese origin, whose family lived in America for several generations. In 1970, DeFunis applied for admission to University of Washington Law School (UWLS). DeFunis, who applied to UWLS, as his first choice of six law schools he applied to, was considered simply "a white male," under the government's definition of disadvantaged students, which allowed him to choose "other" on the race identification box, used by the University of Washington. With an above average LSAT score of 566 (a fifty point improvement on his first score of 512), UWLS denied DeFunis' application. Instead of attending another law school-DeFunis, who was accepted to University of Idaho Law School, University of Oregon Law School and a private law school (he was declined by Boalt Law School at UC Berkeley and one of the private law schools), decided to wait a year, and re-apply again. Taking the LSAT a third time, DeFunis raised his score to 668, thus, placing him in the top seven percent of law school applicants, nationally.[22] When DeFunis applied again in 1971, the University of Washington Law, however, averaged DeFunis' three scores which placed him at 582, again above average, but well below the top tier of applicants. DeFunis was declined a second time, and rather than go to another law school, he filed a civil suit against the University of Washington, stating that he was deprived of his equal protection rights, under the Fourteenth Amendment, because the UWLS had racially classified applicants, and had preferentially admitted members of favored racial groups, who had poorer scores than his. DeFunis was seeking court ordered admission, based on the fact that "special admissions" program illegally established racial preference, as a admission criteria, discriminating against white men in the process.[23]

DeFunis reached the United States Supreme Court in December, 1973, who heard oral arguments, as the UWLS denied it set up a "quota system," because it only sought a "reasonable representation" of "historically suppressed" minority applicants, which it estimated at "15% to 20%" of it's applicants, if "sufficient qualified applicants were available," but hadn't set aside any specific number of seats for the applicants.[24] The U.S. Supreme Court dismissed the *DeFunis* case, because it was seen as moot, since the UWLS had subsequently admitted him, and he was about to receive his degree, as the case was about to start, but it was this case that planted the seed surrounding "racial quotas," by asserting the University of Washington had set up a quota system.

The quota system argument never went away. A few years later, the defining case for "what was a quota" would come to the forefront. The biggest hit affirmative action took in the 1970s was a legal challenge to higher education admissions policy, that became the legal precedent of what affirmative action should be, how it should be interpreted and how it should affect non-protected classes. In 1973, at the University of California, at Davis Medical School (UCDMS), a white student named Allan Bakke applied for admission to the medical program. He was denied. He applied again, in 1974. Again, he was denied. After the second time, he sued the State of California. His claim was "reverse" racial discrimination. Reverse racial discrimination asserted that Whites, who had no proven role in past discrimination, were being penalized, based on the color of their skin, when they were excluded, or passed over, in positions of employment, education and contracts, in favor of minorities.

The *Bakke* case was born of out a challenge to a "set-a-side" system. Developed by UC Davis, its racial set-a-side admissions process allowed a specific number of seats to be held for minority student admissions, in its medical school, as a strategy to increase its minority enrollment. UC Davis' medical school program, started in 1968, in its

339

first two years, had only a regular admissions policy which it had admitted 100 students; 83 Whites, 14 Asians, two Blacks and one Latino.[25] The school's faculty, seeing that Blacks and Latinos only made up three percent of the school's admissions, while Asians-Americans made up three-quarters of the minority applicants, and four-fifths of minority enrollees, decided to create a special admission's program, in 1970, to increase opportunities in medical education for disadvantaged citizens.

The admissions class of 1970 had 50 seats, of which eight seats would be held for disadvantaged minorities. In 1971, demand required that admission open up 100 seats, of which 16 seats would be held for minorities. Under UCDMS's procedures, nondisadvantaged and disadvantaged persons of the preferred minority groups (Black, Latino, Native American-Asian-American weren't viewed as a disadvantaged group, because they were admitted through regular admissions, and overrepresented in the medical student population), were assigned to the regular and special admissions programs, respectively. Preferred minorities could be admitted through either program, while Whites could only be admitted through regular admissions. Both programs together, from 1971 to 1974 (100 seats each years), admitted 64 minorities in the special admissions program (100% of the available seats) and 13% of the 336 remaining seats, in the regular admissions program, meaning that though minorities were only 11% of the applicants, they were awarded 27% of the seats-allowing minorities, in comparison to non-minorities, to have a twice as good a chance for admittance, under special programs, and better than regular odds in the regular admissions program.[26]

When Allan Bakke applied in 1973, he competed against 2464 applicants, for 100 seats. 2173 of them, including Bakke, were in the regular admissions pool, giving them entry odds of 1 in 26 for any single applicant, where for minority applicants-the odds of admission were 1 in 18, in the special admissions pool, plus minorities could be considered for regular admission, where Whites could not, reducing their admission odds even further.[27] Bakke, a Viet Nam veteran, had outstanding academic credentials; a 3.5 GPA (B+ to A-), high MCAT scores (97th percentile on the science test, 96th percentile on the verbal test and 72nd on the general information). Bakke applied to eleven medical schools. Four granted him interviews, Stanford, Minnesota, Mayo UC Davis-but none admitted him, citing an excess of "qualified candidates over the number of space available."[28] Davis was the only one, with a special admission program, that held seats open for minorities applicants. In the Davis admission process, applicants invited to the admission interview process, had a one in five chance of being admitted. An evaluation committee of five interviewed applicants, and gave them ratings based on the interview and non-cognitive factors based on the applicant's file. The baseline score for admission was 470. Bakke interviewed at the end of the fall, 1973 admission cycle, which had started the previous fall.

Under UCDM's "rolling admissions" procedure, automatic admission was accorded applicants with a benchmark rating of 470, and promising candidates with somewhat lower scored were also accepted, but most of the early applicants-including the lower scores, that were accepted early in the application process.[29] Due to his mother's illness, Bakke was not able to complete his application until January, 1973. His interview was not scheduled until late March, a time when three-quarters of the total acceptances already had been extended, and the 470 benchmark was being strictly enforced for regular admissions. Bakke scored a 468, and even though his MCAT scores were well above-and his GPA about the same-many of those who had been accepted, Bakke was declined admission. Between the time of Bakke's first application, and his second application, he wrote a letter to the admissions committee chairman, Dr. George Lowery, questioning the validity of the special admission program, in particular, the racial quota system. Bakke stated that he "believed that admissions quotas based on race are illegal," and that he was considering "formally challenging these quotas through the courts."[30]

By the time his 1974 application for admission came up for interview, the committee was well aware of who he was, and the politics of his application. The application class for 1974 was larger, by more than 50% than the previous year-a total of 3737, with 3100 of those, being considered for 84 regular admission seats, an enrollment to application ratio of 1 admit for every 37 applications. The admission threshold was that an applicant had to score 94 out of 100 in their interview. In 1973, with a score of 468, Bakke scored 93.6. In the 1974 interview, there were six committee members (as opposed to five the previous year), and a top score of 600. The benchmark was a score of 564. Bakke scored a 549, worse than the prior year, with a threshold score of 91.5, with Dr. Lowrey giving Bakke the lowest score on the committee of 86.[31] Bakke was again declined.

In November, 1973, Bakke filed a compliant with the San Francisco regional office of HEW-Office of Civil Rights, alleging he had been a victim of racial discrimination, because UCDMS had adopted a "16% racial quota." On June 20, 1974, Bakke filed a lawsuit in state court against UC Davis, seeking to compel the medical school to admit him based solely on the fact that the special admissions minority program had reduced the number of places for which he could compete-not petitioning the program for all white people, but as an individual, having been violated by a discriminating system.

Bakke was thirty-three years old when he first sought acceptance to UCDMS, in 1973. He filed suit the following year, after his second denial, and the trial court decision came a year later, after he had turned thirty-five. The California Supreme Court ruled in his favor, eighteen months later in September, 1976, and the U.S. Supreme Court ruled in his favor in June of 1978-while partially defending the need for affirmative action-when Bakke was thirty-eight years old. It took five years to determine Bakke's fate, and had he lost, it presumably would have ended his quest to become a doctor. However, *Bakke*, even while it was pending, influenced the race policy landscape, as other cases benefited from this new area of constitutional challenge raised by its plaintiff.

Reverse discrimination was viewed as a legitimate issue and a rolling snowball, as it related to legal interpretations of Fourteenth Amendment rights, and now other students had heard about the racial challenges of DeFunis and Bakke. This was the instance in the case of Rita Clancy. Clancy, a twenty two year old Russian born Jewish woman, applied to UCDMS through the special admissions program, and was denied, because of her race. Though she was a psychobiology major with an A-minus GPA, she was referred to the regular admission's program, placed on the alternate list where she was fourth-moved up to first by the time the 1977 fall semester started, but wasn't admitted.[32] Her claim being even stronger than Bakke's, Clancy filed suit in state court just before classes began, and requested a court-ordered admission, on the grounds of Bakke, or through the special admissions program, which still carried the race-free label of "economically or educationally disadvantaged." She won directed admission in the state court, and when the UC appealed to have the case transferred to the federal district court-the outcome was the same, based on the federal judge wanting to "give the [*Bakke*] decision respect," and to avoid doing harm to Claney, in denying her admission, which the court said, "would be far greater than what the university would suffer if she was admitted despite an adverse ruling (in their favor) in Bakke."[33]

Thus, even before Bakke was settled, Clancey was able to make use of the essential premise of Bakke's claims at UCDMS, "denial of immediate rights," and "harm to non-offending individuals," even before Bakke could. Claims of "denial of rights," and "harm to the non-protected classes of non-discriminating people," resonated loudly among legal theorists. In June, 1978, Bakke's time came.

On June 28th, 1978, the Supreme Court announced the *Bakke* decision. The decision came on a Wednesday, a departure from the usual Monday decisions, because of the courts large case load in the 1977-78 session. The announcement was without warning, but the public and court watchers, had been "waiting on *Bakke*," looking for clues in which way the Court was leaning, watching other Court decisions, and guessing, since early April, when the case would be announced. A clue that something was amiss when a courtroom packed with media, civil rights leaders, the Solicitor General, many court employees, and even five justices' wives, as the outcome of this much anticipated case prompted Justice Lewis Powell, to say-prior to announcing the decision-"Perhaps no case in my memory has had so much media coverage."[34]

Bakke, like *Dred Scott, Plessy, Gaines* and *Brown* before it, received no less public attention than other "race cases" that would have a profound impact on societal behavioral and policy practices. However, the *Bakke* decision lacked the judicial consensus of those prior decisions. In fact, Justice Lewis began the announcement with the statement, "We speak today with a notable lack of unanimity," as the Bakke decision involved an unusual 4-1-4 three way split, that produced three majority judgments on Bakke's admission, UC Davis' special admissions program, and the use of race as an admissions factor. The court split into essentially two blocks, and wrote five different opinions on how they saw the *Bakke* case.

On the first judgment, Justices Stevens, Stewart, Rehnquist and Chief Justice Burger, held that the Davis special admissions program violated Bakke's rights, under the Title VI provision of the 1964 Civil Rights Act, while Justices Brennan, White Blackmun and Marshall upheld the Davis program, as protected by both the Equal Protection clause of the Fourteenth Amendment, and Title VI; Powell added his vote to the Stevens bloc (Steven's wrote the opinion), striking down the Davis program, ordering UC Davis to admit Bakke, and also voted with Blackmun bloc (all four of whom wrote separate opinions), in favor of the right of the University of California to use of race,

343

as a criteria for admission. Both sides made "quotas" the central theme of their opinions, asserting both its legality, and illegality. Powell saw "quotas" as illegal, in the Davis context, but permissible, as a remedy to repair past discrimination and, thus, was the fifth vote in each instance, and the only justice to vote in favor of all three judgments.[35]

Justice Thurgood Marshall wrote the most impassioned defense of affirmative action, stating his cynicism of the state of black America and bitterly cited the Court's historical role in advancing inequality, stating that;

> *"The experience of the Negro in America has been different in kind, not just in degree, from that of other ethnic groups... The dream of America, as the great melting pot, has not been realized for the Negro; because of the color of his skin he never even made it into the pot...[After] several hundred years of class-based discrimination against Negroes, it is more than a little ironic that...the Court is unwilling to hold that a class-based remedy for that discrimination is permissible...I fear we have come full circle...Just as the Court had earlier destroyed the movement toward complete equality (by sanctioning racial segregation), Now we have this Court again stepping in, this time to stop affirmative action programs...*
>
> *The position of the Negro today, in America, is the tragic, but inevitable consequence of centuries of unequal treatment. Measured by any benchmark of comfort or achievement, meaningful equality remains a distant dream for the Negro."*[36]

344

Despite Marshall's objections, the quota argument made by southern segregationists, during the filibuster of the 1964 Civil Rights Act, had made it into the opinions of the Supreme Court. Moreover, discrimination, in reverse, made sense to the Court, and the notion that any black, brown, or any other disadvantaged person of color, could make a blanket claim of "benefit due to historical discrimination," against any white person, whether they discriminated or not, was viewed by a majority of the justices, as illogical, at best, and equally as illegal of historical discrimination, at worse. In the Supreme Court decisions of the immediate *post-Bakke* era, the Court-while remaining conflicted about affirmative action-continuing to uphold its tenets.

In the case of *United Steel Workers v. Weber* (1979), a Supreme Court majority found that "voluntary affirmative action programs," using "a temporary quota system," to eliminate traditional patterns of "conspicuous racial segregation," was permissible under Title VII of the

Civil Rights Act of 1964, where a plant's workforce was less than two percent, while the local workforce was 39% African American.[37] This decision was followed by another in 1980, in the case of *Fullilove v. Klutznick*, where the Supreme Court found that a congressional affirmative action program, requiring ten percent of a federal grant, for public works projects, could be used to procure the services of minority business enterprises. The Court cited that the program did not violate the Fifth, or Fourteenth Amendment, nor the Civil Rights Act of 1964, because the program was within Congress' power to attempt to eradicate past discrimination, as the program targeted failed compliance in federal procurement, that had only achieved a one percent minority participation in federal contracts, when minorities comprised 15% to 18% of the national population.[38]

This would be the last time the Supreme Court would be viewed as "favorable" to affirmative action, as Ronald Reagan, who came into office in 1981, took significant steps to make sure that his key civil rights appointees, as well as his judicial nominees, shared his opposition to-what his 1980 Presidential campaign framed as-"quota policies." Like economic equality, social equality would also take some significant hits as two cases, *San Antonio Independent School District v. Rodriguez* and *Milliken v. Bradley* proved to be frontal assaults on *Brown*, in assuring that disparities in unequal schools would be maintained.

345

In March, 1973, the Burger Court overturned a lower court decision that said the school financing system in Texas, that unfunded poor schools, in the mostly Mexican-American neighborhood of Edgewood in West San Antonio. Demetrio Rodriguez, and his neighbors, challenged the scheme of public schools being financed by local property taxes, that enabled high value and commercialized communities to supplement school revenues, allowing for greater "per student" spending.

A three judge federal panel agreed with Rodriguez, in January, 1971, and ruled that unequal school financing violated the Fourteenth Amendment. The Burger Court disagreed. Led by "the Nixon Four," Chief Justice Burger and Justices Powell, Blackmun and Rehnquist, along with Justice Potter Stewart, made up a new conservative majority, introduced a new era of judicial restraint, by ruling five to four that there was no proof that San Antonio's financing system advantaged any identifiable group of poor people, that the Equal Protection Clause doesn't require absolute equality, or precisely equal advantages, and that school were locally controlled, and not a fundamental interest under the Constitution.[39] *Rodriguez* prohibited the type of centralization of funding and control, that made it impossible to achieve uniform standards, ensuring that schools and districted disproportionately funded, would continue to be, because the ruling made it impossible to remedy the huge disparities in per capita spending between one school system and another.[40]

The same four Nixon appointees and Stewart encored their act a year later, confirming that judicial activism was dead, when they remanded the case of *Milliken* back to the lower courts, asserting that the lower courts had erred, when it said that forced busing outside city limits, or between school districts, was not an appropriate remedy for overcrowded segregated schools in Detroit, and remedies had to be found within the district, keeping poor, overcrowded, segregated districts away from rich, less crowded, well-resourced segregated districts. *Milliken* avoided the question of *de facto* segregation that now allowed residential patterns to be the separation point that law had been during *de jure* segregation, twenty years earlier.

Milliken was the first Supreme Court case to back away from *Brown*, and became the law of the land, as the precedent for protecting the schooling rights of local communities, virtually causing "white flight" exoduses out of central city districts, to avoid busing, and stymieing mandatory metropolitan desegregation plans that now could only include suburban educational plans on a "voluntary basis."[41] Of course, no suburban school districts adopted voluntary educational plans, because Milliken said they didn't have to. The politics of "re-segregation," that fifty years after *Brown* has been much debated, actually began with the case that thirty years earlier, ceased forced busing.

These two cases alone assured that public schools within urban, and rural communities, would be highly segregated and unfunded, while suburban schools that would get away with only token integration programs, would continue to be highly funded, continuing long held inequalities in education. Combined with the new legal interpretation of affirmative action, it had become apparent that government's role in the equality movement was being checked, by both public sentiment and legal reasoning. Furthermore, the limits for judicial activism had been reached, and a new conservative ideology now held a majority on the court, whereby integrationists and equality advocates could no longer rely on the courts to give force to social and economic parity gains, at the expense of the individual rights, political will, and economic standing of Whites. After twenty years of backing equality policies, the Court was giving protection to America's largest "un-protect-ed" class, white people. The "Whites Rights" movement had begun, and affirmative action, more than anything-including busing-had brought it on.

Reverse racial discrimination, and individual rights, became the basis for which Whites asserted their 14th Amendment rights of equal protection under the law, and by virtue of the fact that they weren't being "treated equally," in terms of having an equal chance to access economic and educational opportunities, Whites, on an individual basis, claimed that their civil rights were being violated, by race class, or protected group, discrimination. And just as higher education was used by Houston, Marshall, and the NAACP to expose the inequalities in segregated discrimination, Whites used higher education to challenge, what they called the new "de jure" race policy, racial quota systems. While the Supreme Court affirmed that affirmation action, for past discrimination, was a legitimate policy, given America's racially discriminating history, and upheld the policy, in theory- affirmative action, in practice, became even more convoluted. So did the quandary of how best to achieve racial equality. It was within this quandary that affirmative action, in practice, began its decline. It all started the moment *Bakke*, was decided.

347

14

The Reagan Revolution:
The Return of Redemption and Racial Privilege

There are no good times to be black in America,
but some times are worse than others.

- David Bradley

Here we are in the '80s, practically the '90s, talking
about the same thing we were talking about in the '30s.

- R&B Entertainer, James Brown

Nixon's resignation in 1974, and the subsequent election of Jimmy Carter, created a four-year hiatus for the attack on racial equality. Carter, defeated Nixon's replacement, Gerald Ford-who was appointed to the Vice Presidency to replace Spiro Agnew, Nixon's original Vice President. Agnew, the former Maryland Governor was forced to resign, after being accused of taking kickbacks, while he was Governor of Maryland. Ford, then, became the only President in the history of the United States, to serve in both the office of President and Vice President in appointed capacities, without being elected by the American people.

Carter's election offered equality only a brief reprieve, as Nixon's abuses left America no choice but to make a change. It had to tolerate Nixon's replacement for two years, however, and President Ford was bent on completing the assault, on affirmative action, that Nixon had started. Taking office on August 9, 1974, Ford assured this demise, by giving Nixon a "blanket pardon" for "all offenses against the United States," undermining Ford's "new start" proclamation that promised an administration of "openness and candor."[1] Ford was seen as a team player for conservative Republicans, since he was elected from a "safe district" in Michigan, since 1948, and had been serving as House Minority Leader since 1965. During his tenure as House Minority Leader, Ford delivered 85 to 90 percent of the votes of Republican House members against Lyndon Johnson's Great Society legislation.[2] There was no reason to believe that Ford would be anything other than a loyal soldier, and that pardoning Nixon was just part of the "deal" to maintain Republican control over "quotas" policies and other "social welfare" legislation.

Nixon had contemplated defunding the Office of Economic Opportunity but his staff hadn't completed the paperwork. By the time Watergate came about, Nixon had become too distracted to deal with it. In the stack of unfinished business that Nixon's hasty exit brought about, Ford came across a memo from Nixon's domestic affairs chief, Kenneth Cole, recommending termination of the agency, on the basis that such, "Community Action is more properly a state/local program," that would save the federal government $300 million dollars. On just his fifth day in office, Gerald Ford signed the approval box on the memo, ending the funding for the primary outreach agency of federal government contracting opportunities, to assure economic equality in federal contracts could be achieved.

When violence broke out in Boston during 1975 over the federal courts order to desegregate public schools, Boston Mayor, Kevin White, requested U.S. Marshals, to help enforce the order, and quail the violence-as had been done in Little Rock in 1957. Ford gave a tacit endorsement to mob violence, as an obstruction to equality compliance, by denying White federal protection, saying "The court decision in that case, in my judgment, was not the best solution to quality education in Boston. I respectfully disagree with the judge's order."[3] The Ford administration was willing to allow black children to be put in harm's way, by denying them equal protection under the law.

On the other hand, Ford was prepared to allow a local sub-division to disobey a federal order, by nullifying it under the same premise that Whites had assigned to forced busing, a mythology that described busing, as "the forced exposure of vulnerable little white children to quite hostile and dangerous black environments...that involves "placing that innocent child in a far distant blackboard jungle, with switch-

349

blade knives, stealing of lunch money, assaults in restrooms, and terror, far from the parent's benevolent protection."[4] Despite the same hostilities were, in evidence, present in the white schools that black students attended, busing became a "one-way" proposition in most cities, because *Milliken* gave white parents "an out" in terms of voluntarily sending their children into black communities-while, all the while, still resisting the presence of black children in "their" schools. These were just two examples of how the Nixon/Ford administration's recalcitrant behavior stonewalled policies to end official discrimination against Blacks, at all levels of government. In particular, at the national level, where they even nullified the Supreme Court's mandate, requiring affirmation action to be practiced by all branches of the federal government.[5]

While working class Whites trusted Ford's racial instincts, his insider politics, and still strongly perceived "connection" to Nixon corruption, caused them to turn to a Southern "outsider," in hopes of having someone they could both trust and control. Southerners had trusted Lyndon Johnson's judgment (they didn't like his decisions but knew he was right), but they couldn't control his politics. Johnson too knowledgeable and wily. Southerners controlled Nixon politics, but couldn't trust his judgment-not even when he was Vice President. Nixon always had "trust" issues. Ford showed he could not be trusted his first month in office, through he did his part to hold the party's racial politics in line.

Ford lost a close election to Georgia Governor, Jimmy Carter, who won the election by a coalition composed of working class Whites and Blacks, carrying 90% of the black vote. Carter's only debt coming in, was to former King aide, Andrew Young, who was in the House of Representatives (the first Black ever elected from Georgia), and noted when Carter carried Mississippi, due to a large black voter turnout, "The hands that picked cotton finally picked a president."[6] Carter had won, walking a fine line on the question of affirmative action, by drawing distinctions in what he supported, as affirmative action, saying that he favored "flexible affirmative action programs using goals" and opposed "inflexible racial quotas."

Carter's opponents, as well as his white supporters, seeking a firmer stand against affirmative action, accused Carter of "being fuzzy" in his thinking, but political observers later understood that Carter was purposely ambiguous, in order to maintain connections in his two key constituency bases.[7] Carter reversed the trend against affirmative action, started by Nixon and Ford, by signing the Omnibus Minority Business Act of 1978, which employed set-asides that reserved a percentage of government business for minority firms. Carter also made a significant difference in the racial make-up of the federal courts, appointing eight Blacks to appellate judgeships, and thirty to federal district judgeships.[8] This was in sharp contract to Nixon and Ford, who had not appointed a single Black to the federal courts. Of Carter's judicial appointments, 15% were Black and 16% were women.

The 1970s did provide African Americans some political gains, but fell far short of equality, as the gaps in education, wealth and jobs only narrowed slightly, and by 1975, the most significant indicator of present day equality-income-the one indicator that had narrowed considerably, began to widen again.[9] The real outcomes wouldn't be measured until after Carter left office, but in 1983 (two years later), when white unemployment reached 10%, black unemployment reached 20%, reflecting the widest employment disparity in three decades-since before the *Brown* decision.[10]

The primary reason for the increase in black unemployment was a boon in the black male population. From 1960 to 1982, the black male population over the age of 16 doubled from 5.6 million to 10.73, while the number of employed black men only increased 1.79 million (from 4.15 million to 5.94 million), thus adding 3.4 million black men to the unemployment lines, and dropping the proportion of "BMWs" (black men working-a term that would become popular in the 1990s, as a schism between working black women and non-working black men, impacting the stability of black male-female relationships) from 74% in 1960 to 56% in 1982.[11]

Throughout the 1970s, black unemployment was twice that of white unemployment (a trend that would continue throughout the 1980s and the 1990s), and would be dramatically affected by another socio-economic reality, "white flight." This phenomenon also took hold in the 1970s, as Whites in southern cities, like New Orleans, Atlanta, Houston, Richmond and Memphis, left newly integrated communities, and school systems to "resegregate" themselves, in "suburbs," as did Whites in northern cities like Boston, Newark and Detroit. Detroit became the poster child for white flight, as the city's population was close to two million (1,870,000) in 1950. After the riots of 1967, there was such a mass exodus of Whites from the city, to where the city's census fell from 1,670,144 in 1960 to 1,203,339 by 1970, then fell under a million by 1984, and the city hasn't reached a million in pop-

351

ulation since (as of the 2000 census).[12] Blacks went from being 28.9% of Detroit's population to over 50% by the 1970 Census, to 65% by 1980 (black population is 83% in Detroit in 2004).

As Whites left urban cities, so did the jobs reflecting the failure of national policy, and of the economy, to produce jobs for a growing black population, reinforcing a persistence in the income gap between black families and white families. The median income ratio of black family income compared to white family income, in 1981, black family income was 56% of that of white families, was hardly different than the 55% ratio that existed in 1960.[13] This combination of no jobs, no commerce, no income in highly resegregated communities produced extreme poverty and a social condition that sociologist, Julius Wilson, called "the permanent black underclass," by the end of the 1970s. The central cities in America had been left to fester in poverty, and Blacks were disproportionately impacted, as they were 23% of the nation's central cities population, but constituted 47% of these central cities' poor populations.[14]

Carter did what he could to practice the "politics of inclusion," in four short year, however, poor Whites didn't fair very well under the Carter Administration, and it produced a high level of public disapproval. Carter's presidency was, by and large, seen as a failure, as both the domestic economy, and the nation's foreign affairs policy collapsed, in the face of rising interests, high unemployment, consumer stagnation ("stagflation, it was termed), gas shortages and Carter "lack of action" when Iran took American hostages-deposing the U.S. "propped" dictator, "The Shah of Iran."

As during the Great Depression, racial strife took a somewhat of a backseat to circumstances that affected the whole country. This period, from 1976 to 1980, was viewed as America's "period of uncertainty," as confidence in American industry took a backseat to the rise of Japanese economic and technological advancements, where Japan was viewed, as the emerging economic "superpower." The 1970s had proven that "the Big Red Scare" was a reality as the Soviet Union had engaged in a nuclear arms build-up that far surpassed the American weapons' stockpile, exposed the nation's vulnerability to the oil, and the price demands of the OPEC nations. The world hadn't seen this type of American vulnerability since before World War II. In short, the nation was searching for answers, and it was searching for leadership, and it found it, in the person of Ronald Wilson Reagan.

The 1980 election was a racially orchestrated campaign from

the very outset. Ronald Reagan, the former Governor of California, after presidential runs in 1968, 1972 and barely missing the nomination in 1976, announced his 1980 candidacy for President in, of all places, at the Neshoba County Fair in Philadelphia, Mississippi, the place where civil right workers Schwerner, Chaney and Goodman had been murdered in 1964. There was no mistaking what Reagan was doing, and the racial symbolism he chose to communicate, in going South to announce his candidacy. Reagan calculated that his declaration of "I believe in states' rights," would be a re-signaling of the same codes that were used to end 19th Century Reconstruction, and bring the South-then under the control of the federal government-back under state controlled elections, representatives and traditions.

Reagan also knew that his coded speech would be heard in the South, and ignored in the North, and even those who thought southern strategy was a Nixon ploy of the past, were forced to acknowledge the ferocity for which Reagan had brought it back. This essentially brought forth an endorsement of the Ku Klux Klan, which Reagan was slow to repudiate, and Klansmen in full bed sheet uniform carrying "Reagan for President" signs in Alabama.[15] Carter called out Reagan's race-mongering, as "the stirrings of hate, and the rebirth of code words like 'states rights'," which as a southerner, he knew would invoke racial passions. The media called Carter's comments "mean," never focusing on whether his comments were correct, instead, using quotes, by the conservative hierarchy, to vilify Carter, as a champion of Blacks, and black causes and an enemy of the mostly white, tax-paying, middle class. Carter tried to right his campaign by publishing a "book of Reagan quotes" to show how racially divisive Reagan was on various topics.

On *Brown*, Reagan said, "There was nothing that said there had to be-while it said you could not enforce segregation, it did not say that you had to force integration;"

On the Civil Rights Act of 1964, Reagan said, "bad legislation that went beyond and infringed on the individual rights of citizens;"

On the Voting Rights Act of 1965, Reagan said, it "humiliated the South;"

On Busing, Reagan said, "it isn't a racial issue;"

On affirmative action, Reagan called it, "reverse discrimination."

On other topics like "the Roosevelt coalition," Reagan said "the Negro has delivered himself to those who have no other interest than to create a federal plantation;" and on whether the hearts of minds of Americans could be changed in the area of race relations, Reagan said, "you can pass a law, but you don't change the heart of the individual who is discriminating now."[16] Reagan, on black rioting, after the King assassination, also cavalierly stated, "If the Negroes don't cool it, Martin Luther King will have died in vain," insinuating that no amount of displaced aggression, would move him on the question of racial inequality. This caused first lady, Rosalynn Carter to say, in a public interview, that she didn't like Reagan's politics because "he made people feel comfortable with their prejudices."

So effective was the Reagan spin, and his ability to rise above the emotionalism of race politics, that nothing President Carter, said or did, could turn the nation away from the Reagan message. Carter's adviser, Hodding Carter, another Southerner, called Ronald Reagan, part George Wallace-a cultural whiz at fueling racial sentiment, part Richard Nixon-a closet racist whose demeanor didn't indict him to an undiscerning public, and a better southern strategist than both put together, as pundits, and the public, took Reagan's "friendly racism," as a given part of his personality.[17] But America was eating it up, and as Reagan won the election, America had a new hero.

What had began in 1968, as a protest departure against the Democratic Party's civil rights platform, had become a mass defection of white voters to the Republican Party, by 1980-especially in the South where Whites flocked to the Republicans, either in their vote or by a party switch, transforming a region that had been a Democratic stronghold into "Reagan Country" in the 1980s. These "converts" were known as "Reagan Democrats," and, as historian Dewey Grantham noted, they were made up of mostly white southerners, who had once made up a third of the Democratic Party. Southern Whites made up only a fifth of the Democratic party, by the end of Reagan's term in 1988.[18] Seeing someone who was prepared to protect the individual Constitutional rights of Whites, not being influenced by race politics, sympathetic to the over-taxed middle class, and prepared to redefine "American values," the 1980 Presidential election was a referendum on racial privilege in America, and represented the first real ideological shift in American politics, since the popular referendum on presidential candidate, Franklin D. Roosevelt's "New Deal" liberalism in 1932.[19] Reagan "Conservatism" spread like wildfire, as the new President's policy agenda represented the first modern day attempt, to actively pursue the deconstruction of the gains of the civil rights movement-specifically targeting affirmative action, and dismantling federally funded social programs started in the 1960s. Reagan strategists, like budget director, David Stockman, who didn't accept equality "as a moral principle," played "the race card," at every turn, as Reagan used stories of "welfare queens," and labeling rioters, and "radicals," as street criminals to stigmatize Blacks, in a very codified manner. Stockman played a leading role in the administration's charge from the war on poverty, to Reagan's war on welfare, sending a message that both crime and welfare had a "black face" on it, in Reagan's America, as the party sought to push northern Whites toward the Republicans point of view.[20]

Reagan's impact on America, termed the "Reagan Revolution," or what many called "the Second American Revolution," was felt in three ways; first, in the reorganization of the federal government, and its implementation priorities; second, in the Reagan administration's approach to fiscal policy and; third, Reagan's influence on judicial appointments, all of which had a dramatic affect on African Americans and other minorities efforts, to achieve equality. Therein, lies the magnetism of "the Reagan effect" where his attitudes toward race was seen, as non-descript and nonchalant, but his policy action and lack of political will, toward enforcement of what he called "quota policies," were very racial.

The beneficiaries of Reagan's policies were for "Americans," pure and simple, but they were reinforced in a popular sovereignty that Harvard Law Professor, Lani Guinier, called the "Tyranny of the Majority." Reagan Republicanism advanced an "optimism" about the future that was absent the racial confrontation of the 1950s, 1960s and 1970s. By the 1980s, racial attitudes had changed significantly, not in principle and practice, but in nature and scope. White backlash was as pervasive as ever, but as Whites began to ask the question, "What about my rights?" Reagan responded, by insisting on protecting the rights of the states, and the rights of "all Americans." Reagan shrewdly gave recognition to black rights, extending the 1965 Voting Rights Act in 1985, and even signed the Martin Luther King Holiday bill in 1983 (against the wishes of his advisors). But Reagan also returned the racial privileges of work, of wealth, of rights back to Whites, in a non-confrontational way that rejected overtly racial interjection, to a more widespread subversive racial approach-covert in scope, but passive-aggressive in nature.

Reagan introduced a economic recovery plan in his 1980 campaign, to reduce inflation, and create jobs by using tax cuts, to spur per-

355

sonal savings, and investment that would, in turn, generate consumer activity that would generate productivity, create jobs and strengthen the economy. It was supply-side economics with "a Reagan twist," that was called, "trickle down economics," because the immediate benefits seemed to go to the wealthy, but Reagan argued that the benefits would eventually "trickle down" to the middle and lower classes of taxpayers. Reagan's opponents were highly skeptical of this economic plan at a time, when inflation and unemployment were both in "double digits." Reagan's primary campaign opponent, and eventual Vice Presidential choice, George H.W. Bush, called Reagan's economic plan, "Voodoo economics."

However, when Reagan took office, the term became, "Reaganomics," and it was seen as risky at best. Reagan set out to reorganize the federal government to reduce the size of the federal government, as well as limit the behaviors of what he called "tax and spend liberals." Reagan didn't really reduce the size of government. He just shifted the federal government's spending priorities, cutting $45 billion from various social programs and increased spending in defense proportionately-even though the United States were in peacetime. When Marion Wright Edelman called him on it, accusing him of seeking "to repeal or weaken everything, every single federal child's program, and every program protecting the poor," President Reagan wryly commented, "In the war on poverty, poverty won."[21]

He claimed that Congress was overtaxing the middle class, proposed a $750 billion dollar tax cut that, for all intense and purposes, eliminated any discretionary federal government spending, and created the largest federal deficit in the nation's history, $100 billion dollars in his first year, and $200 billion in three of the next four years.[22] Defense spending increased 40% in the 1980s, from $227 billion in 1981 to $317 billion in 1989, and when questioned about it, Reagan advisors said they only continued what Carter had started (even though Carter had only raised defense spending 14% from 1977 to 1981). By the time Reagan left office, inflation would be in the four to five percent range, unemployment was down to 5.3% (lowest since the Nixon administration), a record 20 million new jobs were created, and 118 million Americans were employed, more than at any time in history.[24] However, the national debt had more than doubled, surpassing one trillion dollars for the first time, and America had borrowed so much debt just to keep its economy afloat and had developed such huge trade deficits that it went from the world's largest creditor nation to world's largest debtor nation by Reagan's last year in office (1987-88).[25]

President Reagan, who was called the "Great Communicator," could have easily been called "the Great Separator," as the largest inequitable division of equality, and the greatest class separation of wealth, occurred under his administration. The Reagan economic recovery brought about massive divides among "the rich" and "the poor." For instance, the Reagan economic "boom" contradicted previous booms, where government surpluses and GNP (gross national product) growth proceed income growth. In the 1950s economic boom, the number of Americans with annual incomes of $500,000 grew 19% from 842 to 1,002, while the 1980s produced a growth from 16,881 in 1980 to 183,240 in 1989, a 985% growth rate; by the decade's end, the wealthiest fifth of the population had the highest portion of income ever recorded for the group, the bottom three-fifths-the lowest, and wealth controlled by the poorest fifth of the population shrank from 5.5% in 1970, to 3.7% by 1990; poverty rose to 35.7 million-the highest since before the War on Poverty in 1964-and more than half of those in poverty, came from working households, creating another 1980s phenomena called "the working poor," that stemmed, in part, from a massive shift in the quality of jobs, as industry cut hundreds of thousands of high paying manufacturing jobs-they were replaced with low paying service sector jobs.[26]

Seven million of the new jobs created in the Reagan years paid less than $7,000 a year, while the number of millionaires, deca-millionaires, centi-millionaires and billionaires were created in unprecedented numbers. The number of millionaires created in the Reagan years grew from 638,000 to 1,500,000; the number of Decamillionaires (persons worth $10 million or more) increased from 38,885 in 1982, to 100,000 in 1989; the number of Centimillionaires (worth $100 million or more) grew from 400 in 1982, to 1,200 in 1989; and the number of billionaires grew from what was commonly acknowledged as just a few (old money like the Vanderbilts, Rockefellers and the [J.P.] Morgans-the real number wasn't known), to "a documented" 51 by 1988.[27] The "wealth explosion," in what was termed "the decade of greed," was a function of Reagan's tax reform that brought tax cuts, tax breaks (shelters), corporate loopholes, that shifted the tax burden from individuals to corporations, dropped millions of low-income people from the tax rolls, and gave income tax benefits that provided the greatest windfall for the wealthiest Americans.[28]

While the rich got richer, at waterfall pace under Reagan, the

357

benefits to the middle class trickled, at the pace of a leaky facet drip. The middle did grow under Reagan, and so did the "Black "upper" and "middle" classes." The black "upper" class grew from three percent in 1969 to nine percent in 1986, while the black middle class grew from 28% in 1969 to 38% in 1986.[29] At the same time, the portion of the black non-working poor grew from 14% in 1969 to 30 percent in 1986, and black male teen unemployment grew from 15% in 1973 to 40% in 1986, causing a "duel track" of economic independence, and sociological dysfunction that bred crime, greater welfare dependency, drug addictions, and fragmented families, as three out of five black children born in the 1980s, was born out of wedlock.[30]

The majority paradigm for the new "black family" emerged, as it was no longer two parents households, or even male headed households. The head of the "new black family" was now a single female head of household. The issues of economic separation, and social disengagement, within the American public, produced calls of class conflict that became the subject of Jesse Jackson Presidential campaign in 1984. It resonated more loudly in 1988, after eight years of "trickle down" economics -without the trickle. This brought forth a second Jesse Jackson/ "Rainbow Coalition" presidential candidacy.

Finally, the most lasting of the Reagan legacy, was how he effectively took control of the justice system, through a combination of "tough on crime" proclamations, ideological favoritism, and executive office persuasion. Reagan's "war on drugs," didn't do much to stop the flow of drugs into the country, particularly into the urban cities, but it caused Congress to produce the most stigmatizing and discriminating public policy since segregation, institutionalizing racism, as it had never been done in the *post-Brown* era.

Reagan advocated for (and got) two pieces of public policy that took judicial discretion away for from federal judges. The first was "mandatory minimums" for first time offenders that gave a five year federal prison sentence to anyone who was caught in possession of certain drugs, or intended to distribute certain drugs. The drug of choice for the Reagan administration, was synthetic or "crack" cocaine, an inexpensive drug that targeted inner city urban dwellers, and gave its user permanent brain damage. The Reagan administration wrote the law to put special emphasis on "crack" cocaine, where possession of a certain number of "rocks" triggered the mandatory minimum sentence of five years. One rock, with a street value of five dollars, was enough to get you arrested. Five rocks, with a street value of $25.00, was enough to get you an "intent to distribute" rap that carried the five years sentence. On the other hand, if one got caught with a pound of power cocaine, one mostly likely get probation on a first offense, and one to three years on a second offense. This was because power cocaine was the drug of choice for the rich and privileged, and thus was not written into the federal law. Possession of crack was a federal crime, while possession of power cocaine wasn't. Those most likely to possess crack were Black, while those most likely to possess power cocaine were White. So the prison population exploded in the 1980s (and early 1990s), with small time drug dealers and drug users, and the streets of urban America became filled with other social ills, such as, crackheads and "strawberries" (women who traded sex for crack), who robbed their neighbors to feed their drug habits.

The second policy involved the use of sentencing guidelines for any federal crime, after 1986 that used a calculation of past offenses, likelihood of rehabilitation, and serious of offenses to determine future sentences. Federal judges effectively hand their hands tied, in being able to use their discretion, in departing from the recommended sentences called out by the guidelines. The guidelines were most punitive on repeat offenders, and was supposed to curb recidivism. It instead swept thousands of unemployed black men, and "gang members," into the federal system. Reagan's "tough on crime" policies disproportionately impacted the poor and disenfranchised.

Reagan's ideological favoritism came in the form of his propensity to appoint mostly those persons of a conservative mindset. Most were ideologues, who many questioned their ability to put aside their biases, while serving the government. The biggest battle came as Reagan tried to appoint his Solicitor General, Robert Bork, to the United States Supreme Court. Bork had been a federal judge and Yale Law Professor, with a very narrow interpretation of the Constitution, which he called "the Original Intent" theory, that said the Supreme Court should interpret the Constitution as the framers intended, not in the way, as Chief John Marshall said, that offers contemporary insight and gives the Constitution life.

The Senate rejected Bork's nomination because he alienated too many people of color (and women) on all fronts, but he also represented the Reagan/Meese Constitutional agenda that sought the "institutional high ground" that "the 60s generation" and its "left liberal culture" in our society commanded, that Bork blamed for blocking his confirmation.[31] The lessons the Reagan administration learned on the

Bork confirmation, opened the flood gates for future judicial picks. By the time the twelve years of Reagan-Bush administration had ended, Ronald Reagan had effectively taken away the one branch of government that could re-interpret equality justly for Blacks-the Judiciary. Congress had been effectively neutralized in the 1980s, but the Courts had been effectively politicized. In Reagan's eight years in office, he made 360 lifetime judicial appointments to the federal bench, including three associate justices, a chief justice, and nearly half of full-time appeals court judges.[32]

George H. W. Bush's administration was seen as an extension of Reagan's administration, and between them, they appointed 837 federal district, appellate, and Supreme Court appointments, including six Supreme Court Justices, and 115 appeals court judges. Reagan and his advisers, which included Attorney General, Ed Meese, developed clear goals in how to achieve a more conservative judiciary, that would rule against abortion, be passive on civil rights, and be borderline cruel on crime policy. Diversity and tolerance of views went out the window, as both Reagan and Bush appointed white males in the mid-ninety percentile, and only two and four percent black nominees, respectively.[33] They were not only white, but elitists as 64% reported net worth of more than a half million dollars, and one-third were millionaires. Twenty-six of Bush I's appointees belonged to clubs that discriminated in choosing members-and none were members of the ACLU. Ideologues to the hilt. A study of the Reagan/Bush judicial appointments by the People for the American Way, caused its president, Arthur J. Kropp, to offered the following analysis;

"The Reagan Bush court-packing effort is unprecedented in terms of its scope and methods. We've seen political court appointments before, but never such a prolonged and blind adherence to strict ideological guidelines. The architects of this court, coming from the Republican Party's right wing, pulled off a judicial revolution in the guise of judicial restraint.[34]

The Reagan revolution offered everything back to white America that had been equalized, or had gotten as close to equal, as African Americans had seen, in the Civil Rights era. America had been redeemed, "optimism" restored, racial privilege redefined. Social and economic equality had been pushed further away, under Ronald Reagan, than it was in 1954.

15

The Assault On *Brown*:
Angry White Men and the Constitutional Rights Movement

*Salvation/or a race, nation, or class must come from within.
Freedom is never granted; it is won. Justice is never given; it is exacted.
Freedom and justice must be struggled for by the oppressed of all
lands and races, and the struggle must be continuous, for freedom is
never a final fact, but a continuing evolving process to higher and
higher levels of human, social, economic, political and religious
relationships.*

- A. Philip Randolph

*Anger made us terribly aware that something is wrong because it does not
spring wantonly out of air: it has an originating cause. But anger also blinds
and therefore limits and weakens; it cripples those who suffer it, and in the
end those who have caused it.*

John Williams, cited in his book,
Beyond the Angry Young Black

The last decade of the 20th Century proved to be the most divisive in terms of struggle for equality, as race, and racial definitions took its most regressive turn yet in the Post-*Brown* era. Ronald Reagan's presidency had consolidated, updated and refined the right-populist, race-coded strategies of George Wallace and Richard Nixon, through the Republican Party's innovative use of powerful new tools of political technology, that included computerized direct mail, tracking polls, focus groups, marketing techniques, and the manipulation of voter lists, of paid and unpaid television, as well as the use of demographic, psychological and geographic data to support ideological positions. [1] Reagan's conservative agenda was structured around the issues of race and taxes that solidified the post-riots "white backlash" polity of the 1960s, into the "embourgeoisement" of a segment of Democratic voters that had become disillusioned with the Democratic Party, picked up Reagan's message, and now re-identified with the Republican Party as a newly created middle-class, anti-government, property holding, conservative base among white voters that brought their "values" (thoughts about merit, race and government facilitated equality measures) and their insistence on protection of their individual "rights" to the public's attention.[2]

This ideological shift, or what many others called-an ideological shock to the right, represented a bold move, from left of center to right of center, enough to tilt the country into a more conservative mode, that allowed the Republican Party to adopt a posture that staked out the conservative side of racial issues, and literally change the nature of how the public viewed race and articulated racial issues.[3] As Reagan administration ended, and the Bush I era offered a four year continuum of Reagan's conservative agenda, racialization of policy issues turned to racialization of public opinion as the 1988 and the 1992 Presidential campaigns offered up racial symbols that both raised racial fears and re-stigmatized African Americans in ways that re-polarized the racial electorate. For all that had been done in the 1980s to eradicate policies, programs and systems that sought to equalize Blacks and Whites, the prior decade would pale in comparison to policies and strategic approaches that would emerge in the 1990s and foster new forms of inequality.

The 1990s, while serving as the decade where the greatest economic boon in the nation's history would occur, would also serve as the decade where racial anger would resurrect itself, and serve as the basis for policy and legal decisions that would do irreparable damage to the prospects of racial equality. Succinctly put, three decades of "white backlash" reached a maturation point in the 1990s where policy-makers, academic discourse, the courts and public opinion came together to formulate the ultimate racial revolt, in a way that hadn't been seen since the "Redeemers" of the Post-Reconstruction period of the 19th Century returned control of the South to southern Whites.

The current day redemption movement sought to capitalize on the "optimism" of the Reagan era, to redeem the nation, a redemption that sought protect the individual rights of Whites, and reject any poli-cies that would benefit "other minorities," at the expense of infringing upon their "right to be equal." This push toward individualism, and the assertion on "individual rights," changed the nature of race politics in America in two ways.

First, it allowed for Whites to re-assert the values of egalitari-anism, whereby the privileges and politics of racial group benefits were downplayed, and individual benefit being part of a "society of equals" was highlighted, as a staple of the American values system. Secondly, it allowed Whites, as individuals, to separate themselves from their racial history, as a group of haters and discriminators-in the collective-in order to assert that they, as individuals, should not be punished for the nation's legacy of past discrimination since, they, themselves, had no involvement in slavery, segregation, and other acts of discrimination that Whites, as a group, had clearly benefited from, as racism became more systemically and institutionally ingrained.

This argument, while artificial in scope-due to the fact that many Whites, and their direct beneficiaries (their children), who were involved in segregation and other discriminatory and racist behaviors were still living-offered cover to a new generation of Whites that very well may have never discriminated against a black person a day in their life, but were the beneficiaries of a society that had, and continued to, unequally distribute social, political and economic resources on mas-sively inequitable terms.

363

Yet, it was not uncommon to hear such rationalizations as "Why should I have to pay for something that happened 100 or 200 years ago." This segment of the white population gladly accepted the benefits of America's race caste system, and the privileges of whiteness that the system provided to them, but didn't want to pay the costs to repair, or repatriate Blacks for the social, economic and political dam-age that had been done. This was the weakness of the individualist's argument, as they attempted to escape the remaining downside of America's inequality politic, retribution-and restitution, if affirmation action can be framed as such, for 300 years of past discrimination.

It turns out that the scare of affirmation action was actually a lot worse than the reality of the "threat" posed to white job security. Polling indicated that at the beginning of the decade in 1990, that there wasn't any real hostility toward affirmative action, as a policy that Whites, in the collective, felt would displace them in their jobs, large-ly because white women, to this point, had been the biggest beneficiaries of this inclusion policy. National surveys, by the National Opinion Research Center of the University of Chicago, reflected a different story than what media pundits, and politicians were advancing, about the threats of affirmative action.

The survey indicated that 70% of Whites polls felt that another white person was likely to be hurt by affirmative action for Blacks, but only seven percent of these same Whites claimed to have actually experienced any form of "reverse discrimination." Only 16 percent knew of someone close to them that had been discriminated against, and only six percent of white women, and eight percent of white men claimed to have been affected by affirmative action policies, in any way, despite their fears about it.[4] Plainly put, the "spin" on affirmative action was actually worse than the effects of the policy itself.

However, the "spin" masters, driving fears of what affirmative action was, or wasn't, were the very ones claiming to be most impacted by adverse effects of the policy. When aggregated according to race and gender, clearly the most hostile segment of the population toward affirmative action were white males who, according to then emerging opinion leaders like Pat Buchanan and Rush Limbaugh, were claiming to be the "forgotten minority" in the redistributive benefits of America's public and free market resources. Nothing could have been farther from the truth. This claim proved to be a false assertion. What reason did white men have to be angry about their societal rank? White males were better positioned than any other demographic in American society.

Despite how white males sought to frame their "exclusion" from the benefits of American society-work, education, wealth and other public enjoyments-no such exclusion actually occurred. The median income for black families, represented as anywhere from 54% to 64% of white families since 1939 (when such statistics started being complied), didn't reach "three-fifths" of the median income of white families until 1966 and by 1994, almost thirty years later, black families median income had fallen back to "three-fifths" or 60% of white family median income.[5] In fact, there was very little, if any, slippage in any of the primary socio-economic indicators for white males. White males were still the top wage earners in the labor force, as in 1990. Black males earned 60 percent of what white males earned, while black women earned 62% of what black males earned, and white women earned 47% of what white males earned; white males represented 26.8% of the managerial and professional occupations (compared to 28.5% for white women, 19.5% of black women, and 14.1% of black males); white employment, from 1980 to 1990, fell 6.3% to 4.8%, while black unemployment remained literally the same, falling only one-tenth of one percent from 14.3%, in 1980, to 14.2%, in 1990.[6]

The only socio-economic indicator that dramatically impacted Whites, also impacted Blacks, the number of persons below the poverty line. From 1980 to 1992, the percentage of white families below the poverty line grew from 10.2% in 1980 to 10.7% in 1992, compared to the percentage of black families, actually grew twice as much (percentage change) from 31.4% to 33.4%. However, the number of white families in poverty grew by almost six million (from 19,699,000 to 25,259,000), while the number of black families grew by more than two million (from 8,579,000 in 1980 to 10,827,000 in 1992).[7] Poor Whites were as dramatically affected by "Reaganomics" as poor Blacks were. If any white men suffered under Reagan, it was poor white males, at the bottom of the income strata, but not for the reason opinion leaders and political pundits asserted.

The issue of economic mobility was complicated in the 1990s, by a huge influx of new immigrants, largely Latino and Asian, that changed America's racial paradigm, from bifocal (Black and White), to multi-focal (White, Black, Brown and Yellow). New immigrants arrived in cities, where economies were restructuring, and globalization created bifurcated labor markets, with labor intensive, low-paying jobs that did not provide a living wage on one end, and a growing sector of knowledge-intensive, good-paying jobs requiring extensive educational credentials, and English language proficiency on the other, creating a labor force where immigrants were "underemployed," meaning forced to accept substandard wages, or occupational over-qualification.[8] New immigrants were forced into a highly stratified racial system that imposed on them a "minority status," with all its disadvantages, something that descendents of European immigrants in the late 19th and early 20th Centuries didn't face, as they become white as a function of upward economic mobility.

As low socio-economic status impeded Blacks and poor Whites economic mobility, it also impeded the new immigrant, and further reinforced their placement in the preexisting, highly stratified, and racialized hierarchy.[9] Meanwhile, not only had white males dominated the economic, political, legal and educational values of American society. They were in firm control of the key roles, and top positions, in all of the major institutions, they had maintained control of for nearly four centuries, while concrete barriers or "glass ceilings" emerged for Blacks,

365

white women and other persons of color. According to several studies in the early and mid-1990s, white men controlled almost every U.S. institution from most Fortune 1000 companies and elite universities, to the presidency, the military. In federal and state legislatures, they made up 95 to 100 percent of those in top positions, which were reinforced by other sources, including; a mid-1990s *Newsweek* report that noted white men held 77% of the House and Senate seats, as well as, 92% of the state governorships; 90% of newspaper editor positions and 77 of TV news executives were white men; 95% of white men held corporate positions, at the vice president level and above, according to a 1990s report of the federal Glass Ceiling Commission, and as late as 1998, not a single one of the Fortune 1000 Companies had a black executive as its head.[10]

So in the 1990s, white males were not replaced in the hierarchy, they were reinforced in a newer, more expanded racial hierarchy that subordinated other people of color in the new global economy, and placed whiteness as the head of the hierarchy. White males were at the top of the economic hierarchy, as the measuring point for which all others had to climb to be accepted-not as rich or poor, but as the middle class, or the "underclass." The multifocal racial paradigm created more competition at the middle and the bottom of the labor markets, than at the top, and displacement of white males anywhere in the labor force, particularly at the top of the economic hierarchy, was the exception, and not the rule.

Yet, the conservative ideologues would have had the nation believe that, due to the loss of income by the lowest one-fifth of white men at the bottom of labor market and income scale, all white men had been disproportionately impacted. Loss of jobs, and loss of income was blamed on the "browning" of jobs in America, and the racial scapegoating that occurred in the prior century (mid to late-1800s and early 1900s), was resurrected again nearly one hundred years later in the early 1990s.

While the loss of income could be attributed to the loss of high paying manufacturing jobs-replaced by low paying service jobs, the issue was framed in the public discourse, as "white jobs" being replaced by "black jobs," or the result of affirmative action programs. Competition for jobs from the new immigrant, and the shift in the global economy, was rarely mentioned, as factors in the early 1990s. Affirmative action was less than 10% of the problem, but took almost 100% of the blame-a case in which, the perception of reverse discrimination had become reality, in the minds of many Whites. In one of the few times there could have been a nationwide dialogue about America's silently emerging class struggle, politicians and pundits always fearing any discussion of class conflict opens the free market systems' "Pandora's Box" on the hidden flaws of capitalism, the public chose instead to discuss the only other salient issue that could offset a national discussion on class struggle, race, and the new equality discussion-equality rights for Whites. Affirmative action could have served as the basis to discuss the class divide, in a way that offered socio-economic solutions to the poor-wage equality, or a fairer income redistribution among those willing to work, and willing to contribute, to the tax rolls for citizens, and immigrants alike, a discussion that is now pervasive in the 21st Century. Affirmative action didn't have to be just about race. It could have addressed generational poverty, in ways the transcended the politics of race and gender.

Instead, affirmative action served as the "bait" to shift the societal discourse, and what took place was the de-emphasis of societal group status, and the prioritization of societal "individual" status that lent a greater credence to support of a merit principle, that advanced the benefits of a "color-blind vision" for America, in ways that race-based preferences did not.

The core elements of the moral support for the principle, according to legal scholar, Christopher Edley, Jr., were; 1) emphasizing merit maximizes efficiency and social welfare, 2) a person's individual entitlement to have decisions made about them based on personal "individual" qualities, rather than social or political conventions tied to group identity, and 3) by emphasizing the first two (merit and individuality), society align the necessary incentives to promote and reinforce both racial autonomy, and personal responsibility.[11]

As Edley pointed out, there were realities to the merit discussion that many failed to see-thus the flaw in the discussion, mainly that there were few places in America, where pure forms of merit were used to hire, or select people, given America's "who you know" societal norms driven by nepotism and cronyism. Merits is a factor, in selection processes, as we tend to look for "qualified" persons or firms, but we then use a whole host of other considerations like, cultural "fit" or environmental compatibility, longevity, non-work related benefits they bring to the table (rolodex, contacts, etc.), to make the final decision.[12] Affirmative action hires only applied to "qualified" candidates, but somehow came to be viewed-specific to racial consideration-as not being about to pass the "merit test," in ways that other preference groups, like legacies in higher education, or women in hiring, passed the test. Race, as Edley surmises, is different, as companies and universities pursued multiple objectives in hiring, promotions and admission decisions because societal interpretations could never be stretched enough to accommodate racial considerations in these areas.[13] However, demands that America return to a merit based society, as the "moral claim" in new array of "American values," set in play new realities that, though theoretically flawed, favored the instructional arguments that "race policies," like affirmative action, undermined one of the true principles of democracy, merit.

The new discourse to dismiss historical discrimination, to ignore existing social and economic disparities created out of racial discrimination, and redirect any discussion of race as counterproductive to the "national interest" (i.e., the individual interest of Whites) brought about what sociology scholar, Lawrence Bobo, called Laissez-faire racism. The change in attitudes by Whites, from "Jim Crow" racism to laissez-faire racism, reflected a change, from one dominant ideology to another, where we witness the disappearance of overt bigotry, demands for strict segregation, advocacy of government enforced discrimination, and adherence to beliefs that Blacks were the intellectual inferior of Whites, to a new ideology that moved past embracing, democratic vision of a common humanity, worth in dignity, and equal membership in the polity for Blacks, instead choosing to incorporate stereotypes, a preference toward individualism, rejection of the group structural accounts of racial inequality, as well as, an unwillingness to see government actively work to dismantle racial inequality.[14]

Laissez-faire racism involved a number of attitudinal, and cultural behavioral shifts, that mitigated race as a consideration in social benefits. In de-emphasizing group benefit for individual benefit, and seeing African Americans as individuals-just like themselves (a unique departure that gives support to being equal, in the present context of individuality), and using the same set of rules to compete for success in the marketplace to achieve whatever gains one acquires, discussion of racial differences are mitigated because no one is viewed as disadvantaged. On the other hand, Laissez faire racism involves subtler, and more covert discriminating behaviors than its predecessor, making it more difficult to directly confront, and is more amenable to the more fluid and permeable set of racial divisions, in the present day social order that asserts that government should be "race-neutral," and committed to anti-discrimination protection for all people, including Whites.[15]

Given that most Americans, surveyed in the 1990s, had finally adopted racial equality-in principle, Whites felt that Blacks should compete as individual equals rather than as members of a group, though they were forced to play in the market, by "rigged rules," used historically to ensure their disadvantage, and white domination, and another set of rules to insure their inclusion solely based on their racial group.[16] While the discourse of white America was edging toward race neutrality, African Americans were experiencing a different type of reality, centered in the recognition that they were not only losing economic ground, but also experiencing a regression in social standing.

A new "black militancy" came about, by the end of the 1980s, that gave recognition to new tools of racial oppression, namely economic redlining, wealth separation and disproportionate incarceration, that caused a new generation of Blacks to reject the "we ain't where we should be, but we ain't were we was" rationalizations of the quickly fading civil rights community. The emergence of Minister Louis Farrakhan, the national spokesperson of the old and resurrected Nation of Islam, as the pre-imminent leader for African Americans in the 1990s, offered a bold and critical analysis of the 1990s social construct that was reminiscent of the Malcolm X discourse of the 1960s.

369

Farrakhan as a focal point in communicating African American misery, caused Whites much distress, as many took to take his message of self-determinative racial consciousness, and called it "black hate," a message that reflected, and interjected, what many Whites viewed as "anti-white" sentiment. Much of the apprehension surrounding the "Farrakhan factor" was a carryover of Whites interpretations of Farrakhan's 1984 statements about the practices of Judaism as Zionism. The messages was simply a continuation of cultural prognosis advocating the "do for self," "be your self," "protect yourself against racial oppression and assault" messages of past leaders in the 20th Century.

The adverse circumstances of the 1990s made Farrakhan's message more popular than they otherwise might have been, had not the Reagan-Bush years created such massive economic disparities, that made Blacks and Whites more unequal than they were in 1960. For instance, in 1960, white unemployment was 4.9% and black unemployment was 10.2%, twice (a 2.08 multiple) that of Whites; in 1990-thirty years later, white unemployment was 4.1 and black unemployment was 11.3, almost three times (a 2.76 multiple) of Whites.[17] In 1960, black men made $669 for every thousand dollars white workers (men and women combined) made. However, black women made $696-$27 more than black men. In 1990, black women's earning had risen to $900 for every $1,000 the median white worker earned, while black men had only risen to $731-only $62 in 30 years and only $27 (from $704 in 1970) in the prior 20 years.[18] The median family income for black families ($21, 423) in 1990 was 59% of white families ($36,915), and more dramatically, households headed by black women grew from 24.4% in 1960 to 58% in 1991 (compared to only 17.95% of white women heading households in 1991),[19] giving credence that Blacks, as a whole, had lost ground, even as both white and black women gained ground, as systemic factors began to purge black men from the workplace, and from society (increased incarceration that started in the mid-1980s).

Farrakhan's most frequent declaration-that Blacks were still slaves, "Corporate working, Cadillac driving, big home living, Rolex watch and diamond wearing slaves," was based on the fact that Blacks, while living better than they once lived, in comparison to Whites, had actually lost ground-a point moderate black leadership failed to acknowledge, and refused to admit. Blacks had lost ground, and equality prospects were fading, fast. Farrakhan's outsider perspective wasn't the only one making the case for the economic justice-his was just the most vocal. Blacks who had worked "in the system," like Dr. Claud Anderson, who was appointed as an Assistant Secretary of the Department of Commerce, who knew, from an inside perspective, that affirmative action had already been dismantled, to the point where its outcomes were negligible. Anderson wrote in his 1994 book, *Black Labor, White Wealth*:

The 20 years between 1969 and 1989, saw the introduction of controversial affirmative action policies, supposedly to compensate black employees for past discrimination in the job market. Conservatives vehemently opposed those policies, charging that affirmative action unfairly advantaged and enriched Blacks at the expense of Whites. However, statistics suggest that affirmative action brought few real changes to the position of black employees. Between 1969 and 1989, black annual income increased by only $22 relative to white income. Moreover, from 1979 to 1989, overall black income increased by only one dollar.[20]

Those who took the time to assess racial equality, in the most measurable indicators available, employment, income and wealth, demonstrated that the outcomes showing that Blacks were displacing Whites in the labor force were not in evidence, and that the equality gap was being made up at the expense of Whites was a false assertion. Even polar opposites in the black socio-political strata, like Anderson and Farrakhan could arrive to the same conclusion-that the benefits of affirmative action were minimal and that Blacks were losing economic ground.

Farrakhan's dissertations, on the realities of racial relations in America, took unprecedented resonance in the 1990s, often drawing stadium size crowds of disenfranchised Blacks looking for an answer to the inequities of their social and economic conditions. Black response to Farrakhan was an indicator of how bad things had actually gotten-while many, in the now antiquated civil rights organizations, were saying that things were getting better. Farrakhan was correct in his analysis, and was often the only one willing to say what lower class Blacks were feeling.

His message, however, was most often taken in the context of the Nation of Islam's separatist views, and the nationalist spiritualism of Elijah Muhammad (causing continual arguments of religion's validity among practitioners of Orthodox Islam), giving the conservative right license to reframe the race discourse-by and large avoided in the 1990s-as black or "reverse" racism, to which Whites themselves needed to be protected from. Many scholars, politicians and activists viewed the "black racist" arguments as false, and artificial, because racism can only occur, when one has the ability to impose their will, and the power to cause harm to another person based on race. Blacks, it was argued, didn't have the ability (even if some had the will) to impose their will, or the power to cause harm to white America.

Thus, you had folk like Coleman Young, a former "black militant," who was elected Mayor of Detroit, and served for 20 years, rejecting the black racist argument, saying that Blacks in the United States could not be called racists, simply because they were an oppressed people, and racism could only be attributed to those who have the power to cause suffering. Though most white people disagreed with this analysis- Coleman raised an important point that most were forced to acknowledge. That point being that few care how powerless people feel when they can't cause harm.

Even if one subscribes to the notion that one does not have to have power to hold racist views, because they seldom cause harm-no one cares because the significance of racism lies in the way the powerful cosigns the powerless to the margins of society, and it is within this context that racism helps crystallize how ideas about equality, inferiority, and superiority, are not simply figments of people's minds, but are sentiment that impact how institutions operate, and how opinions can become self-fulfilling when members of a minority race are viewed in ways that consigns them to subordinate positions, by the will, and the power held by members of the majority race.[21]

This is what opponents of the black racism argument sought emphasize, but it didn't resonate well with an emerging white underclass that could no longer separate themselves from the class status of the black underclass-which Pat Buchanan blamed-starting in the 1992 Presidential campaign, and well into the mid-1990s-on globalism that robbed Whites of the means to live apart from Blacks, and were less likely to be comfortable with sharing space, public resources and political power with Blacks, whom they perceived in two conscripts, morally inferior, and dangerous.[22] From it, stemmed a "white nationalist" voice that urged the "cleaning" of America's cultural institutions of the influence of minorities and advocated for the interests of "a displaced, angry and racially hostile white proletariat," thus, the advocate of the restoration of white racial status[23] -and the birth of the policy agenda for the "Angry White Male." It's targeted policy, affirmative action, more specifically, the end of affirmative action, in an economy where white workers were being squeezed by global capitalism, and technological change, that would allow white males to, once again, claim the lion's share of internal security jobs, as one way of avoiding the dirtiest, least respected jobs in American society.[24] This was far right ideology at its race baiting extreme, but it was a center page in the playbook that led to the rise of the Conservative right.

Complicating the racial agenda of the Angry White Male, which was really the agenda of the conservative right since there really wasn't a displaced white proletariat-just more of an alienated white male proletariat-was the emergence of white youth connecting to African American cultural behaviors associated, with then a fringe musical art form called 'hip hop." Hip hop, which would become America's predominant music genre by the end of the 1990s, "blew up" (gained mainstream popularity) largely due to the attention it drew from suburban white youth that began imitating the dress, language and cultural attitudes of disenfranchised and rebellious urban youth, and caused white youth to bond with Blacks, at least on a musical tip, in a much greater way than when white youth in the '50s adopted rhythm and blues driven, "rock and roll" music that Elvis sung. These youth became known as "wiggers," or "wigga" (rhyming with nigga), and was defined as "perhaps the fastest growing group among teenagers," "want to be black" and open to "new worlds and new ideas," but were subject to the same historical mythologies of other generations of Whites who crossed the cultural lines between the black and white races.[25]

David Roediger compares the modern term as consistent with uses of the historical term, white nigger, in the 19th Century, when Whites broke with "proper behavior" (discriminating behavior) of other Whites such as accepting "nigger work (work considered beneath the dignity of Whites), or showing sensitivity to Blacks (by voting with the pro-equality Republicans, who were opponents of white supremacy initiatives), or Whites who were "wigged out" over the emergence of an earlier black musical art form, jazz (that was called "jungle music" by Whites in the early day of jazz).[26]

While viewed as a transitional phase of white male adolescence (who emulate Blacks in the way previous generations emulated Indians, according to Leslie Fiedler) before settling into a white adulthood, "crossing over" in an manifestly unequal society, is seen as a product of tragic and exploitive forces that materialize and commoditize cultural lines more than blending them.[27] However, acceptance of Blacks, in any context, makes it difficult to contextualize their inferiority, if the majority society (or their children) is following the purported inferior class' cultural norms. It was difficult to frame black youth as disrespecting, hostile, immoral and dangerous, if young white males thought it was "cool" be the same, and defended the behavior.

What white youth didn't know (that their parents did know) was that black youth were rebelling against the conditions that caused them to resort to non-conforming lifestyles that they were singing about in their raps, rhymes and songs. When white youth did, it didn't appear as "authentic," thus the "Vanilla Ice" experiments exposed what the genre was really about, the angry deprivation of black life-that couldn't be emulated by a middle class suburban white boy, who knew no hardships. Still the reintroduction of whiteness, and white privilege, didn't dissuade the politics of the Angry White Male from changing the political landscape.

The emergence of "acceptable Blacks," who didn't view the world in a racial paradigm, sought to counter the image and the mind-numbing thump of rap, and its appeal to "angry" black urban youth.

Nothing did more to counteract the "angry black" image than the "politically generic," "pull yourself up by your bootstraps," conservative rights "black" advocate in the image of Clarence Thomas when President George H. W. Bush nominated him for the U.S. Supreme Court in 1991. Thomas' nomination became a focal point largely because he was replacing the first black Supreme Court justice, the legendary Thurgood Marshall-who only happened to be an iconic figure in 20th Century civil rights lore, having argued, and won, the equality rights of African Americans in the *Brown* decision- and thus came under the inevitable scrutiny of having his own civil rights record critiqued. His nomination's problems stemming from the Anita Hill claims, provided a highly racialized diversion, in what would have been an otherwise mundane confirmation process. Blacks were hesitant to criticize Thomas' civil rights record during his tenure over at the EEOC (for fear that Blacks would lose "the black seat" on the Supreme Court), and Whites really didn't care about his civil rights record (or lack of one).

Thomas became the face of the new "black conservative" in the 1980s, but others like Ward Connerly, and Alan Keyes, would become "the mouths" espousing "race-neutral" rhetoric in ways that white conservative couldn't. Playing "the race card" became the new code word for "don't bring race up" in this conversation-even when race was a legitimate factor. Not being able to discuss race, meant not being able to address group identity, in ways that allowed racial bias, racial discrimination, racial subjugation and racial oppression to be eliminated from the public discourse, giving way to the premise of merit driven individualism, and a new term, political correctness, as the basis for how race should be reference. For old "overt" racist, "Nigger" was part of his regular vernacular, whether it was in private or in public. For the Laissez- faire, or passive-aggressive, racist, the term was not "politically correct" for public use, and "the N word" became its socially acceptable replacement. This is not to say that racist behaviors became politically incorrect because they didn't.

The continuing gap in the racial divide, and the outcomes of social and economic indicators substantiated that racism was still in evidence. The practice of racism just became more subversive, and many-Blacks included-mistook this change in tactic, as a change in practice, thus asserting that race no longer relevant to the public discussion. In essence, there was nothing else to talk about, as far as, race was concerned. Nothing could be farther from the truth, but the new conservative mood of the country dictated time and discourse, and the "black" conservative was a key component in the plan to neutralize race as a salient public issue.

Clarence Thomas' appointment was a paradoxical shift in the imagery of what significance constructive black symbols held to Blacks, and Whites, in American society. Thomas was replacing Marshall, a man of enormous stature who was considered one of the architects of America's "free society," where all men were legally seen as equals. Although, the society may not have necessarily gotten to the point where all men were treated equally. *Newsweek* magazine called Marshall, "a true reformer in the best tradition of the rule of law," and his nomination was seen by Martin Luther King, Jr., as a "momentous step toward a color-blind society."[28] However, the real reason Marshall was appointed by Johnson, was because he was a racial symbol. President Johnson wanted the world to know that he was appointing a black man to the highest court in the land and, other than King, picked the highest profile black in the nation, Thurgood Marshall, whom he had tabbed three years earlier as a federal judge, then as solicitor general in a long term plan to integrate the Court. Then Johnson manufactured a vacancy on the Court for Marshall, in 1967, by naming Ramsey Clark to Attorney General, which forced his father, Tom C. Clark, to submit his resignation to avoid the appearance of a conflict of interest, in having his son as the nation's top prosecutor.[29]

375

When the President let it be known that he was considering a black for the Supreme Court, not letting on that he had already decided his pick, his advisors began submitting names ,and the name, federal judge, A. Leon Higginbotham, Jr., who was considered one of the finest jurist in the lower courts. Johnson replied, "The only two people who ever heard of Judge Higginbotham are you, and his mamma. When I appoint a nigger to the bench, I want everybody to know he's a nigger."[30] Johnson, as politically shrewd as he was, understood what the symbolism of having America's foremost civil rights icon, the legal mind that was handed to the baton from Charles Houston, and carried the fight to kill "Jim Crow" across the legal finish line, on the highest court in the land.

Johnson knew what Marshall meant to black people, as a symbol of the equality movement, and he knew what he meant to white people, who perceived Marshall as the nemesis responsible for the fall of segregation. Marshall was synonymous with *Brown*, and Johnson was about to put *Brown's* biggest symbol, Thurgood Marshall, on the high

Court before the same white Congressional "resistors," who had spent the past dozen years resisting Brown. There was no mistaking what Thurgood Marshall meant to the birth of the civil rights movement, and what his 24 year presence on the U.S. Supreme Court represented, as being a "watchdog" for the rights of the oppressed, even as he, and William J. Brennan, had outlived '"their time" as the last vestiges of judicial activism, in their final years on the Court.

The vacancy created by Marshall's resignation was deemed "the black seat," not because it was held by a Black, or by the only Black that had ever sat on the Court. It became the "black seat," because it was held by the legacy of the equality struggle, from Charles Houston to William Hastie to Thurgood Marshall, as the true "justice seat," in terms of the debt Blacks paid and the justice Blacks had earned to make America live up to the "character of its creed," in striking down segregation. Unfortunately, for the equality interests of Blacks, by the time Marshall had resigned, more conservatives were quoting Martin Luther King, Jr. than those "in the movement," and a notion of achieving a "colorblind society" meant something entirely different in 1967, when Marshall was nominated.

In 1991, the ideology of a colorblind society was about come full circle, in a regressive step away from what King signaled as progress, in Marshall's selection, with the appointment of Clarence Thomas. When President George H. W. Bush had put forward as Thomas' name, as the choice to replace Marshall, he was seen as neither part of a civil right legacy or as a legal scholar. He was on nobody's short list, except that of the far right ideologue in the Republican Party. Afraid that Bush would renege on the "black seat," Clarence Thomas literally got a "ghetto pass" to the Supreme Court, by virtue of *his* skin color.

Thomas was a conservative ideologue appointed by Ronald Reagan, to head the Civil Rights Office of the Equal Employment Opportunity Commission, at a time when Reagan was offering tax credits to Bob Jones University to abandon affirmative action, and Thomas played the role as obstructionist, implementing Reagan's plan to suppress the enforcement of discrimination complaints. Thomas, who had been one the D.C. Circuit Court of Appeals less than a year, would not have even been a consideration, had he been white. But he wasn't. He was black, a beneficiary of affirmative action-but one of its harshest critics, as well as a critic of the NAACP and civil rights. This was seen as conservative ideologues attempt to mock Johnson's politics of symbolism 24 years earlier, with a symbol of their own. Thomas was the "anti-Marshall," in terms of being a symbol for the black community.

Thomas was a relative unknown to the general public before Bush nominated him, and wasn't known to many Whites outside of the far right ideological strata of Republicans, who saw Thomas as just what the Supreme Court needed, their invention of the "colorblind" Black-a 1990s "new Negro." And just as President Lyndon Johnson had politically calculated the symbolism in putting Thurgood Marshall on the U.S. Supreme Court, President George Herbert Walker Bush politically calculated, finding a "blackface" to fill "the black space" on the Court, but one absent of the cultural sensitivities that made race relevant to the appointment.

Clarence Thomas was benign to the historical issues of the civil rights movement, saw himself as race neutral, and offered an ideological perspective inconsistent with protecting the equality rights of Blacks, and any other disadvantaged minority. Bush also calculated (correctly) that Blacks would get so caught up in the racial symbolism of the appointment, that they would not seek to upset the confirmation process solely on Thomas' conflicting ideology. He was right, as the national black populous was highly divided on Thomas' nomination-even in the aftermath of disclosures that Thomas engaged in sexual harassment behaviors.

377

The Anita Hill testimony temporarily side-tracked Thomas' confirmation hearing until he, himself racialized the discussion, by claiming that the Hill allegation was nothing more than a "high tech lynching," to which the all white male Senate Judiciary Committee didn't know how to respond. Thomas' Senate confirmation was the closest on a Supreme Court Justice in American history, 52 to 48, with South Carolina, Strom Thurmond, the ultimate segregationist, who led the States Rights ticket in 1948, opposed Marshall's confirmation for seventy-eight days in the spring and summer of 1967, and was most vocal on the passing of the King holiday bill in 1983, standing in defense of Thomas' nomination. Conservatives in Congress, who were so blinded to Thomas' color, didn't see the black man they saw when Johnson sent them Marshall in 1967. They saw a different symbol this time around, one in support of their political ideology, a fellow ideologue, that would advance a "non-racial" judicial temperament, but still allow them to fill "the black seat," with a black man of their liking. It was a "win-win" for Republicans-a "no brainer."

This is what conservatives meant in advancing equality from a "colorblind" perspective. Thomas was, by no means, Marshall's equal in stature, or prestige. Nor was he meant to be, as Bush sought to replace Marshall with a black who was different in every way, from social views to racial cues, in redefining what new Blacks were to become in what Bush I called, the New World Order. The 21st Century Black was to be atypical and nondescript, as far as, their socio-political views on race were concerned. Clarence Thomas was G.H.W. Bush's joke on black America, because he knew that nobody knew, in 1991, what this race experiment was really about.

By the time Democratic party nominee, Bill Clinton emerged, in 1992, Blacks, and their collective social interests, had been decimated by Republican public policy, and were ready for change. Particularly, given the fact that unemployment in the nation's African American communities had been at an all-time high during the Reagan-Bush years, rising as high as 18.9% and 19.5% in 1982 and 1983 respectively, while white unemployment never rose above 8.6%.[31] Full employment for America is when 95% of the people are employed, and the nation's unemployment rate is five percent, or less.

For the entire 1980s, and the first part of the 1990s, black unemployment was in "double digits" (higher than 10%), and averaged 2.37 times white unemployment (in the 1980s), and had risen to 2.76 times of white by the time the 1990s arrived. Unemployment has often been the most critical problem in the black community, and according to political scientist, Michael Dawson, how high unemployment goes within the black community, is tied to which party is in control of the presidency. On average, a Republican administration in power for two terms causes a rise in black unemployment of nearly 2.5 percentage points, while black unemployment declines by about 2.5 percentage points, when a Democrat occupies the White House for two terms.[32] It stands to reason that if job opportunities are more plentiful when Democrats are President, and jobs are the high salient issue for African Americans, Blacks would be predisposed to supporting the Democratic Party.

Thus, there was the big push to get a Democrat elected in 1992. Bill Clinton emerged as the frontrunner, and appeared to have a high sensitivity to the African American community. However, one episode called into question as to whether Clinton had adopted the tactics of the new Laissez-faire racism, as he sought to negatively stereotype black militancy, in the face of rising assaults on Blacks by police, in urban cities. Rodney King had suffered an unmerciful beating that turned up

378

on video tape, and on national television, in March of 1991. This came about during a renaissance of Black Nationalism, spurred by a series of movies by film-makers. Spike Lee, in particular, made as series of movies that addressed America inter-race politics, and African America's intra-race politics, in the late 1980s, and early 1990s, that included; *Do The Right Thing* (1989), *Mo Better Blues* (1990), *Jungle Fever* (1991) and *"X,"* a long awaited autobiography of Malcolm X, in 1992, that resurrected feeling of pride, militancy and assassination controversies, in the early to mid 1990s. Lee's films were latent with underlining racial and intra-racial messages, that dug at deep seeded racial stereotypes, affecting the black psyche, in ways that created high inter-race and intra-race tensions.

During this time, rap music was making its way into the nation's consciousness, as was its messages. Public Enemy's *Fight the Power*, introduced on Lee's *Do The Right Thing* soundtrack, helped America understand the power of hip-hop, as *Fight the Power* was the signature cut of Public Enemy's landmark album, *It Takes A Nation of Millions To Hold Us Back*. It was an album that sold millions of units, with literally no radio airplay, and has been acclaimed by several music industry critics, and music pollsters, as one of the greatest albums in American music history.

A new underground movement had begun, and rap artists were the prophets of change, and, in many instances, of destruction. They also became symbols for racial attacks, based on their volatile lyrics that called out social conditions of Blacks, and the social structures that were exploiting the masses. The racialization of rap reached a crescendo when "gangsta" rap groups like NWA (Niggas With Attitude) and "gangsta" rappers like Ice Tea, released products that assailed law enforcement. NWA's *Fuck The Po'lice* and Ice Tea's *Cop Killer*, became the focus of national protest, by mostly white male law enforcement agencies. Mostly "angry white male" cops-a major source of abuse, and misconduct, in urban cities-took to airwaves, and protest lines forced record companies to withdraw both products from the market. It also created a new level of alarm for Whites, still war-worm from the urban riots of two decades either, who now advocated for the protection of their rights in the same way oppressed, and disenfranchised masses advocated.

The particularly violent response to the "not guilty" verdicts of the four police officers accused of beating Rodney King, offered the first nationally televised urban revolt, "live" from Los Angeles, in 1992. The

379

revolution "was televised," and offered the rest of the nation a snapshot of what could be anticipated in other cities, if social and economic conditions of America "urban core" were not addressed. This was just the latest opportunity to address massive social and economic inequalities in American society. Instead, it was in this environment that race issues of the 1992 Presidential elections were framed, and rap artists became the racial symbols of the new white backlash-a "silent majority" looking for a political voice.

That political voice came in the form of Democratic candidate, Arkansas Governor, Bill Clinton, when he used comments by rapper, Sista Soulja, to show the nation he could stand up a Jesse Jackson, in assailing her comments at Jackson's Rainbow Coalition Conference in June of 1992. Both of whom had been invited to speak at the conference. Soulja's presentation preceded Clinton's, who had been invited to keynote the conference. In May, 1992, while speaking to a *Washington Post* reporter, Sista Soulja had the most noted "kill whitey" moment (a reference dating back to the pro-Black militancy of the 1960s) of the 1990s new black radicalism, when she commented on the events of Los Angeles riot that had occurred a couple weeks earlier, stating;

"I mean, if black people kill black people every day, why not have a week, and kill white people? You understand what I'm saying? In other words, white people, this government, and that mayor were well aware of the fact that black people were dying every day in Los Angeles, under gang violence. So if you're a gang member, and you would normally be killing somebody, why not kill a white person.?"[33]

Clinton knew he needed to the black vote, but he also needed those "Reagan Democrats" that tended to cross the party line when they felt the Democratic Party was doing too much for Blacks. Jesse Jackson, coming off a huge showing in the 1988 Presidential primaries, where he drew support from a broad cross-section disenfranchised voters at the other end of the Democratic party's factionalized spectrum, was clearly the highest profiled, and arguably, most influential Democrat in the party, having registered two million new voters for the party in the last election-after finishing second to Michael Dukakis among democratic candidates running in 1988, including Clinton's eventual pick-Al Gore, and was refused a place on the Dukakis ticket. Clinton needed Jesse Jackson, but also needed to recapture the support of the party's defectors.

Sista Souljah was not a widely known artist beyond true hip-hop aficionados, and had been invited to do a youth workshop, while Clinton was the conferences keynote speaker. Clearly, both were there for different reasons, to address different target audiences. Still, Clinton used the occasion to show Whites that, not only could he stand up to Jackson, but to address the race concerns of Whites, by condoning black violence against Whites. While there was no evidence that Sista Souljah's comments were nothing more than a bad joke, or a poor example of articulating the abusive extremes of America's race dilemma. It never appeared that she meant to insinuate that Blacks should go out and kill Whites. However, Clinton used a clever debating technique that white conservative ideologues use, where they distort what your target, a black victim of white racism, has said, then compare that black target's views with the views of a white supporter of the oppression of black Americans.[34] Clinton asserted that "if you took the words, white and black, and you reversed them, you might think David Duke was giving that speech," insinuating that the nation's most visible black Democrat was cavorting with black racists, and implicated Jackson in condoning black racism.

In case the white press missed it, Clinton's campaign staff went to great lengths to distribute his comments, which netted him a *Newsweek* cover story, after which time tracking polls showed that the incident became a salient issue in focus groups, and surveys among suburban, and blue collar "Reagan Democrats," who praised Clinton for standing up to Jackson, as well as his strong stand on welfare and capital punishment.[35] Apologizing to Jackson, a few days later, and rationalizing to black youth in Harlem, that queried Clinton on his attack on Sista Soulja, which Clinton excused as an example of how polarized the nation was on the issue of race, when, in fact, Clinton simply had taken a calculated risk that allowed him to hold on to his black voter base, while playing to racial symbolism that connected to white voters, and resonated in a way that, within the next two weeks, moved him from third in the polls to first.

Clinton won the following November, with 43% of the popular vote-receiving only 82% of the black vote, the lowest since the 1960 election, and only 39% of the white vote. The ironic paradox of the 1992 election was that Blacks elected a president, who ran a campaign, in which he tried to distance himself from the very constituency that was responsible for his election, despite the fact it represented the very core of the party.[36]

However, the new politics of "racial symbolism," while starting with Reagan's 1980 campaign, and his "welfare queen" comments, had actually taken took root as a strategic focus in the 1988, George H.W. Bush-Michael Dukakis campaign, with the now famous, or infamous, Willie Horton ad. Conservative strategists were able to draw a nexus between two Republican platform issues, crime and race, by playing to Whites worse fears, "the Nigger Loosed" mentality of the post slavery era, who became a symbol for quintessential "violent black man."

Horton was convicted, along with two other men, of robbery and, the stabbing murder of a gas station attendant where the police couldn't determine who did what, and didn't read the suspects their rights. Sentenced to life without the possibility of parole, Horton served several years of his sentence in a maximum prison, transferred to a minimum security prison, where he had nine successful furloughs, before he fled on the tenth (June 7, 1986), which according to Horton, was because he couldn't get back in time.[37] Horton was picked up 10 months later in Florida, driving a stolen car, and was accused and convicted of assault and rape, on April 3, 1987.

The Bush (I) campaign strategist. Lee Atwater, who said he would make Horton, Dukakis' "running mate," used the Horton incident to frame Democratic challenger, Mike Dukakis, as soft on crime in a television ad, that showed a revolving prison door with black men coming in and black me going out, with the caption under Dukakis' picture saying, "Allowed Murders to Have Weekend Passes."[38]

A second ad ran saying that Dukakis had 268 convicts jump furlough, and even though most were white men, but the Bush campaign continued to use black faces in Bush literature. Dukakis responded much too late, and saw a double digit lead evaporate into a November loss, as racial intolerance and the fear of crime, black crime, caused 61% of white men nationwide, to vote for Bush.

Willie Horton didn't evaporate after the 1988 election, as campaigns nationwide chose the politics of racism, in creating their own "Willie Hortons," and Negrophobia returned to such a degree that even non-threatening black men became suspect in the minds of Whites, as New Jersey Senator Bill Bradley, reminded his colleagues on the floor of the U.S. Senate, stating "the Willie Horton ad" was an attempt to demonize all of black America, and if you don't believe me, ask any African American who tries to hail a cab at night in any American city?"[39] Racial symbolism was now part of the American political landscape. It had also became part of the country's judicial landscape.

In 1989, the U.S. Supreme Court struck down an affirmative

action program in the city of Richmond, Virginia that sought to esca-late the level of minority contracts, by instituting a 30% set-a-side for minority participation in state and municipal contracts, due to the fact that black firms were being excluded from governmental contracts though the city of Richmond's black population was 50% of the total population. The percentage of contracts awarded to Blacks was less than one percent.

The Richmond City Council constructed a definition of the word "minority," based on Congress' definition used in the Public Works Employment Act of 1977, stating that "minority" meant "Blacks, Spanish-speaking, Orientals, Indians, Eskimos, and Aleuts," in terms of who would be entitled to take advantage of the special pro-gram. Known as the *Croson* decision, the U.S. Supreme Court ruled that the Richmond affirmative action policy was unconstitutional, because its set-a-side represented a case of intentional race discrimina-tion by state and local government, and subject to "strict scrutiny," because the city gave justification for the plan, as being a remedy for past discrimination to these protected groups, even though some of them, specifically Eskimos, that had never set foot in the state of Virginia-much less had suffered any historical discrimination.[40]

The most far-reaching aspect of the *Croson* decision was its "proof of past discrimination" declaration, where Justice Sandra Day O'Connor, who wrote the opinion for the majority, stated that calling a plan "remedial" didn't make it so, because the city had no evidence on how much past discrimination had really taken place (none in the case of Eskimos). O'Conner stated that only remedies that could prove "real" past discrimination could stand up to strict scrutiny, and that the Richmond plan didn't qualify, because it was not "narrowly tailored" to overcome proven past racial discrimination.

Croson represented the first time a clear majority of five justices applied strict scrutiny test to a state or local government affirmative action plan, a significant departure because, prior to *Croson*, only two cases had stood up to strict scrutiny since 1944; the first was preferences for Japanese Americans after the federal government interned them during World War II, and courted ordered affirmative action programs in the Deep South states, where legal segregation provided society-wide discrimination against Blacks.[41]

In any other case, the Court had held that government only had to stand up to what was considered rational, meaning under "rationality," that the Court supported government treating citizens un-

383

equal, as long as, it had a rational reason for doing so-race being the exception. If the government singled people out because of race, then discrimination was subject to strict scrutiny-meaning the policy, or law, in question had to be motivated by a compelling reason, and the remedy had to be tailored to achieve a specific purpose.

Dissenters in the *Croson* case, which included Thurgood Marshall, wondered how the Court could allow affirmative action programs in Alabama and Georgia, to survive strict scrutiny, and not allow Richmond, a border state that was the former capital of the Confederate States of America, which was guided by the same segregation laws as were in the Deep South, to survive strict scrutiny. Justice Blackmun, who called out the Court's inconsistency in his dissent, wasn't bothered that there was "no evidence" that most of the groups listed in the plan had ever been discriminated against by anyone in Richmond, Virginia.[42] The fact that state supported discrimination (Jim Crow) existed, that would have historically discriminated against all the listed parties, was compelling enough reason to justify the remedy. However, O'Connor, and the new conservative majority, had reduced strict scrutiny interpretation, from group based, or societal discrimination, to individual discrimination, and used the claim that there was no evidence that the contractors being forced to hire Blacks, and other minorities, had historically discriminated, though it was obvious from the one percent procurement that less than best faith efforts to hire black firms had occurred, as the basis for saying that the Richmond plan failed the strict scrutiny test.

On the 40th Anniversary of *Brown* in 1994, legal scholar Kimberle' Crenshaw analyzed the effects of the *Croson* decision, and its detriments on using affirmative action to achieve black equality, by analogizing the legal reasoning used by this U.S. Court in this case, to the legal reasoning used in *Plessy*. In *Croson*, the Court reached back beyond the 1964 Civil Rights Act, beyond the *Brown* decision to a period when judicial restraint offered simple analogous doctrine to substantiate maintaining the racial "status quo," just as the justices in *Plessy* reached back before the Reconstruction Amendments to reconnect to the underlining reasoning (more extralegal than legal) of the *Dred Scott* decision, because the legal outcome simply served the best interest of protecting the individual Constitutional rights of America's majority populace-Whites. Crenshaw noted that the first thing the U.S. Supreme Court did was review the constitutionality of the Richmond program to determine whether race classifications that burdened Whites would be subject to the same level of review, as traditional classifications that burden people of color-construing race as simply skin color absent of any historical, political or economic value.[43]

Secondly, Crenshaw asserts, O'Connor chose to ignore Richmond's history, as one of the most racially entrenched southern cities in the country, who had often come before the Supreme Court on issues of race doctrine, noting that surely the Court hadn't forgotten that it was Virginia (Prince Edwards County) that resisted *Brown*, and subsequent federal court desegregation orders for five years, then rather to comply with the federal order, chose to close its public schools, in defiance, until 1964.

There was more than enough evidence to document the historical discrimination of the state of Virginia to compel the Court to uphold the City of Richmond's remedy. Lastly, Crenshaw pointed out O'Connor used the *Plessy* defense of Justice Henry Billing Brown's opinion, that just because a white person chooses in their rights of enjoyment to socialize with other Whites, doesn't make Blacks unequal, or in need of federally assisted protection, and that it is not the role of government to legislate equality that might be otherwise attained, as a "result of natural affinities, a mutual appreciation of each others merits, and a voluntary consent of individuals."[44] Reaching back to *Plessy*, Crenshaw assertion was that, in O'Connor's attempt to postulate that Richmond low minority contracting percentage may have had nothing to do with discrimination, and everything to do with Blacks not wanting to be contractors, she gave constitutional protection to the same properties of white privilege that *Plessy* gave, when the Supreme Court stated that property rights were assigned to the dominant race.

In O'Connor's interpretation, affirmative action was designed to correct for social discrimination, and open up the process to the "privilege" of contracting, but not a guarantee to award Blacks opportunities, at the expense of more deserving Whites.[45] *Croson* was landmark, because it reasserted that "sameness" of equality in 1989, that guaranteed that Blacks and Whites be treated "same and separate"- while being called equal-analogous to how it was applied in 1896. *Croson* allowed for legal interpretations of this new formal equality to reinforce conditions and systems of inequality that *Plessy* allowed and insulated the new equality from attack on past discrimination claims unless very specific claims can be proven in the same way that "Separate But Equal" forced those who attacked social and economic disparities of segregation to prove separate was, in fact, unequal. *Croson*, as did *Plessy*, reduced the question of racial to merely a question of skin color, abstracted from history, contract, or the meanings and experiences of black and white that have complicated the question of what's equality in America.[46]

This was the shift in equality thought brought forth into the 1990s, and black business development was going to be setback because of this change in direction in the court. There were similar set-a-side programs in 36 other states, and more than 200 localities, that would now follow Croson's lead, and the drop off was dramatic. For instance, one year later in Philadelphia, black contractors saw their share of city contracts decrease from 25 percent in 1990 to 3.5 percent in 1991.[47] Richmond fell from 25 percent in 1989, to one percent in 1990, clearly demonstrating that diversity efforts were not voluntary, they were mandatory and when not forced to comply, white contractors returned to their pre-affirmative action goal numbers.

The politics of racism had shifted America's cultural behaviors by the start of the 1990s, and Clinton's election didn't necessarily put an end to racial politics. Clinton never fully acknowledged that his "double Bubba" strategy was designed subtly to appeal to southern voters, while at the same time managing racial tensions within his party among the race sensitive, party jumping "Reagan Democrats," as well as the nation, who was now watching everything through racial lenses, after the O.J. Simpson verdict in 1994.

The racially charged O.J. Simpson trial was every bit of the real life "Bigger Thomas" racial hysteria drama that Richard Wright wrote about in *Native Son*, as O.J. Simpson was truly the essence of the nonthreatening black-the native son, if you will, allowed to crossover into white America's world, amidst hidden anxieties that Simpson's propensity to socialize with white women might one day go terribly wrong. Well, like the Bigger Thomas experience, something did go terribly wrong, and America grasped every bit of its 300 year "Nigger loosed" mentality to assail O.J. Simpson on the basis the white male's long held fears expressed in literary form, cinema, and in real life, every time a black man was accused of rape, or assaulting a white woman. The Simpson criminal trial had all the components a highly charged "race" case; a victim, a black man, cloudy circumstances and what's a race case with a bigot up in the middle of the case, convoluting facts.

Former LAPD detective, Mark Fuhrman, stood ready to exploit the worse images of-not just O.J.-but every black person, whom he simply framed indiscriminately as "niggers," in earlier interviews, while denying that he had any racial motives, or biases toward Simpson, during his investigation on night of the murders.

On national television, race-its fears, its motives, its biases, its realities were played out, as it always had in America, except for the conclusion. The ending that had most always played out during encounters of racial hysteria, escaped "the Juice," as Simpson was found "not guilty." Yet, it was Simpson's attorney, Johnnie Cochran, who was accused of, not defending his client-not exposing holes in the prosecutor's case-not exposing a closest racist in Mark Fuhrman, but, playing the "race card" that had freed Simpson. America had played the race card every day of the African Americans existence in America, never playing by the same set of rules. However, though Cochran didn't cheat, didn't manipulate or change the rules, he somehow did less than what the law required him to do, vigorously defend his client. The O.J. Simpson case, in the most grotesque and twisted manner, represented what legal equality could be, minimally, when an African American had the capacity to provide themselves the best defense in a racialized system stacked against them.

The "legal lynching" that Clarence Thomas claimed he was a victim of, didn't occur in the O.J. Simpson trial, nor did the extralegal physical lynching that usually followed the accusations that Simpson faced. In the eyes of many white people, "Bigger" Thomas lives in O.J. Simpson, which is why anywhere he went, and any social conflict he had after his trial, was reported with the same hysteria that drove Birth of a Nation, and Rosewood and Tulsa and Emmitt Till, Goodman, Schwerner and Chaney, and the list goes on and on. A long history of racial hysteria was revisited in mid-1990s that made it hard for Whites to ignore race, or the racial cues that were coming from the media, from Congress, and from the White House.

However, on November 8, 1994, the mid-term elections that were impacted by the convergence of angry white males, low voter turnout, and what was called, the "new nigger syndrome" (Blacks who thought that racism was over, and thus there was no need for civil rights struggle) caused the biggest party shift in the history of Congress. The Republican takeover, of both bodies of Congress, ended 40 years of Democratic party domination, and with their new majority, Newt Gingrich was elected Speaker of the House, and the "new Republicans" immediately rolled out their new policy agenda. Called the "Contract with America," it was a policy "manifesto" that included balancing the

387

federal budget, reducing government spending and changing some of the house rules, it started out as a call for responsible government, but ended up being a referendum on social welfare policy. Within a couple weeks of launching its "contract," the real policy agenda surfaced, as affirmative action, and welfare reform suddenly became two of the "Contract with America's" de facto items, as both issues were used raise racial stereotypes like never before.[48]

The Republican takeover, the "Contract With America," the sudden attack on affirmative action, and on welfare, were caused, in the opinion of political observers, by two things; the big push for "Majority minority" Congressional districts (districts drawn to enhance Black and Latino representation) that led to the tripling of "ethnic representation" in Congress, and backlash from the O.J. Simpson trial. White males didn't riot in the streets of America (as they had done just 80 years earlier). They rioted at the ballot box, and took back "their" government, and now were intent on governing "for the people." "Their" people, but under the guise of governing for all.

President Clinton now had something to think about for the 1996 election. As long as Clinton could appeal to Blacks, without seeming like he was capitulating to Blacks, his "centrist" ideology worked. But the moment he appeared to take any position on any racialized issue, his more conservative constituency base would pull him back to right of center, and negate any benefit African Americans were seeking.

Though, there were other prime examples of Clinton's strategic race policy (including Clinton's refusal to apologize for slavery, and his silent policies on Haiti and the Sudan), there was no better examples of this Clinton "waffle" then on two issues; Clinton's nomination of University of Pennsylvania Law Professor, Lani Guinier, to be Assistant Attorney General for Civil Rights in the Justice Department, and Clinton's "Mend it, don't end it" position on affirmative action. Guinier, a classmate of Bill and Hilary at Yale, had written extensively on how white racial "bloc" voting in America undermines black representation, and offered "winner takes some" proportional elections that overcome the "winner takes all" outcomes of single district representation as possible solutions to inequities in black political representation. Guinier was attacked on both sides of the ideological spectrum, within the Democratic Party, and from without.

The liberal advisors in Clinton's White House saw the nomination as a potential move toward policy concessions for African

Americans, that threaten "the fault line" between Blacks, Jews, women and white liberals, within the Democratic coalition, while the Republicans called her a "quota queen" for suggesting Blacks would gain greater representation in proportional elections that considered their parity in the general population.[49] Caving to pressure on both sides of the aisle, Clinton withdrew her nomination before it could come up in the Senate.

A few years later when the U.S. Supreme Court gave, what many perceived to be the death knoll to minority set-a-sides in government, for the promotion of race based equality, in the case of *Adarand v. Pena* in 1995, Clinton convoluted the affirmative action discussion with his own position, called, "Mend it, don't end it." Caught in the mix between two polarized constituency bases, one calling on Clinton to praise the Adarand decision, the other calling for the condemnation of the decision, Clinton was, at first, silent on the decision. Republicans lauded the *Adarand* decision, as one that eliminated the many minority "fronts" that had begun to spring up in the late 1980s, and early 1990s. A minority front was a business that showed majority minority ownership on paper but was bankrolled (financially underwritten) by white partners, or investors to be able to access business set aside for minorities.

Based on the more egregious cases of abuse in these set-asides, and of contractors just trying to fill "quotas" to keep their contracts, Clinton was considering eliminating some affirmative action programs, using the Supreme Court decision as cover. Jesse Jackson called out Clinton's capitulation against affirmative action, as pandering to the right in the upcoming Presidential election, to which he stated, was "becoming a party of Demopublicans" and threatening to run for President himself, if Clinton tried to end affirmative action.[50] Clinton, trying to avoid the possibility of a Jesse Jackson run in 1996 that could split the party, and possibility do to him, what Ross Perot did to George H.W. Bush in 1992, came out in a limited support of affirmative action in June of 1995, attacking those who would end the policy, as not having done enough, but promising to end all policies that went too far, by becoming racial quotas, a position was largely perceived as moot, given that *Adarand* had already changed the law and Clinton himself altered very few programs.[51] The whole episode gave rise to how much the right had influenced the question of race, and equality, by the mid-1990s, when even the U.S. President winked at equality.

While social and economic equality came to a head in 1995,

389

the year also served as a year of contemplation, and reflection, for the black equality movement. The Black Nationalist movement, and the civil rights movement, who had begun to come together in the early 1990s, participated in a series of events during that year to discuss the "future direction" of the struggle. Maulana "Ron" Karenga, the head of the US Organization, principle co-founder of the Kwanzaa holiday and architect of the Nguzo Saba (seven principles of cultural restoration for Africans to return to their former glory), held a national "Critical Issues" Conference in Los Angeles to address the issues most impacting the collective African in America.

The most noted event to take place was the Million Man March, convened by Minister Louis Farrakhan, in October, 1995, that drew over one million men on the premise of atonement and reconciliation. With he biggest mass demonstration in the history of America, and the broadest African American coalition since the 1960s, the National Parks Service created a controversy when it reported the number of attendees at 400,000, then later adjusted the number to 700,000, and said it would no longer be responsible for enumerating public gatherings in Washington, D.C. Independent demographers and surveyors put the number at closer to 1.8 million attendees.

The march was seen as a referendum against House Speaker, Newt Gingrich, and the policy agenda of Congress' Angry White Men that had passed a major staple of its "Contract With America" policy promise, in getting Clinton to sign a welfare reform earlier in the year. Social and economic conditions of the inner cities had led to high "black on black" violence, 50% unemployment amongst African American teen-aged males, almost a doubling of the incarceration rate of black males, and a massive rise in homeless, foster care and stated supervised children.

The following year, a deluge of cases and events occurred viewed as partly backlash from the O.J. Simpson case, and partly racial hyperbole heightened by the new "shock" jolt of talk radio hosts, led by Rush Limbaugh, that offered daily opinions with racial undertones. Public sentiment didn't, of itself, slide to the right. The fear that a "war" for American culture and American "values," as Pat Buchanan framed it, jump started an ideological shift to the right. Coming on the heels of *Adarand*, the University of Texas (UT) law School, adopted a minority admissions policy that gave preference to disadvantaged students that were underrepresented in the law school.

The most underrepresented were Black and Hispanics, so UT

Law School set up a segregated evaluation process, outside of the regular admissions process, enacted a separate admissions committee made up of minorities, who screened applicants, evaluated qualifications, and made decisions regarding admissions that were final. The problem was that Black and Hispanic students were held to lower academic standards that weren't applied to Whites and Asians, as it was determined that American born Blacks and Hispanics (citizen or alien), were considered "preferred minorities." The median LSAT score for Whites, in the 1992 admissions class, was in the 91st percentile, while the median black score was in the 78th percentile. The median grade point for Whites was an A while the median grade point for Blacks was a B-minus. The University of Texas said it lowered its standard to meet a goal of ten percent (10%) for Mexican Americans, and five percent (5%) for African Americans that was "a target set to overcome the effects of past discrimination and to ensure 'diversity.'"[52]

However, to white students-with segregated admissions policies, segregated waiting lists, and the preferred treatment given to less qualified "preferred minorities"-it was "Jim Crow" treatment in reverse, that could be justified as nothing more than a racial double standard, confirming the worst fears of those who opposed quotas. Four white students filed a law suit, claiming reverse discrimination, and alleging that UT Law School passed over six to seven hundred more qualified white Texas residents, before the first Blacks were denied admission. The lead plaintiff, Cheryl Hopwood, was White and disadvantaged, didn't receive the same considerations, as the black and Hispanics students, because she wasn't in the protected group. In filing a lawsuit after she and three others were denied admission, Hopwood asserted her Fourteenth Amendment rights were violated, claiming that UT was engaging racially motivated state action, and that the purpose of the Fourteenth Amendment was end to all racially motivated state action.

The irony of this claim was that Hopwood used the *Brown* and the *Gaines* interpretation of equal rights, and equal protection, arguments that had long been denied by the Courts. This time in 1996, the Fifth Circuit Court of Appeals gave a very succinct interpretation that went further than the *Bakke* decision, stating that "The law school may not use race as a factor in deciding which applicants to admit."[53] Unlike it did 36 years earlier in the case of *Sweatt v. Painter*, University of Texas accepted the decision and chose not to appeal to the Supreme Court. A Court, that in its 1990s conservative posture, would have most likely upheld the lower court's decision.

391

Still, it was obvious that the University of Texas Law School had no intention of defending "diversity," as vigorously as it had defended segregation almost four decades earlier, when it built a whole law school for one black student. Equality had now shifted in defense of white's rights and there was no need to challenge the Constitution in defense of white rights. The *Hopwood* decision, and UT's acceptance of the decision, in the face of the fact that Blacks and Latino were still underrepresented, because of past discrimination, was only the latest example of the passive defense of a quickly fading policy called affirmative action. Though *Hopwood* wasn't a Supreme Court decision, it had major national reverberations, in how equality would be perceived. This wasn't the only attack on racial equality in 1996.

The most significant attack was launched by then. Governor of California, Pete Wilson, who used his authority, as Chairperson of the University of California Board of Regents, a year earlier to eliminate race, as a criteria for admissions in the state's UC system, considered one of the nation's leading state funded university systems. The next year, he bankrolled a ballot initiative to eliminate affirmative action in all state agencies, state funded educational systems, and state contracts. Calling it the "California Civil Rights Initiative," it represented the biggest act of political chicanery, since the Southern Manifesto. With Wilson raising the money, the state's Republican Party hired black conservative, Ward Connerly, a regent of the University, to espouse the notion that there was no longer a need for race, declaring the country "colorblind," and with "King verse" in hand, Connerly went up and down the state, spouting that it was time to "judge people by the content of the character-not the color of their skin."

Connerly had become the "Anti-Negro," advancing the same artificial arguments that Whites had long advanced, in terms of how preferences and quotas were just as discriminatory as racial segregation, but offered no remedy for how past discrimination would be rectified, other than goodwill efforts of those in authority doing the right thing. One hundred years after the Atlanta Compromise speech that urged Blacks to forsake social equality, identified Booker T. Washington, as the voice of reason for Northern philanthropists, white conservatives had finally found another Booker T. Washington, to urge Blacks to forsake, this time, the economic equality that affirmative action represented, in context of restitution for past discrimination. "Civil rights for everybody" was Connerly's call, but he was essentially the mouthpiece to say the things about race that Whites themselves could not say, which was "protect the Constitutional rights of Whites, by eliminating racial preference programs." Connerly straight up stated that affirmative action discriminated against Whites, and stated on Clinton's advisory panel on race, that the best way for America to move forward was "to take the whole subject of affirmative action off their plate...deal[ing] with the broader subject of race absent the issue of preferences.[54]

The ultimate undermining of affirmative action, as a constructive measure for remedying past discrimination, was effectively undone by a black man, who has never admitted, to this day, that he was nothing more than a "hired gun" in the movement that was a ploy, on the part of conservative think tanks (Heritage Foundation and Claremont Institute), to undermine racial equality, by eliminating affirmative action. Convincing California voters that they were voting for "civil rights," and "equality for everyone," many thought-including 25% of black voters-that they were somehow strengthening equality when, in fact, they were weakening equality by disconnecting the primary remedy for past discrimination and dismantling the policy most apt to arrest racial disparities.

The California Civil Rights Initiative won handily in November, 1996. By the end of 1996, affirmative action had been stripped of all of its compliance and enforcement mechanisms, and with California showing the rest of the nation that "states rights" was the way to follow, in the Supreme Court's new precedents of extremely narrow interpretations of affirmative action applicability, the referendum battle against affirmative action went nationwide. Ward Connerly had a model to introduce to states across the nation, and he would over the next five years get similar measures passed, in several other states. Black student enrollments at all University of California campuses, fell the year following the passing of the referendum. At the University of Texas Law School, admission of black law students in the Fall, 1997 class, fell from 65 black students, in 1996, to six, the year after the *Hopwood* decision.

Affirmative action, as the nation knew it-though distorted most of the time-was as good as dead, and it was almost as if there was an agenda to accomplish this before the end of the year, that represented the 100th anniversary of *Plessy v. Ferguson*. Thirty-two years after *Brown*, *Plessy* rose from the grave to make one last grab at equality, as new judicial interpretations that reached back to past legal reasoning to give it life.

393

Federal jurist, A. Leon Higginbotham, wrote an open letter to the nation on the 100th Anniversary of Plessy by publishing in the *Boston Sunday Globe,* on May 19th, 1996, in a commentary entitled, "100 Years Later, *Plessy v. Ferguson* Still Hurts." After the death of Thurgood Marshall in January of 1993, Judge Higginbotham became black America's foremost spokesperson, on legal and civil rights affairs-though he was still on the bench. Earlier that year, he headed the national search team to identify a new Executive Director for the NAACP, that was five million dollars in debt, on the verge of collapse and had been without a leader, since Ben Chavis was removed for allegation of sexual and administrative improprieties. Higginbotham subsequently convinced Maryland Congressman, Kwesi Mfume, to take the position, to save "an American Institution."[55]

On the *Plessy* Anniversary, Judge Higginbotham noted that *Plessy* was "one of the most retrogressive 'civil rights' decisions ever rendered by the United States Supreme Court" that even present day moderate, and conservative, Supreme Court jurists of the present day high Court (he cited Anthony Kennedy, Sandra Day O'Connor, David Souter and Chief Justice William Rehnquist) agreed "was wrong the day it was decided," and acknowledge Justice Harlan's dissent was the proper rule of constitutional law.[56] He pointed the prior two years had been dangerous as rationalizations to abandon equality doctrine, had been advanced, much of it stemming from the hate filled nearsightedness of the Angry White Male sentiment. Higginbotham, essentially, asserted that America had been down this "colorblind" road before, stating that:

> *"Americans have heard millions of words about what House Speaker Newt Gingrich proclaims is the 'Contract With America.' I, and other persons of good will, listen to the rhetoric surrounding the Contract With America with considerable skepticism. Why?*
> *Because, in Justice Oliver Wendell Holmes's phase, 'a page of history is worth a volume of logic.' We know about the bitter consequences of Plessy, and the Contract With America sounds much too historically familiar."*[57]

Noting that this "contract" was just another example of how past states rights doctrines were used "to keep African Americans poor, and powerless, under the dominance of arbitrary state governments."[58] Judge Higginbotham, as an astute interpreter of the law, understood where folk like Gingrich, and California Governor, Pete Wilson, who became an unsuccessful Republican candidate for President after his UC Regents move against affirmative action, were going and he knew they were not moving forward. They were moving backwards, and taking the equality rights of black people backwards with them.

This would become obvious by the end of the decade, as new manifestations of the racial divide became in evidence. Education, employment and housing divides, as racial comparisons, gave way to more damaging, intergenerational forms of racial discrimination like wealth, inheritance, corporate and technological divides. For instance, the differences in black and white families, could no longer be measured, in just comparative percentage terms. They now had to be measured, in terms of the increase in the gaps between Blacks and Whites, as well as, residual benefits that are created from generations of inequality, what Melvin Oliver and Thomas Sharipo called, "sedimentation of racial inequality."[59]

Sedimentation is based on one principle factor, wealth. The fact that Blacks are born with low levels of wealth-wealth being the best indicator of material disparity between Blacks and Whites-and are impacted by historical legacies of low wages, personal and organizational discrimination, and institutional racism, that essentially effects wealth accumulation over the life of Blacks. Sedimentation of inequality takes into consideration that paradoxical relationship between black poverty and white wealth, where the accumulation of wealth for some Whites is intimately tied to the poverty of wealth for most Blacks, creating "cumulative advantages" for Whites and "cumulative disadvantages" for Blacks that allows the former to pas wealth from generation to generation, while the latter passes less wealth, if any, and falls further and further behind in the equality gap.[60]

In a historical context, almost every circumstance of bias and discrimination against Blacks, has produced a circumstances and opportunity of positive gain for Whites. The most significant positive gain for Whites has been the accumulation of assets. Just as America established an "income" poverty line to establish a minimum standard of living, there is an "asset" poverty line. The asset poverty line is based on whether a family has assets of $4,175 (three months of income at the 1999 official U.S. government income poverty line for a family of four, at $1,392). A family with less than $4,175 in assets, would be considered "asset-poor." At the end of the 20th Century, wealth and assets demonstrated how racial equality had faired, despite the fact that, the

395

1990s economic boon produced enormous wealth (over $8 trillion in stock market equity alone), and record low unemployment. By the end of 1999, 54%, or more than half, of black families lived below the "asset poverty line," while only 25% of white families lived by this asset line. [61] It is a telling disclosure on how separate the economic realities of black and white America are, and how disparately unequal they are. The racial wealth gap is just as telling. By the end of 1999, the median black household earned 59 cents for every dollar Whites families earned, which transcended to an even more disparate inequity in wealth, as those same black families possessed only ten cent for every dollar of wealth that white families possess. [62] By earning less, and keeping less, there is no reasonable expectation to conclude that this racial wealth gap will close any time soon, and that wealth equality can be attained given the massive Black/White income disparity currently in place.

These massive income and wealth disparities produced, by the end of the 20th Century, significant gaps in both net worth, and net financial assets between Whites and Blacks, at all income levels. Blacks in the nation's top twenty percent of income earners, had one-third the net worth (at $43,806) of Whites in the same income bracket ($133,607), and less than 20% of the net financial assets (18%), at $7,448, of Whites at $40,465. [63] Black to White dollars ratios served as a distinguishing baseline, in determining how worth and assets differentials get larger as Blacks and Whites earn less.

For instance, Blacks in the middle twenty percent of wage earners, had less than 30% (29.59%) of the net worth of Whites ($14,902 versus $50,350), and only 12% of the financial assets ($800 versus $6,800). Blacks in the second lowest twenty percent had only 17% the net worth of Whites ($6,879 versus $39,908), and only 7% of the financial assets of Whites ($249 versus 3,599), and of the lowest twenty of wage earners, Blacks had 14% of the net worth of Whites ($2,400 versus $17,066), and only one percent of the net financial assets of Whites ($100 versus $7,400). [64] Only Blacks in the second highest twenty percent of wagers ($39,000-$60,000), come close to having *half the net worth of Whites* (45%), $29,851 to $65,998, but still had only 20% of the net financial assets ($2,699 versus $13,362) of Whites. [65] Fact of the matter is, wage earners at all levels, except the highest wage earners, had net financial assets less than $3,000, by the of 1999, and the lowest income Whites at $7,400, had net financial assets equivalent to the highest income Blacks, at $7,448, and net worth higher than all Blacks except those in the top forty percent of wage earners. This means if Blacks accumulate low net worth and little net financial assets, they have even less wealth to pass on to the next generation of Blacks. This is not the case for white families. Inheritance has become a factor in perpetuating inequality.

Studies in the 1990s documented that one of four white families receive an inheritance after the death of one parent-leaving on average $144,652, versus one in 20 black families-who leave, on average, $41,985, a $102,167 gap in inheritance received at *five times* the rate.[66] Whites not only leave more money to the next generation, they leave inheritances more often. Racial inequalities in income and wealth, of those school age children, who came of age in the *post-Brown* era (Baby boomers born after 1946), will be much larger than those born in the generation born before 1946. The average life time inheritance for white baby boomers will be worth $125,000 (in 2000 dollars), at age 55, where it was only $70,000 for the previous generation that benefited from segregation and other laws of racially preference treatment. Black baby boomer will inherit only $16,000 by age 55, 13 cents for every dollar inherited by white baby boomers.[67]

This means that racial inequality will be perpetuated well into the next generation, and the racial separation borne out of segregation, maintained throughout the second half of the 20th Century, and reinforced by the new "Colorblind" mindset at the end of the century that ignored race and racial disparities, will remain in effect. This is based on the simple fact that there will be a wealth separation between those "who inherit" and those "who don't." By the end of the 20th Century, studies revealed that 28% of white families received inheritance bequests, with an average inheritance of $47,878-though the typical family inheritance was $10,000, compared to just 7.7% of black families, who, on average left $21,796-with a typical inheritance of $798, 8 cents of inheritance for every dollar inherited by Whites (those fortunate enough to receive bequests).[68]

Whether you look at net worth, or net financial assets, or look at the mean (average) or the median, the fact is those who inherit have, minimally three times the wealth of non-inheritors, which translate to higher incomes, than subsequently leads to a better quality of life. So, African American wealth and income, among both inheritors and non-inheritors, are unequal and highly disparate, a racial divide to be passed to the generation. The separation of black and white wealth of the "Separate But Equal" era of America's racial divide, survived the equality movement, and was being covered up by the Colorblind society politic. For all intents and purposed, Colorblindness, in its ability to represent an "equal" society, while covering up a racially discriminating socio-economic reality, is the new "Jim Crow."

16

Brown, Race and Equality in the 21st Century:
Colorblind or Blinded by Color?

"Color is not a human or personal reality; it is a political reality."

- James Baldwin

Racism is still very much a part of the American way of life; we do not live in a colorblind society.

Federal District Judge Damon Keith

"We thought that when we beat segregation that equality would come. We soon found out that segregation was only a symptom of the problem. The real problem of racial equality in America is White Supremacy, and it will only be solved when we rid ourselves of White Supremacy."

Federal Judge Robert L. Carter at the 50th Anniversary of *Brown* Conference, New York University, May 17th, 2004

Colorblindness, or race-neutrality, as a primary social interface, had become the mainstream social construct of the 21st Century. It is devoid of a true discussion about historical racial equality, and allows current discourse on race to be abrogated, for the sake of a more convenient discourse in current day individualism that, in the opinion of its proponents, offers a less divisive, more harmonious social benefit. What Colorblindness offers instead, is a bevy of false arguments that lead to a greater collection of false assumptions, tied to the absence of race being related to the absolution of discrimination, and, thus, more equality rather than less equality. The disparities of the "racial divide" have become such a latent issue in today's society, that racial equality has become separated from the more salient societal issues of age, class, youth and lifestyles. In terms of an emerging civil rights agenda, the "unequal" has become the "unseen," and relegated to being, "un-discussed." "Race fatigue" has become the term used in the 21st Century, for how society excuses not talking about race, in the context of social, economic and political disparities. These disparities have all now become issues associated with the emerging class differences that affect the politics of the rich and the poor.

However, to the exclusion of the poor, American society "class" discussions are almost exclusively framed in context to the pains and progress of the "American Middle Class," in and of itself-a racial cue to what equality has come to represent. Blacks, and other people of color, are disproportionately represented among the poor-even now represented as "the permanent underclass," that is expanding nearly at the same rate that the middle class is shrinking. Yet no one talks about the poor anymore, because it offers an appropriate transition into a discussion on who is poor, and why they continue to be poor, after the greatest economic boon the country had ever known. Why is society not allowed to see these differences in the quality of life, nor allowed to discuss them in the realm of larger societal problems?

Colorblindness allows the societal discourse on the poor to be reduced to individual pain, and individual circumstance, that said circumstances might be inequitably distributed throughout certain segments of the society. Colorblindness also allows race to be separated from all other relevant discourse in our society, and the disparities of race to be swept under a rug of "race fatigue," and social indifference. The term, "race fatigue," is nothing more than a 21st Century codification that society has now grown tired of talking about race, even to the point of suggesting that, race no longer matters, and Colorblindness, as a social construct, offered "the escape" from the social responsibilities tied to racial inequality, whereby no resolution can be offered to address that widening gap in equality.

Because the "colorblind" discourse cannot be reduced to situational generalizations of "group inequities" in society, the sudden declaration that "everybody's equal," after centuries of trying to establish legal and extra-legal inequality, that "everybody has problems" and its our own individual responsibilities to work it out, that "everybody's out of work" and faces the same social and economic challenges, and that "everybody could be doing better" if everybody's allowed to compete in an open free market economy, offers the simplistic analogy of meritocracy, absent of resolution of the true inequities that remain throughout the society. Because race-neutrality discourse doesn't allow for race problems to be adequately addressed, the Colorblind consciousness has caused a different kind of separation that allows society to ignore racial, social, and economic disparities, dismissing them as irrelevant to the total picture of America's current problems. Thus, justification for this book's conclusion, that colorblindness is the latest barrier to resolving racial inequality in America.

This conclusion that Colorblindness is "the new Jim Crow, that has fostered a new "separate but equal" society, is derived from observing social and economic gaps, in America's present day racial divide that are every bit as disparate as they were 30, 40, even 50 years ago. Separate, in terms of the racial differences in America's present day socio-economic construct, but equal, in terms of how society views all persons' social and economic realities-in a strictly individual context. Separate but unequal is really what we see, and is more reflective of the race realities that has returned to American society. Colorblindness doesn't allow us to rationalize the ever increasing disparities of race. The underlining racial tensions associated with trying to achieve equality, and the tensions of its resulting consequences, that we now call "fatigue," doesn't allow society to acknowledge racial inequality-because if one acknowledges it, there is a responsibility to fix it. America doesn't want to fix it because it would require acknowledgement, repentance and reparations. Race, and discussions about race, now blinds society, to the point, that it refuses to address the realities of racial inequality, as well as what is necessary to make up past inequality, and what is necessary to address, and subsequently achieve, true equality.

The *Brown* decision was supposed to represent the end of Jim Crow, accompanied by the demise of explicit ideology of white supremacy. Instead, "Jim Crow" mentality resisted, which brought forth a counter-movement, in the Civil Rights Era, and subsequently caused the formal removal of most barriers of racial symbols-public manifestations of subordination-that reflected white social norms in the first half of the 20th Century. However, instead of those social norms disappearing, and new ones introducing a new social reality that promoted reforms in racial policy, to bring about an attainment of formal equali-

401

ty, we witnessed the persistence of "Jim Crow" mentality and a move to race neutrality. Race neutrality, designed not to see race, that brought about a new White race conscienceness that reintroduced historical white social norms. The same ones that once rationalized racial inferiority, into a submerged popular consciousness, but now legitimizes black domination, through references to an assumed cultural inferiority, that leaves the old racial hierarchy in place, and excuses the deteriorating material conditions of Blacks, remnants of the historical race caste, as self-inflicted circumstances caused by Blacks themselves, not society at large.[1] Instead of separating society on the basis of legally "official" race caste policies that reinforced the pre-*Brown* racial hierarchy, the post-*Brown* racial hierarchy has been reinforced by this concept of Colorblindness presents the same dualities of race superiority, and socio-economic conditions, that historically legitimizes racial subordination and, the same type of white race-consciousness that includes modern beliefs of the same type cultural inferiority, which justified all the same forms of "unofficial" racial discrimination, social injuries and economic neglect-only in a new Colorblind society formally dedicated to equality.[2]

Colorblindness, thus, reinforces beliefs by Whites, in this new Constitutional rights movement, that society is truly a meritocracy, and that the present day racial hierarchy is a function of some legitimate free market correction, impartial to race, producing a social pecking order that is an outcome of fairness, not racism-when it is actually a function of a racial ideology that operates in conjunction within the class (and submerged racial) components of the same "status quo" that reinforced the same white superiority/black inferiority beliefs of America's historical race caste. The elimination of overt symbols of white supremacy, in exchange, for a formal embrace of equality, caused the historical black experience in America to be regarded in race neutral terms, absent of racial barriers that marginalized Blacks, as second class citizens, but did little to alter the hierarchical relationship between Blacks and Whites. The engagement of a new white race consciousness-did little to eradicate the racial norms that legitimate black subordination in the eyes of "colorblind" Whites. Nor does colorblindness do anything to resolve the racial inequalities that came about as a function of societal and, in many instances, government permitted and facilitated discrimination. What colorblindness did do was mitigate government facilitated remedies that offered, not immediate equality parity but, an aggregated attempted to bring about equality over time.

Colorblindness put all of these efforts on pause.

Colorblindness, intended to create a truly equal society instead, created a "blind spot" among Whites that returned privilege to whiteness, and indifference to race. At the turn of the 21st Century, New Jersey Senator, Bill Bradley, in announcing his run unsuccessful run for President of the United States in 2000, spoke of this "blind spot" as he promised to make racial unity a core issue of his platform in recognizing that white skin privilege acted as an organizing principle in American society. This blind spot would rather assert that there is no race problem in America. Race as a "problem," instead becoming a euphemism for "privilege"-white skin privilege as it once had, where the real problem then becomes the social and political construction of race, in a way that advantages Whites over, not just Blacks but, other people of color in economic markets, political institutions, and social policies, whereby the problem of the 21st Century is not DuBois' 20th Century "colorline," but challenging whiteness as ideology, and race reality, in ways that will produce true racial equality.[3]

It is in this race neutral ideology that political conservatives, in the last decade of the 20th Century, sought to correct, in their opinion, policies that, they said, had betrayed the original goals of the Civil Rights Act of 1964, and the Voting Rights Act of 1965, as school busing, affirmative action in employment and college admissions, the creation of Black and Latino majority "minority" voting districts were framed as the result of liberal political elites, civil rights activists and judicial activism who demanded race-conscious remedies that "perverted" the promise of a colorblind society and imposed undemocratic outcomes that drew a deep resentment by America's majority population of Whites.[4] It is this recent history of civil rights law that required reparative remedies that conservatives say caused antidiscrimination policy like *Brown*, the Civil Rights Act and the Voting Rights Act-intended to be colorblind-to be transformed into compensatory policy for minorities that legalized race-conscious policies. Subsequently, it was these race conscious policies, conservatives say, that brought on this dissent to a blind state of "color consciousness" that now dismisses race but reinforces the racial "status quo."

What conservatives dismiss from this rationalization was that it was not the intent of civil rights laws to betray a color-blind principle, but to remedy deep seeded racial disparities caused by white racism, that otherwise would not have been remedied, except for laws that gave force, and compliance requirements, to very specific forms of racial dis-

403

crimination. Anti-discrimination policies knocked down barriers, in the high wall of the white labor market privilege, created some gains-though small-that mattered in the total scheme of things, as economic opportunities for Blacks as well as Latinos, Native Americans and females would have been greatly diminished in the present day had it not been for anti-discrimination laws.[5] Yet, conservative Whites perceived antidiscrimination policies, like affirmative action, and majority black Congressional districts, as an assault, not on inequality, but on their privilege-their whiteness, that produced a set of racially polarized elections in the 1970s, 1980s and 1990s.

This strongly suggested that racism in America was rooted in a sense of group position, rather in a collection of selected bigoted attitudes, as the notion of black progress threatened a perceived superiority, disrupted the historical racial hierarchy, and undermined the normality of whiteness.[6] What the whole philosophy of colorblindness was designed to do was to blind society to the issue of race, thus making sure that many of the race-conscious antidiscrimination policies, that were meant to become "equality-centric" became, in effect, equality-neutral or "race neutral," meaning Whites could no longer targeted, or excluded, in remedying historical discrimination.

Race neutrality, as a policy shift, and colorblindness, as a behavioral shift, became ways to dismiss racial equality from America's socio-political, and legislative agendas, while also causing an ideological shift in the judicial branch of government that brought about a legal shift in the Court's position on race and race equality. Once colorblindness became legally defensible, it became the basis for which color consciousness, or the privilege of whiteness, and its residual benefits, could be reintroduced, without ever mentioning race, as an incentive, or a cause for policy-"separate but equal" without the signs, without laws, and most importantly, without the corrosive, socially debilitating attitude.

Colorblindness, as the new "Jim Crow," offered a new set of social protocols and racial etiquettes that used "formal" equality as a subterfuge to maintaining racial inequality and reordering the racial contracts that represent America's 21st Century unilateral globalism, or as President George H.W. Bush defined it at the turn of the 1990s, the "New World Order's" set of power relations that benefit those in society's superior position. Racial contracts, as a social construct theory, represent that set of formal or informal agreements, between members of one subset of humans, in the case of the United States, Whites, within the overall society that allows the dominate group to categorize the remaining subset of humans, as "non-white," and of a different and inferior moral status, becoming subpersons to the dominant group, so that they have a subordinate civil standing in the white or white-ruled polities Whites already control, whereby the moral and juridical rules normally regulating the behavior of Whites in their dealing with each other, do not apply at all in dealings with the designated subpersons, in this case, non-Whites.[7]

America was founded on the premise of a Western political theory "social contract," between its people, and the government they it would adopt, constituted a powerful set of rules that established a civil society of equals, and a government based on popular sovereignty that is, in essence, between everybody in the society-"We, the People"-in theory. However, among its social and political relations, particularly, as it relates to race-from the outset, America practiced a social contract among just those people who counted, which was really not "We the People," but, "We, the white people of America," which in effect was a racial contract.[8]

Brown attempted to end almost two centuries of racial contracts in American government-not to mention, the two centuries racial contracts existed before the formation of the United States of America. Yet the vestiges of "three-fifths, *Dred Scott*, and *Plessy*, had survived the 20th Century, and made it into the 21st Century, as racial contracts replaced a brief 40 to 50 year period of raceless social contracts, as a model of the actual world, and what needs to be done to reform it.[9] The absence of social contracts in the colorblind society doesn't allow for the opportunity to correct problems for those in the society, when the contract has not been fulfilled. When replaced by the racial contract, within the context of colorblindness, race is de-emphasized, but not forgotten. The racial contract just decolorizes Whiteness, and places it in a parallel universe that could be Blackness, Brownness, Yellowness, or Redness to where race, including Whiteness, doesn't become about color, but a set of power relations that can be maximized in a domain that is already controlled by a dominant subset group, Whites.[10]

There, then , is no reason to mention race, in any context, as the set of power relations that Whites control become the privileges by which social, political and economic benefits are derived. Those who subscribe to colorblind ideology, also subscribe to eliminating race from the public discourse. Becoming blind to the inequalities that remain

405

behind in society, as the racial contract places itself within the mainstream, Colorblindness does not hold people responsible for which they can claim, as individuals, they did not create, and thus, cannot help eradicate, if it means giving up their superior position in the society, or surrendering privileges and benefits that cause the dominant group in society to be equalized.[11]

By eliminating race from the public discourse, colorblindness allowed Whites, even liberal Whites, who often felt uncomfortable discussing the inequalities of race, to no longer view themselves as "the forgotten majority" in American society, and transition racially corrective policies, like affirmative action, into class based approaches, versus race based approaches, in order that the forgotten "poor" and lower middle class White could receive the privileges of any policy set up to benefit any particular segment of society.[12] This was done, even though those Whites who were disadvantaged in society suffer, not because of their race-for Whites in America are not an oppressed people nor are they at risk becoming oppressed-but in spite of their race, as refusing to implement affirmative action as a remedy for racial subordination will not alleviate the class oppression of poor Whites, but reinforce the existing regime of race, and class domination, that leaves lower-class Whites more vulnerable to class exploitation.[13]

While affirmative action didn't institute the same type of racial hierarchies in which all Whites, because they are white, were deprived of economic, social and political benefits-as any and all Blacks were deprived under institutional racial hierarchies, such as slavery and segregation-neither did it reverse the racial hierarchy; instead, affirmative action simply tried to mitigate the racial privilege that such a hierarchy created.[14] Colorblindness, simply created a new justification for the racial hierarchy, despite that fact that its proponents claimed that its ideology hinges upon insuring that no one are discriminated against. However, it does just the opposite.

Like its predecessor, segregation, colorblindness' unintentional, non-discriminatory policies were advanced for the very purpose of discriminating, and to re-engage the privileges of the racial hierarchy, namely the benefits of whiteness, that had been legally erased in the fall of segregation. Colorblindness reconnected the privileges of whiteness, not only rendering race invisible, but in helping society understand what others weren't. Colorblindness re-established what whiteness was and what it would represent in the 21st Century. Colorblindness also rendered the privileges and benefits of race invisible, creating for Whites what scholar, Peggy McIntosh, refers to as an "invisible knapsack" of white privilege that all Whites carry around with them, which afford them, at least, twenty-six skin color privileges that her African American co-workers, friends and acquaintances cannot count on, as they move about American society-most of which speak to various forms of social inclusion, racial exclusion and/or social/moral standards that provide tangible, and intangible benefits, to Whites and provide no benefits and, in fact, penalizes or casts demeaning social aspersions on Blacks.[15] It is within these societal privileges that Colorblindness caused racial disparities of the previous five decades-since the *Brown* decision-to remain in effect, and carryover into the 21st Century.

It is within the emerging scholarship of "critical white studies" that the benefits of whiteness, and its residual privileges demonstrate how explicitly farcical the whole ideology of colorblindness has been, in terms of rationalizing equality, as a function of some in society endorsed as, meritocracy. Most Americans are unfamiliar with the initial chain of presumptions, under which meritocracy in America was founded; the first, being the selection of the "best suited" to form a new elite; secondly, the means of selection being on the basis of intelligence-as a proxy for superior talent-thus merit being defined as a purely intellectual, educational endeavor; lastly, the selection for a paradigm, for which there is a presumed fit for the tasks at hand.[16] The goal of giving opportunity to all Americans was later added to present day meritocracy definitions, as a way of generating public support for a "merit" system that evolved into a more general way of distributing opportunity to millions of people, rather than as an elite civil-service delivery system for the modern bureaucratic state that the founders of the merit system had envisioned.[17]

Affirmative action and other equal access/equal opportunity remedies for past discrimination were "merit-based" remedies that "all things being equal" gave access to those who had been historically excluded. The new meritocracy, under colorblindness, eliminated past discrimination considerations, because those considerations operated counter to the inclusion of America's dominant group-within their own system-in a way that devalued whiteness for the sake of achieving equality. American societal norms doesn't allow for the devaluation of whiteness, in the same ways blackness and other societal sub-groups have been devalued. Thus, there became a need to reassess whiteness in the context of this new multi-focal race paradigm.

Critical white studies, as an emerging area of academic study, has reframed the historical lenses in which equality is viewed. The redefinition of meritocracy suggests that merit infers the selection of the best suited in an open system of the free market competition-regardless of color-which, actually contradicts both the closed, competition-less, racially exclusive histories of slavery and segregation. Merit-based equality now become vessel by which race has become transparent, and merit is offered, in a revisionist kind of way, as a softer argument-minus the negative "supremacy" element-for how Whites access the same opportunities they've always accessed, and how those opportunities should be distributed in America, in a way that not only includes Whites but allows the historical benefits of whiteness in America to be utilized.

Opportunity produces benefits and, in its own right, has become "a right" in American society-the right to compete, particularly where whiteness is concerned. Most Whites, under no circumstances, will be excluded from what they see as entitled rights in "their own country," thus causing theoretical whiteness in the United States to be revisited, and re-studied in order that a new generation of Whites can understand the historical racial hierarchy, advanced in its invisible colorblind paradigm, that will allow tenets of white privilege to survive in the 21st Century.

Colorblindness serves as the same tool that segregation served, inasmuch as the colorblind argument allows society to ignore the present day disparities of unequal-ness, as it did during segregation, as well as ignore the resources, networks, institutions and systems that unequally favor Whites, over any other segment of the population. Diversity, and other forms of political and societal inclusion are marginalized, largely due to the fact that they operate counter to the interest of those who currently hold "individual" positions of power in this country, and require society to address group interest, which run counter to the current "race-less" public discourse of "equality for all" that colorblind ideology advances.

The colorblind argument offers little opportunity to redress societal inequities, in the same way segregation did. Saying "Don't play the race card" today, dismisses queries of racial inequality observations, in the same way, as saying "That's just the way it is" did in yester-year's analysis of why things-i.e., racial differences exist-between Blacks and Whites. This "let it be," or laissez faire attitude regarding race and racial differences is a defining characteristic of colorblindness. Most critically, colorblindness allows the same 19th Century foundations that latently re-established whiteness, as a property right after Reconstruction, to re-establish it in the 21st Century. In a case that laid the groundwork for *Plessy*, the often overlooked *Civil Rights Cases of 1883*, established "the right to exclude" that law theorist, Cheryl Harris, called a central principle, in defining the privileges of whiteness, wherein the U.S. Supreme Court affirmed that "the possessors of whiteness were granted the legal right to exclude others from the privileges inhering in whiteness."[18] As the possessors of whiteness, Whites were legally entitled to create, define and protect White spaces and places in their social economy, a right that Court accepted that gave birth to *Plessy's* "separate but equal" doctrine. Colorblindness allows the same "spaces and places" to be created, defined and protected, only in the 21st Century, while there is no formal legal "colorline," seeing no color has resulted in a widening racial divide. It is a divide facilitated by a voluntary re-segregation, brought on by individualism.

What further complicates this argument is the fact that African Americans are no longer the nation's largest ethnic minority-Hispanics are, and they offer America a different set of policy problems. However, African Americans are still the nation's most negatively impacted minority, and have the longer history of racial struggle within this constitutional paradigm called the United States of America. Colorblindness will allow societal disparities that impact other minorities, in this new multi-focal paradigm, to be marginalized, in the same way it covered up black and white disparities in America's historical bi-focal dynamic.

Colorblindness, as the new "Jim Crow," separates the ability to compare, contrast and remedy racial differences, as demonstrated by the push in several states, in the late 1990s and the early 2000s, to attack race wherever it existed, including moves to eliminate the compilation of statistical data, as it related to race. At this point, some people in America, had become so blinded by color that they didn't know when to stop in their efforts the re-enforce the privileges of whiteness, again-as was the case during segregation. The unequal disparities caused by colorblindness and segregation, in distinctly separate periods, and the racial disparate outcomes they produce are chillingly parallel. Yet the subtleties of their discriminating effects are contrasting inasmuch as one, segregation, was so overt and "in your face" while the other, colorblindness is so subvert and "out of your face"-if you will. However, both were as equally effective, and socially accepted, as strategies to maintain the racial status quo. The colorblind movement had become so blinded by color that it didn't see, and still doesn't see, the limits to the false arguments it has fashioned, and, at times, had its policy unravel because of unsubstantiated claims.

Therein, was the demonstration that colorblindness, and its idiom that "race no longer matters," was full of false assumptions. Colorblindness assumes that everyone will be impacted the same, by a particular law, or policy. However, when a policy requiring governmental agencies to eliminate racial data, as was the case with a Ward Connerly sponsored, Racial Privacy Initiative, those same proponents found out the absence of health data had the ability to negatively impact Whites, as much as (in some instances, more than), it would Blacks, and other minorities, support for the initiative shifted.

The 2003 California ballot initiative assumed that the a law banning race data would negatively impact Blacks, and literally end all ability to track equality progress, if racial data wasn't kept. However, when it was disclosed that such policies would also keep agencies from identifying illnesses and diseases, that not only negatively impacted Whites, but disproportionately impacted them, like occurrences of breast cancer, or heart disease or Alzheimer disease, those policy did not receive the same level of support as previous anti-race initiatives. California's white voters weren't so blinded by color that they couldn't see that their own interest could be impacted. However, they did see race, and reacted differently whenever race was interjected. Whenever racial fairness was argued, as a reason to defeat the initiative, voters favored the initiative. Only when benefits, or the loss of benefits, were argued did the initiative lose favor with the majority of the voters. The initiative eventually lost, but it was only the first anti-race initiative defeated in California. This is just one instance where the false assumptions of colorblindness could be tested. Most have not been tested.

Other false arguments of colorblindness include; 1) that society would be more equal (versus less equal) without racial categorization, 2) the access to all people would be greater without racial designations to create racial barriers, 3) that racial policies promote discrimination and the absence of race policies promote opportunity, and lastly, but most critically, that America never sees the world through a hostilely racial lens. If these arguments were, in fact, correct, and the assumptions behind them were, in fact, true, then it stands to reason that true progress toward eliminating racial disparities in our society would be achieved, as "the color of our skin" became less relevant and the "content of our character" guided society's decisions. Only in the case of rare individual examples, and colorblind philosophy cannot point to very many instances, if any at all, where race-neutral policies produced greater diversity goals, and achieved greater equality outcomes, than race sensitive policies that sought to remedy past discrimination. Instead, the divide has remained the same, and some instances, gotten greater, and the remedies for racial discrimination and racial inequalities, under colorblindness, have been non-existent.

Several studies have analyzed the state of racial equality at the beginning of the 21st Century. The state of black equality in the "Colorblind" era has fared no better than it did in the periods that preceded it; the Post-Civil Rights Era, the Civil Rights Era, the Post *Brown* Era, the "Jim Crow Era-all were periods that maintained hugely disparate gaps in key social and economic indicators. The Colorblind Era was no different. "Colorblind Society" proponents like to quote from Martin Luther King, Jr. and say things like "Keep King's Dream Alive" but little has been done during this era to achieve King's dream of "reaching the Mountaintop" in helping African Americans achieve racial equality. In fact, many in the civil rights and social advocacy communities called the state of black equality at the end of the 20th Century, King's "nightmare."

In 1963, the year King gave what Whites (and most Blacks) call the "I Have A Dream" speech-but what the Rev. Jesse Jackson, Sr. reminded progressive audiences on the lecture circuit in 2003 that it was, in fact, the "America's Broken Promise" speech, the black unemployment was 10.8%, compared to a white unemployment rate of 5% (considered full employment).[19] In 2003, 40 years after America heard King's dream, the black unemployment rate was 10.8%, compared to a white unemployment rate of 5.2%.[20] The fact that black unemployment rate remained unchanged, after forty years doesn't take into consideration that while it fell as low 6.4%, by 1969, and had risen to a high of 19.5%, by 1983, that there was only six years out of the forty years, that black jobless rate wasn't at least double that of Whites-and in years that it was less than double, 1.83 times that of Whites, in 1971, was a low as it fell. Since 1972 (to 2003), the Black-White Gap in unemployment had actually increased.[21]

The year that King was assassinated, in 1968, the wage disparities between black and white were so deplorable that the Southern Christian Leadership Conference, on May 1st 1968, waged a month long "poor people's campaign" called Resurrection City on the Mall of

411

the nation's Capitol to bring attention to the nation's income and wealth divide. In 1968, the median family income of black families ($23,514) was 60% or "three fifths" of white families ($39,206), though actual per capita income between Blacks and Whites was actually less than "three-fifths" as black per capita income ($6,823) was 54.8% of white per capita income ($12,454).[22] By 2002, black per capital income, at 57%, was still less than "three-fifths" of white per capita income, gaining a little over two cents on every dollar earned by Whites in 34 years-while median family income for black families actually fell, in comparison to white families, from 60%, in 1968, to 58%, in 2002.[23]

These decades of wage inequities translate to hundreds of thousands of dollars in pay differential, over the life of the black worker, and the loss of potential revenue for housing acquisitions, business start-up and retirement funds that would create near equality, in the comparative wealth, between Blacks and Whites. Instead, white families' net worth, whether the mean (average) or the median is measured, is six times that of the typical black family. In 2001, white households had an average net worth of $468,200 as compared to $75,700 for black households, while black families had a median net worth of $19,000 (including home equity), 16% of the wealth of the typical white family of $121,000.[24]

The gap between White and African American wealth actually increased between 1989 and 2001, a period that saw the greatest economic in the nation's history and saw the nation's top 1% of the population double its wealth, while African Americans, who represent 13% of the nation's population have only accumulated three percent of the nation's assets collectively. While black wealth rose from five percent of the median wealth of Whites in 1989 to 16% in 2001, it would take Blacks another 98 years, to the year 2099, assuming that all things remained constant (meaning no future barriers of discrimination arose to further exaggerate the racial divide), to reach wealth equality with Whites.[25]

The absence of income and wealth has exacerbated the racial wealth divide, in ways that have maintained racial gaps in other quality of live measures, like poverty and homeownership. The last 50 years since *Brown* have been most telling, in terms of what equality has really meant to Blacks, and how Blacks it sought to achieve equality during this period. While the first 15 years of the *Post-Brown* era was dramatically effected by the politics of the "Southern Manifesto," and the draconian activities of Massive Resistance movement, the last 35 years represented the period, whereby, the truest opportunities for equality could have been achieved. Yet, in hindsight, this period of opportunity only served as a period of re-entrenchment for historical inequalities.

During this time of re-entrenchment, equality opportunities shifted against Blacks, where there was truly a wealth consolidation, and industrial transition (from automation to computerization technology), that created two decades of unprecedented economic boons from which Blacks benefited little, in terms of wealth accumulation and wage equality. African Americans, either stepped up into a marginalized lower middle class, or fell deeper into a poverty class, that created a host of social ills, and economic despair realities. Poverty and homeownership are perfect examples of how equality opportunities shifted in ways that "intimated progress," but where little actually occurred. Prime examples of how, "the more things changed, the more they remained the same."

When President Lyndon announced he wasn't running for re-election in 1968-the year "the Dream" was assassinated-his Great Society programs designed to win the "War on Poverty," had made a dent in the state of black poverty in America. Poverty rates had fallen, from an estimated 50% in 1960, (before official poverty rates were kept by the government), to 34.7% in 1968. In 1968, black poverty (34.7%) was almost three and one-half times (3.47) that of white poverty (10%). In 2002, though, both the black poverty rate (24.1%), and the Black-white poverty gap (3.01) had fallen, 34 years later, black poverty was still three times that of Whites.[26] Equality had made little progress in the area of eradicating the problems of the poor in America.

Homeownership is the primary source of wealth for all Americans. In 1970, 65.4% (almost two-thirds) of white Americans owned their homes compared to 41.6% (a little more than two-fifths) of African Americans owned their homes, but 32 years later in 2002 almost 74.5% (almost three-fourths) of Whites owned their home while 47.9% (less than one-half) of Blacks owned their homes.[27] The black/white homeownership gap was 63% (63 black families to every 100 white families) in 1970, and 64%, in 2002. Literally, an inequality gap that remained unchanged for the past 32 years.

As income, wealth and poverty measures remained unchanged, for the past 30 plus years, a whole set of residual inequalities have manifested themselves in ways that undermined the traditional black family structure, created community instability and further stigmatized the already economically deprived urban core. The results being negatively adverse health status for African Americans, and greater incarceration rates of Blacks, where the percentage of black men, who had been jailed almost doubled from 1974 to 2001 from 8.7% to 16.6%, and the rate at which black men are jailed, already, six times, as likely to be imprisoned than white men, has increased, to where "a lifetime chance" of a young black male going to jail rose from one in eleven for males born in 1974, to currents trends that indicate one out of three black men, born after 2001, will be jailed in future.[28]

The most quoted statistic at the turn of the 21st Century was that "there were more black males in prison than in college," a statistic that was misleading only because it took into consideration all black men in prison (all ages) versus that fact that college aged black men represent a significantly smaller segment of the population. The point was, however, the presence of black men in higher education had significantly shrunk. Incarceration, and another debilitating social ill, black on black homicide, were primary contributors to this phenomenon. The number of Blacks who died to gang and urban violence nationwide in two decades (1980s and 1990s) exceeded the number of casualties America lost, in total, during the Viet Nam War. The estimates are in the tens of thousands. One city alone, Los Angeles, has lost over 15,000 young black men to gang violence from 1985 to 2002. Irrespective of the reasons that black men aren't in college, fact of the matter is that the "college gap" has closed some, from Whites 2.5 times as likely to graduate from college as Blacks in 1968 to Whites to be likely graduating 1.7 times more than Blacks in 2002, but was still 73 years away (to the year 2075) that black college graduation rates would be equal to that of Whites.[29]

In early 2004, the National Urban League released its annual "State of Black America" report, where, in noting the significance of the 50th Anniversary of *Brown*, it sought to explore the state of black equality in what it called, "The Equality Index, a statistical measurement of the disparities that exist between Blacks and Whites in economics, housing, education, health, social justice and civic engagement. Examining "the complexity of black progress," the Urban League report interestingly establishes, as the report's black-white comparison benchmark, that the basis for which equality-as established by the nation's founders-that enslaved Blacks were "three-fifths" or 60% of a white person. After establishing some key sources of racial disparities, such as the fact that Blacks are denied mortgage, and home improvement loans, at twice the rate of Whites; that, on average, Blacks are twice as likely to die from disease, accident, behavior and homicide at every stage of life than Whites; that the quality of education for Blacks are disproportionately impacted by inexperienced teachers with less than three years experience in minority schools at twice the rate they teach in white schools, and, social justice in America is dramatically impacted by sentencing disparities that cause Blacks, on average, to be jailed six months longer (39 months) than Whites (33 months) for the same crime, the National Urban League (NUL) concluded that 50 years after *Brown versus the Board of Education* and 40 years after the signing of the Civil Rights Act, and almost 135 years after the ratification of the Fourteenth Amendment, meant to eradicate the "three-fifths" status of Blacks, Blacks in America are still not equal to Whites.[30]

According to the National Urban League's 2004 Equality Index, the social-economic status of African Americans is .73 or 73% of the status of Whites. So, in a sense, after 216 years, Blacks are no longer "three-fifths" of a person. Blacks are now a little less than "three-fourths" of a white person. While it's not equality, in a sense, some more moderate perspectives, both Black and White, would suggest that this is, in fact, "progress." This is how black inequality is dismissed.

However, there were two very distinguishing revelations in the Urban League's report that was consistent with "State of the Dream 2004" study released by the Racial Wealth Divide Project a couple months earlier; 1) that economic subjugation is still the principle focus, and most discriminating factor, of America's "Black-White" racial divide and, 2) African Americans feels that racial inequities, and old (not new) forms of discrimination have become socially accepted, to the point where efforts to achieve parity are not even attempted-much less addressed.

In the 2004 "State of Black America" report, the most disparate "sub-index" was the economics measure that combined five categories; mean income, employment, housing, wealth formation and digital divide (access to information), all factors that most influence economic success in today's global economy, to determine how equal Blacks were, relative to Whites, in their ability to achieve economic parity in America today.

The outcomes were similar to the "Dream 2004" study. The Urban League report revealed that Blacks were unemployed more than two times the rate of Whites, had homeownership rates that were as

415

disparate, as in "the Dream 2004" called out (less than 50% for Blacks, over 70% for Whites); were denied mortgages and home improvement loans at twice the Whites (.45 index), and black homes were valued at 65% of what white homes were worth-a gap of $42,000, bringing the home index to .63; that wealth formation was a function of Blacks having less, wealth because they own less homes, as a result of being rejected for home loans, at twice the rate of Whites, and the fact that their homes are worth less, allowing Whites to create three times as many businesses as Blacks, by leveraging the wealth of their homes; and an information highway gap between Whites and Blacks of .59 on computer ownership (59 black families have computers in homes for every 100 white families), and .51 on internet access (51 black families have home internet access for every 100 white families), making the index for economic issues at .56, a very sophisticated way of saying what the Dream 2004 study reported, that Blacks earn 57 cents of every dollar Whites earn.[31]

The second revelation made in the "State of Black America" report was the results of NUL Survey Poll conducted between January 28th, and February 10th, 2004, where 700 African Americans, 200 Hispanic Americans and 200 Asian Americans were interviewed about social, political and economic issues affecting their "quality of life." Some of the more poignant responses pointed to countering perspectives of ethnic minorities in America, as the dominant cultural group continues to ignore race, and problem associated with racial inequality. The results included that 36% of the respondents (including 39% of Blacks) believe that race and gender discrimination is widely accepted in the workplace, 52% of the respondents (including 62% of Blacks) believe the country in headed in the wrong direction, and 54% of Blacks feel that things will "remain the same," or "get worse" for them, as a race, in the areas identified in the 2004 report.[32]

The most stigmatizing response in the survey was that 40% of Blacks feel that there has been "very little/no improvement," in the essential indicators for economic and social mobility in America, since 1964. The poll results was indicative of the state of black equality that has been observed on a number of academic and sociological fronts, and consistent with social and economic indicators, year after year. It is no surprise that perspectives on the realities of racial disparities in America's "Colorblind" era reflect the similar perspectives that many Blacks held about race and social change in the Segregation era. Black and white race realities were "Just the way is was" back then, and is "just

416

the way it is" here and now.

It wasn't until the 50th Anniversary of *Brown versus the Board of Education* on May 17th, 2004, and the various conferences nationwide, that the state of equality in America was truly revisited, within the context of the "Colorblind" paradigm. While much of the discourse focused on continuing educational inequality, persistent questions were raised about the success of *Brown*, in terms of its impact on the eventual outcomes on integration, and subsequent re-segregation, of public schools, that often frame the impact of Brown as minimal, at best, and failing, at worse. The fact that *Brown* is iconic, because it was the case that overturned the most legally unjust interpretation of the Fourteenth Amendment, in America's history, and suspended, at least legally, American apartheid, is often marginalized by arguments over whether the tactics *Brown* attorneys introduced, particularly, the sociological tests, were "pseudo-science," and appropriate for courtroom consideration. Lost in the arguments of "legal tactics" was the fact that, for the first time in America history, equality-in its truest constitutional context-was analyzed, argued and correctly defined, for that segment of the population in which it had been most egregiously denied, African Americans. What can be argued is whether the benefits of equality had ever been correctly applied. The answer to that question has to be a resounding "NO." There is no supporting evidence that equality is present in American society or even being attempted in the context of fixing what the American race caste broke. The damage to true equality in America appears to be deep and permanent.

417

The state of black equality, in no way, reflect the gains of the legal correctness of the *Brown* decision, the pains of the Civil Rights movement, and its arguments of moral suasion that said "equal rights" was the right and correct thing to do, nor the minimal reparative gains of the limited successes of affirmative action policies. The state of black equality in America 50 years after *Brown* reflects the historical recalcitrance of racial resistance in America that started from the very day the first government of the United States, the Confederation of the United States-the one that preceded the formation of the Constitution in 1787, sought to exclude free Africans and enslaved Africans from ratification discussions as early as 1779. The politics of equality, and who was more equal versus who less equal, stands squarely within a mindset of the racial superiority borne out of America's slave master/slave relationship that manifested a inhumanely disregard for the rights of a people who, from the very outset of the American egalitarian experiment, wasn't meant to have any rights.

Four centuries of ignored rights for the African, then the American born African, then the Negro, the Colored, the Black, the African American, hasn't allowed Whites, who had guaranteed rights from the outset, to see their black counterparts, as equals, in a society setup for themselves. The conflicts inherent in advancing the notion that America, as the world's first "truly free" society, truly egalitarian democracy, truly judicious social order, engaged its social contract with "the people" in a way that said one thing, and did something else. America's treatment of certain segments of its population reflected an entirely different political reality.

Only in the last 50 years, since the *Brown* decision, has American society been engaged in reckoning with this sort of black "retro-equality" that white Americans, as individuals, and in the collective, have never come to grips with. "Retro-equality," in the sense, that Blacks have been promised equality since 1868, and the passing of the Fourteenth Amendment, but have only been afforded remnants of equality, i.e. freedom of limited movement and freedom of limited enjoyment, 50 years hence-since 1954. Maintenance of America's present day racial inequality became a deep seeded vestige of the pre-*Brown* era when white supremacy was not only the law, it was the American way of life. A way of life that, some in the dominant culture, have yet to let loose of.

418

The state of black equality, and the inequities that still persist, is a function of a predated mindset still pervasive throughout American society. The state of racial equality in America, today is the result of a concentrated effort to maintain a historical racial hierarchy, a failure to address past discrimination, a concerted attempt to ignore the disparities created out of intentional societal exclusion, as well as, a failure to repair the social, and economic damages, borne out such a protracted exclusion. And any attempts to discuss race meets with a new resistance that, in a sense, suggests one is irrelevant in the public discourse for even wanting to interject race. So, how will African Americans, collectively, ever achieve true equality on par with Whites?

Well, it is highly questionable as to whether racial equality can ever be achieved when the tenets of American racism can be hidden beneath a cover of "colorblindness," preventing racial disparities from being recognized, acknowledged, and socially discussed. In not giving recognition to race makes racism hard to define, harder to identify, and harder still to prove. Not being able to discuss what race is (or is not), what race means and, more critically, what racial inequality is (or does) makes it impossible to rectify the problems stemming from inequality, or what to do about it. America is in a quandary over racial equality, because it refuses to deal with it, as a society in the whole. Those who choose to deal with it, in the political diaspora, run the risk of incurring a political backlash that causes a rush to the side that doesn't discuss race-or that provides enough sufficient racial cues that tie into the racial symbols of historically stereotypical views of racial inferiority. Equality in America, is a cued reality that when Blacks move toward it, the social networks, systems and institutions will, in many cases, react against them. And while it is done with a lot less hostility (though racial animus toward Blacks is still quite high), it is done knowing that the interjection of race will be minimalized, due to the fact that Whites know they will not-and cannot-be excluded, and that their superior social networks will function on their behalf to protect their collective group interests. Whites really have no reason to be hostile, in the current racial paradigm, because their interests are more protected, and more secure, than they were in the previous segregation paradigm. It is no coincidence that white conservatives now control all three branches of the federal government.

Race in America is, by no, means colorblind. The country sees race as clearly as it ever has before. It is simply blinded by realities of what true black equality would bring about, a powershare among equals, and an end to racial domination in America. The thought that a racial hierarchy would cease to exist is one experiment America is apparently not prepared to try. Instead, it just chooses to pretend they don't see color, and play blind to the fact that the state of black equality in America is still, separate and unequal, in comparison to what the overwhelming majority of the dominant culture, in the United States, views as guaranteed experiences in freedom, justice and equality.

The "white" American experience has always been, and will be-for at least the foreseeable future-different from the "black" American experience. An experience that is "three-fifths" of the rights, benefits and privileges Whites shared in 1787, and "three-fifths" of the rights, benefits and privileges Blacks received in 2004, 50 years after the United States Supreme Court correctly re-interpreted equality, as stated by the U.S. Constitution's Fourteenth Amendment, and legally abolished racial separation, in the case of *Brown v. Board of Education of Topeka, KS et. al.* What *Brown* did not abolish, and could not abolish, was the inequalities created out of past, present, and continuing

419

patterns of racial discrimination. It is unreasonable to expect that one legal case even could. Brown forced the question of equality, not discrimination.

The state of black equality in America, is a standing tribute to America's continuing legacy of racial inequality, and a continuing pursuit that will take most, if not all, of the 21st Century-or forever-to rectify. It is an important reflection to acknowledge, because equality for the African American has been a protracted struggle, a struggle Whites will not, don't want to, nor have any incentive to, deal with. And it's a struggle that many Blacks have either forgotten-in this era of less overt racial confrontation, and greater material comfort-or have chosen to not to fight, as society tries to convince everyone-who will listen-that race is no longer relevant, and the racial struggle in America is no longer necessary, given the apparent absence of "a colorline."

The colorline that DuBois referred to over 100 years ago, in *The Souls of Black Folk*, is still present. Colorblindness has erased the colorline, but the hush of the last 25 years hasn't removed it. The mantra of the segregation, or the "equal rights" struggle was, "We Shall Overcome, someday." Overcoming racial inequality in the Colorblind era will be more than a notion. Racial inequalities will not go away simply by ignoring them. Achieving racial equality will require every bit of strategic foresight, and planning that defeating segregation took. The first step will be to acknowledge that the colorline still exists, and that there are racial differences to be eradicated. An invisible colorline is still a colorline none the less. The next step will be how best to deal with racial inequalities-and that will be society's next big racial question, a question currently being raised, in the national call for slave reparations.

A similar case could be made for segregation reparations, and now colorblind reparations-once black America figures out how to fully address the racial politics of colorblindness. It's much more difficult to touch, to feel, to see in a society blinded by color, a behavior that is just the latest attempt to ignore the realities of racial inequality in America, and the two centuries of equality promises to African Americans, that went along with previous "broken promises." "Jim Crow" hasn't gone away. It's just taken on a different form-Colorblindness-that now require new, and different remedies before the state of black equality can be considered "equal" to that of the rest of the nation. The state of black equality, and the state of race relevancy in America, as convoluted as both have become under "colorblind" ideology, are now one and the same. Addressing the state of one, addresses the state of the other. However, one conclusion that can be resolved, is that African Americans are continuing a struggle for equal protection under the law, under the Fourteenth Amendment, and African Americans are still in pursuit of racial equality, in America.

NOTES
&
CITATIONS

Chapter 1 Notes and Citations

1 Frederickson, George M., *White Supremacy: A Comparative Study in American and South African History*. 1981. Oxford University Press, New York, NY. P. 31

2 Ibid., P. 45

3 Quarles, Benjamin, *The Negro in the Making of America*. 1987. Touchtone Books, New York, NY, P. 74

4 Rossiter, Clinton, 1787: *The Grand Convention*. 1996. W.W. Norton & Company, New York, NY. Pp. 188-189

5 Ibid., P. 186

6 Quarles, P. 74

7 Packard, Jerrold M., *American Nightmare: The History of Jim Crow*. 2002. St. Martin's Press, New York, NY. P. 27

8 Ibid., P. 28

9 Roediger, David R., *The Wages of Whiteness*. 1991. Verso, New York, NY, Pp. 50-54

10 Ibid., P. 54

11 Bell, Derrick, "Property Rights in Whiteness-Their Legal Legacy, Their Economic Costs," *Critical Race Theory: The Cutting Edge*. 1995. Delgado, Richard (editor), Temple Uiversity Press, Philadelphia, PA. P. 76

12 Ibid., P. 76

13 Conduit, Celeste Michelle and Lucaites, John Louis, *Crafting Equality: America's Anglo-African World*. 1993. University of Chicago Press. P. 79

14 Locke, John, *Two Treatises of Government*. 1690. Cited from *Great Political Thinkers: 15 Plato to the Present*. William and Alan Ebenstein, editors. Harcourt College Publishers, Fort Worth, TX. Pp. 389-390

Jordan, Winthrop D., *White over Black: American Attitudes Toward the Negro, 1550-1812*. 1968. University of North Carolina Press, Chapel Hill, NC.

16 Baker, Jean, "From Belief into Culture: Republicanism in the Antebellum North," *American Quarterly, Volume 37*, Issue 4, *Republicanism in the History and Historiography of the United States*. P. 545

17 Boxill, Bernard (editor), *Race and Racism*. 2001. Oxford University Press, New York, NY. P. 37

18 Gossett, Thomas F., *Race: The History of an Idea In America*. 1965. Southern Methodist University Press, Dallas, TX. P. 44

19 Ibid., P. 48

20 Ibid., P. 42

21 DiGregorio, P. 43-52

22 Meier, August and Rudwick, Elliott, *From Plantation to Ghetto (3rd Ed.)* 1966, 1970, 1976. Hill and Wang, New York, NY. P. 57

23 Irons, Peter, *A People's History of the United States*. 1999. Penguin Book, New York, NY. P. 157

24 Irons, Peter, *A People's History of the Supreme Court*. 1999. Penguin Books. New York, NY P. 159

25 Franklin, John Hope and Moss, Alfred A., *From Slavery to Freedom: A History of African Americans, 8th Ed.* 2000 (Original Ed. 1947). McGraw-Hill, Boston, MA P. 65

26 Finkelman, Paul *Dred Scott V. Sandford: A Brief History with Documents*. 1997. Bendford Books, Boston, MA. P. 20-21

27 Ibid. P. 20

28 Ibid. P. 22

29 Wang, Xi, "The Dred Scott Case," *Race on Trial: Law and Justice in American History.* Annette Gordon-Reed (Editor) 2002. Oxford University Press, New York, NY. P. 27

30 Garraty, P. 83

31 Kaufman, Kenneth C., *Dred Scott's Advocate: A Biography of Roswell M. Field.* 1996. University of Missouri Press, Columbia, MO. P. 184

32 Ibid. P. 184

33 Ibid. P. 185

34 Ibid. P. 186

35 Ibid. P. 186

36 Ibid. P. 186-187

37 Ibid. 188-189

38 Finkelman, P. 27

39 Irons, P. 171

40 Finkelman, P. 27

41 DeGregorio, William A., *The Complete Book of U.S. Presidents (5th Ed.).* 2001. Gramercy Books, New York, NY. P. 219-220

42 Irons, P. 171

43 Irons, P. 169

44 Irons, P. 170

45 Finkelman, P. 43

46 Finkelman, P. 29

47 DiGregorio, P. 114-117

48 Ibid. P. 115-116

49 Patrick, John J., Pious, Richard M., Ritchie, Donald A. (Editors), *The Oxford Essential Guide to the U.S. Government, Berkeley Ed.* 2000. Berkeley Books, New York, NY. P. 316-317

50 Kaufman, P. 204

51 Irons, P. 170

52 Unger, Irwin, *These United States: The Questions of Our Past.* 1999. Prentice-Hall, Upper Saddle River, NJ. P. 331

53 Kaufman, P. 219

54 Ibid. P. 219

55 Ibid. P. 219

56 Finkelman, P. 29

57 Garraty, P. 86

58 Irons, P. 173

59 Ibid. P. 172-173

60 Ibid. P. 170

61 Ibid. P. 172

62 Kaufman, P. 221

63 Ibid. P. 221

64 Irons, P. 172

65 Ibid. P. 172

66 Garraty, P. 87

67 Irons. P. 177

68 Kaufman, P. 222

425

Chapter 2 Notes and Citations

1 Henry, Robert Selph, *The Story of the Confederacy.* 1931. Konecky & Konecky. Old Saybrook, CT. P. 16.

2 Foner, Philip S. (Ed.), *The Life and Times of Frederick Douglass, Vol. 3: The Civil War, 1861-1865.* 1952. International Publishers. New York, NY, P. 141

3 Angle, Paul M. & Miers, Earl S. (editors), *The Living Lincoln: The Man And His Times, In His Own Words.*1955, 1992. Barnes and Nobles Books, New York, NY, P. 502

4 Fredrickson, P. 159.

5 Unger, Irwin, *These United States:The Questions of Our Past.* 1999. Prentice Hall. Upper Saddle River, NJ. P. 348.

6 *American History.*1996. Mark C. Carnes, editor. MacMillan Library Reference USA, Simon & Schuster/MacMillan, New York, NY. P. 199.

7 Meir and Rudwick, P. 153

8 Degregorio, William A., *The Complete Book of Presidents (5th Ed.).* 2001. Gramercy Books. New York, NY. P. 264

9 Thernstrom, Stephan and Thernstrom, Abigail, *America In Black and White: One Nation, Indivisible.* 1997. Simon & Schuster, New York, NY. P. 27. 10 Franklin. P. 228-29.

11 Franklin. P. 361

12 Zinn, Howard, *A People History of the United States.* 1980. HarperPerennial. New York, NY. P. 190

13 Meir and Rudwick, P. 154

14 Zinn, P. 190

15 Meir and Rudwick, P. 155

16 Douglass, P. 141

17 Meir and Rudmick, P. 157

18 Quarles, P. 134

19 Quarles, P. 146

20 Fredrickson, P. 158.

21 Fredrickson, P. 158

22 Meir and Rudmick, P. 158

23 Quarles, P. 136

24 Quarles. P. 137.

25 Quarles, P. 137.

26 Meir and Rudwick, P. 158-159

27 Franklin, P. 233

28 Henry, P. 42

29 Packard, P. 38

30 Meir and Rudwick, P. 159

31 Packard, P. 38.

32 Henry, P. 439

33 Franklin, P. 237-38

34 Henry, P. 492

35 Meir and Rudwick, P. 161

36 Franklin, P. 241

37 Meir and Rudwick, P. 162

38 Henry, P. 338

39 Henry, P. 338

40 Schlesinger, Jr., Arthur M. (Ed.), *The Almanac of American History.* 1983. Perigee Books. New York, NY. P. 293

41 Degregorio, William A., *The Complete Book of Presidents: From George Washington to George W. Bush (5th ed.)*. 2001. Gramercy Books. New York, NY. P. 242.

42 Thompson, Peter, *Cassell's Dictionary of Modern American History*. 2000. Cassell & Co., London, UK. P. 54

43 McPherson, James M., *What They Fought For, 1861-1865*. 1995. Anchor Books, New York, NY. P. 63.

44 Garrison, Webb, *The Lincoln No One Knows: The Mysterious Man Who Ran The Civil War*. 1993. MJF Books, New NY. P. 222

45 Garrison, P. 222

46 DuBois, W.E.B, *Black Reconstruction In America, 1860-1880*. 1935, 1962. Atheneum Books, New York, NY. P.282

47 Ibid. P. 282

48 Conduit & Lucaites, P. 106

49 Gossett, P. 256 as cited in Hodding Carter, *The Angry Scar, The Story of Reconstruction* (New York, 1959), P. 52

50 Gossett, P. 257-258.

51 Rabinowitz, P. 34

52 Ibid. P. 34

53 Ibid. P. 34

54 Grant, Page 141

55 Grob, Gerald N. and Billias, George Athan (Editors), *Intrepretations of American History, Volume I to 1877: Patterns and Perspectives*. 1967. Free Press. New York, NY. P. 480

56 Gossett, P. 257

Chapter 3 Notes and Citations

1 Conrad, Earl, *The Invention of the Negro*. 1966. Eriksson Books, New York, NY.
P. 134

2 Ibid. P. 140

3 Unger. P. 377

4 Ibid. P. 375

5 Ibid. P. 375

6 Sefton, James E., *Andrew Johnson and the Uses of Constitutional Power*. 1980. Brown, Little and Company. Boston, MA. P. 109

7 Adams & Sanders. P. 200

8 Ibid. P. 200

9 DuBois. P. 276

10 Jackson, Jr., Jesse L., *A More Perfect Union: Advancing New American Rights*. 2001. Welcome Rain Press, New York, NY. P. 143

11 Zinn, P. 193

12 Camejo, Peter, *Racism, Revolution, Reaction, 1861-1877*. 1976. Pathfinder Press, New York, NY. P. 58

13 Ibid. P. 159

14 Jackson, P. 138

15 Smith, J. Owens, *The Politics of Ethnic and Racial Inequality. A Systematic Comparative Micro-Analysis from the Colonial Period to the Present*. 1992. Kendall/Hunt Publishing, Dubuque, IO. P. 131

16 Mandle, Jay R., "Black Economic Entrapment After Emancipation in the United States," *The Meaning of Freedom: Economics, Politics, and Culture After Slavery*. Frank

McGlynn and Seymour Drescher, Editors. 1992. University of Pittsburgh Press, Pittsburgh, PA. P. 77

17 Franklin. P. 260

18 Mandle, P. 77

19 DuBois. P. 282

20 Ibid. P. 282

21 Ibid. P. 283

22 Ibid. P. 283

23 Gossett. P. 257

24 Unger. P. 378-79

25 Berry, Mary Frances, *Black Resistance, White Law: A History of Constitutional Racism in America*. 1971, 1994. New York, NY. P. 69.

26 As cited in Amendment XIV in The Constitution of the United States of America.

27 Unger. P. 383

28 Ibid. P. 383

29 Packard, P. 50

30 Zinn, P. 206-246

31 Allen, P. 262

32 Winant, Howard, "Racial Dualism At Century's End," cited in *The House That Race Built*. 1997. Wahneema Lubiano, Editor. Pantheon Books. New York, NY. P. 90.

33 Roediger, David R., *The Wages of Whiteness*. 1991. Verso Books. New York, NY. P. 59

34 Ibid. P. 59-60

35 Loury. P. 95-96

36 Comer, James P., *Beyond Black and White*. 1972. Quadrangle Books, New York, NY. P. 165

37 DuBois, P. 280

38 Douglass (Foner), Vol. 4, P. 31

39 Ibid. P. 31

40 Roediger. P. 52

41 Ibid. P. 55

42 Fredrickson, P. 208-210

43 Dawson, Michael C., *Behind The Mule: Race and Class in African American Politics*. 1994. Princeton University Press. Princeton, NJ. P. 51

44 Franklin, P. 293

45 Lott, Tommy L., *The Invention of Race: Black Culture and the Politics of Representation*. 1999. Blackwell Publishers, Malden, MA. P. 28-32

46 Roediger, P. 116

47 Ibid. P. 116

48 Ibid. P. 117

49 Adams & Sanders, P. 206

50 Ibid. P. 206-207

51 Douglass (Foner) Vol. 4, P. 35

52 Packard, P. 52

53 Douglass (Foner) Vol. 4, P. 35

54 Packard, P. 52-53.

55 Douglass (Foner) Vol. 4, P. 36

56 Adams and Sanders, P. 207

57 Packard, P. 54.

58 Horton, James Oliver & Horton and Lois E. Horton, *Hard Road To Freedom: The*

Story of African America. 2001. Rutgers University Press. New Brunswick, NJ. P. 190

59 Ibid. P. 19

Chapter 4 Notes and Citation

1 Franklin & Moss, P. 255
2 Ibid. P. 257
3 Ibid. P. 263
4 Adams & Sanders, P. 204
5 Ibid. P. 204-205
6 Gillette, William, *Retreat from Reconstruction, 1869-1879.* 1979. Louisiana State
  University Press, Baton Rouge, LA. P. 22-23.
7 Franklin, P. 267
8 Ibid. P. 269
9 Ibid. P. 268
10 Ibid. P. 266
11 Gossett, P. 260-261
12 Zinn, P. 233
13 Gossett. P. 261
14 Unger, P. 394
15 Ibid. P. 394-395
16 Rabinowitz, P. 266
17 Ibid. P. 267
18 Ibid. P. 259
19 Ibid. P. 268-275
20 Ibid. P. 274
21 Ibid. P. 274
22 Gillette, P. 191
23 Ibid., P. 191
24 Ibid., P. 191
25 Ibid., P. 188
26 Ibid., P. 186
27 Ibid., P. 189
28 Ibid., P. 192
29 Ibid. P. 192
30 Ibid. P. 193
31 Unger, P. 395
32 Trelease, Allen W., *White Terror: The Ku Klux Klan Conspiracy and Southern
  Reconstruction.* 1971. Louisiana University Press, Baton Rouge, LA. P. 3
33 Ibid. P. 4.
34 Ibid. P. 4
35 Ibid. P. 4
36 Trelease, P. 13.
37 Ibid, P. 11-12
38 Ibid, P. 14
39 Ibid, P. 19-20
40 Ibid, P. 20-21
41 Ibid, P. 21
42 Ibid, P. 15

43 Ibid, P. 16
44 Gossett. P. 260
45 Ibid. P. 260
46 Ibid. P. 260
47 Adams & Sanders, P. 207-208
48 Unger. P. 395
49 Adams & Sanders, P. 208
50 Ibid, P. 208
51 Horton, James Horton & Horton, Lois, E., *Hard Road To Freedom*.2001. Rutgers University Press, New Brunswick, NJ. P. 193
52 Adams & Sanders, P. 212
53 Gillette, P. 25
54 Ibid, P. 26
55 Horton & Horton, P. 193
56 Adams & Sanders, P. 220
57 Horton & Horton, P. 193
58 Meier & Rudwick, P. 189
59 Gillette, P. 193
60 Ibid. P. 193
61 Frederickson, P. 213-214
62 Ibid. P. 214
63 Ibid. P. 214
64 Franklin, P. 263
65 Horton and Horton, P. 194
66 Adams & Sanders, P. 220
67 Ibid., P. 223
68 Ibid. P. 223
69 Gillette, P. 322
70 Adams & Sanders, P. 224
71 bid, P. 225
72 Ibid, P. 225
73 Ibid., P. 225
74 Allen, P. 57
75 Ibid. P. 57
76 Adams & Sanders, P. 226
77 Ibid., P. 226
78 Allen, P. 265
79 Ibid., P. 265
80 Williamson, Joel, *The Crucible of Race*. 1984. Oxford University Press. New York, NY. P. 57-58
81 Conduit and Lucaites, P. 103

Chapter 5 Notes and Citation

1 Williamson, P. 50
2 Ibid., P. 50-51
3 Packard, P. 63
4 Ibid., P. 63

5 Ibid., P. 63-65

6 Lofgren, Charles A., *The Plessy Case: A Legal-Historical Interpretation*. 1987. Oxford University Press, New York, NY. P. 23

7 Ibid., 23-24

8 Ibid., P. 25

9 Williamson, P. 51-52

10 Malcomson, Scott L., *One Drop of Blood: The American Misadventure of Race*. 2000. Farrar, Straus and Giroux, New York, NY. P. 351

11 Ibid., 351

12 Packard, P. 64.

13 Williamson, P. 52

14 Packard, P. 70

15 Lofgren, P. 20-21

16 Williamson, P. 58

17 Ibid., P. 111

18 Ibid., P. 113

19 Ibid, P. 115

20 Malcomson, P. 352-353

21 Williamson, P. 116

22 Ibid. P. 115-116

23 Wsetin, Alan F., "The Case of the Prejudiced Doorkeeper," *Quarrels That Have Shaped The Constitution*," John A. Garraty (Editor). 1964. Harper & Row, New York, NY. P. 129-130

24 Ibid. P. 132

25 Ibid., P. 132-133

26 Ibid. P. 133

27 Ibid. P. 130

28 Lofgren, P. 20

29 Lofgren, P. 21-22

30 Williamson, P. 224

31 Garraty, P. 134

32 Ibid., P. 134-135

33 Ibid. P. 135-136.

34 Ibid., P. 138

35 Cohen, William and Varat, Jonathan D., *Constitutional Law: Cases and Materials (11th Ed.)*. 2001. Foundation Press, New York, NY. P. 1117

36 Garraty, P. 138

37 Ibid, P. 146

38 Ibid., P. 147

39 Ibid., P. 147

40 Davis, Thomas J., "Race, Identity, and the Law," *Race on Trial: Law and Justice in American History*, Annette Gordon-Reed (editors). 2002. Oxford University Press. New York, NY. P. 66-67.

41 Ibid., 67.

42 Ibid., 67

43 Ibid., 69

44 Fireside, Harvey, *Separate and Unequal: Homer Plessy and the Supreme Court Decision the Legalized Racism*. 2004. Carrol & Graf Publishers, New York, NY. P. 17

45 *Race on Trial.*, 69

46 Malcomson, P. 355

431

46 Ibid., P. 355
47 Ibid., P. 356
48 Garraty, P. 151
49 Garraty, P. 151
50 *Race on Trial*, P. 69
51 Garraty, P. 151
51 *Race on Trial*, P. 69-70
53 Ibid. P. 71
54 Fireside, P. 194-195
55 Ibid. P. 195
56 *Race on Trial*, P. 71
57 Ibid. P. 71
58 Ibid. P. 71-72
59 Lofgren, P. 178-179
60 Fireside, P. 209
61 Ibid., P. 208-209
62 Ibid., P. 209
63 Ibid., P. 216
64 Ibid., P. 216
65 Ibid., P. 216
66 Ibid., P. 217
67 Ibid., P. 219

Chapter 6 Notes and Citations:

1 Woodward, C. Vann, *The Strange Career of Jim Crow, 3rd Edition*. 1974. Oxford University
   Press, New York, NY, P. 7.
2 Ibid., P. 18
3 Ibid., P. 18
4 Massey, Douglas S. and Denton, Nancy A., *Amercan Apartheid: Segregation and the Making of the Underclass*. 1993. Harvard University Press, Cambridge, MA. P. 25-26
5 Packard, P. 15
6 Woodward, P. 84
7 Lord, Walter, *The Past That Would Not Die*. Harper & Row. New York, NY. P. 21
8 Ibid. P. 24
9 Woodward, P. 85
10 Lord, P. 25
11 Ibid., P. 25
12 Fairclough Adam, *Better Day Coming: Black and Equality, 1890-2000*. 2001.
   Viking/Penguin Books. New York, NY. P. 52
13 Fairlough, P. 52
14 Packard, P. 91
15 Logan, Rayford W., *The Betrayal of the Negro: From Rutherford B. Hayes to Woodrow Wilson*. 1997. Da Capo Press, New York, NY. P. 370
16 Ibid., P. 327
17 Quarles, P. 194
18 Meir and Rudwick, P. 218
19 Ibid., P. 219

20 Fairclough, P. 44
21 Ibid. P. 49-51
22 Meir and Rudwick, P. 219
23 Fairclough, P. 44
24 Franklin, P. 301
25 Quarles, P. 197
26 Franklin P. 304
27 Ibid., P. 305
28 Ibid., P. 305
29 *Webster's New Explorer Dictionary*. 1999. Springfield, MA. P. 175.
30 Packard, P. 93
31 Ibid., P. 90-93
32 Ibid. P. 92
33 Williamson, P. 213
31 Fairclough, P. 27
35 Gossett, P. 269
36 Ibid., P. 269
37 Ibid., P. 270
38 Williamson, P. 189
39 Ibid, P. 117
40 Ibid. P. 186
41 Ibid., P. 188
42 Gossett, P. 270
43 Williamson, P. 282
44 Ibid. P. 187
45 Cowan, Tom, Ph.D. & Maguire, Jack, *Timelines of African American History*. 1994. Perigee Books, New York, NY. P. 219
46 Williamson, P. 187
47 Packard, P. 94
48 Ibid., P. 95
49 Packard, P. 96
50 Ibid., P. 97
51 Frederickson, P. 249
52 Ibid. P. 223
53 Ibid. P. 223
54 Ibid. P. 226
55 Meir and Rudwick, P. 232
56 Packard, P. 95
57 Ibid., P. 95
58 Frederickson, P. 188
59 Lord, P. 30
60 Adams & Sanders. P. 243
61 Ibid. P. 244
62 Ibid. P. 244
63 Ibid. P. 244
64 Logan, P. 365-366
65 Ibid., P. 367
66 Ibid., P. 366-367
67 Adams and Sanders, P. 249
68 Fairclough, P. 24

69 Bishop Alexander Walters, *My Life and Work* (New York, 1917), p. 257

70 Fairclough, P. 56

71 DuBois, W.E. Burghardt, *The Souls of Black Folk: Essays and Sketches* (Chicago, 1903)

72 Logan, P. 352

73 Ibid., P. 352

74 Ibid., P. 354

75 Franklin, P. 353

76 Ibid., P. 353

77 Fairclough, 72-73

Chapter 7 Notes and Citations

1 Wilson, Sondra Kathryn (Editor), *In Search of Democracy: The NAACP Writings of James Weldon Johnson, Walter White and Roy Wilkins (1920-1977)*. 1999. Oxford University Press, New York, NY. P. 17

2 Carnes, Mark C. (Editor), *American History, Macmillian Compendium*. 1996. Simon & Schuster Macmillan, New York, NY, P. 590

3 Cowan, Tom and Macguire, Jack, *Timelines of African-American History: 500 Years of Black Achievement*. 1994. Perigee Books, New York, NY. P. 219

4 Wilson, P. 3-4

5 Wilson, P. 15

6 Fairclough, P. 79

7 Wilson, P. 14

8 Bennett, Jr., Lerone, *Before The Mayflower: A History of Black America*. 1984. Penguin Books, New York, NY. P. 518

9 Bennett, P. 521

10 Packard, P. 147

11 Brophy, Alfred L., *Restructuring The Dreamland: The Tulsa Race Riot of 1921*. 2002. Oxford University Press, New York, NY. P. 24-25

12 Brophy, P. 12-13

13 Packard, P. 146

14 Ibid., P. 146

15 Ibid., P. 146

16 Ibid., P. 148

17 Meir & Rudwick, P. 240

18 Packard, P. 148

19 Ibid., P. 149

20 Brophy, P. 51-52

21 Packard, P. 149

22 Brophy, P. 60

23 Packard, P. 149

24 Appiah, Kwame Anthony and Gates, Jr., Henry Louis (Editors), *Africana*. Basic Books, New York, NY. P. 1637-1638

25 Maclean, Nancy, *Behind The Mask of Chivalry: The Making of the Second Ku Klux Klan*. 1994. Oxford University Press, New York, NY. P. 4-5

26 Ibid., P. 6

27 Ibid., P. 5

28 Ibid., 6-7

29 Ibid. P. 46

30 Ibid., 136-139

31 Ibid., 139

32 Ibid. P. 53

33 Ibid., P. xiv

34 Packard, P. 128

35 Maclean, P. 27-28

36 Fairclough, P. 100

37 Packard, P. 128

38 Maclean, P. 9-10

39 Ibid. P. xiii

40 Davis, John P. (Editor), *The Negro Reference Book.* 1970. Prentiss-Hall, Englewood Cliffs, NJ. P. 111

41 Frederickson, P. 221

42 Ibid. P. 226

43 Smith, P. 150

44 Hacker, Andrew. Two Nations: *Black and White, Separate, Hostile, Unequal.* 1992. Ballentine Books, New York, NY. P. 101

45 Comer, P. 105

46 Ibid., P. 105

47 Adams and Sanders, P. 256

48 Ibid., P. 257

49 Packard, P. 112

50 Smith, P. 153

51 Packard, P. 82

52 Ibid., P. 82

53 Franklin and Moss, P. 360

54 Meir and Rudwick, P. 239

55 Davis, P. 64

56 Ibid, P. 63

57 Ibid, P. 63

58 Franklin, P. 364

59 Davis, P. 615

60 McNeil, Genna Rae, *Groundwork: Charles Hamilton Houston and the Struggle for Civil Rights.* 1983. University of Pennsylvania Press, Philadelphia, PA. P. 45

61 Ibid., P. 45

62 Ibid, P. 64

63 Ibid., P. 64

64 Ibid., P. 65

65 Ibid. P. 53

66 Meier and Rudwick, P. 242

67 Quarles, P. 208

68 Fairclough, P. 83

69 Davis, P. 69

70 McNeil, P. 100

71 Ibid, P. 100

Chapter 8 Notes and Citations

1 McNeil, P. 60

435

2 Ibid., P. 62

3 Ibid., P. 63

4 Ibid., P. 64

5 "Before Brown/Beyond Boundaries: Comemorating the 50th Anniversary of Brown vs. Board of Education," The Association for the Study of African American Life and History (ASALH), Inc. 2004., African World Press, Trenton, NJ. P. 7

6 McNeil, P. 64

7 McNeil, P. 66

8 "Before Brown/Beyond Boundaries" ASALH , P. 7

9 McNeil, P. P. 68

10 Ibid. P. 69

11 Ibid. P. 70

12 Ibid., P. 70

13 Ibid., P. 79

14 Ibid., P. 75

15 Egerton, John, *Speak Now Against The Day: The Generation Before The Civil Rights Movement In The South*. 1995. Alfred A. Knopf, New York, NY. P. 150

16 Kluger, Richard, *Simple Justice*. 1975. Knopf Books, New York, NY. P. 162

17 Ibid., P. 162

18 Ibid., P. 162

19 Ibid., P. 162

20 Ibid., P. 163

21 Wilson Sondra Kathryn (Editor), *In Search of Democracy: The NAACP Writing of James Weldon Johnson, Walter White, and Roy Wilkins (1920-1977)*. 1999. Oxford University Press, New York, NY. P. 260-261

22 Rowan, Carl T., *Dream Makers, Dream Breakers: The World of Justice Marshall*. 1993. Little, Brown and Company, Boston, MA, P. 63-64

23 D'Angelo, Raymond, *The American Civil Rights Movements: Readings & Interpretations*. 2001. McGraw-Hill/Dushkin, New York, NY. P. 167

24 Wilson, P. 263

25 Egerton, P. 150

26 Rowan,. P. 61

27 McNeil, P. 115

28 Tushnet, Mark V., *The NAACP: Legal Strategy against Segregated Education, 1925-1950*. 1987. The University of North Carolina Press, Chapel Hill, NC. P. 26-27

29 Ibid., P. 27

30 Ibid., P. 27

31 Ibid., P. 28

32 Kluger, P. 169

33 Tushnet, P. 113

34 Ibid., P. 114

35 Tushnet, P. 17

36 Ibid., P. 26

37 McNeil, P. 115

38 Fairclough, P. 198

39 D,Angelo, P. 179

40 Tushnet, P. 32

41 Ibid., P. 17

42 McNeil, P. 116

43 Ibid., P. 117

44 Ibid., P. 116
45 Ibid., P. 120
46 Kluger, P. 200
47 D'Angelo, P. 179
48 Egerton, P. 152
49 Ibid., P. 152
50 Goldwin, Roger (with David Gallen), *Thurgood Marshall: Justice For All.*1992. Carroll & Graf, New York, NY. P. 31
51 Kluger, P. 267
52 Ibid., P. 31
53 D'Angelo, P. 179-180
54 Fairclough, P. 199
55 Ibid., P. 199
56 Goldman, P. 31
57 Ibid., P. 181
58 Wilson, P. 237
59 Ibid., P. 239
60 Klarman, Michael J., *From Jim Crow to Civil Rights: The Supreme Court and the Struggle for Racial Equality.* 2004. Oxford University Press, New York, NY. P. 116.
61 Ibid., P. 116
62 Ibid., P. 115
63 Ibid., P. 116
64 Higginbotham, Jr., Leon A., *Shades of Freedom: Racial Politics And Presumptions Of The American Legal Process.* 1996. Oxford University Press, New York, NY. P. 159.
65 Ibid., P. 159
66 Higginbotham, Jr., P. 164
67 Tushnet, P. 71
68 Ibid., P. 71
69 Higginbotham, Jr., P. 164
70 Klarman, 115-116
71 D'Angelo, P. 182
72 Higginbotham, Jr., P. 165
73 McNeil, P. 150-151
74 Tushnet, P. 75
75 Ibid., P. 77
76 McNel., P. 149
77 Fairclough, P. 199
78 Klarman, P. 135
79 Fairclough, P. 200
80 Ibid., P. 200
81 Klarman, P. 253
82 Baker-Motley, P. 66
83 Myrdal, Gunnar, *An American Dilemma: The Negro Problem and Modern Democracy.* 1944. Harper & Brothers Publishers, New York, NY. P. ix
84 Tushnet, P. 119
85 Myrdal, P. 573
86 Ibid., P. 587-588
87 Ibid., P. 577
88 Ibid. P. 577
89 Ibid., P. 577

90 Baker-Motley, Constance, *Equal Justice Under Law*. 1998. Farrar, Straus, Giroux. New York, NY. P. 68

91 Tushnet, P. 120

92 Baker-Motley, P. 68

93 Tushnet, P. 120-121

94 Tushnet P. 121

95 Kluger, P. 325

96 Klarman, P. 205

97 Tushnet, P. 111

98 Klarman, P. 261-262

99 Ibid., P. 262

100 Vose, Clement E., *Caucasians Only: The Supreme Court, the NAACP and the Restrictive Covenant Case*s. 1959. University of California Press. Berkeley, CA. P. 199-200

101 Ibid., P. 200

102 Ibid., P. 199

103 Ibid., P. 205-206

104 Kluger, P. 327

105 Ibid. P. 327

106 Ibid., P. 238

107 Ibid., P. 335

108 Ibid, P. 335-336

109 Ibid., P. 336

110 McNeil, P. 199

111 Ibid., P. 188

112 McNeil, P. 189.

113 Ibid., P. 190

114 Ibid., P. 200

115 McNeil, P. 200

116 Patterson, James T., *Brown v. Board of Education: A Civil Rights Milestone and Its Troubled Legacy*. 2001. Oxford University Press, New York, NY. P. 14

117 Kluger, P. 340

118 Ibid., P. 341

119 Ibid., P. 348

120 Ibid., P. 348

121 Ibid., P. 348

122 Ibid., P. 348

123 Ibid., P. 353

124 Ibid., P. 354

125 Ibid., P. 355

126 Klarman, P. 254

127 Tushnet, P. 136

128 Whitman, Mark, *Brown V. Board of Education: A Documentary History*. 1993, 2004. Markus Wiener Publishers, Princton, NJ. P. 40-41

129 Patterson, P. 25

130 Ibid., P. 25

131 Whitman, P. 40

132 Ibid., P. 42

133 Whitman, P. 42

134 Patterson, P. 32

135 Kluger, P. 470

136 Patterson, P. 32

137 Kluger, P. 497

138 Whitman, P. 42

139 Kluger, P. 498

140 Whitman, P. 50

141 Ibid., P. 43

142 Patterson, P. 28

143 Whitman, P. 44

144 Patterson, P. 28-29

145 Wolters, Raymond, *The Burden of Brown: Thirty Years of School Desegregation.* 1984. University of Tennessee Press, Knoxville, TN. P. 177

146 Patterson, P. 30

147 Wolters, P. 177

148 Patterson, P. 31

149 Wolters, P. 177-178

150 McNeil, P. 209-210

151 ASALH, P. 83

152 Cottrol, Robert J., Diamond, Raymond T., Ware, Leland B., *Brown v. Board of Education: Caste, Culture and the Constitution.* 2003. University Press of Kansas, P. 138

153 Ibid., P. 138

154 Ibid., P. 139

155 Klarman, P. 292

156 Rowan, Carl T., *Dream Makers, Dream Breakers: The World of Justice Thurgood Marshall.* 1993. Little, Brown and Company, Boston, MA. P. 194

157 Ibid., P. 194-195

158 Klarman, P. 294

159 Ibid., P. 295

160 Ibid., P. 296

161 Ibid., P. 296-297

162 Ibid., P. 297

163 Ibid., P. 298

164 Friedman, Leon (Editor), *Brown v. Board: The Landmark Oral Argument Before The Supreme Court.* 1969, 2004. The New Press, New York, NY. P. 177-178

165 Cottrol, Diamond, and Ware, P. 144.

166 Ibid., P. 145

167 Klarman, P. 301

168 Ibid, P. 302

169 Gray, Ed, *Chief Justice: A Biogrphy of Earl Warren.*1997. Simon & Schuster, New York, NY. P. 118-121

170 Friedman, P. x

171 Klarman, P. 302

172 Ibid., P. 302

173 Egerton, P. 586

Chapter 9 Notes and Citations

1 Gray, P. 287

2 Ibid., P. 287

3 *Brown et al. v. Board of Education of Topeka, et. al. (347 U.S. 483)* cited in Friedman, P. 330.

4 Bolling v. Sharpe (347 U.S. 497) cited in Friedman, P. 332

5 Ibid, P. 333

6 Gray, P. 281

7 Rowan, P. 218-219

8 Bartley, Numan V., *The Rise of Massive Resistance: race and Politics in the South During the 1950's.* 1969, 1997. Louisiana State University Press, Baton Rouge, LA. P. 68

9 Wilhoit, Francis M., *The Politics of Massive Resistance.* 1973. George Braziller, Inc., New York, NY. P. 28

10 Ibid., P. 30

11 Ibid., P. 239

12 Packard, P. 238

13 Bartley, P. 76

14 Ibid., P. 77

15 Wilhoit, P. 43

16 Ibid., P. 44

17 Ibid. P. 44

18 Ibid., P. 23

19 Ibid., P. 23

20 Ibid., P. 23

21 Ibid., P. 44-45

22 Ibid. P. 52

23 Ibid., P. 57

24 Ibid., P. 86

25 Ball, Howard, *A Defiant Life: Thurgood Marshall.* 1998. Crown Book Publishers, New York, NY. P. 143

26 Ball, P. 143

27 Bartley, P. 85

28 Ibid., P. 85-86

29 Ibid., P. 84

30 Ibid, P. 82

31 Ibid., P. 82-83

32 Ball, P. 143

33 Bartley, P. 86

34 Ibid., P. 91-92

35 Sarratt, Reed, *The Ordeal of Desegregation.* 1966. Harpers & Row Publishers, New York, NY , P. 209-210

36 Ibid., P. 96

37 Ball, P. 143-145

38 Belknap, Michael R., *Federal law and Southern Order: Racial Violence and Constitutional Conflict In The Post-Brown South.* 1987. University of Georgia Press, Athens, GA. P. 28-29

39 Bartley, P. 82

40 Belknap, P. 32

41 Ibid, P. 31

42 Belknap, P. 53

43 Ball, P. 147

44 Bartley, P. 116

45 Sarratt, P. 41

46 Bartley, P. 116-117
47 Congressional Record, 84th Congress, 2nd Session, March 12, 1956, in full text as cited in Wilhoit, Appendix, P. 285-287
48 Packard, P. 238
49 Ball, P. 139
50 Ibid., P. 138-139
51 Gray, P. 262
52 Packard, P. 239
53 Ibid., P. 239
54 Wilhoit, P. 150
55 Ball, P. 147
56 Ball, P. 147

Chapter 10 Notes and Citations

1 Ball, P. 147
2 Packard, P. 246
3 Packard, P. 248
4 Ibid, P. 248-249
5 Ibid., P. 249
6 Williams, Juan, *Thurgood Marshall: American Revoluntionary*. 1998. Times Book, New York, NY. P. 252
7 Ibid., P. 252
8 Packard, P. 249
9 Fairclough, P. 235
10 Ibid., P. 235
11 Ibid., P. 238
12 Moses, Greg, *Revolution of Conscience: Martin Luther King, Jr. and the Philosophy of Non-Violence*. 1997. The Guilford Press, New York, NY. P. 148
13 Ibid., P. 149.
14 Feagin, Joe R. and Vera, Hernan, *White Racism*. 1995. Routledge. New York, NY. P. 45.
15 King, Jr., Martin Luther, "Letter from Birmingham City Jail," cited from *The American Civil Rights Movement: Readings & Interpretations*, D'Angelo, Raymond. 2001. McGraw-Hill Dushin, New York, NY. P. 320-321
16 King, Jr., Martin Luther, "I Have A Dream Speech," August 28, 1963, cited in *The African American Archive: The History of the Black Experience Through Documents*, Kai Wright, Editor. 2001. Black Dog & Leventhal Publishers, New York, NY. P. 578-79
17 Sarratt, P. 53
18 Schlesinger, Jr., Arthur M., *A Thousand Days: John F. Kennedy in the White House*. 1965. Houghton Mifflin Company, Boston, MA. P. 967
19 DeGregorio, P. 557
20 Sarratt, P. 54
21 Ibid., P. 55
22 Ibid, P. 50
23 King, Jr., Martin Luther, *Where Do We Go from Here: Chaos or Community?* 1968. Beacon Press., Boston, MA. P. 80 Ball, P. 147

441

Chapter 11 Notes and Citations

1 Sarratt, P. 66
2 Ibid., P. 66

3 Ibid., P. 193
4 Baker-Motley, P. 182
5 Ibid., P. 183
6 Sarratt, P. 165
7 Patterson, P. 105
8 Belknap, P. 29
9 Ibid., P. 47
10 Patterson, P. 110
11 Belknap, P. 48
12 Ibid., P. 49
13 Ibid., P. 50
14 Patterson, P. 107
15 Ibid., P. 107
16 Sarratt, P. 167
17 Ibid, P. 196
18 Ibid. P. 167
19 Schlesinger, P. 964-965
20 Ibid., P. 966
21 Mitau, G. Theodore, *Decade of Decision: The Supreme Court and the Constitutional Revolution, 1954-1964.* 1967. Charles Scribner's Sons, New York, NY. P. 198
22 Sitkoff, Harvard, *The Struggle for Black Equality, 1954-1980.* 1981. Hill and Wang, New York, NY, P. 128
23 Fairclough, P. 274
24 Mitau, P. 198
25 Ibid., P. 198-199
26 Packard, P. 268
27 Fairclough, P. 275
28 King, Coretta Scott, *My Life With Martin Luther King, Jr.* 1969. Holt Rinehart and Winston, New York, NY, P. 218
29 Sitkoff, P. 128
30 Fairclough, P. 310
31 Packard, P. 268
32 King, Coretta Scott, P. 233
33 Belknap, P. 119
34 Mitau, P. 225-226
35 Ibid., P. 226
36 Ibid., P. 68
37 Ibid., P. 204
38 Ibid., P. 206
39 Ibid., P. 206
40 King, Coretta Scott, P. 229
41 Ibid., P. 121
42 Stern, Mark, *Calculating Visions: Kennedy, Johnson, and Civil Rights.* 1992. Rutgers University Press, New Brunswick, NJ. P. 161

43 Sarratt, P. 43
44 Ibid., P. 73
45 Adams & Sanders, P. 277-278
46 Ibid., P. 278
47 Mitau, P. 223
48 Patterson, P. 124
49 Belknap, P. 129
50 Sarratt, P. 44
51 Ibid., P. 44
52 Patterson, P. 124
53 Rowan, P. 286-287
54 Olson, Lynne, *Freedom's Daughters: The Unsung Heroines of the Civil Rights Movement From 1830 to 1970.* 2001. Scribner Books, New York, NY. P. 315
55 Belknap, P. 147
56 Mitau, P. 199
57 Olson, P. 315
58 Horton, James Oliver & Lois E. Horton, *Hard Road To Freedom: The Story of African America.* 2001. New Brunswick, New Jersey. P. 299-300
59 Olson, P. 318-319
60 Ibid., P. 320-321
61 Ibid., P. 324
62 Horton and Horton, P. 302
63 King, Coretta Scott, P. 254
64 Ibid., P. 256
65 Ibid., P. 264
66 Ibid., P. 259
67 Ibid., P 260
68 Belknap, P. 207
69 Ibid., P. 209-210

443

Chapter 12 Notes and Citations

1 Cashman, Sean Dennis, *African-Americans and the Quest for Civil Rights*, 1900-1990. 1991. New York University Press, New York, NY. P. 173
2 Sitkoff, P. 211
3 Wolfenstein, Eugene Victor, *The Victims of Democracy: Malcolm X and the Black Revolution.* 1993. Guilford Press, New York, NY. P. 313-314
4 Breitman, George (Editor), *Malcolm X Speaks.* 1966. Grove Press, New York, NY, P. 33-34
5 Cone, James H., *Martin & Malcolm & America.* 1991. Orbis Books, Maryknoll, NY. P. 183
6 Cashman, P. 169
7 Rubio, Philip F., *A History of Affirmative Action, 1619-2000.* 2001. University Press of Mississippi, Jackson, MS. P. 144
8 Adams and Sanders, P. 302
9 Rubio, P. 144-145
10 Cashman, P. 182
11 King, Coretta Scott, P. 271

12 Cashman, P. 208

13 Cashman, P. 208

14 United States. Kerner Commission, *Report of the National Advisory Commission on Civil Disorder*.1968. U.S. Government Printing Office

15 Ibid.

16 Ibid.

17 Ibid.

18 Ibid.

19 Cashman, P. 211

20 Horton & Horton, P. 319

21 Sitkoff, P. 200

22 Ibid., P. 200

23 O'Reilly, P. 257

24 Cashman, P. 215

25 Silk, Leonard, *Nixonomics*. 1973. Praeger Publishers, New York, NY. P. 32

26 Coles, Jr., Flournoy A., *Black Economic Development*.1975. Nelson Hall, Chicago, IL. P. 14

27 Silk, P. 32

28 Quarles, P. 331

29 Rubio, P. 150

30 Ibid., P. 153-154

31 Ibid. P. 153

32 Franklin, P. 553

33 Grant, Joanne (Editor), *Black Protest: 350 Years of History, Documents and Analyses*. 1968. Fawcett Columbine, New York, NY. P. 490

34 Rubio, P. 159

35 Ibid., P. 159

Chapter 13 Notes and Citations

1 Feagin, Joe R. & Vera, Hernan. *White Racism*.1995. Routledge, New York, NY, P. 16

2 Sidanius, James, "The Psychology of Group Conflict and the Dynamics of Oppression: A Social Dominance Perspective," *Explorations In Political Pyschology*, Shanto Iyengar and Willaim J. McGuire, Editors. 1993. Duke University Press, Durham, NC. P. 196.

3 Feagin & Vera, P. 16

4 Sidanius, P. 196

5 Ibid., P. 196

6 Feagin & Vera, P. 24

7 Sidanius, P. 207

8 Ibid., P. 207-208

9 Ibid., P. 208

10 Ibid., P. 209

11 Williams, Linda Faye, *The Constraint of Race: Legacies of White Skin Privilege in America*. 2003. The Pennsylvania State University Press, University Park, PA, P. 165

12 Rowan, Carl T., *The Coming Race War In America: A Wake Up Call*. 1996. Little, Brown and Company, Boston, MA, P. 44-47

13 O'Reilly, Kenneth, *Nixon's Piano: Presidents and Racial Politics From Washington To Clinton.* 1995. The Free Press, New York, NY. P. 318.

14 Ibid., 318-319

15 Rowan (1996), P. 44-45

16 Ibid., P. 43

17 O'Reilly, P. 308

18 Ibid., P. 320-321

19 Ibid., P. 325

20 Cohen, Cari & Sterba, James P., *Affirmative Action and Racial Reference: A Debate.* 2003. Oxford University Press. New York, NY. P. 194

21 Ibid., P. 194

22 Sindler, Allan P., *Bakke, DeFunis, and Minority Admissions: The Quest for Equal Opportunity.* 1978. Longman, Inc., New York, NY. P. 38

23 Ibid., P. 40

24 Ibid., P. 90

25 Ibid., P. 50

26 Ibid., P. 55

27 Ibid., P. 67

28 Ibid., P. 66-67

29 Ibid. P. 69

30 Ibid., P. 70

31 Ibid. P. 76

32 Ibid. P. 86

33 Ibid., P. 86

34 Ibid., P. 292

35 Ibid., P. 294

36 Ibid., P. 299-300

37 Cohen and Sterba, P. 195

38 Ibid., P. 195-196

39 Patterson, pp. 177-178

40 Fairclough, P. 329

41 Patterson, P. 181

Chapter 14 Notes and Citations

1 Ashmore, Harry S., *Civil Rights and Wrongs: A Memoir of Race and Politics*, 1944-1994. 1994. Pantheon Books, New York, NY, P. 254

2 Ibid., P. 255

3 Ibid., P. 256

4 Clotfelter, Charles T., *After Brown: The Rise and Retreat of School Desegregation.* 2004. Princeton University Press, Princeton, NJ. P. 95

5 Ashmore, P. 256

6 Adams & Sanders, Pp. 306-307

7 Ibid., P. 307

8 Rowan *(Dream Makers, Dream Breakers)*, P. 308

9 Fairclough, P. 327

10 Taylor, William L., "Access To Economic Opportunity: Lessons Since Brown," *Minority*

Report: What Has Happened To Blacks, Hispanics, American Indians, & Other Minorities In The Eighties, Leslie W. Dunbar (Editor). 1984. Pantheon Books, New York, NY. P. 41

11 Taylor, P. 41

12 U.S. Bureau of the Census-Decennial Census Reports, Population, 1900-2000

13 Taylor, P. 41

14 Ibid., P. 93

15 O'Reilly, P. 305

16 O'Reilly, P. 352

17 O'Reilly, P. 355

18 Fairclough, P. 331

19 Edsall, Thomas Byrne and Edsall, Mary D., *Chain Reaction*. 1992. W.W. Norton, New York, NY. P. 24

20 O'Reilly, Pp. 360-61

21 Ibid., P. 359

22 DeGregorio, P. 653

23 McKenzie, Richard B., *What Went Right In The 1980s*. 1994. Pacific Research Institute for Public Policy, San Francisco, CA. P. 260

24 DeGregorio, P. 653

25 Phillips, Kevin, *The Politics of Rich and Poor*. 1990. Random House, New York, NY. P. 7

26 Patterson, James & Kim, Peter, *The Second American Revolution*. 1994. William Morrow and Company, New York, NY. Pp. 74-75

27 Phillips, P. 239, Appendix A

28 DeGregorio, P. 653

29 Patterson & Kim, P. 233

30 Ibid., Pp. 232-233

31 O'Reilly, P. 268

32 Rowan (Dream Makers), P. 308

33 Ibid. P. 309

34 Rowan *(Dream Makers)*, P. 309

Chapter 15 Notes and Citations

1 Edsall and Edsall, Pp. 10-11

2 Ibid., P. 11

3 Ibid., P. 13

4 Patterson, Orlando: *The Ordeal of Integration: Progress and Resentment in America's "Racial" Crisis*.1997. Civitas Counterpoint, Washington, D.C. Pp. 148-149

5 Pinkney, Alphonso, *Black Americans (fifth ed.)*. 2002. Prentice Hall, Upper Saddle River, NJ. P. 97-98

6 Ibid., P. 92

7 Ibid., P. 100-101

8 Zhou, Min, "Contemporary Immigration and the Dynamics of Race and Ethnicity," *America Becoming: Racial Trends and Their Consequences, Volume I*, Smelser, Neil J., Wilson, William Julius, Mitchell, Faith, (Editors). National Academy Press, Washington D.C., P. 224.

9 Ibid., P. 228

10 Feagin, Joe R., *Racist America: Roots, Current Realities & Future Reparations*. 2000.

Routledge, New York, NY. P. 184

11 Edley, Jr, Christopher, *Not All Black and White: Affirmative Action and American Values*. 1996. Hill and Wang, New York, NY. Pp. 142-143

12 Ibid., P. 143

13 Ibid., Pp. 146-147

14 Bobo, Lawrence D., "Racial Attitudes and Relations at the close of the Twentieth Century," *America Becoming: Racial Trends and Their Consequences, vol. 1 ed.* Neil Smelser, William Julius Wilson, and Faith Mitchell, National Academy Press. Wash, DC. P. 292

15 Ibid, P. 292

16 Shapiro, Thomas M., *The Hidden Costs of Being American American: How Wealth Perpetuates Inequality*. 2004. Oxford University Press, New York, NY. P. 101

17 Hacker, Andrew, *Two Nations: Black and White, Separate, Hostile, Unequal*. 1992. Ballantine Books, New York, NY. P. 103

18 Ibid, P. 101

19 Ibid, P. 68

20 Anderson, Claud, Ed.D., *Black Labor, White Wealth*. 1994. Duncan & Duncan, Edgewood, MD. P. 190

21 Hacker, P. 29

22 Andrews, Marcellus, *The Political Economy of Hope and Fear*. 1999. New York University Press, New York, NY. P. 157

23 Ibid, Pp. 157-158

24 Ibid., P. 159

25 Roediger, David R., *Colored White: Transcending the Racial Past*. 2002. University of California Press, Berkeley, CA. P. 221

26 Ibid., Pp. 224-226

27 Ibid., Pp. 227-228

28 Williams, Juan, *Thurgood Marshall: American Revolutionary*. 1998. Random House. New York, NY. P. 333

29 Ball, Howard, *A Defiant Life: Thurgood Marshall & the Persistence of Racism In America*. 1998. Crown Publishers, New York, NY. P. 194

30 Dallek, Robert, *Flawed Giant: Lyndon Johnson and His Times, 1961-1973*. 1998. Oxford University Press, New York, NY. P. 471

31 Hacker, P. 103

32 Dawson, Michael C., *Behind The Mule: Race and Class in African-American Politics*. 1994. Princeton University Press, Princeton, NJ. P. 177

33 Mills, David, "Sista Souljah's Call to Arms" The Rapper Says the Riots Were Payback. Are You Paying Attention?" *Washington Post*, May 13, 1992, p. B1

34 Feagin & Vera, P. 125

35 Smith, Robert C., *We Have No Leaders: African American in the Post Civil Rights Era*. State University of New York Press. 1996. State University of New York Press, Albany, NY. P. 269

36 Marable, Manning, *The Great Wells of Democracy: The Meaning of Race In American Life*. 2002. Basic Civitas Book. New York, NY. P. 81

37 Feagin & Vera, P. 120

38 Ibid., P. 115

39 Ibid., P. 122

40 McWhirter, Darien A., *The End of Affirmative Action: Where Do We Go From Here?* 1996. Birch Lane Press. New York, NY. Pp. 107-108

447

41 Ibid., P. 11

42 Ibid., P.108

43 Crenshaw, Kimberle' Williams, "Colorblindness, History, and the Law," *The House That Race Built*, Wahneema Lubiano (Editor). 1997. Pantheon Books, New York, NY. P. 284

44 *Plessy v. Ferguson (163 U.S. 537, 16 S.Ct. 1138, 41 L.Ed. 256 (1896), cited from Constitutional Law: Cases and Materials (11th Ed.),* Cohen and Varat (Editors), P. 704

45 Crenshaw, P. 285

46 Ibid., P. 285

47 Pinkney, P. 93

48 Mfume, Kweisi, with Ron Stodhill II, *No Free Ride: From the Mean Streets to the Mainstream.* 1996. One World/Ballentine Books. New York, NY. P. 351

49 Mayer, Jeremy D., *Running On Race: Racial Politics In Presidential Campaigns, 1960-2000.* 2002.
    Random House, New York, NY. P. 255

50 McWhirter, Pp. 259-260

51 Ibid., P. 260

52 Thernstrom, Stephan and Thernstrom, Abigail, *America In Black and White: One Nation Indivisible.* 1997. Simon & Schuster. New York, NY. P. 419

53 *Hopwood v. Texas*, 78 F. 3d. at 962

54 Pinkney, P. 237

55 Mfume, P. 360

56 Higginbotham, Jr. A. Leon, *Shades of Freedom.* 1996. Oxford University Press, New York, NY. P. 188.

57 Ibid., P. 189

58 Ibid., P. 189

59 Oliver, Melvin L. & Shapiro, Thomas M., *Black Wealth/White Wealth.* 1995. Routledge Books. New York, NY. P. 50

60 Ibid., Pp. 50-51

61 Shapiro, Pp. 37-38

62 Ibid., P. 47.

63 Ibid., P. 50

64 Ibid., P. 50

65 Ibid., P. 50.

66 Ibid., P. 67

67 Ibid., P. 67

68 Ibid., P. 69

69 Ibid., P. 49

70 Ibid., P. 67

71 Ibid., P. 55

72 Ibid., Pp. 109-113

Chapter 16 Notes and Citaations

1 Crenshaw, Kimberle' Williams, "Race, Reform, and Retrenchment: Transformation and Legitimation in Antidiscrimination Law." 1995. *Critical Race Theory: The Key Writings That Formed The Movement*, Kimberle' Crenshaw, Neil Gotanda, Gary Peller, Kendall Thomas,

editors. The New Press, New York, NY. P. 115

2 Ibid., P. 116

3 Ibid., P. 118

4 Williams, Linda Faye, *The Constraint of Race: Legacies of White Skin Privilege.*
2003. Pennsylvania State University Press, University Press, PA. P. 367

5 Ibid., Pp. 367-368

6 Brown, Michael K., Carnoy, Martin, Currie, Elliott, Duster, Troy, Oppenheimer,
David B., Shultz, Marjorie M., Wellman, David, *White Washing Race: The Myth Of
A Color-Blind Society.* 2003. University of California Press, Berkeley, CA. P. 161

7 Ibid., P. 187

8 Ibid., P. 212

9 Mills, Charles, *The Racial Contract.* 1997. Cornell University Press., Ithaca, NY. P. 11

10 Ibid., P. 3

11 Ibid., P. 120

12 Ibid., P. 127

13 Ibid., P. 126

14 Teixeira Ruy, and Rogers, Joel, *America's Forgotten Majority: Why the White
Working Class Still Matters.* 2000. Basic Books, New York, NY. P. 162

15 Harris, Cherly I., "Whiteness As Property." 1995, from Critical Race Theory, P. 289

16 Ibid., P. 289

17 McIntish, Peggy, "White Privilege: Unpacking the Invisible Knapsack." 1988, from
White Privilege: Essential Reading on the Other Side of Racism, Paula S.
Rothenberg, Editor. Worth Publishers, New York, NY. Pp. 98-99

18 Lemann, Nicholas, *The Big Test: The Secret History of the American Meritocracy.*
1999. Farrar, Straus, Giroux, New York, NY. P. 344

19 Ibid., P. 344

20 Harris, Cheryl I., "Whiteness As Property," from Critical Race Theory, P. 283

21 Hacker, P. 103

22 Bureau of Labor Statistics, Employment Situation, Historical Table A-2.

22 Muhammad, Derrick, Davis, Attieno, Lui, Meizhu and Leondar-Wright, Betsy, "The
State of the Dream 2004: Enduring Disparities in Black and White." January, 15, 2004.
Published by United for a Fair Economy-Racial Wealth Divide Project, Boston, MA. P. 4

24 Ibid., P. 6

25 Ibid., Pp. 6-7

26 Ibid., Pp. 8-9

27 Ibid., P. 8

28 Ibid., P. 10

29 Ibid., P. 14

30 Ibid., P. 20

31 Ibid., P. 26

32 "The State of Black Equality: The Complexity of Black Progress," Executive Summary,
compiled by the National Urban League, March, 2004. New York, NY. P. 5

BIBLIOGRAPHY
&
REFERENCES

Books

Anderson, Claud, Ed.D., *Black Labor, White Wealth*. 1994. Duncan & Duncan,Edgewood, MD

Andrews, Marcellus, *The Political Economy of Hope and Fear*. 1999. New York University Press, New York, NY

Angle, Paul M. & Miers, Harl S. (editors). *The Living Lincoln: The Man And HisTimes, In His Own Words*. 1955, 1992. Barnes and Nobles Books, New York, NY

Appiah, Kwame Anthony and Gates, Jr., Henry Louis (Editors), *Africana*. BasicBooks, New York, NY

Ashmore, Harry S., *Civil Rights and Wrongs: A Memoir of Race and Politics, 1944-1994*. 1994. Pantheon Books, New York, NY

Baker-Motley, Constance, *Equal Justice Under Law*. 1998. Farrar, Straus, Giroux.New York, NY

Ball, Howard, *A Defiant Life: Thurgood Marshall & the Persistence of Racism InAmerica*. 1998. Crown Publishers, New York, NY

Bartley, Numan V., *The Rise of Massive Resistance: race and Politics in the SouthDuring the 1950's*. 1969, 1997. Louisiana State University Press, Baton Rouge, LA

Belknap, Michael R., *Federal law and Southern Order: Racial Violence and Constitutional Conflict In The Post-Brown South*. 1987. University of Georgia Press,Athens, GA

Bennett, Jr., Lerone, *Before The Mayflower: A History of Black America*. 1984. Penguin Books, New York, NY

Berry, Mary Frances, *Black Resistance, White Law: A History of Constitutional Racism in America*. 1971, 1994. New York, NY

Bishop Alexander Walters, *My Life and Work* (New York, 1917)

Boxill, Bernard (Editor), *Race and Racism*. 2001. Oxford University Press, New York, NY

Breitman, George (Editor), *Malcolm X Speaks*. 1966. Grove Press, New York, NY

Brophy, Alfred L., *Restructuring The Dreamland: The Tulsa Race Riot of 1921*. 2002.

Brown, Michael K., Carnoy, Martin, Currie, Elliott, Duster, Troy, Oppenheimer, David B., Shultz, Marjorie M., Wellman, David, *White Washing Race: The Myth Of A Color-Blind Society*. 2003. University of California Press, Berkeley, CA, Oxford University Press, New York, NY

Camejo, Peter, *Racism, Revolution, Reaction, 1861-1877*. 1976. Pathfinder Press, New York, NY

Carnes, Mark C. Editor, *American History*. 1996. MacMillan Library Reference USA, Simon & Schuster/MacMillan, New York, NY

Cashman, Sean Dennis, *African-Americans and the Quest for Civil Rights, 1900-1990*. 1991. New York University Press, New York, NY

Clotfelter, Charles T., *After Brown: The Rise and Retreat of School*

451

Desegregation. 2004. Princeton University Press, Princeton, NJ

Cohen, Can & Sterba, James P., *Affirmative Action and Racial Reference: A Debate*. 2003. Oxford University Press. New York, NY

Cohen, William and Varat, Jonathan D., *Constitutional Law: Cases and Materials (11th Ed.)*. 2001. Foundation Press, New York, NY

Coles, Jr., Floumoy A., *Black Economic Development*. 1975. Nelson Hall, Chicago, IL

Comer, James P., *Beyond Black and White*. 1972. Quadrangle Books, New York, NY

Conduit, Celeste Michelle and Lucaites, John Louis, *Crafting Equality: America's Anglo-African Word*. 1993. University of Chicago Press

Cone, James H., *Martin & Malcolm & America*. 1991. Orbis Books, Maryknoll, NY

Conrad, Earl, *The Invention of the Negro*. 1966. Eriksson Books, New York, NY

Cottrol, Robert J., Diamond, Raymond T., Ware, Leland B., *Brown v. Board of Education: Caste, Culture and the Constitution*. 2003. University Press of Kansas

Cowan, Tom, Ph.D. & Maguire, Jack, *Timelines of African American History*. 1994. Perigee Books, New York, NY

Daliek, Robert, Flawed Giant: *Lyndon Johnson and His Times, 1961-1973*. 1998. Oxford University Press, New York, NY

D'Angelo, Raymond, *The American Civil Rights Movements: Readings & Interpretations*. 2001. McGraw-Hill/Dushkin, New York, NY

Davis, John P. (Editor), *The Negro Reference Book*. 1970. Prentiss-Hall, Englewood Cliffs, NJ

Dawson, Michael C., *Behind The Mule: Race and Class in African American Politics*. 1994. Princeton University Press. Princeton, NJ

DeGregorio, William A., *The Complete Book of U.S. Presidents (5th Ed.)*. 2001. Gramercy Books, New York, NY

DuBois, W.E. Burghardt, *The Souls of Black Folk: Essays and Sketches* (Chicago, 1903)

DuBois, W.E.B, *Black Reconstruction In America, 1860-1880*. 1935, 1962. Atheneum Books, New York, NY

Edley, Jr, Christopher, *Not All Black and White: Affirmative Action and American Values*. 1996. Hill and Wang, New York, NY

Edsall, Thomas Byme and Edsall, Mary D., Chain Reaction. 1992. W.W. Norton, New York, NY

Egerton, John, *Speak Now Against The Day: The Generation Before The Civil Rights Movement In The South*. 1995. Alfred A. Knopf, New York, NY

Fairclough Adam, *Better Day Coming: Black and Equality, 1890-2000*. 2001. Viking/Penguin Books. New York, NY

Feagin, Joe R., *Racist America: Roots, Current Realities & Future Reparations*. 2000. Routledge, New York, NY

Feagin, Joe R. & Vera, Heman. *White Racism*. 1995. Routledge,
  New York, NY

Finkelman, Paul, Dred Scott V. Sandford: *A Brief History with Document*
  1997. Bendford Books, Boston, MA

Fireside, Harvey, *Separate and Unequal: Homer Plessy and the Supreme Court
  Decision that Legalized Racism*. 2004. Carrol & Graf Publishers,
  New York, NY

Foner, Philip S. (Ed.), *The Life and Times of Frederick Douglass, Vol. 3:
  The Civil War, 1861-1865*. 1952. International Publishers. New York, NY,
  P. 141

Franklin, John Hope and Moss, Alfred A., *From Slavery to Freedom:
  A History of African Americans, 8th ED*. 2000 (Original Ed. 1947).
  McGraw-Hill, Boston, MA

Frederickson, George, *White Supremacy: A Comparative Study in American
  and South African History*. 1981. Oxford University Press,
  New York, NY. P. 31

Friedman, Leon (Editor), *Brown v. Board: The Landmark Oral Argument
  Before The Supreme Court*. 1969, 2004. The New Press, New York, NY

Garrison, Webb, *The Lincoln No One Knows: The Mysterious Man Who Ran
  The Civil War*. 1993. MJF Books, New NY

Gillette, William, *Retreat from Reconstruction, 1869-1879*. 1979. Louisiana
  State University Press, Baton Rouge, LA

Goldwin, Roger (with David Gallen), *Thurgood Marshall: Justice For All*.
  1992. Carroll & Graf, New York, NY

Gossett, Thomas F., *Race: The History of an Idea in America*. 1965. Southern
  Methodist University Press, Dallas, TX.

Grant, Joanne (Editor), *Black Protest: 350 Years of History, Documents and
  Analyses*. 1968. Fawcett Columbine, New York, NY

Gray, Ed, *Chief Justice: A Biography of Earl Warren*. 1997. Simon & Schuster,
  New York, NY

Grob, Gerald N. and Billias, George Athan (Editors), *Interpretations of
  American History, Volume I to 1877: Patterns and Perspectives*. 1967.
  Free Press. New York, NY

Henry, Robert Selph, *The Story of the Confederacy*. 1931. Konecky &
  Konecky. Old Saybrook, CT

Hacker, Andrew, *Two Nations: Black and White, Separate, Hostile, Unequal*.
  1992. Ballantine Books, New York, NY

Higginbotham, Jr., Leon A., *Shades of Freedom: Racial Politics And
  Presumptions Of The American Legal Process*. 1996. Oxford University
  Press, New York, NY

Horton, James Oliver & Horton and Lois E. Horton, *Hard Road To Freedom:
  The Story of African America*. 2001. Rutgers University Press.
  New Brunswick, NJ

Irons, Peter, *A People's History of the United States*. 1999. Penguin Book,
  New York NY.

453

Jackson, Jr., Jesse L., *A More Perfect Union: Advancing New American Rights*. 2001. Welcome Rain Press, New York, NY

Jordan, Winthrop D., *White Over Black: American Attitudes Toward the Negro, 1550-1812*. 1968. University of North Carolina Press, Chapel Hill, NC

Kaufman, Kenneth C., *Dred Scott's Advocate: A Biography of Roswell M. Field*. 1996. University of Missouri Press, Columbia, MO. P. 184

King, Coretta Scott, *My Life With Martin Luther King, Jr.* 1969. Holt Rinehart and Winston, New York, NY

King, Jr., Martin Luther, *Where Do We Go from Here: Chaos or Community?* 1968. Beacon Press., Boston, MA

Klarman, Michael J., *From Jim Crow to Civil Rights: The Supreme Court and the Struggle for Racial Equality*. 2004. Oxford University Press, New York, NY

Kluger, Richard, *Simple Justice*. 1975. Knopf Books, New York, NY

Lemann, Nicholas, *The Big Test: The Secret History of the American Meritocracy*. 1999. Farrar, Straus, Giroux, New York, NY

Lofgren, Charles A., *The Plessy Case: A Legal-Historical Interpretation*. 1987. Oxford University Press, New York, NY

Logan, Rayford W., *The Betrayal of the Negro: From Rutherford B. Hayes to Woodrow Wilson*. 1997. Da Capo Press, New York, NY.

Lord, Walter, *The Past That Would Not Die*. Harper & Row. New York, NY

Lott, Tommy L., *The Invention of Race: Black Culture and the Politics of Representation*. 1999. Blackwell Publishers, Maiden, MA

Loury, Glenn C., *The Anatomy of Racial Inequality*. 2002. Harvard University Press, Cambridge, MA

Maclean, Nancy, *Behind The Mask of Chivalry: The Making of the Second Ku Klux Klan*. 1994. Oxford University Press, New York, NY

Malcomson, Scott L., *One Drop of Blood: The American Misadventure of Race*. 2000. Farrar, Straus and Giroux, New York, NY

Marable, Maiming, *The Great Wells of Democracy: The Meaning of Race In American Life*. 2002. Basic Civitas Book. New York, NY

Massey, Douglas S. and Denton, Nancy, *American Apartheid: Segregation and the Making of the Underclass*. 1993. Harvard University Press, Cambridge, MA

Mayer, Jeremy D., *Running On Race: Racial Politics In Presidential Campaigns, 1960-2000*. 2002.Random House, New York, NY

McKenzie, Richard B., *What Went Right In The 1980s*. 1994. Pacific Research Institute for Public Policy, San Francisco, CA

McNeil, Genna Rae, *Groundwork: Charles Hamilton Houston and the Struggle for Civil Rights*. 1983. University of Pennsylvania Press, Philadelphia, PA.

McPherson, James M., *What They Fought For, 1861-1865*. 1995. Anchor Books, New York, NY

McWhirter, Darien A., *The End of Affirmative Action: Where Do We

Go From Here? 1996. Birch Lane Press. New York, NY

Meir, August and Rudwick, Elliott, *From Plantation to Ghetto (3rd Ed.)*. 1966, 1970, 1976. Hill and Wang, New York, NY

Mfiime, Kweisi, with Ron Stodhill II, *No Free Ride: From the Mean Streets to the Mainstream*. 1996. One World/Ballentine Books. New York, NY

Mills, Charles, The Racial Contract. 1997. Comell University Press., Ithaca, NY.

Mitau, G. Theodore, *Decade of Decision: The Supreme Court and the Constitutional Revolution, 1954-1964*. 1967. Charles Scribner's Sons, New York, NY

Moses, Greg, *Revolution of Conscience: Martin Luther King, Jr. and the Philosoph of Non-Violence*. 1997. The Guilford Press, New York, NY

Myrdal, Gunnar, *An American Dilemma: The Negro Problem and Modem Democracy*. 1944. Harper & Brothers Publishers, New York, NY

Oliver, Melvin L. & Shapiro, Thomas M., *Black Wealth/White Wealth*. 1995. Routledge Books. New York, NY

Olson, Lynne, *Freedom's Daughters: The Unsung Heroines of the Civil Rights Movement From 1830 to 1970*. 2001. Scribner Books, New York, NY

O'Reilly, Kenneth. *Nixon's Piano: Presidents and Racial Politics From Washington To Clinton*. 1995. The Free Press, New York, NY

Packard, Jerrod M., *American Nightmare: The History of Jim Crow*. 2002. St. Martin's Press, New York, NY

Patrick, John J., Pious, Richard M., Ritchie, Donald A. (Editors), *The Oxford Essential Guide to the U.S. Government, Berkeley Ed*. 2000. Berkeley Books, New York, NY.

Patterson, James & Kim, Peter, *The Second American Revolution*. 1994. William Morrow and Company, New York, NY

Patterson, James T., *Brown v. Board of Education: A Civil Rights Milestone and Its Troubled Legacy*. 2001. Oxford University Press, New York, NY

Patterson, Orlando: *The Ordeal of Integration: Progress and Resentment in America's "Racial" Crisis*. 1997. Civitas Counterpoint, Washington, D.C.

Phillips, Kevin, The Politics of Rich and Poor. 1990. Random House New York, NY

Pinkney, Alphonso, *Black Americans (fifth ed.)*. 2002. Prentice Hall, Upper Saddle River, NJ

Quarles, Benjamin, *The Negro in the Making of America*. 1987. Touchtone Books, New York, NY. P. 74

Roediger, David R., *Colored White: Transcending the Racial Past*. 2002. University of California Press, Berkeley, CA

Roediger, David R., *The Wages of Whiteness*. 1991. Verso Books. New York, NY

Rossiter, Clinton, *1787: The Grand Convention*. 1996. W.W. Norton & Company, NewYork, NY.

Rowan, Carl T., *The Coming Race War In America: A Wake Up Call*. 1996. Little, Brown and Company, Boston, MA

Rowan, Carl T., *Dream Makers, Dream Breakers: The World of Justice Thurgood Marshall*. 1993. Little, Brown and Company, Boston, MA

Rubio, Philip F., *A History of Affirmative Action, 1619-2000*. 2001. University Press of Mississippi, Jackson, MS.

Sarratt, Reed, *The Ordeal of Desegregation*. 1966. Harpers & Row Publishers, New York, NY

Schlesinger, Jr., Arthur M., *A Thousand Days: John F. Kennedy in the White House*. 1965. Houghton Mifflin Company, Boston, MA

Schlesinger, Jr., Arthur M. (Ed.), *The Almanac of American History*. 1983. Perigee Books. New York, NY

Sefton, James E., *Andrew Johnson and the Uses of Constitutional Power*. 1980. Brown, Little and Company. Boston, MA

Shapiro, Thomas M., *The Hidden Costs of Being African American: How Wealth Perpetuates Inequality*. 2004. Oxford University Press, New York, NY

Silk, Leonard, *Nixonomics*. 1973. Praeger Publishers, New York, NY

Sitkoff, Harvard, *The Struggle for Black Equality, 1954-1980*. 1981. Hill and Wang, New York, NY

Sindler, Allan P., *Bakke, DeFunis, and Minority Admissions: The Quest for Equal Opportunity*. 1978. Longman, Inc., New York, NY

Smith, J. Owens, *The Politics of Ethnic and Racial Inequality. A Systematic Comparative Micro-Analysis from the Colonial Period to the Present*. 1992. Kendall/Hunt Publishing, Dubuque, 10

Smith, Robert C., *We Have No Leaders: African Americans in the Post Civil Rights Era*. State University of New York Press. 1996. State University of New York Press, Albany, NY

Stem, Mark, *Calculating Visions: Kennedy, Johnson, and Civil Rights*. 1992. Rutgers University Press, New Brunswick, NJ

Trelease, Alien W., *White Terror: The Ku Klux Klan Conspiracy and Southern Reconstruction*. 1971. Louisiana University Press, Baton Rouge, LA

Themstrom, Stephan and Themstrom, Abigail, *America In Black and White: One Nation Indivisible*. 1997. Simon & Schuster. New York, NY

Teixeira Ruy, and Rogers, Joel, *America's Forgotten Majority: Why the White Working Class Still Matters*. 2000. Basic Books, New York, NY

Thompson, Peter, *Cassell's Dictionary of Modern American History*. 2000. Cassell & Co., London, UK

Tushnet, Mark V., *The NAACP: Legal Strategy against Segregated Education, 1925-1950*. 1987. The University of North Carolina Press, Chapel Hill, NC

Unger, Irwin, *These United States: The Questions of Our Past*. 1999. Prentice-Hall, Upper Saddle River, NJ

Vose, Clement E., *Caucasians Only: The Supreme Court, the NAACP and the Restrictive Covenant Cases*. 1959. University of California Press. Berkeley, CA

Webster's New Explorer Dictionary. 1999. Springfield, MA

Whitman, Mark, *Brown V. Board of Education: A Documentary History*. 1993, 2004. Markus Wiener Publishers, Princeton, NJ

Wilhoit, Francis M., *The Politics of Massive Resistance*. 1973. George Braziller, Inc. New York, NY.

Williams, Juan, *Thurgood Marshall: American Revolutionary*. 1998. Random House. New York, NY

Williams, Linda Faye, *The Constraint of Race: Legacies of White Skin Privilege*. 2003. Pennsylvania State University Press, University Press, PA

Williamson, Joel, *The Crucible of Race*. 1984. Oxford University Press. New York, NY

Wilson, Sondra Kathryn (Editor), *In Search of Democracy: The NAACP Writings of James Weldon Johnson, Walter White and Roy Wilkins (1920-1977)*. 1999. Oxford University Press, New York, NY

Wolfenstein, Eugene Victor, *The Victims of Democracy: Malcolm X and the Black Revolution*. 1993. Guilford Press, New York, NY

Wolters, Raymond, *The Burden of Brown: Thirty Years of School Desegregation*. 1984. University of Tennessee Press, Knoxville, TN

Woodward, C. Vann, *The Strange Career of Jim Crow, 3rd Edition*. 1974. Oxford University Press, New York, NY

Zinn, Howard, *People's History of the United States*. 1980. HarperPerennial. New York, NY

Published Articles, Speeches, Reports and Research Papers

Baker, Jean, "From Belief Into Culture: Republicanism in the Antebellum North," *American Quarterly, Volume 37, Issue 4, Republicanism in the History and Historiography of the United States*.

"Before *Brown*/Beyond Boundaries: Commemorating the 50th Anniversary of *Brown vs.Board of Education*," The Association for the Study of African American Life and History (ASALH), Inc. 2004., African World Press, Trenton, NJ

Bell, Derrick, "Property Rights in Whiteness-Their Legal Legacy, Their Economic Costs," *Critical Race Theory: The Cutting Edge*. 1995. Delgado, Richard (Editor), Temple University Press, Philadelphia, PA.

Bobo, Lawrence D., "Racial Attitudes and Relations at the close of the Twentieth Century," *America Becoming: Racial Trends and Their Consequences, Vol. 1 ed.* Neil Smelser, William Julius Wilson, and Faith Mitchell. 2001. National Academy Press. Wash, DC

Crenshaw, Kimberle' Williams, "Race, Reform, and Retrenchment: Transformation and Legitimation in Antidiscrimination Law." 1995. *Critical Race Theory: The Key Writings That Formed The Movement*, Kimberle' Crenshaw, Neil Gotanda, Gary Peller, Kendall Thomas, editors. The New Press, New York, NY

Crenshaw, Kimberle' Williams, "Colorblindness, History, and the Law," *The House That Race Built*, Wahneema Lubiano (Editor). 1997. Pantheon Books, New York, NY

Davis, Thomas J., "Race, Identity, and the Law," *Race on Trial: Law and*

457

Justice in American History, Annette Gordon-Reed (editors). 2002. Oxford University Press. New York, NY

Harris, Cheryl I., "Whiteness As Property." 1995, from *Critical Race Theory*.

Locke, John, "Two Treatises of Government," 1690, *Great Political Thinkers: Plato to the Present. 2000 (Sixth Ed.)*. William and Alan Ebenstein, editors. Harcourt College Publishers, Fort Worth, TX.

King, Jr., Martin Luther, "I Have A Dream Speech," August 28, 1963, cited in *The African American Archive: The History of the Black Experience Through Documents*, Kai Wright, Editor. 2001. Black Dog & Leventhal Publishers, New York, NY.

King, Jr., Martin Luther, "Letter from Birmingham City Jail," cited from *The American Civil Rights Movement: Readings & Interpretations*, D'Angelo, Raymond. 2001. McGraw-Hill Dushin, New York

Mandle, Jay R., "Black Economic Entrapment After Emancipation in the United States," *The Meaning of Freedom: Economics, Politics, and Culture After Slavery*. Frank McGlynn and Seymour Drescher, Editors. 1992. University of Pittsburgh Press, Pittsburgh, PA

McIntoish, Peggy, "White Privilege: Unpacking the Invisible Knapsack." 1988, from *White Privilege: Essential Readings on the Other Side of Racism*, Paula S. Rothenberg, Editor. Worth Publishers, New York, NY

Mills, David, "Sista Souljah's Call to Arms" The Rapper Says the Riots Were Payback: Are You Paying Attention?" *Washington Post*, May 13, 1992, Bl

Muhammad, Derrick, Davis, Attieno, Lui, Meizhu and Leondar-Wright, Betsy, "The State of the Dream 2004: Enduring Disparities in Black and White." January, 15, 2004. Published by United for a Fair Economy-Racial Wealth Divide Project, Boston, MA

Sidanius, James, "The Psychology of Group Conflict and the Dynamics of Oppression: A Social Dominance Perspective," *Explorations In Political Psychology*, Shanto Iyengar and Willaim J. McGuire, Editors. 1993. Duke University Press, Durham, NC

Taylor, William L., "Access To Economic Opportunity: Lessons Since *Brown*," *Minority Report: What Has Happened To Blacks, Hispanics, American Indians, & Other Minorities In The Eighties*, Leslie W. Dunbar (Editor). 1984. Pantheon Books, New York, NY

"The State of Black Equality: The Complexity of Black Progress," Executive Summary, compiled by the National Urban League, March, 2004. New York, NY

Wang, Xi, "The *Dred Scott* Case," *Race on Trial: Law and Justice in American History*. Annette Gordon-Reed (Editor) 2002. Oxford University Press, New York, NY

Westin, Alan F., "The Case of the Prejudiced Doorkeeper," *Quarrels That Have Shaped The Constitution*, John A. Garraty (Editor). 1964. Harper & Row, New York, NY

Winant, Howard, "Racial Dualism At Century's End," *The House That Race Built*. 1997. Wahneema Lubiano, Editor. Pantheon Books. New York, NY

458

Zhou, Min, "Contemporary Immigration and the Dynamics of Race and Ethnicity," *America Becoming: Racial Trends and Their Consequences, Volume I*, Smelser, Neil J., Wilson, William Julius, Mitchell, Faith, (Editors). 2001. National Academy Press, Washington DC

Legal Cases

Adarand Contractors, Inc. v. Pena, 515 U.S. 200, 115S. Ct. 2097, 132 L.Ed. 2d 158 (1995)
Boiling v. Sharpe (347 U.S. 497)
Briggs et al. V. Elliot et al., 98 F. Supp. 259 (1951)
Brown et al. v. Board of Education of Topeka, et. al. (347 U.S. 483) (1954)
Brown v. Board of Education of Topeka (Brown II) 349 U.S. 294 (1955)
City of Richmond v. J.A. Croson Company 488 U.S. 469, 109 S. ct. 706, 102 L.Ed. 2d 854 (1989)
Civil Rights Cases 109 U.S. 3 (1883)
Davis v. County School Board of Prince Edward County, 103 F. Supp. 337 (1952)
DeFunis v. Odegaard, 416 U.S. 312, 94 S. Ct. 1704, 40L.Ed.2d 164 (1974)
Dred Scott v. John F.A. Sanford, 60 U.S. (Howard 19) 393 (1856)
Gebhart et al. v. Belton (Gebhart v. Bulah) et al., 91 A. 2d 137 (S.C. of Del., 1952)
Hopwood v. Texas, 78 F. 3d. at 962 (1996)
McLaurin v. Oklahoma State Regents for Higher Education 339 U.S. 637 (1950)
Milliken v. Bradley, 418 U.S. 717 (1974)
Plessy v. Ferguson (163 U.S. 537, 16 S. Ct. 1138, 41 L.Ed. 256 (1896)
Regents of the University of California v. Bakke, 438 U.S. 265, 98 S. Ct. 2733, 57 L.Ed. 2d 750 (1978)
San Antonio Independent School Dist. V. Rodriguez, 411 U.S. 1, 93 S Ct. 1278, 36 L.Ed. 2d 16 (1973)
Shaw v. Reno, 509 U.S. 630, 113 S. Ct. 2816, 125L.Ed.2d5H (1993)
Sipuel v. Board of Regents of the University of Oklahoma, 332 U.S. 631(1948)
Smith v. Allwright, 321 U.S. 649 (1944)
State ex rel. Gaines v. Canada, 305 U.S. 337 (1938)
Sweatt v. Painter, 339 U.S. 629 (1950

459

Government Documents

The Constitution of the United States of America.
Congressional Record, 84th Congress, 2nd Session, March 12, 1956
U.S. Bureau of the Census-Decennial Census Reports, Population, 1900-2000
U.S. Bureau of Labor Statistics, Employment Situation, Historical Table A-2.
United States. Kerner Commission, Report of the National Advisory Commission on Civil Disorder. 1968. U.S. Government Printing Office

INDEX

461

467

468

ABOUT
THE AUTHOR

Anthony Asadullah Samad is an author, columnist and scholar known for his fiery analysis of social, political and economic issues that impact American society. As one of the most read featured columnists in the African American press over the past 13 years, Samad's various weekly editorial commentaries contribute to newspapers and cyber websites that appear in over 100 U.S. markets.

An Associate Professor of Political Science and African American Studies at East Los Angeles College, Samad has a Masters of Arts in Public Administration (Public Finance specialization) from the University of Southern California, a second Masters of Arts Degree, in Political Economy, from the Claremont Graduate University's School of Politics and Economics, and is currently a Doctoral Candidate at Claremont Graduate University, completing his doctoral study, with a dissertation, entitled, "Legal and Policy Interpretations of the Fourteenth Amendment in the Post *Brown* Era: A 50 Year Case Study on the Policy Implementation Challenges of *Brown v. Board of Education.*"

Samad is also President of Samad and Associates, a strategic planning/ urban affairs firm, specializing in the assessment and management of public policy, economic development, urban, social and race issues. His firm's 15-year efforts have generated over $300 million in economic development opportunities in urban and rural communities nationwide. Mr. Samad is also currently the managing director of the Urban Issues Forum of Greater Los Angeles, and is the author of two books; the Essence magazine bestseller, *Souls For Sale: The Diary of An Ex-Colored Man* (Kabili Press, 2002), and his current release, *50 Years After Brown: The State of Black Equality In America* (Kabili Press, 2005).

Anthony Asadullah Samad, his wife and family, currently reside in Southern California. His current writings and commentaries can be read at www.AnthonySamad.com.

470